A Biography

THOMAS SEWELL INBORDEN

Early Educator Of Color

A Biography

Thomas Sewell Inborden

Early Educator Of Color

by

ROBERT EWELL GREENE

R.E. Greene, Publisher
Fort Washington, Maryland, 1996

Copyright © 1996 by Robert Ewell Greene
ALL RIGHTS RESERVED
Published in 1996 by R.E. Greene, Publisher
Fort Washington, Maryland

Library Of Congress Catalog No. 95-081770
ISBN-0-945733-13-5

To a very wonderful and gracious lady a daughter and aunt whose personal desire and love for her family's genetic heritage and an unswerving love, respect and remembrance of her father has made a dream come true; a biography of her father. May God continue to bless you, Dorothy Inborden Miller and keep you in his everlasting love every hour, day and years to come.

TABLE OF CONTENTS

AUTHOR'S PREFACE

ACKNOWLEDGMENTS

CHAPTER	PAGES
1 The Early Years	1
2 Genesis Of A School	18
3 Brick's Beginning Years	23
4 Challenging Years	69
5 Demise Of A Landmark And A Gallant Resurrection	116
6 Final Retirement Years	145
7 Epilogue To An Early Educator Of Color	166

APPENDICES 169

A PICTORIAL REVISIT 329

NOTES 429

BIBLIOGRAPHY 447

INDEX 451

AUTHOR'S PREFACE

The year was 1865 and that was the birthday of Thomas Sewell Inborden. Thirty years later he would have survived the young life of a mountain boy in Virginia and known the trials and tribulations of poverty. He had completed successfully studies at Oberlin College, Ohio and graduated from Fisk University, Nashville, Tennessee. One hundred years ago, Inborden was the founder and architect of the curriculum of a Normal school for his people of color in North Carolina. The school was named in the honor of Joseph Keasbey Brick, the husband of its benefactor, Julia Elma Brewster Brick of New York. This year, 1995, is the centennial of Brick's founding. When we view the present state of the African American community with the conversations and writings about topics such as the black youth's learning abilities, morals, culture, the black family and affirmative action, I believe that it is more than a necessity to reeducate some African Americans and white people and others in our multiracial society that African Americans have always been an industrious and determined people whose past and present achievements refute the allegations and misinformation, we hear today. Unfortunately, American history books for the majority of Americans still do not reflect the actual lives and achievements of many black persons such as the life of Thomas Sewell Inborden. This book will give the details of Inborden's life and the institution he founded and also depict through many pages and pictures the true history of black Americans, who lived in eastern North Carolina and were eager to obtain an education and survive the dehumanizing effects of separation and inequality in their respective communities. Their living and surviving have brought their descendants thus far to the present year of 1995. I have included in this book many names of people, articles, and papers that will present events that occurred in Inborden's life and Brick Normal School. Because I have been able to have an historian's wish and that is primary sources, oral testimonies, papers, letters, speeches and articles of Inborden during the period 1880-1950, I have included in this book the detail information about the life of Inborden. This book will be a valuable biography and reference for the family, history collectors, educators and historians. Thomas Sewell Inborden was an early educator of color who demonstrated in his life, the fruit of the spirit, love, joy, peace, long suffering, gentleness, good faith and meekness. Inborden and some member of his family were fair enough to be mistaken for whites or Caucasians, however they choose not to do. Many of them married husbands and wives of darker skin complexion, Inborden once stated that *Colored blood must be powerful blood*. It has been my intention since 1980 to write a biography on Thomas Sewell Inborden. I must thank you many times Mrs. Dorothy Viola Inborden Miller for preserving your father's personal papers and above all making it possible for the pages of this book to resurrect the life and times of your father. I pray each day that our merciful Lord will continue to bless and keep you beyond his first promise of three scores and ten so you may gracefully approach your 99th birthday and eventual 100 years.

Robert Ewell Greene
August 20, 1995

ACKNOWLEDGEMENTS

I wish to express my sincere gratitude to Janice Lucile Wood Hunter for her caring, patience, understanding and supberb administrative and immense stenographic contributions to this manuscript.

I sincerely thank Viola F. Smith for her outstanding scholarly expertise in the grammatical, editing and proofreading of this manuscript.

I also wish to express my sincere gratitude to the following people for their contributions in making this manuscript possible:

        Bill Grant
        David A.F. Greene
        Janice L.W. Hunter
        Kimberly Cherie Hunter
        Frances Gordon Kent
        Tom Mackey
        Dorothy Inborden Miller
        Viola F. Smith

My appreciation is also hereby expressed to the wonderful persons who have assisted me and may have been inadvertently excluded.

                                                              R.E.G.

Thomas Sewell Inborden 1

CHAPTER 1

The Early Years

One hundred years ago on Friday, January 6, 1865, Congress was discussing the 13th amendment and the military campaigns of the Civil War were concluding. Also on this day in the beautiful area of the Blue Ridge mountains surrounded by Loudoun and Fauquier counties, a baby boy was born and named Thomas Sewell Inborden after his maternal uncle. The family home was located in the recesses of the mountain, four miles from the town of Upperville, Virginia, and sixteen miles from Winchester, Virginia. Thomas Sewell was born to Harriet Proctor Smith, a free black who had an interesting family background. She was the daughter of Levi and Hannah Proctor. Levi was born in 1797 and Hannah, 1801. Levi and his brother escaped from their master and were placed in a jail in Leesburg, Virginia. While in jail, Levi's meals were brought to him by a sixteen year old slave girl, Hannah. The drinks were carried in a distinctive pitcher. On the side of the pitcher was a picture depicting George Washington receiving the sword of Cornwallis at Yorktown, Virginia during the American Revolution. Levi was able to prove that he was a free man and was released from jail. Later, he purchased Hannah from slavery and married her. They were the parents of five mulatto children, Caroline, born 1822, Harriet, 1829, Jane, 1835, Thomas Sewell, 1843 and Nathaniel, 1846. Hannah's maiden name was Rector. She was related to one of the distinguished first families of the local area. Hannah died at the age of 81 years from pneumonia contracted during the winter of the big snow of 1881. Levi Proctor had an occupation of burning wool coal and making whiskey. There were more than a hundred coal pits in Loudoun County, Virginia. When Levi was making whiskey in 1855, it was not considered moonshine or bootleg business. The man who made the best whiskey received more money for his services and the whiskey sold on the markets. Levi used the ingredients of buckwheat, rye, oats and persimmons for his whiskey. Levi Proctor died in 1888 at 91 years. The Loudoun county newspaper wrote that Levi had an exemplary life and had many descendants. Harriet Proctor Smith was the mother of Faunce Grigsby, Thomas Sewell Inborden, Mary Smith, Turner Smith, Edward Ashton Smith, Cecelia Smith and Dorsey Spinney. Faunce, Thomas Sewell, and Dorsey had different fathers. Faunce became a minister and lived in Delaware. His physical description was similar to his white father. Cecelia remained at home with her mother prior to her marriage. Edward Ashton lived in the Upperville - Paris, Virginia areas until his death. Edward Ashton was born August 8, 1870 and was a farmer. He was quite fond of his horses, pigs, poultry and garden. Edward Ashton was the father of Edna Smith Lewis, Nellie Smith Young, Sarah Smith Ramey, Frances Smith Freeland, Mary Smith Murray, Mattie Smith Cabell, Rosella Lee Smith, Virginia Smith Howard, Robert Edward Smith, Thomas Clarence Smith and Sarah Smith Rainey. He also had many grandchildren and great grandchildren[1]. Harriet Proctor Smith was a lady of refinement, industrious and believed in the education of her children. She required that all of her children attend school. When the public school was closed, she enrolled her children in a private school. Harriet was as insistent that the white people in the community should send their children to school as she was that black people should send theirs. Harriet and her daughter, Cecelia worked as midwives in the local community.

During the Civil War many of the Confederate officers of the Upper Virginia contingent would pass through the mountains near her home. She would cook their meals and at times hide more than a hundred gallons of scotch rye and barley in the stone piles and fences to keep the Confederate officers from over indulgence. Harriet was able to observe some interesting sights as the Union and Confederate troops would confront each other in military actions. On a beautiful Sunday morning Harriet went out to the side of a hill to see if some strawberries were ripe. Suddenly, she heard something flying over her head and in several minutes she heard horses coming up a path in the mountain. There was a rattling of chains and excitement What Harriet thought was honey bees were minnie balls buzzing over her head. The Confederate soldiers were fleeing from some Union troops. Some of the men were wounded and bleeding. Harriet treated some of their wounds with cloth from her loom and juice from vines to ease their pain. The Confederates were seeking safety in the recesses of the mountain. Harriet was able to see a mile down the mountain where an eighty acre field was covered with what was called General Oliver O. Howard's Union White Horse Cavalry covering the large field. Harriet had her personal views about John Singleton Mosby and his men. She believed Mosby caused great trouble for the Union soldiers and did not fight fair. She said that he would hide in the mountains and make surprise attacks on unsuspecting groups of Union men as they marched along the road. Harriet once delayed a large contingent of soldiers passing along the Old Winchester and Alexandria Pike crossing the mountain at Ashbey's Gap. Harriet Proctor Smith was a very good seamstress. She used her spinning wheel to weave the wool into cloth. The wool was obtained when the sheep left the wool sticking to the briars and when they were killed by the dogs. The wool was washed, carded, spun and woven into cloth. She made clothes for the children. The girls' clothes had red, white and blue stripes.[2]

Thomas Sewell Inborden (hereafter referred to as T.S. Inborden) did not openly know about his Caucasian father. Because of historical accuracy and an analysis of primary and secondary sources to include the oral tradition. I have decided to present the known available facts about the possible identification of T.S. Inborden's paternal heritage. The following will include some inferences and researched accounts from letters and interviews using the oral tradition. In June 1985, Dorothy Inborden Miller, daughter of T.S. Inborden stated in an interview that she was attending a family reunion in Middleburg, Virginia and decided to ask her first cousin who was her grandfather? She asked Nellie V. Corie Smith Young, the daughter of T.S.' brother, Ashton. Nellie replied without hesitation, that *he is the son of Robert E. Lee* and was surprised that Dorothy Inborden Miller did not know. Mrs. Dorothy I. Miller informed me that it was not her desire to have Robert E. Lee as her grandfather. I decided to pursue this allegation as near as possible. I made numerous visits to county court houses, towns of Middleburg, Upperville and Paris, Virginia. I also interviewed several people who believed General Robert E. lee of Confederate fame was indirectly related to them. I have developed some inferences and a scenario that will reveal that Robert E. Lee possibly was involved in some intimate relations with some females of color, especially a family that has some direct relationship to T.S. Inborden. After some 15 years of researching this allegation, I sincerely believe that Robert E. Lee was not T.S.Inborden's father. However, there is a great possibly that Robert E. Lee's sons or Lee had some intimate relations with a female closely related to Inborden. I will present some evidence in my discussion that will show that. T.S. Inborden possibly knew the identity of his father. I was not able to ascertain where the name Inborden originated. There was a Confederate officer named General John Imboden. There were present in Inborden's personal library some books written on the subjects of Robert E. Lee, and the Civil War. Several books had their pages folded and some pencil marks reference paragraphs pertaining to General Imboden. These books had T.S.' name stamped inside the front covers. These manuscripts are: *Treason of Major General Charles Lee, 1858, Robert E. Lee a Biography, 4 Volumes, 1936, Recollections and Letters of General Robert E. Lee, 1904* and *Jeb Stuart 1934*. T.S. Inborden had clipped a picture from a newspaper, The *News and Observer, Raleigh North Carolina*, January 17, 1937. The picture was of Robert E. Lee on his horse, Traveler and the caption read *Tuesday January 19, marks the 130th anniversary of the birth of that great Southern gentleman and leader in the Confederacy Robert E. Lee*. I have posed the question to Dorothy I. Miller several times, why would her father have a personal interest in books on Robert E. Lee and the Civil War?

In November 1993, I had an interview with, Ashton E. Smith's great granddaughter's husband. He stated that there were discussions in the family that they could be related to Robert E. Lee. He also told me about a lady that lives in Chatham, Canada whose family was also related to Robert E. Lee. I made a telephone call to a Mrs. Connie Travis and she informed me that her family was related to Robert E. Lee. She sent me a letter dated November 10, 1993 and later sent a book on the history of the early black community in Canada after the Civil War. After reading the contents of the letter and the book, I was able to learn the following facts about her alleged relationship to General Robert E. Lee. Mrs. Connie Travis said that the story has passed down to family members through the years by the oral tradition from her mother and father, Martha Watts, daughter of Horace Black, her grandmother, Julia Black and her Aunt Julia Black Chase. There was a young girl named Martha who worked as a slave on the Kentucky plantation of Asher (or Ashton) Lee, a cousin of Robert E. Lee. She worked in the kitchen of the plantation house. General Robert E. Lee was apparently visiting his cousin Asher's plantation and as a southern custom, Martha was offered to Robert E. Lee to satisfy his sexual desires. This intimate relationship was possibly the biological conception of a baby who was named, Horace Lee. Horace was sent from Paris, Kentucky as a substitute for his master's son during the Civil War and served in the Union Army. After his discharge from the army and receipt of his freedom, Horace Lee changed his last name to Black. Horace Black decided to travel to Canada and purchase some land. He purchased crown land in Raleigh Plains, Kent County, located near the Elgin settlement where some former slaves found freedom prior to the Civil war. Horace's name appeared on the assessment rolls of Raleigh township as early as 1874 for 100 acres of land. Horace Black was married twice. His first wife was Maria Poindexter, a hair dresser from Detroit, Michigan. Their children were William Herbert Black, Cleveland, Ohio; George Poindexter Black, Allentown, California; Horace Greely Black,

Harriet Anderson, and Martha Watts, Canada. Horace's second wife was Julia Watts and their children were Edith Ella Smead; Arnold Black, Omaha, Nebraska; Charles Black, Detroit, Michigan; Stanley Black, Cleveland, Ohio; Gladys Riddle, Ann Arbor, Michigan; Sidney Black, Canada, Julia Louis and Gordon Black, Canada. Mrs. Connie Travis said Horace received a bullet wound in the thigh while in military service and he received a pension. His widow received forty-two dollars a month until her demise in 1938. Mrs Travis also stated that some photos of Horace Black did resemble pictures of Robert E. Lee. The information that I received from Mrs. Connie Travis about Robert E. Lee enhanced the possibilities that Lee did have an affinity toward intimate relations with women of color.[3] I called a very graceful lady around the age of 80 years in 1993 to discuss Robert E. Lee. Ironically, during our discussion, I learned that my late Aunt's husband was this lady's brother-in-law. I felt quite relaxed and received a very warm and helpful responses from her during our telephone interviews. She lives in the area of Upperville - Middleburg, Virginia. She stated that there was a lady named Hebie Fisher who married a Waynefield Fox. It is believed through the oral tradition that her father was Robert E. Lee. Hebie was born around 1840, she lived to be 103 and died in 1943. When Hebie Fisher was twelve years old, she worked for a Colonel Delaney in the Upperville area. Her physical description was blue eyes, straight hair and a mulatto complexion or white appearing skin. The known children of Hebie Fisher and Waynefield Fox were Henry, Curtis, George, Waynefield, Daisy, Hebie, Leslie and Rose. Waynefield Fox had a sister, Lillie, she married an Al Spinney. Caroline Fox, another sister married Oscar Sanford and they had a daughter, Alcinda. There are some known relatives of color of Hebie Fox and Waynefield Fox that are living in Middleburg, Virginia today.[4] One of the daughters of Hebie and Waynefield Fox was Daisy Fox. She lived in New York City during her adult years. Daisy's physical description was blue eyes, course straight hair, mulatto skin complexion and quite stout. I learned from her niece that when she visited her Aunt Daisy in New York many years ago, she heard her say *I am related to Robert E. Lee, he is my grandfather and sometimes I am mean like him*. At times, Daisy Fox would pass as white when traveling on a train or bus, especially when traveling in Virginia or the south. Sometimes she would wear a veil over her face. Daisy Fox left New York City one day to visit her relatives in Upperville, Virginia. When she arrived in Washington, D.C. she changed buses. She boarded the bus for Upperville and found a seat next to a white man from Upperville named Jim Kenslow. He did not recognize her. Daisy and Jim carried on a conversation and he assumed she was a white lady riding in the section of the bus reserved for whites. Kenslow offered Daisy some chocolate candy from his box of chocolates. She practically ate all of his candy by the time the bus reached Upperville. When Daisy disembarked from the bus, she told the gentleman goodbye and walked swiftly toward her family's house. Mr. Kenslow never recognized her as Daisy Fox. This was a true example of how she would pass as white at times.[5] The story of Hebie Fox and Daisy Fox has some relationship to Thomas Sewell Inborden because within this manuscript will be some letters that Inborden received from a lady in New York named Daisy Fox and she would write *Dear Uncle Sewell and sign her name, Daisy, your niece*.

I was able to locate several letters where T.S. Inborden did mention about his genetic inheritance. In a letter written to his daughter, Dorothy, T.S. stated:

> I am Indian for a large part. I have at least half white aristocracy which has given me the spirit of independence and an attitude of the equality of any man who walks the face of the earth. I have some French and Dutch extraction. These inherent qualities have given me tenacity and personality that has made me more than anything else except perhaps my environment. In all my life, I have never cared for the cheap and trashy element of people. I have had to mix with a great many of them. I have always tried to put myself with those who were looking upward and onward, especially those who wanted to be somebody. When I come into a bad environment and cannot remake it, get out of it. The one thing to consider is whether one course will lead us to wealth or woe.

In 1930, T.S. Inborden wrote a letter to his daughter Julia and said:

> I have never said nothing about my father. He died not an old man with Brights disease (Kidney disease). I have seen him on several occasions when he has come to my mother's house. He was one of the cleanest and finest dressed men I ever saw. He was a typical southern gentleman. He was well educated and had the finest cultural bearing. He had one son whom I remember very well for he clerked in Conrad's store in Upperville where we all traded. I never went there but I was the recipient of the best delicacies to eat and sometimes to wear which the store had. I was too young to understand it but all of this was the tragedy of the old days for which none of us seemed responsible. This my half brother was undoubtedly the finest looking man I ever saw in my life and I make no exceptions to nobody. Destiny did not decree that he should live very long. Some physical incipiency had perhaps already reached his blood stream and given the unusual facial expression which so often leads itself to beauty.

In later years, there was a student who graduated from the school where T.S. was a principal who said he always thought Inborden was a white man passing as a colored man.[6] After reviewing thoroughly T.S. Inborden's letter to his daughter Julia, I was convinced that Robert E. Lee was not the father of Inborden. I tried very diligently to locate any information concerning the presence of a Conrad's store located in Upperville during the period 1870-1885 and records of the employees. This information would have revealed the identity of T.S.' half white brother and possibly the name of his father. This biography of T.S. Inborden will reveal the wholesome, productive and interesting life of an early educator and administrator of color who chose once he left the mountains of Virginia to live and identify himself as a person of color. I deeply believe that in view of the discussions presented, inferences and oral traditions, and information that T.S. Inborden knew his father's name but he also was well knowledgeable of his multiracial genetic heritage of African, Indian and European. He lived and died as a black man and he used the genetic talents of his tripartite of rich genes to achieve and help for many years in the south his black brothers and sisters to obtain upward mobility through the pursuit of excellence in education. T.S. Inborden's early childhood in the Blue Ridge mountains of Virginia served as a rich background for his successes in life, especially his knowledge of working with his hands, agriculture and botany. Harriet Proctor Smith was very adamant about T.S. attending school. T.S. went to school for three months during the winter. His mother also hired a teacher for several months to tutor him. T.S. never went beyond the third grade in the county schools. He used the third grade reader. Inborden walked six miles up and down the mountains to go to school a total of twelve miles a day. Sometimes T.S. made fifteen cents a day working and his mother would hire him out to do work for three dollars a month. Harriet Proctor Smith grew broom corn and T.S. helped her to make brooms, doormats and straw baskets. Inborden worked as a cooper, making mattresses, and brooming chairs with white oak splits. While working in the mountains T.S. learned how to cut logs for the saw mills and make rails, shingles and wagon spokes. As a young child T.S. Inborden was able to study and observe the plants, flowers, trees and animals that were present in the mountain environment. He was able to find apples late in the spring which had wintered in the leaves under the snow. He was able to observe how the blight had killed practically all the fine old chestnut trees, and black locust. T.S. was able to locate in the dark recesses flowering plants and ferns of rare varieties. He also saw hunters bagging squirrels without moving from their positions, hunting coons at night and hunting possums, rabbits, ground hogs, pheasants, wild pigeons and wild turkeys. When T.S Inborden was a small boy, he would see growing in his mother's garden on the side of the mountain, white strawberries. He knew nothing at that young age about mutants (changes) or unusual varieties. The mutation had affected the strawberry fruit which was creamy in color and most delicious in taste but also affected the caring of the leaf and its bordering. T.S. noticed that when the garden was worked year after year with no special attention given, eventually the white strawberries disappeared never to be seen again.[7]

In 1882 at the age of seventeen years, T.S. Inborden made a decision to leave the mountains of Virginia in order to better his conditions in life and receive an education. His mother was hesitant at first because at one time T.S. tried to run away. She finally supported his desire to leave the mountains. In later years, Inborden stated that he wanted to leave his mountain home because it was a dream that would come true. He said, *I did not flounder around and just happen to float into a drift that carried me to success.* T.S. honestly believed that he wanted to create something fundamental and necessary in the life of great masses of his people, the Negroes in the south, with these visions at a teen age, onward to Cleveland for T.S.

Descent From the Mountain On To Cleveland

T.S. Inborden left his mountain home at 1:00 a.m., on April 1, 1882 with thirteen dollars and seventy-five cents. He was accompanied by Oscar Sanford and another young man. These two young men returned home. Inborden was familiar with the name Cleveland, Ohio because he had read in a newspaper that President Garfield had been killed and was buried in Cleveland. Inborden had never been 25 miles away from his home and never on a train. He was quite sad about leaving. Hampton Institute, Virginia was the only black school he had heard about from friends. T.S. walked until he found his money would carry him the rest of the way to

Cleveland. Inborden traveled across the Blue Ridge mountains and the Shenandoah River to Boiseville where he boarded a Baltimore and Ohio Train to Cleveland. Inborden arrived in Cleveland, Ohio and was able to find a job at the Forest City Hotel. The proprietors of the hotel were Mr. Ingersoll, and Mr. Terrell. A Mr. Payne was the head clerk. T.S. discarded his old clothes and appeared for his job wearing patent leather toed shoes, a white suit and a double bosom ruffled shirt. He later threw away his old satchel. The headwaiter at the hotel told T.S. that when he was used to walking on the hardwood floors as a bellboy, he would take him in the dining room and teach him how to wait tables. While working in Cleveland, T.S. was very interested in improving his education. He wrote his mother and asked her to send him his arithmetic book and dictionary. He probably did not realize that the books could be purchased in Cleveland. T.S. would use his free time to study his books. One day a hotel visitor observed T.S. studying and decided to ask him some questions. The visitor was a graduate of Oberlin College and had invited T.S. to the 50th anniversary of the founding of the college. When T.S. returned to Cleveland from the interesting and informative visit to Oberlin, he was very motivated about continuing his education.[8]

An Oberlin Student

T.S. Inborden was impressed with Oberlin College and decided to leave Cleveland for Oberlin. When he arrived in Oberlin, he enrolled in the College's preparatory school. T.S. was placed in the lowest course, and used a fourth grade reader. Inborden had saved 150 dollars while working in Cleveland. He used 150 dollars to pay the school entrance fee, purchase books, rent a room, and buy a couple tons of coal and some kerosene for his lamp. When his money was depleted, he found a job at the town's hotel and earned some money for his board and meals. T.S. could purchase all of his materials for school. He believed he should purchase everything the teacher said was needed. During the summer months at Oberlin, T.S. would return to Cleveland and worked for Mr. Ingersoll and a Mr. F.S. Chisholm of the old East Cleveland Screw works. Sometimes in the winter it was necessary for T.S. to walk the floor of his little room with an over coat on and without heat when the temperature was ten degrees below zero. Inborden attended a Methodist Church in Oberlin. He was the superintendent of the Sunday school even though he was trying to read a fourth grade reader.

T.S. Inborden and two friends, Hunter and Loeb, decided to share some rooms in the home of an Oberlin family of color. Hunter later became a physician in Lexington, Kentucky and Loeb became a lawyer. They lived in the home of a free man of color and his family, Wilson Bruce Evans. Evans was born in 1824 in Orange County, North Carolina. He had a brother, Henry Evans and sisters, Corrie, Rosa, and Delilah Evans. Henry Evans requested several friends in 1854 to write Governor Reid of North Carolina to ensure his family's safe passage to Ohio. Henry Evans, his brother Wilson and their families and some friends were able to leave North Carolina. They traveled by Ox teams, stage coach, boat and a Baltimore and Ohio train prior to reaching Oberlin, Ohio.[9] When the Evans brothers settled in Oberlin, they started a business. Henry was an upholsterer and Wilson was a cabinet maker and an undertaker making wooden coffins. The Evans brothers had a shop on East Mill street (later named Vine). Later, they purchased Walton Hall, a two story building on south Main street, The building previously was an Oberlin College Men's dormitory. W.B. Evans buried an early white Oberlin pioneer, Hiram A. Pease. One day Alexander Graham Bell visited W. B. Evans' carpenter shop and had some earphones made out of wood for his receivers.[10]

Wilson Bruce and Henry Evans participated in the Oberlin-Wellington Rescue in 1858, the rescue of a John Price, a fugitive slave of John G. Bacon of Mayslick, Kentucky. Bacon had given power of attorney to Anderson Jennings to apprehend Price in the Oberlin area and bring him back to Kentucky. As he was being transported to Columbus by way of Wellington, several miles from Oberlin College, students and some citizens gathered to rescue him. Price was rescued and sent to Canada for safety. Later, a federal grand jury at Cleveland indicted thirty-seven persons for the violations of the fugitive slave laws. Among those indicted were Henry and Wilson Bruce Evans along with other free men of color, Charles Langston, O.S.B. Wall and John Scott. They were confined in jail briefly. On July 6 1859, the citizens of Oberlin gathered to welcome their faithful and honored men who were protesting against a law that they thought was unjust.[11]

Wilson Bruce Evans served during the Civil War. He volunteered at the age of 40 years in Ohio Volunteer Units and was assigned to company D, 178th Ohio Volunteer Infantry as a private September 1, 1864. Evans served with the Post Commissary, Tullahoma, Tennessee. He was discharged on June 29, 1865 and received a bounty of one hundred dollars.

W.B. Evans was a tall well built man, white hair, hazel eyes and complexion, mulatto. He was often asked by photographers and artists to pose for pictures. It has been said that his features were similar to Longfellow. W.B. Evans was also a direct descendant of General Nathaniel Greene of revolutionary war fame. Evans was a deacon of the Second Church in Oberlin, Ohio. W.B. Evans build his home a hip roofed brick house (Italian style) at 33 Vine Street (in 1856, Old Mill Street). The home has been placed on the National Register of historic Places by the United States Department of the Interior, Family Home of Wilson Bruce Evans.

Henry and Wilson Bruce Evans were the patriarchs of two successful and distinguished families. The brothers married two sisters, Henrietta and Sarah Jane Leary. Henry Evans married Henrietta Leary. They were the parents of Elizabeth, Julia, Matthew, Anna, Sarah, Mary Patterson, Delilah, John, Wilson, Jane and Sheridan Evans. Their daughter Anna married Daniel Murray who was an Assistant Librarian of Congress, Washington, D.C. for many years. Their children achieved numerous goals within their respective vocations: Daniel Murray Jr. was a violinist, George Henry Murray, a lawyer and business instructor, Cardozo High School, Washington, D.C., Nathaniel Murray was a science instructor at Armstrong High School, Washington, D.C. (while a student at Cornell University, Nathaniel participated in the founding of Alpha Phi Alpha Fraternity at Cornell), Harold B. Murray was an engineer in Brazil and later of paper in Mexico. Anna Murray was instrumental in introducing the Kindergarten concept in the public schools, Washington, D.C.

Henry and Henrietta Evans' son Wilson Bruce Evans graduated from Howard University's college of Medicine, class of 1891. However, he pursued a career in education and was responsible for the founding of Armstrong High School, Washington, D.C. Evans was honored in later years with the naming of Wilson Bruce Evans, Junior High School, Washington, D.C. in his memory. He married Annie Brooks and they were the parents of Joseph H. B. and Lillian Evans. Joseph H. B. worked in the insurance business and federal government. He married Hilda Johnson and they were the parents of Hilda Evans Lewis whose husband was Clarence Lewis. They were the parents of Hilda and Clarence. Lillian Evans married Roy W. Tibbs. They were the parents of Thurlow Tibbs Sr., the father of Thurlow Tibbs Jr. and Elizabeth Tibbs. Lillian (also known as Lillian Evanti) was an internationally known acclaimed lyric soprano. She was a graduate of Howard University. She continued her musical studies in Paris, France; Milan, Italy; and Munich, Germany. Lillian Evans has performed in France, Italy, Germany, Switzerland, Austria, Mexico, Haiti, Rio de Janeiro and Buenos Aires. Evans also triumphed in the operas of *Opera la Traviata*, *Barber of Seville*, *Romero and Juliet*, *Hamlet*, and *Die Entfuhrung*. She had given a command performance at the White House for former First Lady, Eleanor Roosevelt.

Sarah Jane Evans and Henrietta Evans had a rich heritages from North Carolina. Their grandparents were Jeremiah O'Leary of Irish and Croatian descent and Sarah Jane Revels, black descent. She was related to Hiram Revels, the first black senator from Mississippi. Revels was born in Fayetteville, North Carolina. Sarah Jane Revels' father was Aaron Revels, a free black that served in the American Revolution. Jeremiah O'Leary and Sarah Jane Revels were the parents of Matthew Nathaniel born on February 15, 1802, in Sampson County, North Carolina. He spent his early childhood in Cumberland County, North Carolina and learned the trade of harness maker and saddler. Matthew Leary was successful in purchasing his freedom and started a business. He was a Whig and later a Republican. He was also interested in abolition and freedom for slaves and gave money to purchase their freedom. Leary assisted in organizing the St. Joseph Episcopal church of Fayetteville and organized the first choir in the church and taught vocal music. In 1825, Matthew Leary married Juliette Anna Meimoriel, a French woman born in France and brought from the French West Indies to Fayetteville, North Carolina by her mother, Mariette Colostic Williard Meimoriel. Matthew Nathaniel and Juliette Anna were the parents of Matthew Nathaniel Jr., Mary Elizabeth Lewis Sheridan, Henrietta, Sarah and John Leary. Matthew Nathaniel Leary Jr. was a manufacturer, politician and government worker in Washington, D.C. He was the father of Libby, Sarah, Lucy and John Leary. Mary Elizabeth Leary married Dallas Perry, an architect and builder. She was an organist at St. Joseph Episcopal Church of Fayetteville, North Carolina. Their children excelled in their educational pursuits. Matthew Nathaniel IV was a physician in Fayetteville, North Carolina. Mary Elizabeth II was a music instructor at Fayetteville, North Carolina Teachers College. Dallas Leary Perry was a pharmacist and John Sinclair Leary Perry, a physician in Washington, D.C. John Sinclair Leary married Nannie B. Lathan. John was a very successful lawyer and politician. He was dean and founder of Shaw University's Law department. Leary served two terms in the North Carolina state legislature. John and Nannie Latham Leary were the parents of Hattie Beatrice, Henrietta Davis,

Nannie Ethel Syphax, Rose Graham Love, Matthew Nathaniel Leary IV and John S. Leary Jr.

Lewis Sheridan Leary, the son of Matthew Nathaniel Leary Sr., was born on March 17, 1835 in Fayetteville, North Carolina. It has been stated that when Lewis Sheridan observed a white slave master whipping his slave, he intervened and began to whip the white slave master. After this incident, Matthew Leary Sr. advised Lewis to leave Fayetteville, North Carolina. Immediately, he left for Oberlin, Ohio and began a trade as a saddler and harness maker. In 1858, he married Mary Simpson Patterson who was born in Fayetteville, North Carolina. She came to Oberlin to attend the Preparatory school of Oberlin College in 1857. When John Brown arrived in Oberlin to recruit some men for his Harpers Ferry Raid on October 16, 1859, one of his eighteen men was Lewis Sheridan Leary. Leary was wounded at Harpers Ferry and died from his wounds. His widow, Mary Patterson Leary in later years married Charles Langston, brother of former Virginia Congressman John Mercer Langston. Charles Langston assisted her in raising her daughter Louise or Lois whose father was Lewis Sheridan Leary. Leary was accompanied to Harpers Ferry by a close friend, John Anthony Copeland Jr. Copeland was the son of John Anthony Copeland Sr. and Deliah Evans, a sister of Henry and Wilson Bruce Evans. John Sr. was a carpenter and joiner from Raleigh, North Carolina. He worked on the North Carolina State House. John Sr. migrated to Oberlin, Ohio with his children in 1843. He and Deliah raised eight children. Two daughters were teachers and two sons were carpenters. A son William studied law and was a policeman in Little Rock, Arkansas. Deliah died in 1888 at 79 years of age. John died in 1894. John Anthony Copeland Jr. assisted his father and received an adequate education which enabled him to attend Oberlin's Preparatory department during the years 1854-1855. Copeland Jr. was a member of the Oberlin Anti-Slavery Society. He also participated in the Oberlin-Wellington Rescue. John Anthony Copeland Jr. survived the first stage of John Brown's Raid at Harpers Ferry. However, he was captured, tried by a jury and sentenced to be hanged. On December 16, 1859, John Anthony Copeland Jr. died of strangulation after being hung for his participation in the Harpers Ferry Raid.[12]

I have included the above discussion of the Leary-Evans families because it is the desire of the oldest known descendant of Wilson Bruce and Sarah Jane Leary Evans. They were the parents of Frances, Sarah Jane, Elizabeth, Julia Ann and Cornelius Evans. Frances and Elizabeth did not live until adulthood.

Sarah Jane was an outstanding student in high school and college. She graduated from high school in 1886. The graduating exercise program read:

Oberlin High School
First church
Friday June 11, 7 O'clock
Graduates of Classical course, ten students and
Graduates of Literary course, six students

The program consisted of organ, prayer music and student presentations.

One presentation was *The companion of Books by Sarah Jane Evans*. Sarah Jane graduated from Oberlin College in 1890. Her professor of Latin, L.B. Hall said that her years of training would fit her for successful work as a teacher. Sarah's professor of Moral Philosophy, John M. Ellis wrote that Sarah Jane Evans was a member of the fourth year class in the literary course. He said that she was a faithful student with the knowledge and acquirements of the course pursued. Sarah Jane had attained excellence in her pursuit of higher education and was prepared to obtain her desired goals in life.[13]

The Evans family was well respected in Oberlin's social circles as well as in the south among white and black friends. Wilson Bruce and Sarah Jane Leary Evans received several invitations from relatives and friends.

Wilson Bruce Evans' daughter Julia was a graduate of Oberlin and one of her class friends was a Mary Eliza Church. Wilson Bruce and his wife, Sarah Jane received an invitation from Mr. Robert R. Church of Memphis, Tennessee. The invitation read:

Mr. Robert R. Church requests your presence at the marriage of his daughter Mary Eliza to Mr. Robert Heberton Terrell, Wednesday, evening October, twenty-eight at six O'clock. 362 Lauderdale Street, Memphis, Tennessee.

A card was enclosed with the invitation that read:

Mr. and Mrs. Robert Heberton Terrell
at home 1415 Corcoran Street, Washington, D.C.[14]
Wednesday after November fifteenth

Thomas Sewell Inborden was living in the house of an industrious and distinguished family, the Evans. T.S. received a favorable response from Wilson Bruce Evans when he asked him for the hand of his daughter, Sarah Jane. T.S. and Sarah Jane were engaged on Saturday, July 2, 1887. During the summer of 1887, T.S. worked at a summer resort, Beebe House near Lake Erie, Put-In Bay Island, Ohio. The resort was owned by H. Beebe and sons and they accommodated four hundred guests. Inborden affectionately, referred to his future mother-in-law as *Mother Evans*. He wrote her a letter from the resort on September 5, 1887. T.S. said that he had received her card and that he was writing the letter in this office, because he wanted to give it to the bellboy for the evening mail. He was excited about a fishing boat trip that morning because he caught a very fine fish for her. His friends Hunter and Loeb were coming the next day and wanted him to go to Cleveland. However, T.S. said he would leave on the five O'clock train. Thursday, for Oberlin. He concluded his letter wishing the family well.[15] The cold winters in Oberlin were affecting T.S.'s health. It was necessary for him to leave Oberlin. Mr. Ingersoll of Cleveland gave T.S. half of his train fare to Nashville, Tennessee.

A Fisk Student Inborden arrived at Fisk university with only one dollar and twenty-five cents in 1887. On October 21, 1887, T.S. wrote a letter to Mrs. Sarah Jane Leary Evans. The letter read:

I suppose you have heard of my successful arrival. I like it here very well so far. Everything seems pretty much as Oberlin. The teacher and students are very sociable. The college is situated in a very pleasant place upon a very high hill. We can look over the entire city from the dormitory of our building (Livingston Hall). We do not have to go out of the building for anything except our meals and it is very pleasant. I am a freshman here. The class is very small consequently, we get the benefit of the recitation. We have had very good weather since I came here. The sun does not shine all the time, but it is warm. The mosquitoes are very large and are about to carry me off. They came near taking me out from under the bed clothes one night. I have to take care for my own room here. I am becoming an expert in domestic affairs. There is nothing here but prohibition all the time. There is one other student beside my self in the institution who is not a pro. I am lonesome here without the boys and my association there I felt like leaving home when I left there to come here. I think I shall always regard Oberlin as one of my dearest homes. I will not burden you with a long letter. Give my love to Mr. Evans, Dock, Sarah and all the boys. You must not work too hard this year and be sick again. Let the boys attend to their own rooms as I am doing. Tell Sarah to not study too hard. Tell Dock he must raise a big crop of corn in two years, I will come up and help him cut it. Write soon, your most respectively, T.S. Inborden.[16]

T.S. Inborden learned some good habits of thrift while studying at Fisk University. During his first year, he knew what it was to buy a dozen postage stamps. His sister sent him ten cents worth of stamps. Later, T.S. was able to find some work. In the summer he taught school in Davidson County, Tennessee and one summer he worked at the Beebe summer resort at Putin-Bay, Ohio.[17] In June 1888, T.S. attended a graduation exercise at Fisk. There was a week of activities for the graduates. Some of the activities were exhibition of the Senior Preparatory class, anniversary exercises of the literary societies, Missionary sermon, Baccalaureate sermon, Chapel worship and examination of classes, graduating exercises of Normal Department and Anniversary of Alumni Association, the Twenty-First Annual commencement exercises were held on Wednesday, June 13, 1888 at 10:00 a.m. One of T.S.'s classmates was a graduating senior. He was a young man who spoke on *Bismarck*, his name was listed on the program as William Edward Burghardt DuBois. In later years, DuBois would become a distinguished educator, historian, activist and scholar.[18]

Harriet Proctor Smith could not provide financial support for her son at Fisk but she did give him a mother's love and concern. On June 16, 1888 she wrote him a letter from Upperville, Virginia. She said that she had received his letter and was glad to hear from him. She further wrote:

I am glad to know that you were getting along so nicely with your school. Some days I feel for you while you are in school these warm days. It is very warm here now. I would have answered your letter before this time but Cecelia has been very busy in the cornfield here and the corn is looking nicely. We had it plowed over once and it is now ready to go into it again. I have not had to buy any corn this year. I was up to see Mary last Sunday and the children. They send their love to you and also they said that they received a letter from you but had not read it over. They said when you write to them again, please write it in plain English language because they do not understand any other language.

I received a letter from Ashton. He is well and doing well driving James Quackonon's carriage. He expects to come home this fall. His address is Edward A. Smith, Highspeed Dauphiniste, Pennsylvania. Did you know that Cecelia is twenty-one years old? Write soon. Yours, H. Proctor.[19]

Inborden was a very successful student at Fisk. The university issued his standing on a report card on September 5, 1889. The report card read:

Standing of T.S. Inborden

Arithmetic - written material	8 1/2
Grammar	9
Geography	7
U.S. History	9 1/2
Reading	9 1/2
Orthography	9
Penmanship	9

A.M. Cahill for Fisk University
Rev. E.M. Cravath, President[20]

T.S. Inborden had read a Missionary Magazine at Fisk University and prior to his graduation he wanted to engage in Christian work for the American Missionary Association. The American Missionary Association (AMA) was founded in 1846. Some of the early founders were William Jackson of Massachusetts, George Whipple, Ohio, Lewis Tappan, New York. The Executive committee members were Arthur Tappan, Theo S. Wright, Simeon S. Jocelyn, Amos A. Phelps, Charles B. Ray, S. E. Cornish, William H. Pillow, William E. Whiting, J.W.C. Pennington, and Edward Weed. Cornish and Pennington were free men of color. The AMA believed that all peoples must live by bodily labor and must be taught and trained to work, learn to do things by doing them and develop mental discipline. There was also a belief that the school was the mind, conscience and heart. The AMA felt people were in need for a race and the elevation of a race through Christian learning and education. In its early days, AMA started missions in Africa, Sandwich Islands, Jamaica, Siam, Egypt, Canada, and North America. When the Civil war ended, AMA had 532 Missionary teachers for blacks. The association believed that blacks needed an education that would eventually lead toward having their own educators and leaders. The AMA felt that no race should be dependent upon another race for its ultimate development. The association established a school under the protection of Union troops at Fort Monroe, Virginia for blacks after the Civil War. The AMA in its early days was able to establish industrial training, agriculture and handicraft programs for blacks. The AMA had organized many schools for blacks. Schools were opened for former slaves at Norfolk, Newport News, Portsmouth, Suffolk, and Yorktown, Virginia. There were schools opened in Beaufort, Hilton Head, St. Helena, and Port

Royal, South Carolina. Schools were also opened in Talledega, Alabama, Memphis, Tennessee, New Orleans and Port Hudson, Louisiana, Vicksburg and Natchez, Mississippi, Little Rock and Helena, Arkansas, Wilmington, North Carolina, Savannah, Georgia, Jacksonville, Florida, and Atlanta, Georgia. There were institutions of higher learning established by the AMA. Some of them were: Fisk University, Nashville, Tennessee, Atlanta University, Georgia, Avery and Straight Colleges, New Orleans, Louisiana, Tougaloo University, Mississippi, Howard University, Washington, D.C. and Tillotson Institute, Austin Texas. The association organized some normal schools at Charleston, South Carolina, LeMoyne School, Memphis, Tennessee, Gregory Normal, Wilmington, North Carolina, Lewis Normal, Macon Georgia, Emerson School, Mobile, Alabama, Beach Normal, Savannah, Georgia, Normal School, Lexington, Kentucky, Storks Atlanta, Georgia, Trinity, Athens, Alabama, Warner, Jonesboro, Brewer, Greenwood, South Carolina, Dorchester at McIntosh and Burrell at Selma, Alabama and Normal School at Williamsburg, Kentucky. This rich history of the American Missionary Association made a profound impression on T.S. Inborden because his future life would be centered around a dedicated and personal mission to follow the goals of this association.[21]

A Fisk University professor published a pamphlet in the early 1900's recognizing some outstanding graduates of Fisk in recent years. T.S. Inborden was included. There were the names and brief sketches of some of the women and men who were present at Fisk during T.S.' four years. They were possibly his friends or casual acquaintances. They were: W.E.B. DuBois, Thomas Julius Calloway, James Nathan Calloway, Maggie Murray Washington, James Dickens McCall, Thomas Washington Talley, Frank Gatewood Smith, Emma Jean Terry, Harriet F. Kimbro, Susan M. Harris, Henry Hugh Proctor, Matthew Elliott Stevens, John Lemuel Barbour, Andrew Piphney Neill, Thomas Porter Harris and John Turner Warren.[22]

After four years of study working part time, Inborden was able to attain his goal of receiving a college education. He had received an inspiration while living on the farm in Upperville, Virginia. T.S. wanted to improve his condition by studying and earning more money than fifteen cents a day. When T.S. arrived in Oberlin in 1883, in less than three months he was converted to a different view of life. Thomas Sewell Inborden, a former young man from the farm and mountains of Virginia who left home for Ohio at seventeen years of age with a third grade education proved not only to himself but to others that hard work and faith could overcome all obstacles that were before him. Inborden received the Bachelor of Arts degree from Fisk University in June 1891. T.S. was in debt to the university for books which nearly every teacher had furnished him. He had only 35 cents to pay his board for a week. This lasted five days as he brought five cents worth of cakes a day. When these provisions gave out, T.S. walked ten miles into the country to receive some assistance from friends. The Reverend Dr. A.F. Beard, Executive Secretary of the AMA asked Inborden to accept a position in Beaufort, South Carolina. T.S. accepted the offer. However, prior to leaving for South Carolina, he had a very high priority personal task to perform. T.S. Inborden had received enough finances to travel to Oberlin, Ohio, after his graduation. On September 24, 1891 was a blessed day for two young people who had prepared themselves academically, morally and spiritually to repeat their vows of matrimony. Sarah Jane Leary Evans and Wilson Bruce Evans were very proud to see their daughter marry a young intelligent man that the family had known. Sarah Jane Evans and Thomas Sewell Inborden were married in an Oberlin church by a former college professor and Ambassador to the Republic of South America. Rev. James Monroe. After the wedding, Sarah Jane had accepted a teaching position in the south. She taught briefly at a school in Greenwood, South Carolina and was the only black faculty member. T.S. returned to Nashville where he prepared to leave for his assignment. Dr. Beard had written the treasurer of Fisk University and asked him to give Inborden traveling expenses to Beaufort, South Carolina.[23]

A Young Missionary

Even though T.S. Inborden was not an ordained minister of the gospel, he was assigned to a congregational church in Beaufort, South, Carolina as pastor. He preached there for three months. Dr. A.F. Beard was a very influential Executive Secretary of AMA. Beard was a good speaker, had pastored a church in Bath, Maine and had met Senator Charles Summer in 1859. The Reverend Dr. Beard asked T.S. to accept another position because he wanted him to serve as principal of a school in Helena, Arkansas. Inborden, after reorganizing the school in Arkansas, was asked to go to Albany, Georgia, seat of George Chitauqua and serve as principal of the AMA school. The Fisk Herald, October, 1893 had a statement about T.S.'s new position:

Mr. Inborden goes to Albany, Georgia. He called on us on his way down and renewed his subscription. Mr. Inborden will be assisted by Mrs. Inborden. He has a promising future before him and we are confident of his success.[24]

Inborden needed someone to teach the little children in the Albany School. He wanted to employ a lady named Mrs. Alice Davis of Oberlin, Ohio. When T.S. was a student at Oberlin, she gave him board for morning devotions. He was also given a job to make some money by Mrs. Davis' brother-in-law. It was a time when T.S. was not too well and needed money. Inborden said that he had made up his mind that if ever the chance came, he would thank her for her kindness. When he was visiting Oberlin after graduation from Fisk, he learned that Mrs. Davis' husband had died. She was in great need and her education was limited in finding a good job. T.S. recommended Mrs. Davis to the AMA New York office to teach the young children. The AMA headquarters did not want to appoint her because of her education and no experience in the class room. T.S. boarded a train for New York and met his superiors and insisted on the appointment of Mrs. Alice Davis. He stated that Mrs. Davis could perform the job, she was refined and had an excellent cultural bearing. He was successful in receiving approval of her appointment. Mrs. Davis served at the Albany school for four years and later would work for T.S. Inborden at another Normal school for twenty-eight years.[25] T.S. was able to find time in his busy schedule at Albany, Georgia to have some concerns for his family in Virginia. He received a letter from his niece, M. Saunders, the daughter of his sister Mary. She thanked him for a beautiful dress he sent her and had received it in time for the opening of her school. His sister and her family lived in Markham, Virginia.[26]

T.S. Inborden, during the early days of his career, had the experience of learning how some so called liberal whites dealt with educated blacks. He was attending the AMA's Forty-Eight Annual meeting at the First Congressional church, Lowell, Massachusetts in October, 1884. Inborden happen to explain a situation that occurred in a letter he wrote to his wife from Massachusetts, October 24, 1894.

My Dearest Sarah, it is now about 11:00 p.m. and as sleepy and tired as I am I must drop you a few lines. Today has been a great day. I was made so mad this afternoon that I was sick by Dr. Beard and Woodbury. If I am a Negro, I am not going to be humiliated. I told Mr. Ryder that I was not going to make a fool of myself up here in Massachusetts before the AMA where the newspaper men six or eight were putting down every word.

I prepared a paper to be read on the subject as requested by Dr. Beard. Just before I went to sit upon the platform with all the speakers both of these men, one at a time came to me and told me that they wanted me to speak off handed. All the other speakers spoke from their papers, even Dr. Beard and President Cravath, who preceded me and so did I. I am Inborden North and South. But I have in consolidation that I made a big hit. The house applauded me three times and President Gates came to his feet almost and emphasized a certain point in my paper and that part he read again. I received high congratulations from men whose judgement means something. Dr. Woodbury took my paper as soon as I was seated to have it published. I send you papers every day, you will find it in some of them especially the one that comes out in the morning. I ordered it to be sent to you. Love to all, kiss the baby, Your own, T.S. Inborden.[27]

While in Massachusetts in 1894, Inborden met Frederick Douglass, the distinguished abolitionist, orator and statesman. T.S. spoke from the same platform with Douglass. While Frederick Douglass was speaking, T.S. overheard a white man say *Faith, if a half Negro can make such a speech when one or a whole Negro can not.* That was probably the stereotype or mental thought of some white people as early as 1894 and in the New England so called liberal states.

The Georgia Congressional Association held its sixteenth Annual session in Thomasville, Georgia, November 14-18, 1894 at the Bethany Congressional church, pastored by Reverend Charles F. Sargent. Inborden appeared on the program along with Reverend J.H.H. Senstacke, Savannah, Georgia and Reverend H.H. Proctor of Atlanta, Georgia.[28]

T.S. Inborden received a very heartbreaking letter in June, 1895, from L. J. Saunders, his brother-in-law. He had to inform T.S. of the death of his sister, Mary. The letter details the possible causes of her demise. Saunders wrote:

Dear Brother, with feelings of deep emotion, I have to inform you the death of my dear and beloved wife who departed this life on the morning of June 1st about 2:40 a.m., after having been sick about two weeks. It is impossible to give an intelligent account of her illness. As my feelings are too much lacerated to attempt to do so. But will do the best I can.

Mary was confined on the 10th of May and gave birth to a fine healthy child and all seemed accomplished with best results. But on the eleventh day after, she was suddenly stricken with what the doctor pronounced, milk leg and her suffering may be better imagined than told by me. She however, bore her troubles well and grew much better, and the doctor was telling us she was on the road to recovery and that in time would be well again. But on or about midnight of May 31st, the disease took hold of the right leg. She could not stand this extra misery and died in about 28 hours after. The doctor tried to give me an explanation of the cause of her death taking off which is of course but little comfort.

The doctor said that my darling had some little heart trouble being too weak to stand the extra duty forced upon it death was inevitable. She was buried at her old home, yours as well on Sunday evening last. We had no time nor convenience to preach the funeral. I have left it to your mother to appoint a day to have this done as to select the preacher Gabriel Bannister, I think will be the right man. Now Sewell I have given you as well as I can the sad side of this more than sad story. Now let me give you what you must consider with me the bright and beautiful side as well. My poor darling died as happy as it is possible for any poor mortal to die. She left us proclaiming her redemption by the Savior and she was married to Jesus, ready and willing to die. Oh, while my soul was harrowed to witness her great suffering, it was also delighted to behold her happiness. She called all the children each by name to her bed side, and shook hands and kissed them. She bade them be good and honorable and try to meet her in heaven.

My pen fails me to my feelings and all this was done between gasps for breath and the most intrinsic torture I ever witness who put one resurrected from perdition by an almighty power and have done this love a thousand years. I shall never forget this scene. Please come and see us when you come to Virginia. Mother has the baby which was three weeks old at its mother's death. Your brother, L.J. Saunders.[29]

T.S. grieved very deeply over the death of his sister Mary. In a letter to his wife, Sarah Jane, he told her that he knew Mary was better off and he did not see why it hurts him so to think of her as gone. But he had some pain relieved when his mother wrote him and said that Mary had died with hope in Christ.[30]

CHAPTER 2

Genesis of a School

While Inborden was continuing his work at the Albany Normal School, there were some chain of events occurring that would affect the future years of his life in a most challenging way. A Mrs. Julia Brewster Brick was in attendance at Clinton Avenue Congregational church in Brooklyn, New York and heard a Sunday morning guest speaker. He was William Sinclair of Fisk University and was the financial agent for Howard University, Washington, D.C. After the benediction, she introduced herself to Mr. Sinclair and congratulated him on his address *How Negroes Were Eager For an Education*. She told Mr. Sinclair that she owned a farm in North Carolina and wanted to use the land to build a school for poor *colored* children who could not attend other schools. Dr. Sinclair informed her that he would discuss the matter with President of Howard and former Union Army General, Oliver Otis Howard. General Howard visited Mrs Brick in Brooklyn, New York and informed her that she should contact the AMA. Howard arranged a meeting with the AMA treasurer, H.W. Hubbard and Mrs. Brick. The meeting was successful because Mrs. Brick agreed to develop a plan for AMA to accept her financial contributions and real estate. Her lawyer, George Ingraham prepared the documents to transfer the real estate (farm 1129 acres) to the AMA and a cash contribution of $5,000 dollars. Mrs. Julia Brick was a widow. Her late husband, Joseph Keasbey Brick was an electrical engineer who had acquired his wealth mainly in the south. He built reservoirs and permanent structures in the area of Enfield, North Carolina. Mr. Brick invested his money into municipal and public enterprises and the value had increased greatly by 1895. Mrs. Brick was a caring, well read, informed, poise and a dedicated person. She was a philanthropist who supported several hospitals in Brooklyn. She was not a college graduate. Julia Brick obtained this land through her generosity in assisting a relative. It was during the Civil War that a Union General Estes assigned to General O.O. Howard's command had marched through the cities of North Carolina, Fayetteville, Raleigh, New Bern, Kinston and Rocky Mountain into the area of Enfield, North Carolina. Estes was fascinated by the scenic surrounding and the land. After the Civil War, General Estes returned to Enfield and purchased the Garrett farm, 1429 acres for $60,000 dollars. The farm was owned by Charles, Paul and Joe Garrett. Paul was a manufacturer of the Virginia Dare extracts and prosperous banker. The land had previously been owned by a Mason Wiggins.

General Estes cultivated cotton, corn, peaches, strawberries and vegetables. He used a railroad side track to ship his products north. The farm venture was unsuccessful for Estes. He became heavily in debt and asked his relative, Mrs. Brick for assistance. She gave him thousands of dollars and later it was necessary for her to assume ownership of the farm. The farm included a mansion, overseer house and twenty dilapidated one-room cabins.[1]

A young dedicated educator of thirty years of age in 1895, was selected by the AMA's Executive Secretary Beard to become the founder or architect of a school three miles from the town of Enfield, North Carolina. His superb performance in Helena, Arkansas and Albany, Georgia, definitely contributed to Beard's wise choice and of course, this man was Thomas Sewell Inborden. The town of Enfield, North Carolina had few stores in 1895. The citizens were still using kerosene oil to light lamps. Later the area would get electricity from the Virginia and Carolina Electric plant. The streets were winding with some mud holes. The population was around 300 citizens. On August 1, 1895, T.S. embarked from train 81 around noon at Enfield, North Carolina. He had a light lunch of sardines and crackers at S. Meyer's store. The Meyer store sold dry goods, groceries, hardware, and wearing apparel. The store was located in the old Aesop Brick Building. Mr. Meyers displayed a great interest in the newcomer to Enfield. He escorted T.S. to the Estes farm in his horse and carriage. T.S. could observe an unfinished building as they approached the farm. This was the first constructed building for the future school. It was about two-thirds finished. There were no windows, or doors, just holes and walls. The first night at the farm. T.S. slept on an old dining room table on the second floor of the building. In the immediate area he could see snakes, cats, wild dogs, and there were many mosquitoes. At night he could hear dog fights, cat squalls, screeching owls, whippoorwills and mosquitos songs. In 1895, there were eighteen tenant farm houses on the farms. The majority of the inhabitants were infected with malaria and typhoid fever. T.S. found in the old wells, water melon rinds, frogs, terrapins and snakes. He purchased a briar scythe and cleared the weeds and bushes. Inborden also purchased some shovels pipes and pumps to fill up the cess pools and installed sanitary pumps. T.S. learned that there was not a single black within five miles of the farm that owned their land. After the first building was completed T.S. made a trip to new York to obtain equipment at a reduced rate. The local merchants had told him that they could not do business with him for less than five percent deduction. He was able to obtain a better percentage in New York from large stores and wholesale houses. A carload of equipment was shipped to Enfield for the school. While visiting New York, T.S. had the opportunity to meet Mrs. Brick for the first time. He was invited to her residence at Lafayette and Vanderbilt Streets, Brooklyn, New York. T.S. met a very gracious lady who conversed with him as though she had known him for years. He realized that this first meeting had eliminated all fears and anticipations. Mrs. Brick asked T.S. what was the final cost of the first building minus equipment, he replied six thousand dollars. She then gave him some more money for the school. A decision was made to name the new school in honor of Mrs. Bricks' late husband, Joseph Keasbey Brick Agricultural, Industrial and Normal School. Mrs. Brick asked T.S. about the Enfield community, churches, race relations, farms and available public schools for black children. Upon his return to Enfield, Inborden made arrangements for a post office that would be called Bricks, North Carolina. The AMA office in New York sent T.S. five teachers to assist him in the opening of the school. The teachers were cooperative, loyal and sacrificing. The school had fifty-four students the first year.

Mrs. Julia B. Brick was able to visit the school in 1896 with Dr. Beard, AMA Executive Secretary and her niece, Miss Lydia Benedict. She was quite impressed with the progress made by Inborden. Mrs. Brick observed how the one building was being used for the boys, girls, and teachers' dormitory, laundry, kitchen, dining and class rooms. This was quite inadequate for her. She saw many ignorant people in the surrounding community. After seeing the school's one old mule standing outside in the cold, she suggested that some barns and stables were needed. On a second visit to the school, Mrs. Brick believed the school needed a recitation hall and a boy's dormitory. She gave ten thousand dollars for the construction of Brewster Hall and later gave twelve thousand dollars for the building of another hall. Mrs. Brick's lawyer, Attorney Ingraham donated five thousand dollars for the construction of Ingraham Chapel. T.S. was also fortunate to obtain money for the construction of some other buildings in later years.[1] The landscape of the developing campus was improved when Mrs. Brick sent plants and seeds that she believed could grow there. The physical plant of Brick School would eventually include Benedict Hall, a girls dormitory located in a former cotton field, Elma Hall, for recitations, built in the exact spot occupied previously by the former masters of some 200 slaves, Ingraham Hall, the Chapel, and Beard Hall, which housed 82 students, offices, a library, store houses for vegetables, and storage space for light tools, and wagons. There was also constructed a manual training shop where tools were pressed for work in wood and iron. Students were required to attend classes once a day in the shop.[2]

In the fall of 1895, Inborden was presented with a tax bill for the school's property, 57 dollars from officials of the county. T.S. realized that the AMA and the new school was a philanthropic organization and not a profit venture. He believed the school should be exempt from taxes. At the time T.S. received the bill, he was ill in bed with malarial fever. He sent his farm manager, Mr. J.L. Watkins to Tarboro Court House to meet the County Board of Commissioners and explain to them the objectives of the school. T.S. had learned that the political elections for the city and county officials were to take place and there were many conscientious office seekers. Surprisingly, most blacks were enjoying their citizenship prerogatives at the voting precincts. After a church service one night, twelve black citizens met with Inborden around 11:00 p.m. at the resident of John Jones. Jones was a graduate of Oberlin College, class of 1856. He had worked in the gold mines in British Columbia and was well versed on many subjects. They discussed at the meeting politics and the school's tax problem. Inborden stated that if he could not reach the boss directly he knew the way to the back door and could talk to the cook, because the cook always had the ear of the boss. T.S. was comfortable at the meeting because he had confidence in his friends and he knew the background of John Jones. Jones was a fine northern bred man who knew how to adapt to the conditions of the south. His wife was an Oberlin graduate and the aunt of the distinguished violinist and composer of color, Clarence Cameron White. The black citizens of influence that were present at the meeting assured T.S. that he had their fullest support. They also gave him advice on how to approach the all white members of the Board of Commissioners on the school's tax problem.

Inborden had a meeting with the commissioners and they suggested a compromise. A suggestion was made to tax all the farm area and exempt only the classroom equipment and tax 500 acres of land east of the county road. T.S. did not accept these suggestions. He told the commissioners that every inch of the farm was to be used for school purposes as much as a map hanging on the walls and if they taxed any part of it they would have the same right to tax all of it. Inborden said that if he did not collect rents from the tenants, he could not continue operation of the school. When the AMA in New York learned about the tax problems, they hired Attorney Thomas of New Bern, North Carolina to represent Inborden. Thomas and the County's lawyer, John Bridges were able to reach an understanding of the tax problem. They believed that taxing the school was a hardship, however, the AMA would pay the taxes if necessary. Inborden did not agree with this decision and he decided to meet personally with some board commissioners, namely Orman Williams, Chairman, Joshua Horne Jr., Winfield Ruffin, and Mark Battle. Williams said that he would consider T.S.' request. Horne promised Inborden that he would support his proposition and try to convince the other members. Ruffin owned a farm near the school. The school had purchased corn from Mr. Ruffin and paid him immediately. T.S. believed Ruffin would support a motion to exempt the entire school farm from taxation. However, Mark Battle was a direct opposite of Ruffin who represented the *Boss Class* and had a limited education. Battle was a real aristocrat and well educated. He was a cousin of Attorney Tom Battle of New York and Dr. Kemp Battle of State College, North Carolina. Mark Battle was married to a lady who was a Garrett. The Garretts owned land at Crowder Mountain and Kings Mountain. It was during the Civil War that livestock was driven from the farms and hidden in those mountains. T.S. remarked that he personally met one of the former slaves who helped to drive the cattle to the mountains. While discussing the family background of the Battles, T.S. wrote that Dr. Beard of the AMA office was visiting Brick school and it was mistaken identity when he met one of the Battles. Beard was sitting in a room with one of the teachers, Miss Dowell and Mark Battle's son Cullen Battle. During the conversation between Mr. Beard and Cullen Battle, Beard was talking to him as though he believed he was talking to a black person. Miss Dowell became concerned and told Beard that he was talking to a white man. Dr. Beard replied and said yes, yes, I understand, he could be a colored man and still be Mr. Mark Battle's son. This was quite an observation in 1895 because the statement by Mr. Beard was a realistic fact. T.S. continued his discussion about Mark Battle in stating that the Civil War had caused Battle to lose everything but his farm and his aristocratic spirit. When the school wanted to buy some Jersey cows and heard Battle had some they purchased the cows from him and also chickens and butter. Therefore, using his tact and his method of approaching these commissioners T.S. was able to approach them as a friend and a business customer. Inborden persistence paid off because Chairman Williams said the matter was a clear case of charity and that the entire school should be exempt from taxes. Then Joshua Horne Jr. made a motion and Mark Battle and Winfield Ruffin concurred. Brick school paid no taxes to the county for the next forty years.[3]

   The Executive Secretary of the AMA was visiting some of the schools and churches of the association in 1896 and he was impressed by the progress at Brick School. He expressed his thoughts in an article in the Association's publication, *American Missionary*. He wrote that it is a long journey from New York to Enfield, North Carolina where one will not find a New England village. When we leave the Weldon and Wilmington Railway, it is quite another part of the world. Beard said a ride of four miles among plantations and cotton fields will bring you to the latest born of the Association's school, now one year old, Brick School. He also gave a sketch of its founder T.S. Inborden in the article.[4]

During the organization of the school, T.S. had another important responsibility and that was giving time and love to his family. On August 10, 1893, Sarah Jane and T.S. Inborden were the proud parents of their first child, Julia Ella Inborden. They also purchased a house in Oberlin in 1894. The house was next door to Sarah Jane's family home. They rented the house to the Champ family for many years. A baby boy was born to the Inbordens on November 12, 1894 and unfortunately died on February 12, 1895. In January 1897, the Inbordens were blessed with the birth of a healthy baby girl on the 28th day. They named her Dorothy Viola Inborden. Sarah Jane Inborden received a letter from her mother in Oberlin, Ohio on December 21, 1897. Her mother had received her letter and the black eyed peas. She said that Sarah's father, Wilson Bruce Evans was not too well. Sarah Jane's mother was concerned about baby Julia Ella. She reminded her daughter to be careful about taking the baby outside unless she has her wrapped very well with warm clothes. She was also saving some pennies for her grandchild. The letter included a hand made linen dolly. The dolly is still in good condition 98 years later.[5] A baby boy, Sewell Evans was born on July 28, 1898 and he died on May 18, 1899. However, as the Inbordens were saddened by the death of their baby boy, joy did come in the morning. Because on August 15, 1898, a blessed event did occur, the birth of a healthy son that they named Wilson Bruce Inborden.[6]

Reverend George A. Moore wrote an article for the *American Missionary*. The article stated that the Joseph K. Brick School at Enfield, North Carolina had celebrated its 4th anniversary in 1899. Moore mentioned that many changes had taken place at the school since his last visit to Enfield. He said several buildings were added to the physical plant. They were a large three story boys dormitory equipped with bathrooms, and reading room. There was also the constitution of a teachers home, a two story brick workshop for carpentry and blacksmithing, and a large equipped frame barn. George A. Moore was able to see how the students work on the farm during the day and attend school at night.[7]

The Inbordens started the new century with some sadness. A baby boy name George Martin was born on October 20, 1900 and he died on April 12, 1901. Another baby boy was born on November 6, 1901 and died as an infant[8].

CHAPTER 3

Brick's Beginning Years

The Joseph K. Brick Normal and Industrial school had been operating for five years in 1900. T.S. and his staff had prepared a curriculum and operating plan that was showing improvement each year. There was a climate of discipline, morals and culture that was present at the new school in Enfield, North Carolina. The school was now identified with its own location name, Bricks, North Carolina.

T.S. had stated that the purpose of Brick was to teach students how to do things the best way in the community where they may live and he stressed agricultural education along with a basic academic curriculum. Inborden prepared a detailed brochure for prospective students. The brochure contained some interesting information about the school and expectations and requirements for the students. The curriculum in 1901 included an academic program, domestic science, manual arts, agriculture and education courses. The grade levels were primary (1-3), Intermediate (4-5) grammar (6-8) and Normal (9-12). There was a night school and three terms, fall, winter and spring. The primary courses available were reading, numbers, language, writing, drawing, music, arithmetic, nature studies, geography, oral language, and writing compositions. The intermediate courses included the subjects of reading, spelling arithmetic, geography, writing, United States history, health sciences, and classical literature for eight grade students. The students were required to improve their communications by presenting declamations, recitations and writing assignments on current events. T.S. emphasized that there must be quality rather than quantity. Students on the secondary level (9-12 grades) could select some of their subjects. They were able to select courses in dress making, cooking, gardening, horticulture, laundry techniques, agriculture, carpentry, and mechanical drawing. T.S.'philosophy of the importance of daily attendance and the priority of learning was that anyone coming to Brick in bad faith takes the place of someone who might come in good faith. If you can not come in good faith, remarked, Inborden, do not come. This philosophy could be used today, 1995 in many of our schools. The brochure informed students that they must include with their application, references indicating their reputation for honesty reliability, truthfulness and good morality.[1]

Inborden and his faculty had a rigid time schedule for the students and it supported a goal for teaching the students responsibility, punctuality, and the importance of time. A Reverend R.R. Johns wrote an article in the American Missionary, *What They Ring For*. He quoted Edgar Allen Poe and said *Bells, bells, bells, bells, bells, bells, bells*. T.S. Inborden's bell schedule for the Brick school was:

5:00-9:30 p.m. - The students and faculty adhered to this schedule.
5:00 a.m. - A waking bell.
6:00 a.m. - Second bell, the student went to breakfast and

	after their meal, they returned to their rooms and prepared for daily morning chapel services.
7:30 a.m. -	Students were allowed a half hour to prepare for study recitations.
8:20 a.m. -	A five minute bell for students to report to the chapel. They would march into the chapel to the music played by Mr. A.H. Brown. In the chapel, the students would sing a song, recite a prayer, and there receive a brief message by Principal Inborden or the school chaplain. At the conclusion of chapel services, the students, would march out of the chapel and proceed to their classrooms.
11:45 a.m.	A bell rings for the young farm students to report to the dining room for dinner.
12:15 p.m.	A bell summons the students and teachers to the dining room for dinner.
1:00 p.m. -	A bell rings for the students to report to classes for recitation and manual labor classes.
3:00 p.m. -	A bell rings to announce the end of classes for the day. Students would participate in some sports activities after classes. They would enjoy baseball, basketball, croquet, tennis, cycling, and boating.
5:30 p.m. -	A farm bell rings for the farm work students to conclude their day.
6:00 p.m. -	A bell rings for all students and faculty to report to the dining hall for supper.
7:00 p.m. -	A bell rings for all day students to participate in a two hour study hall. The night students would report to their respective classes.
9:00 p.m. -	The ringing of this bell dismisses the night school students from class and day students from their study hours.
9:30 p.m. -	The last bell of the day rings for all students in the dormitories to cut off all lights in their rooms.[1]

The significance of the bells at Brick school is that all of the students were able to develop a sense of discipline, responsibility and punctuality during their matriculation at the school. These were the characteristics of Inborden's philosophy of education and his method of management of the school.

The Brick students extra curriculum activities were musical programs, public rhetoricals and socials in which the local townspeople were invited. The young ladies participated in the young women training union and the young men had a bible class. On Sunday, all students were required to attend Sunday school and church services at 11:00 a.m. As early as the 1900's, T.S. Inborden required all students to pay their board and tuition monthly. Some students could use work credits for their tuition and board. Students of sixteen years and over were allowed to work. The daily record of their work hours were maintained by their supervisor. The night school program started by T.S. was an early concept of the present day night classes or continuing education. The young ladies performed work duties in the dining room, kitchen, laundry and general housekeeping. The young men performed work duties in gardening, farming, campus cleaning and custodial tasks. Brick students who traveled to Enfield, North Carolina by train would use the Atlantic Coast Line trains. They stopped at Bricks on signal. Trains 80 and 89 would stop by the special authority of the train dispatcher. The young ladies were not permitted to stop enroute to or from school except for train connections.[2] This was definitely an early form of discipline that students were required to respect.

Sarah Jane Inborden received a letter from Jeannette Norvell Keeble on April 27, 1901. Mrs. Keeble was Sarah Jane's colleague at Albany Normal School in Georgia. Keeble expressed her sorrow about the death of the Inborden's baby in 1901. She hoped the family liked a jacket they received from her for little Dorothy Viola. Mrs. Keeble suggested that Julia Ella Inborden should begin training in music as soon as possible. Ironically, Julia Ella did mature in later years as an accomplished musician. Keeble closed her letter by stating that Mr. Inborden had always been kind to her and that she could never forget him and felt that she could not do enough for him or anything that belong to him.[3]

T.S. Inborden was able to have some very illustrious people to visit his campus in 1902. On May 27, 1902, the faculty and students were honored with the presence of Mrs. Mary Church Terrell and later they had a visit by George Eastman, the photographic magnate. Eastman owned a hunting lodge fifteen miles west of Enfield, North Carolina.

Inborden often would tell the story of three children whose sincere desire for an education was portrayed in their walking eight miles daily to Brick school. Later, the family was able to move on the school tenant farm area. The children attended school daily and worked their parents' crops at night. This family had one cow which furnished sufficient milk to pay their children's tuition and books for six years. T.S. said in a humorous manner, the same cow gave milk for nine consecutive years without a vacation. One of the children was able to enroll at Talledega College, Talledega, Alabama.[4] Enfield, North Carolina is a considerable distance from Cementville, Indiana. However, Sarah Jane Inborden and her sister, Julia A. (Pet) Inborden Johnson were able to communicate with each other through the writing of letters. Julia or, Pet, as she was affectionately called, wrote Sarah Jane a letter on March 16, 1903. She was concerned about the family's estate in Oberlin, Ohio. Their parents had died five years prior to 1903 and their Uncle Cornelius (or Neal) was living in the house. Pet stated very emphatically that she wanted the house sold or Uncle Neal could purchase the estate. She wanted her share immediately. Ironically, this did not occur at that time, because T.S. and Sarah Jane were able to keep in contact with Uncle Cornelius and upon his death, T.S. continued paying the yearly taxes. Today at this writing and in 1995, this family estate in Oberlin, Ohio is a National Heritage Home and the summer residence of T.S. Inborden's surviving daughter, Dorothy Viola.[5] T.S. was interested in assisting the local farmers and in 1900, he had a farmers' meeting and was able to learn how some of them were using different farm methods. He was surprised when several farmers stated that they were using ox teams to plow their lands. The farmer said they used oxes because they did not have to feed the animals because they would turn them loose in the woods to roam for food.

The year of 1903 started with an unfortunate message that was received by the Brick family. The distinguished and grateful benefactor of this maturing school, Julia Elma Brewster Brick had died. Inborden told the faculty and students of Brick that Mrs. Julia Elma Brick had contributed eight years ago to the birth of the school. He said her sincerity, interest, concern and humility all contributed to her earnest desire to improve the conditions of black people in eastern North Carolina. T.S. stated that her philanthropies were the joy of her declining years, and her life was not an accident and she was in union with the spirit of Christ and the school.

T.S. Inborden and the faculty at Brick School published a school paper, the *Joseph K. Brick News*. The school paper contained information on diverse subjects. The articles in the papers have been very helpful in learning about the school's early years of activities. An article written by Inborden in 1904 gave an inventory of the farm's productive season. Some of the tenants owned their horses, cows, hogs and poultry. The school farm was able to produce 350 barrels of corn, valued at $1,050, 996 bushels of peanuts, $796, 379 sweet potatoes, $190, 23,401 pounds of fodder, $192, 187 gallons of syrup, $78, and garden produce consisting of cabbage, turnips, white potatoes, peas and beans. There were 110 pigs, valued at $660, 7 cows, 11 horses, and mules, 80 turkeys, valued at $80, 839 chickens, $210, 303 dozen eggs, 15 cents a dozen. The farm workers planted 500 fruit trees of peaches in 5 years.[6]

Brick school was receiving publicity and recognition from newspaper and magazine articles. The Guardian newspaper of Boston, Massachusetts published an interesting article about Brick school. The editor of the newspaper was an outstanding journalist and activist, Monroe Trotter. The April 23, 1904 edition printed a front page article on the Tar Heel State, North Carolina. The article included a picture of T.S. with the caption.

A capable and energetic principal of Joseph K. Brick School. The article said North Carolina is unique from the fact that there are more high grade colleges and universities for the higher education of the Negro than in any other state in the Union.

The Guardian newspaper included a very praise worthy assessment of Brick School and its principal. The article read:

The Joseph K. Brick Agricultural and Industrial Normal School at Enfield, North Carolina of which T.S. Inborden, one of the ablest graduates of Fisk University is principal. This is a young school, being started in 1895 by Principal Inborden. But it has had a marvelous growth. It owns a farm of 1129 acres of land and with the exception of Union University in Richmond, Virginia has finer buildings than any other colored school in the south. With an able and practical representative of what the higher education can do for a Negro, the school has the finest graduates of Oberlin and other leading southern colleges and universities of the south and a graduate of the University of Chicago as teachers. There treasurer is Isadore Martin. The school received an endowment of a quarter million dollars, the generous bequest of Mrs. Julia Elma Brewster Brick. The possibilities before the school are almost unlimited. Although trained in Greek and Latin,

Principal Inborden has been a successful organizer of several schools and superintended the construction of the great school windmill and water tank. Where he got his mechanical skill, he replies studying Greek and Latin at Fisk University.[7]

A distinguished clergyman, Francis J. Grimke wrote some prophetic news about the future of Brick school in the May, 1904 *American Missionary*. Grimke and his brother Archibald Henry were the children of a white wealthy planter from Charleston, South Carolina, Henry Grimke and a slave woman, Nancy Weston. The Grimke brothers received their education in the north. Archibald graduated from Harvard University's Law school and Francis James graduated from Princeton Theological Seminary. After graduation, Francis J. Grimke became the pastor of Washington, D.C.'s prestigious 15th Street Presbyterian church. In later years, two white women who were abolitionist in Boston, Massachusetts acknowledged the fact that they were the aunts of the two Grimke brothers, because they were the sisters of Henry Grimke, Archibald stayed in the residence of Angelina Grimke Weld when he was attending Harvard and also visit his other Aunt Sara Moore Grimke. Francis Grimke was one of the founders of the American Negro Academy in 1897. He was married to Charlotte Forten. This outstanding minister wrote these remarks:

On a visit to Brick School, I was impressed and believed the school is a blessing in the part which it is destined to play in the solution of the vexed race problem. It will help to educate men and women of the colored race to become intelligent and worthy citizens of the republic and of the state and will also help by the character of the work which it is doing. The school is modifying public sentiment in the south in regard to the capabilities of the Negro and his fitness for citizenship. It is impossible to plant such a school in a community without affecting favorably both classes of citizens the whites as well as the blacks.[8] Ironically, Grimke's last sentences supported the earnest efforts that Inborden was doing, accomplishing some wonders that did affect both communities in their separate societies.

T.S. wrote an article on the *Facts On Joseph K. Brick Agricultural and Normal School in 1904*. He stated where the school was located and gave some descriptive characteristics of the community and people. He said a minister told him that he never encouraged his congregation to purchase a home and to educate their children for those who did so would not support the gospel. Inborden wrote that some black graduates from the best schools of the south do not support them as they should, not from lack of loyalty but because they too are trying to get comfortable homes. T.S. said most educated Negroes tried to get a home and have better things. Inborden explained how the white community reacted when Brick school started. He stated that there was a great deal of prejudice against it on part of both races. One white friend told the school faculty recently that he thought it would be a mess, possibly he said this because he had only communicated with some rude elements of the race and his prejudices were born on convictions. T.S. said the prejudice hurt the school very much. Inborden described some accomplishments of the school. He wrote that there were seven renters on the farm and their wives were hired out as cooks. The students have been very industrious. They hauled materials for the buildings, raised corn, and feed for the farm animals, provided wood, hauled coal, performed janitorial chores, cultivated gardens, cared for the cattle, cooked and completed house cleaning duties.[9]

In 1995, many black leaders are sensitive to the recent Supreme Court rulings that will affect the African American especially in view of the legislative gains that have been accomplished since the 1960's. However, in 1903, black leaders throughout the country were concerned about the race problem in America and an understanding between the races. The National Sociological Society convened a Washington, D.C. Conference on the race problems in the United States. Sessions were held at the Lincoln Temple Congregational church, Nineteenth street Baptist Church and the Metropolitan A.M.E. church, November 9-12, 1903. T.S. Inborden was a member of the Committee on Education, National Sociological Society. He was present at the meeting and delivered a brief speech. He told the audience that Brick covers considerable territory, 1,429 acres and had 24 head of horses and mules, students have made 210 gallons of molasses, and grown potatoes, turnips, onions and other produce. He said they teach the youth how to farm, manual training, young ladies how to cook, sew and we do not neglect book work. T.S. reminded the society members that they teach temperance, and the moral life. T.S.' Inborden's picture and a full page of information on Brick School was present in the published proceedings of the conference. The information on the full page stated that Brick was organized with five teachers and one student and the total enrollment for 1903 was 230 students with 140 students boarders and the school had 20 buildings.[10]

Thomas Swell Inborden was a correspondent in the sense that he wrote letters very frequently. His letters were brief and lengthy at times. He wrote to his family, friends, parents, students, AMA officials and new acquaintances. T.S. was a good and interesting writer. His letters would portray his message to the writer, inform and educate others on his recurring experiences at Brick school. These letters have a rare primary source in telling the Inborden story as it really happened. Some of the letters date back to 1880. T.S. would write his frank and earnest thoughts and sometimes he was very direct if he was asking for a personal request that would benefit Brick school. This characteristic of Inborden was evident in a letter he wrote to the photographic magnate, George Eastman of Rochester, New York. T.S. wanted some financial assistance for the school, another building and he wanted Eastman to provide the money needed for construction and name the building in Eastman's honor. Inborden stated his request very clearly in a lengthy letter to Eastman:

I came here yesterday morning with the express purpose of taking the boat in the afternoon to enter the Harvard sumner school. I brought with me plans for the new dormitory to take place of Brewster Hall, that burned. When I presented the plan to the secretaries of the office of the AMA, I was told that the insurance was only eight thousand dollars on the building and that they would not build our dormitory and the domestic science hall.

We need the dormitory and a domestic science hall. I was told that if both halls were built, I must raise five thousand dollars for the domestic science hall. We have realized from Mrs. Brick's estate about

90,000 dollars. We can not use the principal and as a business man you will readily see that this is a nice nucleus of an endowment and to use it would cripple the future of the school. The interest amounts to be about four thousand dollars. We want to add this to the eight thousand dollars received for insurance so that our new dormitory will be in harmony with our other dormitories.

I have already told you of the personal history of the school. We are now paying insurance on nearly 75,000 dollars worth of property.

Our farm of 1,419 acres is one of the best in the state. If you would have our business record examined, you would find them absolutely correct and up to date. The principles that dominate our work are Christian. The work itself is along the lines approved by the best educators both north and south. You already know that the influence of the school has changed very radically public sentiments of the community for better conditions.

I have given you these facts to let you know or see that whatever money is put into our school will be permanent and go a long way into the future in the way of making character and citizenship. The leaven at Enfield will effect directly a race, ten million people, when we have gone to our long home. The white community of Enfield has been greatly benefitted by our school. It was there that they got the inspiration to put up the graded schools of Enfield and in fact in a half dozen other small towns in eastern North Carolina.

Now, I hope you will not be abashed at what I am going to say. We want an Eastern hall in which to house the domestic sciences of our school and the home economics. It will cost five thousand dollars exclusive of furnishings. If you feel that you can take up the matter, I shall be glad to come up and talk it over with you. It may be possible to interest some of the friends who were with you last spring. They seemed interested in Hampton and Tuskegee and I am sure they would be no less interested in Enfield if they knew about our work.

I hope Mr. Eastman that you will not think that I want to annoy you but I have really felt that you would like to do something in this line that would be far reaching in its influence in southern life and southern conditions. I shall be here only a few days and would be very glad to hear from you. I am very truly, T.S. Inborden, Principal.[11]
Unfortunately, Mr. George Eastman did not respond favorably to Inborden's request. However, Eastman did contribute to the construction of several other schools for blacks in the south and did donate a cow to the Brick farm.

T.S. was very adamant and confident when conferring with the AMA headquarters in New York in school matters. He wrote Secretary Beard on December 9, 1904 about his concerns on the completion of Beard Hall. He said construction should not stop and asked permission for Mr. Fletcher, the builder to continue. He also expressed his beliefs about the employees competency. T.S. stated that he did not believe in making excuses for people's failure. He had told his faculty that they must do their work clearly and well. If they can not do it, they must leave and permit some one else to do it well as it should be done wrote Inborden.[12]

Inborden replied to a letter from Miss Julia Lowe, of Edgefield Junction, Tennessee when he was visiting in Springfield, Massachusetts. He stated that he has enjoyed his visit and stayed in New York City for one week. He also mentioned his trips to Long Meadow, Chicopee, South Hailey Falls, Hadely, Holyoke, North Hampton, Indian Orchard and Palmer, Massachusetts where he delivered some speeches about the progress of Brick school.[13]

While visiting Indian Orchard, Massachusetts, he was given a reception at Reverend W.E. Mann's church and stayed at his home. T.S. wrote Mann a letter to express his appreciation. The letter read:

It certainly gave me a great pleasure to tell your people the endeavors of our work. I only had to look the audience in the face to see that I was speaking to people who were in accord with what I was saying. They were very appreciative.[14]

The missionary visits to New England in 1904 were very successful for Inborden and definitely increased his self confidence. He was invited to participate in a Missionary's meeting where some fifty missionaries from over all the world were present. Each speaker was allocated two minutes. When T.S. completed his brief remarks, Chairman Moody was elated with the applause and asked T.S. to speak for several more minutes. Inborden was the only speaker who was invited to speak twice.[15]

Sometimes the letters of Inborden would contain information about the school's faculty and recent happenings at the school. He wrote a letter to Miss Annie Upperman, who was living at 430 College Street, Washington, D.C. on October 17, 1904. T.S. said that he was glad to receive her letter and that he has just returned from his summer trip north. He was pleased to tell her that there were six new teachers on the faculty and they were occupying the dining hall. T.S. always would tell his friends about the successful graduates of Brick. He told Miss Upperman that a student named Ausby had made the freshman class, Hattie Green was at Fisk University, and Joseph was in the freshman class at Talledega College, Alabama, and a sophomore standing in Greek. T.S. remarked, we count this very good. Inborden had to relate some grievous news to Upperman. He wrote that George Bullock accidentally killed his grandmother. T.S. said Bullock had gone hunting and was returning home and shot at a bar post that entered into the cow pasture. Inborden stated that Bullock's grandmother was going fishing and was walking down a small path when one ball from the weapon went through the bar post and another ball struck the post and went off at an angle two thirds. Inborden said people thought that was the ball that hit the grandmother causing her to fall immediately near the bridge. T.S. concluded his letter by saying Bullock came immediately to him and told him what had happened and obviously Bullock was quite upset. The grandmother was shot unfortunately, in the right temple.[16] This event was a most sorrowful burden for the Brick family to experience in 1904.

Although Inborden did not participate directly in the political issues of the day, he was quite aware of the recent effects his brothers and sisters of color were confronted with when they wanted to participate in the voting process in their immediate communities. He expressed this when he wrote a letter to Mrs. Brick's niece, Lydia Benedict in Brooklyn, New York. T.S. said that he had traveled from New York to Long Branch, rested there four days and then went to Lincoln City, Delaware. Inborden stated that tomorrow, November 8, 1904 was election day and you would not know it, unless the papers said nothing about it. He then told Miss Benedict that he gave his students a brief talk on the significance of the election. However, no colored people here will vote, there will be very many white votes for Roosevelt in Delaware remarked T.S. as he closed his letter.[17]

After returning from a productive trip to the New England states, Inborden had the responsibility of selecting some new faculty members and preparing for the approaching fall semester at Brick. He sent letters to Dr. H.B. Frissell, President of Hampton Institute, Virginia and Dr. Wilson Bruce Evans, Washington, D.C. his wife's cousin. He asked them to assist him in obtaining a Domestic Science teacher for the fall term 1904. His request stated that the lady must be a Christian, positive in Christian life and who has the ability to work with other people. He said that her salary will be twenty dollars a month to start and she will be given traveling expenses to school and back home, free washing, ironing, room with heat and light and board. T.S. asked Frissell and Evans if they could find such a person and please ascertain if they will come to Brick, and write a letter stating their age, complexion, school graduated from, teaching experience, and letters of recommendations.[18]

T.S. Inborden would personally answer all the letters that he received in reference to school information from parents, students and inquirers. He actually found the time in his busy schedule to respond. In 1904, he received letters asking for applications, catalogue's circular printed material on the *school* and copies of the school paper. Inborden would write notes when answering the correspondence about the school's facilities, classes, items that were furnished the students, soap, bedding, towels, health care available and things they must purchase such as books. Inborden received letters from these people who were living in different geographical sections of the state and some out of state. Lincolinia G. Hayes, Dallas, Texas; Robert Richards, Weldon, North Carolina, Johnnie Long, Weldon, North Carolina, Thomas Ramsy, Weldon, North Carolina; Charles L. Hawkins, Weldon, North Carolina; Joseph Valentine, Tillery, North Carolina; Richard Cox, Greensboro, North Carolina; Charles Barber, Smithfield, North Carolina; Benjamin Nyes, Talledega, Alabama; Ernest Ingraham, High Point, North Carolina; Jennie Colts, Pinehurst, North Carolina; Gracie Davis, Wilmington, North Carolina; Betsy Joyner, Garysburg, North Carolina; John McLean, Broadway, North Carolina; Banta Ausbey, Crowells, North Carolina; Leonard Price, Highlands, Massachusetts; Eva V. Johnson, Washington, D.C.; Rose Grasppie, Fayetteville, North Carolina; Willie Gossett, Thomasville, North Carolina; Mary Sloan, Richmond, Virginia; Cordelia Coldwell, Charlotte, North Carolina; Mary Reed, Gastonia, North Carolina; Eva Coleman, White Plains, Virginia; William R. Boddie, Nashville, North Carolina; Louise Robbins, Quincy, Illinois; Ransom Harris, Aurora, North

Carolina; James Edmonson, Scotland Neck, North Carolina; Mary Young, Raleigh, North Carolina; Noah Hill, Sparrows Point, Maryland; Laura Battle, Battlesboro, North Carolina and Theresa Johnson, Alexandria, Virginia.[19] Inborden received donations and gifts of clothes, bedding and books during his summer travels from people who wanted to assist Brick school. T.S. wrote letters thanking them for their interest in the mission of Brick. He wrote letters of appreciation to: Reverend T.H. Hanks, Springfield, Massachusetts; Alfred Swan, Palmer, Massachusetts; Herbert S. Rainey, Springfield, Massachusetts; Mrs. M.L. Hastings, Warren, Massachusetts; Reverend William Excell, Livenis Center, New York; Reverend John Luther Kicbon and Park Congregational Church, Springfield, Massachusetts; Miriam C. Smith, Cleveland, Ohio; Mrs. L.P. Putney, Atlanta, Georgia, and Eleanor Little, Pembroken, West Bryn Mawr, Pennsylvania.[20]

Inborden could not forget the Christmas season that was approaching when he wrote a letter on December 13, 1904 to Dr. Beard in New York. He asked him to have the secretary Miss Emerson to go over to a store in New York and purchase some Mackintosh coats for his daughters, Julia and Dorothy. T.S. enclosed a check for eight dollars and said their sizes were for girls 13 and 9 years old.[21]

Inborden wrote an article on student labor in May, 1905. He said working habits must be previously formed and the teacher must use patience, tact, judgement, good temper in order to make contact between the student and their future school days. T.S. believed that at the beginning the student's work is unproductive because their primary object is being present in school to study books and not to do labor chores. Inborden wrote that no one can succeed at their best unless their entire mind is on that particular goal. T.S. realized that students must work at manual labor simply because they have no other way to remain in school and pay their bills but they still have on their mind the class work. Inborden's overall message to the students was that you must place a priority on your class room subjects and also do manual labor at times.[22]

A former third grade student at Brick school in 1899 wrote a letter to the school newspaper in 1905. Richard Battle worked briefly as a poultry man in Baltimore, Maryland prior to his enlistment in the U.S. Army in 1900. He described in his letter interesting experiences in the military and his realization of the importance of receiving an education. The lengthy letter was published as an article:

My unit left the United States on October 1, to the Philippines. We were aboard the transport, USS Hancock. The ship docked at Honolulu, and Island of Guam before reaching Manila Harbor on October 28. We saw some disabled vessels which were bombarded. Upon disembarkment, we relieved some white troops. Restrictions were enforced, possibly due to possible attacks. There were several native prisoners in the guard house. Their wives and daughters visited them three times daily to bring extra meals. Our unit occupied the town of Dasa for nine months. The senoritas bade the soldiers farewell on June 28, 1902. We traveled from Manila to Yokohama, Japan where the ship was loaded with some coal. The ship was in a quarantine station. The command was called to attention, then the great voice of a dark man announced that the National Anthem was to be sung. Many voices with one accord sang the song. Following the singing, many shots were fired from six inch guns on the ship as a salute. The quarantine station was located between Manila and Yokohama. The distance from Manila to San Francisco, 7,000 miles. On August 1, 1902, I arrived in San Francisco, California and went to camp at the Presidio and later boarded a train to Nebraska. My enlistment expired in April, 1903. However, I decided to reenlist for the Signal Corps and I was sworn in on September 3 and given a two month furlough. I visited North Carolina and Virginia and then was transferred to Fort McDowell, California from Fort Myer, Virginia. I had an ear operation at Benicia Barracks, California. The unit had a military exercise at American Lakes, Washington. Some troops participated along with some men from the 9th U.S. Cavalry Colored regiment, the remainder of the troops were white. I am happy to announce that I was selected permanent orderly for the Chief Signal officer during maneuvers, and was stationed at our division headquarters. The 9th Cavalry regiment band furnished music and orderlies for the staff officers. The Signal Corps consists of men whose intelligence is above the average soldier. Because his duty is to construct lines, transmit intelligence and receive messages. I was a telegraph operator and learned telegraphy and mastered the alphabet and was able to receive a message. I transmitted at a rate of twenty words per minute. I love to associate with my comrades who are well prepared for their work. It makes me want to do higher things. I hope to continue my service in the Signal Corps, should I do so someday. I will be able to do as others are doing being successful. The want of an education is the only barrier to my advancement and were it practicable, I would return even now to school. I cannot reconcile my self to the error of leaving Brick. Let me impress upon my good friends the great need of an education that you may endeavor all the more. Since my service in the Army, I have been almost excluded from religious experience. Yet, providence has increasingly caused me to prosper and advance in proportion to my ability. Therefore, I am greatful to every one who shall read this article, I invoke their sympathy in my feeble attempts at writing for I was a third grader when I bade you farewell five years ago.[23]

Inborden was very pleased to receive Battle's letter and published it in the Brick News, trusting that the letter would be a motivator to the students to complete their education.

A commencement exercise at Brick school in 1905 was more than just a typical exercise. Inborden and his faculty developed a first class cultural program that was complete with guest speaker and student participation. Excerpts from the May 1905 commencement exercise are as follows:

Speakers, Professor Kelly Miller, Howard University, Washington, D.C.

Easter Sunday religious sermon delivered by Reverend R.B. Johns on "What Christ Has Done For Women". April 22, 1905, Guest was Fountain W. Ragland, graduate of Talledega College, Alabama.

Visit by Frances Yeomans, Fisk University

Founders Day Ceremony, May 1, 1905. A Remembrance to the Great Philanthropists an Address by the Honorable E.A. Johnson, Raleigh, N.C.

An athletic activity, a baseball game between Brick young men and the Heathsville Team.[24]

The students of Brick participated in programs of public rhetorical, declarations and recitations during the commencement program. The participants were:

>   *Piano Duet, Julia Inborden*
>   *Declaration, "The True Spirit of Decoration Day,*
>   *Silas Arrington*
>   *Recitation, The Drunkards Dream, Daisy Arrington*
>   *Declaration, Devotion to Patriotic Duty, Lafayette Hill*
>   *Recitation, "Aunt Tabitha Way", Nannie Whitaker*
>   *Vocal solo, Voices of the Woods, Julie Smith*
>   *Declaration, "The Young Scholars Hope", Benjamin Powell*
>   *Recitation, "The Volunteer Organist, Lydia Baskerville*
>   *Recitation, "Highlights On The Coast Of Lincolnshire"*
>   *Minnie Cogdell*
>   *Recitation, "The Christening", Lillian Summerill*
>   *Recitation, "A Maiden Resolve", Sadie Bobbitt*
>   *Declaration, "What is a Minority?", Frederic Moore*
>   *Declaration, "Courting Times", Isaac Bunn*
>   *Declaration, "The American Union, A Geographical*
>   *Necessity", Benjamin Bullock*

The competent and capable faculty members at Brick School in 1905 were:

>   *Isadore Martin, Treasurer and Bookkeeping*
>   *Miss Lucy C. Storey, music, Latin and English*
>   *Mrs. Sarah Jane Inborden, Algebra*
>   *Miss. M.V. Little, Preceptress, Girls Hall*
>   *Mrs. M.V. Martin, Sixth Grade teacher*
>   *Miss M.A. Roberts, Fifth Grade teacher*
>   *Reverend R.B. Johns, Chaplain and Charge of Night School*
>   *Mrs. Alice Davis, sewing, Matron, Brewster Hall*
>   *Miss J.M. Harding, Matron of Dining Hall*
>   *Miss J.A. Sadgwar, Primary Department*
>   *J.J. Fletcher, Manual Training*
>   *E.L. Falkener, Superintendent of Farms*
>   *H.G. Forney, Garden and Poultry Manager*[25]

The white community had their fears and apprehensions when the Brick School was organized in 1895. T.S. received a letter on April 20, 1905 from a white physician, Dr. A.S. Harrison, county superintendent of schools and also a druggist. Harrison wrote:

> With some misgivings, I have watched the growth and development of your school from its infancy. I recognized that it was an experiment and that the result depended largely upon the management by those actively in charge. I am convinced that the experiment stage has passed and that you are doing a good work for your race and I think I voice the sentiment of the community generally. I have observed that you teach the heart as well as the head. Morality as well as religion. You teach the work of the hand as well as the brain. Thereby putting brains in the hands and you know the combination of brains and muscle in proper proportions is almost sure to succeed, mentally, physically and financially. I note that your pupils are taught that politeness to each other to the white race is elevating rather than degrading. Honest work makes one more highly thought of especially by the white men. I observed also that you teach cleanliness, a thing most generally lacking in your race. You teach the students to keep their rooms clean and neat. As a physician, I have noticed a very mark improvement in the healthfulness of the place since your occupancy. Which I attribute very largely to your clean surroundings and also to your observance of the ordinary rules of hygiene. As superintendent of public instruction for the county, I am glad to say that some of the best teachers have received their training at your school. May you live long to continue this good work and what your assistants are doing for your people. You may rest assured that so long as you continue your present policy, you will have the good wish and moral support of the community in which you live.
>
> A.S. Harrison[26]

T.S. Inborden and the Brick family were saddened when an accident occurred in a fishing creek near Brick on May 30, 1905. A student, Bascomb Arrington drowned in the creek. Arrington together with several boys went down to the creek to swim. As Arrington was swimming across the stream, he sank where the current was the sharpest. He was buried in the old plantation cemetery on the school farm.

Brick College attracted several distinguished visitors to the campus in May, 1905. The renowned violinist and grandson of Frederick Douglass visited Brick. Joseph Douglass of Washington, D.C. gave a violin recital in the school chapel. The students received an inspiring lecture from Mr. W.A. Hunton, International Secretary of the YMCA. On April 9, 1905 some Brick young men attended a Baptism rite at the Rocky Mountain, N.C. church where sixty-five persons were baptized by a former Brick student Reverend A.S. Croom. T.S. received good news again when Joseph Hill, a graduate of Brick was demonstrating excellence in his studies at college. Hill received a 1905 winter term average of 91.89.

Brick College had a wealth of programs in the 1900's, ten years after the founding of the school. These programs depicted the cultural and writing abilities of the student. Inborden had arranged for these motivated and eager students to participate in commencement week activities. Some of these participants were members of the Adelphian Literary Society:

Piano Duet, "Peter Schmoll Overture", "Weber", Miss Storey, and A.J.
    Rhodes
Declamation, "Waterloo", H.W. Long
Recitation, "Mary The Mind of the Iron", Pearl Johnson
Recitation, "The Immigrants Story", Gertrude Coats
Declamation, "Duty of Literary Men to America", E. Green
Male Quartet, "Loves Old Sweet Song", George Bullock,
    J.S. Jones, William McLaurin and H.W. Long.

The Brick Primary Grades were under the direction of Miss Sadgwar and Miss Jones, who had the students perform in a play, "Anderella In Flowerland". The characters were played by: Julia Smith, Maggie Hilliard, Daisy Long, Katie Coleman, Bonnie Bee, Morris Bullock, Dorothy Inborden, Gertrude Whitaker, and Zollie Powers. The Intermediate Grades presented a program under the leadership of Miss M.A. Roberts. The students were: Julia Inborden, piano solo, Bessie Davis, recitation, and Joseph Bullock, declamation. The students participated in activities called exhibitions of the various grade levels. The exhibition of the grammar grades were organized by Mrs. M.V. Martin. The students were: Nannie Whitakers, recitation, "Blue and Gray"; Frederick Moore, declaration, "A Political Stump speech"; Sadie Bobbitt, "Mrs. Duffy On Baseball"; and Hilliard Long, bass solo. The seventh grade exhibition teachers was Miss M.V. Little and her students were: Fred Phillips, declamation, "The Destruction of Troy"; Lois Johns, recitation, "Mrs. McWilliams and The Lightning"; Joseph Saunders, declaration, "How Reuben Played", and recitation by Ella Reed, "The Sleeping Sentinel". Mrs. Sarah Jane Evans Inborden was the eight grade teacher. Her students were: N.H. Lee, declamation; J. Baskerville, recitation; Cary Pittman, declamation; Lucy Tillery, recitation, and Lida C. Baskerville, recitation. Inborden extended invitations to several renowned artists and speakers for his cultural programs for the school. Visits were made by: Mr. George Moore, Field Missionary, A.M.A.; Mr. Jesse Moorland, Secretary, International Committee, YMCA; Clarence Cameron White, Richard Harrison (played the Lord in the Broadway Production of Green Pastures) and Lillian Evanti (opera singer). The Jamestown Exposition and celebration committee asked T.S. in September 1907 to serve as chairman of the Advisory Board of Awards for the Jamestown Negro exhibit. Other members of the Advisory Board were W.D. Crum, Mary Church Terrell, J.C. Napier and T.B. Williams.[27]

Inborden wrote an article on Suggestions For The Teacher in April, 1907. The article discusses his personal view and some childhood experiences. The article read as follows:

Do not nag students. As a child and country lad wearing a woven suit with boxed toed shoes, a ruffled bosom shirt and flaxen hair red pants dyed to harmonize with the season was my attire when I arrived in Cleveland, Ohio. My speech was the typical Virginia mountain brogue. I stepped not agile and quick but in strides of leaps. I thought a free boy had to ring bells and that a waiter had to sit and simply wait. I knew more about the plow and wagon than I did about the tray. I could handle a four horse team with one line better than I could bring from the kitchen meals for four people. I was an expert at cutting corn and taking up wheat beside a cradle. But I would almost break my neck daily walking over marble floors in the hotel. I could maul rails all day in the woods, but I couldn't walk from one end of the dining room to the other end without liability of hooking into someone's feet. When a gentleman asked for syrup, I would just as soon give him a bottle of Worcestershire sauce and argue with him that was what we served molasses in. Was I nagged? What did I know about a silver syrup pitcher, I never saw one before in my life. I was nagged and nagged. Had it not been for the super human ambition I had for an education, I would have gone back to the country a thousand times. I never was quite so blessed as I was one morning about 23 years ago (1884) in Cleveland, Ohio when I picked up a morning paper and found that my chief nagger had gotten himself in trouble and had been sent to the state prison for two years. It was certainly a good relief to me when he left. While we worked together I was reminded daily that my hair was curly, that my dyed pants needed a little syrup on the bottom to hold them down and that I had not lost my Virginia brogue. They also reminded me that I had fallen in the dining room a dozen times and that on one occasion the second waiter had to help me. I know how it feels to be nagged. As a student, I knew what it was to fail to make a recitation and have to appear before the teacher on Saturday to make up five zeros instead of getting five percent marks. I got the six zeroes with advice from the teacher. There are some students in the class who would make better ox drivers than scholars. I took it all to myself without passing back any retort because I know too well that I was a first class teamster but that was no reason why I should not at least try to be a scholar. About the only consolation that I had was the fact that there were others in the class who had all the advantages and when I went to make up the zeroes, I found them doing the same thing. The teacher was a splendid woman. She meant well but made mistakes not known. When she saw that I meant to stay, she came to me and asked me to give her a place as teacher in the Sunday School which I was superintendent. She taught most acceptable and I was glad to have her in our Sunday school, because of the opportunity it gave me to come into contact with her outside of her own classroom. This was in the town of Oberlin, Ohio in a colored Sunday school and she was a white lady. In all of my study under her, she never knew me until she came to the Sunday School to teach. It was here under these circumstances that we came to know each other as only student and teacher should know each other. My success under her tutorship after this was assured. You cannot nag students when they are doing their best, molding lives of other's failures.[28]

T.S. and Sarah Jane Inborden were a very happy and loving couple. Their letters would help to keep them communicating with each other when they were apart from each. In August, 1908, Sarah Jane and two of the children were visiting up north. Julia remained at Bricks with her father. Inborden wrote Sarah Jane:

My dearest Baby, Mr. Martin, Mr. Forney, Mr. Phillips and I went up to Mr. Sloan's to dinner. We drove by for Mr. Phillips and went from his house to Mr. Sloan across the county. We left here at 8 o'clock and did not get there until eleven. The roads were bad. Sloan was glad to see us. Mr. and Mrs. Bunn, Mrs. Pittman, Mrs. Brantley's mother and some half dozen others were there. They had a fine dinner, had pig, cabbage, cooked fine ham, potatoes, butter beans, biscuits, cornbread, chicken pie which was about the best I ever ate, apple and pecan pie, ice cream and water melon. The boys made some sweet cider and I drank some of that. The apples were ripe and clean and the cider was very nice. We left about four o'clock and arrived home at supper time. Fred met his father here and took him home. He was the happiest man you ever saw. He told Mr. Sloan that when he came to his house that he was going away. He did not think that there was a colored man anywhere in the county fixed as well as Mr. Sloan. The trip had a great effect on him. He said that he was going home and go to the word. He told me he never spend such a pleasant day. Mrs. Phillips was down sometime ago and I gave her some of those old shoes for the children. So when I came back, I put all of them in a sack and was glad to get them out of the way. She said if I would let her have them, she would take the rest of them and have Fred fix them for the grandchildren. She said that if she raised a single turkey, I should have it for Christmas. She was very thoughtful. Joe has been sick with fever but he is up and at work. Mrs. Davis decided to go next week. She thought that she would stay until the next matron came but the next matron is not coming. The people are having a great time in their meetings. They pass here every night going to town to the meetings. Mrs. Forney had peach sherbet last night and I ate three dishes. She makes it every Friday. Julia and I usually get our share. Mr. Forney said that he knew he had a brother up there but he did not know where as he had written him, but could not hear from him. I received the pictures you sent. I suppose they were taken by the new photographer. Julia seized on them for her album. I hope you are well. I thought I would go to town this afternoon and get some medicine for Julia's face. It is broken out so very badly. Please make the children keep their teeth clean. I am your own with lots of love and sweet kisses. I dreamt of you last night. Your own, T.S.I.[29]

Industrial education was considered by many educators in the south in 1908 as primary curriculum for black students. There were some schools that would place a high premium on industrial subjects over an academic curriculum. Inborden's personal philosophy was that there should be a value and limitations of industrial education. He stated Industrial Training cannot be of value without a certain amount of academic instruction among Negro Youth. T.S. believed that young students must have a preparation of arithmetic, grammar, reading and drawing. He gave some references and examples of his views on the subject from his own teaching experiences. T.S. said some years prior to 1908, while he was a teacher in a southern school, he noticed that some of the teachers had problems correcting students who were using ungrammatical English phrases. Some years later, he wrote that a distinguished white educator was speaking at a school and he said that you can take a boy right out of the woods and in two or three years, they can make steam engines and later become contractors and leaders of their people. Inborden asked the educator, why it was that in order to take a course in any of the best trade schools of the country it was necessary to have a college preparation or at least a first class high school education? The white gentleman replied, Oh, your people do not need that sort of preparation, evidently they were not born with some qualities to learn. This was the feeling of many white educators in the 1900's. Inborden realized that the course of study for industrial leadership should be as thorough and as extensive as that prescribed for leadership and any less preparation means slipshod work, inefficiency and failures. He also said some ignorant Negroes have had antipathy to industrial training because they did not know what it included. Some thought it was simply to use a plow, wash, scrub and to do ordinary labor chores with some degree of skills, so that they might be better servants. T.S. stated that on the other hand, a large number of intelligent and ignorant blacks thought the missionary teachers, philanthropists and the state legislatures had formed a huge combine to keep Negroes in a sort of servitude. Inborden stressed the true fact that around 1906, the state schools had reduced the course of study for Negroes to the most elementary branches. The result he wrote was that blacks sent their sons and daughters to the denominational schools which was decreasing very much the enrollment of state public schools. T.S. said the blacks knew what they wanted and sent their children where they could get it. This is an interesting fact because some 89 years later, parents of all races are looking for better schools for the education of their children in 1995 and the private and parochial schools are increasing their enrollment. Inborden asked the question, how do we begin to help the student who comes from a different home atmosphere than others? He said one must start with home development, especially when you realize that some students are still living in a log cabin. T.S. stated that some boys and girls' parents plow with an ox, sweep their floors with a bunch of brushes, and use fruit cans for cups and sauces. When the students come to Brick, said Inborden, they must be taught the simple manner of sweeping floors, and other household tasks. He discussed some specific examples that must be taught to young people when they arrive at school. Inborden said it is a step by step method. There were classes on working in the kitchen knowledge of the foods of the season and use of special dishes. In the sewing room, girls learn techniques of plain sewing, and dressmaking.

T.S. said the young boys were taught modern methods and machinery, how to harness a horse and hitch it to a wagon, correct way to plow and the use of tools. Inborden said many black youngsters go north and leave the south where the woods are full of game, creeks, and rivers full of fish and where they grow everything they want to eat with little cost. However, wrote Inborden, what inspiration is there in an ox, bobtail mule? The young man wants to be somebody and needs a change. T.S. believed that there is inspiration in a plow drawn by the horses and there is allurement and fascination in a mowing machine that cuts the grain, and binds it. The young men go north, said Inborden, because they wanted to learn new improved methods.[30] T.S. Inborden in 1908 was possibly thinking of his early child hood and truthfully wanted his students to follow a path of upward mobility and as he left the mountains to improve his living condition and obtain an education. He encouraged his students to do the same. Inborden was a believer in using the talents of your hands along with the talents of your brains.

A Joint Missionary Campaign was sponsored by the Congregational Home Missionary Society, the American Missionary Association, Church Building Society, Congregational Education Society, The Sunday School and Publishing Society and the Congregational Board of Ministerial Relief in February, 1909 in Lincoln, Nebraska. The theme of the Missionary

Campaign was "For Our Country and the World. The Western District meetings were conducted at the Lincoln, Nebraska First Congregational Church, located on the corner of I and 13th Street. The local committee members were Reverend Charles H. Rogers, Professor Edgar L. Hinman, Rev. M.A. Bullock, and Rev. S. Hanford. Some of the Congregational churches in the Lincoln area that were represented, Lincoln First, Plymouth, The Vine, Butler Avenue, First German Zion, Salem, Emmanuel Swedish, Havelock, Hallan Beatrice, Princeton, Cortland, Syracuse, Waverly, Rokeby Verden, Milford and Ashland. This Missionary campaign was most comprehensive. Some distinguished speakers were Cornelius H. Patton, Home Secretary of the American Board, Boston, a Yale and Amherst Universities graduate, Miss Miram L. Woodberry, New York City, Secretary of the Woman's Department of the Congregational Home Missionary Society, and Rev. Thomas Gray of Micronesia, Missionary of American Board Congregation, Foreign Mission. He was stationed on the Island of Ponape in the Carolina group. Some other speakers were Rev. Edward Evans Jr. of Hyannis, Massachusetts, he worked with the Home Missionary Society; Rev. Charles T. Riggs of Constantinople, Turkey graduate of Princeton University and Auburn Theological Seminary. There was also another distinguished speaker and he was Principal Thomas Sewell Inborden of Bricks, North Carolina. T.S. was honored to be a speaker in an afternoon session. He gave an address on Monday, February 22, 1908 at the First Congregational church[31].

The American Missionary Association demonstrated a high regard and respect for T.S. Inborden in view of the day and time in America, with segregation legally sanctioned by the Plessy Versus Ferguson court ruling of 1896. Inborden was frequently attending integrated meetings and conferences. On April 5 and 6, 1909, T.S. was invited to attend a Joint Missionary campaign in Mansfield, Ohio. The meetings were hosted by the Middle District and First Congregational church. The local committee chairman was Rev. Bernard G. Mattson. Some participating churches were: Ashland, Bellevue Berlin Heights, Castalia, Ceylon, Clarksfield, Fitchville First, Second Florence Greenfield, Greenwich Isle St. George, Kelly's Island Lexington, Lucas, Lymie, Mansfield First, Mayflower, Marble Heart New London, North Fairfield, North Monroeville, Norwalk Verimileon, Ruggles, Sandusky, Wakeman and Washington Riley. Some of the speakers were: Samuel B. Copen, Cornelius H. Patton, Charles C. Creegan, Rev. Daniel Greene, Rev. John P. Jones, Rev. James L. Barton, Charles S. Mills, Hubert C. Herring, Miss Miram L. Woodberry, Mr. William E. Lougee, Rev. A.E. Ricker, Charles H. Richards, Avery H. Bradford, Charles Jackson Ryder, Rev. William Rice, and Rev. Edward S. Tead. Inborden and Professor Kelly Miller of Howard University were the only people of color present at the meetings as speakers. Inborden was listed in the program as a "Colored Orator of Power". T.S. spoke at an afternoon session and also gave a brief address at the supper evening session.[32] While traveling from Richmond, Virginia to Durham, North Carolina, T.S. wrote a post card and mailed it to Sarah Jane. He wrote that he had been waiting for the train to Oxford, and will be home soon. He said that he had a good time. Inborden would always think of his family when travelling.

The American Missionary published an article on Abraham Lincoln written by Inborden. T.S. realized that Lincoln was considered the Emancipator by many blacks. Inborden wrote that Lincoln saw the signing of the proclamation as test of character, an expedient never before tried in the history of any race. T.S. said it was faith joining hands with the eternal and well may it be said that this emancipator was an exigency of war. T.S. explained this statement when he said *God is the author of the exigencies of war as much as he is the exigence of peace and if his will power and spirit cannot be transmitted by man through the exigencies of war.*[33] Inborden had a very great interest in assisting the black farmer in eastern North Carolina. He held a Farmers Day at Brick in 1910. The farmers who attended were interested in growing cotton, corn, peanuts, potatoes and the raising of hogs, cows and poultry. T.S. had a farmers meeting in 1908 where only seven attended. There was a nice representation of farmers in 1910. Inborden examined the progress of the black farmer in the Brick area community in a detailed paper he wrote in 1911. T.S. referred to the area community as Halifax, Nash and Edgecombe counties, North Carolina. Halifax was one of the largest counties in the state at that time. 681 miles with over 30,000 people. It was the part of the state that was referred to as the black belt with black constituting two-thirds of the population. Many of the blacks worked as farm wagers and share croppers. T.S. wrote that after the Civil War many blacks received their freedom and some were given land by their former masters. However, according to T.S., many blacks were not able to confront the responsibilities of ownership due to their years of deprivation as a slave and trained only to accomplish certain tasks as directed by the slave owner. T.S. continued by saying the possession of land brought responsibilities which their former training had not enabled them to assume. They were uneducated and worked with their competitors to a great disadvantage. They had to do their own thinking and were not accustomed to think through some responsibilities. Even though there were a few farms in 1911 still in the hands of some of the slaves families who were given the land, T.S. believed that those who were able to retain their land, had superior mental ability and ancestral endowment. This was evident with thousands of acres of land owned by blacks. Inborden wrote that in Halifax county, there were 53,947 acres of land owned by Negroes and valued at 377,236 dollars. T.S. stated that these blacks owned 353 town lots and houses, valued at 161,175 dollars and they had 1,407 horses valued at 110,000 dollars, 875 mules, valued at 72,949 dollars, 3,119 cattle, valued at 50,465 dollars, and 6,802 hogs, valued at 20,620 dollars. The figures represented only the taxable property of one thousand blacks of Halifax county. T.S. said the figures may appear small when compared with the great wealth of the county, but it was great when one thinks that it is the valuation of land and of stock of only one thousand farmers who started in 1866. Inborden sincerely thought that blacks had half the opportunities and half the encouragement which their white neighbors had. Inborden viewed the three most progressive townships in the county as Scotland Neck, Weldon and Enfield, progressive stations on the Atlantic and Coastline railroads and the outlet with the Roanoke river for Weldon and Scotland Neck, provided the farmers a national advantage over those in other sections of the county. According to Inborden, in 1911, the blacks in Enfield owned land valued at 57,125 dollars, some 12,392 acres, 52 town lots, valued at 19,000 dollars, 146 horses, valued at 7,550, 144 mules, valued at 10,000, 295 cattle valued at 3,899 and 676 hogs valued at 1,482 dollars.

The farmers' meetings provided T.S. some valuable information. He learned that many of the farmers owned their farms and had sheep, goats, turkeys, chickens and colonies of bees, clean and neat living areas with houses painted white or washed and plastered inside. T.S. was impressed with some farmers who had telephones, were subscribers to the church papers and agricultural papers, they were learning to read and think for themselves. He was also concerned about some of the share croppers who were not making progress toward individual self sufficiency and upward progress toward ownership of their land. Inborden was fascinated with how many of the black fathers were able to obtain their land and make unusual progress against the odds, racism and economic obstacles. He wrote some true stories to support the above statements. Inborden stated that there was a man who owned two farms, 182 acres. He had a six room weather boarded house on each farm and shelter for his stock, tools and equipment. He also operated a store to furnish his immediate community with supplies. This farmer had eleven children. Inborden said that there was a farmer named Richard Sanders. Who had a farm of 36 acres. He had a modern six room house. There were farm buildings for his stock, tools and supplies. He had a small store and had a private school house for his own children. The farm's crops were clean of weeds and the ditches were also clean. T.S. wrote about a farmer who had 148 acres under good cultivation and had a six room two story house. He also had a secret order, hall for the convenience of its members. There was also a young farmer who had 45 acres of land and a six room house. He had two horses and his family consisted of his wife and seven children. The farm was part of a 600 acre tract of land that was previously owned by this farmer's former master.

Many articles have been written about the black migration to the city by southern blacks. However, Inborden believed that if blacks could not get the best advantage in the community in which they lived, they should move to the cites and towns because it makes good sense. He also said that good public roads will help to keep the best Negroes in the county. T.S. said equality in the administration of the laws will also help to retard the migration of blacks to the towns. Inborden stated that if blacks could buy small farms of 20-100 acres it would have been good because there were thousands of acres of land that were not in cultivation and could be divided into small farms.[34] T.S. Inborden was again using his experience of farming as a young man and now as an educator and leader. He was really able to understand and communicate with the farmers. He knew something about farm life and he was learning daily about how the North Carolina farmer was progressing and some of the problems and obstacles he confronted.

In 1912, Inborden could reflect on the progress that had been made with the Brick school farm tenants or renters and their families. The boys and girls were taught the use of tools, students helped with the cooking in the kitchen. The steam laundry had some girls helping in the washing. Students also assisted in the maintenance of campus, roads, and bridges. The tenants would pay their rent sometimes in crops produced. The renters replaced lights and did minor repairs. T.S. said the tenants exhibited good business methods, harmony with each other and displayed good morality. There was no intoxicating liquors in the house, no promiscuous, shooting at night and gambling. Inborden was pleased with the renters' decorum at all times. The renters did not hunt or fish on Sunday. The children of the renters were very successful, wrote Inborden. After graduating from school, some started their businesses and several enrolled in college pursuing courses in agriculture and manual training.[35]

T.S. had maintained good relations with teachers in the surrounding commuunities. In 1912, he compiled a list of some teachers. They were:

Scotland Neck, N.C.

Charlotte Simmons
Edward A. Taylor
James A. Smith
Maude E. Lawrence
Angina Higgs
George M. James
Mattie L. Howard
Leah Shields
Mellissa Smith

Enfield, N.C.

Mollie Collins
Eleanor Fox
Fannie Marriner
Mamie Arrington
George Day
Estelle Phillips
Susie Bradley
Clara Yates
Iowa Bellamy
Thaddeus Johnson

Little John, N.C.

Catherine Price
G. Ellis Harris
Mary Harris
Mercedes Harris

Brinkleyville, N.C.

Hallie Williams
Attie Williams
Geneva Hardy
Foler Brinkley
Beverly Hardy

Halifax, N.C.

Annie Mitchem
Aola Reynolds
Annie Williams
Almita R. Neville
Cleve Hargrove
Eleanor Pittman
Dollie Johnson
Annie L. Cheek
Cosey Arrington

Aurelian Springs, N.C.

Sallie Johnson
Lucy Brown
Lizzie Brown
Maggie Brown

Lillie Lynch -   Essex, North Carolina
Salina Harvey -   Airlee, North Carolina
Bertha Boone -   Ringwood, North Carolina
Frankie Myrick - Ringwood, North Carolina
Emma Marriner -   Tillery, North Carolina
Daisy Pittman -   Heathville, North Carolina
Beaulah Daniel - Heathville, North Carolina
Annie Lee -   Hobgood, North Carolina
Mary Boyd -   Hobgood, North Carolina[36]

The white citizens of the eastern North Carolina communities began to appreciate the presence of the Brick School in 1913. When the Brick Jubilee Club gave a performance At Rocky Mount, Elm City and Wilson they were well received by both white and black citizens. Inborden said that when they arrived at Elm City, a white politician and businessman invited the group to his private office. The singers were asked to sing a few selections among them by special request, "Nearer My God To Thee". The white gentleman greeted them stated Inborden on behalf of the city and the mayor and as they were leaving his office, he said "Professor Inborden, here is my car, my son is driving it and he's at your service while you are in this town. T.S. said the young women singers were ushered into the automobile and driven to the city school where after a short talk he gave and the Jubilee club performed in concert. The white politician made some remarks at the conclusion of the program and considered making a generous contribution to Brick School. There were some concerned white southerners in 1913 who wanted to assist blacks in their quest for an education in a legal separate society.[37]

Inborden was more than just a fund raiser, he was a realist and was frank and to the point when he needed financial assistance for the school. He would ask for it in plain direct terminology. On December 19, 1913, T.S. wanted to obtain funds for the school library. He sent a letter to presidents and trustees of selected educational institutions. The letter explained that Brick as an American Missionary Association school was attempting to organize and develop a library. T.S. said the letter was a personal appeal and their contributions could provide several volumes of books and there was a need for standard works in literature and technical or scientific books.[38]

The Brick school continuing success through the years was due to the dynamic leadership of T.S. Inborden and above all his highly qualified and efficient faculty and staff. During the years 1915-1920, Inborden was fortunate to have the following dedicated and competent women and men as part of the Brick family's leadership: Benjamin Taylor, treasurer; R.J. Elzy, science; Sarah Jane Inborden, mathematics; Ada L. Hurlong, sixth grade; Pearl Johnson, fourth grade; Lucille McLendon, Primary department; Anna E. Brown, history; S.A. Allen, Latin and English; Juanita Barry, music; Walker D. Miller, business manager; Janet Whitaker, primary grades; Sarah Edwards, music; Joseph Fletcher, manual training; E.F. Colson, agriculture; H.G. Forney, farm manager; Alice Davis, sewing and matron; Mary V. Little, matron and dining hall; Lillian Hall, clerk and assistant postmistress; and Alice Vassar LaCour, matron.[39]

In 1915, T.S. attended the National Conference of Congregational Workers at New Haven, Connecticut. He also visited his home in Upperville, Virginia and Hampton Institute prior to returning to Brick, T.S. visited Miss Lydia Benedict, Mrs. Brick's niece in Brooklyn, New York. He also spoke at Dr. W.N. DeBerry's church in Springfield, Massachusetts.

The school newspaper, "Brick News" that was published during the years 1915 to 1920 contained articles and descriptive accounts of the activities that occurred at Brick School. These news accounts portrayed the effectiveness of the educational climate that Inborden had developed and managed since 1895. These accounts of students, faculty, events and school programs all resurrect the true spirit of Brick School and its industrial and academic successes twenty years after its founding. The school paper had an article on alumni from 1902-1914. Some members of the classes were: 1902 - James C. Ausby, Hattie L. Green and Joseph J. Hill; 1905 - Annias S. Croom; 1907 - George Bullock, Mattie Hilliard, Paul Johns, and James S. Jones; 1903 - Isaac Bunn, Anna J. Rhoden Sublette; 1909 - Samanna J. Cooke, Elisha Greene, Jennie C. Hopkins and Nathaniel H. Lee; 1910, Ida B. Arrington, Charles Battle, James W. Croom, John D. Fields, Mary E. Dunston Cooke, Joseph P. Harrison, Frederick Phillips and Joseph Saunders; 1911, Susan Adams, Eula Dunston Fields, Caleb Richmond, and Lucy Richmond,; 1912, Lillian Hall, Gertrude Leipsie, and Pearl Johnson, and Dunie Wright Lewis,; 1913, Lula Bullock, Joseph M. Bullock, Etta Cofield, Maude Chisholm, Tezzie G. Dodson, and John R. Murrain,; 1914, Victoria Pegram, Minna Reed, Zenobia Ross, and Wimberly Richard.[40] It was reported in the Alumnae news section of the paper that Joseph Harris and James Croom participated in the wedding of Miss Eula Dunston and Mr. John D. Fields in Kinston, North Carolina. The Young Mens' Christian Association (YWCA) had a very active program at Brick School. The 19th annual banquet of the YMCA was held in the school's Domestic Science Hall on Saturday, March 27, 1915. An inviting menu was served - salmon croquettes, green peas, potatoes, rolls, sweet pickles, chicken salad a la Brick, cake and coffee. The toastmaster of the program was Harmon Taylor and other participants were J.W. McCleod, J.P. Chessom, R.J. Elzy, J.W. Porter, M.S. Simmons, Alexander Sessoms, E.F. Colson and Dorothy Inborden. The YMCA band provided the music. Inborden believed in providing the students with a wholesome environment on the campus. He had a very good athletic and recreation program for the students. The Brick baseball team and tennis team played other schools in competition to include St. Paul's School in Lawrenceville, Virginia.

The alumni of Brick School had a sense of loyalty and love for their Brick Alma Mater. A recent graduate, Lula Bullock wrote an interesting and motivating letter to the school. Her letter included the importance of advantages of college work and spiritual values. She wrote that there is much to be gained from the study of mathematics that leads to accurate thinking, expression and action. Lula Bullock stated that the study of biology, chemistry, zoology, physics, and literature all bring us in closer contact with the forces of nature and indeed the forces of God and of the world when the whys of the every day phenomena of life are more clearly understood. Bullock said students must learn to appreciate the beautiful both in word and deeds as we become close observers. She asked the question, how much is lost when our minds are not alert and responsive to the beauties of nature. She also thought about those who might not be fortunate to receive a college education by stating that for those who never come to college, there is much to be gained in the study of nature. Because trees are symbols of unity, basic of social organization, nature, gives imagination and creative and constructive abilities. Lula said the beauty, harmony, symmetry, life and freedom of nature fill the mind with high ambition and serve to shape the noble character. Lulu Bullock concluded her inspiring letters to the students by writing to those who live in the city there are great opportunities in school visiting the library, reading magazines and daily papers, all making for a broad life. But to those who live in the country there seems to be more vast opportunities, books are good teachers and travel is education. Those thoughtful words of Brick graduate, Lula Bullock in 1915 definitely would be a positive motivating agenda for many of our young people in 1995. She was realistically thinking in the same philosophical arena of T.S. Inborden's beliefs for attaining excellence in the pursuit of one's goals in life.[41]

The commencement exercise at Brick School for 1915 included an active participation of the students. There were dramatic readings by Marie Davis, Anna Johnson, Jacob Porter, and orations given by Matilda M. Peyton, Lucinda Pitts, Livera Arrington, C. Lea Arrington, L. Castella Powers, J. Bernard Williams, H. Tobais Taylor, H. Inez Little, Dorothy Inborden, and O. Narcott Peyton. There was the crowning of the Gypsy Queen and the participants were Murvin Sumner, Margaret Jones, Alfred Leach, Dorothy Inborden, Willie Blow, Charles Ryals, Thelma Parker, Harold Hargrave, Marion Davis, Ida Johnson, Alex Sessoms, Otis Davis, Chris Dobbins, Mason Davis, Wilson Inborden, Mary Davis and Mary Arrington. The commencement address was delivered by Reverend Louis Berry of Stamford, Connecticut and the conferring of diplomas by T.S. Inborden.[42] Programs and activities of personal Christianity were initiated at Brick School by Inborden. He was able to have young students involved in Christian Youth organizations, YMCA, YWCA, young boys Christian club and Sunday school. Every Sunday morning the YMCA conducted Bible class under the direction of men teachers and attendance was voluntary. The Young Women's Christian Association (YWCA) conducted their meetings on Sunday afternoons. Progress was evident in the improvement of the industrial and academic curriculum at Brick School in the mid 1900's. Inborden had made significant strides in accrediting the school and preparing students to enter college. The normal school's major industrial curriculum was: agriculture, practical farming, manual training, woodwork, iron, steel, mechanical drawing, sewing, dress making, domestic science, practical housekeeping, cooking, mechanical drawing, home management, horticulture, raising poultry and farm mechanics. The major academic subjects were primary level - reading, language, spelling, hygiene, music, Bible, writing, geography, history, and grammar. Students on the high school level were required to study English, reading, literature, grammar, composition, mathematics, geography, physical science, agriculture, home economics, civics, biblical history, economics, chemistry, physiology, Latin, and geometry. T.S. introduced a teachers training course to improve the teachers knowledge of selected subject. The course subjects included English, biology, elementary school techniques, household arts, mathematics, hygiene, experimental cooking, millinery and dress making, home structure and furnishings, practical gardening, domestic animals, advanced shop work and practice teaching.[43]

Inborden was very pleased about the successful farmers day that was held on the Brick campus, Saturday, February 20, 1915. At 9:20 a.m., T.S., school treasurer, teachers and students marched to the tunes of the YMCA band to the school train station. They met the visiting farmers and escorted them to the Ingraham Chapel. There were exhibits and displays at the farmers' meeting. Some of the exhibits were: sewing items, dresses, shirts, collars, food, cakes, candy, bread, boiled ham, garden produce, potatoes, turnips, butter, sausage, bacon, all the food was raised on the school farm. The opening program consisted of some remarks by T.S. and he introduced Mr. and Mrs. Garren of Agronomy Division, North Carolina, Department of Agriculture. A student, Hattie Little, rendered a song, "Lead Me To The Rock and the Jubilee group gave a beautiful rendition of "I Want To Be Like Jesus." Mr. Garren talked about "Being A Thrifty Farmer" and Mrs. Garren spoke on the home and importance of the kitchen, the attractiveness and the necessity of well prepared foods. Round table discussions were conducted and the farmers explained their methods of farming, problems, and they exchanged ideas about improving farm life. There were distinguished guests present, Sadie Delaney, supervisor of Domestic Arts, Wake County, Public Schools, R.H. Lightener, Mortician, Raleigh, North Carolina, Berry O. Kelly, President of Colored Fair Association and Dr. M. T. Pope, Raleigh, North Carolina. A delicious and well prepared dinner was served in the dining room of Domestic Science Hall. In order to understand the tune, energy and expertise in the preparation of the dinner meal, the following menus with specific ingredients are necessary: approximately 500 people enjoyed the

Brunswick stew (100 gallons). The stew was composed of *twelve old chickens, three-four hog ears and feet, 20 lbs of beef shank 25 pounds of crackers, well ground, 100 quarts of tomatoes, 50 pints of corn, salt and pepper to season and water to make up the amount of one hundred gallons, cook stew slowly for six-eight hours.*

There was a corn bread recipe:

1 quart of meal
1 cup of flour
1 teaspoon full of sugar
2 tablespoonful of lard
2 tablespoonful of baking powder
1 egg
milk enough to make a stiff batter

Mix and sift the dry ingredients all except the sugar, add the sugar to the lard and eggs, beat thoroughly mixing all ingredients and bake over twenty minutes.

There was a Salad Dressing recipe:

Yolks of two eggs
1 spoonful of salt
1 spoonful of mustard
1/8 spoonful of pepper
1 tablespoonful of apple vinegar

Stir vigorously, adding gradually a small can of cottonseed. One can make a sandwich by buttering the bread, then use salad dressing and add a few slices from an apple and will make a good sandwich.

Inborden concluded the meeting by giving a special message to the farmers. He discussed the diversification of a large variety of crops in order to produce better corn, peas, wheat, red, cloves alfalfa, cabbage, turnips, onions and potatoes. T.S. said that if you grow more of something to eat, you will have more to pay less. He also said that chicken meat is as sweet in January as in June. The pork will keep all the year and is sweeter from one's tub than when it comes 2,000 miles from the west. T.S. remarked that home beef and veal are just as delicious when properly dressed. He said cabbage can be made into sauerkraut, tomatoes, corn, peas, beans, pumpkins peaches and apples may be canned. He stated that the wheat can be put into your farm animals or sold for cash and the result will be more independence and more real happiness.[44]

One of the qualities of a leader or administrator is to identify the problems and also develop a reasonable solution. T.S. possessed these qualities. On July 10, 1915, he wrote a letter to Miss Beam at the AMA headquarters on a matter that he wanted to be discussed with the AMA treasurer, Irving C. Gaylord. The letter addressed fuel, coal, that was being used by the school causing smoke and dirt on some areas. T.S. said that he observed in the kitchen and dining room dirt and the accumulation of smoke from morning to night due to the use of Pennsylvania soft team coal. Inborden wrote that the flues and drafts of the kitchen range are clogged causing smoke in the kitchen and heat instead of going to the bottom of the range and working in a normal manner, but brought to the surface of the range and the result was a kitchen with a temperature of 120 to 130 degrees. T.S. said it affects the students working there all day. Inborden stated that he asked Mr. Taylor how long he expects the condition to exist and Taylor replied, until we can do better." T.S. said the soft coal would solve the problem, and suggested purchasing the coal in Wilmington, North Carolina. Inborden concluded his letter by writing the school is almost twenty years old and they have been very successful and this situation should not continue.[45] H.P. Douglass, corresponding secretary, AMA, replied to T.S.'s letter on September 7, 1915. Douglass said that the problem would be discussed with the Executive Committee and if T.S. could not persuade Mr. Taylor that his judgement is right, then he should consider dismissing Taylor. Inborden had requested a new surrey or buggy. Douglass said if he needed a surrey, they would honor his request and send the money.[46]

It was necessary for Inborden to forward a detailed letter explaining his annual budget requirements and also justification. T.S. wrote a very detailed and lengthy letter to Secretary Paul Douglass, AMA in October, 1915. T.S. said their year's enrollment was 300 students, and the enrollment could be lower due to the farmer's selling cotton at low prices. He advised parents to grow the things they need to eat and recommended that they grow peanuts, cabbage, sauerkraut, beets, cucumbers for pickles, tomatoes, beans, corn, peas, and sweet potatoes and also use broom corn to make brooms. He mentioned that some land was cleared and rented bringing in an income of one thousand dollars. T.S. said four new homes were built on land adjacent to the school farm in the last three years and Mr. Bullock who lived on the school farm for 15 years, brought 83 acres and his sons who are graduates of Brick built him a beautiful home costing two thousand dollars. He also wrote that a lady about sixteen miles from here has purchased 30 acres and the Bullock young men built her house. The lady rents it to a school teacher in the county. Another gentleman bought 22 acres from the Neville farm west of Brick School and built a home. T.S. discussed in his letter about recent purchases. He wrote that the school purchased two mares, ten milk cows, purchased a red Poland to mix with Jersey cattle. He said they need at least four more farm machines. Inborden said they planted 100 fruit trees of various kinds, apple, peach, plum, cherry, fig trees, shrubbery and improved the lawn and garden around the teachers cottage.

Inborden stated the classes made contributions to purchase additional books and magazines for their 3,000 book library. Some of the newspapers and magazines were: *The Independent, Scientific American, Worlds Work, Goodhousekeeping, Mothers Magazine, Washington Post, Southern Workman School Arts Magazine, Boston Guardian newspaper, Crisis, American Missionary magazine, Sunday School Times and the Enfield news.*

T.S. said that he corresponds with churches in the local communities. Some of the churches were Shiloh, Swift Creek, Heathsville and Morning Star. T.S. had presented Mr. Douglass with some information on the operations and productive activities at Brick School.[47] On November 12, 1915, Brick School had a cultural presentation by Madame Ada Bell Griffin of Worcester, Massachusetts. She presented tragic scenes from Quo Vades and Ben Hur's Chariot Race in her readings.

Inborden hosted an educational meeting at Brick School on November 18, 1915, for educators from within the state. There were some public officials and farmers present. Mayor L.F. Tillery, Rocky Mount, N.C.; Oscar Creech, superintendent of Public Instruction, Nash County, N.C.; A.E. Akers county superintendent of Education, Halifax County, N.C.; H.M. Finch, Railroad, YMCA secretary, Rocky Mount; F.A. McNier, Principal of High School Whitaker, N.C.; N.C. Newbold, State Agent Colored Schools, N.C; Miss Havens Carroll, Rural school supervisor, Edgecombe, County, N.C.; A.M. Proctor, superintendent, graded schools, Roanoke Rapids, N.C.; Miss E. L. Vines, Home Demonstration Agent, Edgecombe, N.C.; W.W. Vicks, Deputy Sheriff and member board of Education, Edgecombe, County, N.C.; Member Board of Education, Cicerco Denton, Michael Whitaker, and E.K. Neville, J.W. Bailey, Ex deputy Sheriff, Edgecombe County, N.C.; Miss L. Beam, assistant superintendent of Education, AMA and Dr. Paul H. Douglass, corresponding secretary of AMA. Some other participants in the meeting were Reverend George W. Hinman, Western Work, San Francisco, California; AMA, P.W. Moore, inspector, Public Schools, N.C.; Alberta Desmukes, Gonzales, Texas; Mary Battle, Colored Supervisor, Green County Schools, N.C.; E.V. Bryant, Colored Supervisors, Rural Schools, Edgecombe County, N.C.; and Samuel Arrington, former Brick student from Weldon, N.C. The principal speakers at the meeting were Mayor Tillery, Rocky Mount who stated that he was pleased with Brick School's progress, Oscar Creech, Nash County Superintendent who complimented Brick School and said the best colored teachers in his county were from Brick. Mr. A.F. Akers, Superintendent, Halifax County Schools who said Brick has a great influence in the community.

The visitors to the Brick campus inspected some of the school buildings and observed exhibits prepared by the students under the direction of Mr. Colson. On display were peas, beans, corn, collards, sweet potatoes, home made syrup and honey. There were some articles made in the sewing department on display. A Miss Little displayed her students; canned products to include peaches, peas, apples, pears, beets, beans and garden peas. The meeting ended with a band selection, Jubilee songs and brief remarks by T.S. Inborden.[48]

The concept of family unity, love, and the pursuit of higher education were all values, and goals for Inborden's three children. Sarah Jane and Thomas Sewell Inborden stressed the importance of their children achieving a college degree. The three children were enrolled in colleges between 1915 and 1920's. After graduation and years later, they would all achieve excellence in their respective fields of study. A daughter would continue the descendant line of the Inborden and Evans family. Today these descendants have achieved and are continuing to achieve in a most outstanding manner of performance. Inborden believed that it was best to send his oldest child, Julia Ella to Nashville, Tennessee, to complete high school at Fisk University's Preparatory school. She was able to enter the University later as a freshman and received her bachelor's degree in 1917. While studying at Fisk, Julia met a very studious young man, John Henry Gordon, who received his degree in chemistry and after serving in World War I, did some graduate work at the University of Chicago, Illinois. Julia returned to Brick School and taught there and later in surrounding school districts. Her interest was in music. John Gordon taught science at Brick School. Julia Ella and John Henry Gordon were united in marriage. They became the parents of three lovely children, Frances Camille, John Newton and Julia Evans, affectionately called 'sister'.

Frances Camille Gordon graduated from Brick School and then attended Hampton Institute for one year. She then transferred to Howard University where she graduated with honors, majoring in business in 1940. Frances enjoyed a very productive career in the U.S. government and also in business. She worked as a secretary for the National Youth Administration in Brick, N.C., supervisor for Signal Corps, Washington, D.C. supervising personnel clerks at U.S. Census Bureau, Suitland, Maryland, Staffing Assistant at NASA Goddard Space Flight Center, (assisted in the hiring of engineers, mathematicians and procurement officers), and a Personnel Staffing assistant, Navy department, where she retired in 1984. T.S. oldest granddaughter married Dr. Edward Early, a physician. They are the parents of Camille, Doris and Edward Early Jr. Frances owned and operated a business, Crystal Grill in Williamston, N.C. After the death of Dr. Edward Early, Frances later married Shakespeare Kent, a World War II veteran. They were the parents of Sylvia Kent. Frances' daughter Camille Early Grooms is the mother of six children, Catherine, Zayne, Nina, Ivan, Ian and Jerry Alvarez. Camille attended Howard University and so did her divorced husband, Dr. Henry Grooms, a civil engineer. Their children have been very successful. Katherine Dorothy Grooms received a degree in accounting from Howard University and a masters degree from the University of Maryland. Zayne received a masters degree from the University of California. Nina is a college graduate, and Ivan and Inor are pursuing a college degree.

T.S. would be very proud of the outstanding achievements of his great granddaughter, Doris Early Hughes. She was born in Washington, D.C., graduated from Calvin Coolidge High School and received a B.S. degree from Tuskegee and a Doctor of Veterinary Medicine from Purdue University. Hughes has had exhibits at art galleries at Lincoln University,

Pennsylvania, Georgetown University Hospital, Howard University, Edinburgh Town Festival, Virginia, Garden Show, Eta Phi Sigma Sorority, Art In The Park exhibit Holton Arms school, National Conference of artists and American Art League Gallery. Some of her selected portraits are "Mrs. Brick, Rev. Douglass Moore, Frank R. Williams and Thomas Sewell Inborden. Dr. Hughes' professional career in veterinary medicine has been commendable. She has been the vice president, Hughes Research and Development Company, Kalamazoo, Michigan, commissioner, Toxic Substance Control Commission, state of Michigan (appointed three terms by Governor Milliken); assistant professor, Morgan State University and Board qualified in Clinical Pathology. She is currently Director Veterinary Clinical Laboratory, College of Medicine, Howard University. The late Sylvia Laverne Kent who was born in Washington, D.C. and was a very industrious young lady who believed in the work effort. At the age of fifteen years, she worked after school as a typist for an insurance company. After graduation from high school, she attended Los Angeles Valley College for 2 years and received an Associate degree in Psychology. She worked briefly as an administrative assistant for a business. Later, she returned to Washington, D.C., and entered Howard university where she received a B.S. degree in Human Ecology in 1972. She also completed some graduate courses at American and George Washington Universities. She worked as an associate administrative Specialist prior to her demise in 1983. Frances Gordon Kent and her children and grandchildren are continuing to achieve excellence in their pursuits in professional goals and education.

John Newton Gordon was the second child of Julia and John Gordon. John Newton graduated from Brick School. He attended Howard University and was a member of the Reserve Officers Training Corps (ROTC). During World War II, John served in the military from March 31, 1943 until 1946. He enrolled at Lincoln University of Pennsylvania and received a B.S. degree in biology. He was a kind heartened person, generous and showed kindness to his family. John died in 1988. The youngest child of Julia Ella and John Gordon was Julia Evans Gordon. After graduation from college she worked as a social worker. Later, she married and traveled abroad with her husband to include Africa. Julia Evans Gordon Jordan died at an early age. She was a very talented daughter and granddaughter.

Honor thy mother and father and thy days shall be long upon this earth which God has given. This biblical reference definitely applies to the beloved, thoughtful, caring and responsible daughter of T.S. Inborden, Dorothy Viola Inborden Miller. The preservation of Inborden's personal papers, the Evans and Inborden homes in Oberlin, Ohio and a most unusual love and dedication of family heritage has all been made possible by T.S.' devoted daughter, Dorothy. She is a graduate of Brick School and an honor graduate of Fisk University, class, 1919, and Dorothy Miller has taught at Brick School. She always has had a desire to learn and attend school. As a child, 5 years of age, she would run away from home to be with her sister Julia in the classroom. Her mother went to the school to bring her back home. Immediately, she would run away again, back to the class room. It was necessary for her mother to enforce her instructions with some discipline methods. Finally, she was permitted to begin school at a very early age. Upon graduation from High school, she was class valedictorian and honored with her picture along with other honor students published in the Crisis magazine, 1915. Dorothy was quite happy because her picture was included with some high school alumni, Marjorie Shepherd and Jack Atkins. When Dorothy entered Fisk University, her sister called her a joiner. She joined the Mozart Society which she had to be examined to qualify by singing a hymn, one that she had never seen before. Dorothy practiced orations in college, joined the Henry O. Tanner art club which also required an exam for admission. The Temperance club was also one of her favorite clubs which she tried to encourage others to join. T.S. Inborden's ambitious daughter enrolled in a volunteer class to learn how to teach school and was permitted to substitute in the public schools of Nashville, Tennessee. Her practice teaching was in the elementary school at Fisk University in the subject, geography. Dorothy's first teaching assignment was in Home Economics at Joseph Keasbey Brick School. She also taught Home Economics, reading, spelling on the eight grade level and had time to conduct the school band.

In the fall of 1926, Dorothy Miller was teacher trainer in home economics at Winston Salem, North Carolina Student Teachers College. She was appointed home economics teacher at West Virginia State College in 1929 and later promoted head of the department at West Virginia State College. During the summers, she would study at Columbia University, where she received a master's degree. Dorothy Miller was the head of the Department of Home Economics, Division 10-12, District of Columbia Public Schools, 1933-1943. Her outstanding teaching and administrative experiences were definitely instrumental in her selection as principal, Margaret Murray Washington Vocational school. She held that position until her retirement in 1966. At her retirement ceremony, one speaker remarked that Dorothy Inborden Miller has been a distinguished leader, having received awards the Distinguished Ladies in Education Award, by the National Federation of Colored Women Clubs, 1962, and a service award from the Federation of Civics Association Community Award in 1959. She was also praised for establishing a practical nursing and business program at the vocational school. Dorothy I. Miller married the late Walker Doyle Miller, a former business manger at Brick School, and Finance Secretary at West Virginia State College, Bluefield, West Virginia until his demise. Walker D. Miller was a field clerk in World War I with service in Europe. He was a graduate of Oberlin Business College and Talledega College, Alabama. He is buried in Arlington National Cemetery.

The only son of Sarah and Thomas S. Inborden to reach adulthood was the late Wilson Bruce Inborden. Wilson graduated from Brick School and entered Howard University in 1917 and was a member of the Student Army Training Corp, (SATC). Later, he transferred to Fisk University and was promoted to a corporal and assisted in training Fisk students. At the close of the war, he returned to Howard University to study Civil Engineering. He continued his musical interest in college. Wilson Bruce played the clarinet and coronet in the band at Brick School and at Howard University, he played the saxophone. He was quite fond of his Howard sweater with the Lyre. When Howard University's band played and marched in the inaugural parade for President Calvin Coolidge, Wilson later became very ill with pneumonia. His mother and father came to Washington immediately to be with him and when he recuperated enough to travel, they accompanied him back to Brick, North Carolina. Wilson Bruce graduated from Howard University with a degree in Civil Engineering. He completed graduate classes in mathematics at Catholic University, Washington, D.C. and advanced classes in Engineering at Columbia University, New York City. He was employed as an Engineer at Aberdeen Proving Ground, Maryland during World War II. He has taught in the public schools of Raleigh, North Carolina and St. Augustine College, Raleigh, North Carolina. Wilson was married to Nan Bradford who graduated from a college in South Carolina. She worked at Tuskegee Institute and was employed in the Finance office at Brick School. Later, she worked at St. Augustine College. Nan and Wilson Bruce Inborden are buried in the Raleigh, North Carolina Biblical Garden Cemetery.[49]

Julia Ella and Dorothy Viola Inborden would write letters frequently to their parents while studying at Fisk University. Their letters portray many of their experiences at Fisk and show the strong family bond that always existed between family members. Dorothy Inborden wrote a letter to her parents on January 2, 1916. The letter read:

Dear Mama and Papa, Hope you are well. There has been a coldwave here since Christmas. I received the pamphlet on bees. We had a watch party New years night. When I got back from a Mozart meeting the other night, Sister Julia was frying sausage and I had some and grape juice. We enjoyed the walnuts, green tomato pickle, peaches and Mrs. Little's cakes. The matron of our hall is a very nice lady and was formerly in YWCA work. Last night I went down to Ryman auditorium to hear Dr. Bowen of Atlanta speak. He spoke at the President's inauguration. The colored people of the city had a parade and a program, but we could not go to that event. The program at night was fair. The Meharry Glee Club sang with a clarinet accompanist and were out of tune. An adorable quartet from Roger Williams University and a lady from Normal State and Fisk performed. A Reverend J.W. Porter read an original poem about a slave Garrison near Nashville. Dr. Bowen's speech was fine. We had a temperance meeting tonight. They said that the beef extract that Dr. Harrison gave Papa had alcohol on it and contained no food value. They had a big argument about it. Love, your daughter, Dorothy[50].

T.S. would write articles for the Brick News that would deliver an informative and motivating message to the students on values, morals, and discipline. In January 1916, he wrote that one must realize that they bring children into the world and you cannot excuse yourself from the burden and necessity of education and training them any more than you can excuse yourself pleasing them. You brought them here and you are responsible to God for starting along intellectual and moral lines that will make them efficient in any sort of endeavor. These words of Inborden written in 1916 could assist many parents in 1995.

T.S. would attend local teachers meetings to provide his support and assistance. In 1916, he spoke at the monthly meeting of Halifax County Teacher's, Superintendent Akers was present. The aim of the meeting was to encourage larger educational activity. The Brick Quartet sang old Negro melody songs and Inborden talked about his childhood, sacrifices at Oberlin and Fisk.

On February 6, 1916, T.S. and Sarah Inborden received a post card from Sarah's brother, Cornelius B. Evans. They were told that Fred Copeland, a relative died recently.

Dorothy Inborden wrote a letter to her parents on March 5, 1916. She wrote:

Dear Papa and Mama, I received the papers and money. I am glad the Farmers Day was a success. A Jewish Rabbi from St. Louis spoke in Chapel. The students enjoyed the talk very much. The local Rabbi in Nashville invited him to Fisk. I have had the first two examinations in the Sunday School Training Class, Wednesday night. I got 92 on my papers. A Miss Cutler (white) one of the secretaries of the YWCA is here now. She has given a number of talks. She is also a preacher and finished from some theological seminary. The Freshman rhetorical is Friday night. The class selects two and Miss Scribner and the rhetorical teacher will speak. There was one speaker who had not had freshman English and could not speak. All of the speakers said something from Shakespeare. The training school gave a program Friday night. The program was very good. The little kindergarten children were the best. They had a little flag drill and dance. Mrs. Crosthwait told me to take my note books and catalogues to the domestic science teacher here to see if I can get credit on my freshman work. She is rich and works for nothing. I think she studied abroad. She looks like a toad frog dressed up. She wears the littlest hats. She knows her work though. We are making a raffia pillow in the handicraft class now. We have just finished making waste baskets out of reed. We have them in every shape. Dr. Jefferson has fixed my teeth. Love, Dorothy.[51]

T.S. would clearly express his personal thoughts and analysis of blacks, their conditions of poverty, education, and how the white majority should not always view the unfortunate status of some blacks, but to look at results of progress and the desire of many blacks and their institutions of learning attempting to improve the conditions of his people. Inborden wrote an article in March 1916 and he stated:

Many things are stated about the Negro and every phase of his life has been exploited in public address, in literature and upon the stage. So much has been said against him that the name suggests the worst features of the race. He has been caricatured in every conceivable way. We should learn to discriminate between the worth and worthless of all races and to condemn any classification that includes the good with the bad, it is unjust. You missionaries who go south are good people and worthy of all praise but often they come home and inadvertently leave a sad picture. They do not mean to do so but they do. They tell you about the one room log hut where the family of ten cook, eat and sleep and that room without a window, they tell you about the crude way in which everything is done, they tell you about the quack lawyers, doctors, preachers, and teachers. There are log huts in the south by the thousands, quacks in every profession and apparently few change in the methods of doing things. Millions of dollars have been spent in 55 years and the lives of the best men. Men you have for the word and still these conditions exist. If I were supporting education work in the south or anywhere else and had only the saddest pictures presented to me as rewards of my philanthropy, I would get discouraged as doubtless as some of you have done. I want to show you a brighter side. Take for example, Fisk University organized nearly 50 years ago. Her graduates have gone out into the world and created public sentiment, changed the conditions of life, established schools, preached the gospel instead of a merely emotional religion. They are teachers of a very high order in every part of the south. Instead of one room huts, they are building cottages with rooms ranging from 4 to 12. What is true of one school is equally true of many of the other AMA schools. These schools have a purpose of the moral and intellectual advancement of the Negro. One cannot get the knowledge of the progress made in the south by riding through the country on trains and know nothing about the masses of Negroes. You must know the plantation and home quarters, real conditions. A ride through the country will give you an external view of the log cabins and a sight of a crowd of children with appearance of poverty. Many of these Negroes are discouraged but still some have the highest form of chastity and virtue. There are three difficulties encountered in the educational problems of the Negro. One is discouragement. Some Negroes feel they are only intended for cotton fields and house servants. To meet this difficulty the work must begin with the mother and father in their cabins face to face with their little ones. The rural schools teach people general agriculture and home economics. The mother meetings and the farmer conference are teaching these discouraged people to look up and have confidence in themselves. To be discouraged is the worst affliction that can come to man or beast. The beast lies down to die. Man loses all hope and cares not whether he lives or dies.

Another difficult is the popular prejudice on the part of great many white people against Negro education, what ever nature. It is only intensified. The third difficulty we have is a financial one. The system of land tenure in the south makes it hard for the poor man colored or white to rise far above the obsolete necessities of life because of problems, especially for blacks, discriminatory laws and juries. Negro intellect is as active and capable of high attainments as that of any other nationality in the world. The lower the scale of general intelligence of the masses, the higher should be the attainment of the leaders in intelligence morality, temperance, virtue, loyalty, truth and patriotism.[52]

A visit to college campuses today is an exciting and informative experience. The dress styles, laughter and fun of the students, somewhat characterizes this day and time on college campus. Many are still serious about their academic achievements. However in 1916, college life was quite different. Sarah Jane and T.S. Inborden were able to receive an interesting scenario of how college life was at Fisk from the descriptive letters from their daughters, Julia and Dorothy. On Sunday evening, May 8, 1916, Julia wrote her parents:

Dear Papa and Mama, I have been helping Miss Moore address and mail envelopes and circular letter all afternoon. It was quite a job. We finished at 7:00 p.m. Lula Bullock got back tonight. We made her come back. We are all very glad because she would have had a time making up this last month's work. It is getting very hot here. This is the eleventh of May and on the seventh of June at this very hour, I will be waiting for the train to pull in and out of Nashville. The kindergarten teacher was ill and had to go home and left another girl and myself in charge of the department for the remainder of the year. I have got to train the kindergarten children for the festival in June. Love, Julia[53]

Dorothy wrote her parents a letter on May 9, 1916 and the letter read:

Dear Papa and Mama, your letters were received and also the check. Lula came back Sunday from Salisbury, North Carolina. We went down to the movies Sunday afternoon. Friday night there was an exhibition in the gym. The boys did some hard exercises. The hardest was when one fellow turning over a bar very slowly displacing both of his shoulders and then turning back putting them in place again. They had boxing wrestling and other games. Saturday, there was a little baseball game between the fellows here. After which was the concert. This was the best program or senior concert given. The girl plays so pretty and easy not stiff. The first girl that gave a senior concert was sent home this week. She cannot finish even after she has given her concert. The president said that it was perpetual lying which caused her to be sent home. I do not know what about.

One day this week the president was going up the Livingston Hall steps and someone poured a bucket of water on him. The students that saw it said it was funny. But the students had a meeting and expressed to the president that it was not premeditated or known by any of the student body. I guess they fixed it up with him. He was angry and so were some of the seniors. But it was funny to me. I am just a crab or freshman. Yet so, I could not have so much dignity that it was not funny to me. The freshman are going to have their class day Friday. Friday night, there is going to be a lawn fete given by one of the clubs. Saturday, the Teacher Training Class is going to have a picnic. I got 99 percent on an final exam. The Saturday after the Botany class, I went to a picnic and later studied. We do not have any more Sunday night suppers. They give us a bag lunch. Love, Dorothy.[54]

In 1916, T.S. was still corresponding with Lydia Benedict, Mrs. Brick's niece. Miss Benedict wrote T.S. and said she had received his letter and was sorry to hear about the death of his mother. Miss Benedict said she must have been a wonderful lady of good character to live to a good old age and did a vast amount of good in the world. She comforted T.S. with these words about his mother. *Your mother has left a rich heritage behind her for all her relatives to follow after and she must be greatly missed.* Lydia Benedict thanked T.S. for the article he had written about his mother. Miss Benedict discussed some other matters in her letter. She wrote, I have not sold my house and have had the signs up and they do not seem to do much good. I hope to sell some day. Miss Emerson wrote me and said she was very interested in Brick School and thought you were doing a find job there and in the community. I am glad she went there.

Lydia Benedict asked about his children, she said the children must all be grown and I suppose I could not hardly recognize them. She closed her letter by asking about Mrs. Inborden.[55]

Dorothy Viola Inborden wrote her parents a letter on March 25, 1917 and told them about the speakers who had visited Fisk and a new uniform rule that was in effect. Dorothy wrote:

Dear Papa and Mama, you letters were received and I am glad to know that you are getting along all right. We are not having many speakers here now. The President is away. Ex-President Taft was in Nashville today and was to speak at the auditorium, but none of us went. Dr. Morrow told our psychology class that he did not believe in colored people going to things where they were segregated into one corner, so he did not encourage any of the students to go. He tried to get Taft here this afternoon during his tour of the city. But he did not come. Taft previously had laid the cornerstone of our library. The concert was Friday night and it rained and the crowd was not as large as last year. The concert was for the new colored YMCA of this city. They gave the YMCA 4,000 tickets to sell for the concert and sold only 30 tickets, so you see. Tell Wilson to start a garden so I can have something to can and cook next summer from our own garden. The school has a new uniform sale. The girl must wear tailored thin shirts waists and white skirts every Sunday. They can wear white uniforms and dresses only to socials. They said that we would have to wear shirts and skirts to the concert. But the Dean let those who did not have them wear dresses if they did not have a bit of lace on them, so I could wear that dotted Swiss dress. On Monday, Dr. Proctor spoke in the Chapel and also today. Dr. Proctor and her wife and Mr. Cox are here to attend the funeral of Mrs. Proctor's mother. There are more folks dying here now. You all be sure to take care of your health, Love, Dorothy[56].

Dorothy wrote a letter to her parents on May 6, 1917. She discussed the training camp for army officers and the young men's interest in volunteering for military service. The letter read:

Dear Papa and Mama, Received your letter and the money, thank you. I went with Marjorie Shephard to town and got my slippers. Shoes have gone up, 2.98 at the store. I will room with Marjorie next year. Her sister finishes Durham this year. I am sending a program of the concert Friday night. Mr. Cohen is a Fisk music graduate and finishes from Oberlin Conservatory this year. Saturday, Cora Boulder gave her graduate recital. The senior picnic was also yesterday. Julia took Murvin to the picnic. A man from Howard University came here Friday and signed up fifty young men for the training of colored officers. Howard paid his way to Fisk and Fisk had to pay his way somewhere else. The government promised to give a colored camp if they got 250 men. Now they refuse to unless they get up to 1000 men. This fellow said that they have now over 800 men. Fisk numbers over 50 signed men. The man said that the government was going to pay each man 100 dollars a month to go to the camp. That seems impossible. 600 out of 1,000 are to go to the front in France if they get the camp. There are to be 14 camps in the U.S. and one will be colored. Zeigler signed among the first to go and Murvin did too. They say there may be a slip about the pay but they would rather be volunteers than drafted men. Miss Walker, the domestic science teacher gave three parties last week one for freshman, one for the senior prep and one for her senior domestic science classes. She invited me to the freshman party. Mr. White, the new secretary of the AMA stationed at Chicago made a good talk in the Chapel Friday. A Mrs. Flower from the city brought a lady to speak to the Temperance Society here tonight. A man from Canada, the editor of the Globe largest paper in Canada had been a speaker at Vanderbilt for a week. On Monday he spoke in our chapel and told us about Canadian troops in France. He was Mr. McDaniel, the editor of the Toronto Globe. How is Sarah getting along with the commencement speech? What is her subject? Julia told me about a position offered her. Yours, Dorothy.[57]

George Edmund Haynes, Professor, social science, Fisk University wrote T.S. a letter on May 17, 1917 requesting Julia to work as a supervisor on a playground during the summer. Haynes had discussed the offer with Julia and he wanted T.S.' concurrence. Professor Haynes explained to T.S. about the job and the work environment. He wrote that the school cooperates with a settlement house supported by the Women's Missionary Council, Methodist Episcopal Church, South and the city of Nashville provides a playground on a lot adjoining the settlement house. The supervisory position pays 20 a month and Julia has been selected for the position said Haynes. Haynes stated that Julia would have her board and room in the house with two other women, one of them an elderly widow, whom everyone loves and revere as Mother Sawyer. He told T.S. that the house is under the supervision of an employed officer, a Christian white woman with whom the students have worked with the past four years. Professor Haynes said the playground was limited to children under 16 years of age and that they are under the general supervision of the director of the settlement house. Haynes believed Julia would have no exposure to city temptations but she would be in close association with three or four of the Christian women of the community. Haynes concluded his letter by saying, Julia would like the job if it was alright with you.[58] The letter from Professor Haynes to Inborden in 1917 shows the personal involvement of teacher and parent in the development process of young children. Haynes took the time to write a letter about T.S.'s daughter's agreement to accept a job position that would require her from being away from home several months, but he wanted to assure her father that she would be safe and in an environment that would continue to offer her the best guidance and protection as a young lady. In 1995, some of those responsibilities and caring for young people's future growth in morals, culture and values of 1916 are definitely needed in communities throughout the United States.

Sara Jane Inborden received a letter from her brother Cornelius Evans on June 19, 1917. He was asking her would she be visiting Oberlin during the summer. He said that he had made some profit on some goods recently. Lard that cost him 16 1/2 cents was selling for 30 cents a pound, profit of 13 1/2 cents, and pancake flour that cost him 1.60 a carton was selling for 2.70 a carton. Evans told his sister that he had a large amount of goods on hand and if she decided not to come, he would dispose of it at once. He said it has been a great awakening for him in preparing for her coming. Because the garden on the west side of the lawn has potatoes, cabbage and beans. Cornelius Evans made some interesting remarks about people's thoughts about patriotism and World War I. He stated that if anyone says anything against your son about being in the ROTC, remember one Negro in Sandusky said it was no colored man's country and would not register. Another colored man killed him with a pick handle. Evans completed his letter by writing everything is war and keep your mouth shut.[59]

Sarah Jane Inborden was a very caring mother who frequently gave her children sound advice. She would write letters to her daughters at Fisk, give them the latest news and advise on how to confront some realities of life. Her children learned it at a young age how to always be respectful have concern for others, be thrifty and maintain high standards of morals and values. Sarah Jane was a disciplining, loving and protective mother. Even though she worked as a teacher in Brick School, she had time to raise her daughters along with T.S. and always sustained her beliefs in culture, family heritage and the importance of education in preparing for their adulthood. Sarah Jane wrote a lengthy and most informative letter to Julia Ella in October 1917. The letter read:

I know you are thinking that mother has forgotten you. I have been very busy this summer canning and pickling that we may be a little bit independent of the grocery store this winter. Everything is so high that a dollar goes only a little ways in purchasing either food or clothes. I was away for about eight days during the latter part of August and I left Dorothy and Wilson to look after things. Your Dad and I went first to visit Laura Pouris then to Matthew Martins from Laura by auto. We stayed only one night at each place. The Martins have a nice home and nicely furnished and very comfortable. He has his home and store both lightened by acetylene gas, the nearest to electric light which it is possible to have in the country area. When I fell back in Martin's auto it was like falling into a soft feather bed and the cushions were so soft. He took us back to Weldon, N.C. to take the train to Seaboard. Here we stopped at Mrs. Coats who was a visitor to Bricks. Coats asked about you and Mrs. Coats wants you to spend some time with her when you come home next summer. She lives with her husband's people. They are more than good to her and are only glad to have her friends visit her. I should like to have stayed longer but I was with your Dad and had promised before leaving home not to interfere with the schedule laid down before leaving home. We were three days at Zenobia's and there we found a greater lack of conveniences than anywhere we had gone. We made her house our headquarters, but spent most of the time either in Norfolk or sightseeing and visiting. Chessom had us at his home in the country for Sunday dinner. His people are richly fixed and the dinner was fine.

We have had to send Dorothy some sheets and pillow slips. We did not get your letter saying that you had taken some bedding. Dorothy found out, she wrote us for more and your Dad sent her three sheets and four pillow slips by mail. I am sending you in this letter a check for 15 dollars and hope you will have no trouble in getting it cashed. I have written the check addressed to Miss J.E. Inborden, because in dealing with those people especially the white people, do not tell them that you name is Julia. They will be calling you by your first name instead of Miss Inborden which is due you. If there is need to use more than the term Miss, I tell them my name is S.J. Inborden, therefore you tell them you name is J.E. Inborden. If they persist in trying to find out more, then tell the white people or other people that is what you are to all but your most intimate friends. I am taking my dinner now in the dining room and preparing our own breakfast and supper. I have a boy and two girls to sweep and scrub, and help in other things about the house, but I do the most of the cooking. With Love, Mother.[60]

It is unfortunate that the real personal lives of black people from a most serious and factual presentation sometimes is not available to some non whites and blacks in 1995 devoid of humor, fiction, song, dance and comedy. Yes, the psychologists, sociologists and fiction writers present otherwise analyses and interpretation of the so-called common or majority of black people years ago and derive at interpretative results. These results are depicted in reports, television news and articles in the newspaper. However, we must admit the African American biologically and socially and some culturally is one of the most diverse groups of people. I often raise the question to medical experts what is a black American disease in consideration of the differences in genetic material in blacks today? What is the percentage of genes other than African in blacks? Do these logical inferences refute data in controversial publications in 1994, and 1995 about black Americans collective intelligence? I ask these questions individually when attending science meetings and I am in the presence of more than just a medical practicing physician. What I am saying is that many years ago and even today the culture and personal values of blacks in America are different. It is amazing to realize that many blacks in the 1800's and mid 1900's regardless of their education level had a high self confident personality and respect for themselves and their children regardless of the legal and enforced segregated laws in America. They demanded respect using many necessary means. Sarah Jane and Thomas Sewell Inborden very adamantly instructed their children how to sustain their respect for themselves even when confronting the segregated climate in America. I am only writing that it is unfortunate that some black, white, Hispanic and Asians and others do not have the factual picture of the black experience beyond what is made available to them whether a student, professional or a general worker in society. Because many of them that are living today and have never confronted African American in a social or personal situation. A recent news item posed the question what is Black Talk? Even the legal and professional honorable experts believe to a certain extent that all blacks talk alike. Of course if they have never visited classrooms that did conform to the dictates of Brown vs Board of Education ruling in 1954, then they would observe young black children talking just like their white classmates or if they have never communicated with some Africans from former colonial dominated countries by the British then they could understand that all black people do not talk the same. Even though a large number might use a characteristic so called "dialect", all blacks do not talk the same.

The Inbordens and many of the students at Brick School during a period of 45 years in eastern Northern Carolina a part of the state's black belt did not conform to the stereotypes and misinformation of black people as some people at this writing really believe that there is one module or format to characterize black people within one circle. Brick School and its agenda was refuting this in 1917. The invitations to visitors to come to Brick to participate in cultural programs was still being offered by Inborden in the years of 1915 to 1920's. The YMCA field worker, Max Yeargen lectured to the students on his experiences in India and East Africa. Author, Dr. Frank T. Lee lectured on the Bible; Channing Tobias, student secretary of the YMCA visited the campus. Dr. Homer C. Lyman, superintendent of the International Sunday School Association gave an address to the Brick family. Other visitors and speakers were Rev. Baldwin, pastor Congregational Church, Dudley, North, Carolina; (his daughter was attending Brick), George Hayes, professor, Fisk University, spoke on educational values, and Dr. H. Paul Douglass, secretary of the AMA. The noted violinist, Joseph Douglass made a return visit to the campus and delighted the students with a violin recital. His selected compositions were "Fantasie Caprice, Meditation from Thais Schon Rosmarin, Deep River, Valse Bluette, Liebes Freud, Ave Maria, Minuet and Scene from Czarda.[61] The excellent results of teaching and preparing students to establish goals of attaining education beyond the normal school level were personal accomplishments to Inborden and each member of his staff and faculty. Because some graduates of the classes of 1916, 1917, 1918 and 1919 were enrolled in colleges and universities. Those achievers were: Bessie Broadnax, Shaw University; Nellie Baldwin, Pratt Institute; Martha Harrison, Fisk University; Harold Hargrove, William Sessoms, Murvin Sumner, Chester Phillips, Wilson B. Inborden, P.J. Chessom, Olive Bond and Jessie L. Bullock, Howard University. Lillian Martin, Helen Staten, Naomi Anthony, Joseph Bullock, Alex Sessoms, and Richard Wimberly all were pursuing college courses.[62] There was always an open invitation to welcome new students to Brick School. This was a priority and purpose of the school. Those eager students who arrived in 1918 were: Sallie White, Richmond, Va.; Sara Burns, Dunn, N.C.; Mitte Lee, Dunn, N.C.; Emily Moore, Ashland, Va.; Marie Cowser, Hopewell, Va;, Pearl Roscoe, Norfolk, Va;, Mary Edwards, Durham, N.C.; Goldie Lunsford, Rougemont, N.C.; Maude F. Linsley, Wadesboro, N.C.; Alice Rains, Durham, N.C.; Hattie Branch, Enfield, N.C; Cherry Wheaton, Lynnhaven, N.C.; Annie Lauren Exum, Battlesboro, N.C.; Annie Askew, Farmville, N.C.; Victoria Walker, Charlotte, N.C.; Josephine Christmas, Richmond, Va.; Olivia Anderson, Greenville, N.C.; Rosa L. Johnson, Henrico, N.C.; Eleanor Wainwright, Portsmouth, Va.; Geneva Wiggins, Zebulon, N.C.; Callie Riddick, Norfolk, Va.; Beatrice Peebles, Rosemary, N.C.; Annie Saulter, High Point, N.C.; Fletcher Atkins, Haywood, N.C.; N. Louis Ellis, Farmville, N.C.; Grandison Garrett, Washington, D.C.; Robert E. Rogers, Raleigh, N.C.; and Robert A. Garris Jr., Gilmenton, Va.

The Brick News published some interesting accounts of what was happening at Brick during the school year 1917-1918: The YMCA Brass Band extended its talents by participating in a local rally at Shady Grove School in January 1917. The YMCA established a reading room in Beard Hall and fifty books and nine newspapers were donated. In 1918, Mary Putney spent a few days at home to attend the marriage of her sister Esther to Robert Whitehouse. Miss Putney was working in the school's post office. There were some new teachers who were on the faculty, Ethel Carr, English, Laura Smith, librarian, Lucille Gilbert, domestic science, Sadie Mitchell, sixth grade, Maude Taylor, fourth and fifth grades, and

Sarah Washington, primary grades. In 1917, students of Brick School showed an interest and were members of a select English club. The Club's objective was to promote the use of correct English. Is this information in 1995 delivering a message to some of our youth today?[63]

People of color have served this country with fidelity, bravery and dedication from its earliest days. Blacks have fought in defense of their masters during the Civil War and fought for their own individual freedom. Black military men and women as well as civilians have demonstrated their patriotism and devotion to America. It was during the years of 1917 and 1918, World War I that the students, young men of Brick college demonstrated their loyalty and patriotism. Some of them served in the army and were shipped over seas. There were alumni of Brick who, served briefly in their colleges, Student Army Training Corp (SATC), especially at Howard and Fisk Universities. T.S. Inborden showed his outstanding leadership and patriotism when he was able to get the support of black civilians in the immediate communities to purchase U.S. Savings Stamps for the defense of our country. The brave and patriotic Brick men who served during World War I were: Benjamin Hayes, Chester Phillips, George McLean, McKinley Lyons, Alfred Leach, Alexander Sessoms, Luther Arrington, John Colson, Harrison T. Taylor, Otis Davis, Joe Blount, James McWilliams, J.W. Porter, Wilson Inborden (SATC) and Edward Boykins, (SATC). Inborden was able to have the black citizens in Edgecombe and Nash counties to purchase over forty thousand dollars worth of U.S. Savings Bonds and stamps.[64]

T.S. wrote a letter to his friends to explain in more detail how the communities in East North Carolina and the school contributed to the war effort. The letter read:

The great World War I is over as you know but the cost is not over. Our boys with others handled the guns on the front lines with magnetic skill and precision while you and I fed them shot and shell and powder with reinforced goods of comfortable clothes, flour, meat and condiments from our own tables and we did it. The Christian and social workers we sent over there have brought daily cheers into our lives. We did that too, your liberty bonds. Your war stamps furnished the material for this victory. The money you paid to the United War Work Campaigned furnished medicine, nurses, doctors, books, reading matter, and kept up the morale of our men over there. It will also make them physically morally and mentally fit to come home when all the peace conditions have been established.

Colored citizens of Eastern North Carolina, listen, our state allotment was 48 million dollars worth of stamps. We have paid for 37 million dollars worth. Our people have gone over the top in pledges. We must help to make good the balance of 11 millions of dollars by redeeming every pledge made and in addition we must add to our subscriptions at least one more war stamp. The influenza has taken scores of our pledges and we must make good for them. Will You? It is the best investment that any man, woman or child can make. You are not giving it to the government, but you are lending it and it will come back increased when you will need it very much more than you do at this time. I have been appointed by the state Director, Colonel F.H. Freer,

Winston, Salem, N.C., to stimulate interest in Edgecombe, Nash, Greene and Lenoir counties and in any other places where I can help. We must go over the top with our subscriptions by redeeming every dollar pledged. Signed T.S. Inborden, Principal, Brick School.[65]

One of the principal requirements for a college president especially in private funded institutions, I believe is to possess the administrative and managerial abilities to raise funds for their institutions. T.S. Inborden had unusual superb qualities in raising money and obtaining financial support for Brick School from philanthropists and the common people in our southern states mainly who were in need. In March, 1919, T.S. wrote many friends to solicit funds for the school. He reminded the friends of Brick that in 1916, funds were being solicited for the erection of cottages for married teachers and they raised about 3,000 dollars, that was more than half of what was contributed by friends in the immediate community. He then wrote that with five teachers cottages and now we have the need to erect a guest cottage and some friends of the community have pledged 1500 dollars. Inborden stated that the foundation has been built and the war scare has cut off some of our pledges and also higher prices. He ended his letter by saying that our northern friends had given us over the years two buildings costing 22,000 dollars, will you help?[66]

Farmers Day was still a priority for Inborden to have on his yearly schedule. On March 26, 1919, a farmers day was held at Brick School and Inborden told those in attendance that we are living in a new era and that the object of this meeting is to help every farmer to meet these new conditions and to square up with every obligation imposed by the national government and by the community we all live. T.S. explained to the audience that the general farm products, cotton, peanuts, corn, tobacco which they have been growing are affected by the price of these commodities. He also remarked that the labor problem is still acute but the state and national government is trying to make an even distribution of farm help so that every emergency on the farm can be met economically. Inborden complimented the farmers and their experience in the community. He told them that their status in the social industrial and economic world is being fixed and it is of the utmost importance that you line up with the best tradition of the country in knowledge and industry. T.S. reminded the farmers that they cannot be a fixed entity unless they get squarely in line with progressing idea. At this time Inborden was a member of the Negro Workers Advisory Committee of the Department of Labor.[67]

Dorothy Inborden wrote her parents on May 12, 1919 and told them of events that had taken place at Fisk, and plans for her graduation. The letter read:

Dear Papa and Mama, Papa's letter and money was received also the packages of the skirt and waist. I thank you for all of them. I have plenty of money to last until Mama comes so don't send anymore. When Mama comes she can use some of the folk's there suit cases and we can take them back home. Ask Mrs. Forney if she is going to stay in the hall. As rooms are limited here and I would have to make arrangements early for her if she plans to stay. Please send the names of the folks to whom you want me to send invitations and their address because they should be out now. Julia sent me cloth to make a white voile dress with lace and buttons and also a silver chain with beads on it. I don't think I will have time to make it before commencement. The Junior-Senior banquet was Friday night. Judge McMundy, one of the trustees and his wife just gave the University fifteen band instruments. He was present at the banquet. The pupils' speeches were great and also the music and service. Mrs. Jefferson, dining room matron said that she had never heard or seen a banquet go off so smoothly, Everybody had a big time. Saturday night, Major Dr. Moton of Tuskegee, Alabama spoke and also Judge Munday on Sunday morning. Thomas Jesse Jones preached and Sunday night Mr. Napier and Mr. Paul Cravath spoke. They all left last night after the service. Today Lieutenant William Dawson of Albany Georgia (the late Congressman William L. Dawson who was born in Albany, Georgia and attended the Albany Normal School, that T.S. was principal) spoke in the chapel. He is studying or has been studying law at Chicago, Illinois before he went to France. He finished in Mr. Elzy's class. Lt. Dawson's speech was one of the best that has been made lately. He spoke of what we as students must do to overcome prejudices which is so strong now. The students applauded a great deal. The president did not seem to like the tone of his speech and got up and made a few remarks which indirectly hit his speech. Everybody got his point but they could not help but face facts as they were and as Lt. Dawson put them, it was a fine speech. Dr. Moore is here. I went down to see him. Wilson sent me four carnations to wear on Mother's day, but he did not have one so I gave him one back to wear himself. Did Miss Little get her veil that I sent to her? I hope that you are all well. Your, Dorothy.[68]

The letter Dorothy wrote her parents in 1919 is most historical because she has mentioned the names of some distinguished personalities that she had the opportunity to meet or hear speak at Fisk University in her most beautiful life time of 76 years ago which are probably still memories now of her experiences of yesteryears.

Secretary George L. Cady of the American Missionary Association wrote a praise worthy article *Planting Ideals in Soil and Souls* about Brick School and Thomas Sewell Inborden in 1920. The article posed the question, what and who and where was Brick and Inborden? Cady stated that during a tour of black schools in the south, he told Mr. A.A. Ward of the American Board of Mission in Ceylon that with the idea of finding a school which could be used as a model in Ceylon, he reached a conclusion. Ward found out that the school that came nearest to being a model for the school in Ceylon was Brick Normal School. Cady discussed in his article that under the leadership of T.S. Inborden, the eleven acres of the former Estes' plantation was transformed from a waste with no productive value to the great agricultural experimental station and training school. Cady said that Inborden from the school's beginning made himself an expert in eery branch of progressive agriculture and had demonstrated the best method for growing cotton, corn, peanuts and sweet potatoes. Secretary Cady stated that T.S. was also a consulting expert in analyzing soils, and rotation of crops. He was also an authority in high grade cattle. Secretary Cady was quite aware of T.S. knowledge of bee culture which he had learned from his father-in-law, Wilson Bruce

Evans when he lived in Oberlin, Ohio. Cady said that there was probably no one of his own race and few white men who knew more about bee culture than Inborden. Cady also praised T.S's expertise in botany and wrote that excepting the expert botanists of the State Universities, it is doubtful if anyone there about can so accurately give the Latin name of all the flowers of that region. The article mentioned that the Brick Industrial School had taught the best methods of agriculture and a domestic science. Cady stated that he was impressed when he visited a domestic science class conducted by Inborden's daughter, Dorothy Inborden Miller. He also remarked that the Brick School played a great influence within the community and he observed a tract of 4,000 acres of land owned by blacks. There were residents who were inspired by Brick School. Cady gave an example. There was Mrs. Silver and her husband who was a successful minister and business man. They owned many acres of land. Mrs. Silver used to come to Brick and exchange blackberries and blueberries for old clothing which had been sent to brick by northern benefactors. There were many successes similar to the Silvers all who were inspired by Brick School. The article said the Federal Farm Loan Organization had been helpful to some farmers in the area. T.S. was quoted about his personal views on the subject of farm loans.

T.S. Inborden said, only live and wide away farmers may take advantage of this loan. The man who has owned and lived on a farm for a number of years and has not made improvements, kept up repairs and made payments on the farm, would not qualify for the loan. He must not only make improvements and payments on his farm, but he must have his children in school if he has any children. The borrower must stand for something substantial in the community as a citizen. Many farmers cannot qualify on making the first application, but after several years when they have learned what the requirements are, often apply again and are received by the local organization and granted a loan. They learn that to be a progressive farmer, one must step up into a different class.

Secretary Cady stated that in 1920, a report revealed that there were 200 accredited white high schools in the state and seventeen for the black children. The head of the state educational department in an interview stated when it came to real public high schools North Carolina did not have a single one for the black race. He was referring to those schools who awarded fifteen credit units the same as the white schools. Cady said that the combination of the practical, educational and spiritual has made T.S. Inborden's twenty-five years of investment in Brick School enviable in its rich rewards and brought children in the respect of every man of every race in his region.[69]

Secretary Cady wrote a great testimony to T.S. Inborden highlighting numerous attributes of T.S.' diverse abilities and his most outstanding accomplishments in the leadership of Brick School in twenty-five years. Cady was an AMA secretary who actually gave T.S. credit for what he was doing and praised him in a most unbiased way, because in later years, some of the AMA secretaries either were not aware or possibly forgot about the many contributions that Inborden had made to Brick School and several county communities in eastern North Carolina.

T.S. Inborden wrote some definitive thoughts on education and some of his ideas could be applied today for many of our schools which are in desperate need of change and more structured programs. T.S. wrote:

> A college education should not make one haughty and stuck up or give one an air of superiority or an air of self importance, it should make one self respecting, it should give one a spirit of humility, it should give one an air of refinement and culture, it should make one the master of the conditions of his environment, it should be productive of the material, intellectual, moral and spiritual good of the community in which one lives. One whose ethical nature has been trained sees beauty in people. He sees the hand of God in the formation of the firmament, the stars, the moon, the sun, the clouds, the contour of the earth, the courses of the rivers and streams, in all vegetation and the growth of things generally. He sees a picture with new vision. The printed page is a revelation as well as an evolution to him and her. They have not the time to sit about the streets, railroad stations, hang out at public places or to engage in community gossip, or other mischief that sets the community ill at ease and makes work for lawyers, judges and juries. He finds the sweetest companionship in the best literature, paintings, music and art. One appreciates the finest adjustments of mechanical operations of any sort. It gives me a keen sense of discriminator and beauty. Someone says, If you educate all the people, who are going to do the work? The object of education never was intended to delete any class of people from work. It ought to create better conditions of work and give one a better attitude toward work. Intelligence ought eliminate most of the drudgery. All work by which one must earn a living ought to be honorable. It may always be pleasant. However, some work is irksome and tiresome when one's attitude is out of harmony with it. He is a happy man be he rich or poor who has a job and finds his greatest pleasure in it if his attitude is right.[70]

Inborden wrote an article about a successful family that lived on the Brick farm property. He was quite fascinated about the achievements of this family and their quest for education and a more prosperous life. Ironically, a daughter of this family is living today near Washington, D.C. and is blessed with 95 years.

The family was the Bullocks of Brick, North Carolina. Mr. and Mrs. George Bullock were the parents of four boys and four girls. All of the children attended school at Brick Normal. The subject of T.S.'s article was *Does It Pay?* Inborden wrote that the children had to walk eight miles to school prior to the family moving on the farm. Some of Bullocks' friends, told him that it would be impossible to feed and cloth his children, run a farm and at the same time give them an education. T.S. said the Bullocks met every discouragement but they kept their children in school. Inborden stated that all of Bullock's possessions were under a mortgage for rations, farm implements and supplies. However, under the Brick School system, Bullock was able to pay off the mortgage and afterwards buy his provisions in cash and as the opportunity came he purchased a farm with 83 acres. Inborden discussed in the article how the Bullock children were successful in their chosen endeavors. A son Benjamin, graduated from the University of Minnesota with honors, a son,

Joseph was a training teacher in an Episcopal school in Charlotte, North Carolina and later became a dentist. The oldest daughter studied at Brick and later married a minister of one of the largest Baptist churches in the state, Reverend A.S. Croom of Salisbury, N.C. A daughter married a merchant in Salisbury, N.C. She had finished Brick with a major in sewing and became a dressmaker. A daughter Lula was a graduate of Brick and Fisk University. Another daughter, Jessie was a Brick graduate and also a graduate of Howard University. She became a teacher in home economics and the wife of the late Dr. Robert A. Thornton, a distinguished physicist and master teacher who had studied with Albert Einstein, the noted physicist. Inborden raised the question Does It Pay? because he had observed that the Bullock boys came home one summer and built a house for their parents. They drew up the plans and worked out every detail in the construction of the house. The house cost about 2,000 dollars. The only cost outlay was the material. T.S. said that the house was not only built well, but was furnished largely by the boys themselves and was constructed on their own farm. Inborden said it does pay to do the progressive things. T.S. said their experiences were a transition from the small cabin but the mother was a woman of natural endowment and she knew how to take care of such a house in the style in which it is built. While it is three miles from town, it was lighted with electric lights within a year. He replied by saying that if enumeration is to be in the accumulation of a beautiful home like this with 80 acres surrounding it with sufficient horses to work the farm with implements and other necessities for farm life, it pays. T.S. said the enumeration does not stop here. Here are the boys who have mechanical skill, agricultural knowledge and academic training which has given them eminent successful life. The girls of the family are serviceable in their sphere. T.S. concluded his article by saying the process of the Bullock's children training has given them an ethical conception that is invaluable in any community in which they may live.[71]

The Bullock story portrays how many black families in the south, especially North Carolina were able to survive, receive an education and obtain monumental attainments in life in their respective professions. They were faced with the walls of oppression and forced segregation, but it did pay for them to have faith, belief in God and they saw happiness in the morning. I ask the question today why cannot the young people of today have the self discipline, inspiration, motivation and the initiative to achieve excellence in all of their endeavors. The Bullocks did it so well. There are some descendants of the Bullocks today who have made outstanding contributions in their professions. As T.S. would say it has paid for them the descendants of the Bullocks of Brick, North Carolina.

On January 4, 1920, Julia Ella Inborden Gordon wrote a letter to her parents. She and her children were in Chicago with her husband, John Gordon, who was studying at the University of Chicago. She asked her parents to look for a farm for them with less than 150 acres. She thanked them for some cake and honey that was received. Julia Ella said her husband wants to raise peanuts, and hogs and they wanted some literature on peanuts, hogs, forestry and walnuts, hardwood trees, sheep and turkey. She had a note for her sister Dorothy which thanked her for a cake and some silver.[72]

The year of 1920 brought some sorrowful news for Sarah Jane Inborden. She received a telegram from Jeffersonville, Indiana that her sister Julia A. Evans Johnson had died and the funeral would be held in Oberlin, Ohio.[73] Some of Julia A. Johnson's descendants are living today. She was the mother of one son and four daughters. A daughter Daisy Viola Richardson had an extended family and also her sister Susan Sunbean Watkins.

T.S. had a very good friend, Reverend Dr. George W. Moore, a graduate of Fisk and Theology Oberlin College. Inborden learned about Moore's demise on March 14, 1920. T.S. was saddened by Moore's death and he decided to write a letter and also a news article acknowledging Rev. George Moore's good work in the ministry and also a missionary for the AMA. Inborden wrote that he was sunshine and happiness all the time and everywhere. To know him was to love him. He said Moore's wife, Ella Shepard Moore, a graduate of Fisk, was one of the original Jubilee Singers. She had died in 1918. Inborden stated that Moore leaves two sons and a niece and he had died at Fessenden Academy in Florida where he spent the winter months. He ended his letter by writing that George Moore was a national figure in the church and civic social work.[74]

T.S. was grateful for the continual northern support he would received for the school. The AMA wrote T.S. and sent checks for 100 and 50 dollars each for scholarship money for two students, William and Harold Lazarus for the school year, 1920-1921. The money was sent by a generous friend, Mr. E.M. Van Dycke from Brooklyn, New York.[75] The corresponding secretary of AMA, wrote T.S. and informed him that AMA sent a letter to Ford Motor Company asking if it would not be of mutual interest for them to place a Ford Tractor on the Brick farm. The tractor would e used for demonstration purposes for the black farmers in the community. Cady told Inborden that he did not make a plea on basis of charity or missionary but merely as a matter of business, putting it up to them that it was for their interests, advertising purposes as well as for the school's benefit. T.S. was pleased with assistance for the school.[76]

Sarah Jane Inborden's health was beginning to fail in 1920. Her daughter Dorothy had her to visit New York and a physician prescribed insulin injections twice a day for diabetes. Dorothy I. Miller was studying at Columbia University when her mother visited. She was staying in one of the University's dormitory for the first time. Because they had opened a seven room apartment for the black students. Her roommates were a Mrs. Eaton from Henderson, N.C., and a Miss Everett from Indiana who was teaching at the State Normal School, Nashville, Tennessee. Dorothy had a single room facing 122nd Street and her rent was 205 dollars a year. She was completing the requirements for her masters degree.[77]

CHAPTER 4

Challenging Years

In the summer of 1921, T.S., Sarah Jane and their son Wilson travelled to Hampton, Virginia. Inborden attended a ministers' conference at Hampton Institute. When T.S. visited Wilmington, North Carolina in 1921, he made some observations and later wrote an article for the American Missionary. He said while soliciting money for an institution in the city, that he was advised that ninety percent of teachers in the counties were from that school. Yet raising money was an unpopular proposition in the community among a large class of people who had the educational touch. The best of us get poor when you ask for money for an educational institution said Inborden. T.S. wrote if one does not have a vision of the needs of his children and race, he does not give. Most play poor. Inborden said the best colored people in Wilmington will agree that the town has gone backward, because I was shown some of the finest residence in the town and told that they were built by colored contractors. They are all gone now. T.S. was told that no more than four colored youth went from the city to college in 1920. There was not a colored high school in the county, yet the community had a Negro population of 14,000. At one time, the city was an important seaport and vessels came from all parts of the world. Inborden stated that he had written the article to show and call attention to the background behind farming interest. The historic city has good roads. Colored people own land, one-ninth of the land in the county. T.S. said a few own farms, however there are thousands of acres of land not productive. Most of the land is owned by one individual. Inborden emphasized that farming operations could be profitable in the area. However, Negroes will work the soil under most adverse conditions if there is an opportunity for them to own the land. These were some of my observations in Wilmington, N.C., wrote T.S.[1]

Inborden would purchase supplies for the school from a friendly grocer in Enfield, Mr. Meyers. Meyers slogan was *Everything for Everybody, Never a day without bargains,* Meyer The Hustler. T.S. would purchase soap, meal crackers, oranges, bananas, lemons, sugar, powder, butter, seed feed, fish, shoes and flypaper from the grocer. The YMCA was very active on Brick campus. On Sunday March 27, 1921, there was a program commemorating the 26th anniversary of Brick YMCA. The program included a hymn, scripture reading, prayer. Titt Phillips gave a clarinet solo *Angle Serenade.* There was installation of officer and announcements by T.S. Inborden.[2]

The future of the farmer was always a concern of T.S. He wrote an article in the school newspaper on farm life. The article expressed some views on farming that would help to improve the farmers condition. T.S. stated that the mortgage business is a bad business for the average farmer to enter into partnership. The farmer must become educated, read agriculture papers and magazines, visit county and state fairs. Organization will help the farmer to get the best price for his products, cooperate with fellow farmers. Inborden said the farmer must utilize the services of the Federal Farm Loan Organization and Tri County Federal Farm Loan organization. T.S. gave some direct suggestions that farmers must consider seriously. They were, the farmer must buy modern machinery for his farm such as corn planters, cotton planters, gang blows and tractor engines. T.S. said a farmer who can buy an automobile ought to be able to buy a tractor engine. Although farming is a complicated and diversified occupation, one must learn the correct procedures. Remember, wrote Inborden, that it takes a horticulturalist to grow apples to perfection, it takes a dairyman of the best type to place milk and butter on the market and to meet state and county inspection and public approval. T.S. said it takes a mechanic of the highest quality to keep up the repair on the farm of fences, houses and machinery. It takes a bookkeeper to keep farm accounts and records. A farmer must be something of a wall street broker to keep up with market prices, so that he will know how and when to sell his farm products. T.S. was trying to tell the black farmers that they must prepare themselves to be competent and aware of various duties they will have to perform. He wrote that the farmer must be an electrician, an engineer as well if he is going to compete with his neighbor who lights his house with a Delco light and runs all of his machinery with power. Inborden said the farmer needs necessary information for special treatment and expert knowledge about cattle, cows, sheep, hogs, horses, poultry, bees and different strains. To be a first class farmer one must be a chemist of the first magnitude knowledge of chemicals in production of crops, fertilizers, grades, plant diseases and insect life affecting crops. Inborden's message to the farmer was simply be diversified, a generalist and a specialist in some areas in order to succeed, compete and survive financially in the business of farming.

In 1922, Inborden was able to write an article on some progress in rural life in North Carolina. He said Edgecombe County located in eastern North Carolina had 19,000 Negroes with 4,000 owning their farms and homes with 17,000 acres of land. The school population of the county is 7,000 with an enrollment of 5,000 and there is a black supervisor. Halifax county has an area of 681 square miles with a Negro population of 30,000 and own 70,000 acres of land. The school population of 10,000 has an enrollment of 7,000 average attendance of 3,000 children. T.S. wrote that the people meet every condition for erecting school houses and a few months ago, they had raised their part for twelve Rosenwald schools. Their homes are clean. Well constructed and give an appearance of thrift and happiness. T.S. said that in counties where there are rural supervisors for school and farms, he noticed a marked difference in the material progress of colored farmers. Inborden wrote that the progress was farmers with better work animals, improved machinery, out houses more orderly constructed, better pumps and well fixtures, screen windows and doors, homes painted and the planting of flowers and fruit trees. T.S. realized that education is the key. He believed that a trained mind and a trained hand and heart are indomitable. He also said an unlettered man is living in isolation and he cannot appreciate the world in which he lives because there is no progress and a static mind atrophies.[3]

An unusual experience for T.S. occurred when he was visiting in Chicago in February 1922. He made a statement in writing to the police department. He wrote that upon arriving in Chicago, Illinois with two pieces of luggage, he was walking on 32nd Street toward Forest Street when he was stopped by two men. They began to use rough language and

T.S. said he thought they were talking to someone behind me and in looking back I saw no one. Inborden said one of the men grabbed him by the arm uttering all sorts of language and they told me to follow them. I told them they had no right to hold me up on the street. T.S. stated that he saw two colored men across the street and he called them and said that he was being held up and asked them to call the policemen for help. The men cam across the street toward T.S. and at this time, the two men who were holding Inborden, suddenly pulled out badges, identifying that they were policemen. The policemen said that they were looking for bootleggers and that T.S. should not have resisted them. T.S. told them that he had no whiskey and showed them his card name and business and then the policemen tried to humiliate him in every possible manner by cursing him. Finally, the insulting experience was resolved. But Inborden's visit to Chicago would become a remembrance of how some northern law enforcers treat people whom they possibly misidentify possibly. Chicago was a visit to never be forgotten for T.S. Inborden.[4]

The AMA had selected Inborden to take a five month trip in 1922 traveling in northern states, New England states and Western states, on a Missionary journey. He gave addresses and attended conferences and meetings. A detailed report of his trip is included in Appendix 17. *A Trip To California*, the trip was most informative and educational for Inborden. He was very inspired and motivated by the experience. On February 14, 1922, T.S. wrote Sarah Jane a letter from Los Angeles, California. The letter read:

I am 36 hours out from San Francisco in an old Mexican city. I left San Francisco Monday morning at 7 o'clock and stopped late in the afternoon at Fresno for the night. I was impressed with scenery in one of the parks. I was located in Collins Hotel across from the park and walked and enjoyed the trees and plants. We travelled several miles in the San Joanquin Valley - San Waukene. It is a pretty valley miles and miles of oranges, figs, olive trees and grape vines. The fields were very clean. The trees are full of oranges. The cold weather has hurt the fruit very much but they sell everywhere for five cents a piece. They ship million of dollars worth of fruit from the community of Fresno. You see a great preparation for packing and shipping. The irrigation projects are great, canals and ditches. The valley was perfect level. The water is run by the gravity from the higher levels. We were near out of sight of the mountains and snow. I spoke to a Baptist church and also met old man Hargrove at Fresno and a dozen people from Charlotte and Salisbury.[5]

T.S. Inborden had a cordial relationship with other educators of black schools. He had made a visit to The Palmer Memorial Institute and was greeted by its president, Charlotte Hawkins Brown. She wrote T.S. a letter and stated that she was glad he enjoyed his visit to her school. She said that she had been seriously ill for nine weeks, but God has blessed her and she is back on the job. She was trying to raise 1,000 dollars for a project and asked T.S. if he would like to help her.[6]

In 1923, T.S. wanted to purchase some necessary equipment and improve the physical plant of the school. He appealed to the community for assistance. T.S. wanted a new cowbarn, water and sewer systems, a girls dormitory, a teacher's cottage, cement walks, and electric lights for all the buildings. Inborden used his unique and convincing approach to ask people to contribute in order to match whatever funds the AMA would allocate for these projects. T.S. told his potential donors that every dollar you put into this school helps you to build your own monument, because your money has value only as it stands for an investigated life. He also reminded the people that some of them had made pledges several years previously and their pledges have not been made good. T.S. said the institution is still growing, but without you, I do not know anything better for anyone to do than to live with a progressive and growing institution. Your pledge means sacrifices. Remember, reminded Inborden, that no one can live next year from what we ate last year. We have only a few days and we shall be glad to hear from you and accept your gift to Brick. There were some immediate responses to his request. Some very faithful and thoughtful people were: W.P. Grant, Shields, N.C.; Moses Haywood, Shields; Charles Exum, Whitakers; William Draugham, Whitakers; W.L. Lyons, Whitakers; Ransom Martin, New Haven, Connecticut; Benjamin Williams, Brinkleyville, N.C.; J.W. Whitehead, Ringwood, J.D. Boone, F. Williams, J.L. Lewis, all of Ringwood; Willie Smith, Battleboro, N.C.; Blair Bullock, Enfield; David Sessoms, Nashville; Lafayette McDaniel, EnField; Phyllis Washington, Whitakers; James Bryant, Battlesboro; Charles Simmons, Whitakers; Edward Arrington, Nashville; W.L. Austin, Enfield; and E.S. Dancy, Nashville, N.C.[7]

 Inborden wanted his friends and citizens in the community to know about the wonderful progress of Brick Normal School when it was 28 years old. He sent them a letter where he highlighted the outstanding improvements of the school's advance in the administration, management, curriculum and immediate needs. Again he asked the interested people to contribute to the future stability of Brick. T.S. wrote that some of us are called to places of administration, responsibility, and leadership. Others are called to keep the door or simply to cheer the firemen. Both must answer for his native or acquired ability. The school has sought all these years to fill the most important place in the life of the community. Inborden stated that it has influenced the farmer and teacher as much as the boys and girls. He reminded the people that the mission of Brick has not been a failure, absolutely not. All of eastern North Carolina can testify that the institution has been a potent factor in every good thing. T.S. said if you want to change the conduct of men you change their psychology, that is all. Take away your Christian institutions and you take away the most vital assets for good that a community can have. Inborden remarked that Brick does not stand still it must move upward and outward or it will retrogress. We are the watch tower, to point out to you the signs of progress. Our personal sacrifices are not sufficiently large to meet the financial needs of our educational institutions. Inborden outlined the needs of the school. He wrote a kitchen will cost less than 3,000 dollars. We have been promised one thousand on condition that one raise 1,000 dollars. This ought to be an easy job. We are not excusing anyone from accepting a part of this responsibility. T.S. again explained to the people that the value of their dollars have a more powerful investment and interest. He stated that every dollar you put into this school is a legacy to your children and grandchildren. Money has value only as it stands for a substantial worthwhile return. There are more than a hundred thousand Negroes in this community needing such an investment. T.S. said it is only as we divest ourselves of ourselves that we are best able to serve the times and communities in which we live. If we do not add to the advancement of the civilization in which we live, Inborden reminded the community that if we do not add to our posterity a better spirit, a better mind, and a larger opportunity for service then we have lived in vain and to have lived in vain is worse than not to have lived at all. Inborden asked the readers of his letter to act on their own impulse of their best thought.[8]

Brick School had a Farmers Day in February, 1923. The major theme was *Live At Home*. There were discussion groups on the topics of growing corn, raising hogs, poultry, family cows, home making and home orchards. T.S. had invited speakers from the State Department of Agriculture.

T.S. Inborden had been honored when he was elected president of the North Carolina Industrial Association. T.S. had some definitive ideas and plans for a scheduled fair and composed a letter to the members of the Association because he had made a study of the conditions about the proposed fair from inside and outside. He said that except for the association's executive committee, he had some criticism. Inborden wrote that we must meet these criticisms if we expect to have a fair that will meet the approval of the public whose interest we must have and whose interest we must serve, and we also must remember that these problems did not exist at the last fair. Inborden outlined the things that he thought must be accomplished in order to have a successful fair and consider the wishes and support of the people. T.S. wrote that some have criticized about the Fair's awards and prizes. With some people never receiving them. The criticism false or true makes enemies and keep people and exhibits away and hurts our interest. The Executive committee must correct this and there is also a lack of organization because one man cannot run a fair. The committee should be composed of some of the largest hearted men in the state, some of biggest and some of the best. If they fail to function, drop them from the committee and put in those who will function. T.S. was writing about possible solution for problems that many leaders face today and unfortunate do not apply direct and swift solutions as Inborden did so eloquently in the mid 1900's. T.S. even referred to the organization's constitution. He stated that it should be very explicit on these changes, and the fair should be a democratic event with the people making decisions. I think the officials of this organization must change their policy. A few men should not be allowed to control the organization neither by proxy or by personal holdings. Had the constitution been explicit, these things would not have occurred. The greatest criticism that has come to me since I have been a member is that it is run by a few men. Whether this is true or not the criticism has influence with the people and we as officers must meet the criticism.

Inborden said the four organizations of the county have grown wonderfully in the estimation of the people and our business and policies must have public approval. If they do not the state will have cause to withdraw its interest and support. In view of these larger interests in every part of the country and the continued growth of public opinion, I would make a few suggestions which I think should be taken into consideration. Inborden's suggestions were that: The financial interests should be pooled and all stocks placed on the market and sold. The stock held by anyone man should be limited. The secretary of the Fair should be paid for his services by the year. The secretary and the treasurer should be responsible for all money received and paid out on accounts of the fair and they should be under bond for at least 5,000 dollars. This is a guarantee to the people as well, a measure of the business thing to do. T.S. continued with his suggestion when he wrote: All expenses of the Fair should be paid immediately after the fair from receipts in hand. The stock brokers should be paid a percentage on their investment. We must select a place of our own to use as the fair ground rather than pay an increase amount to the city for the space. We need at least ten acres and a well constructed building. A reserve fund should be banked every year to meet the cost. This proposition could be a large asset to the organization and people. The remuneration paid your fair officials should be fixed by the Executive committee, because if you have men on this committee who are not progressive and who do not see the visions of larger things, then they should not remain[9]. T.S. Inborden portrayed his dynamic leadership, business qualities and above all his recurring interest and love for the people, the hard working common and innocent citizens of his community. This letter illustrated T.S.'s characteristic of being able to challenge others to think about and do the right thing or do not belong to a progressing organization.

The state of North Carolina decided in December 1923 to place under their direct control all elementary classes in private school. There would be an elimination of all grades below the seventh grade level in private schools. When T.S. learned of these plans he sent a letter to the community. Inborden told the patrons of the school that he wanted them to attend a meeting on December 28, 1923. He said that the state was contemplating to taking over all elementary work in our private schools and if this is done it will mean that we shall eliminate all grades below the seventh grade. T.S. stated that in 1922, they employed two additional teachers. This year we have one teacher. It will be a hardship to eliminate all in these grades but we must cut off those who will not be full time, and those who could not progress in their work, please attend the meeting and be on time.[10]

The North Carolina Negro Farmers Congress had their semi annual meeting January 22-23, 1924 at the Court House in Clinton, North Carolina. There was a big free barbecue dinner each day and a fine display of public school work in Sampson County and an elaborate exhibition of farm and garden products. The theme of the meeting was *Better Living and More Money On The Farm*. The program included a devotion, secretary's report, semi annual address, and singing. The meeting's discussions were *The Importance of Fertile Soil,* the best uses of commercial fertilizer and a boll weevil specialist, J.A. Evans gave a speech. There were also discussions on good seed and how to get them, some common plant diseases and how to control them. The Secretary of the Congress was John D. Wray. The meeting was honored with the annual address delivered by the President of the Negro Farmers Congress, Thomas Sewell Inborden.[11]

The American Missionary's February 1924 edition published an article on "*State Cooperation with Joseph K, Brick School In North Carolina* by Mrs. Dorothy Inborden Miller, Teacher. The daughter of T.S. wrote that for many years higher education in North Carolina has largely been left to private institutions. There are only six private institutions in the state that offer to Negroes courses higher than those of high school rank. Mrs. Miller said the number of accredited high schools for Negroes in North Carolina are 24, and only eight are public high schools. The figure tends to recognize the tremendous contribution of private institutions in the past and present time in promoting the growth and expansion of intelligence in the state. Dorothy I. Miller said the AMA had three high schools located in North Carolina. At the close of 1922-1923 class sessions, only one of the schools was accredited. The only accredited school was Brick Normal school. She explained that Brick maintained a four year course of study with an eight month school year exclusive of holiday. The recitation periods were 45 or more minutes in length and 15 units were needed for graduation. Mrs. Miller stated that there were four full time teachers for the high school who possessed a bachelor's degree from a recognized college. The school library is expected to be completed and will contain reference books, periodicals, encyclopedia, modern fiction, standard literature, vocational and historical books, maps, charts, slides and laboratory facilities. Mrs. Miller said that the private schools in North Carolina have been pioneers in Negro education.[12]

The article by Dorothy Miller clearly shows the real importance of Brick School in eastern North Carolina as well as the state. Brick School was providing a paramount service to the black community when the priority of public schools for all black children was not on the agenda of the white ruling majority of North Carolina politicians in the 1920's.

The AMA had a group of missionary trained observers who traveled in foreign countries and in the southern states. They were called Members of the Deputations who came under the supervision of Secretary Cady. One of the trained observers was Reverend Henry S. Leiper. He had lived in Tennessee and North Carolina and had seen progress in Negro education. Leiper was very impressed by reports from Mr. Newbold, superintendent of Negro Education in North Carolina and the Negro principals and faculty member. He wrote in his report to the AMA that the kind of educational work the AMA is engaged in in the south produced profound faith in the mental, moral, and spiritual qualities of leadership in the colored race and is being brought to light by such a man as Principal Inborden at Enfield, N.C. Leiper said Inborden revealed himself to us in our brief visit as a man of amazing resources, unfailing energy, transparent honesty and a degree of unselfishness rarely met anywhere. The impress of his personality upon the community was everywhere manifest. Leiper stated that T.S.'s energy and skill in managing a large enterprise was evidenced by the discipline, neatness and efficiency to be seen on the campus. The outreach of his life as invested in that school was manifest when we visited the homes of people who had come in contact with him to appreciate the value of education for their children. Leiper wrote that after the children have received their training under Principal Inborden, they go out in the world to make a success of their lives in broad fields of human science. Rev. Leiper as an outsider was able to observe those magnificent qualities of T.S. Inborden as an educator and manager who gave the kind of leadership which others could compare. Leiper wrote that Principal Inborden is an outstanding example of the kind of leadership for which one who has had the privilege of knowing Booker T. Washington, Dr. Moten, Dr. Proctor, Dr. Garner and Dr. Lawless who also worked increasingly among the colored people. Leiper was simply saying, I can compare Inborden with those great men because his qualities are also as good as their leadership or even better. This was a great attribute of T.S. Inborden.[13] I was quite surprised to read Rev. Leiper's remarks on biological genetic diversity in 1924 when he wrote about his views on the mingling of white and Negro heredity in the south. Leiper said he had seen government statistics showing that one fourth of the Negroes in America today (1924) have some white blood in their veins. This is an interesting reflection by Leiper in 1924 because in 1992, I was discussing a science matter with a very qualified geneticist and physician who is a professor at a very reputable university. He told me that there has been research in recent years that produced results alleging that the majority if not all of African Americans in the United States today have at least 25 percent of European genes. I then posed the question that the percentage could increase depending on the varied genetic heritage of the individual's family to include Indian, white, Asian and others over the years. He agreed that would increase the percentage of genes other than African. Of course, this is a subject that people today do not like to discuss because they only see two colors black and white and in this respect genetic diversity is invisible to them and not a significant factor to consider, especially when people say medically this is a black disease. I always say to the scientists what about the varied genes in people who are not just black. Always, I receive no response. Therefore, Rev. Leiper's observations in 1924 were interesting, because he went on to write that it never came home to him about Negroes with white blood in their veins until he visited the black schools and sat and counted a room full of 150 to 200 students where a minority who could by any stretch of the imagination be considered pure Negro. Leiper said he saw a moral obligation of his white race toward the Negro race when you consider two and half million of sons and daughters or grandchildren of black mothers and white fathers are present today (1924) in our land.[14] Rev. Leiper was discussing a real true factor of the residual sexual effects of slavery as far as miscegenation occurred. I am sure that his visits to the classrooms of Brick Normal School also gave him some thoughts on the subject that he probably never realized.

There was some jubilant news and a great prophetic vision in 1924 when the results of a North Carolina State Survey Board on black education presented some recommendations. The Director of Negro Education recommended that Brick Normal School add a grade each year until it became an accredited Junior College. The vision became a reality on May 14, 1925. The Executive Committee AMA voted that Brick Normal School should become known as the Joseph K. Brick Junior College. The Executive Secretary also initiated action to begin the reduction of the land acreage at Brick. They agreed to deed two acres of Brick Property to the County Board of Education for a Rosenwald School to be constructed. When the new Brick Junior College opened its doors on September 25, 1925, many citizens of color in eastern North Carolina were happy. Twenty-two freshmen enrolled the first year. There were twenty from North Carolina, 1 from Georgia, and 1 from Virginia. The college was accredited by the state and also the high school. The college had a library, 3,300 volume, chemical laboratory, sports facilities to include tennis courts, basketball courts, volleyball and croquet grounds, cross country hikes, fishing, netting and YWCA and YMCA activities. The Junior college's basic curriculum included courses; namely pre-medicine, commercial, and teacher training. The sixty-four semester credits included the subjects, English (12), algebra (3), trigonometry (3), history (12), chemistry (10), and twenty-fourth electives in education, French, Latin, biology, analytical geometry and differential calculus. The pre-medicine course include English (12 credits), French (12), chemistry (15), zoology (4) physics (8), and electives (13).[15]

Throughout his professional career T.S. Inborden was interested in the farmers and the improvement of their conditions. He was a school principal who did not sit in an office, give orders, and conduct meetings. He moved among his faculty and students and above all he had a sincere personal and loving concern for the people, the farmer and their families. Frequently, T.S. would write speeches and articles on the farmer and their farms. In 1925, Inborden wrote about the farmer's progress and things that must be accomplished for their continued existence. T.S. wrote that in 1895, one hundred percent of black farmers were tenant farmers. But in 1925, there was a change because over the years, the black farmer had faith, hope and worked hard to improve his condition from a tenant farmer to a farmer that owned his land, his house and had productive crops. T.S. said that there was a man who lived 40 miles from Brick, and was able to purchase 150 acres of land. He built his house, had a cotton gin, and cleared his land for tobacco crop and was able to receive the highest price for his crop. T.S. told the story about a black man who lived in a one room log hut under an umbrella tree around 1900. He came to the farmers meetings and went back home with inspiration. He bargained for the farm on which he lived and hired several men to clear the woods. Several white men came along and laughed at him for trying to clear the woods to plant corn. The farmer told T.S. that he had been selling corn and almost everything for several years and eventually was able to purchase the farm, built a house and lighted it with acetylene gas. He was also able to purchase a saw mill and country store. Inborden was quite impressed with the man's progress because he was able to educate his five children at Brick and several went to college. Inborden wrote that ten miles from Brick School is a farm of 2,300 acres and it was advertised to be sold. One Negro in the community who could read a little saw the advertisement and organized a few of his neighbors to provide the rest of the payment for the farm. The white owner had no idea that these ignorant Negroes would ever pay for it and they would have to foreclose. A little while after the first payment, said Inborden, a lumber company came along and paid them for the lumber which they received a large amount, more than the cost of the land. They had enough money to finish paying for the farm and some left which they divided among themselves. T.S. believed that if a farmer owns his land and handles it intelligently, he will always be in a position to shoulder a man's responsibility in the community.

When the Federal Farm Loan Organization was established, T.S. had a meeting with several farmers and organized a local farm loan group. It was two years before they were able to satisfy the Federal qualifications. Fortunately, the black farmers in the local group were able to get loans totalling some 180 thousand dollars for farms. T.S. said the Federal Farm Loan Organization assisted some black farmers by giving them a chance that the banks and private leaders did not. Within a twelve year period, only one man failed. Inborden stated that many applicants did not qualify at first and were refused a loan and informed why they did not qualify. After 2-3 years, that same farmer would improve his property, install window lights, rebuilt his porch and steps, white wash, the outhouse, paint his living qualities and have several children in school.[16]

Inborden was able to assist some farmers in eastern North Carolina, not a great amount, but under those conditions of the day and time, segregation poverty, ignorance and the white financial institutions refusing loans to blacks, he was during almost the impossible. One must also realize that economic equality for blacks in 1925 was unheard of and there was no affirmative action to excite and intimidate some so called white liberals and conservatives. T.S. was ahead of his time by penetrating the walls of opposition by using federal assistance programs for blacks in a southern state where officials really had no desire to see black economic upward mobility, especially the poor and in some cases the illiterate black farmer.

In 1969 and in the 1990's Howard University, Washington, D.C. experienced several student unrest or protests on the campus. However, in 1925, the prestigious AMA school in Nashville, Tennessee, Fisk University had a student unrest and protest. The Fisk alumni and concerned citizens of color in Nashville, Tennessee played an integral part in resolving the problems. Several honorable historians have written books and articles on campus unrest but they normally develop their discussions around a particular individual or situation. Unfortunately, they do not go into the detailed discussion of individual participants and the role they performed during the campus unrest situation. In the case of Fisk University, Thomas S. Inborden was a principal participant in an investigation of the student unrest. There was a storm of protest brewing on the campus of Fisk University in 1924. The distinguished historian and writer, W.E.B. DuBois visited the campus to attend the graduation of his daughter, Yolanda. He made some remarks about the alumni being bitter and disgusted, that discipline at Fisk did not mean the abolition of rights and students should have an athletic program, student newspaper and their freedoms. The students wanted a change in policies and some regulations at Fisk. Du Bois had written articles in the Crisis about conditions at Fisk. He had provided some motivation and inspiration to the students and he would later applaud the students for their actions. On February 4, 1925, approximately 100 young men independently of any adult influence including Du Bois decided to ignore the student curfew of 10 p.m. They began some singing, chanted slogans, broke windows, and overturned chapel seats. One of the verses they would sing *Before I will be a slave, I will be buried in my grave*. When the situation became very tense, the president of the university, Dr. McKenzie decided to call the Nashville policemen. The policemen were instructed to arrest several young men and it was alleged that during the arrest, one student was kicked and another clubbed by the police. Also one student was told to leave the city of Nashville immediately, by the next train. When the remaining students on campus learned about this incident and the presence of some fifty police on campus, the student unrest was in full force. There were some students who participated in a walkout did not attend classes, went home or to friend's residence in the city of Nashville. The students presented their demands and wanted an audience with the president of the university. President McKenzie had instructed the students on the night of the major incident to report to his office and sign a document stating that they denounce the protest and if they did not sign, they would be withdrawn from school.[17]

The Vice Chairman of Fisk's Board of Trustees, L. Hollingsworth Wood spoke to the students in Jubilee Hall on Monday, February 12, 1925. He told the students that it is with great regret that such scenes of disorder and defiance of constitutional authority of the university have taken place. There can be no excuse in my opinion and I know that I voice the opinion of the trustees for such an outbreak. Wood said the trustees stand absolutely behind President Fayette Avery McKenzie in his unflinching stand for the maintenance of law and order. Wood called upon the alumni and student body to support the president and trustees in their effort to uphold the fundamental of educational progress. The trustees expect the students to promptly return to their classes and endeavor to support the administration. At the time Wood delivered his address, there were only 84 students in attendance in the dining room. The Fisk alumni and the Board of Trustees formed a Greater Fisk Committee whose purpose was to inquire into the whole controversy and suggest possible solutions. The members of the committee were: James N. Robinson, Cincinnati, Ohio; Miss Sophia Boaz, Chicago, Illinois; F.A. Stewart, Nashville, Tennessee; John H. Gandy, Petersburg, Virginia; Thomas S. Inborden, Bricks, North Carolina; Rev. Henry R. Proctor, Brooklyn, New York; J.C. Napier, Nashville, Tennessee; Mrs. Margaret Murray Washington, Alabama; L. Hollingsworth Wood, and F.A. McKenzie, Nashville, Tennessee.[18]

The first meeting was called to order at 10 a.m., February 16, 1925 by L.H. Wood, Chairman. Wood organized five groups, a local group headed by Rev. Proctor; Graduates, T.S. Inborden, Group of white people who are interested, F.A. Stewart; not enthusiastic citizens group, J.C. Napier; and Fisk supporters Group, Mrs. Margaret M. Washington. The Greater Fisk Committee advised the parents whose children had left school to return to their classes. The committee examined and discussed the student's grievances and demands, they were: an athletic association, fraternities and sororities, student publications, and changes in some of the rules and regulations of the university and more student freedom. Another meeting was convened on February 17, 1925 and the members were led in prayer by T.S. Inborden. The Greater Fisk committee allowed individuals to come before the committee and expressed their views either in support of the students or President McKenzie actions. The Dean of Women, Miss Collins told of the difficulty in securing responses from students in the past year about their problems. Dean Graham said the students should have larger liberty and he felt the trouble that occurred could have been averted firmly but kindly. A Miss Boyston remarked that the students wanted self government, a student council and warned that the boys would keep up noise until McKenzie's hair turned white. Mr. Isaac Fisher admitted he saw the clouds and knew the trouble had to come. A Dr. Phillips stated that an institution is greater than one man. Professor

Caliver said the students have ground for disaffection and colored people are not discredited in the city. Dr. Parks stated that President McKenzie has the most delicate sensibility. Miss Streator said one must live on the campus to understand the problems. The students have been in a state of insurrection since October even though they do have some privileges.[19]

Charles S. Lewis, senior student gave his view points to the committee. Lewis said students wanted an athletic association, fraternities and sororities, student council and student publications. Professor T.W. Talley, a professor for 22 years at Fisk stated that he tried to adjust to the administration of President McKenzie and sometimes McKenzie's policies did not command themselves to his best judgement. The attorney for the university, J.H. Dewitt told the committee that actions of McKenzie were done in no vindictive spirit. Mr. J.L. Leventhal, representing the white citizens of Nashville, talked about the manly stand and good initiative of President McKenzie among the white citizens of Nashville. The Chicago Fisk Club represented by Mr. Henry H. Proctor Jr. and Dr. Clarence H. Payne requested a change of administration. Dr. Jefferson, Dental Examiner at Fisk said a shot was fired over his head and he supported McKenzie and warned him of difficulties. Rev. Baker, school Chaplain said he heard four shots fired and believed President McKenzie was justified in calling the police. Professor A.L. Small, psychology department, said the students had all the liberties they needed. Miss A.F. Sweet, instructor for 18 years at Fisk in Latin and Spanish said she was in sympathy for President McKenzie and he should be retained as president. The members of the Negro Board of Trade were introduced at the meeting. They were Dr. Maryland, Dr. W. Ford, D. Wesley Crutcher, Dr. J.T. Phillips, and T. Clay Moore. Mr. Crutcher said the President had failed to act as a father in that he resorted to the police in the recent emergency. The Board of Trade members felt the alliance of President McKenzie with white organizations in the city had unfavorably affected his usefulness among colored people of the community as head of the school. Professor A.W. Partch, had taught physics for 8 years at Fisk said the president should remain and had given money from his private funds to assist students. Professor Brumfield, 7 years teacher of religion, stated that McKenzie would be unable to regain confidence of the students. Two alumni of Fisk sent a message to the committee stating that they believed McKenzie should not have called the police. They were Charles Wesley and J. Altson Atkins. A telegram was received by the committee from Sterling Brown, Howard University. Brown stated that you must urge young people not to use liberty for licenses but to respect consecrated authority to reestablish better relations to the school. J.C. Napier, local attorney and member of the Board of Trustees and Greater Fisk Committee remarked that W.E.B. DuBois had a personal grievance. Dr. A.W. Davis, Tuscambia, Alabama wrote a letter and said as parent of a daughter at Fisk, that they thank President McKenzie for his intervention in calling the police to quiet a riot before it raided Jubilee Hall.

George White, Principal Burrell Normal School, Florence Alabama stated in a letter that his personal investigation at the request of a student and parents revealed that the students left President McKenzie no alternative but to summon the police to protect lives and property.

White believed McKenzie had not been accorded the treatment of good sportsmanship or fair play. Chicago Urban League Director, A.L. Jackson wrote an editorial condemning the actions of President McKenzie. A Professor Shaw said the removal of President McKenzie would be a set back to Negro education all over the country because of the violent methods used to bring about it. Mr. R. Augustus Lawson, class 1895, musician, sent the committee a statement. Lawson wrote that he was spending several days on Fisk campus in connection with a piano recital. I have endeavored to get at the facts of the present situation at Fisk University and as far as I have been able to do this, my opinion is I cannot condone the abuse of law and order. I am sorry for the students who have had to suffer because of the lawlessness of a few disgruntled who attempted to disturb the peace and quiet of the university. Lawson said Dr. McKenzie should be upheld in his strong desire and effective effort to move Fisk, all should be in every good way, and my children are remaining at Fisk. The students at Fisk were given support from the local community, Meredith G. Ferguson, bookkeeper at the black owned Citizens Savings Bank and Trust Company, Nashville, used his own savings and cashed the student's check. The Louisville Fisk alumni, student council, Howard University sent letters in sympathy for the students' demands and actions. Mrs. Margaret M. Washington once said, *In order to help people you must love them and if you do not love them, they will soon find it out.* These words somewhat reflected her views on the Fisk protest by students.[20] President McKenzie made some remarks before the Greater Fisk Committee on February 19, 1925. McKenzie said that when he arrived at Fisk, the school was a wreck (1915), and I made improvements and kept faith with the students. In a chapel talk, McKenzie mentioned the names of the students arrested. Streator, Lewis, Anderson, Taylor and Gordon. In court, McKenzie made a plea for leniency which was misinterpreted. McKenzie remarked that he was opposed to the Ku Klux Klan (KKK) and he had refused the assistance of the Klan in the disturbance. He told the committee that with the cooperation of Trustees and the alumni that he could bring things together again and ensure the future of the university.[21]

T.S. Inborden attended the meetings of the Greater Fisk Committee and was head of the Graduate group and corresponded with other committee members and received letters from people supporting the students and President McKenzie. The principal of Brick School played an integral and significant role in helping to change the leadership of Fisk in 1925 and paving the way eventually for a president of color to assume the helm of leadership of the south's acclaimed Fisk University. S.I. Daniel, class 1914, wrote Inborden and stated that the Trustees should be elected by the alumni. On February 25, 1925, H.H. Proctor wrote T.S. and acknowledged he had received his confidential letter. Proctor said he was in agreement with what T.S. wrote and that they must stand as firmly as we did before. If we do that I feel quite sure matters will come out as we desire.[22] A faculty member who was in support of Dr. McKenzie's actions wrote T.S. a letter on February 26, 1925. A Miss Addie Sweet said she was called before the committee and she desired to express a few statements about her convictions with regard to the present problems. Sweet stated that McKenzie's opponents do not understand him, and failed to appreciate his exceptional qualities as a man and an educator. They have loss their perspective and cannot with fairness judge his career as a whole. The do not see that here is a man who has served them with the utmost devotion. Sweet said that she was convinced that the colored people have no more loyal friend than Dr. McKenzie. He believes in the ability of our students to maintain as high standards of scholarship as white students that he has succeeded in convincing others of their ability and thus he has built up a large body of friends for the school. Miss Sweet said the extent to which McKenzie has personally aided needy students though unknown until recently to most or all of us indicates how deep is his interest in their welfare. The importance of this school as a bond which unites two races cannot be overemphasized. Such is McKenzie wrote Sweet because he stands in Nashville and throughout the country that if he were able to be driven from the presidency of Fisk, the cause of Negro education must greatly suffer and that which has already been achieved in the way of better race relations must face serious loss.[23]

T.S. Inborden along with H.H. Proctor and some other committee members believed in March 1925 that McKenzie should resign as president of Fisk University. Committee member F.A. Stewart wrote T.S. on March 7, 1925. He told Inborden that he was working on some important testimony that he will present to the committee. Stewart said that T.S.' suggestions were fine and he believed Inborden should follow his suggestions through. Inborden wrote Chairman Wood a letter on March 27, 1925. He stated that he had received the minutes and read them along with his own notes and was pleased with Proctor's accomplishments. T.S. said that he had a feeling since the day he left Nashville that we have made a serious mistake. Our committee, wrote T.S. was not appointed to go to Fisk to settle an internal disruption. Our mission was a large mission Inborden said that he believes the president of Fisk and those associated with him should have taken their primary action in settling the particular trouble. After they had gone to the limit of their power and authority and the matter still unsettled, they should have appealed to the Executive Committee of the University. A word from the chairman of that committee should have settled every question. I mean a direct word not through the president of the university but from the committee itself. Then if the students could not abide by the decision, let them sign up orderly and leave. Inborden said they only asked for a thing and I see no reason in the world why they should not have been allowed to have an athletic association. All schools have some type of an organization. T.S. stated that at Brick, they have less trouble when the young people are spending their physical energies in athletic activities. The testimony received in our minutes states that athletics were never refused the students. A thing so vital to student life in all of our institution should have the fullest endorsement of the administration of these institution. They should have entered into it with enthusiasm, no decision was made except in unchanged policy.

T.S. was expressing in his letter his personal ideas and of course support for the student's demand. He wrote that the students wanted to publish a student paper. T.S. then referred to his student days at Fisk. He said forty years ago we published the Fisk Herald and the faculty got behind it with all their might and made it pay for the expenses. Proctor was the editor of it for several years and I was on the staff. T.S. stated that his younger daughter, Dorothy, was on the staff just a few years ago, when she was at Fisk. I would hate very much to think that after 35 years, the students of Fisk University would not have the mental poise to edit and publish a small school paper.[24] T.S. sent a copy of his letter to Wood and to Dr. F.A. Stewart. Stewart wrote T.S. on April 4, 1925 and said he read the letters twice with a great deal of care and interest. He congratulated T.S. on the stand he had taken and on the splendid way in which his points were presented. Dr. Stewart wrote that he felt it was not the thing to do to state what the committee findings were until they had heard all the proof and had been given an opportunity to discuss with the committee the different phases of the testimony. Stewart asked the questions. Is it intended? Have we had our say? and, Have we discharged our full duty? Stewart wrote that in reply to Mr. Wood's letter asking for my findings that he and Proctor might have time to digest them, I stated that I had very definite ideas as to what the findings of the committee should be. But more proof should be introduced at the next meeting. I desired that no findings be formulated until we meet again. Wood replied and said that he felt our next meeting should be held in New York City. Stewart differed with T.S. on how to submit the recommendations. He wanted the recommendations made to the board.[25]

T.S. received a letter from Mary E. Chamberlain expressing her views about President McKenzie. She wrote T.S. that the next morning after the meeting was adjourned of the Greater Fisk Committee, she went over to Jubilee Hall to see him, but he had left. Chamberlain said she wanted to know T.S.'s position on the problem. She stated that T.S. was a leveled head man and a Christian and school man and hoped both his head and heart will guide him right. Miss Chamberlain said the whole affair is the strangest thing I ever heard of. Here is Dr. McKenzie, one of the finest men God ever made, the target of criticism and slander. His character is above reproach in every way. He has no race prejudices. She stated that McKenzie has for years devoted himself to Fisk because he has faith in the possibilities of the Negro race and felt that he could invest his life on a good way. He has won a host of friends for the cause of Fisk through his own enthusiasm. He is the friend of all, having done so much. Miss Chamberlain said McKenzie has a wonderful program for Fisk and his ideals give the students some freedom. His experience tallies closely with that of our Lord have given himself wholly. He is rejected by those whom he longs to benefit figuratively speaking. He is cussed and spit upon. All manner of false charges are trumped up against him and some are crying away with him, and truly they know not what they do. Mary Chamberlain pleaded with T.S. to do what he could to straighten and blot out the misunderstanding about McKenzie, for the good record of the Fisk alumni.[26]

The Greater Fisk Committee met on April 18, 1925 and made their final report which was submitted to the Board of Trustees and director from the American Missionary Association. There was tremendous support by many white citizens and faculty and some people of color for President McKenzie to remain at Fisk University. However, McKenzie decided to submit his resignation as President of Fisk and probably evaluated all of the opposition against him to include the Greater Fisk Committee. The Board of Trustees established a temporary administrative committee to direct the university affairs until a new president could be selected. The committee recommended and permitted a student newspaper, an alumni was named to the Board of Trustees and some specific student proposals were accepted. There were new regulations on discipline, fraternities, and sororities were organized on the campus. The students returned to class.[27]

After a six month search a white missionary who possessed the qualities of Christian zeal, fund raising skills and academic competence was selected. Many blacks wanted a black president. The new president of Fisk University was Dr. Thomas Jesse Jones, Quaker Pacifist, founder of the American Friend Service Committee who had worked with foreign missions in Japan. Jones was instrumental in the development of a social science department under the leadership of Dr. Charles S. Johnson. Jones agreed with some of Dr. W.E.B. DuBois views on black higher education. President Jones served as president of Fisk University for 25 years.[28]

The final outcomes of the 1925 Fisk Student Unrest included the genesis of a new attitude by AMA leaders and white college presidents toward their past attitudes and views on leading a black institution especially in the 1920's. Although Fisk University would not receive its first black president until 1950, T.S. Inborden and the members of the Greater Fisk Committee heard the student's cry demanding respect, self confidence and freedom in their academic environment. Inborden and his colleagues came to the rescue of the students and reaped many benefits toward their future matriculation at Fisk. T.S. Inborden had proven to the white majority and some blacks in 1925, that his rich knowledge and experience at Brick since 1895 definitely qualified him as an outstanding contributor to the Greater Fisk Committee and Fisk University in resolving the problems of the student unrest and protests of 1925.

The Semi-Annual meeting of the North Carolina Negro Farmers Congress was held at St. Augustine School, Raleigh, N.C., July 30-31, 1925. The theme of the meeting was *Home Ownership Through Better Farming*. The officers of the Congress were: President, T.S. Inborden, John D. Wray, Secretary. The Executive Committee consisted of C.R. Hudson, Chairman, T.S. Inborden, John D. Wray, secretary, H.R. Phillips, B.F. Bullock, L.H. Roberts, Matthew Martin, R.J. Beverly, L.E. Hall and Frank Lytle, Dr. F.B. Buford, President, North Carolina Agricultural and Technical College made some brief remarks. Board and lodging was free and the registration fee was one dollar. The farmers were greeted by the Mayor E.E. Culbreth. T.S. Inborden and the Executive Committee had prepared a very excellent program for the meeting. Some major highlights of the program were: Selective speakers and their interesting topics. I.O. Schaub, Director of Extension Service spoke on the *Negro's part in North Carolina's Agriculture*. The editor of the Progressive Farmer delivered a speech on *Successful Methods in Modern Farming*. Professor C.D. Matthews, a horticulturist's topic was *The Year Round Garden in the Feeding of the Family*. Dr. M.L. Townsend, Director state Health Department gave a talk on *The Fruit in the Diet*. George McDonald, St. Augustine School, spoke on *Utilization of Milk Products on the Farms,* District Agent L.E. Hall talked on *Pastures and How to Make Them*. S.L. Kirby spoke on *Pork as an Important Meat,* F.B. Latham spoke on *Farm Tenant Plans* and C.R. Hudson, state agent gave a brief speech. J.P. Kerr gave a talk on *How to Get More Poultry and Eggs On The Farm* John D. Wray, state agent for Negroes spoke on the *Use of Farm Boys and Girls in Farm Agriculture*. T.S. had invited some motivating speakers to the meeting. They were J.P. Pierce,

Field agent, Hampton Institute, and Major R.R. Moton, President Tuskegee Institute, Alabama. The Semi-Annual Farmers meeting was not an all male event, because T.S. and his colleagues included the women in the program. They had their speakers who discussed subjects of interest. Mrs. Sarah L. Williams presented a canning demonstration. The Home Demonstration Agent, Miss Emma McDougold spoke on *Farm Women's Problems and How To Solve them. Miss Esterbrook, N.C., Department of Extension Service talked about* Clothing and Mrs A.W. Holland, a state farm supervisor, spoke on *Women's Place in the Farm House.*[29] The careful planning, selective subjects and a diverse group of speakers at the meeting in 1925 gave the farmers current information, how to apply correct techniques and methods on the farm. The black farmer was developing his expertise and general knowledge in his profession and as an economic provider. T.S. was leading the way and challenging farmers to improve their conditions.

F.B. Latham, Circle Grove Farms, Belhaven, North Carolina extended an invitation to T.S. and some farmers to visit his farm on August 20, 1925. When Latham wrote T.S. he told him to take a route from Tarboro either by Williamston or Greenville to Washington. Then route 91 by Belhaven to the farm. Inborden and at least nine other people were able to see farm breeders of registered Hereford cattle, Shropshire sheep, Duroc hogs and the growing soy beans, double ear corn, and peanuts.[30] T.S. would take advantage of these opportunities to continue to educate the black farmers and expose them to the latest improvements in farming.

The AMA asked Inborden to serve as a Home Missionary Representative and attend the Annual Western Association of Congregational churches in Helena, Montana, September 20-27, 1925. The Helena Newspaper said Inborden will have a prominent place on the program and will discuss the problems of education in North Carolina. The article also include a brief sketch of T.S. During his visits, T.S. was asked to speak to some of the congregations. He attended the Mussel Shell Association meeting and it was held at a congregational church. He also spoke at a Fellowship Supper at Silver Grill. T.S. spoke during a morning session at the First Congregational church, Third Avenue, North of Ninth St., Great Falls, Montana. Inborden told the audience that he was a member of North Carolina Interracial Relations Committee and president for several years with the Negro Fair and Industrial Convention. T.S. also had speaking engagements at Morning Mill and Mullan, Idaho. He took pictures of areas. He had visited, the Bluffs, Yellowstone River and Wallace Idaho[31]. There was a flyer announcing a Church Business and World service at the Congregational Church in Montana on November, 1925. The flyer included a picture of Thomas S. Inborden, Home Missionary Representative Brick, N.C. Inborden had visited Broadus, Alazada, Ekalaka, Plevana, Custer, Redlodge, Plena, Billings, Lone Rock, Arlee Dixon, Missoula, Montana. In November, 1925, T.S. was on a team with missionaries who traveled to the towns of Verdale, Newport, Colville, Westminster, Colfax, Walla Walla, Dayton, Pasco, Yakima, Everett, Seattle, Bellingham Pleasant Valley, Anacortia, Fairmount, Kirland, Poligrim, Taconia, Waslougala, Kalama, Poshastin, Torjasket and Brewston. There was an article in the *Seattle Enterprise* newspaper about T.S. Inborden. The article stated that the principal of Brick School, Brick, North Carolina would be giving a series of lectures in the states of Montana, Idaho, and Washington. He is representative of the National

Mission Organization of the Congregational church. The commission composed of the biggest business and church men of the country. They represent the work of AMA and societies of the Congregational Church, which operates in foreign and home fields, said Professor Inborden. T.S. said the AMA has 140 Negro Congregations in the south, and in Northern Carolina the education program is unique, because during the past few years 500 modern school houses have been built with a capacity of 60,000 children.[32]

S. Meyer, the Enfield grocer remembered T.S.'s birthday, January 6, and sent him a birthday card. The News and Observer (Raleigh) published an article on Brick School written by H.W. Kendall. Some of the highlights of the article were: that Brick School had 26 buildings and 350 students. He said the flower beds, walks, drives, grass and trees all attractively placed on the campus making it a scene of great beauty. Kendall was impressed by the cleanliness of the place, there was not a piece of paper or trash to be seen on the campus. The interior of the buildings and classrooms were spotless and the large kitchen and dining room looked as though they had just been scrubbed and polished. Kendall made a very excellent remark about Brick when he wrote that in the various white schools which he has visited, he had never seen one which could touch this colored institution, Brick, for cleanliness. Kendall was impressed with the school's activities, he wrote the school's choir, glee club and orchestra appeared before the Kiwanis Club of Rocky Mount and on several occasions they gave concerts at the Rocky Mount theatre. T.S. told Kendall that at Brick they have not only tried to stimulate the farmer but have tried to make more intelligent housewives. He said their kitchen, dining rooms and laundry were open for the training of our young ladies who perfect themselves in the household arts.[33] Inborden stated that his students are dexterous with the needle. They can make their own clothes. T.S. said a doctrine of discipline and Christian character must be taught by every teacher.

There were some farmers who traveled 50-80 miles to attend Farmers Day meeting at Brick, February 19, 1926. Some 400 people were in attendance. The guest speakers were J.B. Pierce, Attorney Griffin, Professor Snowden and Mrs. Charlotte Hawkins Brown. As usual, the citizens of the local community would assist Inborden in his programs. Some of the contributors were: Isaac Bunn, Sandy Lyon, Enfield Grocer Co., S. Meyer, S.D. Hilliard, Daniel Brown, Henry Lyons, Charlie Adams, C.F. Bowen, T.H. Hines, Lucy Grant, John Fobbs, Wallace Williams, Henry Myrick, Lucille Pittman, Lucius Pittman, W.Y. Harrison, Mack Sloan, Jim Daniel, Professor Louis Gregory and Max Myer.[34]

Occasionally T.S. would receive requests for student's summer work in the north. On April 19, 1926, a Mrs. Cresap wrote Inborden and she said Edward C. Beard recommended T.S. Mrs. Cresap wanted a graduate student to cook and possibly remain a while. She wanted a young lady who was fond of children. T.S. learned that the selective student would have no laundry work and she would receive forty dollars a month. Her travel money would be sent. Mrs. Cresap lived in Scarsdale, New York. T.S. responded to Mrs. Cresap by letter on April 23, 1926. Inborden said that he had found two nice young ladies. They are freshman students. The color description was used when T.S. wrote these are nice yellow girls and they are quiet and refined. Their names are Jessie Mae Gidney and Lossie Mae Gidney. Both were graduates of the school at King Mountain, North Carolina.[35]

The year of 1926 was not a favorite year for T.S. The AMA had plans to ask T.S. to retire. H.H. Proctor, pastor of the Nazarene Congregational Church, Herkimer Street and Troy Avenue, Brooklyn, New York wrote T.S. a letter March 18, 1926. He discussed the recent appointment of Fisk new President, Thomas Elsa Jones. Proctor remarked that he had been in close contact with Jones, and was convinced that he is the kind of man Fisk needs in the present crisis. He desires for Fisk to be a representative of the colored race and seek the earnest cooperation of the Alumni. Proctor wrote that Jones comes to us broadened by contact with the Japanese people and desires to be ambassador of friendship from the white to colored people. Proctor also wrote that Mrs. Jones is a woman of culture and is deeply interested in her husband desires and ambition for Fisk. It seems to me, said Proctor, that the only draw back to the million dollars is the financial problem we face. I trust therefore, you will do all you can to interest people in our district to contribute to Fisk.[36] Several of T.S.' friends wrote him about the changes at Brick. On May 1926, T.S.' long time friend, Rev. H.H. Proctor wrote T.S., I understand AMA is endeavoring to put something over on you, and kindly write me the fine facts. I will see what can be done at this end. There is not a single secretary of AMA that has done as much for the organization as you have.[37] Alice Davis wrote T.S. from Oberlin, Ohio and said remember there is one who watches over all and not even the sparrow falleth. You have felt this, perhaps you were too secure. Have you plans for the future? Only wish you had left Brick long ago and not waited for this. It is that way all over, always someone to take one's place. I could not have stand to see this change down there. Do not lose the faith.[38] Clarence H. Wilson wrote T.S. on May 24, 1926 and he acknowledged T.S.'s brief note. Wilson said he learned to think so highly of your work and after your visit to my church and home, my opinion of you so amply confirmed that I hoped you would retain your connection with my church for many years to come. I did however, have some intimation that trouble was brewing, said Wilson, but never dreamed that it would come to this.[39] T.S. received a note from Ida B. Arrington and she wrote I am standing still on principle and I want you to know I will hold up your hands and all just righteous hands until death.[40] Maggie Young of Battleboro, N.C. wrote T.S. on May 25, 1926 and she said I have heard about the trouble you are having there and I am very very sorry. Young stated that there is not one graduate or student of Brick School who is favor of your being treated so unjustly. She said that she would help to see that T.S. is given justice.[41] Dr. F.A. Stewart was concerned about T.S.'s position at Brick. He told Inborden that he had a conference with Mr. Napier and they would write a letter to AMA suggesting that you remain at Brick as principal.[42]

Inborden wanted to see a hospital present at Brick School and college. He wrote a letter to Dr. N.C. Newbold, who was the director for Negro education in North Carolina. T.S. wrote that he had meetings in Chicago with Mr. Rosenwald. T.S. said he was a wonderful man and has done a wonderful job in the south. Inborden told Newbold he was writing in reference to efforts for a hospital at Brick. Some years ago, 1913, T.S.

said he tried to have the AMA to have a hospital at Brick as a part of their general work. One of our local white doctors went as far as to have a conference with our officials and then put himself on record in a lengthy letter which I afterward ran in our school catalogue. We never got any further with the matter. I had traveled as much in this section of the state and have seen so much suffering on the part of the masses. I have wanted to do something to relieve the situation of the suffering. The agencies already in operation are not meeting the necessities of the people. T.S. said that they have organized a hospital at Brick, Enfield, and Dr. Dubissete has been conducting this privately for several years. Recently, a group of men have been advising him of a larger possibility. We have put our plans on paper and these are now being prepared with reference to getting a state charter. We do not know of a better way to get things done as they should be done. Inborden wrote that they are housed in a rented building in a section not too well adopted for our purpose. We have only eight beds and they are usually filled all the time. I am not sure yet, where we shall make it a permanent home. Personally, I would like to see it here at Brick. I think it is the logical place for it. T.S. said he was enclosing these articles of incorporation for Newbold to read and at the same time you know the field and the needs. We thought that under the second inquiry by Mr. Embrie's letters raised the question of financing, our methods of financing thus far is to get a large membership and to charge a fee which be nothing like the amount of work to be done. We have dreamed of having a hospital fitted with rooms for a physician, dentist, and nurses. T.S. said the equipment and materials would be some medicines and cots. T.S. said Dr. Dubissette has already had correspondence with the State Health Department and they have somewhat considered the proposition. T.S. said that he asked Dubisette to put it in writing and discuss the proposition from a point of view of a physician. Inborden said that wherever we locate permanently and wherever we build must be thoroughly in accord with the best practice here. I am sorry, wrote Inborden, that we have not had the organization incorporated due to the fact that we had the articles drawn up but they did not appear to us to be in good form and we had it done over. At the same time we want to cooperate with any of the state departments. To the end we shall strive to accomplish the goal of having a hospital in the Brick community.[43]

A letter dated May 31, 1928 was written by Inborden to a friend. Professor W.A. Robinson, Raleigh, N.C. T.S. discussed some of his personal family concerns and also his views on education among blacks. T.S. wrote, Wilson, my son took his civil engineering degree at Howard University. When he was there, I advised a white man in a high engineering position about Wilson receiving his degree. The white engineer told Inborden there were jobs available in engineering positions. When Wilson returned to Brick, he made application to the North Carolina Highway Commission and never heard from the agency. T.S. wrote our colored people are buying expensive cars and it seems that the educated and trained men who can qualify should be able to fill positions along the line of their qualifications. T.S. said he had made some good connections in the north, New York, Cleveland and other places. I do not want Wilson to go there for work when he is due to be employed in his own state. He can go anywhere in the north and pass for white and get by it as thousands are during. But I do not want him to do that. Inborden wrote that white people must be willing to share the responsibilities of jobs requiring higher and technical skills, who have made special preparations for their jobs. If whites are willing to do that, then our students must be qualified, enter into politics and be prepared to obtain better jobs. T.S. said every educated man who leaves the south because he is economically pinched takes a chance for better employment in the north. Inborden wrote that all of us who are in education work should look into these matters. We need some type of organization to assist many blacks to prepare for technical and mechanical positions and also have a good academic background. T.S. said there will not be so much unhappiness when people are properly adjusted to their economic environment.[44]

Attorney R.C. Dunn of Enfield, N.C. was a friend to T.S., Inborden frequently would write letters to Dunn. On January 7, 1928, T.S. wrote Dunn, I am having trouble in getting my son Wilson in the type of work he prepared for in college. T.S. asked Dunn if he could provide some help. T.S. said he had no pull with the local politician. I am not disposed to go about it in this way. I think I have some consideration at the hands of men who are in command of large public affairs. Inborden told Mr. Dunn, you know my record here for 33 years. I do not wish to recount my work here at the school and what I have stood for all these years in racial matters and community issues. During the war, I offered my services freely without a red copper and made many trips to state meetings without one cent, for car fare or anything else. Where token praise and medals were presented, I did not even get one of them. You may know that I was asked to be responsible for the war stamps sales program in Edgecombe County. Inborden remarked that he was all over the countries of Nash and Halifax asking people to participate in the war effort. I was told that in Edgecombe County alone they had totaled up 48,000 dollars worth of Liberty bonds and stamps. We collected some 8,000 dollars in Nash township. Inborden continued informing Dunn about his accomplishments. He wrote that for eight years he had been president of the State Farmers Conference. I am a member of the local committee on Race Relations. T.S. said that his son, Wilson had taught wood, iron and mechanical drawing at Saint Augustine, Episcopal school in Raleigh. Wilson has reached the age now, when he needs something permanent. If he cannot find work in N.C., then he will be leaving for the north where he can get something to do even at the expense of sacrificing his racial identity to do it. This none of us want. Wilson has a cousin in Cleveland, Ohio and one in Chicago, Illinois. They probably could assist him in finding a job. However, I would rather Wilson to stay in North Carolina, said T.S. He was born in N.C., his grand parents and their parents for a hundred years back to their relative, General Nathaniel Greene who fought in the American Revolution. T.S. told Attorney Dunn that what he was saying about Wilson might be said about a great many North Carolina black young men. If all the aspiring young ladies and young men leave the state after they are educated, what will you have left after a hundred years. You are going to need more than farm labors to solve the problems that are going to confront the people in the country and southland. There are thousands of young students graduating from the colleges in the state and there still will be a stream of them as the years go by who must be placed where their education best fits them. If our students are to be educated then the education should be utilized for the good of the state. T.S. asked Dunn, Do you know there are a few colored women in the United States who hold master degrees in Domestic Arts. North Carolina has not a single one. My daughter is one of the three. She is teaching at a college in West Virginia. The state did not pay 5 cents on my daughter's account at Columbia University. What I did not pay, she worked for the remaining amount. She would be in the state of North Carolina today if the conditions here were compatible.[45]

T.S. wrote a letter to the Norfolk and Guide Newspaper (Virginia) on the subject of *Stimulate Farm Life and Unemployment*. Inborden wrote that he has read daily articles in various newspapers and it amused him to see what city folks are doing to feed and warm their dependents. T.S. said some people that he has met in Halifax, Edgecombe, Nash and Martin Counties, N.C. do not have to worry about not having a job nor about their board or where they are going to keep warm. Inborden said that he had not seen a single soul picking up coal along the railroad or begging bread except in the case of perhaps a few aged and unfortunate people who have to be at the county home because of physical infirmities. T.S. wrote some examples of programs among black farmers in North Carolina. He said in Martin County, farmers, John Cherry, C.W. Slade, W.T. Anderson who have their own farms are interested in better schools, and churches.[46]

Katheryne Redding wrote T.S. a letter on June 28, 1928 from Chicago, Illinois. She told T.S. that she was enrolled in school and was studying harmony theory, sight reading, swimming, folk dancing, singing games and rhythm and a member of a physical educational class. Redding was interested in a job at Brick's Junior College. She wrote your Dean said that he was looking out for the best interest of the school and since I did not warm up to him, he would not recommend me for reappointment. So, I am too kicked out. It does not matter though. I hope that you are well and enjoying a pleasant summer. The AMA was successful in their plans to have Inborden retire and appointed another as their choice as administrator of Brick Junior College. T.S. had been warned by his friends earlier. In 1928, T.S. had accepted his new title as *Emeritus*. Inborden wrote letters to his friends and told them about the situation at Brick School. T.S. confronted some issues, the planned community hospital and some problems that arose concerning Dr. Dubissette, a physician of color.

T.S. wrote a letter to a Mr. Petway about Dr. Dubisette, the letter read:

> *Dr. Dubisette feels very strongly that he might not have been understood and is anxious to go over the matter with you or any other person and get it straight. Dubisette has the most loyal feeling as far as he knows on the part of Enfield's white people and wants to put our program with their cooperation and support that will greatly help the town of Enfield. In his enthusiasm for the project, he may overstated his best judgement but I myself thinks his mistake, if he has made one, is more of the head than the heart. Dubisette is a young man and yet not so young, who wants to do real constructive work for the alleviation of a people who have not had great opportunities. He has asked me to serve with him on his board who consist of residents of the community. These men would not endorse for one minute any*

attitude on the part of anyone connected with the institution that would bring trouble to the people of the community. We have already made selections tentatively of three or four white citizens of Enfield, to be on our advisory committee. We are feeling our way like every new organization but with the best advice we can get from those who have had great experience. In our meetings, we have discussion on how we can obtain the interest of our white friends in this proposition. I am very sorry that the information has gone out that some of the white doctors are not in accord with our establishing a hospital. I do not believe seriously that there is a white doctor in Enfield or in the community who really oppose the hospital. I know all of them very well and I have the utmost confidence in them. There is not one of them whose office I cannot go into and talk as freely as I would to you in your office and they know that I think well of them. I do not think the objection is against the hospital but could be Dr. Dubisette. A better acquaintance with him may remove some objections. In the first place. Dubisette was not born in America, and may not know all the traditions that we practice. He is a very fine scholar, having been educated in some of the best schools. He knows his profession and has added very much to his profession of medicine. I have been following him among the people for a year and have been in all sorts of gatherings and have the first time to hear him make any expression in the public that was not in its entire accord with the best spirit of the community. His relation with the white doctors have been few. Dubissette is neat in his personal appearance and that is correct if he is going to the bedside of his patients. He does not hang about the streets promiscuously. There is very much in his favor. He has a nice home in Wilson where his wife lives during the winter when the children are in school. I have seen her in Wilson and Enfield. She is a great asset to the doctor. Dubissette has been offered a job in a New York hospital. He would be paid quite well and would not have to depend on a country clientele. But the colored people here need a doctor. They need him in Enfield, Rocky Mount, Smithfield and Wilmington would like to have him practice in that city.[47]

There were some progressive and economic minded African Americans in 1926 who organized an Insurance company in N.C. The company was called the Eagle Life Insurance company. The home office was in Raleigh, N.C. The company had three branches, Raleigh, Winston Salem and Wilmington, N.C. with a total of 35 agents. The initial officers of the insurance company were : Dr. A.W. Pegues, President, C.E. Lightener, Vice President, T.S. Inborden, 2nd Vice President, and General Manager, L.E. Graves. The company's physician was Dr. Rufus N. Voss, and the attorney was Roger O'Kelly. When Dr. A.W. Pegues died in 1928, T.S. Inborden was made President on August 8, 1929. When T.S. assumed the office of president, the Eagle Life Insurance Company had some 12,000 policy holders, stock was sold at 37.50 per share. With 150 stock holders, Inborden became very interested in the company and sent letters to many people explaining about the insurance policies. Unfortunately, the Eagle Life Insurance was not successful in maintaining the financial growth and the company ceased to operate in 1930. Although the company failed, T.S. was able to receive a valuable experience about the insurance business and its operation.[48]

Sarah Jane Leary Evans Inborden was a very kind, gentle lady whose Christianity was exemplified in her daily life. She attended rural churches and had respect for their congregation. In 1928, the angels of the Lord greeted Sarah Jane and escorted her to the beautiful paradise called Heaven. She had completed a life in the flesh and it was well done. Her remains were viewed in the chapel at Brick School prior to burial in the family plot, Westwood Cemetery, Oberlin, Ohio. Services were conducted in Oberlin at the Second Congregational Church. Dr. Frank Hugh Foster was the minister. The Inborden family had loss a mother, grandmother and wife and all the members of the family mourned for the demise of their loved one. One of Sarah Jane's granddaughters remarked, Mrs. Brick has a very nice little home for grandmother in Heaven.

Howard University, Washington. D.C. has an outstanding research center for books manuscripts and papers. The name of the center is Moorland-Spingarn Research Center. Jesse Edward Moorland gave Howard University a large amount of books on the black experience around 1929. T.S. Inborden was a friend of Moorland and received a letter from him on April 22, 1929. The letter read:

My dear friend Inborden, received your letter. I was shut in with bronchitis and it seems to take me a long time to catch up with my work and also to get the spirit of work going on. It is fine for friends to keep their connections. I am convinced that there is a great weakness in human nature. It seems aggravated unless there is some selfish reason or routine duty which is part of the days work. Very few colored men show more than passing evidence that they are friends. I have not had time to master the meaning of those masters, Cicero and Emerson. Your letter means more than the written page to me. It appears that you are going strong everything you sent me has been read with interest and your comments on the YMCA is very interesting. I shall be glad to see every printed matter you may have on the movement and to have in written form anything which place light on Brown and Hunton and the association in early days. It can not be too trivial of help to me. I shall write a history of the movement. I have most of the material gathered for it. Mrs. Moorland is well and we enjoy life very good. I am devoting the most of my time to real estate business. I am with a good firm downtown and I am able to help a good number of people. I am carrying my course in law for culture and business sake. I am now the oldest living trustee of Howard University in point of service. I go to Washington monthly in the interest of the University. I am on the building committee and on the Board of Trustees of Dr. Proctor's church and secretary of the YMCA Retired Secretaries in and around New York. I must slow down a bit from now so I can have time to do some writing and other things I am doing. Why don't you come to see us. Some people say Brooklyn is a good place to sleep. You better hurry if you want peaceful rest. I think you are doing some of your best work now. You have the great outdoors at your hand with your beloved flowers and birds. How about the Buffalo head? One of your boys, A.J. Sessoms is on our Board of Trustees. He is a fine boy and has high regard for you. I brought John Moore from Washington in 1920 to do the carpenter work on my house, which I remodelled. So I have been an investor in the Brick securities. I hope to hear from you, beg my pardon for the delay in making a reply to your kind letter. With very good wishes, I am your friend, J.E. Moorland. P.S., I know you are President of the North Carolina Historical Association, have you any data you could send me? I am interested on this subject as you may know. I gave Howard University a large library on the Negro.[49]

In view of his dedication, interest and years of hard work to mold Brick Normal school and later Brick Junior College into an outstanding institution, the AMA made a decision in 1928 to close Brick School. A federal team in 1928 recommended that the academic program at Brick be reorganized into a continuous senior high school and junior college. Brick students had been very successful in their academic studies at Howard University and other colleges. T.S. had expressed some of his views on the reorganization of Brick School as early as 1922. He said that because of money and family influence of status quo. Brick never had a Board of Trustees and did not share in the governance of the school. AMA managed the school directly from New York. Secretary Brownlee thoughts were that Brick should be consolidated. The AMA had made no improvements since 1922, T.S. said there appears to be no regards to the local black community needs. Earlier the AMA had made a decision to eliminate the school's work department and eventually the enrollment declined. The youth of the communities were able to attend school and also work. Secretary Brownlee of the AMA believed that it was the responsibility of the white local boards to govern and make decisions for the future of black education in the region.

In July, 1929, some of T.S.'s friends wrote him to express their concerns about the future of Brick School. L.E. Graves sent T.S. a copy of a letter that was forwarded to Mr. Charles B. Austin, New York City. The letter read:

Dear Mr. Austin, I am certain Mr. Inborden's attitude and influence will greatly improve the spiritual tone of the college. I know of no person in the entire state of North Carolina who would be of larger service than Mr. Inborden. During the past two years I have been very closely associated with Mr. Inborden and even under the very trying situation that had come, he has clung to the hope that he may again be active in the development of Brick College. Of course, he feels that he has been unjustly dealt with but he does not place the blame on anyone. Mr. Holloway who he maintains cultivated an attitude which has caused the officials to think the worst all of which was a studies program to discredit him and his work. In this he is not entirely wrong. I see the situation there from both angles. I feel Mr. Inborden will give to any administration there a support that it could not get in the state of North Carolina from any other person.[50]

Charles B. Austin replied to Mr. Graves's letter by stating that Graves was touching upon a question of administration in one of AMA schools and he was not free to reply to the points which were raised in the letter. However, Executive Secretary Fred L. Brownlee would have to respond to the questions if he cared to do so.[51]

Many books and even movies have been made available to the public to learn about the Ku Klux Klan. One thing about a primary source is that its contents are factual and leaves no doubt if there is of its authenticity. On July 18, 1929, a letter was sent to T.S. Inborden at Brick School. The letter read:

> *Professor Inborden, It is with regret that we find it necessary to call your attention to this matter and warn you thus. We find that for recent months you have been taking up considerable time and make a close associate of one Dr. M.E. Dubisette. After having given his record a thorough investigation, we find that his policies, principles and activities are very undesirable. He is a treacherous and dangerous character. One who is designed to create and cause trouble both in his own circles and among races. If you value your past record and standing in the community, your future, for yourself and family and the welfare of your people. We advise you here and now and urge that you put a stop in your association with or coming under the influence of Dr. Dubissette. Accept this warning and save further trouble in the future. Knights of the Ku Klux Klan.*[52]

The letter from the Ku Klux Klan definitely supports the fact that they were present in the area of Enfield, North Carolina in 1929. It is believed that Inborden continued his interest in the hospital project that was being planned by the black citizens in the local communities.

When the Brick School was organized into the Junior College there were changes in the administration and curriculum of the school. The Brick Bugle catalog for 1929-1930 gives a descriptive picture of the faculty, Curriculum and activities of Brick Junior College and High School. The college faculty were: Thomas S. Inborden, President Emeritus, William H. Holloway, Dean; Irving C. Tull, Treasurer; John H. Gordon, chemistry; Chauncey L. Elam, biology; William H. Robinson, mathematics, M. Gertrude Leigh, French, history; Cyril Price, English; J. Leon Hawkins, education; Louise R. McKinney, librarian; Mabel L. Robinson, piano and harmony and Ruth B. Douglas, stenographer. The high school faculty were: Rubye B. Lyon, geography and history;, Ruth Brown, Latin and English; L. Zenobia Coleman, arithmetic and language; Ruth E. Buckingham, home economics; Joseph W. Saunders, manual training; Eugene B. Hunt, sixth grade; Thelma L. Black, fourth, fifth and sixth grades; Ernestine Saunders, first, second and third grade; Mary V. Little, matron and dining room; Florida P. Robinson, Preceptress, Benedict Hall; Ruby Price, Preceptress, Brewster Hall; Alice J. Tull, Preceptress, Beard Hall; Lula Baker, supervisor, laundry; and Inez Albritton, music.[53] Brick students were assessed a fee registration, library, athletics, artist series, shop, sewing and cooking, diploma. The total tuition for college students was $46 and high school $40.50 dollars. Some students would reduce their fees by enrolling in the student work programs. The Brick Junior College curriculum for 1929-1930 was: English, foreign language, science, algebra, plane geometry, history, a total of 10 units. Electives were physics, chemistry, civics, economics, education, home economics, manual arts, general science and biology. There were also courses in teacher training, liberal arts and pre-medical courses, which include biology, zoology, health, sanitation, and general biology. The chemistry courses included inorganic, organic, qualitative and analytical. Physics courses include mechanism, heat, magnetism, electricity, sound and light. The education courses included class management, educational psychology and children's literature. Elementary teacher courses included primary reading, language, geography, arithmetic, English, composition, rhetoric, argumentative and debating, public speaking, English and American literature, history, math, analytical geometry, differential calculus, and religious education. The high school curriculum was accredited by the state of North Carolina. The curriculum included the subjects of geography, manual arts, cooking, sewing, biblical history, music, French, chemistry and physics. The music courses included voice, piano and harmony.[54]

There was a student strike at Brick Junior College under the administration of Dean Holloway. The students challenged the enforcement of some rules. Dean Holloway suspended several young men, Ernest Broome and Harry Holmes in the spring 1929. They were suspended for leaving the campus without permission. The students protested this action by staging a meal time walkout from the dining hall. The faculty was surprised. The students organized a committee of 17 to lead a protest and informed students not to attend classes. A Kate Lassiter was the student leader. The students set up guards to guard campus entrances and buildings for the purpose of enforcing the strike. The teachers had to ask the guards for permission to enter their classrooms. The second night of the strike, lights were shut off and Dean Holloway left the campus. The college administration responded by informing parents that the students could be expelled for striking. Some parents wrote to their children and told them to come home. Several students wrote the AMA in New York and they received a telegram from Executive Secretary Fred Brownlee and an attorney from the New York office. The officials met the students in the library and talked to them individually, continuing the meetings day and night to find a solution to end the strike. Finally, the AMA mediators decided that the school authorities should rescind the suspensions of Holmes and Broome and that no student who returned to class within 48 hours should be penalized. The victorious students shared the platform with Brownlee, an attorney and college administrators. Ironically, a few months after the strike, Dean Holloway was replaced as President of the college.[55] It should be noted that Inborden did not experience a student uprising as serious as the one that confronted Holloway. The AMA in 1929 awarded T.S. the title of president Emeritus and an annual retirement salary of 1,000 dollars and life long use of the campus home with a promise of 25 acres of land. Holloway's successor was John Clarence Wright who was born July 27, 1881 in Glendower, Albermarle County, Virginia. He was a graduate of Oberlin College. Wright was married to Addie Lee Street and they were the parents of four children. Wright had taught at St. Paul College, Lawrenceville, Va.; Tuskegee Institute, Alabama; and Florida A&M College, John Wright also had experience as president at Edward Waters College, and as Vice President at Daytona-Cookman Institute. Secretary Brownlee, AMA, wrote T.S. and told him that he appreciated the cordial welcome that John Wright received.[56]

Inborden still showed great interest in the possible hospital for Enfield area for blacks. He expressed his views in a letter to his friend R.C. Dunn. T.S. said:

The colored people have taken the lead and pledged 1400 dollars and a guarantee of faith for the health organization. The Trustee Board will function as soon as the Ku Klux Klan flare which had its inception and prejudice is cleared up. Albermale in Stanley County is a little town of 3,000 people with a small Negro population. They received a few days ago, the sum of 35,000 dollars from the Duke Foundation for a Negro hospital. I do not know of any accession that would be a better asset to the town of Enfield and community. We should have such an institution and have white men and women on a board as this would give it the greatest stability and poise. The southern white people send missionaries to Africa and glory in it and it is fine but here in our very midst, in the closet proximity in our kitchen, yards, sleeping chambers and nurseries here is an opportunity inconceivable for the highest expression of human life. People cannot rise higher than their environment. This institution would certain add very much to the local Negro environment. I want to see an institution manned and operated by our people, it can be done.[57]

On September 25, 1929, T.S. travelled to Raleigh, N.C. with President Wright, Professor W.H. Robinson and J.W. Saunders to attend an alumni meeting. The meeting was called to order by Inborden at 5:00 p.m. Mr. Graves presented former graduates and friends. Others who were in attendance included Pearl Schmokes, Ruby Williams, Frank Dunston, and Berry O'Kelly.

T.S. Inborden wrote Dr. Carnegie, Rocky Mount, N.C. about the desired hospital for Enfield. The letter read:

There are more than 200,000 Negroes in eastern North Carolina who do not have adequate health protection. The state cannot furnish all hospital facilities except in special diseases. In a white hospital, the Negro patient has a serious mental reaction to his environment. We would like to establish a hospital in this community under the care and supervision of our people who are prepared to handle such an institution and whose interests are identical with our race traditions. This would be an advantage to white physicians who have Negro clientele. Eighty to ninety percent of colored have white physicians.[58]

On October 1, 1929, T.S. sent a personal note to Dr. Dubissette and told him that there was serious friction with some Enfield people white and colored, according to C. Pittman. Inborden said, if there are whisperings we should know what it is and meet it. *If the white doctors make charges of unprofessional practice against you, I think they should call you and give you a chance to clear yourself.*[59]

Inborden had second thoughts on the future of the hospital project and recurring problems that were preventing progress toward having a hospital in Enfield. T.S. decided to write a letter to the members of the Executive Committee Health and Hospital Board on October 5, 1929. The letter read:

Gentlemen, the object of this letter is to give you notice of my resignation as head of your organization. There is too much confusion on the part of our group for effective work and I see no use in my worrying about a proposition in which there is no unanimity of cooperation. The organization is all right but the machinery for pulling it together is not in accord. In the first place we have an executive committee composed of the charter members. A very small group of men who cannot workout the simplest working principles. We are supposed to have a Trustee Board in whom is vested the larger affairs of the organization. This board has not been appointed. There is some cross firing and misunderstanding and personal differences that should be settled. I can not settle them. I do not want to be mixed up in an unpleasant situation.[60]

When Inborden's daughter, Julia, was ill in a Richmond, Virginia hospital, he wrote her a very personal and interesting letter. The letter read:

Dear Julia, when it comes to health, I have to leave myself in hands of others when I am physically out of condition. If I fail to observe the best laws of health, when on my feet and apparently well, I must suffer. I say, if I fail to observe I must let the things human system requires and take time to feed my mind on the sort of food and stimulant necessary for growth and development. Nature and human waste have given us here a beautiful environment even though human atmosphere may not all the time have been the best. We are hoping that your physical condition, teeth and feeling will soon be all right so that you can come home rejuvenated in spirit and health. Then we want to get a big tent and go to the seashore and mountains and get into a new environment and forget and see new face and have new experiences and that you will like. When Gorum was in the hospital in Enfield, Dr. Dubisette said his condition was not bad but Gorum would not do anything for himself to help his condition. The Bible says that as a man thinketh so is he. That is true. We are what we think we are. You are too intelligent a woman to brood or become melancholy over things that can be eliminated in our daily lives. The mind can control the material and what we think must control our bodies. If we build up our physical condition we must let our mind dwell on the things that contribute to health. If you find yourself getting nervous or worrying about anything, just close your eyes and say "Get behind me Satan, forget and take a nap. You must be the master of your destiny and you have too much at stake to give up. It seems to be in the nature of your family to fight the doctors. As a result, we have all waited too long to be advised. We discount his advice and think we know more about our physical condition than the best experts. I speak with very definite knowledge. I have been on the verge of a nervous breakdown my self and it was with the best advice from the best doctors here that I did not have a complete collapse. I was taken ill in Richmond at the fair where I went to throw off the things that brought me down but I went away too soon. Nothing can do you more good than to help the medicine so to speak with your best mind. One must be consigned to the care of the doctors and nurses and always stay in the best mental attitude. It is your faith that will make you a whole. There must be faith in yourself, faith in your medicine and in the sincerity of your physicians and nurses. Years ago, I had a serious operation performed on my throat for tonsil trouble. My whole system was affected by it and they thought I had consumption but it was toxic poison from my tonsils. When Dr. Harrison removed the trouble I got well. If my mental attitude toward the doctor was against the operation and was negative, you would never grow up to the friction of womanhood because your mother wouldn't have been equal to the task of raising you alone. I had too much to think about and too much to do to give up. There were three children to raise and Brick School to build from absolutely nothing. Here was a community of a hundred miles in area to influence with a beneficial spirit and helpful inspiration. When I graduated from Fisk, they said I would not live too long to do much harm, because of a physical condition but I got out, ate decent food, read books and read the best papers. Today, I will challenge the most brilliant student who has ever gone out from any Negro school, Hampton, Howard, Fisk and Talledega, Straight and all the rest to make a better showing for the almost 40 years I have been in the educational field. Money as you know, has never been my goal so I have not much money, barely enough to meet the necessities of life. I have put all that into making you, Dorothy and Wilson fit to carry on when we have quit. It is what I have done for the inspiration of our own people. A few days ago, Mr. Holsey, Tuskegee, said to a small group of men, not in my presence, that Mr. Inborden is one of the most outstanding Negroes in the south today. If I am it, its because I have dared to stand for right conduct and principles of life and especially so in dealing with uneducated people and a large student body here for almost 40 years. Then in order to put in over my work here, my work on the public rostrum has brought me into contact with the best white people of the entire country from the Atlantic ocean to Pacific ocean. I have been told by the Tuskegee teacher that Brick School had influenced the community which it was located.[61]

Augustus Field Beard, former Executive Secretary of AMA celebrated his 100th birthday in February 1933. Fred Brownlee wrote Inborden and asked his participation in establishing a living tribute to Beard, an Endowment Fund. T.S. agreed to assist in the tribute and contacted many of his friends and former students to become donors to the Beard Memorial. Inborden was able to receive responses from white and black citizens of North Carolina and also in other states. Some of the possible donors were: white donors - Lawyer R.C. Dunn, Enfield, N.C.; Simon, Joe and Sam Meyers, Merchants, Enfield, N.C.; Sam Pierson, Enfield; Walde Whitaker, banker and farmer; Walter Holiday, farmer; Lee Whitaker, farmer; Billy Neville, farmer; and Ivy Watson, banker. The black donors were: Matthew Martin, Thelma, N.C.; former Brick student, Edward Martin, Pendleton, N.C.; Dr. George E. Davis, Dr. R.R. Robinson, former Brick student; Rev. A.S. Croom, former Brick student, Durham, N.C.; William Miles, farmer; Garysburg, N.C.; Dr. J.A. Tinsley, Weldon, N.C.; Julia Sadgwar, Wilmington, N.C.; Rev. J.R. Moorland, Brooklyn, N.Y.; Joe Martin, Albany, Ga.; Minnie B. Quinn, Oberlin, Ohio; Carry Sadgewar Manley, Alexander Hughes, Hattie L. Greene, Brick graduate; Susie Adams, Brick graduate; Annie Murray, Washington, D.C.; and Carie S. Shepherson, Bristol, Tennessee. In the 1930's, T.S. also raised money for buses to transport students to the school from Halifax, Nash and Edgecombe counties. Inborden was successful in receiving contributions from citizens in the county. Nash county citizens contributed 356 dollars, Halifax, 500 dollars and Edgecombe 450 dollars. The AMA sent T.S. 575 dollars. Inborden personally gave credit to Flossie Parker, James Eaton, Wade Allen, H. Dickens, Walter Quinitcheet, James Tucker, Elizy Battle, and Oscar Debreuax.[62]

On April 25, 1930, T.S. received a letter from Walter White acting secretary, NAACP. White was requesting support for the Moorfield Story - Louis Marshall Memorial Campaign. The letter stated that there was an invitation to a number of outstanding colored men and women to show their appreciation to Mr. Storey and Mr. Marshall. White said there would be a honor roll listing those contributions and to show the families of Storey and Marshall how the public generally felt in extending the Negro's gratitude to these men. The letter include a quote from Kelly Miller, *The Negro pays for the thing he wants, But begs for the things he need.*[63]

F. Banks, manager, Bay Shore Hotel, Buckroe Beach, Virginia wrote T.S. a brief note on May 19, 1930. Banks stated that we sincerely hope you are including a stay at Bay Shore Hotel in your vacation plans this year. We are deeply thankful for your patronage in the past and hope you have been pleased with our service.

T.S. wrote a personal letter to his friend L.E. Graves in Raleigh, N.C. on May 30, 1930 and discussed the subjects of education, business and the future. The letter also expressed some of T.S.'s philosophy. The letter read:

My Dear Mr. Graves, I have just heard from Mr. Miller. Please write him and see if he is interested in a business. I am sure he does not expect to stay in the educational field and business will suit him better. He has a good paying job now and his brother is at Talledega. I wish it were so that several of our family could put our mite together and make up a thousand dollars. I am looking toward the future which is uncertain and can not take chances if you call it that with my small holdings and certainly not with that of others who are more dependent than myself. My personal income has been small considering I have done a good day's work to educate others. I am not as young as before. I pride myself on my activities, my youthful activities, I might say. I cannot look at the future as I did 20-30 years ago. Mine is behind me. When your children come into life one looks forward to obtaining something solid for them. We build an institution here at Brick so that others might step in and continue to carry on when we have retired, but the devil stepped in and upset all our plans. They are all left in the world to scramble with the rabble as best they can and others less capable are reaping the harvest, and they have not sown a single seed or made a single sacrifice and service. We build this institution out of the swamps. I was hoping to leave my successors a heritage of achievement for them to continue. Graves, you are comparatively a young man in the prime of life yet, working like a deuce to make a place in the sun for yourself and your children. After you have spent forty years building up the company and making it worthwhile, the best institution in the country, the pride of the whole organization, then let a set of men come in and say to you they are going to change the whole administration, attitude and personnel and want none of your advice and interference and keep your hands off, you would feel like a fool. Can you put yourself in that position? An expert analyst is a poor constructionist you are not making the sacrifice, you are making to build up an organization for the fun of it. You see in independence for your children and a bigger opportunity for others. In this, you could not have a larger vision. When you spend days and days without suitable meals, half the nights on the roads and in all sorts of weather with cusses and abuses, and this is the price you are paying. Your incentive is higher than the patience you get out of it in dollars and cents. A finer incentive never dominates the mind of man. If I had the money as some of our men have, you would not have to go to another man for advancement.

Now I want to say a word about the educational business. I think there is no higher calling if one can make the sacrifice. It is the only profession into which the masses of our graduates can go and three fourths of those who are in it are not fitted by nature to do the work. Sometimes when I meet the teachers in their convention, I see nothing in it but contentions, troubles, fusses, strife and fury. I dare say that 75 percent of all the Negro teachers at least are away from home and you cannot build up a happy homogeneous group who are away from home two thirds of the time. White men have thousands of jobs to every one the Negro has. The life of our teachers are the life of rovers. There is no stability any where. We cannot shape our own policies on education. We are slaves to the system imposed from without. Many are less capable of directing the system than those who directing now. I cannot with any degree of confidence advise any of my children to go into the educational field as a life work. At best it is a makeshift. Nothing is a success that is regarded as only a stepping stone. Only a few can be regarded as permanent futures in any of our institutions. Here is a word of praise to you, Graves. You have all the attributes for success. You have courage, you have faith, you will not take no for an answer. Console yourself with this fact that you are engaged in doing a piece of constructive work that means more for humanity than any other enterprise in the world. Death brings into the home the saddest of sad experiences and when a life insurance man can come in and alleviate this sadness with financial responsibility, reimbursement is the best sort of sympathy. This letter is not a lamentation nor have I sought to express a complex, T.S.[64]

T.S. Inborden was given the responsibility to execute the Exum estate. He wrote a letter on April 15, 1930 to Benjamin Exum, Route 1, Whitaker, N.C. He stated that he had sent checks and letters to all beneficiaries to the Exum estate and he wanted Benjamin's mother to sign her mark in the proper place on each check and mail the letters to the parties to whom addressed, and return the list to T.S. Inborden said that he and Mrs. Priscilla Exum, Executors went to the court house and arranged for the clerk of the court to use 2,000 dollars of the estate in settling claims of the heirs so that they may have immediate use of this in their work this year. Mrs. Exum had ten heirs and they would received 200 hundred dollars each and 1,000 dollars should be retained in the bank to meet contingencies for next year. The balance would be divided according to the will. The Exum family included Lugenia Exum, Rolista Exum Wimberly, Molesta Exum Atkins, Mary Exum Whitaker, Rebecca Exum Grant, Benjamin Exum, Olivia Quinchett, and William Exum.[65]

L.E. Graves, Secretary and Manager, Eagle Life Insurance Co., Raleigh, N.C. wrote T.S. a motivational letter on June 3, 1930. The letter read:

As long as one brick is left on another at that school the name of Inborden will be synonymous with education. What an enduring monument? Children will be singing Inborden, Inborden. What if dreams are not frictions? Is not the dream eternal? What if worms spoil the fruit? That is the way of the worm but the tree blossomed and beauty shone, the earth is made blessed by the tree. All man's course thumb and finger failed to plumb all instincts immature, all purposes were thoughts hardly to be packed into a narrow way, fancies that broke through language and escaped all. I could never be all me ignored in me, this I was worth to God. Then look not thou down but of the best is yet to be. The joy of creation makes you kin to God. Those who follow set a salary and some prestige but kinship to God in the highest recompense for your labor, dark nights. Swamps, and muddy roads, he who pushes past them all with the flaming desire to be and to be is the worthwhile man. You are guided by this spirit, I fight on till I may apprehend that for which I was caught and with which the gad fly stung me. I am glad for your words of encouragement, few men alive have written that letter better. From you it sends me out again in the storm to push forward. If I may reach the high calling of fine service.[66]

James C. Evans was a professor at West Virginia State College, Institute, West Virginia and in later years was the Civilian Assistant to the Secretary of Defense for Manpower and Reserves. Evans was instrumental in race relations in the military service in the 1950's and 1970's. Evans wrote Inborden a letter on June 20, 1930. The letter read:

Received your letter and expect to meet you in Petersburg. I was there a few days ago and I advised President Gandy that I expected to be there from start to finish. I cannot at this time write you anything of value on the topic that interests you. I am very greatly interested and the topic is of great importance. I think one of the biggest mistakes we have made in our more recent course of studies in all of our installations is our departure from practically all technical education. In the few schools that still have the courses, they lack the emphasis in equipment and personnel. A couple of weeks ago I spent almost a whole day in the trades building at Hampton Institute with the superintendent, a very nice white man who was thoroughly interested in putting over a very technical proposition in that institution. That sort of thing the way he is doing it appeals to me very much the way it is done at Hampton.

When the boy or girl graduates and is informed that the job they desire is a white man's job and Negroes need not apply, we have got to meet that sort of prejudice and fight it in the open and in the press where it will be effective. I am not a trade student but I have an acute appreciation for the best in every vocation. A teacher who is without character cannot express art in anything. I am talking now about personnel. Then the best trained man cannot do his best work with the inferior complex. He must feel that his field is no secondary field but that it is the most important work on the school campus. When he speaks it must be with authority and with a background or achievement. Just a few other words. No school let it be technical, trade or any other sort, can do its best work with school politics dominating from head to foot. I want to tell you we have had not many Negro schools but too many of our teachers are giving too much of their time placating to somebody in order to hold their jobs and too little time to do that work. The atmosphere of the campus and in the halls does not lend itself to the best work of our institutions. The spirit on the campus that keep teachers ill at ease all the time is not the best professional spirit. The short tenure of office cannot lend itself to efficiency in technical education any more than it can to the purely academic side of education. The University of Minnesota dominated for years and years by an undominated spirit of Dr. Northrop. The New London Polytechnical School founded by Fred L. Hitchcock, all are the finest expressions of the high art of teaching people how to do things. I know these institutions and I know some of their products. They are high colored products. They can deliver the goods, and take care of themselves in any exigency. The education that this is worthwhile. The teacher who has not the imagination to see art in the raw material, let it be wood, iron, straw, copper, lead, clay, rock sand and lime or cement in the human being has no business in the school rooms. He must make the students see it.[67]

T.S. Inborden wrote a letter to his daughter-in-law, Nan, Wilson's wife, on December 8, 1930. He told her that several years ago he went up in the mountains of Virginia to spend the winter with his brother and after a few weeks there, he received a letter from Mr. Graves asking him to come to Raleigh as soon as possible. T.S. said that he lost no time in going to Raleigh. Graves wanted him to help with the Eagle Life Insurance Company. My influence greatly assisted the company. I thought the company was a good thing. I recommended and put the first agent in the field, J.B. Herren, who put a thousand dollars in the stock at once and bought a new car with to do business. Everywhere we went in the east, I was asked if I had stock in the organization and when I replied, yes, people would buy stock. I worked hand in hand with Graves. There were times I would go without eating until I got home. I also kept Graves in the house and looked after his every want and asked no pay as I wanted to get the organization on its feet at once. Graves sold stock almost solely on presence. When the agents were knocking him, I stood by him and tried to defend him and told him so. He had lost some of his best men because he did not seem to be able to adjust his differences with them. He owes no living soul more than he owes me for the publicity and prestige he has had in this section where most of the stock has been sold. T.S. told Nan that Dorothy and he had taken out about one thousand dollars worth of stock in the company and he had not recovered one red copper for his time and investments. Inborden remarked how he had travelled to several board meetings at his own expense. Graves is a bright fellow and tried to adjust as manager, but he has not been fair or equitable. T.S. told Nan, remember this, I will call it number one or how people can change or forget what others have done for them. Inborden said that he had other friends that you can cash in on. When Dean Turner graduated from Shaw University, I was one of three oratorical judges to go to Shaw and act as judge in an oratorical contest which Turner won and which brought him much prestige. I brought great disrepute to myself by the other contesting schools because I would not put myself to vote carte blank to give the verdict to other schools,

Virginia Union or Petersburg. Turner and Dr. King won it and I gave it to them. They should never forget me. T.S. discussed another situation with Nan when he wrote Craver was coming into his own in the work in which he was engaged for years. I am the man who threw open our doors here to give him entrance at all times and without limit of time or money when it was needed. I suppose they count it all in the day's work. I will call this number 2. T.S. said that before a single Rosenwald school was built in this section of North Carolina, that he was the one to round up the first bunch in Halifax County in the interest of such a school and I have had a hand in practically every one of the other schools built. I prepared the minds of the people for them. I might give an incident after incident. Just one incident was one day when I drove sixteen miles to Tarrapin Point to interest the people in education and I drove that distance in a buggy. After getting three miles from the place of meeting, I changed horses and took a preacher to the tobacco barn with a lantern. The meeting was held in a tobacco barn and we asked the people for the money that went into one of the first improved schools in that section. After they had contributed all they were asked to, I was allowed to make an appeal for the erection of a teacher college here and they gave me forty dollars that night. Later, I addressed in one spring more than 10,000 people in churches and schools in the interest of better schools and teachers. T.S. concluded his letter to Nan by writing, Dr. G.E. Davis, the Rosenwald school's state agent spoke with me. I was helping to make a job for him at the same time. The activities opened up the word for Miss Molver, County supervisor. They had a nice reception.[68]

On January 2, 1931, T.S. responded to a request from Fisk University. The University wanted a photograph and a one hundred word sketch of alumni who graduated prior to 1900. George M. White gave a lecture at Brick School in April, 1931. He talked about his visits to Angola and Portuguese East Africa. White was the brother of Walter White, executive Secretary of the NAACP.

Inborden would try to help students who were in need by asking assistance from friends. He sent a letter on April 21, 1931 asked for contributions to assist two girls. He wrote in the letter that two girls were helping in chores at his house and had been at Brick for six years. One girl was in the 11th grade and one was in first year, junior college. Panzy was the youngest and the oldest was Gossie. Gossie had finished high school and was accepted in a nursing program at a Richmond, Virginia hospital. She had assisted her father to retire his debts and had only 15 dollars not sufficient money to purchase uniform and entrance requirements at the school. Her parents had five small children and were share croppers near Scotland Neck, N.C., 30 miles east of Brick. The father would send some vegetables and fresh meat at Christmas time. T.S. had overheard the girls talking and Panzy said that she had only one pair of stockings and she had to wash them at night to have them fit to wear the next day. She had some clothes. Later T.S. went to the store and purchased four pair stockings for the girls. Inborden stated that he needed thirty dollars to assist the girls in preparing for school. T.S. Inborden wrote a letter to Charles Austin, Mount Vernon, New York on August 15, 1932. He wrote that he had visited his relatives in Upperville, Virginia and was accompanied by his daughter, Dorothy and her husband. T.S. said he visited Elizabeth City and was interested in the work of Principal Bliss. His work students had assisted in canning 8,000 cans of fruit and vegetables. Bliss had helped T.S. at Brick. Inborden said that he does not know of anything better than teaching young people how to do things with their hands. T.S. told Charles Austin that he had never seen farms look better than they now look in eastern, North Carolina and if farm people should have to beg for bread it will be because they get nothing for their crops. But they will not beg for bread if they get nothing for tobacco and cotton and peanuts because they are growing hogs, corn, tomatoes, potatoes and other things to eat. They may not have the money but they will have what is better, something to eat. They may not have fine clothes but they can have full bellies. T.S. said that he had received letters from all over the country telling him about people out of work and out of money who have fine brains and college education. They were all dressed up and no where to go so to speak. The people in Mr. Forney's class will not be begging for bread. The efficiency of one's philosophy is the efficiency of its product. There is no other test if you plant corn and plan the undeveloped grains at the end of the year, you should get 50 percent yield, perhaps but if the farmer just keeps making the same or he is only a fool. T.S. said Benjamin Bullock is the best possible example of what I am thinking about. I want you to go out there sometime and see what he is doing.[69]

Reverend Henry Hugh Proctor, pastor of the Nazarene Congregational Church, Brooklyn and secretary of the National Convention of Congregational Workers Among Colored People was in the south making a special investigation of the courses and results of Negro migration from the south in August, 1931. The New York Herald Tribune published an article on some of Proctor's findings during his tour of the south, especially in North Carolina. The title of the article was *North Carolina Striving to Better Negro's Status, A Race Investigator*. Rev. Proctor stated that North Carolina has good roads, schools and good race relations. He said Winston Salem has 71 millionaires and in 1931, one was a Negro, and 5,000 blacks were employed by the Reynolds Tobacco Company who provided insurance for all of its employees. Proctor wrote that the National Negro Business League had initiated a chain of colored merchants's association stores. He also remarked that the only bus line operated by Negroes in the United States exists in North Carolina with a capital stock of 100,000 dollars, 51 buses and employed 72 persons. Rev. Proctor stated that despite some progress, prejudice still was present in North Carolina. He cited an example, when Mr. Spaulding, President of the North Carolina Mutual Life Association, Negro Insurance company was visiting in Raleigh and went into a white cigar stand located in a building belonging to a Negro man and purchased a bottle of soda water which he started to drink in the back of the store. The clerk ordered him out of the store. Mr. Spaulding was assaulted, and his teeth was knocked out. His assailant was arrested and released on a 25 dollar bond and later fined 15 dollars. The article written by Rev. Proctor discussed Brick School. Proctor stated that the Joseph K. Brick School located near Enfield has been of great service to the region. The school was under the leadership of Thomas Inborden for more than a quarter of a century and it has proved to be a veritable Tuskegee and its Principal Inborden is another Booker T. Washington. There were pictures of C.C. Spaulding, president of North Carolina Mutual Life Insurance Company and

Thomas Sewell Inborden

Professor Thomas S. Inborden with the caption, he has been called the *Booker T. Washington of North Carolina.*[70]

The President of the Baltimore Afro American Newspaper, Carl Murphy wrote Inborden a letter and asked him to write a 200 word essay on the "Greatest Moment In His Life" and to include a photograph. T.S. wrote following essay.

The most outstanding day in any man's life is the day he makes a momentous decision, the result of which everything else hinders. The greatest moment of my life was the day I made the decision to leave the mountains of Virginia in order to better my condition in life and to help ameliorate the sad condition of ten million of my people in the south. This was a dream before I had yet entered into my teens. I did not flounder around and just happen to float into a drift that carried me to success. I never had a thought except to create something fundamental and necessary in the life of the great masses of Negroes. I only wanted the opportunity. I had faith in the future and in men to believe the opportunity would come if I prepared myself. I was born the last year of the civil war and am therefore sixty-six years old. I first saw the light of day from the eastern slopes of the Blue Ridge Mountains, over looking the beautiful and fertile valley of Virginia, some sixty miles south west from Washington, D.C. The whole valley had just been devastated by the ravages of the Civil War. The relics of these ravages are still very much in evidence. The first seventeen years of my life were spent on the mountain farm in an environment that had been rent with all the viscids of a great war for freedom. In these seventeen years of mountain life, I had mastered all the industries and some of the evils common to mountain life. The environment lacked inspiration except the mountains still higher and the beautiful valley below. These have always held an enhancement for me. I left home the first of April 1882 and my first stop was Cleveland, Ohio and I walked part of the way. I worked sixteen months in a hotel and saving up one hundred and forty dollars and then proceeded to Oberlin, Ohio. It was only a few months before the last cent was gone and I found myself working in another hotel for my board. I made the necessary sacrifice for four years and declining health forced me to go south and I enrolled at Fisk University, Nashville, Tennessee. After graduation, I went to work for the AMA. I have been in educational work for forty years under the auspices of the AMA. At the time of my retirement, I had been in the service of this organization longer than any other person except one and strange to say we are both drawing a monthly stipend for Christian and educational services rendered all over the south during the most hectic period of its reconstruction. Of course, there have been other outstanding events in my life as in every human life. I had to shear my life and soul of the attitudes that were incompatible with the highest and best things I had set out to do. I have always had a mind of my own and follow largely by my own beckonings when I know I am correct. The efficacy of any philosophy is in the efficiency of its product. That is the measure of success. T.S. Inborden, President Emeritus, Brick Junior College, Brick, North Carolina.[71]

Thomas S. Inborden served occasionally as a diplomat or mediator. The article about Brick School and T.S. in the New York Tribune was read by the wife of a distinguished attorney and suffragist leader for Negro rights, John E. Milholland. Milholland founded the Republican state party in New York, and he was a pacifist. He also played an integral role in the founding of the NAACP. Later, he served as Treasurer, Executive committee and served as a member of the board of directors. He was also interested in women's rights, prison reform and federal and state education. There were times when Milholland and W.E.B. DuBois did not agree with some of the philosophies of Booker T. Washington of Tuskegee, Alabama. However, he did assist Tuskegee Institute on numerous occasions. Inborden received a letter from his wife Jean Milholland of Meadowmount Lodge, Waham, New York in August, 1931. After reading the letter, T.S. realized that some of the contents referred to Tuskegee Institute and he decided to write a letter to his friend, Dr. R.R. Moton, President of Tuskegee. He told Moton that he had received the letter and that the original was in Mrs. Milholland's own hand and he was copying it and sending it as a suggestion and possibly Moton would know how to handle it to his advantage. Inborden said he was copying only the part with reference to Tuskegee. The letter to Dr. Moton read:

My Dear Professor, In reading about your wonderful work in the New York Sunday Tribune, August 23, 1931, I immediately began to recall the days when John E. Milholland and Booker T. Washington were so friendly and regret so much that Tuskegee, the one of Mr. Milholland's favorite schools seems to be the only one among all those he delighted so to help, has no reminder there of him. Howard University and the NAACP's crisis in New York have busts, but somehow there was never any effort made at Tuskegee. Some time you might ask Emmett Scott (former secretary for Booker T. Washington) about Mr. Milholland and what he did for them. I should like so much to have that school above all others see that his bust was there.[72]

When Dr. M.E. Dubissette left North Carolina for New York, he asked Inborden to act as his agent for some business matters. On September 23, 1931, an agreement was made between Mr. and Mrs. Benjamin Fobbs who purchased some furniture that had belonged to Dr. Dubissette. The furniture consisted of one room heater, 35 dollars, one dining room suite, 25 dollars, and a double bed, 30 dollars. The agreement stated that payments would be five dollars each month.[73] Inborden wrote Dr. Dubissette a letter on September 29, 1931, and said that he had received a letter from Mr. Mann and that he went over to see him and used the school truck to obtain the remaining things and that he had made agreement with the Fobbs for the furniture. T.S. said that he had brought two book cases and eight chairs to his house.[74]

T.S. Inborden wrote a letter to President Wright, Brick Junior College and expressed his views about a situation. T.S. wrote Wright that he was concerned about children who needed to be in school. He said that he had helped many students in the past and families on the farm in one way or another, but there must be a limit. Inborden stated that he recently had a concerned parent who was trying to enroll her daughter in school. T.S. said Wright must try to extend them the courtesy of credit where their guarantees are good until they get their crops on the market, because in case of the croppers, you have nothing to lose as their crops and products are under your control for the sake of getting the children in school. I would not mind underwriting any of their obligations but it is not my job. T.S. said in 1930, he placed two dollars in the account of two girls in addition to their board and heat. I brought them clothes and shoes.[75] many students are making sacrifice and they also need some assistance if possible.

    T.S. wrote his daughter-in-law Nan a very detailed letter about some of his thoughts and personal dealings with people and their appreciation. He stated that a Mr. Berry O'Kelly spoke at the school. He had sold fertilizer and feed and flour to the school. O'Kelly could give fine advice and tell you how and what to do. But he is strictly a *white man's Negro*. T.S. said he had no back bone and he would get what he wanted by acting the *Uncle Tom*. He could get you a job at once if he wanted to do so but sometime he would forget those who helped him. Inborden told Nan that Mr. Hudson of A and M College could put you in line for almost anything you wanted. He was in charge of the County agents. T.S. had worked with him for ten years when he wanted to locate agents at Brick, T.S. went along with him, and was able to collect 400 dollars to the farmer's credit. T.S. said he went before the County Commissioners and obtained more money for the agents. T.S. also wrote that a Mr. Hall enjoyed his good offices more than all others. He was with T.S. when he went to the Board of County Commissioners and they authorized him to be personally responsible for the people to pay 300 dollars for the agent's salary. T.S. said he made the appointments and Hall was with him. Unfortunately, because some white faces did not keep him from speaking his thoughts. Hall is not scared of God nor the devil when you catch him wrong. When he was dropped, T.S. said he went to Raleigh with 18 men in his interest and had him reinstated. When he was dropped the last time, T.S. wrote all the state officials in his interest including Dr. E. C. Brooke, president of the college. But it appeared that Hall was self assertive and they did not want a Negro who knew too much and this was characteristic of most white men. Inborden stated that he had to deal with them all his life. He said that when he had a misunderstanding with Secretary Brownlee, AMA, Hall was the one Negro outside of my daughter, Dorothy, that delivered himself to the fullest and Brownlee will always remember him. He does not want Hall in his business. Hall would be the best man today to handle Brick School. At one time said Inborden, the Ku Klux Klan beat Hall unmercifully for nothing but they never conquered his spirit. T.S. told Nan about short memories of people. He cited an incident when he invited Dr. R.R. Moton of Hampton Institute to speak at Brick School. After his address, he was invited to a luncheon and reception in his honor. A few weeks later T.S. and the treasurer went to Hampton Institute and were shown to several rooms in the Indian student barracks. There were no towels, bedding chairs, and wash basins. The treasurer was not pleased and he left for home the next day. T.S. remained. Later, he told Dr. Moton that he had only a bare room with a bed and mattress. T.S. was changed to a place where he should have been at the beginning. Moton had forgotten when he made his visit to Brick. I had met him at the station, remarked T.S. and handled his luggage and took him to the best room on the campus and gave him the best we had including a stand of fruit on his dressing table in his room and accorded him every consideration. T.S. told Nan that his major goal has been to make Brick School the best school in the country. Sometimes you will not receive full support from everyone. He wrote that Nan and Wilson have good qualities that are an asset to their character. He told Nan that they may have set backs here and there but in the end, you will get ahead. He closed the letter by writing, I have had to study hard everything and it has been helpful.[76]

Many black farmers in eastern North Carolina were thankful for T.S. Inborden. He would write letters and approach the white bankers to consider helping some of the black farmers. On February 12, 1932, T.S. wrote a letter to a B.D. Mann. He discussed the problems of a black farmer, Isaac Bunn. He said that Bunn was having some difficulties with the Commercial and Farmer Bank. T.S. said Bunn had worked hard for his education and home. But he received nothing for his crops recently. The Red Cross and the National Government are spending millions of dollars to help thousands of people who are less worthy than Bunn. The fact is the farmer who can qualify to receive help from the National Organizations do not need it and those who do not qualify are the fellows who need the help most. T.S. wrote that he was a man who believed that a man who is willing to work the land, who is able to work, should own a little land of his own. This class of people make the best citizens, lest they be white or colored.[77]

Inborden wrote T.S. Jackson a letter on February 21, 1932 and discussed some of his philosophies and things that he had accomplished at Brick School over the years. T.S. wrote that he had canned himself 400 quarts of fruit and tomatoes and later he gave them freely to some people in the community. He said that he is receiving daily lamentations from various sources relative to the way some landlords are treating the tenants. He said a man brought mules several years ago and tried to pay for them together with other furnishings for two years and all he has made has gone into the landlord's pocket. But he could not pay out reduced fees for his crops which has always been good. A few days ago, the landlord came to his house and took everything in sight that was of any value. T.S. stated that the tenant is absolutely stranded. Inborden wrote about another man who worked for one man for several years but could not pay even though the landlord took everything in sight and ejected him from his house. The tenant had to beg among his friends and the last report T.S. received was that he was planning to go to the county seat for support. T.S. wrote about a land lady who was quite wealthy and had taken every mule, cow, horse, chicken and pig from her tenants. Many whites wrote Inborden obtained their wealth from the Negroes and the confiscation of their farms. T.S. said a few years ago, he went to this wealthy white land lady for a small contribution for the school. But she told T.S. she could not help because she had to pay her taxes. T.S. wrote about a black farmer who was paying taxes on more than 50,000 dollars worth of property. For seven years the farmer has found it impossible to pay his bills. The prices of the crop fell lower and lower and the interest on his loans higher and higher. T.S. went to Durham with the farmer to see if some of his black friends in the business world would help the farmer. But the men told T.S. they had the money but were not allowed to use it on real estate. Eventually the farmer's property was advertised and sold.

T.S. said that he had heard from another source that his house was taken by the landlords. He had ten children and was trying to educate them. The past summer when he should have been canning fruit, he was growing many crops with which to clear his debts, but he was getting further in debt. Inborden had to give this farmer 20 quarts of fruit. The house in which the farmer lived, and his barns he will have to pay rent on them if he remains on the farm.

T.S. related another example of the farmer's problem to Mr. Jackson. He wrote that there was a man who graduated from Brick some years ago. He left the school and later purchased 250 acres of land and paid it in full. He ditched the land, subdrained it and bought machinery, a farm house and made some permanent improvements. This man went to a business man and obtained a loan for sixteen hundred dollars to include a ten percent interest. When the 1930 depression occurred, this farmer had a debt of 2,000 dollars. However, the banker wanted him to make payments on his mortgage immediately. The farmer could not make a payment and the mortgage holder took everything the farmer had. T.S. wrote about his assessment of the black farmer's conditions in the south. He said the environment that produces the disadvantages for the people is itself the criminal. Inborden remarked that he had travelled far and wide, all over the country and had contact with white people in every part of this country. T.S. said that he had studied with white boys and girls, slept in their homes, eaten at their tables, spoken with them in their churches and halls. Their refinement and great culture is absolutely beyond measure of description. However, how some white people can do the things they do without absolutely any compunctions of conscience is beyond my conception. Inborden continued by saying that he was born in the south, lived in the south all my life, all of my traditions are southern all of my best friends are in the south all my relatives on both sides of the race line are southern. Yet, this race complex puzzles me more than any expression I can make. I get on the train anywhere I wish so long as they know I am white, but soon as they see I am colored I am prescribed to every inconvenience. Inborden stated that prohibition is counted a failure because it began at the wrong end, with the law instead of with the cradle, in the Sunday school and in the pulpit. If race prejudice is ever rooted out as it never will, it must begin with the cradle and in the home about the fire side, in the Sunday school and churches. Respect must begin with human personality. Graduations are formed by natural aptitudes. The one solvent is Christianity. T.S. closed his letter to Jackson by writing, If we cannot solve the problem of our generation, our philosophy is wrong and we would do well to analyze the whole situation, ourselves and change our philosophy.[78]

On February 28, 1932, Inborden wrote a letter to Lawyer Andrews. T.S. discussed an article in a newspaper on *The Carpet baggers, Negro and the Constitution of North Carolina*. Inborden stated that when one reads the white man's history, he gets the idea that Negroes did nothing that was good in the reconstruction days. The truth will leak out here and there. There is only one thing that will save us now and in the future if we are to figure in the future development of this country and in his own future as a citizen. Forty years ago the Negroes were counted as a factor to be recognized more than he is now. T.S. said our position today is one of complacency, we are jim crowed in every hand because we accept it and have no power. A few days ago, I wrote Professor W.G. Jackson and discussed some things very hard. Jackson is the Chairman of Interracial Relations Committee and I expect he will think I am impatient. I told him in a lengthy letter that the laws were not made by the riff raff of the country but by the most intelligent men of the country and these lawyers were elected on the ground of their fitness and then those laws circumscribed the activities of a whole race that whether they were right or wrong, the most intelligent people of the state gave assent to them. Inborden wrote how some white people calling themselves superior can do the things that most of them do is beyond my comprehension. We meet in conferences, farm meetings and various other gatherings to hear a lot of what I call purely palaver. We are asked to meet them halfway in settling race relations. When we have always met them two-thirds and three fourths of the way, we must let them dole out what they want us to have in the way of social matters, and public places of influence. T.S. told Attorney Andrews that he is an eminent lawyer, but he can get all the law that Blackstone ever knew or be as great as the greatest lawyer in the country, you need not ever expect to be a judge in the south or a solicitor. Inborden said that he was in the Supreme Court of North Carolina in Raleigh recently, and he was blessed if he could not make a better speech than some of those men and reason better. T.S. said that at the next meeting of the state relations committee, they should have some of the black lawyers to include you and Rich to draw up an indictment against our complacency and I might say against the complacency of the whole race relations committee for not developing a more radical program for absolute human rights. T.S. wrote that he with all his education and background of achievement for the past forty years had no more rights than his mother who was born in a low environment reared under the conditions of human slavery though not a slave herself. Our school teachers are on less salary and other semi school officials are on less than white people would receive doing less than the same work. Our complacency give an assent to it. I move about among farm people almost daily and it would interest you to know perfectly subjected, they are to conditions imposed on them by their superior whites. T.S. said he was making inquiries to Washington, D.C. to see how this class of Negro will be handled in the newly organized Reconstruction Finance Corporation (RFC). If left solely to the southern white man's administration and especially the small county banks and landlords, it simply means a better tool with which to exploit the Negro and poor white man. Inborden stated that he went to a bank and they knew nothing about the RFC. It is to their advantage to keep the Negro in all the ignorance they can. I am going to get all the information I can and will use every opportunity to give this information to the Negro farmers. T.S. remarked how he was attending a meeting at Chapel Hill, N.C. Only at noon an announcement was made as the time and place for lunch. We were advised after some little excitement and my inquiry that we would have to go down to a certain street and in a specific building, and the YMCA secretary would tell us where to go and the cook might give us a handout. There was to have been another meeting after lunch. We found our car and went to Hall's hotel in Raleigh. When we got to our car, we found a red tag saying call at Police headquarters. We went to Police headquarters and waited but no official was to be found. I learned the officials were having court and I went over there to where I found an officer, to whom I explained my predicament. We had gone to the university in a special invitation and had parked on the school campus near the building where the meeting was held along with other parked cars. The officer was nice, after seeing that we were completely at his mercy. He advised us that since we were out of town to forget it. The point was not that I was doing all the talking and I took all the responsibility for the situation but that he thought that I was a white man. I have been caught in that sort of mesh before. I do not think the angels in heaven can be nicer than some white people I have met as I move about from place to place. They seem to be the embodiment of everything fine, culture, refinement, education, religion, free from every semblance of race prejudice. Yet one does not have to go very far in any direction without their showing the cloven fact. There only are only a few whites one can meet and talk to as one man should talk to another. He shows intuitively his superior complex and most of us blacks feel that we ought to take off our hat and put it under our left arm while we talk to them. I never go into a court house, said T.S. where there are Negroes but that I have to tell them to keep their hats on in the halls and lobbies unless white men have theirs off. The background for this tradition is bad and is still the common white man takes as humility in his presence. He thinks it is obeyance to him.[79]

The President Emeritus former Principal Thomas Sewell Inborden in 1932 was very sincere and adamant about his observations and experiences of the black status in the southern states and the power-ruling dominance by white people in subjugating blacks to an inferior status, politically, economically and socially. Inborden was not a politician or known black leader giving speeches without any direct results. He was a man who understood his people, the common black man and woman and their children. He knew poverty, ignorance and the continuing imposition the whites placed upon blacks. He was displeased with a so-called North Carolina Race Relations Committee. In 1932, T.S. Inborden wrote his friends and expressed so eloquently the situation and some possible solutions. I sincerely believe Inborden was quite conscious of the race problems in America.

T.S. Inborden wrote President J.C. Wright, Brick Junior College a note, dated June 24, 1932 concerning his observations. T.S. wrote that there was some unrest and nervousness on the campus and I do not know what is in the air. T.S. said that he advised two girls in his house that he did not want them mixed up in any unpleasant situations or they would have to find new boarding places. Inborden stated that one of the girls was present in a meeting with some students and they were obtaining signatures for some document that was to be sent to Dr. Brownlee in New York. She says she did not sign it. The running of an institution is not a student's job. T.S. told Wright that this note was for him personally and absolutely for no other eye.[80]

Inborden believed in direct action, not just words spoken about something. He sent a letter to Governor O. Max Gardener, North Carolina on October 26, 1932. He told the Governor he wanted to call his attention to several matters that this office might offer some assistance. T.S. discussed relief. He said that a number of people have complained that there was partiality shown among those seeking immediate help and that there was great differences shown between the white needy and the colored needy. One party called on me last night and said flour and meal were only a very small part of our needs. The people here need clothes, shoes, and medicine. T.S. said just how to get these things they do not know. A few days ago, I was in certain communities and I was advised that some of the colored farmers a little better fixed than others were bearing this extra burden themselves. They cannot buy clothes, sugar, coffee, medicine or meet the doctor's bill as there are inevitable in every family and in all communities. The schools are opening for the children now in a few days and there will be a book bill which those needing it cannot obtain, No man can bear a family numbering from five to eight earning thirty-five cents a day or even sixty-five cents a day. Earning this as a day's work. When he can get work, all the things named might be available in certain channels but ignorance, in fear, and very strong racial complex are awful handicaps. T.S. told the governor that Negroes have a very personal pride and are reluctant to let their best friends white as well as colored know their needs if they are in serious need. Not long ago, I called on two families remote from the public roads who were in the lowest squalor. They were parching peanuts for their dinner and that was all they had in the house. They were sleeping on pine straw mixed with old rags and fertilizer sacks. There was a man who died from starvation and want of care. At the last minute, the community came to help, but it was too late. His children were bound out.[81]

Inborden was quite concerned about the welfare of his people. During the months of October and November, 1931, he organized a community welfare committee. The individual efforts of T.S. were actually paramount when he received considerable support from citizens in the community. Pledges were received from Wade Allen, 5 bushels sweet potatoes, package peas, and 25 pounds pork, Moses Pittman, 10 bushels, sweet potatoes, 2 bushels corn and 25 pounds pork, Divan Reed, one help bushel potatoes and corn, Dave Tillery, bushel potatoes, gallon syrup and others scheduled to pledge were William Exum, Bennie Exum, and Walter Quinichelt. Assistance was given to residents in Edgecombe County, Township No. 6 and the Enfield community. T.S. and the concerned citizens were able to assist 78 children in need of clothes. His committee consisted of Bettie Pittman, Fannie Hunter, Mrs. Neely, Professor Pullen and H.C. Cofield.

The Governor of North Carolina decided to answer T.S.'s letter in an indirect manner. He had his Director of Relief, to prepare a response to T.S.'s letter. The director Fred W. Morrison wrote T.S. on November 21, 1932. He suggested that Inborden should contact Mrs. Winnifred Y. Wiggins, superintendent of Public Welfare of Edgecombe County, Tarboro, N.C., to assist in direct or work relief. Morrison wrote T.S. that he did not think that there was a continuous effort to make distinction between white needy and colored needy in the administration of relief throughout the state.[82]

Inborden learned from a newspaper clipping that his friend, Dr. H.H. Proctor had died. T.S. wrote his widow a letter and expressed his deepest sympathy. He also wrote that the way of death is the way of mystery. It is quiescent and eternal. We never know why such an imposition is made upon our lives. All nature is ever dying and ever producing, death is a process of eternity. Just a half dozen years ago

I had the experience that has now come to you. The demon of sadness, melancholy, dejection and either loneliness must be fought with continuous activity of some sort. There is no use in giving up but fight to the end. It is not all of life to live, it is a mental and spiritual struggle. T.S. also reminded Mrs. Proctor that her husband was a good friend and former Fisk classmate.[83]

A Lucinda Smith, case worker, Travelers Aid Society, Richmond, Virginia sent a letter to Inborden concerning a young black boy, William Wooten, who was stranded in Richmond. She stated that the boy was a former Brick student and had been reared in the orphans home at Concord, North Carolina. Miss Smith requested T.S. to write her and verify his legal residence in North Carolina. Inborden answered her letter and wrote that William Wooten was raised in the Colored Orphanage operated in Oxford, North Carolina by the Honorable H.P. Cheatman. T.S. said that when he visited the orphanage a year ago with nurse Winnie Neely, he became interested in Wooten and asked permission for him to attend Brick School. The boy had stated that he could not yet work as planned at Brick School. T.S. said he had nothing to do with school affairs at that time. He went to see the nurse and she was made responsible for him. The school program changed, said T.S. when he retired.[84]

R.C. Luciuis was a white childhood friend of T.S. in Upperville, Virginia. He wrote T.S. a friendly letter in 1933. The letter read:

Dear Sir, Excuse me for not answering your letter sooner. I am glad to hear from you and what do you think of the N.R.A and the depression. I hope it may workout all right for the poor people. I never see your brother Ashton now. He has strayed off from me now, from some courses, unless I meet him in the road. People are curious, don't you think so? I often think of the old horses you mentioned one and the boys who use to help me work them. One was as trifling as the other one. I don't like to say which one. I thought one was the best as I don't want to show partiality to the least. How do you like the term prohibition has taken, we will have plenty of whiskey now. The Blue Ridge has taken on its autumn here. I often look up there and think of my friends, your father and grandfather, Chappele, Mileys and Slacks all gone. Where the woodbine turneth. The old lady is alright, except can't walk and my legs are beginning to get a little feeble also. Good bye, R.C. Luciuis, Upperville, Virginia[85]

In 1933, Inborden was still forcibly expressing his views in writing about the status quo of his people. He wrote a letter to Dr. W.C.Jackson, Dean, School of Public Administration, University of North Carolina, Chapel Hill, and stated that we are not fighting with the bayonet and the sword, but with the most enlightened public opinion. The Negro has been a constructive force since the first cargo landed on the eastern shore of the country. He is not a Bolshevik nor a pacificist, nor a communist and there are absolutely no zangaras among us. The Negro has spoken in the biggest colleges of the state and notable changes have been going on quietly. The public press have been charitable and showed some sentiment.[86]

The death of Maggie Speight caused Inborden to write a letter to her children on March 31, 1933. T.S. told the children that he has known them since childhood, they had been present at Brick School and they must believe that their mother will never die as long as one lives who recalls her ministrations. Inborden wrote that she will never die as long as they should live or one of the grandchildren or one of the great grandchildren who shall yet be born into the world. We have read somewhere that sounds turned loose on the electric waves of the air never again come to rest. It is so with the human soul. The body in the shell for the abiding spirit, like all things material, the body wears out and disintegrates. After disintegration, it may appear in some life form again unrecognizable but perfectly natural in nature. T.S. said they must realize that every breath, every pain is a process of disintegration. It is reincarnated into what we call everlasting life. The soul that sins, it shall die. Inborden said, I knew your mother for thirty-eight years, she had a radiant spirit and I commend you to the Savior for inspiration.[87]

Inborden participated in the Program of the Fifty-Second Annual meeting of the North Carolina Negro Teachers Association, Raleigh, N.C. The convention theme was *No Step Backward*. T.S. gave several brief speeches. Some highlights of his speeches were: On April 14, 1933, he honored N.C., Newbold by stating that best eulogies are usually written after the subject has been re-incarnated into another life. However, they may be embarrassed when the subject is present in person. This is not intended to be a cadence of words to bring emolument to the writer, for he has been where he is going, neither to any member of this organization. I am not an artist in the portraiture of human character. That person is dumb indeed who cannot appreciate the outstanding qualities of a man who has given by his voice and pen for twenty years to the highest ideals applied to the Negro. He has championed the cause for the Negro. T.S. said Newbold was a counselor who championed iniquity and every inequality. In most different places he has spoken with great discrimination, tact and judgement. He has shown virtue. It never occurred to any of us that he had one standard of culture for one group of people and another for another group, a lower standard. Newbold was born into the faith that education makes all men better citizens, better home makers, better neighbors, and it also harmonizes our racial differences.

T.S. Inborden had the greatest respect and appreciation for the AMA outstanding leader Dr. A.F. Beard. On May 9, 1933, T.S. wrote Beard a letter of congratulations on his 100th birthday. Inborden wrote that he had read that one is never any older than he thinks he is and no one is no older than the youngest cell of the brain. The cells keep young by use. When one stops using the cells, they atrophy. This law has been wonderfully verified in your longevity. T.S. said that the last time he saw Beard that he was still thinking. His articles in a magazine were evidence of his continuous thinking. Inborden wrote that Beard has been a pioneer in an unknown field of research, the Indian in the west, Eskimo in Alaska, the mountain white in Virginia, Kentucky, Tennessee and North Carolina, and the Negro all over the south. These people owe their better life and their inspiration to Dr. Beard his wise administration, genius and constructive statesmanship. T.S. said that it has been forty years since Beard had handed him his passport to the service of the AMA.

For as many years, I have owed obedience to no other organization and no other group of men, association, fellowship, respect, affection and love. These are steps Dr. Beard, by which you have inspired my life and my attitudes. T.S. recalled an address by Beard at Lowell, Massachusetts and also those of Dr. Lyman Abbott, Dr. E.M. Cravath, Frederick Douglass and Dr. C.J. Ryder, all were still ringing in his ears. T.S. said that he sat on the platform also and read a paper on Southern education, some thirty years ago. yes, Dr. Cravath was so overcome for it looked as if Fisk University might have to close its doors for financial reasons, that he paused long enough to wipe the tears from his eyes. Inborden reminded Dr. Beard that it was his words that brought many tears from the audience. Also Frederick Douglass said that he was not present to make a speech, but to put himself on record, he threw his manuscript over to the newspaper people in front of the speakers stand. T.S. told how a Dr. Merrell E. Gates stopped him in the middle of his paper to comment on something he had said which had brought a great applause from the audience. T.S. ended his letter by telling Dr. Beard that it was a great meeting and a new impetus was placed in the work of the AMA.[88] The interesting letter written by Inborden documents the fact that the principal from Brick, North Carolina really did appear and speak on the same platform with the most distinguished statesman and abolitionist of color, Frederick Douglass.

T.S. received a wedding invitation on May 31, 1933 to the wedding of his friend's daughter. Mr. and Mrs. Nathan Benjamin Young extended an invitation to T.S. to attend their daughter, Julia Balkey's wedding to Dr. William Mason Sessoms at Rocky Mount, N.C.[89] In June 1933, Inborden had traveled to Washington, D.C. to attend the 64th Annual Commencement Exercise, Howard University, at the University stadium. While in Washington, D.C., T.S. visited his friend, Reverend Marsh, but did not find him at home. Inborden stayed at the famous Whitlow Hotel, located at 13th and T Streets N.W. that was owned by people of color. The first night in Washington he had stayed at a Girls dormitory at Howard University. After leaving Washington, T.S. visited his relatives in Upperville, Virginia for the weekend prior to returning to North Carolina. During his interim retirement, T.S. would receive letters from friends who wanted his assistance. Mrs. Eliza W. Coel of Baltimore, Maryland wrote T.S. on June 14, 1933. She told him that her husband, Reverend Coel had a nervous condition and was sent to John Hopkins University Hospital in Baltimore. A determination was made that he was insane and he was sent to an asylum in Crownsville, Maryland. Mrs. Coel told Inborden that she needed help. Her daughter Mildred K. Coel who had received her B.S. degree from Virginia State College, Petersburg, Virginia, needed a job. She wanted T.S. to assist her if possible.[90]

CHAPTER 5

Demise Of a Landmark and A Gallant Resurrection

Three years after the 1930 Depression, Brick Junior College was closed, possibly due to the financial problems of AMA. The AMA's New York office believed the state of North Carolina should or could assume the educational responsibilities of Brick School. After some serious consultations with the state of North Carolina and AMA, the three counties, Edgecombe, Nash and Halifax agreed to pay the salaries of teachers for a centralized high school at Brick. The Brick faculty, students and citizens of the surrounding communities were dismayed. T.S. strongly opposed the closing of the school. Many citizens, friends and local business people expressed their discontent in letters to T.S. Inborden and he in turn wrote letters about his personal opinions and thoughts on the demise of a historical and significant land mark that he founded and nurtured since 1895. James Sanford was concerned about the Brick School situation and wrote T.S. a letter from Madison, Wisconsin on July 7, 1933. Sanford wrote that if the AMA had kept Austin out of the picture, you, Miller and myself could have worked out a program for Brick. The story would have been very different from every angle. Sanford said he believed that the state would have cooperated and black and white people would have supported their plans. James Sanford wrote that they knew the job analysis and the needs of Brick. The same thing that has broken Brick asunder will eventually break the rest of the land grant colleges under Negro management. These whites are liberal minded, but not enough to admit the actual requirements of the Negro's needs. I am again working out here with the people that God made and they are all of that and more. As you very well know one may go in any hotel, restaurant, lunch or cafeteria regardless of conditions or previous servitude, since you dressed as a gentleman. Sanford said the farm crops in Wisconsin were late. Mrs. Sanford is well and, joins me in love to all.[1]

Fred L. Brownlee, Executive Secretary, AMA wrote T.S. on July 12, 1933 and discussed some facts on the AMA's situation and the closing of the Junior College. Brownlee wrote that there would be reductions in salary and that there was an accumulative debt of 80,000 dollars and the general income for AMA 1933-4 was reduced by approximately 350,000 dollars. The secretary stated that Allen Normal School, Thomasville, Georgia, a school at Caphasic and the Rio Grande Institute were closed. He also wrote that the work at Brick College has been suspended pending an increase in income and the state of North Carolina would have to assume the education responsibility of lower grades. Brownlee said that a school district will be established and a free public school from the first grade through high school and bus service will be established. There will be some 500 children in attendance, pending the securing of sufficient funds from the county. The AMA writes Brownlee, will permit the counties to use such facilities on the college campus as needed. In addition, 70 positions have been discontinued throughout the field.[2] Inborden had received this information and was now knowledgeable of the state and AMA's plan to duplicate if possible the efforts of the years of successful educational plans that produced the outstanding and successful students of Brick Normal School and College. Inborden initiated some immediate action reference the school's future. He wrote a serious letter to the county superintendent of Edgecombe and other county officials on July 15, 1933. He discussed the historical background of the school, its past and present importance and its overall successes. T.S. also included some suggestions and recommendations. T.S. stated that he came to Enfield 38 years ago 1 August and lived on the campus and managed the school as its principal for 31 years. I retired seven years ago. Mr. Joshua Horne, of Rocky Mount was on the Edgecombe Board of Commissioners and knows very much of our struggles at the very beginning of my work and he has kept up with the growth of the school over the years during my administration. Mr. Orman Williams was Chairman of the Board and through him the board gave me every consideration and every encouragement. Had it not been such support the school would have been short lived. T.S. said Mr. Winfield Ruffin and Mr. Mark Battle were also on the board about the same time and they both lived on the adjoining farm and were among our best friends and of course were able to speak for the work we were doing. When I retired all of Eastern North Carolina was a witness to the efficacy of my educational philosophy. My programs were too well known for me to try now to recite or delete. Every intelligent white man and colored man in the three counties knew the program and what I stood for. Inborden wrote that Mrs. Julia Elma Brewster Brick of Brooklyn, New York gave our AMA the farm and 5,000 dollars to start the school. When I went to New York, to buy equipment for the first building, I met her at her home and she gave me one thousand dollars to pay a deficit. She then told me that she did not expect to give any more money because she was interested in hospitals in Brooklyn which were taxing all of her income. As a matter of fact she came to Brick on a short visit and saw what had been done in a few months, then she began to get very interested in our work. Every year for eight years afterwards, Mrs. Brick gave a building for the campus. At the time of death, she had given about 150,000 dollars to Brick School and in her will left approximately 250,000 dollars for the continuation of the school. Some of the money was used for building repairs, permanent improvements on the farm and salaries. T.S. said that there was never a year when he did not register from 300-400 students from all the county and especially eastern North Carolina. I have yearly catalogues covering the students and events. He wrote that the subjects taught covered the regular academic courses, the same as the state of North Carolina. There were classes in wood, iron shops, mechanical drawings, practical and scientific agriculture, home economics, cooking and sewing.

T.S. remarked how the farmers met once a year with a large attendance of one-two thousand farmers from all over eastern N.C. The speakers for the farmer's meetings were sent to Brick from the Raleigh, Department of Agriculture. Inborden said Brick teachers were from the best colleges and their farm manager was a product of North Carolina A&T College, Greensboro. T.S. wrote that he has been in educational work for 42 years and he knows that it takes a great amount of work to have an attractive program that included class room mannerism and good morals. T.S. said that for a week he went over eight counties in this section with a county official in the interest of the continuation of Brick School. I did this in order to save the school for the people who needed it the most. Although the AMA New York office and local officials have discussed a program of continuation and procedure for educating the students said

T.S., I am taking the liberty of saying that I would like to suggest at least one person who might make a good head of the institution. He is a product of Fisk University, was in World War I in France, and has done some work on his masters degree at the University of Chicago. He would have completed his degree requirements but the climate in Chicago was against his health. He has been here for eleven years and served as a science teacher, registrar and school lecturer. This man lives on campus with his wife and children. I refer to you Mr. John H. Gordon. Inborden wrote that his white and colored friends have advised him to go on record by writing his suggestions. I have written this letter with the hope that it may help you to solve the problem.[3]

When T.S. Inborden received the news of N.B. Young's demise, he wrote a letter to his widow and family members in Tallahassee, Florida. T.S. wrote that he and President Young and he were friends and roommates when they were students in Oberlin College. He said that he has always followed N.B. Young's progress and his attainment of eminence. There is no Negro who has left Oberlin so highly respected than N.B. Young. His achievements in the area of education are outstanding. He was an educator of the first magnitude and life and achievements are comparable with the most outstanding men of his age. Inborden wrote that Young had kept up with all the outstanding movements of the country that had a bearing on Negro achievement. I will always remember N.B. Young as a scholar, clear thinker and speaker. His passing is a distance loss to all of us.[4]

T.S. Inborden did not exhibit any outward desires or hints that he was interested in serving as Principal of the new county school. However, some influential citizens of the community were interested in recommending T.S. to serve as principal. County superintendent A.E. Aker wrote superintendent J.A. Abernathy, Tarboro, N.C. He said a Mr. R.C. Dunn of Enfield called him and stated that the high school had been set up at Brick and the superintendents from Halifax, Edgecombe and Nash counties would select the principal and suggested T.S. Inborden. Aker said that he approve enthusiastically the suggestion and if I may not be presuming, I should suggest to you and Mr. Inscoe and urge that you employ Inborden. I have known him for many years and consider him one of the fittest Negro in the state. I believe that Inborden can do more to keep the spirit between the races on an even keel than any man we may select.[5] A dental surgeon in Weldon, N.C., Dr. W.L. Horne wrote R.C. Dunn of Enfield on July 27, 1933. Dr. Horne said that he was a former Brick student, born in Nash County and reared in Rocky Mount. He said that he had traveled throughout the state and knows both white and colored in eastern North Carolina. Many of them agree with me that Brick School has served a most unique part in the industrial training among my people in not only this county but also in surrounding counties. Horne stated that he had been advised that the former principal has been suggested to head this institution under the new organization. I am proud of that if it is true and I believe every alumni and the people of my race are too. We do have a man whom I believe carries as great respect and esteem of both races as Professor T.S. Inborden and who can organize and harness up as many of my people for their common and civic good. Dr. Horne said I do not believe a man can be named who will roll up his sleeves and go in the fields and in the homes as this man, Inborden has done. He has worked with the humblest and most insignificant ones in their agricultural economic and domestic problems. He has done it and never refused to assist in any righteous cause. Horne continued his long letter by writing there is nothing that can be told to anyone who has lived around here any length of time about Mr. Inborden. His life and work has stood out eminently and as a former student and realizing the good work previously done by him. I am taking the liberty of asking a favor yet, in behalf of my people at large in the interest of the institution itself that you lend your influence and help in having Professor T.S. Inborden named as principal of Brick School. Dr. Horne stated that whatever is done must be through men like you and you most certainly are the logical one upon which my race might call. You know the school and if your full power is placed behind this request, I feel that something good will occur. This letter is written out of my own interest, said Horne and not on solicitation of Professor Inborden. I feel that I am quite right when I tell you this community is unanimous in the sentiments favoring appointment. Many citizens have expressed how they have missed him and his good work in their communities and allow me to say this. If Brick is to be revived again, I do not think you could find the better person than its former head Professor Inborden.[6]

A.N. Rice, Garysburg, N.C. wrote R.C. Dunn a letter, July 28, 1933. He wrote that he was writing concerning the entire community and Negro race. He said that he has been a patron of Brick School for sometime and it has served a useful purpose to my race. It has been a great asset. If it is true that Professor T.S. Inborden is being considered for the head of a new organization of this institution, I want to assure you that the people of this community will be astonishingly proud of that fact and will show him every possible help, cooperation and support. I believe this be speaks of all Northampton County. Rice stated that he wrote the letter because he knows of Mr. Dunn's long interest in the school. Your help and assistance will be appreciated by the people of my race. The Reverend J.W. Blackwell, Garysburg, N.C., wrote R.C. Dunn and said that news having reached us that the counties of Halifax, Nash and Edgecombe will be in charge of Brick School and that a principal must be appointed. Blackwell said we are asking you to consider the first principal of the school, Professor Inborden whom we feel will meet the approval of the greater part of Negroes in eastern, North Carolina. Blackwell was the moderator of the Neuse River Association.[7]

Inborden wrote a letter to Professor W.W. Saunders, Louisville, Kentucky and suggested that before the closed session of the National Association of Colored Teachers, something should be mentioned about the passing of President N.B. Young in Tampa, Florida. T.S. said Young received his college degree at Talledega College and graduated from Oberlin, Class of 1888, there were 29 men and 41 women. Inborden stated that Young was born in Tuscalossa, Alabama and taught at Decatur, Tuskegee and was head of the state college of Alabama. However, through some chicanery and trickery on part of some politicians who governed the school, he lost his position as President and then served briefly as President at Lincoln University, Jefferson City, Missouri when he met the same fate as in Alabama. Young was interested in the organization and perpetuation of the National Negro Education Association. He was a fine scholar, excellent writer and forceful speaker. T.S. wrote that had it not been for Young's influence over me as to my own health and the need to leave Oberlin for a warmer climate, I would probably not be writing these lines about him today. Inborden said N.B. Young's life was an inspiration to him and has been to all who knew him. Had he been a white man, he would have been a congressman, senator or a member of the presidents cabinet. T.S. was very fond of N.B. Young as a friend and educator.[8]

Support was continuing for Inborden as Principal of the new Brick School. On July 31, 1933, Joseph L. Peacock, Tarboro, N.C., sent a letter to Mr. Dunn. He said that he had written his friend Abernathy to do what he can to have Professor Inborden appointed principal of the new county Brick School. I surely believe in Inborden. He never should have been retired.[9]

T.S. Inborden had future plans in mind for the Brick estate for farming purposes. He shared them with a Mrs. Bratcher that he wrote to on August 4, 1933. He stated that the 1129 acres of land/farm over the years were used to rent large tracts of land to tenants with a financial return of more than 5,000 dollars a year. T.S. said they had a large number of tenant houses and all were occupied. There are now seven tenant houses. The tenants had a written contract, terminated when their conduct and attitude were out of harmony with the purposes and interest of the institution. Some tenants paid for their rent in one thousand pounds of lint cotton for each horse or mule. They could grow anything they wished except tobacco because that was costly to produce and we did not have the wood for curing or for barns. The school kept up home repairs, barn repairs, pump and half ditch work. When T.S. went before the county Board of Commissioners, the strongest argument was that income from the farmers renting land had to go in operating the school and agricultural expenses. Mr. Forney's management of the farm was excellent with farm returns of cotton, vegetables, and fruits. The students had worked for two months in the summer. Inborden wrote that prior to 1895, General Estes grew peaches and shipped them to Baltimore, Maryland. T.S. remembered when there were 27 plows running on the farm. The farm manager had to know the soil. There were particular soils, some was sand, clay, gray loam, some black, rich and shallow. There are swamps back of the school barns. In the near future said Inborden, they could afford pastorate for two hundred or more hogs. The land could be very useful and repairs made to the old store houses, barns and buildings. T.S. said that he would like to see the county obtain the entire plant so that it can utilize the farm income for the education program. Mrs. Brick gave the land for educational purposes and the AMA would be happy.[10]

The possibility of Inborden becoming the principal of the new Brick School was more a reality in August 1933, Mr. Dunn received a letter from Attorney Cooley in Nashville, N.C. and he said that he had discussed the matter with L.S. Inscoe, superintendent and that it was Inscoe's opinion that Inborden was the proper man for the principal of Brick School. Surprisingly, T.S. received a letter from Helen B. Smith, Sparrows Point, Maryland, recent graduate of Shaw University in home economics who wanted a teaching position at Brick School.[11]

During the discussions and negotiations on a principal for the school, T.S. still had the time to write Dr. James E. Hilman, Raleigh, N.C. and discuss a favorite subject of botany. T.S. wrote Dr. Hilman that during all of his school administration that he had taught 3-5 classes daily to include advanced arithmetic, algebra, history, biology, psychology, social service, political economy, botany, French, Greek and agriculture. Inborden stated that his hobbies have been honey bees and he has harvested as much as 5,000 pounds of honey. He has conducted six week courses in agriculture to include field of human knowledge and science and he developed a course in agriculture for the colored state schools in 1913 and he helped North Carolina A and T College. T.S. had studied type setting and printing and remarked that he did all the printing for Brick School. Inborden told Dr. Hilman that he loved botany and his collections have been gathered from all over the United States except Florida, Maine and a few of the south western states, the number would run into the thousands. T.S. said that he had exchanged specimens with the Botanical Societies of Massachusetts and Boston. The Society of Boston furnished many of the specimens to the botanical departments of Oberlin College, Ohio. T.S. stated that a German botanist, Dr. Gottenger of Nashville, Tennessee wrote up the flora of Tennessee and in Inborden's collection at Fisk University, Dr. Gottenger came across one specimen which he did not know grew in Tennessee. He wrote T.S. Inborden when he was spending the summer on the islands of Lake Erie, to locate the plant for him. T.S. said he located the plant description for Gottenger. Some 20 years later, while visiting the Botanical Society of Massachusetts, he was shown a book on the flora of Tennessee by Dr. Gottenger and there was his name as the original authority on the plant he had described. Inborden related to Dr. Hilman that in North Dakota a violet with a leaf like a cactus leaf for storing up water in dry weather was growing in the area and was quite unusual. He also discussed some flora found in southwest Washington state, as polypod six-eight feet tall, a very beautiful fern. He also found the same polypod near Washington Lake adjacent to the grounds of the University of Washington between Bellingham, just south of Vancouver, British Columbia. T.S. said that he found more of these polypods in the city park of San Francisco, California. He also observed in San Francisco, a real fern tree he had never seen before. He wrote about a Scottish broom that he had never seen until 1933 when he was on the old York road leading from Newport News to Willimsburg, Virginia, and found it in the woods. T.S. said he also observed a migrant plant in Virginia that had come over in the hay which was fed to the British horses during the revolutionary war.

During the discussion of botany, T.S. said that North Carolina is rich in the flora from the mountains to the sea. He was not aware if anyone had written about it. Every year he found new plants that were not recorded in any of the old class books covering northern or southern flora. He was able to find new plants, hybrids and mutants. T.S. said he found a new plant on the side of Crawley's mountain in western North Carolina in 1933. He also found a new plant ten miles west of Murfreesboro and neither were mentioned in his class books. T.S. concluded his letter to Dr. James E. Hilman by writing that the last few years of his administration at Brick, his wife Sarah Jane was librarian. He was able to have mounted and labelled his pressed plants. When he retired they unfortunately overlooked the plants and left them in the cabinets. Inborden said when he looked for them later, the plants had been piled up with thousands of magazines and old books and were burned. He said he still have most of the names of his collection.[12] This talented characteristic and knowledge of Inborden's accomplishments in botany was not known to many people. It is fortunate that his preserved letters to others have revealed another attribute the former mountain boy from Virginia who traveled to Cleveland, Ohio for upward mobility on to Oberlin and Fisk University and a life's dedication to educating and assisting his own people of color.

Jeannette Keeble Cox, a friend of the Inborden's also had heard the news about the possibility of T.S. being appointed principal of Brick School. She wrote Inborden on August 5, 1933 and said that it might be different when he gets the job to consider the appointments of many of his friends. She told T.S. that he would have to consider card playing and dancing in the teacher's home. Also some of the men smoke in the dormitory but they are modest and respectful about it. Mrs. Cox said the county officials will probably give less favor to some restrictions than the AMA might have done. She told T.S. if he has read the current issue of the Norfolk Journal and Guide newspaper, he would see what Hampton Institute and the Virginia State College are doing. Each school in August is having state and national tennis tournaments and bridge and dancing are second features. The world is changing.[13] T.S. received a letter from President John W. Davis, West Virginia State College, Institute, West Virginia. He was discussing the financial problems in his state and trusted the college would not suffer.[14]

The news was spreading through newspapers, letters and by individuals that Brick School in North Carolina was reopening. Many people wrote T.S. inquiring about job positions or for their friends. Inborden's daughter-in-law Nan, wrote him and said her young friend, Helen C. Latimer, a graduate of South Carolina State College wanted T.S. to use his influence to assist her in getting a job at Brick.[15] While Lugenia G. Exum of North Carolina was attending Chicago University, Illinois she wrote T.S. and inquired about a job teaching English or history at Brick.[16] Evelyn Forney wrote T.S. a letter from Cincinnati, Ohio and stated that she wanted a job teaching physical education or science and also enroll the ten year old daughter of a school physician in Jacksonville. He does not want her to attend the public schools in the city because the training there does not equal that in the boarding school and the children are so very bad. Mrs. Forney said that she met a Professor Bluford of Lincoln High School in Kansas City, Kansas and he knew T.S. very well and his wife's home is Weldon, N.C. The year was 1933 and some people wanted their children to attend well disciplined and good structured curriculum schools. Ironically, sixty-two years later, people are echoing the same words and thoughts.[17] President J.H. Bias of the State Normal School, North Carolina Teacher Training School, Elizabeth City, wrote T.S. and stated that he was pleased to see that his friend, founder and maker of Brick School would be head again of this grand school.[18] W.A. Holmes, Mount Olive, N.C., wrote T.S. and wanted a position teaching English and social studies at Brick. Inborden received a letter from Jefferson R. Snype, Brooklyn, New York on August 20, 1933. Snype told T.S. that he was glad to learn that the school would have the right man for the job and none is capable of a better leadership and future success for his dear Alma Mater than Inborden. Snype told Inborden that he had made the school and can still make it a greater school.[19] Julia P. Johnson, Washington, D.C. wrote T.S. and asked for a teaching position in history, English, art or physical education. She was a graduate of Howard University. She also had a Masters degree in secondary education from Teachers College, Columbia University, New York. Mrs Johnson listed as her references, Dean Oliver W. Holmes, College of Education, and Dr. Charles Wesley, professor of history, Howard University.[20]

T.S. Inborden wrote a letter to Dr. J.L. Peacock on August 25, 1933 and discussed the opening of Brick School, of an experience in Virginia that he probably has discussed in other letters to friends and his personal thoughts about Mr. R.C. Dunn. T.S. thanked Dr. Peacock for his excellent judgement. He wrote that Mr. Dunn had informed him that the school would be managed by three counties and they wanted him to be the head. Inborden told Peacock that he had advised the county superintendent to use him, and he wanted Dr. Peacock to know that he had demonstrated the interest of black people at Shaw University who some did not know how to appreciate Peacock's good officers. Ignorant leaders of many people do silly and foolish things. T.S. mentioned about Holloway who was at Brick when T.S. retired from the school. He told Peacock that Holloway was the man who made so much trouble come to Brick. Correct one, said Inborden, he never did a real constructive job in his life and made an absolute failure here. He was dropped from the school, left the denomination and joined the Presbyterian church and has gone into politics. T.S. said that last Saturday night some one came to his door. He opened the door and who should it be but the same man with his little daughter seeking a place for the night. I told him he did not need to go any further that I had five beds and all were made ready for company or occupancy and absolutely no one else was in the house. T.S. said he told Holloway that he was welcome and gave him some food. Prior to his leaving, Holloway told T.S. that he had made a great mistake and if he had to do it all over, he would do it different. Inborden related to Peacock a story about an experience in Virginia. T.S. wrote that there was a white man in Virginia who owned at one time many slaves before the war and 250 acres of land. His wife was a cultured white woman and very refined. They were the parents of five daughters. They also died before the old man's demise. T.S. said that he had worked for the old man and carried cool water for the family during their illness. There are two brothers living. Both are my kindred by marriage said Inborden. When the land was divided, the old man drank up part of his money and married again and began life as a tramp. There was a neighbor of this old white man who also had some slaves. After the war he gave eight acres of land to a black that was called *Uncle Robert Taylor* with title to house and land for life. The old white gentleman remarked Inborden was incensed that this old Negro man should be given land and a home at the close of war. As the years passed by, Robert Taylor became a Methodist preacher. On one cold afternoon in the winter Taylor observed a man stepping over his fence toward a stack of wheat straw. Taylor watched him as he was trying to find a warm place to stay. Along with him was his six year old son. Robert Taylor decided to go out to the wheat stack and he recognized the old man and his son as his former neighbor and the same man who did not like him. The old white man asked Taylor if they could stay in his house for the night. Taylor responded and said that they could stay in the best room he had and his wife Lizzie would cook a warm supper for them. T.S. told Peacock, that the point of the story was that people ought to be careful. The whole world is upset right now and nobody wants to take the blame. T.S. repeated again his famous saying, *The efficacy of any man's philosophy is in the efficiency of its product.* If he finds his product is not efficient then he had better change the philosophy. T.S. said most people are willing to change. Inborden informed Dr. Peacock that he is looking forward for a program at the school that will involve hard work with a good appeal. He also said the teachers must be willing to sacrifice what they might call a good time to do the job. You do not have and cannot build an institution when teachers are playing cards half the night and are present in public dance halls. T.S. ended his letter to Peacock by writing his praises about Mr. Dunn. Inborden said that Dunn was a good speaker who mastered the pieces of diction, and poetic art. At one time he was begged to join the Ku Klux Klan. He told the KKK that he was a Baptist, Democrat and a Mason. In recent years, he had given every expression of his life and he did not need to join the Klan.[21]

The AMA had expressed quite vividly their impressions about Inborden remaining as head of the school when they asked him to retire some years ago. However, T.S. did write a letter to the Executive Secretary, AMA on August 25, 1933 and told him that he has been asked to head the new Brick School. Inborden wrote Brownlee that he made it plain that he was not entering any competition with anybody. T.S. said that he was making no addresses anywhere to get the job, and taking no papers to be signed by anybody. T.S. also remarked that he would not take the work under any circumstances unless Mr. Gordon, his son-in-law was appointed to assist in the registration and classification. T.S. had brought Gordon back from Chicago, Illinois where he was making about 800 dollars a year while working for his Masters degree and at the same time when we could not pay him that amount. Inborden told Brownlee that he would like to hire some of his former teachers, namely, Mr. Killingsworth, music, and Evelyn Forney. However, J.D. Killingsworth had accepted a job as head of the music department at Clark University, Atlanta, Georgia.[22] Job applicants were writing to T.S. in September, 1933 requesting jobs. Inborden had received letters from Emma L. Marrow, Scotland Neck, N.C.; Hopie N. Dawson, Raleigh, N.C.; Elizabeth Hardin, McIntosh, Georgia; Helen Smith, Baltimore, Maryland; Sallye J. Taylor, Abbevine, South Carolina; Maggie E. Highsmith, Wilmington, N.C.; and C.H. Williamson, Henderson, N.C. T.S. also received letters from Mamie Dowtin, who was going to visit Brick and Frankie Myrick, a former Brick student who wanted a letter of recommendation.[23] On September 2, 1933, T.S. wrote Mr. J.W. Pittman and informed him that the three counties would be operating Brick School as a tri county elementary and high school as with other free high schools under state auspices. There is no charge except for books and maintenance. The different communities which have children to send here are working out their own transportation under county direction. Inborden wrote that Mr. Gary Pittman could explain about the planning in his section. T.S. remarked that the dormitories will not be open unless sufficient applications are received. The overhead expenses must be met and arrangements are being made to take as many young people who wish to come to live in the cottages where there will be several teachers to supervise the girls.[24] T.S. received a letter from Secretary Brownlee,

AMA with instructions about the transfer of Brick School to the State of North Carolina. Brownlee wrote that AMA would permit five acres of the land with a cottage for use by the vocational agriculture teachers. All chemical material and equipment is to be stored in the chemistry lab, also all biological and physical equipment except that which is used for high school work. The AMA's typewriters and adding machines are to be stored. The school can have free use of classrooms, charts, and maps. The grand piano in the chapel is to be removed for use in the auditorium. The specific buildings were listed by Brownlee as the elementary school, some shop buildings, Young, Peters, Gordon, children's, and Austin cottages, laundry building and the administration building. Brownlee said the county would assume responsibility for the care and order of the school campus, tenant farm, and school farms. The property was placed in the custodianship of Mr. L.W. Hemmons who would live for one year on the campus.[25] Mary V. Little wrote T.S. a letter from Demopolis, Alabama and wished him success in his new position at the Brick School. She said that her sister and family sends their love.[26]

T.S. Inborden sent a detailed letter to friends and patrons of Brick School announcing the opening of the school. He stated that the school will no longer be operated by the AMA but by the three counties, Nash, Halifax and Edgecombe. There will be an elementary and high school with academic courses and also home economics and vocational training. The plant will be valued at 400,000 dollars including 4-5,000 books, a science laboratory, equipment for elementary work, separate buildings for elementary and high school students, small cottages for teachers and some students, three large dormitories and a spacious dining room for 300 students and if needed some 1100 acre farm with farm buildings and farm cottage for agricultural activities. T.S. stated that the physical plant will be leased to the state for one dollar. There will be no tuition fee. A full board if desired will be charged sixteen dollars a month and places will be found on campus for them. The live in cottages will be under teacher's direction. Those in close proximity of the school will walk to school and others will come daily in their own cars or on buses. Inborden wrote that the social, religious and athletic activities will be wholesome inspirational and character building. They must be in accord with the most enlightened thought and in harmony with community interests and not at variance with religious and Christian activities. T.S. said questionable attitudes will not be tolerated. Those who can not and will not conform to the best and approved standard in the best home should not apply for entrance here. Your future will depend largely upon the inspiration you get from good selected teachers. T.S. concluded his letter by writing that the child makes a record every school day and unless he or she is here, the record cannot be made.[27]

Cora E. Black Grant wrote T.S. a letter to congratulate him on his new position of principal. She stated that I am sure you have merited it from your success in the past. The state and the community need you to carry on in the educational field. Ms. Grant told Inborden that she appreciates the interest that he had manifested in her in a tangible way years ago at Brick.[28] The North Carolina Department of Education wrote T.S. about his teaching abilities for certification. He replied by stating that he has taught since 1891. He had taught twelve months in Tennessee, public school work, and organized schools in Helena, Arkansas and Albany, Georgia where he taught for 2 years. T.S. also wrote that he organized Brick School in 1895. Inborden stated it very precise when he wrote my work here at Brick School is my certificate and I had received a state certificate in 1925.[29]

In October 1933, T.S. reflected on some past memories and looked toward the future as far as Brick School was concerned. He wrote a letter to a Dr. Thomas and shared his feelings. He wrote that he had not doubted for an instant the sincerity of Thomas' appreciation for him and his life's work at Brick. T.S. stated that he did not want the place and gave his reasons for not wanting it. It was not a question of compensation because our great AMA had amply provided for absolute necessities of life, that is food, a place to live and clothing. I also have nephews and nieces living in Virginia, Maryland and Delaware and a house in the best of repair in Oberlin, Ohio, and I could live with daughter, Dorothy and her husband in West Virginia, or at my old home in the Blue Ridge mountains of Virginia where he was born 68 years ago or a place in Enfield. T.S. continued his letter by writing that Brick School had orders to close May 15, 1933. I heard it on the streets of Enfield. I was very much perturbed and could not sleep, for at two in the morning I would go and write the college president a letter, advising him what course to take, but my suggestions were turned down, remarked T.S. Inborden said he visited county officials and traveled over eight counties and wrote hundreds of letters to offices, friends to save the school because 60,000 blacks in three counties and 200 or more thousand in eight counties. I did not want to head the school. I told everybody that want me. T.S. wrote that the men who succeeded him had nothing to do but move off on a road or highway that had been well established. They wanted miscegenation, social equality, liberty, liberalism and such idea that were incompatible with the best educational and most rational continuity at that time of southern life, they failed.[30] When T.S. wrote the above words in 1933, one cannot set aside that he was living in a time that was the way they were and it was common sense and sometimes conformity to existing laws and rules established by the white majority which were necessary for survival and continuance of a program plan and institution to people of color of who experienced the worst of evils and ostracism that their fortunate successors and descendants of this day do not have to confront. The actions and sometimes disciplines that men and women like Inborden had to impose or conform to have brought their survivals thus far first by faith and the desire for upward mobility through education and hard work. T.S. Inborden was thinking of the past tribulations and tranquil occasions when he wrote a letter to Mr. Robert Elzy on October 8, 1933. T.S. wrote that through the efforts of many, especially former Bricklites the doors of Brick School will be kept open. T.S. said that the troubles with most people who make failure is that they are bull headed. They think they are right when they are wrong. They will not listen to argument and reason. History teaches them nothing, the romance and fiction readings are exciting and at the same time they are passive. T.S. said that most of us learn by hard knocks and failures. We never admit the failure. We look for an alibi and always have one at hand. Inborden told Mr. Elzy that the richness and greatness of Brick as a learning institution with such loyalty on the part of students and teachers had people saying that this school was the garden spot of eastern North Carolina. T.S. said that at the end of his administration the school had a property value of 500,000 dollars and that its greatest value was not in the physical assets but in the investment of our attitudes and thought in a better manhood and womanhood in fine citizenship. The white and colored communities were the beneficiaries.

T.S. Inborden wrote that everywhere he would go, he could find Bricklites practicing medicine, dentistry, teaching education, economics, preaching and teaching in great numbers in Washington, D.C., Chicago, Cincinnati and New York and of course over all the south. Some Brickites were raising honorable families, buying farms and homes of their own, all imbedded with the traditional spirit of their teachers. T.S. said they never preached to the students, but gave them inspiration to succeed as many did enroll at Fisk, Talledega and Howard. Those who did not go were forced into the military service because of economic conditions. T.S. discussed in his letter to Elzy how he drove the mules to have lumber for the buildings over roads, 20 miles to and from the saw mills and helped to clear the swamps dug ditches to carry away the waste and water. He said he built walks and carried food from Enfield on his own back for the teachers's breakfast and made other trips before breakfast. He would walk six miles to carry sacks of flour, meal, and groceries. Inborden stated that now as to the present set up at Brick in 1933, he has no control of the farm or the tenants. He said that he had only the use of a few cottages for students and teachers. T.S. said he would use certain rooms in the administration building for high school work and the shop building for elementary classes. He said the science equipment would be restricted and the chapel would be used for special occasions. Inborden said that Mrs. Forney and some neighbors have promised to assist him after they finish getting their peanuts and cotton picked. The state will only be pay for academic work, remarked T.S. Inborden said that his hands were on the throttle and he knows exactly what it takes to do a good job and he was equal to it. He believed that he had the support of every county and state official except a person named Spruill who wanted Wright as principal. T.S. said he had every farmer and all the white collar men in eastern, N.C. and all the Negroes who have contributed. T.S. said he had received congratulations from everywhere and he had made no application for the job and practices no politics, no chicanery and no trickery. Inborden stated that when he found out what work Wright was doing in trying to get the position, he decided that at any cost that someone else should have the position and not necessary himself. Wright had tried to get you Elzy said T.S. off the campus and also Gordon and Saunders and me. Inborden remarked that he was not as powerful as Napoleon but he knew his strength.

T.S. was still receiving praise and acceptance for accepting the position of principal of the new Brick School. The graduates and former students of Brick School living in the metropolitan area of New York met at a mass meeting and sent best wishes for the scholastic year to T.S. and the school. They also said that they rejoiced in the new constructive plan for reaching leadership for Brick School. The letter was signed by Robert Elzy, Chairman, Samuel A. Allen, secretary, Susie Adams Langston, Estelle Campbell, Martha Harrison-Bares, B.T. Hayes, Harold Proctor, P.L. Phillips and F.B. Frederick.[31] T.S. received a warm consoling letter from a friend, Reverend G.T. Thomas, pastor Wentz

Memorial Congregational church, Winston-Salem, N.C. Thomas told Inborden that he had received his letter with a great deal of personal satisfaction and inspiration. I truly thank you for all that you have said and done above all for your taking me into your confidence. God bless you and you should ever live in the heart of the people. Rev. Thomas wrote that he fully read between the lines and T.S. had verified his opinion, because he told his wife all along that the school closed to get rid of the man and the pity is he did not know it. Thomas said that he was of the opinion that the enrollment of the school fell off more as a protest against T.S. retirement than the incompetency of Wright and yet, it had its tremendous weight. Thomas said the people are bound to have what they want. He told T.S. that he knew that his standing in the community among both races and great work is known all over the country and Brick School is T.S. imperishable monument. The school is erected in the hearts of its people more strongly than the walls of the institution which you have established in this vicinity wrote Thomas. Rev. Thomas told T.S. that he was certainly kind to Holloway who came in and spent one night and a day with him. Thomas said he was glad Holloway saw his mistake even though late. Thomas wrote that he liked T.S.' philosophy and he shall never forget Inborden's words. "For the sake of our work and our people we must make some sacrifices if we live in the south and we must sacrifice some opinions as well as some of our liberty".[32] The above quotation of Inborden emphasizes again as I have previously stated that T.S. Inborden was a tactful man who believed in achieving the best for his people and the necessity for survival and at times there were sacrifices he did not like but had to make in view of the increasing tactics of the white ruling majority. It is unfortunate that in 1995 that people of color do not have more men and women leaders who are made of the stuff that Inborden was especially a sincere and first priority, his own people. B.T. Bullock of Spelman College, Atlanta, Georgia wrote T.S. a letter, October 17, 1933. Bullock wrote that his eyes were filled with tears of great joy and his heart was rejoiced to know that the King had gone back to rebuild the walls of Jerusalem. Bullock said that T.S. has the inspiration that many loyal sons and daughters of Brick and believers in your philosophy of life are praying that Brick may not only return to its former place of usefulness in that community, but under T.S. leadership the school will have a new birth and thus fill a new need in this day of tremendous stress and strain, not only physical but mental and spiritual stress and strain. Bullock told T.S. that Brick School is an institution in North Carolina of educational leadership that should remain. On November 1, 1933, T.S. received a very encouraging letter from L.S. Inscoe, superintendent, Nash County Schools. He wrote T.S. that he was glad to receive the report on Brick School and the enrollment in the high school department was better than expected. Inscoe said that they have been making plans for sometime to have a larger school population among the colored schools. He told T.S. that Brick School fits into their plan just fine and is going to assist in speeding up the realization of their aim, that every boy and girl, white or colored in Nash county will have the opportunity to receive a high school education without leaving their home area.[33] T.S. experienced a one day strike at Brick School on March 26, 1934. He was successful in containing the situation by immediate actions. It appeared that there was some discontent by some farm tenants and a crowd of people assembled at the front of the school chapel for more than hour.

Eventually, order was restored and the crowd was dispersed. Executive Secretary Brownlee, AMA, wrote T.S. and discussed some findings from a recent meeting in Washington, D.C. He told Inborden that the Rockefeller Foundation was contemplating making some funds available through the Southern Interracial Committee that would be used for a preliminary survey of the Brick property and future possibilities. Brownlee said that if the subsistence homestead committee would approve the preliminary study, money could be made available. He said members of the Interracial Special Committee were Clark Foreman, Chairman, Calvin Hoover, Mr. Hunt, Mr. Murchinson, Mr. Forrester, Brownlee and they would appoint Inborden as a member. Brownlee was hoping that these actions would help to ensure the future of Brick School.[34] A graduation program was conducted at Brick School on May 23, 1934 at 10 a.m. The program consisted of the processional, invocation, introduction of the speaker by T.S. The speaker was former Governor, R.T. Fountain. A solo was rendered *Rose In The Bird*, awarding of certificates, announcements, and the benediction. At times, local communities would extend invitations to Inborden to participate in their services and programs. In November 1934, T.S. was invited by the pastor and members of the First Baptist Church, Weldon, N.C. to participate in an installation service. Pastor J.W. Wiley Jr. asked T.S. to give charge to the service.

President Thomas E. Jones, Fisk University sent T.S. a letter of recognition from his Alma Mater, 27 April 1935. The letter read:

Fisk University in recognition of the distinguished and meritorious services rendered by Thomas S. Inborden, A.B. Fisk University 1891, in the field of education, community organization and race relations. He has been a moving spirit in the establishment and development of business enterprises, farming interests and better homes among Negroes in the state of North Carolina, does hereby attest to that fact and further endorse and approve the high standards which he has taken in all matters of vital concern to the people of his state. Wherefore, the seal of Fisk University hereunto set this 27th day of April, 1935. Thomas E. Jones.[35]

A commencement exercise was conducted at Brick High School during the week of May 19-22, 1935. A Baccalaureate sermon was given on May 19 by Reverend J.W. Wiley. The primary school exercise *Mid Summers Eve* was presented 8 p.m., May 20. On May 21, the seventh grade exercises were held at 2 p.m. with an address by Professor J.E. Bowen Jr., from Hollister, N.C. At 8 p.m. the Senior Class Day program gave two one act plays. The major commencement exercises were conducted on May 22 with an address by Professor C.H. Hamlin, head department sociology, Atlanta Christian college. At 1:30 p.m. a two act operetta *Sunny of Sunnyside* was presented. A baseball game was held at 3:00 p.m.[36] Occasionally community people would request to use Brick facilities for their events. A Miss M.E. Hawkins wrote T.S. July 8, 1935 and ask T.S. if the Nautilus Club of Halifax could have a picnic at Brick, August 16. She said there would be 40-50 high school students. Dr. C. Hawkins Brown, president, Palmer Memorial Institute, Sedalia, N.C. wrote T.S. reference a Eugene A Bruce, Wildwood, New Jersey who was interested in employment at Brick School.[37]

A conference was held in the office of N.C. Newbold, Department of Education, North Carolina in Raleigh on July 19, 1935. The persons present were N.C. Newbold, H.M. Trigg, State High School Inspector of colored schools, N.C., N.E. Gresham, superintendent, Tarboro County, A.E. Akers, Roanoke Rapids, N.C., Halifax County School superintendent, H.W. Mitchell, District Manager, County Farms, S.B. Simmons, State Supervisor of Vocational Agents, Professor Hamilton, N.C. State College, Secretary Brownlee, AMA, and T.S. Inborden. These members formed a committee, permanent Chairman was Brownlee, Newbold, Vice Chairman and Inborden was Secretary. A vote was taken to call the permanent committee the Sponsoring Committee. A sub-advisory committee consisted of Mr. D.F. Lowe, Greensboro, director of County Home Agents Demonstration work, Mrs. Johnson, Enfield, representing Halifax County and representative from Nash and Edgecombe counties. Secretary Brownlee remarked that the AMA has a thousand dollars to assist the betterment of rural life through health, better homes, vocational activities and religious programs. Brownlee said that in order to meet these objectives, county agents could assist by working with local farmers. The committee stated that there should be a combined effort to reach the citizens of the communities through the efforts and assistance of home agents, nurses, and home economic teachers.[38]

T.S. Inborden wrote a letter to Joseph H.B. Evans, special advisor to the director, Resettlement Administration, Washington, D.C. on October 9, 1935. Evans was the cousin of T.S.' wife, Sarah Jane. T.S. discussed some problems on the homestead project. He wrote that some government men visited Enfield and he escorted them to the Tillery Rehabilitation project and they were pleased with what they observed. T.S. said that he had not found a single objector to the project among the community land owners who would object on any grounds. Mr. E.K. Neville joins us on the west side and is the only large land owner near us whose land we would like to have some 600 acres. He has expressed himself to me personally as being in accord with the project. When asked by me if his land might be available, he replied that the land has been his source of income for forty years. He would want a substantial amount of money if he sold the land. Inborden said that there is about a thousand acres on the Brick farm. The wood farm is already under the Welfare officials and has been offered to the project for some acres. I have no doubt that there are those who object to any settlement. Thousands of acres all over the country and this land would be not worth anything to them if they had no Negro labor and poor white labor to work the land. This class of people are exploiters for the interest of the big land owners and they cannot help themselves, the condition of the poor whites is as appalling as that of the Negro stated Inborden. Both should be given a better chance in the economic field. T.S. wrote that one of the whites was at his door recently begging for food and clothes and sometimes entire white families come from the highway begging. Just a few hours ago, four colored men came requesting food for their families. T.S. said he knew everyone of them and took them to Enfield to the grocery store and purchased sixteen dollars worth of meal, flour, meat sugar and coffee. The store merchant asked me if I knew that I was playing a losing game. T.S. told him. No, I was not, these people will repay me, because somewhere down the road if it is to be, there is the next generation that might be a little better.

Inborden wrote that he called on a white friend who had a large family. On the bed in his house was a beautiful spread, the girls had made. He told me to take the spread and see what I could get for it so that he might have some of the income to feed and cloth his children so they could go to school. T.S. also discussed a situation where a family of ten children lived near the school. The parents were ill in bed, had no medicine or money and asked T.S. to go to the drugstore and get them some medicine. T.S. said he drove 26 miles and reported the case to a county worker. She gave him a form and advised him to go back and get it filled out and then bring it back to the county seat and they would have a case worker to investigate. Inborden decided that if the case worker from another town was getting her carfare and paid for the services, he should let her handle the situation. T.S. made an inquiry about the family later and learned that the children were not in school and were practically nude without sufficient clothes. Inborden sent one of his teachers to the children's home and they were taken to Meyers store in Enfield and fitted out with 13 dollars worth of clothes. T.S. said the emergency relief people still had not initiated any actions to assist the family. Inborden told Mr. Evans that these are the sort of things that have influenced him to try to get some government money into the Negro community to improve their living conditions. T.S. said these classes of people must learn how to live, clean their homes, and improve their immediate family environment.[39] If these conditions existed in many black communities and some white communities in the south some sixty years ago and some form of public assistance was available through tremendous paper work being filed, how much progress has really been made in solving the economic situation among poor people to alter their condition from poverty to self subsistence through a reasonable paying job?

T.S. Inborden explained the real purpose of the Homestead project that he believed in through a letter he wrote to Professor J.D. Reid, Wilson, N.C. on September 23, 1935. T.S. first discussed the background. He wrote that in October 1933 the depression had really affected the people of color very seriously as well as some white people. They were begging for bread and sleeping wherever they could find a place, in the woods, old shacks and under bridges. T.S. said he advised some leading white citizens about the problems. They were not able to help too much. He talked with an Enfield lawyer about land being made available for the people. T.S. said a Dr. Roy Brown of Raleigh visited Brick along with a Mr. Oxly, state welfare officer for colored people. T.S. said that he suggested to Dr. Brown that a thousand acres of land adjacent to the Brick area be made ready for possible habitation. The land cold be divided into small plots, cleared and build small houses from the lumber cut and give people a deed for the land. T.S. stated that the lands were owned by large land owners who could not pay taxes. Some of the acres were Roanoke River, Tar River, Showan River, Fishing Creek and Swift Creek. There were also areas from Weldon, Rocky Mount, Wilson, Fayetteville and a hundred or more miles before reaching the Atlantic Ocean. T.S. said the soil is 100 feet deep and productive. The land could be drained and exterminate the mosquitoes and swamp pests. T.S. wrote that the government's money is simply pamperizing the great masses who receive it and no self reputing Negro wants to see his race pauperized. In our cities when land is needed for public utilities, it is condemned and utilized. Those large areas in the south might be handled the same way. T.S. had suggested this to Dr. Brown. Brown told T.S. that he would review some of his suggestions. T.S. told Professor Reid that recently Secretary Brownlee was visiting Brick and he told Brownlee about his suggestion on the Homestead project. Inborden and Brownlee went to Raleigh to discuss the project with Dr. Brown and was assured that Brown would discuss the project with officials when he goes to Washington. Inborden wrote that he began to work on the local project by discussing the plans with J.W. Mitchell, state farm agent and S.B. Simmons, state district vocational teacher. T.S. had dinner at his home and talked about the project with Dr. Bruce Melvin, Homestead Division, Dr. Roy Taylor, Interior Department, Dr. Clark Foreman, advisor on Negro Affairs, Rosenwald Fund, and others in attendance were several men from Duke University and Chapel Hill, and some distinguished men of color. T.S. had a meeting with Judge Kerr, Warrenton, N.C. and he appeared interested in the project. T.S also inquired how whites felt about the project and also some blacks. Decisions were made on vegetables that would be grown, type of houses with electricity. Soil tests were made, and rainfall checked for the last 20 years. T.S. remarked that they were running into some obstacles. An official from North Carolina visited Washington to speak with an official on the project and when he arrived he was told that the official was not in after making an appointment and he had to return to N.C. without a hearing. There were times that letters were not received by respective officials. Inborden stated that he had written a letter to a Dr. Pynchon and told him that the law applied to rural and urban population and they were interested in becoming part of the Rehabilitation project. T.S. said that out of 40 projects submitted, they had the best of them. Under the Resettlement administration they were advised that 18 projects in view and the Enfield project appeared promising. T.S. said they had to prepare new data and were attempting to receive 5,000 acres of land. When the government surveyor came to obtain the new data, some were concerned about it being a Negro project.[40] T.S. Inborden had found the time from his busy schedule as school principal to become directly evolved in a land resettlement project that would benefit many poor citizens of eastern North Carolina. T.S. was an outstanding educator but also a very exemplary statesman in interceding through legislative and political obstacles to secure a better life and conditions for his own people of color.

On September 24, 1935, T.S. received a reply from his letter to Joseph H.B. Evans. Evans wrote T.S. and told him that the information he sent was just what he desired and he could use when he presents the matter before some officials. He stated that the bulk of funds in the Rural Resettlement program was being used in connection with rehabilitation of families in place to include provisions for livestock, farm supplies, farm equipment, repairs, taxes, subsistence and community cooperative services. Evans said that it has been impossible to obtain information concerning to which extent Negro farm families have been participating in the program and that he was writing T.S. and other Negro leaders asking them to make an effort to secure definite information as what is being done for the black families. Evans told T.S. that if he was able with the assistance of extension agents and others please find some definite cases where Negro families are being aided. I should like to know the nature of this assistance for each individual case and it is needed at once, wrote Evans.[41] Joseph B. Evans sent T.S. a note on

September 27, 1935 and said that he had talked with the regional director for N.C. and he mentioned that there was some difficulty in obtaining suitable land at a fair price. He is not discouraged. However, said Evans, we feel that we should be able to locate something desirable. T.S. Inborden planned a trip to Washington and wanted an appointment with Congressman J. Reid of North Carolina. Reid wrote T.S. on October 5, 1935 and told T.S. that he would try to have the Speaker of the House meet T.S. and Mr. Meyers and you must be in the Capitol at 8 a.m. so you can see him before he is occupied with other business.[42]

Inborden participated in the county affair in Edgecombe County on October 9, 1935. Other participants from the community were Mrs. Wharton, Mrs. Spellman, Miss Cruise, Mrs. Bowen, Mrs. Bettie Draughan, Mrs. Eaton, Mrs. Maggie Grant, Miss Fannie Laurence and Julia Gordon. In 1935, T.S. was still receiving good community support on special projects. He was pleased with the assistance he received to help the camp girls. Some of the persons who provided their help were: Will Pope, Alice Pope, Thomas Pope, Ralph Pittman, Bloomer Pittman, Hyman Pittman, Lester Hunter, Ella Hunter, Curtis Taylor, Daniel Williams, Luther Williams, Willie Williams, Avant Bullock, Marion Hopkins and R. Wade Exum.

Joseph H.B. Evans wrote T.S. on October 9, 1935 and discussed the land project. He told T.S. that he is anxious to establish a program there and especially where the Resettlement region office will work just as hard for the development of Negro projects as they will do for whites. Evans said that he felt a great deal better over T.S.' letter because it advises him that the land situation is clearing up and it looks as though there will be enough available acreage to carry through our regional plan. Evans told T.S. that he knew that he was working hard and unselfish to bring the development to the people in his vicinity. There is a possibility that we shall be able to place through our regional office, a field worker to cover the state in connection with the Debt Adjustment Program wrote Evans. Evans stated that there will also be a need for women who have training and development experience in home economics and home management to work with the Rehabilitation program. He asked T.S. if he had any persons in mind who were qualified. Evans told T.S. that he would like for him to send their names and addresses with a brief statement as to their training and experience.[43] T.S. wrote Mr. Newbold in Raleigh and told him that it looks as though they would get the homestead project. Inborden said that the officials in Washington said they need a field worker to cover the state in connection with the Debt Adjustment Program and also need a high calibre businessman and experienced women for a Home Economics program. T.S. said there are plans to locate about 200 people in small farms and they must learn to cooperate and live together.

T.S. Inborden had the abilities and qualities of a weatherman when he assumed his weather bureau tasks. With the assistance of his family, especially his children they performed daily tasks as weather observers. Some of their significant duties were the measuring of water using rain gages at different sites on the campus, in front of their home and near Fishy Creek. His son Wilson walked a mile daily to measure the water in the creek. His daughters Julia and Dorothy would determine the direction the wind was blowing in the morning and check the amount of rain from the gage in front of the house. In later years, T.S.' granddaughter, Frances had some duties of recording the results. Inborden performed his duties as a weather observer in an outstanding manner over the years and in 1936 he was given credit and praise for his accomplishments. The office of the chief, United States Department of Agriculture, Weather Bureau, Washington, D.C., sent T.S. a laudatory letter. The letter read:

> Mr. T.S. Inborden, Cooperative Observer, Weather Bureau, Enfield, North Carolina. Dear Mr. Inborden, It is with great pleasure that I note from our records that you have, in the capacity of Cooperative Observer at Enfield furnished this bureau with valuable weather reports for more than 25 years. As you know, there are at the present time from coast to coast nearly 5,000 Cooperative Observers of the weather bureau. But comparatively few have to credit such long and distinguished service as yours. We fully realize what it means in the way of inconvenience and bother to make these weather observations day after day, year in year out and with the years accumulated to the imposing number you have served without monetary compensation. The matter becomes so outstanding fitting these words of personal greeting, congratulations and assurance of appreciation thereof. Your contribution to the climate of North Carolina and the work of the Weather Bureau in general is of great value and we are glad of the opportunity to recognize it in this personal way. There comes to you with the message the sincere hope for many years of health and for your continuance through them as a valuable number of our official family in the capacity of Cooperative Observer at Enfield. Sincerely yours, W.R. Gregg, Chief of Bureau.[44]

> Eat thou honey because it is good sweet
> to the taste and health to the bones.
>
> *King Solomon*

T.S. Inborden had learned the art of maintaining bee cultures and producing honey when he was in Oberlin, Ohio from his wife's father, Wilson Bruce Evans. T.S. was fascinated about bees and honey and at one time maintained 65 colonies and was successful in selling all of the produce. He would ship orders to friends in glass jar containers and buckets. T.S. would order some of his honey supplies from Dadant and Sons, Hamilton, New York, York Bee Company, Jessup, Georgia, White Apiarist, North Carolina, and A.L. Root Company, Norfolk, Virginia. Inborden would order honey supplies consisting of bee wax, gloves, cartons, honey labels, hive tools, glass containers, veils, wax presser, and uncapping machines. Inborden's son, Wilson assisted him in bee honey making and his daughter, Dorothy assisted him by placing labels on bottles filled with honey. Throughout the years while T.S. was at Bricks, N.C., he supplied many people with honey requests at a minimal price. Some of his regular customers were: Reverend J. Allen Russell, Principal, St. Paul Normal and Industrial School, Laurenceville, Virginia; Rev. H.H. Proctor, Nazarene Congregational Church, Brooklyn, New York; Principal G.C. Shaw, Mary Potter Normal School, Oxford, N.C.; Arthur P. Holmes, Architect, AMA, Jacksonville, Florida; Quentin Gregory, Halifax, N.C.; P.R. Davies, Washington, D.C.; Ruth Beebe, Connecticut; Louise H. Allyn, Athen, Alabama; Judge Keech, Tarboro, N.C.; L.R.

Reynolds, Enfield, N.C.; Ivey Watson, Enfield, N.C.; and his good friend, William Pickens, NAACP, New York City, New York. T.S. frequently extended invitations for the N.C. State Extension Apiarist to visit Brick School. Bee culture and honey was another interest and talented task that was characteristic of the diversified abilities of T.S. Inborden.[45]

Christmas, 1936 was a very pleasant season for T.S. He was host to his brother, Ashton Smith from Upperville, Virginia. T.S.'s niece in Swarthmore, Pennsylvania, Virginia Mosley wrote him on January 2, 1937 and acknowledged that she had received a package of honey and peanuts. She also wished T.S. a happy birthday.[46] Inborden had continued his cultural programs for the students, in the new Brick School. Katherine Green, pianist was presented in a recital on Monday, May 10, 1937. She was accompanied by Eugene H. Brice, Tenor. Their repitore included *Still as the Night, The Lords Prayer, A Spirit Flower, Over Jordan, Sinner Please, Manhattan Serenade, Country Gardens, Blue Are Her Eyes* and *In a Russian Garden*.[47] Doris M. Dubissette wrote T.S. from New York City on May 11, 1937 and said that she had written to Dr. Dubissette about the prospect T.S. had for the house occupied by a Cad Davis. She said Dr. Dubissette suggested that Inborden should go ahead with the deal if it seems reasonable and will net an amount proportionate to the valuation of the property. Doris Dubissette informed T.S. that Dr. Dubissette appears to live in Grenada and was adjusting himself to it quite satisfactory.[48] Inborden was still active with the farmers in the area in 1937. Dr. G.W. Bullock, Rocky Mount, N.C. invited T.S. to the farmers picnic that was held on Friday, July 2 at the providence Township School.[49]

The continuous practice and enforcement of segregated activities in North Carolina was quite evident when N.E. Gresham sent a letter to the black and white school principals. Superintendent Gresham's letter read:

A janitors school for white janitors who have not attended more than one school will be conducted in Raleigh July 19-23 and one for Negro janitors at Greensboro July 26-30. The county will furnish transportation and expenses paid by the state.[50] The state agent for Cooperative Extension work in agriculture and home economics, state of N.C., C.A. Hudson invited T.S. to participate in a meeting at Wilson, N.C. He asked Inborden to talk about things that would benefit the farmers. T.S. was able to share experiences of many years with the farmers at their Negro Farmers Institute at the court house in Wilson on July 15, 1937.[51]

During the so-called separate but equal period in America. T.S. would have to use his managerial and financial skills to obtain needed equipment for the school. In September 1937, he wrote a letter to the superintendent of schools, Tarboro about obtaining seats for the school auditorium. He asked for an appropriation of 250 dollars to purchase the seats. Inborden told the county official that he did not desire to have his students seated about in windows and on stair. In November 1937, T.S. was asked by Superintendent N.E. Gresham to serve as chairman in his community for the American Red Cross.

T.S. Inborden displayed a very sincere interest in helping the people in the surrounding communities. When he was asked about pensions for World War I Veterans, he wrote a letter to Congressman John H. Kerr. Kerr responded to T.S. request on November 18 and stated that information on pensions for widows of veterans of the World War are contained in many statues and laws, therefore he would need some specific information or requests. When the political agenda of some parties in America today are very concerned about welfare and orphanages for children, they should realize that black people have been addressing these subjects and their responsibilities for many years, as late as 1883. A colored orphanage of North Carolina was founded in 1883. In 1937, T.K. Borders was the superintendent. He conducted a state wide drive for funds to assist some 154 children in Oxford, N.C. Borders wrote T.S. to help during their fund raising drive. Many white children were sent to an orphanage supported by a Masonic group.[52]

T.S. Inborden had developed and organized a successful curriculum and programs for the Tri-County Brick School during the years 1933-1937. The academic and social climate was excellent and indicative of Inborden's expertise and leadership abilities in operating the new Brick School. Through the assistance of his faculty and selected students, there was a revival of the distinguished school newspaper, *The Brick Bugle*. The staff of the paper consisted of editor, Eddie Draughn, assistant editor, Burnetta Branch, campus-news editor, Julia Gordon, sports writer, John Gordon, campus comedy writer, Clara Whitaker, circulation manager, Chauncey Belle, business manager, Woodrow Walston, and faulty advisors, Eugene H. Brice, James W. Eaton and Gladys Hammond. Some members of the school faculty were James W. Eaton, Minetta Eaton, Gladys Hammond, Eugene Brice, Julia I. Gordon, Annie Ruth Cruse, Esther V. White and Katherine Mae Green. Inborden supported and welcomed the various programs and activities that the students and faculty had organized. A Dramatics Club was started under the supervision of Miss Hammond. The members were Charity Whitaker, Marina Collins, James Hayes, Willie Harrison, Eddie Draughn, Mittie Clark, and Clara Whitaker. Movies were shown on Thursday nights in the Brick Chapel. A sports program for the school included a girls baseball team and its members were Julia Gordon, Ruby Nelson, Beatrice Lyons, Nell Bowens and Geneva Harrison. There was a football team for the high school in 1937. The team played against schools in Wilson, Spring Hope, Rich Square and Nashville. The efforts of students and faculty through socials, entertainments and contributions were able to purchase equipment for the football team. Some members of the team were Jessie Tucker, George Adams, Woodrow Walston, and Spencer Battle. The football was cheered on toward victories by the Brick Cheerleaders. They were Gaston Pittman, Julia Gordon, Marina Collins, Eddie Draughn, Clara Whitaker and James Boddie. Basketball was also present at Brick, the Green Panthers under Coach Bob Earl. The members of the team were *Tank* Watson, Horace Tucker, *Bo* Gordon, Mingo Fobbs, George Adams, Matthew Whitaker, Gaston Pittman, and Andrew Howington. There was also one active girls basketball team consisted of Ruby Nelson, Beatrice Lyons, Nell Bowens, Julia Gordon, and Geneva Harrison. The senior class of Brick High School sponsored a carnival in November 1937 under the supervision of their sponsor Miss Gladys Hammonds. The main features of the carnival were punching for candy, bingo, fortune telling, pecan throwing, pennies in a tub and bobbing for apples. Some prize winners were Beatrice Lyons, Olive Draughn, Jessie Tucker, Julia Gordon, Edward Anthony, James Boddie and Woodrow Walston. The teachers at Brick High school under the guidance of T.S. Inborden developed a lecture series on various subjects for the students. Their purpose was to provide the students with practical information about life. Inborden was able to demonstrate his finest and community relations in obtaining support from the local merchants by advertising in the Brick Bugle paper. Some of the cooperative advertisers were Meyers' Fashion Shop, Young Men's Shoppe, department stores and groceries, Enfield, Harrison Drug Co, Enfield, Daylite Bakery, Rocky Mount, Rocky Mount Furniture Company, Kimble Hardware, Enfield, Epstein's Clothes, Rocky Mount, Southern Dairies Ice Cream, Rocky Mount, M System Stores, Enfield, M. Cohen's Enfield Store, Bellamy and Enfield Oil Company and D.J. Edwards' store, Rocky Mount.

Inborden initiated a program in 1937 involving the students and their parents when the New Farmers of America was organized at Brick School. The members were Eddie Draughn, John Gordon, James Hayes, Harold Belle, Percy Battle, Benjamin Exum, William Clark, and their advisor was Mr. Rogers. Some of their activities included a father and son Banquet and a Thanksgiving program. The patriotism of Brick students was observed when they celebrated Armistice Day on November 11, 1937. The participants were members of the Junior class. They were Isaac Smith, Clara Whitaker, Fannie Lawrence, Jennie Draughn, Geneva Harris, Elizabeth Lowe, Carthinia Dixon, Orlanda Itovall, Nell D. Bowens, Carthinia Dixon and Mingo Fobbs. T.S. Inborden was hospitalized briefly on August 6, 1937 in a Rocky Mount hospital due to a hip condition. His daughter-in-law, Nan, Wilson's wife, wrote T.S. a letter and stated she understood that services for colored people were quite poor.

Inborden recalled his first Thanksgiving dinner in Enfield, N.C., 43 years ago in 1938 when he read an article *His Masters Body*, in the State Newspaper, Raleigh, N.C. The article was discussing an old colored woman who lived for more than 65 years in the town of Battleboro. When a confederate, Dr. Joe Phillips, was at Fredericksburg during the Civil War, this colored woman's father Ned Green of Edgecombe County was present as Phillip's bodyguard. The newspaper article stated that when it was safe to do so Ned Green went into the battle lines and brought his master to a place of safety and made shelter for him. Green dressed the wounds of Phillips and found something for him to eat and drink. When it was safe, Ned Green started south, some 200 miles away to help his master to travel to Battlesboro. The article stated that when Dr. Phillips died, in later years, his will provided land for each of Ned Green's four children, 25 acres each. The will also stated that if any time Ned Green's children or grandchildren should need professional services, Phillips' children or grandchildren would help them and provide the service without cost. Ironically, in 1918, Ned Green was very sick and Phillip's children were at Green's bedside until he died. They also made preparations and paid for the burial. Inborden remarked that the saga of Ned Green showed the finest tribute the Phillips's children gave for Green's years of patriotism and loyalty to their family. T.S. said he had his first Thanksgiving dinner in North Carolina in the home of Ned Green.[53]

The state of North Carolina Governor's office sent a form letter to the Negro High schools. Governor Clyde R. Hoey signed a letter stating that the state department of education was planning to have seventeen group conferences with Negro principals of high schools, T.S. received a letter on January 15, 1938.[54] The colored public schools, Spring Hope, N.C. held a dedication of their new gymnasium on January 23, 1938. Their guest speaker was T.S. Inborden who spoke on *Physical Education In Community life*. D.A. Thomas was the principal of the school. The Tri-County Cooperative Extension service, Home Economics and Agriculture held a meeting at the Parmelee School in February 1938. The theme of the meeting was *More Money and Better Living on the Farm* T.S. was asked to summarize the discussion and make comments on things that were learned. He was invited by state agent C.R. Hudson who recognized and appreciated Inborden's vast experience and knowledge in the areas of education and agriculture.[55] Members of the National Organization of Negro Farmers of America made T.S. Inborden an honorary member in March 1938. President William John Clark, Virginia Union University wrote Inborden on March 31, 1938 and thanked him for the information concerning Reverend Junius Cofield of Enfield. Cofield was continuing his education at Virginia Union University. Clark told T.S. that he would see if he could find some means of helping Cofield to obtain an education.[56] The Meyers family of Enfield had been friends of T.S. since his arrival in 1895. Inborden decided to visit Sigmund Meyers of Enfield who had a law office in Durham and was seeking his candidacy for Judge of the Recorders Court. Meyers sent T.S. a letter on April 6, 1938 and thanked him for writing several friends and he was sure that Inborden's efforts on his behalf were increasing his changes of getting into the second primary.[57]

There is a German proverb that says *Counsel is for the elder and action is for the young one*. Many institutions in society, political and private have their leadership performed by senior citizens ranging from 65-75 years and their abilities are respected and their performances are commendable. There are some people in our society who believe that young leadership is needed in various professions where individuals who are older have been there for years. Especially in the field of education, over the years very capable and efficient men and women have been asked to retire and make way for some new and young leadership. Somehow people are not interested or really do not care about one's years of dedication, loyalty and continued successes in a particular job once they reached the age of 65 or 70 years. These trends of thought existed yesterday and even today. Sometimes the decisions are intertwined with political, personal and individual motives to have capable persons to submit their resignations. The outstanding dedicated and loyal commitment to Brick School by Thomas Sewell Inborden was challenged and a decision made by those powers to be that he should retire in 1938. There had been a storm brewing in the past, the AMA had benefitted from his service, they appreciated it but, it was time for Inborden to retire especially in the mind of Brownlee. It is believed that his behind the scene actions gave some kindling fuel to the combustible decision that came. Many citizens of eastern North Carolina did not agree with the decisions by the politicians, some superintendents and individuals who believed Inborden should retire. T.S. Inborden did not greet the decision mildly and expressed his thoughts in numerous correspondence that he wrote. Many of his loyal friends and supporters also displayed their feelings and support for T.S. There was an initial demise of Brick School in the late 1920's, then there was a resurrection in the early 1930's but in 1938 it was finished. Yes, many courageous years of a loving, sincere and unselfish service to his people, the common one, middle class and upper class, he talked, walked and was there with them all to give his very best, all of this ended with a letter that was probably very hard for T.S. to write but he complied to his critics request.

On May 1, 1938, T.S. Inborden wrote a letter to Professor N.E. Gresham and the County Board of Education of Edgecombe County, Tarboro, N.C. The letter read:

Gentlemen, I hereby give to you my resignation as principal of the Brick School to go into operation at the close of school and when all reports have been made out and passed to your office. When I accepted the principalship under the state auspices and county supervision it was entirely through the solicitation of Lawyer R.C. Dunn in Enfield and your own Dr. J.L. Peacock in Tarboro. These are two outstanding men in this community and for whom I have the most profound respect and the highest possible admiration. I will mail a copy of this letter to our office in New York. T.S. Inborden.[58]

T.S. also sent a personal note to N.E. Greshman and told him that when he accepted the job in 1933, he asked no one for the position. I unbarred the doors and windows and got busy. T.S. also said that he had conducted the school under state and county auspices and increased the enrollment. He also added a home economics teacher and vocational instructor. I was also successful in obtaining three buses for the school, remarked Inborden. On June 4, 1938, T.S. wrote his friend Professor Newbold and told him about the school being closed for the summer and being called to Tarboro along with Mr. Eaton and was informed that their services would be terminated. T.S. said the implication was that Secretary Brownlee in New York objected to T.S. being principal of the school. The superintendent told Inborden that they had correspondence with Brownlee and he was not willing to put any money into Brick if T.S. is managing it. T.S. said some of his friends told him not to resign because the New York people could not dictate who runs the schools of North Carolina. Inborden told Newbold that he went to see Dr. W.W. Green, Tarboro and asked him about the situation. Green stated that he had no correspondence with Brownlee and had no information from anyone on the matter.[59]

Fred Brownlee wrote T.S. on June 9, 1938 and told him that he had written Mrs. Mable Davis Artist, the daughter of the late Alice L. Davis and asked for some interesting information about her mother for an article in the Missionary magazine. Brownlee requested T.S. to provide him some information on Mrs. Davis. T.S. as usual responded to the request. He wrote the following about Mrs. Alice L. Davis.

Mrs. Davis spend thirty years in Missionary service in Georgia, Florida, North Carolina and Virginia. She died at Oberlin, Ohio on Saturday, June 4, 1938. In 1891 she assisted T.S. Inborden in organizing the AMA school at Albany, Georgia. She was the mother of two daughters and a love for all children. She served at Brick Normal School for 30 years as a Matron and teacher. Her academic training was limited but she was well read and was an excellent conversationalist.

She also taught sewing classes at Brick. Mrs. Davis was a refined and cultured person and an embodiment of what she taught. She had a fine background and had been raised in a fine old family of white people. She experienced the loss of her daughter and husband in the early years. Alice Davis is gone but not forgotten by those she taught.[60]

Superintendent N.E. Greshman of Tarboro wrote Attorney R.C. Dunn of Enfield on June 25, 1938 reference T.S. resignation. The letter read:

Replying to your letter of June 20 in which you enclosed a petition signed by the friends of Professor Inborden, I am writing to say that I shall be very glad to present the petition to the Board of Education at the next meeting. I wish to thank you for your interest in Professor Inborden and the Tri-County school. You asked me to write you frankly to Professor Inborden's chances of remaining principal. I do not think the Board of Education will be inclined to change its decision it made some two months ago. All of us realize that this man has rendered a very high type of service to the colored people of this section for many years. On the other hand, we feel that Professor Inborden having reached the age of 73 years should retire. Dr. Brownlee, Executive Secretary of the AMA advised this change and the Board of Education cooperating with the AMA asked Inborden to resign. This decision was made sometime ago. N.E. Gresham.[61]

T.S. was very fortunate to have his white friend, R.C. Dunn to share the above letter with him and be able to know the true facts surrounding the white board of education and the white executive secretary of AMA agreeing to a decision to have T.S. retire. It was unfortunate that the responsible black citizens in eastern North Carolina did not play a role in the white controlled decisions concerning the needs and future of black education in their communities. The white majority in 1938 perpetuated segregation and made the rules and call the shots for the destiny of people of color within their segregated society.

After his resignation, T.S. wanted to recommend his friend Mr. James Eaton for the position of principal, Brick School. On June 18, 1938, Inborden wrote a letter to Professor Trigg about a possible successor and his retirement. T.S. said that he had learned that Secretary Brownlee, AMA did not want to make any repairs to the school as long as he was principal. Eaton was able to talk with the superintendent at Tarboro but no decision was made. T.S. told Trigg that Eaton was a Talledega graduate and was well prepared for the job and he is a very loyal person. T.S. said there were eleven teachers at the school, graduates of different colleges, yet there has been perfect harmony and sharing and respecting each others opinion in all school matters. The teachers and students have contributed a hundred percent to every financial interest the county has presented. Inborden asked Trigg to write Supt. Gresham about Eaton's possibilities of becoming principal. T.S. said Gresham is in good faith on some matters.[62]

Inborden's reputation in the community was still respected and the citizens would continue to call on T.S. for advice and assistance. On June 26, 1938, a group of people went to see T.S. about some problems they were facing with land resettlement project which was now called the

Tillery project. After the meeting with the citizens, T.S. wrote a letter to Joseph H.B. Evans in Washington, D.C. Inborden told Evans about the meeting and that he was able to have the group to state in their own words their grievances. T.S. stated that the people had organized and there was a Board of the Tillery Mutual Association and the board was not functioning to the full extent of the office. Inborden explained to Evans that the secretary-treasurer of the board would sign all blank checks and knew nothing about the money that was being paid out. The association's general manager should have had this authority. Other problems cited were, the store supplies need to be improved and there were problems in making annual payments to the Farm Security Administration. T.S. said the people have worked for a permanent warehouse and cotton gin. They would also prefer a colored manager. T.S. told Evans that the group that called on him represented some very intelligent farmers. Inborden wrote that one of the local white men who has to deal directly with the Tillery Project is full of prejudices against educated colored people and said that when a Negro is educated he forgets his place. T.S. said that those feelings on the part of any administrator engenders trouble, let him be white or Negro, northerner and southerner. Inborden also stated that men who hold administrative positions where justice and fairness is expected irrespective of race should be the broadest possible men or women. T.S. wrote that he heard criticism from some white people about blacks managing their own business, and believed some whites should be present to accomplish the tasks. T.S. said our country is a democracy but at times we fall short of living up to our creed. Inborden told Evans about a situation that occurred recently that shows how black people must constantly confront oppressive actions by some white people. T.S. wrote that a black woman went to the court house to make an application for a job. Inborden had escorted the lady and drove 22 miles to the courthouse. At the court house he was told the lady would have to go to another place to obtain the application which was 18 miles in another direction. They went to the place and talked to the white man in charge and he informed them that the colored applications were processed in another part of the city. Inborden and the lady went to this office and received an identification card and were instructed to travel the 18 miles back to an office that they had previously visited. They arrived at that office and waited for one hour for a white lady to open her office. She then began to talk to someone else and finally turned to the black woman and asked what she wanted. She told them to go to an office several blocks away. When T.S. and the lady arrived at this office, they were informed that the lady they wanted to see was out of town and no one knew when she would return. T.S. told Joseph H.B. Evans that he had driven a total of 80 miles used eight gallons of gasoline, a quart of oil and a full day had been lost. T.S. said these events might be irrelevant to some people, however, these are the facts and conditions that black people faced in eastern North Carolina and possible other areas of the south.[63]

There were some friends of Inborden who still were interested in his being reappointed as principal. M.V. Barnhill, state of North Carolina Supreme Court replied to a letter C.M. Eppes, Greenville, N.C. had written. Barnhill wrote that he has very high regard for T.S. and would like very much to see him continue in the position as principal. However, the matter was not called to my attention until after the County

Board of Education had already acted and retired Inborden. Barnhill said that he was interviewing different people in this section to ascertain whether we can get the action of the County Board revised. I am satisfied that the trouble is due to the attitude of Secretary Brownlee and AMA and some local officials. Barnhill stated that Professor Inborden is one of the outstanding Negroes in the state and he has always used his influence to bring about cordial relations between the races.[64] The letter written by Barnhill adds support to the facts that Brownlee and the AMA were interested in Inborden submitting his resignation. As stated previously this is another example how the white majority would dictate and reach their conclusions concerning the lives, future and personal business of people in color in those days that we must not forget segregation in "America the Beautiful". I believe that we are experiencing some of these same tactics in a covert manner in phases of institutional racism and bias in our society today which has not reached a desired pulse of color blindness among our multi-racial population.

T.S. Inborden wrote Attorney R.C. Dunn and thanked him for helping him. T.S. wrote that the county superintendent admits that he is being influenced by someone in New York. He also admits that my administration has been given every satisfaction. T.S. told Dunn that there is not a single charge that could be brought against him or his work and relations with the outside community. Inborden said that he had obtained buses for the school and increased the enrollment. He said that he begged for lunches for the students, got outside toilets and received support from teachers and white people in the community. T.S. said that when he arrived in North Carolina, there were some Negro politicians. There was George White, the Congressman and also a race riot had occurred in Wilmington. Some of my teachers wanted to resign and go home. T.S. said that he was asked to speak all over the county to Negro churches. He was asked by the editor of the Commonwealth Newspaper at Scotland Neck. T.S. realized that the white people were using him to assist in quelling the disorder. He also knew that there had been several lynchings in Halifax County. Inborden told Dunn that an article was published in the *Enfield Progress Newspaper* and was edited by a Mr. Alsop. Some of the articles kept Negroes in fear. T.S. said he decided to write several articles to the newspaper and delivered them to Mr. Alsop. He also visited him one afternoon at home and sat on the front porch and advised him that he should take the wise course and stop writing ugly articles.[65]

T.S. Inborden at times was a mediator, advisor and possible peace maker between the races. However, Inborden was very conscious of the racial climate in North Carolina and America. He would often remark in his writings his views on whites and some of their unfair treatments of his people. But in reality, he communicated with both races on the critical subject of racism and used his tactical ways to exist and for his race to survive under the unfortunate condition of the time. Today in the United States we have many honorable, well qualified women and men of color who profess or are elected as leaders in their respective communities. Their tactics vary from appeasement, self survival quest for monetary advantages, and they use high level rhetoric and appearances before the television cameras. These individuals in 1995 do not possess in many instances the sincerity, dedication and personal involvement to go among their own people and really understand what they are really confronting a so-called integrated society. T.S. Inborden was with and among his people in their trials and brought them when it was possible toward a brighter future with the greatest tools needed for survival, respect for themselves and others and educate themselves and improve their living conditions through economic upward mobility. T.S. plan of leadership should be emulated by some of our so-called black leaders in all professions today.

We must also realize when we reexamine the minds of many leaders years ago that they would take various positions on major topics within their communities. There were some black leaders to include Booker T. Washington who believed in maintaining black institutions and improving possibly without offending the white majority as far as ideas of integrated schools at that time. There was a time when the NAACP was very active in North Carolina and along with the support from some black educators were contemplating of filing legal suits against the state in relation to the unequal black schools. Many educators of color believed that these suits could create a spirit of oppressive tactics by the whites that could make conditions worse in some ways. This was before the Brown vs Board of Education, 1954. It is a great possibility that T.S. Inborden could have had mixed emotions on the NAACP's planned actions. He did not voice them outwardly but I believe that in his position with the AMA and the conciliatory impressions that many white leaders had of him in the community and above all the results and past accomplishments that Brick School had made, he did not want any interference offensive wise from the white community. As I reflect today in 1995 and visit the classrooms of major cities, public schools and never see a white or others present in the classrooms, and I am aware that there is a most crucial need for the sustenance of black colleges and universities. I ask the questions, how far has America really travelled as far as integration in our elementary, secondary and collegiate institutions. I also pose the question, are some black Americans and others not making the decisions that Inborden and black educators had to make years ago. They were decisions that were devoid of methods that are used today. Unfortunately, many black leaders today carry their own agenda minus considerations for the common person. They do not attack the real problem, our polarized society and some of the conditions in our black communities are similar to yesteryears.

T.S. had learned that a Mr. Wiley had written Mr. Newbold, State Director of Negro Education, Raleigh, N.C., when T.S. saw Wiley, he asked him about the letter and he denied writing to Newbold. Later, T.S. was told that Wiley was appointed principal by the county Board of Education in August. T.S. heard that Wiley was dismissed from a job because he used his influence with blacks to vote against a white man who was running for political office. Inborden said that he thought well of Wiley and did all he could to help him when he was in Enfield and at Garysburg. When Wiley was trying to obtain a job at a church in Weldon, I wrote to all the members of the church and asked them to give Wiley an opportunity, remarked T.S. He does not know today that I helped him said T.S. Inborden, and stated that Wiley had said that he never wrote anyone in Raleigh for the principal's position. T.S. also realized that J.W. Wiley had written him a letter on July 6, 1938 and said that he was grateful T.S. had thought of him to head the school at Brick, but Wiley wrote that we should not rush the matter. At the time Wiley wrote the letter he definitely had some assurance that he would be the next principal of Brick School. However, he did not tell Inborden. T.S. would appreciate the letters of encouragement and consideration of his past labors at Brick School. Queen E. Lyons, North Carolina College for Negroes, Durham wrote T.S. on July 27, 1938 and told Inborden that it was a pleasure for her to write to someone who has done so much for our race, especially in the educational field. Lyons said that T.S. has given his life to the work of helping others and that he fought a good battle and the victory is his.[66]

T.S. wrote a letter to his friend, Mr. Dreyden about his bee colony. He said he made a visit to Dreyden's farm. All the colonies were in fine condition for the winter except three colonies. These colonies were late swarming and had not had time to build up in strength without being a little late. It would take about forty pounds of sugar to carry them through the winter. Inborden told Mr. Dreyden that he would take his own feeder and use them for the bees, or show someone how to use them. T.S. said that he would ask the colored county agent to go out to Dreyden's farm and give some advice as how to feed his laying chickens. The agent also promised to assist a Mr. Johnson at the farm in treating the trees, and soil. Also Mr. Johnson must lengthen the stands on which the colonies are setting so that they will be at least two feet from one colony to the other. Because when the boxes are too close to each other the bees make an error often and go into the wrong hive. T.S. stated that this often happens with the queen when she goes out as she does sometime. Inborden told Dreyden that he would cut and dress around the hives with pollen because often they strike the weeds and grass and lose the pollen.[67] Inborden could find the time and had the patience and desire to help others using his vast knowledge of bee culture. Thomas Sewell Inborden approached his retirement years with an active and busy schedule. He enjoyed residing at his home on the campus of Brick School and used his time wisely. T.S. accepted invitations to speak and participate in various civil programs in the community. There was also ample time to work with his bees and fill honey requests that he received frequently from his friends. Inborden corresponded with many friends during his retirement. He wrote to his relatives, especially his nieces and grandchildren. It was necessary for him to move to Washington, D.C. around 1949 to live with his daughter, Dorothy I. Miller. He continued to reply to letters from his friends and relatives. T.S. strenuous efforts and persistent actions in helping to bring the Tillery settlement to eastern North Carolina was appreciated when the Farm Security Administration honored him and two other black leaders. The leaders were honored when streets were named after them. T.S. Inborden received this unique distinction along with the Rev. Joseph Silver, minister in the community over 50 years and N.C. Merrick, founder of the North Carolina and Mutual Life Insurance Company, Durham. The streets were named Silver Lane, Merrick Road and Inborden Drive.

CHAPTER 6

Final Retirement Years

The Roanoke Island Historical Association celebrated its 353rd anniversary of the Birth of English Colonization in America in August, 1939. T.S. received an invitation from the President D.B. Fearing, Manteo, N.C. Inborden was asked to be present on Friday, August 16, *Negro Day at Old Fort Raleigh*. Fearing told T.S. that the day was endorsed by all Negro college Presidents of North Carolina and Governor Clyde R. Hoey, Dr. Frank P. Graham President, University of North Carolina and state superintendent, Clyde R. Irwin, and other prominent educators. Fearing also said that Negroes only will participate directly in the program on Negro Day and there will be a special welcome address by a prominent official of Dare County. T.S. was recommended to participate by his friend President Trigg of Elizabeth State College. The Negro Day program would include music by the Excelsior Band of Norfolk. There would be an old fashioned fish fry and special music to be provided on the Hammond organ by James Hart, Lost Colony organist. A chorus of 40 voices directed by Mrs. Neil Hunter of Durham would sing spirituals and solos. The program also scheduled remarks by C.C. Spaulding President of North Carolina Mutual Life Insurance Company and other prominent Negroes would be introduced to the audience.[1] During the years 1939-1940, Inborden received numerous requests for honey and correspondence from his nieces and granddaughters, Louis M. Hickman, Board of Home Missions, Congregational Church asked for a 10 pound bucket of honey. L.R. Reynolds, Richmond, Virginia wrote T.S. for some honey and his friend, William Pickens frequently requested honey. Inborden received a letter from his nieces, Rosa Lee, Alice Grigsby and Daisy Fox. In December 1949, his niece Alice wrote him from Philadelphia, Pennsylvania and thanked him for a nice gift. She told T.S. about the wonderful gifts she received. Some of them were, silver, cocktail glasses, bed spreads, clothes, perfume, stockings, rain cape and some money. Alice also told T.S. that she had made some ice cream and saw the movie Gone With The Wind for seventy-five cents. Inborden's niece Daisy Fox, wrote a letter and thank T.S. for some peanuts. She wanted some honey and inquired about Mrs. Pittman. T.S. Inborden's granddaughter Julie, wrote him some interesting and descriptive letters while a student in college. Julia was affectionately referred to as Sister. She thanked him for some eggs and said that while in Washington, D.C., she met a former student at Brick, Percy Battle from Battlesboro, N.C. While studying at North Carolina College for Negroes in Durham, Sister wrote for the student publication *The Eagle*. She told her grandfather that she was very pleased with her recent article about a book exhibit in the college's library. The theme of the exhibit was Good Books, Good Friends Encourage Reading For Recreational Purposes. Sister described in her article the categories of books on display. Frances Camille Gordon was one of Inborden's very close granddaughters. She would write her grandfather quite often. She believed in excellence in scholarship and would always share with others her accomplishments. Frances told T.S. that she had been busy with her college examinations, but was happy about receiving final grades of three A's and 2 B's. She wrote that she was attending night school at Cardozo School, Washington, D.C. and where she was enrolled in a typing class and shorthand class. Frances mentioned to Inborden that she had received some praises about his honey. She said that when she received her honey, some was given to her friend who was a secretary at Howard University for Dr. Emmett Scott. Frances said that Dr. Scott was invited to the secretary's family's home for Christmas dinner and tasted the honey. Dr. Scott remarked that it was the best honey he had tasted recently and wanted to purchase a jar of honey. Frances Camille sent T.S. a very important invitation and that was to her graduation at Howard University. Inborden was very happy to know that his granddaughter would receive a BA degree with the coveted honor of Magna Cum Laude.[2]

William L. Pickens, a director of branches at the New York office NAACP, wrote T.S. a cheerful letter on January 3, 1940. He told Inborden that his friend was not forgotten, because he told his wife recently that he must write T.S. and learn how he entered the *New Year*. Pickens extended regards to T.S. devoted housekeeper, Mrs. Grant. He concluded his letter by reminding T.S. that *Life Goes on, an Adventure of Consequence*. Inborden answered Pickens' letter on January 10, 1940 and told him that he was feeling good at age 75. William Pickens answered T.S.' letter and said that it is bad to learn about the trouble in North Carolina on the resettlement project over the matter of a colored manager for the cooperative store. Pickens wrote that he hoped T.S. and others would be able to keep the black manager on the job, and if he needed NAACP assistance to contact him. Pickens said economically the Negro is more ruthlessly opposed than in any other area.[3] That is a very interesting statement by William Pickens, because in 1995, we read about various instances where blacks confront economic opposition; in real estate, mortgage loans and opportunities for financial assistance to compete in the majority dominated economic arena in our so-called color blind society by political enthusiasts and possibly misinformed honorable gentlemen and women about the real inner circles of black deprivation economically in these United States in the late part of the decades of the 1990s.

While in retirement T.S. Inborden would write his reflections on many subjects during his fruitful years of experience in North Carolina. He wrote some notes on the boll weevil epidemic, the farmer and the middle class black. T.S. mentioned about evolution in human life or just progress, being a change from old methods to new ones. But he said the change to new methods sometimes is not progress. He said that while attending a meeting in 1900 at Kittrell College, there were a thousand colored farmers present from, Granville and Vance Counties. It was his first introduction to Negro farmers in North Carolina. He said many of them came on horseback, some with entire families in ox carts, buggies as they were styled as Big Negroes of their community especially if they appeared in a two horse or mule carriage. Inborden said they were the aristocrats of their community with children at Kittrell College. Some wore big bandanna handkerchief decked around their heads and beautiful colored ribbons. T.S. said that even some of their horses wore ribbons about their shoulders. Inborden wrote that the ladies walking or riding were dressed to match the other colors. The procession was headed by a brass band and the United States flag. It was a gorgeous display and at a certain signal the riders dismounted from their carriages and in a single file were escorted to an assembly area. Inborden said there was plenty food to include barbecue. T.S. assessed the situation by writing that a program was best adopted by a group of teachers. The dinner was the biggest attraction to the farmers. It was the inspiration more than the information they received in the meeting. T.S. said anyone who could gather such a large number of Negro farmers even with a good dinner was an agricultural benefactor.

Inborden stated that the boll weevil had decimated from a half to three fourths of the cotton crop in the state of Texas. People were migrating northward. They had to cross Mississippi, Arkansas, Alabama, Georgia, South Carolina and North Carolina. These were the cotton areas of the country and the cotton output was the greatest source of the south's wealth. T.S. said to save the south's economy, something must be done. Inborden wrote that a Dr. Seaman Knop, an influential man from the Department of Agriculture in Washington went to Texas and called together the farmers and bankers to develop a program of eradication of the boll weevil. The experiment was a success. T.S. said that government officials and state legislators throughout the south saw at once that to save the south, a large army of workers scattered all over the south and money was needed. They realized that to lose the cotton crop meant the loss of income. T.S. said the less of two evils was to enlist enough county agents to fight the pest under Dr. Knop's experiment. Inborden stated that the next infection was world wide and that was World War I. The war threatened civilization and created an economic scare to include minimal food supplies and the depletion of some food production. T.S. wrote there was also a fruit infection condition that created an emergency. The government responded and money was appropriated to combat the problem. T.S. said that all of these problems did affect the Negro farm and there were some white people who were against the appointment of Negro County agents. They believed it would create racial antipathy. Inborden said there were aggressive efforts of some concerned people of both races appointed some Negro county agents and educate the black farmer of the latest discoveries and innovations in the field of agriculture and health. These accounts that T.S. recalled happened in many cases and possibly other states but normally these detailed experiences cannot be found in many popular American history books today. I am simply saying that there were many people of color in the south and especially North Carolina who believed 60-70 years ago in self respect, self confidence, economic empowerment and a better life for their families. Many of these blacks were known as the Negro farmer.[4]

Corneluis King, special assistant to Governor, North Carolina on problems of Farm Credit Association visited the Brick campus in February, 1940. He was appreciative that Inborden who made his visit enjoyable and said in a note to T.S. that it was a pleasure to talk with him. During Negro History Week in February 23, 1940, the Hartford County Farmers sponsored a ham show and farmers school at the Ahoskie Colored High School. Their theme was "Raising the Low Factors of Production". The farmers recognized their true founder of Brick School and invited him to make some remarks. C.E. Dean, local advisor to the Agricultural Association at A and T College, Greensboro, North Carolina, invited T.S. to speak at their program, March 25, 1940. During my senior year at Lincoln University of Missouri, I resided in the men's dormitory that was named Tull Hall. Probably like many students I did not know who Tull was and possibly could have cared less. Ironically, while researching the Inborden story, I learned that a man named I.C. Tull was an outstanding educator and a very good friend of T.S. Inborden. In April 1940, T.S. had learned of the unfortunate death of I.C. Tull and wrote a letter to his widow to express his sympathy. Even though Inborden was in retirement, he would still receive requests from people about matters relating to Brick School. On April 14, 1940, he received a letter from Richard Battle, Washington, D.C., Battle wanted the record that would show his attendance at Brick School as a night student during the year of 1899, because he was trying to verify the correct date of his birth. He believed his birthdate was August 25, 1881.

Emily Mae Daniels, Winston, N.C., visited Brick School in April, 1940 and was very impressed with the school. She wrote T.S. that her visit was a real education. Daniels said she appreciated the splendid bee industry and it was a lesson for her. She gave T.S. a most outstanding tribute when she told him, Brick is a beautiful place and is a monument to you.[5] T.S. Inborden's first assignment for the AMA after graduation from Fisk University was at a church in Beaufort, N.C. During the research of T.S. life and many conversations with his daughter Dorothy, there is no knowledge or documentation that supports the fact that he was an ordained minister. However, he was assigned to the church for a brief period. Ironically, almost 50 years later Inborden received a letter from N.C. Calhoun, Beaufort. Calhoun wrote T.S. that he trust things are going well with him. He told Inborden that he does not know him in person. However some of the Beaufort people told him that T.S. had supplied the Congregational church of Beaufort for a while. Calhoun said that he was the pastor of the same church at the present. He told T.S. that he was looking for the principalship of a good school. He stated that he has 5 years of teaching and served four years as a principal. Calhoun said that he would appreciate any assistance T.S. would give him[6]

T.S. was happy to hear his grandson John Gordon, deliver the valedictory remarks. The students at this special graduation exercise for T.S. Inborden were: James Edward Boddie, Pearl Rene Cherry, William Henry Clark, Rosa Lee Cofield, Minnie Evelyn Collins, Idonia Archeline Dixon, John Newton Gordon, Ellen Ruth Harrison, John Willie Harvey, Annie Beulah Hedgepeth, Julius A. Hunter, Bedelia Belle Hynes, Gertrude Delois Jones, Lulie Lee Lane, Valeva Lyons Olive, Lucile Mason, Willie McWilliams, Louise Emily Phillips, Fred Clyde Pitt, Mary Jean Pitt, Lark C. Powell, Flora A. Speight, Mary Elizabeth Tucker, Geraldine Almeta Wade, Doris May Whitaker and Mary Whitaker.[7] T.S. Inborden had a brother-in-law, C. Evans who lived in Oberlin, Ohio. T.S. received a letter from one of Evans' neighbors, Susie Green. She wrote that she had received T.S.' letter and that Mr. Evans was not too well. Green mentioned that Mrs. Minnie Quinn was in Cleveland with her daughter and Mrs. Dave Quinn was in the Old Folks Home in Cleveland. Some of the other news was Rust Church had its anniversary and she asked about Mrs. Grant.[8] On July 18, 1940, T.S.' niece Daisy Fox wrote him a letter. She wrote that she had a terrible burden, her sick sister, but with God's help, she will bear it out. She told T.S. that she did not want to complain for if she was in the same condition, she would want someone in her family to help her. Fox said that she bears it with a smile and tries to do her best. She also said that her mother was very feeble in Virginia. Daisy Fox asked about Mrs Grant, Julia and the children. She told T.S. to keep her in his prayers and love from Lesley. Daisy Fox and her family as stated previously were possibly related to General Robert E. Lee.[9]

T.S. received a letter from his brother, Ashton Smith, in August 1940. He thanked T.S. for the package he sent. He also told T.S. that on August 8, he would be 70 years of age. Smith said the children were well and he was sorry to learn about Mrs. Pittman's death.[10]

Inborden was still concerned in 1940 about the people of color in eastern North Carolina and would continue to assist them in any way possible and especially writing letters to high officials in local and state government. A recent flood condition in the immediate areas of Enfield incited T.S. to write a lengthy letter to Clyde R. Hoey, governor of North Carolina. The letter read:

My Dear Mr. Governor, when flooded areas of this section, Tillery area was under extreme water conditions, someone called from Tillery for help. I and three men arrived within seven miles of the resettlement area and were not allowed to go any further by policemen, we were going to offer services of our large dormitories for refugees and as many Enfield trucks as would be needed. Later, one of the men got in the flooded area after the policemen left his station. He returned about nine o'clock at night and reported the conditions and stated there would be several trucks in two hours loaded with people fleeing from their homes. Some of the people had nothing to eat and they were given a lunch after arrival. I went to Enfield and purchased some food and by 11 p.m. the people were housed in a comfortable building and lunch was cooked and served at 12 a.m. The children were having the times of their lives on the lawn in front of the dormitory. The people were coming in trucks all night and all day Monday to the number of more than 200 people. Very early, Monday morning, one of the county lady workers and I went over to Enfield where I called to see the head of the Red Cross. I showed them what purchases I had made last Sunday night. He thanked me and appreciated what I did for the people. He said that he would take care of the bills and advised me to get whatever we needed to carry them for at least two days. This we did. Some of the merchants gave me clothes which were given to the welfare workers from the Tillery resettlement for distribution. When the white ladies of Enfield and the community found out the situation, they made a personal canvass for wearing apparel so that these refugees might be clad again. Most of them had no time to get any clothes. Everyone I met on the streets of Enfield, white men and women who offered their services in anyway possible. They have always done this in every emergency we have had and the colored people are grateful. The state welfare official from Raleigh, Mr. William R. Johnson, called at my house and I went with him to spend the entire day looking over the stricken communities adjacent to the Roanoke river. We spent some time going over the situation about Weldon and then we went many miles down the river and the miracle is that so few lives were lost, only one in that area. One truck load came here about three o'clock Monday morning. The water surrounded the people's homes and they started out in a wagon drawn by two mules. They wandered three miles in the woods with the water over the backs of their mules and the mules were swimming part of the time. When they reached the high grounds a truck picked them up and brought them here. The Northhampton county area we visited, there were two churches and they were cooking dinner in large old time pots and the camps were spotless clean. White and colored people were working together. People were bringing vegetables, meat and clothing for the poor destitute families who had lost all of their things. Their belongings, mules, cows, hogs, poultry had all gone down the river and their homes were unfit for occupancy.

I cannot think of anything finer than such a manifestation of good feelings on the part of all the white people who have talked to me about the problems. I am sure the same spirit is characteristic of all of the white people in this grief stricken area. Mr. Johnson took copious notes and I am sure in due time will give you the fullest account of what we saw today. I don't know what the state or other organizations have done outside of the Red Cross in Enfield. Mr. Johnson can go into that in his report. I am sure what the Red Cross in Enfield did was to fill an immediate emergency. When a group of people are hungry and clothesless, they become desperate but not so with these refugees. I have never seen about 500 men, women, children, happier in my life in any such adversity. In 1892, I saw the Mississippi river ninety miles below Memphis, thirty-six miles wide and after the flood thousands left the area for Oklahoma never to return. Many of them spent nights in school yard. They were sad, not so with these people here in Enfield along the Roanoke river. They are going back to the old farms to begin life all over again. I never saw a tear except a few very small children crying for their bottles of milk. I think they did not cry long for I heard that 25 gallons of milk would soon be there at that particular camp. Dr. B.M. Nicholson, head of Red Cross in Enfield deserves very much credit for his immediate authority without any red tape to make whatever purchases were necessary to meet absolute necessity. The county Negro agents and their wives have done wonderful in getting up food and helping to alleviate the distress among these people. I am very truly, T.S. Inborden[11]

Inborden's brother-in-law, C.B. Evans of Oberlin had a friend to write T.S. A Mrs. Mattie Burwell wrote that C.B. Evans wanted to spend the winter with his niece, Dorothy Inborden Miller at her home in Washington, D.C. He had spent one winter in Oberlin at a rest home on East College Street, but he preferred to come to Washington for the winter 1940.[12] T.S. answered Mrs. Burwell's letter and wrote that his daughter Dorothy was visiting him and will not return to Washington until later. Inborden stated that as soon as he read her letter that he passed it on to Dorothy and she said that she had not made any special contact with her Uncle Neal or special arrangements. T.S. said all she did once was to give him an invitation to come to Washington to spend the winter with her in a comfortable warm house. Inborden wrote that his daughter said that the invitation is still good. Last winter, she spent with Julia's girls, Julia and Frances. Since Frances has graduated from Howard University and Julia or Sister will be going to a school in North Carolina, the only person that will be with Dorothy is Julia's son John Newton Gordon. T.S. said Dorothy has plenty of room and if Uncle Neal wants to come to Washington, she will be glad to have him.[13] Dorothy I. Miller did care for her uncle a brief time when he came to Washington, D.C.

T.S. received a letter from his brother Ashton on September 1, 1940. Ashton said he was glad to hear from T.S. and that Edna and Frances were down to see him recently. He told T.S. that he wanted some honey and to write soon.[14] On September 5, 1940, T.S. received a letter from Governor Clyde R. Hoey. He wrote T.S. that upon his return home, he found T.S.' letters of August 22, giving a full report of the flood situation in his territory and of the various services rendered in attempting to relieve that situation. Hoey told T.S. that he has received the full reports from the officers but I wish to thank you for the intelligent and detailed statement which you sent covering the situation.[15] Minnie Gregg, T.S.' niece wrote him a letter on October 9, 1946. She said that she was in Upperville, Virginia and had been sick. Minnie stated that her children took good care of her and that she wished he would come to see her. She said that she was over to Morgan College in Baltimore recently because her granddaughter is there. She sent her love to Julia.[16] William Pickens wrote Inborden and said that it was interesting that they drafted the teachers to go to a neighboring town and register the people who were enlisting in the military. Pickens remarked that it was very unAmerican that the whites denied those teachers the use of restrooms in the schools where they were working. Pickens believed that some protest should be made against that type of treatment. You are correct that this is a great country and a great effort at democracy wrote Pickens, but we have to fight continually to keep that effort going. The NAACP is a great judgement for democracy in my opinion. Pickens told T.S. it is interesting to hear that there is no draft dodger so far, as we know yet among the colored people.[17]

T.S. wrote a white politician Thomas Pearsall and congratulated him on his election or appointment to succeed a Mr. Fenner to the general assembly. He wrote that Pearsall has a good reputation and fairness. He mentioned a Mac Braswell and said that he traded with some farm tenants. He also said Maggie Grant, daughter of Ned Green has spoken to him about Braswell and said he was interested in the welfare of colored people. Inborden stated that he was 5 years old and that he learned a long time ago that we do not live for ourselves alone. Our greatness and happiness comes when we share that joy and happiness with others. You learn that by experience. T.S. told Pearsall that the annual gathering of colored and white people once yearly on his picnic grounds has been of the finest type. Inborden wrote that 30 years ago Mr. Fletcher Parker, Enfield, Uncle of Judge Parker was elected to the general assembly of North Carolina and I called at his office and congratulated him remarked T.S. Inborden said he suggested that Parker should introduce some education bills to assist the colored schools. T.S. invited him to visit Brick so that he could speak with authority on what the school was doing. Inborden stated that he was making a suggestion for Pearsall to do the same. T.S. said that there are a number of colored colleges in N.C. and are doing fine. T.S. remarked that the newspapers write often about educational problems in the state that are discussed in the general assembly and advised Pearsall his life's work thus far has not brought him in close contact with the educational problems. Inborden informed Pearsall that the state of North Carolina is too great to be allowed to lag behind in its most adequate provision for its colored people. North Carolina has the reputation of being ahead of all the southern states in the education of the black population. T.S. wrote that the private black institutions have been a great asset in the educational work of the state. The city of Raleigh has been a pioneer in education but they cannot do all of it being church schools. The quality of work the schools are doing are superb. T.S. told Mr. Pearsall we should not have one boy or girl going to a northern school to get the type of education that is available in North Carolina. T.S. said please take a few hours from your schedule and visit North Carolina A and T College at Greensboro and the College at Durham. The colleges are not just for the present but also the future.[18] Ora Brown Stokes, Washington, D.C. visited Brick School and was grateful for T.S.' hospitality and courtesy. She wrote T.S. that she was happy to find T.S. alert as usual and enjoyed his delicious honey. Miss Stokes was employed by the National Youth Administration in Washington, D.C. T.S. received a request from former Brick student, Mrs. Marge Hockaday Clarke of New York City. She was interested in obtaining a catalogue about the school. She had two children ages 15 and 17 who would like to attend Brick School. C.L. Spellman invited T.S. to participate in a Negro Achievement Day Program in Wilson, N.C. at the Darden high school. Mr. John Mitchell, District Farm Agent for North Carolina also wanted T.S. to be present at the program. Inborden had a great respect for senior citizens in his community who were not too well. He would often visit them and offer his assistance. Olivia Street, Washington, D.C. thanked T.S. for visiting her mother in North Carolina during the Christmas holidays. T.S. escorted Street's mother to observe the decorations in the city.[19]

Inborden wrote Howard Gordon, Regional Director, Region 4, Department of Agriculture, Farm Security Administration, Raleigh, N.C. about the Tillery settlement. T.S. wrote Gordon that he has a personal interest in the settlement project. T.S. said that there has been some unhappiness at the settlement and one of the problems have been leadership. Inborden suggested that they need a Negro man to head up the colored division. The people had suggested Mr. H.E. Sutton who is a fair and honest person. T.S. said that he was a Virginian by birth, educated at Oberlin College and Fisk University. He stated that he had taught at schools in Arkansas, Tennessee, Georgia and forty years in North Carolina. Inborden told Gordon that he knows the southern attitude as well as the Negro attitude in particular. There is no group of people who can advance when they have grievances which they fear to express. This accounts for the fact that a great mass of Negroes move from farm to farm every year. T.S. said a few years ago thousands from every part of the south left and migrated to various parts of the north. I have met them in New York, Chicago, St. Paul, Seattle, Portland, Sacramento, and San Francisco. T.S. stated that these people wanted to go where they could work out their own salvation under compatible conditions. Inborden wrote that he thought the resettlement organization when established would have ideal conditions under which to live and people could work out their salvation and I think with some minor adjustments that there is still time. T.S. said that when the law was passed creating the Federal farm Loan Organization, we at Brick perfected a loan organization at Brick School which had 225,000 dollars of federal funds in savings and kept Negro farms from the auction block. T.S. said the organization which Gordon was heading in the state now has even more potentialities.

Inborden told Gordon that the Negro is demonstrating every day and all over the country and in every proposition projected by the government has loyalty to the country and the flag. Inborden wrote that when the Negro is in his own home, eating the fruit from his own planting, educating his children and attending the church of his choice, only then is he best fitted to fit into the American life. T.S. acknowledged that the U.S. Government has done a wonderful job in creating laws to help every man, boy, girl and woman whether white, colored, Indian or what not to try to improve their living conditions. T.S. believed that we can try to work out conditions compatible to that end. T.S. told Gordon that recently he had sat in the gallery of the House of Representatives in Washington, D.C. and left after listening for four or five hours with one general impression too much lost motion.[20] T.S. Inborden was writing and talking about problems that people of color were facing economically forty-fifty years ago and the federal and state government's efforts to help to resolve them. He also wrote about the black's ambition and initiatives to help themselves. Inborden was informing white officials that there must be some equitable decisions made to resolve some of the problems that were existing in a segregated society. T.S. was asking for action from those who had the authority and power to remedy the situation. Inborden was a leader who would take pen in hand and document his thoughts and ideas and passed them on to the white majority and made it clear that people wanted the same things that whites and other were enjoying. The Women's Baptist Home and Foreign Missionary Convention Of North Carolina, Meuse River Baptist Association and Department of Religious Promotion, Shaw University sponsored a Missionary Training Institute at Brick School. Inborden was invited to participate in the institute. T.S. gave a lecture on the heritage of the Brick community.

T.S. Inborden received the sorrowful news of his brother, Edward Ashton Smith's demise on March 31, 1943 at Paris, Virginia in Loudon County between the town of Upperville and Paris. Inborden prepared a written eulogy for his brother's farewell services. T.S. wrote that his brother was born August 8, 1870 in Loundon County, Virginia and was a farmer who loved his horses, pigs and poultry and garden. He stated that Ashton lived in the old home farm of small acreage to which he added an additional one hundred acres. The farm was located near Mount Weather, United States Weather Bureau. T.S. wrote that his brother left to mourn his loss ten children. They were Edna Lewis, Mount Vernon, N.Y.; Nellie Young, Upperville, Va.; Sarah Ramey, Clarksburg, Maryland; Frances Freeland, Bronx, N.Y.; Mary Murray, New York; Mattie Cabel, Dickerson, Maryland; Rosella Lee, New Rochelle, N.Y.; Virginia Grigsby Mosley, Willie Smith, The Plains, Va.; Walter Smith, Leesburg, Va.; Luther Smith, Frank Smith's brother-in-law; and Agnes Hall, Middleburg, Va. T.S. wrote in the eulogy that Ashton Smith had two ministers officiating at the services, Reverend Wilson, former pastor of Falls Church and Reverend Jackson, pastor of the Paris church. The funeral director was Mr. Charley Walker, a life long friend of Upperville who provided splendid services in every way. His brother was buried in the old burial ground at their old home on the mountain. T.S. wrote that *A Man's life is the sum of his ancestral inheritance.*[21] There are many of the descendant lineage of Ashton Smith living today who possess the genetic diversity from the Harriet Proctor line, the mother of Ashton and Thomas Sewell.

T.S. received an informative letter from his friend and former colleague, Mrs. Jeannette Keeble Cox. She wrote that she was glad he was fine and did not like his being in the house alone at night at Brick. She wished him a happy birthday and many returns and wished she was there to help in the celebration and how they would talk. Mrs. Cox told T.S. that she wanted to express her appreciation for all his kindness and consideration. She recalled how she came to Brick as a young and inexperienced teacher and a foolish frivolous girl. She said sometimes I don't see how you stood me. But you were always encouraging. No one has ever encouraged me as you and my mother did. Cox stated that each of you made me feel I was worthwhile and I could do some things. She also wrote that until this day I remember particular instances where words from your lips brought balm often to a discouraged soul. Cox said that she tried to present a happy exterior but all my life I knew the other side. Cox told T.S. that she often wondered how she got along, but everything is so much better now. Jeannette Keeble Cox discussed in her letter some of the pleasant moments of her life. She wrote that we have made no money but what has come our way we have taken care of. We have a nice home, better than I expected to own. We had it built by a South Carolina carpenter at a reasonable price. Cox stated that they had their house built in a way that they would be able to take in roomers, which had helped their living income. They lived very near Meharry Medical Center and its students take rooms in the neighborhood. They had all the students their house could hold. Mrs. Cox mentioned in her letter about Holloway who was at Brick School. She wrote that Holloway started the school downhill and not one of his successors could start it again. God wanted no liberal arts college out there and they never heard a word from Holloway. Inborden was elated when Mrs. Cox praised his daughter, Dorothy. She said Dorothy inherits her extreme loyalty from her father. She has been magnificent in your hour of trials and see how God has blessed her. Cox told T.S. that she was sending him a photograph of how she looks now with her hair whiter than her mother's and said she weighs 140 pounds. She told T.S. that he was not the only one feeling the infirmative of old age approaching and remarked that she too was stiff with arthritis. Mrs. Cox informed T.S. that her two younger boys were studying dentistry at Meharry College. Her elder son would finish in March of the year. She stated that her younger daughter was in Richmond, Indiana with her sister. She also wrote that the husband of her eldest daughter was a physician and was doing very well.[22]

T.S. had written several articles that he decided to send to some of his friends in 1944. W.G. Clark, owner of a fertilizer and general merchandise business in Tarboro, N.C. thanked T.S. for a copy of the article. He wrote T.S. that he has done a great service to his people and that it has been a pleasure knowing T.S. over the years. Superior Court Judge, R. Hunt Parker told T.S. that he had read his article *Civics and Art* with great pleasure and complete agreement. Every line shows your scholarship and sound ideals of life remarked Parker. The judge stated that T.S.' quotation from Plato is eternally true. The great Greeks for twenty centuries have delighted and inspired the people of Europe and America. Parker said that he believed the present generation is neglecting the noblest of all literature except possibly some of the great English writers. He noted that T.S. was an admirer of writer George W. Cable.[23]

When I visited Enfield, North Carolina I was pleased to see a school that bears the name Inborden School, I trust that it will always be a lasting memory to a man who loved his people of color from eastern North Carolina and who was able to communicate with members of the white race who would listen to him even though at times some of them would disagree with T.S.' remarks. The Reverend F.L. Bullock, St. Paul Baptist Church, Enfield, N.C. wrote T.S. on May 2, 1944 and said that it is with much appreciation and respect that we the citizens of Enfield and the community desire to have your name in a monument by having our school named in honor of you. Bullock wrote that it is out of the fruits of your life that you have done good. Your fine type of citizenship you have stood for during the many years of faithful service you have rendered the community. Bullock said we appreciate the many lives you have touched and the many men and women you have helped to the road of success by your stern examples of living. Bullock said he wishes T.S. many more years of faithful service to his people and the community.[24] I am sure that many students and parents, people passing by still only see the name Inborden inscribed on a building, but is the sincere intent and most important desire by his daughter, Dorothy I. Miller and this writer that the people of Enfield, people of North Carolina and the world know the identity of the genius of an educator of color, especially an early educator who lived and walked among both whites and blacks and shared his gifts of talent of loving, giving and helping others. Yes, he was the man from the mountains, Cleveland, Oberlin, Fisk none other than Thomas Sewell Inborden.

Julia *Sister* Gordon loved to write her grandfather when she was away in college. Her letters relived the day and time that young people like her were experiencing as college students and some of the problems they met, some fifty years ago. She affectionately referred to T.S. as Grandpa. She wrote T.S. on September 23, 1944 from North Carolina College for Negroes, Durham. She told T.S. that they had just arrived from Washington on a plane trip that was only one hour and 15 minutes flight time and four dollars more than the cost of a train ticket. She said that they observed a bridge on the southern railroad that was washed out and it took some of the students 34 hours to travel on a train to Durham. Julia said that she saw a Mr. Amey who inquired about T.S. She informed Inborden that she had enrolled in sociology, economics, mathematics and industrial arts classes for the semester.[25] Julia Gordon wrote T.S. and told him about a racial incident that occurred when some students visited the state capitol. She said some college students had been invited from her school by the speaker of the state house who was speaking for a democratic primary. When the students arrived to hear a discussion on the white primary the guards came and said, *All you darkies get out of here.* Young people today use the latest technology in computers and observe and use many automatic devices. However, some fifty years ago, a young college student would write her grandfather and describe her amazement and delight interest in an automatic washing machine. Sister wrote T.S. and said that some washing machines were installed in the dormitory. She said you place your clothes in the machine, drop a dime in a slot and the clothes wash and rinse three times without your having to do anything. The water runs in and out of the machine automatically. Sister said be sure to tell Dad about it. Julia Sister Gordon was an ambitious young lady and she had a major goal in mind and that was to graduate from college. She wrote T.S. and said she had enrolled in a great number of classes and was very busy. However, she did find time to work in the dormitory as a receptionist and earn two dollars a week. She was pleased to tell Inborden that she had received the grade of A for her work at the Juvenile court. In 1947 sister was married and had received a twenty-five dollar gift from her brother John Newton Gordon. Sister told T.S. that John had asked her not to tell anyone so she wanted T.S. not to tell him he knew. Julia wrote that her class was scheduled to visit Warm Springs, Georgia, the Infantile Paralysis Rehabilitation Center to observe the patients. She also stated that her vocational class would visit Tuskegee Institute in Alabama. Julia was eagerly awaiting graduation in June 1947 and told her grandfather the details about the commencement activities. She had also enjoyed several invitations to the home of some of T.S.' friends. Sister said she enjoyed a good dinner at the home of Mr. Trigg. His son, Harold was home from New York City where he is completing his internship at Harlem Hospital.[26]

T.S. Inborden's granddaughter Frances who was married would always write her grandpa. She wrote Inborden a letter from Williamston, N.C. and talked about her little daughters Camille and Doris. She said Doris talks almost as well as Camille. She was also happy about Camille's progress. Frances said Camille is becoming quite smart, knows how to dry the dishes almost as well as a grown person and she loves to help me after each meal. She also takes her little broom to sweep. Frances told T.S. that the little boy was growing quite fast and weighs 16 pounds now She said Camille has a large stuffed cloth doll and Doris has a teddy bear and the baby has a rattle. Frances informed T.S. that she had joined the literary guild and Book of the Month Club and was doing more reading. Frances wrote T.S. a letter in 1947 and her discussions were of course her cherished children and T.S. great grand children. Frances thanked T.S. for some money he had sent for the children to purchase some ice cream. She had explained to them what the money was for and she said Camille actually understood. Frances stated that all three of the children were growing fast and both Camille and Doris knew how to count to ten. She said Doris learns very fast by imitating Camille. She said the baby stands up and holds on to the side of the cribs and walks. Frances wrote that sometimes she asks Doris is the baby sweet and every time I ask her, she replies that she is sweet too. So I tell her that she is sweet too. Frances told T.S. that she and her husband had plans to build a soda shop on a lot they owned. She wrote that Camille likes to play with large cardboard boxes. Tonight when I went into her bedroom after she had gone to sleep, I found that she had placed her toys in the card board box on the bed beside her and fallen to sleep. Frances was very proud of her children and she told T.S. about them playing together so well and that Camille knew her prayers and Doris was learning hers.[27] The mutual correspondence between T.S. and his grandchildren was most beneficial in maintaining a family unit and a continual expression by the eldest member to reinforce the principles of values and be abe to learn how they have been applied in the maturation of his grandchildren. I believe the family principles, caring, value systems, morality and love that was so prevalent in the black community 50 years ago need to be revived and those qualities that have brought us thus far are needed to be emulated to carry on out of the present status quo on to the successes that are awaiting us in the future years ahead. Fay McDowell, Bureau of Medical Social Services, County, Los Angeles wrote T.S. to inquire about a former Brick student, Edward Richardson. T.S. responded and told Ms. McDowell that he remembers Richardson as a former student. He also sent her a history pamphlet on Brick School.

In 1945 at the age of 80 years, Inborden was hospitalized with a prostate problem It was necessary for his physician to use the medical procedures and knowledge that was available for the treatment of abnormalities of the prostate gland. He was admitted to the hospital because of a diagnosis of urinary retention and an enlarge spongy prostate gland. His physician drained him using a urethral catheter for five days. After a cystoscopic examination, a decision was made to perform a suprapubic puncture and sutured in an indwelling mushroom catheter which had been placed for period of a number of weeks. His urea was normal for two weeks. The physician said T.S. received the usual forcing of fluids, sweating and drainage for his uremia condition. Inborden was progressing quite well, until he developed pneumonia. The doctors were considering additional operative procedures. However, one physician stated that those procedures are probably contraindicated. The physicians had considered a transurethral resection. But they thought at that present time, it would be safer to leave the catheter in the bladder for one month. T.S.' physicians were able to treat the pneumonia and his condition improved and he was released from the hospital. The doctors suggested that the bladder should be irrigated with a boric acid solution daily. Inborden's physician wrote a note for his family doctor and said T.S. was an exceptionally fine patient and hope you will give him every attention.[28] It is interesting to consider, that T.S. probably had a benign prostate and it was observed frequently under the care of a physician and he would not die in later years from the prostate condition that he had in 1945 and of cost the advanced medical knowledge that is available today was not present forty years ago.

T.S.' niece Daisy Fox wrote him and hoped that he was feeling better. She told him that he must take care of himself and do not worry about trying to send people honey. The sales manager of A.1 Root Company, Medina, Ohio, Charles G. Tollafield wrote Inborden in 1946. He told T.S. that they were not able to provide some information on bee keeping in Liberia. However, the rubber companies may have attempted to do something along this line remarked Tollafield. He also wrote that some missionaries may have attempted bee keeping using articles of Italian bees. Tollafield also stated that the new minister at Monrovia might be aware of modern bee keeping in the country. There is also some type of bees there because of bees wax brought to the coast from time to time.[29] Lela Gordon from Nashville, Tennessee sent T.S. a letter and said that she was glad his grandson John Newton was with him. She also had sent him a fruit basket. Lela said that she trust the Lord will let your Dorothy live for a long time because I believe she will do what she can for you. It is most interesting that Lela Gordon stated in her letter some fifty years ago that she hoped Dorothy I. Miller would live a long life. The power of the Lord can be manifested through faith and the actual revelation we see as living in the flesh. Because God has blessed Dorothy I. Miller as she now approaches her 99th birthday. The biblical verse *honor your mother and father and thou days shall be long upon this earth and* Dorothy Miller did honor her parents so faithfully and devoted with love.[30] A friend of T.S. Inborden had a tremendous idea in 1946 and that was writing the history of Brick School and the life of T.S. John W. Mitchell wrote T.S. from Hampton Institute and said he was interesting in writing about Brick School and T.S. Inborden. He stated that he do not know just when he will undertake the task. Because if he would write it entirely it might have to wait until he retired. He told T.S. since he would not be retiring for many years T.S. could do the job for him and he would get the credit. Mitchell nor did T.S. accomplish writing the book.[31] Rose Mary Leary Love, Inborden's wife's relative wrote T.S. in March 1946. She said that some years ago, T.S. had sent her mother a pamphlet concerning the Leary family and Sarah Jane Evans Inborden. Rose Mary said her family has prized the pamphlet but somehow it has been misplaced. She wanted T.S. to send her another copy if he had one. Leary told T.S. she was anxious to read the information again. She reminded T.S. that she is the daughter of the late Honorable John S. Leary, of Fayetteville, North Carolina. Lillian Evanti, the cousin of Sarah Jane Inborden sent T.S. a card during her recital concert tours. She wrote that she had a brilliant success in Fort Wayne, Indiana and St. Louis, Missouri. She also sent her love to Dorothy I. Miller.[32]

The *Enfield Progress*, a newspaper in Enfield, North Carolina published an article written by Ivey Watson describing the old Enfield in 1896. The article mentioned that Watson arrived in Enfield from Warrenton, N.C. in 1896 and worked as a bookkeeper with a tobacco company. He wrote that the merchants in the town were J.L. Britt, George B. Curtis, Simon Meyer, J.B. Pierce, H.C. Atkinson and Dempsey Bryant. He said the local attorneys were David Bell and S.S. Alsop. Watson stated that the local physicians were J.A. Collins, A.S. Harrison and L.T. Whitaker, and Jesse De Berry, barber. The article also said the first public school established in Halifax County was in Enfield in 1901. Realizing that the article was written in 1946 and considering the separate but equal period in America the beautiful was quite active in North Carolina, the newspaper article had no reference to a private school that was started in the county in 1895 by its founder T.S. Inborden and through the philanthropic gratitude of Mrs. Brick. As many whites would do in those days of segregation, people of color were insignificant and possibly did not exist in their mental world and reasoning. Therefore mentioning of Brick college was not news of that day to the white majority of Enfield, N.C.[33]

On September 20, 1946, Executive Secretary Fred L. Brownlee wrote a letter to T.S. from the Board of Home Missions of the Congregational and Christian churches. The letter head listed the Director of Race Relations as Charles S. Johnson who later would become the first person of color to serve as President of Fisk University. The letter stated that they were celebrating the American Missionary Association Centenary Week, for contributions to their fund raising goal of 300,000 dollars.[34] In a letter that Inborden had written to a friend he revealed some interesting history. T.S. wrote that he had a number of friends in Chicago. Lawyer H.K. Lord and lawyer W.L. Martin, both were his roommates in Oberlin. T.S. said they roomed at the home of Mrs. Evans. Inborden stated that he has a very rich white friend in Chicago. His name is George P. Dreyden, president of the Chicago Rubber Company.

Inborden said Dreyden owned 3,000 acres of land not far from Brick School. He also had a summer home 12 miles from Brick School. T.S. said Dreydon's wife was the sister of photographic magnate George Eastman of Kodak photographic company. T.S. said some of the boys at the school had worked for Eastman in New York. Silas A. Artist an elocutionist from New Haven, Connecticut wrote T.S. and told him that he visited Dr. and Mrs. Bullock in Hartford. Later, he visited his first cousin Reverend J. Westray, a Howard graduate in Pittsburgh, Pa. Artist told T.S. that he was sorry about his eye condition and suggest that he should see an eye specialist. He sent regards to Dorothy, Julia and Wilson.[35] T.S. received a letter from his niece, Daisy Fox and she was quite upset about her ill sister Leslie, she had been in a hospital for four years. She told T.S. they have taken her out of the hospital and that she is with her sister Hebe in Jamaica, New York. Daisy asked T.S. to send her 5 gallons of honey. She told T.S. that she would be visiting the Washington area soon.[36] Jesse Stoudmier from Chicago, Illinois had visited T.S. She is the relative of Sarah Jane Inborden. She wrote T.S. and told him she arrived home safe and enjoyed the time she spent with him and sent regards to his daughter, Dorothy.[37] Maggie Grant, Battlesboro, N.C. wrote T.S. and told T.S. that she thanked the Lord that she was up and about. She was glad to know that T.S. was fine. Mrs. Grant wrote that her husband had been very sick with asthma but was better.[38]

John Mitchell, Hampton Institute, Va., wrote T.S. on January 4, 1947. He told Inborden that he remembers T.S. telling him some years ago that he did not send Christmas cards or greeting cards but instead wrote his friends letters. Mitchell said therefore, I am writing you and want you to know that if there is anyone who could be depended upon at all times for real friendship then it is you, T.S. Mitchell said it would be hard for anyone to convince him that T.S. is anything but a genuine friend. John Mitchell wrote that he often thinks about the splendid service that T.S. has rendered such people as himself who are struggling along with the farm program and to the thousand of farmers along with their families that he has helped. Mitchell said that he was glad that Inborden has lived to see the fruits of his labor.[39] T.S. who was now living in Washington, D.C. at his daughter, Dorothy's home, wrote Mr. J.W. Reid in Whitaker, N.C. about his bees. He said that he has not been able to give attention to his bees since he has been in Washington. T.S. told Reid that a Mr. Owen Bellamy wants all the bees and that he was a good bee man. Inborden said that there was a man in the Washington City Market that wants the bees. This man has 1,000 colonies in Virginia and Maryland and receives sixty cents a section. T.S. told Reid that his three colonies were behind the house at Brick. Inborden said the letter is not done well on account of his eyes. T.S. was still typing his letters a the age of 82 years. Reid wrote T.S. later and said that he would go over to T.S.' Brick home and see what he could do about the bee colonies.[40]

T.S. wrote Mrs. Anna Evans Murray a letter in 1947. Mrs. Evans was the daughter of Sarah Jane's uncle Henry Evans of Oberlin. T.S. wrote that he wanted to congratulate her for her long years of service and great usefulness to her people. He told Anna Murray that she had certainly been a great inspiration to many people both young and old. T.S. said he has kept up with her activities for many years and I know what you have done. Inborden said that he knew her parents even before they left Oberlin, Ohio and that he had visited their home many times after they moved to Washington. T.S. said Anna Murray's work in Washington has been very outstanding. Inborden said that Anna Evans Murray has lived in an age when the world has made its greatest liberty and progress. Also you have made a great contribution to this age. T.S. said that she has lived long enough to see at least part of its freedom to some citizens.[41]

T.S. Inborden had unusual pride and love for his friends. He believed in telling others the good news when he wrote his letters. In a letter to Executive Secretary Brownlee, AMA, T.S. boasted in a proud manner about his wife, Sarah Jane Evans Inborden's distinguished relatives. He told Brownlee that recently he was invited to a reception given in honor of one of his cousins, Mrs. Annie Evans Murray who celebrated her 90th birthday. He wrote that Annie Murray began life when A.F. Beard heard Lincoln speak, Dr. James Fairchild, President of Oberlin, Dr. Finney and others were preaching what they thought was right. T.S. said that Mrs. Murray's father was Henry Evans and his brother Wilson married the two Leary sisters from North Carolina and they all moved to Oberlin to have freedom and education and were pioneers in the town. T.S. said Mrs. Murray founded the kindergarten schools in Washington, D.C. in 1895 and that her husband, Daniel Murray was an assistant librarian for some 50 years at the Library of Congress. Ironically, in 1970 when I was researching for a manuscript, I was writing, I was able to review the Murray collection of books in the Library of Congress that were in the process of being integrated into the regular library collection. During his many years at the Library of Congress, Murray would collect any book that was published on the Negro or blacks and they were placed in a separate area for storage and availability.[42]

When Brick School was closed, somehow the records were in disarray and students would write T.S. to see if he could assist them for information as late as March, 1947. T.S. received a letter from Mrs. McMillon, from Pittsburgh, Pa. She wrote that he had been recommended for her to write about her record at Brick Junior College, high school division. She stated that she had written Mr. Wiley several times for 9-10 months. Finally, he answered remarked McMillon and said the records had been destroyed. Mrs. McMillon told T.S. that she attended Bricks High School from September 1928 until June 1930 and had completed the eleventh grade. She said Mrs. Robinson taught her geometry and Mrs. Ruth Brown was her Latin teacher. McMillon said she was born in Carnegie, Pa. and also attended Francis Junior High school in Washington, D.C. Edna Lewis, T.S.' niece wrote him from Mount Vernon, New York on April 4, 1947. She was discussing her health. Edna said she had arthritis in her limbs and her blood pressure was very high. She told T.S. that she recently visited cousin Daisy Fox. Edna also told Inborden about her brother Thomas who was in the hospital in Long Island, New York. She wanted T.S. to know that she would be celebrating her 54th birthday and extended her best to Dorothy.[43] Jeannette Keeble Cox from Nashville, Tennessee sent T.S. a note and told him about her family. She wrote that her husband was well and that all her children are married now. Helen married a physician, specializing in radiology and they lived in Cleveland, Ohio.

She said another daughter and her husband were teaching in Leaksville, N.C. Cox said her two sons are dentist in Michigan.[44] Daisy Fox wrote her uncle on April 16, 1947 and told him that she had received a letter from Ella and Flora and they were well. She said Eva was crippled with arthritis. Daisy said there was brief scares about an increase in small pox and many people were being vaccinated. She wrote that she received a letter from Rose and that all were well in Upperville, Virginia.[45] O.H. Bellamy of Enfield, N.C. wrote T.S. about his bees. He said he had visited Brick and found the colonies in very bad shape, and some hives were turned over. Bellamy gave T.S. an offer to sell his bees and equipment. He told T.S. that it was a shame to leave them neglected.[46]

On August 17, 1947, the county treasurer of Lorain County, Elyria, Ohio made a deed for the ownership of T.S.' house and lot on East Vine Street which he had purchased June 15, 1896. The deed was transferred to his daughter, Julia E. Gordon, who was teaching in North Carolina. In later years the property was transferred again to daughter Dorothy I. Miller. This 99 year old house is occupied today and recently received a paint job. The house is next door to the heritage home of Sarah Jane Inborden's father and has been maintained in its original state since 1855. The credit must be given to T.S.' daughter Dorothy because she has been responsible for the personal care of both properties.[47] Nan Inborden, T.S.' daughter-in-law wrote him a letter on August 25, 1947 from Raleigh, N.C. She said her brother Henry had just completed his work for the Ph.D. degree at the University of Chicago and would be teaching at the Kentucky State College. T.S. made a visit to Upperville, Virginia in 1947 to see some of his relatives. His niece Minnie sent him a note and told him that she enjoyed his visit. Daisy Fox wrote T.S. and said Edna was in New York to visit her. She said Edna has a husband and does not have to work but she must go to work. Isadore Martin of Philadelphia, Pa, was a former business manager at Brick School. He wrote T.S. a letter on September 4, 1947. He told T.S. that he had read an interesting article about Brick School. The article mentioned that a fine job was been done there. Martin stated that he was happy to know that because he hated so much to see the fine buildings fall to pieces and the beautiful grounds that are grown with weeds. Martin said he was going to spend a few weeks in New York. He told T.S. that his son, Max was in the Army and assigned to the Finance Branch. Martin said his son was the disbursing officer and signed all government checks issued from his office at Fort Huachuca, Arizona.

The Brick School memory was still alive in 1947-48 because there was a Washington, D.C. Brick Alumni Club. They were graduates from Brick School and Brick Junior school. Some of the members were Eddie Anderson, William Anderson, Ruth Bryant Arrington, Lucille Ward Artist, Fletcher Atkins, Molester Exum Atkins, Eula Hilliard Baines, Dr. Gilbert Battle, Richard Battle, Ruth Barnes Battle, Fred Blue, William Bowens, Fannie Burt, Evelyn Henderson Cannon, Booker Carpenter, Roderick Cheek, John Cox, James Dew, Martha Archer Crichlow Grant, Massie Battle Elliott, Lugenia Exum, Louise Fobbs Hargrave, James Harrington, Luther Hemmons, Emma Atkins Holmes, Harry Holmes, Milton Holmes, Queenie Lyons Mayo Holmes, Belinda White Hicks, Connie Howen, Jehu Hunter, Ola James, Charles Jones, Leonard Jones, Julia Gordan Jordan, Earl Lassiter, Alfred Leach, Beatrice McDowell, Mattie Bullock Owens, Exel Powell, Beatrice

Lyons Redman, Ada Ford Reid, Naomi Anthony Saunders, Emma Battle Shepard, Alice Warwick Smith, Gerald Smith, Charlotte Smith, Ola Stancil Smith, Clarence Stancil, Annie Tillery Steele, Murvin Sumner, Harmon Taylor, Ernestine Fenner Taylor, Wilder Taylor, Harry Terry, Ann Jenkins Thomas, Ivan Torrain, Eleanor A. Murray Venture, Phoenix Watson, Odie Williams and Dorothy Latham.[48] Fred L. Brownlee, AMA, wrote T.S. on October 28, 1947 and said that there had been another fire at Brick, the house located to the rear of T.S' house. He said the buildings and contents were completely destroyed, however, the family was able to escape without injury. Brownlee said the tenant family that was living in the house would be housed in Benedict Hall. Brownlee asked Inborden if his furniture could be stored under Mrs. Gordon's supervision in Benedict Hall, locked and secured. Secretary Brownlee wanted to use T.S.' house as temporary quarters for a Yates family.[49] This was probably the beginning of Brownlee's tactic to eventually have T.S. vacate his house at Brick. Flossie Parker, Tarboro, N.C. wrote T.S. for a letter of recommendation. Inborden had known her family for years. Ms. Parker was a county supervisor for schools in Edgecombe County, N.C. Julia Inborden Gordon wrote her father on October 31, 1947 and said that she did not know about the fire at Brick. She would contact her daughter Frances and see if she could use some of the furniture. Julia stated that Frances had purchased a lot with a house and they plan to remodel it and she might be able to use your desk. Julia said she had read in the *Journal and Guide* newspaper that Fred Brownlee will make the final address at the installation of Dr. Charles S. Johnson as President of Fisk University.[50] A post card was received by T.S. from his niece, Edna Lewis who wrote that she has not been so well and that Thomas was very ill in the hospital. She said he was paralyzed on one side and could not talk. T.S. received greeting cards during the 1948 Christmas season from Nettie Pinchback, Dorothy Dunston and family, Brick Club of Tidewater, Virginia and Lugenia G. Exum. Nora E. Morgan, Baltimore, Maryland wanted some information about the family of the late Mrs Fannie Arrington and wrote a letter to T.S. in 1948. She stated that she was the widow of the late Essex I. Hicks who was Mrs. Arrington's brother and she wanted to find some of his relatives who were still in North Carolina. Mrs. Morgan asked T.S. to please help her if he could. She told T.S. that she often think of the nice time she had when she visited North Carolina. Morgan said that she realizes that Brick is a small place, but she really would like to visit again. Mrs. Morgan inquired about T.S' family and asked if he still had his bees.[51] John Gordon wrote his grandfather and enclosed a money order for ten dollars with a note. The note read enclosed is the money I borrowed and give my regards to all and please write sometimes.[52]

Edna Lewis wrote her uncle in 1949 and was still complaining about her arthritis, especially in her hand. She also stated that she was taking insulin for her diabetes. Edna said that her brother Thomas was still in the hospital and that she had a visit from her mother's sister who lives in Harrisburg, Pa. She spent three weeks with us. Edna Lewis closed her letter by telling T.S. that she hopes to see him soon.[53] Inborden's faithful and devoted house keeper, Mrs. Grant died and she was buried in North Carolina and the funeral services were held at the First Baptist Church, Battlesboro, N.C. on November 21, 1948.

A letter was received by T.S. from G.E. Davis. He told T.S. that he had learned from Dr. George Evan's brother in Washington, D.C. that T.S. had a daughter, Dorothy I. Miller who was a principal in Washington, D.C. Dr. Evans lived in Greensboro, N.C. Davis said your Dorothy is a devoted loving daughter and my Gladys is the same, she is also a school principal. Davis wrote T.S. that among the pleasant and cherished memories of many yesteryears are the frequent visits with you at Brick and the many trips we made around that part of the state. He also recalled the trips that were made to Kill Devil Hill at Kitty Hawk. Davis stated that T.S. and he had made their contributions to the uplift of their people in North Carolina. G.E. Davis said T.S. did more than any single man in the section. He also wrote that acclaim goes to the politician and workers, however, what will remain in the hearts of people, Halifax, Nash and Edgecombe is that they will never have a man to do what you did in your service while at Brick. Davis continued his letter by writing that he read with pleasure T.S.' article on Civics and History which has grown out of T.S. experience and travel. It is a classic. Davis told T.S. that God and ourselves have been good to us in extending our lives. G.E. Davis recalled that he taught Judge Armond Scott four years at Biddle school. He is a fine fearless man. Davis said that he lived right on the corner near A&T College, Greensboro and that he goes there often. Davis ended his letter by telling T.S. that there are few now who go to the people with a message of inspiration and love. *The old order perisheth.*[54]

Myrtle L. Forney wrote T.S. on February 13, 1949 and said her father had asked her to write to T.S. and thank him for sending the inaugural edition of the Washington Post, newspaper. I enjoyed it more than Papa, remarked Forney. She said she took the paper to school and used it in her classroom and she had already asked her students to listen to the radio version. Forney wrote that she travels home frequently to visit her parents. She said she saw Dr. Sessoms recently and he asked about T.S. She stated that the doctor looks much better because for a while he was not able to continue his practice. Ms. Forney said Benjamin Bullock was home to work on his farm. She stated her father is well and keeps very busy. The Forney family members attended Brick School.[55] The beautiful campus of Brick School had been kept in an attractive manner over the years. Around 1949, this could have been the beginning of Brick's campus losing its past perpetual treatment that was necessary to maintain its beauty and splendor that was frequently noticed by its students and visitors. Julia Inborden Gordon wrote her sister Dorothy I. Miller and told her that she did not know how to tell Papa the things that were occurring at Brick. Julia wrote that she saw some men working in Papa's yard near the garage and at the back. They were cutting trees. She said she told Mr. Richard Garrett who was cutting a tree that her father did not want those trees cut down. He replied that they were cleaning up and would only cut a few. Julia then said that he should only cut the hedge bushes and the vines. However, the next day she observed they were still cutting the trees and very few hedges were cut. They had cut down a pear and a plum tree near the garage and the yard was full of tree stumps. Julia told Dorothy that she hoped that they would not cut any more trees near the house. T.S. was living in Washington, D.C. at this time and Julia was away sometimes teaching school. There was no one present at the home at times to prevent the men from cutting down many trees and shrubbery that Inborden had planted and cared for over the years.[56]

T.S.' frequent writer his niece, Daisy Fox, wrote him on September 18, 1949. She wrote that she was glad that he was away from Washington, D.C. for awhile during the hot weather. She said Leslie was the same somewhat lifeless as a baby but she tries to be cheerful. Daisy said that she had received a letter from Uncle Jim Cross' son Grayson and he lives in Alexandria, Virginia on 323 South Alfred Street and so do not be surprised if he and his sister Mary comes to visit you. I told them where you live. You will know Grayson and you will see that he is the image of his father. Daisy said that she was sorry that Dorothy had some contact with poison ivy because she know how it can irritate one. She told T.S. that she wrote Maggie Jones recently. Daisy Fox told T.S. to give her love to Dorothy and God will bless her because she is so nice to you. Daisy said that she will visit Washington soon.[57] T.S. received a letter from Edna Lewis and she wrote:

Dear Uncle Sewell, I visited Thomas last week and took him some fried chicken and cake, because he enjoys his meals. I heard from my sister Mattie and she said that they went up to visit the old house in the mountain. Edna said they had to walk from the school house to the home place and the area was covered with bushes and weeds. She told T.S. that she hoped to see him sometime soon.[58]

During the years of 1950-1951, T.S. Inborden was getting a little weaker and his eyes were beginning to fail him at the blessed age of 86 years. He was very fortunate to be at home with his daughter Dorothy and receive the best care that one could ask. Although Dorothy was performing her duties as Principal of Margaret Murray Washington Vocational School, she still had sufficient time to devote to the attention of her ailing father. T.S. would write some letters when he could and would see friends and family that visited him at his daughters comfortable home in Washington. As the year of 1951 would approach, T.S. would suffer a serious fall at his daughter's home and would eventually require hospitalization at Howard University's Freedmen's Hospital, Washington, D.C. Thomas Sewell Inborden, a loved father, grandfather, uncle and educator of his people won his victory unto Christ on Saturday, March 10, 1951. He was blessed with life in the flesh for 86 years and his time spent living those years were productive and fulfilling in the love and caring that he gave to many people. His Christian ideals and faith in God was his motivation that made his living so wonderful. Thomas Sewell's family and friends in Washington D.C. were able to say farewell to him at his daughter's house where a viewing was held prior to his final burial in the town that captivated him as a young man to seek an education and prepare for the missionary work to help others in his future life. Yes, he was taken to his second home Oberlin, Ohio. He was buried beside his loving and faithful wife Sarah Jane Evans Inborden in the family plot at Oberlin's Westwood Cemetery. Thomas Sewell's victory unto Christ was felt as a sorrow to all of those who knew him and loved him even though his leaving them was a spiritual joy for his work that was done so well. There were many family members and friends who visited his home, some sent telegrams cards and even made phone calls to express in their sympathetic way their condolences to a man that was known by some as T.S., the Professor, Mr. Inborden, The Bee Man, in North Carolina and above all the founder of an institution of learning for his people of color that was called Brick School. The following people knew and appreciated their acquaintance with Thomas Sewell and so humbly paid their last respects to him in many ways. They were: Gladys Houston, Carrie Young, Edna Lewis, J.C. Bias, A.F. Wilder, Lorraine Pinchback, Ethel Dunlap James C. Evans, Eula Arrington Williams, Fred Brownlee, Harold Trigg, Thomas Cofield, Daisy Fox, Lillian Evanti, Garnett C. Wilkinson, Cato Adams, Lucille Dodd, Alice Grigsby, Cora E. Black Grant, Nathaniel Murray, Agnes Hall, William C. Syphax Jr. Minnie Griggs, Olive Polk, J.R. Phillips, Meyers Family, Brick Club of New York, John W. Mitchell, Clifford Johnson, Ruth Morton, Brick Club of Tidewater, Va., Lora Phillips, P.J. Chesson, J. Thomas Hamlin, James Eaton, Newton Gordon, Sally A. Phillips, and the Washington Fisk University Club.[59]

I believed in a mystical way that the spirit of Thomas Sewell Inborden was escorted to the beautiful paradise of God's heaven on March 10, 1951, by the angels and our master greeted him and said Thomas Sewell now that you have come to the end of your journey in earthly life, a job well done.

CHAPTER 7

An Epilogue To An Early Educator of Color

The guns had silenced, and a treaty of peace and tranquility was signed at Richmond, Virginia between the Gray and Blue forces of the war between the states, commonly known as the Civil War. The year was 1865 and in the beautiful splendor of the recesses of the Blue Ridge Mountains near Loudon and Fairfax counties of Virginia was born a baby boy who was given the name of Thomas Sewell after his maternal uncle and a family name of Inborden. His mother was an industrious loving and caring woman who was Harriet Proctor Smith descended from the distinguished Rectors of Virginia. Her family were former slaves but she and her siblings were born free. She served as a midwife and also prepared the food and healed the wounds of many of the high ranking officers of the Confederate Army possibly to include Lee's Lieutenants. The name of the baby boy would carry the name of Inborden. As stated previously in this manuscript, his Caucasian father was a well cultured and stately southern gentleman. The mystery of his actual identity will possibly always remain. However, in consideration of some inferences, circumstances, testimonies of family members and some researched facts, there is a strong possibility that Thomas Sewell Inborden was the illegitimate son of General Robert E. Lee or some southern gentlemen of equal status. Regardless of who was his paternal father, Inborden was able to overcome all residual effects from his state of poverty, illegitimacy and ignorance and leave the mountains of Virginia and accomplished monumental success in some sixty years of his adult life. Thomas Sewell traveled to Cleveland, Ohio on to Oberlin, Ohio and then to Fisk University, Nashville, Tennessee in his determined quest to obtain excellence in the pursuit of an education. He was given an early exposure to the Christian ideals and disciplines of one's self during his years at Oberlin College. His learning experiences at one of the most prestigious colleges of the American Missionary School's Fisk University gave Inborden the opportunity to receive an academic education of the highest standards. He was able to meet and communicate with future black leaders who would challenge the world with their expertise, namely W.E.B. DuBois and Margaret Murray Washington. Thomas Sewell was offered his first job and assignment by Dr. Beard of the AMA to pastor a church in Beaufort, South Carolina for nine months even though he was not an ordained minister of the faith. I believe that Dr. Beard and the Congregational Church could perceive the genius in this young man from Oberlin and Fisk who would be able to preach the Christian doctrines and serve as a missionary to the people of color in Beaufort. As the AMA was increasing their missionary private schools in the south, Inborden was selected to go to Helena, Arkansas and Albany, Georgia to establish and reorganize two schools. A Christian and philanthropic Brooklyn Caucasian lady named Julia Brewster Brick became interested in giving her money for the establishment of a school to educate poor black students in eastern North Carolina. She asked the AMA to assist her and they again selected a man they believed in and he was Thomas Sewell. If we would review the number of schools one hundred years ago that were founded, organized and sustained for a period of some forty years by one man, I do believe there would be few. Inborden was the founder of Joseph Keasbey Brick School in Enfield, North Carolina in 1895. That was his monument for his life's work not only as an instrument for the AMA but for the salvation and survival of his people of color who were reared from the same conditions he had come from in rural Virginia.

Thomas Sewell Inborden believed in the diversity of knowledge he was not a specialist in education but a generalist who would use his many talents in a transfer learning method in many of the disciplines he taught. Inborden's curriculum at Brick School encompassed the ideas of DuBosis' talented tenth and Booker T. Washington's agricultural expertise. Thomas Sewell believed in teaching Christian ideals, morality, academic, work effort, home economics and agriculture. He believed in the economic progress of black people through their knowledge of the soil, the farm, its products and raising of the animals. Inborden believed that the farmer must be progressive, educated and use the latest technology for success. Inborden was able to go among the people, walk with them, talk with them and solve their problems, if possible, immediately. He was a leader of the people in Eastern, North Carolina but not in the sense of a politician or ambitious person whose agenda was his personal gains. He was there to render his services as a missionary to the poor and illiterate and to improve their status. Thomas Sewell had his hobby, some were productive in an economic way such as his love for bees and honey production. He was a self taught botanist who was well respected by the professional scholars of that science. Inborden was quite aware of the dictates of the famous ruling one year after the start of his school, the Plessy vs Ferguson ruling of 1896. He was not subservient to the demands and appeasement of the white majority. Inborden would respond to them in a tactical and intelligent manner and did not compromise his people's demands and request for upward mobility. His name was not known to many of the popular politicians of color of that day but in the field of academics both white and black knew of Thomas Sewell Inborden. He knew what it was to receive a letter from the Ku Klux Klan to warn him against doing things they did not like, but that did not stop him for doing what he thought was best for his people of color. Thomas Sewell Inborden did so many things so well and the results have been exemplary. The graduates of Brick Normal School and Brick Junior College through the years have had some impact on their lives that can be attributed to their studying and experiencing the good curriculum and environment that Brick School offered them under the most outstanding leadership of an early educator of color, Thomas Sewell Inborden. The descendants of former graduates and students of Brick School have benefitted from their parents and grandparents's presence at Brick at one time or the other. Their possible successes and achievements in life were the results of their family member who were given their upward mobility motivation from Brick School and Inborden.

There are many examples that would support the above statement. However, I will cite a few. There were members of the distinguished Sengstacke family who were students at the Albany Normal School, Georgia. At one time when a Sengstacke member was the editor of the *Chicago Defender* newspaper, he sent his son and nephew to Brick Normal School. The late Congressman William Dawson of Illinois was a student at Albany Normal School, Georgia. There is a possible family connection of a student who attended Brick School in its early years who was named Guthrie L. Turner to the first African American General of the United

States Army Medical Corp, retired Brigadier General Guthrie L. Turner. A well respected scholar in science named Jehu Hunter of Washington, D.C. is the son of the late Jehu Hunter of North Carolina who was a student at Brick School. There was a very good student at Brick School in the early years named Ida Battle. Inborden would receive numerous requests from white supporters of the school in the New England states. They were interested in having young ladies to work for them during the summer months and assist them in their tuition expenses. Dr. Beard, AMA Secretary for many years, asked Inborden to recommend several young ladies to work for his family in Norwalk, Connecticut one summer. One of the young ladies was Ida Battle. She spent several summers working for the Beard family. After graduation she decided to move to Norwalk, Connecticut. In later years, while attending the Negro Baptist Church in Norwalk, she met a very talented young man named Aaron Archer who played the piano and organ at her church and also the other black church in town, the African Methodist Episcopal Church. Ida Battle and Aaron Archer were married. Their daughter Martha Archer Crichlow Grant graduated from Brick Junior College's high school in the 1930's. There are family names in eastern North Carolina, Washington, D.C., Virginia, New York and many areas of the United States who can trace a lineage back to the classrooms of Brick School.

History many times records the names of selective persons who appear in a more wider limelight of the news and more geographically known. However, there are and have been many individuals of the same quality and achievements who never become part of the annuals of historical preservation. The name of Inborden warrants a place not just in North Carolina history, not just in black history, but in American history that is taught at the majority schools of our multiracial society. I trust and hope that someday Thomas Sewell's Alma Mater Fisk University will claim his greatness in their perspective and evaluation and honor their son posthumously in some manner.

I am most grateful and privileged to have had the greatest primary source through the oral tradition available, the presence of Thomas Sewell's beloved daughter, Dorothy Inborden Miller to assist me, recall and provide the information about her father. Mrs. Miller graduated from Fisk University, 76 years ago, Magna Cum laude and she exemplified so wonderful the belief of her father, the pursuit of excellence in education. One hundred years ago, 1895, Julia Brewster Brick had a vision and a dream. Thomas Sewell Inborden fulfilled them when he nurtured for forty years what was sowed and so abundantly reaped.

                                            Robert Ewell Greene
                                            Fort Washington, Maryland
                                            August 19, 1995

APPENDICES

    I have somewhat deviated from the norm in the writing of this manuscript by including a vast amount of T.S. Inborden's writings. However, I feel that 100 years ago a man without a modern day computer system and typewriter or recording machine was able to document his experiences in the founding and administration of an educational institution. Therefore, I am including as "valuable historical appendices" Thomas Sewell Inborden's writing that were typed in most instance by himself and through the caring and understanding of their richness preserved over the years by his surviving daughter Dorothy Inborden Miller. I sincerely believe that there have been very few people who have documented their accomplishments and somewhat daily tasks as Inborden did so well from 1880s to the 1950s. His writings to include philosophies, accounts, records of student enrollment, friends and other subjects of interested warrant a place in the legacy of his history, Brick's history and the numerous history of families and people he met during his time living in North Carolina and performing duties as an educator and architect of Brick School. These valuable historical appendices should not dwell within a file drawer but should be included within the pages of this manuscript. I trust that his writings will help some one along the way in the futurity of years to come because yesterday can provide some thoughts and directions for a successful tomorrow.

                                                                               Robert Ewell Greene
                                                                                June 4, 1995

APPENDIX 1

Dorothy Inborden Miller
Memories Of Her Mother and Father

I have had the most unique pleasure of knowing Mrs. Dorothy Inborden Miller for 18 years. In 1979, I was able to publish a book on her maternal family from Oberlin, Ohio and North Carolina. Mrs. Miller assisted me in the research of *Leary-Evans Ohio's Free People of Color*. We were able to research together material for a small pamphlet that was prepared for her paternal family reunion in Virginia in 1980. It was at that time that I told Mrs. Miller that someday I would like to write a thorough biography on her father. During the last fifteen years, I have interviewed and discussed with Mrs. Miller many events and experiences of her childhood at Bricks, North Carolina and about her mother and father. I have selected some interesting stories from tapes and notes that I have accrued over the years relating to the many conversations that we have had. The true stories or memories of Mrs. Miller about Thomas Sewell Inborden and her mother reflects the richness, guidance and family support that was given to her and the other Inborden children from two caring and responsible parents. Dorothy I. Miller recalled how her mother and father was interested in an early accreditation of Brick School and preparing their graduates for college entrance exams. They had introduced courses in Greek and Latin. The AMA intervened and stated that the children in that part of the country, Enfield, North Carolina need agriculture and not Greek and Latin. Her parents were very disappointed with that decision. There was a very good student named Hattie Green who was preparing to enter Fisk University upon graduation. Mrs. Sarah Jane Evans Inborden gave her private lessons in Greek in order to prepare her for the entrance exams at Fisk. When the agriculture course was introduced into the curriculum, many of the students, especially young ladies did not welcome the course. A visitor from the AMA went into the classroom of young ladies and asked one student what was the meaning of agriculture. The student replied it is a branch of mathematics. Mrs. Sarah Jane Inborden had told that to the students previously in a humorous way to express her disagreement in having the agriculture course to replace her Greek or Latin. Dorothy Inborden tells the story about her mother's first teaching position upon graduation from Oberlin College in 1890. The AMA offered her a position in the south. She sent her application with picture and was accepted to teach at a school for poor white children in South Carolina. She taught there for one year and it is believed that they never knew she was a black lady.

George Eastman, the magnate of Kodak Photographic Company visited Brick. He came to Dorothy Miller's classroom and was shown her demonstration exhibit and the student's tables were neatly arranged and the drawers all had their contents orderly arranged. Mr. Eastman was surprised when he opened the drawers of each table and asked Mrs. Miller do all the students keep it this neat all the time? Dorothy Miller said her father had distinguished visitors to visit the school and some of them were W.E.B. DuBois, Channing Tobias and Jesse Moorland. Mrs. Miller said her father would order school supplies from Richmond, Virginia and they would be shipped by rail on the Atlantic Coast Line railroad. Dorothy Miller stated that a small cemetery was on the farm and that her parents had buried the young Inborden boys that died. There were seven children and only three lived to adult age. T.S. Inborden had the school's kitchen to include in their menus, cornbread quite frequently because they had plenty of corn and wheat on the farm. The students also enjoyed a bread they called short bread. The bread was baked in large sections and then it was sliced as a square and served. When Dorothy Inborden was studying for her masters degree at Columbia University, New York City, she visited the courthouse and learned that Mrs. Julia B. Brick's will included $250,000 for the future operation of Brick School. It was Mrs. Brick's intention that the school would always be for the education of poor black students in eastern North Carolina.

Mrs. Miller recalled when her father took her and Wilson to visit his old family home in Upperville, Virginia. When they arrived in Washington, D.C., they missed the stagecoach to Upperville. They were able to obtain a ride with the mailman. They sat on their father's lap. Upon arriving at Upperville, they had to walk six miles up the mountain to the home. She recalled that the house was a two story building with a loft. They slept on feather beds and enjoyed their visit with their grandmother and Uncle Ashton. Mrs. Miller said her parents did not smoke nor drink alcoholic beverages. Her father would make apple cider from apples.

There was an occasion where Sarah Jane Inborden and her children were returning from Oberlin, Ohio, when they arrived in Richmond, Virginia, they changed trains for North Carolina. Mrs. Inborden approached the Jim Crow car for colored and was about to enter the doorway when the conductor said *lady, you getting on the wrong car*, Mrs. Inborden replied, *I know where I am going, to this car*. The conductor let her proceed. She was not trying to pass for white. Thomas Sewell and Sarah Jane Inborden instilled the principles of obedience and work effort in their children. Dorothy learned to sew in the fourth grade and the art of embroidery. One time her father purchased some cloth material for her to make three dresses. She finished them very quickly and asked her father for some more material. He told her slow down because it was getting expensive. When Dorothy and Julia went to Fisk University they worked for four years in the school dining room in order to receive free meals. Dorothy worked in the home economic classrooms, cleaning them and mopping the floors for money to help with her expenses. Dorothy and Wilson would help to pick black eye peas on the farm at a very young age. Wilson was only six years old. As a teenage Wilson Inborden would plow the field working all day for one dollar in wages. He would tell Dorothy to prepare him some oat meal in the morning because it would hold him until the noon meal. T.S. Inborden's favorite breakfast meal was pancakes with his delicious honey. He loved his hobbies of bee culture and also raising chickens especially the Rhode Island Whites and he had excellent eggs that were laid. The honey hobby was also a business venture that assisted the family's income since the AMA did not pay very much to its missionary teachers.

T.S. Inborden used the help of his children and grandchildren in the chores of his bee honey culture and weather reporting. Julia and Dorothy would check the rain gauges in front of their house and also determine which way the wind was blowing. When the water level was more than an inch, T.S. would send a telegram to the weather Bureau in Raleigh, North Carolina. Dorothy stated that her father was often called Mr. Bee Man of North Carolina for his delicious honey that his bee colonies produced. The Brick campus did not require the local law enforcement officers from Enfield to come on the campus to maintain order. T.S. Inborden was able to have the students and faculty to obey and respect the school's rules and discipline measures. T.S. Inborden taught his children to always strive for excellence. During her four years at Fisk University, Dorothy was able to maintain an average over ninety and graduated with honors, Magna Cum laude. She did not like to give speeches and really did not want to make a speech at graduation. Dorothy Inborden recalled that when she entered Fisk as a freshman that she received 100 in her math and spelling entrance exams. However, she received a failing grade in English. The English teacher asked her what was wrong because normally the young ladies do not make a 100 in math but they do well in English. Dorothy told her that the test consisted of two questions that were weighed at 20 percent and she had not been taught what a participle adverb was. The teacher asked her what English book did she use at Brick. Dorothy said we used the Harvard Grammar. The teacher then replied, well that book does not contain the participle adverb. Dorothy was given some material to study and in a few days she was retested and made a grade higher than 90 percent. Secretary Brownlee, AMA, told T.S. that he could live in his campus house for life upon his retirement. He also offered him 20 acres of land. T.S. did not accept the land. However, in the 1940's Brownlee asked T.S. to vacate the house and he did not keep his promise of the late 1920's. I asked Mrs. Miller what did she think about Brownlee's action. She replied he did not keep his word, he was a nice man and made a successful record. Therefore vengeance will be the task of our Lord for Brownlee's actions. I thought that was a very Christian reply from Mrs. Miller who the Lord has blessed with many fruitful years of life. The Inborden children were taught music at a young age. Dorothy and Julia played the piano and Wilson played the clarinet and saxophone. They were permitted to play only classical music and they were given eight volumes of the world's best music. One day T.S. Inborden's friend, a minister and his two young daughters visited the Inborden home. The young ladies were invited to play the piano. They were playing very fast and somewhat swinging type music or as one would say literally, they were tearing up the piano. When they finished, Mr. Inborden applauded them for their performance. Then he looked toward his two daughters and said I have spent all this money for your lessons and you do not play that fast and good. Dorothy replied, Papa, they were playing ragtime music and you do not permit us to play ragtime.

On February 18, 1991, I asked Mrs. Miller what were some of her father's sayings. She recalled that when they were young, he would walk down the hall to wake them up in the morning. He would be reciting one of his favorite verses from Psalm 19 on the creation and covenants of God, To the Chief musician a Psalm of David. She was able to recite for me at the blessed age of 94 years, the first two verses of the song. Some of the favorite verses of T.S. were: Verses 1,2,3 and 4.

The heavens declare the glory of God; and the firmament showeth his hand, work. Day unto day uttereth speech and night unto night showeth knowledge. There is no speech nor language where their voices is not heard. Their line is gone out through all the earth and their words to the end of the world. In them hath he set a tabernacle for the sun. Mrs. Miller said they would learn verses from the bible by listening to him recite them in the morning.

APPENDIX 2

T.S Inborden decided to send a letter to his friends to express a great shock and amazement when the officials at the American Missionary Association demanded that he should retire. The founder of Brick School wrote what he called a Declaration.

A DECLARATION

Dear Friends:

This is to say that the greatest shock I ever received in my life came to me several weeks ago when the Secretary, Dr. Fred L. Brownlee, of the American Missionary Association and Mr. George E. Haynes, the colored member of the Executive Committee of that organization asked and demanded of me my retirement from the principalship of this institution, which I am forced by them to accept. The ground for this request was that for many years I have not functioned with Executive Committee and that the organization has a larger and more progressive programme for this institution and I stand in the way of it. I do not need to go into any details of that part of the situation. I have been working under the auspices of the American Missionary Association for thirty-five years. I have been in the active service of the American Missionary Association longer than any other man connected with it except one. I started this institution thirty-one years ago. I do no need to recount what has been done here. It is an open book. You read it every day you pass up and down this country. The institution has stood for definite a fundamental principles of human conduct and human life It has had its vicissitudes as other institutions have had but the direction has always been upward an onward. It has not been a follower in Negro education and community uplift but decidedly a leader. You, your homes, your sons and your daughters have been a witness to the inspiration you have received here these thirty-one years. Your co-operation and the fine inter-racial relations are also a witness to the same philosophy which we have sought to teach and live here.

During all these years, I have had a decided hand in helping to shape every progressive movement in this state that had for its object the uplift of Negro life and Negro progress. For five years, I was Secretary or President of the North Carolina Teachers Association. This is the oldest educational Negro institution in the South. I was chairman of the Jury of Awards for the Negro Building in the Jamestown Exposition. I have been president five years of the Negro Farmers' Congress of the state. During World War I, I was given credit for influencing the sale of forty-eight thousand dollars worth of War Stamps to Negroes in this community. During that awful period, I was the one to speak in practically all the school houses, churches and court houses in the entire community covering an area of two thousand square miles. I was the one to inspire confidence and patriotism in our cause when it was very much needed. I have received several honorary appointments from the various governors of the state and the commissions came to me under state seal. I have never betrayed a single trust that came to me. For two years, I was president of the North Carolina (Industrial Association) State Fair Association. I have been asked to be the president of two state institutions at a salary very much more than I was receiving as principal of the Brick School. I was invited by the state and county officials, several years ago, to speak to ten thousand children in Halifax County alone. My organization. as a recognition of my services, sent me to California several years ago and paid all of my expenses and I was away five months. This trip was written up in a booklet of almost a hundred pages. It is a tribute to you and to the organization that sent me. Fifteen years ago, I was delegated to speak in the interest of Congregational benevolences in the following states: South Dakota, North Dakota, Iowa, Illinois, Minnesota, Ohio and Pennsylvania. This work took me away three months in the coldest part of the Winter. I gave ninety-six public addresses. Last Fall, I was called away again for three months to the far West including Montana, Idaho and the great state of Washington. This time, I was speaking in the interest of all of our ten National Organizations under the auspices of the Commission on Missions of the Congregational Church with headquarters in New York City. I gave one hundred and two public addresses to all sorts of organizations in the northwest, braving all conditions of weather and all hazards of travel to do it. I call your attention not to laud my self but to let you know I have not only been active in school work but I have given my services in every constructive way in the community and over the country.

Friends and Patrons-Listen:

My motto has been "Come on" and not "Go on." "you cannot teach what you are not." The greatest lesson any teacher can transmit is the lesson of personal conduct. It is the lesson of his personality. The student will forget the books but he will never forget the attitude and personality of the teacher. There is not one soul anywhere who can say that I ever asked or received usury for any loan I ever made on account of their tuition, board or any other account. I have never asked a patron for interest on any loan I ever made to them to tide them over any hard place. Every penny that has ever been given to the school directly or indirectly can be accounted for by receipts checks and office records. When I leave this institution I leave to it and to the American Missionary Association an unearned increment worth hundreds of dollars in the way of fruit and nut trees that came from my own pockets and my own muscle. This will never be paid for and never be duplicated in another thirty-one years I now leave an institution whose standard of excellence, scholarship and Christian influence for thirty years has not been excelled. The institution is happily located, well founded and should demand your fullest support. It has background that challenges the best in you. It is in the heart of the black belt of the state. If private philanthropy cannot give it adequate support for the largest possible programme you should see to it that it gets state funds if under the state control. This institution should serve the people of Eastern North Carolina. I want to see a thousand students here under the best possible auspices and control. The education should fit them for the *most honorable and useful places in the life of the community. Let me say very emphatically, that whoever has the control of the institution there should be a local advisory board composed of the best white and colored men in Eastern North Carolina. The men should be broad minded in matters of education and most sympathetic in racial affairs and Negro uplift.*

T.S. INBORDEN
Brick, N.C.

APPENDIX 3

In 1995, some sociologists, psychologists and many laypersons write and discuss about the significance of environment and its implications with the maturing and development of individuals. Many years ago a very perceptive and concerned educator, Thomas Sewell Inborden had his views and inferences on the importance of environment in the shaping of character. Inborden wrote an early paper on Negro Life and character.

AN ESTIMATE OF NEGRO LIFE AND CHARACTER

ENVIRONMENT

One element to take into account in our estimate of Negro Life and character is environment. There are certain animals that do well in the polar regions and others that thrive best at the equator. Oranges which grow to perfection in Florida and California, in other states are sour and imperfect. Animals as well as plant have their habitat and in that they thrive best. I am interested in botany, and I am always surprised to find the great differences in the same species when I find them in the various states. The difference is in the size or color, or in some other development. You will not find whiter people anywhere than in the northern countries, nor blacker people anywhere than under the equator. Between these points may be found all the other colors. The features of the Irish peasantry are rough because they live a rugged life. The American Indians have projecting cheekbones because their food is game and largely raw. The Indian is a marksman because upon that depends his living. The lips of the African are large because of the difficulties for centuries in pronouncing the words of their language; their nostrils are large because they live in a hot climate and they are necessary to supply an abundance of fresh Air for the lungs. You know the man from Boston or New York as soon as he arrives; he walks vigorously, and is full of life and action. If you wish to confer with him you must prepare your address before you get to him. He may give you a few minutes if you have some money to spend with him; if you stay too long this may soon become apparent. In this region, if one wishes to hire a man it may take several days to find the man, another day to make a bargain and it may be several days to collect the money when the work is done. Here, everywhere one sees idleness. These are the general impressions that come to one as he tries to take in the situation. One cause of all this difference is in the environment. In the North the climatic condition requires men to be active all the time. The summers are short and the winters are long and cold, and men must work and not wait. In other words, the conditions do not encourage idleness. Improved machinery, transportation facilities, a desire to excel, business methods, freedom of opinion and of utterance, freedom of the press, good laws, public and private education and general public sentiment all make conditions. These conditions have made for earnestness and industry until these have become marked characteristics of the people.

On the other hand, in the South there is every temptation to languor and idleness. Many servants, little pay, small demand for the best labor and the best products, cheap living, long summers, mild winters, little competition with the outside world, lack of educational interest and a general depreciation of values and time all have influenced southern life and character. Life here is not "strenuous." To say "the Negro was born to idleness," therefore, is not stating the whole truth. The Negro was born in the midst of these environments and was a factor in this environment. The present upheaval all over the country with respect to the Negro is simply a movement towards a normal adjustment of abnormal conditions. The conditions are changing and men are beginning to get adjusted to them. Facts do not sustain the accusation that the Negro is a hindrance to southern society and southern progress. He has tilled the soil of the southland, cleared the swamps and woods, ditched the low grounds and river bottoms, laid all the railroad beds, nursed, waited on the largest part of the southern population and put up nearly all the houses before the war. The fact that the Negro is paying taxes at this time on over four hundred million dollars of property, that over fifty percent of the Negro people can read and write, that several under a thousand have been educated in excellent schools, show that the environment is changing for the better. There are yet many things for the Negro people to do; but now they are buying land, are building themselves homes and churches, are going into business for themselves and are educating their children. Most who have had any chances to better themselves are tying to create a healthy public sentiment for honesty, industry, regard for labor and for good environment. If I read history aright these are the things that count in the progress of any society. The Negro today assuredly is one of the greatest industrial factors south, and he is to be such. Absolutely no one has been found to take his place on southern soil nor will be. He can live luxuriously enough when his means allow, or as poorly as a hermit when necessary.

As a people we have gained much since freedom found us with nothing and living unlettered and poorly clad, with no home, no land, no conception of the value of money or business, nor with any conception of the value of the virtues necessary to true manhood. Since the best life and character result are to be expected. Bad influences, contaminating and destructive conditions are to be changed if you would change the moral tone of the people. Not long since I met a planter who was lamenting because there were so many empty houses and so much cotton in the fields to be picked and all the Negroes gone. I explained to him the cause of their leaving: "You have several sons and daughters. Your house has a kitchen, dining room, sitting-room, and a sufficient number of bedrooms for all. Now, many of these colored men whose services you desire and whom you wish to retain on your plantation have families as large as yours. You give them only a one or two-room cabin. Their families need privacy as well as yours. Give them a fraction of the home facilities you have and they will not leave you." This man thought there might be truth in this; and many of the large planters are realizing that it is necessary to furnish better houses for their renters. This is not a good thing for the planter, but it means a better day for the Negroes who live in these improved conditions. These are some of the environments from which the Negroes are emerging. If he is not progressing as fast as he should, then the conditions should be made more helpful. Those who can do most to change the conditions are those who own the land, who build the houses, who teach in the schools and colleges, who make and enforce the laws, and those who set the pace for public sentiment the editors of the newspapers.

Reference to our own methods may not be out of place. The Joseph Keasbey Brick Agricultural, Industrial and Normal school, located at Enfield, North Carolina, has 1,429 acres of land. Every foot of this land is used strictly for educational purposes. That part which the students cannot cultivate is rented out to colored families. We have eight of these families on the farm. Every renter who comes, signs a printed contract pledging himself that he will abstain from all forms of intoxicants. He also signs that he will engage in no immoralities, nor in any conduct out of harmony with the spirit and work of the school. The results after seven years are most gratifying. The renters pay as much rent as they did under the old conditions. They came in debt, and now they own from one to three horses, their wagons and buggies, plows and hoes, grow most of their own provisions, and can get credit anywhere they want it. They have nearly thirty children in our school, for whom they promptly pay tuition, and buy their books. These children are wearing good clothes; they attend preaching services, Sunday school and prayer meetings regularly. The school provides for these renters three and four-room cottages. You will find their rooms decorated with flowers and pictures, and not with whiskey and cigarette advertisements. They also have flowers in the yards. The houses are whitewashed and the yards are kept clean. In the summer time they live largely from their own gardens. They raise corn, peas, cotton, poultry and hogs. It was a sacrifice for them not to "grow tobacco," which we do not allow but they were willing to give this up for the sake of the educational advantages for their children. The school "advances" nothing but the ground, and a little advice when necessary. I have seen the children who attend school all the day working in the field at nine o'clock at night by the light of the moon, and I have seen the mothers at the washtub at three and four o'clock in the morning in order to keep these children in the school. There is mutual help and sympathy on the part of us all. There is no trouble at the end of the year at "settling time." We start right at the beginning of the year "with the contract," of which each party has a copy, which accounts for our ending right at the close of the year. Thus, the people who own the land and rent the houses have as much responsibility in solving this problem as anybody; I am not sure but that they have more.

Those who teach have their part also to perform. There are teachers of high rank in this southland who are teaching that the Negroes are anything from a monkey up. This sort of teaching engenders a bad spirit. Nothing but the kindliest feelings should be inculcated in the youth of each race for the other. To allow race prejudice to intercept our view is to make us incapable of correct observation. We must learn to overlook the little faults in each other. We must look for the higher, the beautiful in the life of every man and every race. In this we are not pulled down but our lies and characters are made better. If we are not pleased with our inheritance and our environment we should not be discouraged God is just and He is still on the throne. He holds the reins of governments and thwarts the plans of men. He cannot be dethroned. Every race has "problems," as well as every community and every family. We gain strength by struggle. Every difficulty overcome make the next one easier to be overcome. The harder the problem the better disciplined will be those who succeed in working it out. Education must be considered in our estimate of Negro life and character.

The great missionary societies of the country, the educational boards which have recently organized, and the philanthropic spirit of rich men have a meaning and a mission beyond our present comprehension. Injustice and ignorance cannot live very long under the searchlight of intelligence and education. There are some who are working on this problem who see in it a solution chiefly in the acquisition of money. Money certainly means power, but money is not the greatest thing in the world, note the "problems" of our large cities and some of the states like Delaware, and observe how money in the hands of unscrupulous men has thwarted good government and blocked the channels of progress. Money alone will not solve the "problems." We are often told in the South that the "new Negro" needs "more manners" and more self-respect. It is true. manners and self-respect are very important, but these alone will not solve the "problem." I know of nothing that will add to the solution of this problem more or quicker than a *Christian* education. By *Christian* education, I mean that form of education in which Christ is a teacher and his truth fundamental in the life and work of the teacher, in which the Christ-life is magnified in the subject taught, whether it be geology, botany, Greek, Latin, English, blacksmithing, carpentry or farming. In this light and truth, the student gets a greater vision of the ideal life and catches an inspiration that sees God himself full of his glory, beauty and power, and in every thing. It may be called common education, primary education, secondary education, higher education, or industrial education, but if it is not Christian education, it is without the guarantees of power to meet the problems before us. Christianity without education lacks moving, living, active and intelligent permanent efficiency. The missionary societies of the North realized the importance of Christian education when they sent the Yankee schoolteachers into the South with the speller in one hand and the Bible in the other. It would be difficult to conceive what the conditions of the South would have been had it not been for these two regenerating influences of education and Christianity backed by the lives of those early teachers. *They set the standards of life for us.* With the surety of Christian education the money problem, the industrial problem, the franchise problem, the morals and manners problem, the self-respect problem and all the other problems will be rightly met and equitably "solved." A great deal is being said as to some particular kind of education which the Negro should have. Some hold that he should have an industrial education first, that he should do the ordinary things well before he begins with books. When the first settlers landed on American soil the first thing they did was to clear the woods as a matter of necessity, but, at the same time, they built a college. They have planted New England with colleges. They have scattered them all through the West and South. They will continue to do this. They honor labor and they honor learning. I think in this New England spirit, we have our model. Let us labor and learn. We can do both, and since many Negroes from the southern plantations have gone to the northern colleges and carried off many prizes the assertion that he cannot use the higher education has gone to the winds. We have men among us who magnify industrial education, and those also who plead for a higher education. The serious aspect of the discussion between them is that these are often made antagonistic to each other. This antagonistic spirit has divided educators, invaded the homes of the givers and even influenced legislation. *What is needed is all kinds of education.* The Negro certainly needs the higher because he needs educated leaders; needs lawyers who have the education and the manhood to rightly interpret the laws and to protect the oppressed; needs doctors, not quacks, but full-fledged men. The Negro needs educated preachers and educated teachers also. One or two comparatively small colleges can not turn out these leaders for eight or ten millions of people. The Negro needs the education of the best schools in the country. Nothing, absolutely nothing should be done to discourage progress along these lines. This should not be ridiculed as it sometimes has been. We certainly need industrial education also. We need to know how to do things, how to build houses, make brick, to work in metals, to make all sorts of furniture, to do any kind of planning, to put up every kind of machinery; and we should know how to make that machinery. *We need to know how to do anything any one else does, and to do it well.* The marts are full of ordinary men. The colleges should train leaders and exceptional men. To be a leader in any kind of industrial work one must be a draftsman. To be a first-class draftsman one must know how to draw lines and make finer distinctions and calculations than those made in arithmetic. This required a knowledge of higher mathematics and often a knowledge of another language. These two branches that are absolutely necessary even for a very first-class mechanic are a part of what constitutes a high education in most of our college. If one is to be an educated agriculturist he will be lost without chemistry, and here again he must have mathematics. The education to make one a first-class chemist in the line of agriculture will class him in the best colleges. My contention is this, if we are to be educated in any line we should seek the best there is in that particular line, not because we are Negroes but because we are men. American conditions have made the Negro in America what he is. He is here, by no choice of his own, but he is a native, to live and to work out his destiny on American soil. His life must co-ordinate with that of the community. His moral and mental instruction must be along the same lines. It is against reason and against the teachings of history to suppose that all the Negroes are to be only caterers, and that forever. They will accept no teaching and no theory of life that will separate them from the rest of men and decree them as a class to a life of drudgery. They have the common rights of man which all good people will finally acknowledge, and it is right that the Negro should stand for these rights. If, e.g., the college has made my white brother what he is, it will make my black brother what he should be. If the various technical schools of the country will give the hand of my white brother dexterity they will do the same for his black brother. I think it incompatible with God's thought of the brotherhood of man that there should be a differentiation in the occupations based on color. No, give each an equal chance, whether in school or out, in the work of life. Let us aspire for the best that can be secured. If the Negro boy is a real student and wants to go to college, encourage him to get ready, help him on and send him on. If he has mechanical skill and the mind to master the intricacies of mechanics, encourage him, help him on and send him to the best technical school you can, for the race needs leaders in every kind of work. The higher the education of every kind, and the better the training, the better will be the leadership.

APPENDIX 4

In 1931, T.S. Inborden wrote an article on the agricultural conditions in the south after the depression and some effects it had on the black farmer. He was encouraging the farmers of color to continue to farm, if possible, and never acknowledge defeat.

"A MESSAGE TO THE FARMER"
BY
THOMAS SEWELL INBORDEN
BRICKS, NORTH CAROLINA, 1931

The biblical injunction says, "Line upon line and precept upon precept." It might have said with equal emphasis that example is better than precept. The present depression has given rise to as any nostrums as there are individuals and from all the nostrums there is not yet one cynosure. One guess is as good as another. So, here we go. Since the present and most efficient incumbent has filled the governor's chair in Raleigh he has put on a programme to, "Live at Home". His gesture has been much in the form of a personal demonstration on the part of all the state salons. I do not know of any programme anywhere in the South that has been more constructive or better obeyed. There never has been more food stuff produced in eastern North Carolina than has been produced this year. I have traveled far and wide in this section and every where there are prodigious crops of white and sweet potatoes, turnips greens, tomatoes, field and garden peas, beans of all varieties, oats, corn, molasses cane, a varied assortment of odd vegetables, peaches, apples, grapes, hogs, sheep, grapes that are native to North Carolina and still great fields of cotton, peanuts, and tobacco. There never has been such a yield of peanuts. Nature ha been lavish in spit of the idiosyncrasies of the weather. The departure from the normal year is the great amount of fruit and vegetables canned for Winter. Those who could not buy the jars have dried it out in the baking sun. I visited one school, the State Normal School at Elizabeth City, where they had canned eight thousand quarts from only eighteen acres of land and expect to butcher twenty-five thousand pounds of pork. I saw the hogs in preparation for this slaughter. From this small acreage, has gone all over the state and I expect throughout the country inspiration and hope. This project has been of double value. it has helped to keep the students in school and has helped them to get in a most practical way the lesson of economy. They have also learned by doing. They are sure to pass this information along to their parents. I later visited many homes in a radius of one hundred miles and found thousands of cans of all sizes and mechanism filled with canned foods of every sort. Here were gallon crocks, half gallon jars, quart and pint sizes, tumblers, bottles filled with apples, peaches, pears, berries, tomatoes, grapes, figs, etc. indicating that there will be no hunger in that cabin or cottage this Winter. That is correct. Add to this that bunch of porkers out there near the water melon patch and you have a double guarantee against a growling stomach. Tobacco and cotton should be legislated out of commission since their voluntary reduction and efficient marketing can not be controlled. They have been an alibi that have gotten the farmer barely enough to eat and to wear. Their production taxes all of his physical resources and reserve, keeps his children in ignorance, defeminates his wife and daughters and devitalizes every refined and social instinct in the home. The greatest beneficiary is the speculator and the fertilizer man. There are thousands and thousands of farmers who have worked from dawn until long after dark preserving this ancient tradition who will have absolutely nothing to show for their labors but a writ of ejection from the time merchant, the fertilizer man or the landlord. Nor a bright picture I assure you. We must admit there is great utility in cotton. There is no fabric so generally utilized in every industry. Three-fourths of the world's population is not today half clad. This proves the futility of the argument of over production. If cotton sold in eastern North Carolina today for fifteen cents, the merchants' stores would be depleted in ten days and the trains could not bring dry goods from the factories fast enough to meet the demand. No, it can not be over production. It is rather due to manipulation and laws. We need higher up a Theodore Roosevelt who is willing to express the opinions of his convictions. Well, the least I say about tobacco the better I am liked. It has its use the same as other poisonous herbs Its use is greatly abused. The Satanic Majesty could not have devised a better instrument with which to devitalize the mental and physical stamina of our youth. The only hope of speeding up production and prices is to put more of our children and girls to using it. I have no apology to make to friend or foe for the stand I take against its use. The efficacy of your philosophy is in the efficiency of its product. Examine yourself and see if the use of it has not retarded your efficiency. No real farmer in eastern North Carolina is expecting to beg bread this winter. They are far above the bread line. If the smaller farmer and share cropper is in the bread line, it is because he has worked under conditions for which he is not alone responsible. He has inherited a tradition that is certainly national in the South. Nothing short of a revolution in methods of farming and farm procedure will change it. We are undergoing that revolution at this time. The highways are full of tramps. They are men, women and children. Most of them are day laborers and industrial workers. They are poorly clad and hungry. Their facial expression gives rise to their inward thoughts and their anguish of soul. It is not their fault that they are hungry and tramping and begging. Twenty-five cents a hundred pounds for picking cotton can not feed a family. The average pickers can not earn more than fifty cents a day. Fifty cents will not buy one good meal for one working man. These prices simply produce thieves, highway robbers and burglars. It means a run on YOUR poultry house, your hog pen, your person and home. DO YOU BLAME THEM?

The farmer is the back bone of the country. The farmer enjoys the least the luxuries of his own production. He enjoys the least the luxuries common to our civilization. His house is ill planned, poorly built, the least furnished, and his family usually half clad. Things generally have a ramshackle appearance, his hours of labor are as long and irksome that he has no spirit for cleaning up or for domestic enjoyment at home. If he reads, he is too tired to get much help because he is too tired to digest what he reads. The radio and the music box only puts him to sleep. So, he grows old, decrepid and nausea. For him, the whole social and industrial fabric are out of joint and need to be recast. Here and there nomic conditions seem to be propitious to a few. But for the average farmer the condition is disquieting. What is the best help for these industrialists and day laborers who line the highways and who are becoming a menace to organized society? Eastern North Carolina abounds with sluggish rivers, creeks, marshes, small streams, malarial swamps and what not. Create a condition by which these people can be given work clearing up these recesses and cess pools and sluggish streams and thus, bring this waste land into practical use. Again create conditions by which these same people can buy this land and build themselves homes. Here they can work out their salvation. If the public must feed them, feed them to good purposes. In idleness, we must feed them in jail or out. It is cheaper to feed them out of jail and give them a chance to eventually feed themselves. These tramps are not all trifling and lazy. They are simply the victims of an economic situation for which they had no part. Society and the controlling element at large are responsible for the present condition. Most of it is bound up in the political issues of the day. Alleviation must come from the same sources. These poor devils did not make the laws and they had little to do with electing the men who did make the laws. Supply and demand are always supposed to dictate prices but here is an incontrovertible fact that here are millions of bushels of wheat, millions of bales of cotton millions of pounds of tobacco, millions of bushels of corn. Three-fourths of the earths population without clothes and food. All these people needing the necessities of which there is an over production but no money with which to buy. The trouble is in the political manipulation with home and foreign matters.

A few words to the farmer in conclusion

You grow the things first that you must have to sustain your family. The less traditional money crops you plant the better off you will be, plant now for next year. Put in small grains for your poultry, your hogs and other farm stock. Get another cow or one better than you have. Prune your fruit trees this Fall. Spray the same before cold weather. Spray again next Spring after blooming season. Get your hot bed ready for tomatoes, cabbage and sweet potato plants, and be the first on the market. Your products must be superior in quality and early on the market. I know men who will come to your door for your vegetables and pay you the cash before leaving but your products must have superiority. If you do not know how to get quality, the national Government and the state government will furnish you the men and printed matter on how it is done. The bulk of our population is urban and less than one third of us are furnishing all the food for this vast herd of people. Millions of dollars worth of food stuff is coming from the far west to our seaboard cities because we fail to meet the competition right here at home. You who live in the midst of the population have failed to do your duty. If conditions over which you had no control cause you to lose your farm, let her go and buy another, a smaller farm, and keep on fighting. Never, never acknowledge defeat. A busy man is always a safe man. Smile and keep going.

APPENDIX 5

T.S. Inborden wrote an article on "The Progress of Negro Farmers in the Community" in 1911. I pose the question how many farmers of color can be found in the same areas of the North Carolina Community in 1995?

THE PROGRESS OF NEGRO FARMERS IN THE COMMUNITY
BY
T.S. INBORDEN
BRICK, NORTH CAROLINA, 1911

By this community, I mean Halifax, Nash and Edgecombe counties, North Carolina. Halifax County is one of the largest counties in the state comprising 681 square miles. It has a population of over thirty-thousand. It is a part of the black belt of the state and it is safe to say that the Negroes constitute two-thirds of the population of the county. They are engaged in the various occupations but the community is particularly a farming section. A very large proportion of the Negroes are working for wages on the farms. Another portion of them are share croppers, this means generally, that the Negro furnishes the labor and the land lord furnishes the land, teams, implements and food. This is subject to various modifications. The exact agreement often depends upon the integrity and ability of the contracting parties to make a bargain. Another portion of this Negro population owns it farms and farms on its own account. It is this portion of the population to which we wish especially to direct our attention. It would be interesting to know how many farms in these three counties were owned and controlled by Negroes at the close of the war. It would be most unnatural if there was a single one. It is not strange to know that when the colored people were given their freedom, some of those who were loyal to their owners, were also given a home. This home was not limited to forty acres and a mule. As we have studied the matter we have found in various sections farms comprising from two hundred to a thousand acres which were left to some of the colored people by their owners. I have found many farms so left but which have since gone into the hands of other people. This fact is not strange either, these people had been working under the direction of a master mind who directed every kind of work that was to be done. Their part was simply to do as told. When they were given land, that brought responsibilities of another sort. They did not always know what to do next. The possession of land brought responsibilities which their former training had not enabled them to assume. They were unlettered and worked with their competitors to a great disadvantage. They had to do their own thinking and it was not their habit to think through such responsibilities as the ownership of land had brought. Here and there are a few farms intact in the hands of those to whom they were left. The men who have held their farms all these years are those who have superior mental ability and ancestral endowment. This fact, to begin with, put them in a class by themselves. The most interesting fact we have to contemplate is the thousands and thousands of acres owned by Negroes who started with absolutely nothing. In Halifax county, there are 53,947 acres of land owned by Negroes and valued at $337,236. This land could not be bought today for double that amount if sold at private sale. These Negroes own 353 town lots and houses valued at $161,275. They have 1,407 horses valued at $110,765. They have 875 mules valued at $72,949.

They have 3,119 cattle valued at $50,465. They have 6,802 hogs valued at $20,620. This includes only the taxable property of one thousand Negroes of Halifax county. This may seem small as compared with the great wealth of the county, but it is great when one thinks that this is the valuation of land and stock of only one thousand farmers who started forty-five years ago with nothing. Not only that, if Negroes had half the opportunities and half the encouragement which their neighbors have had, their real estate value would be three times what it is today. The three townships which are probably the most progressive of any in the county are, Scotland Neck, Weldon and Enfield. Weldon and Scotland Neck townships are located on the Roanoke River. The three towns are prominent and progressive stations on the Atlantic Coast Line railroad. This outlet with the Roanoke river for Weldon and Scotland Neck gives the farmers and others a natural advantage over those in other sections of the county. We have been particularly interested in the statistics of Enfield township. The Negroes of this township own 12,392 acres of land valued at $57,125. They own 52 town lots valued at $19,000. They own 146 horses valued at $7,550. They own 144 mules valued at $11,661. They own 295 cattle and cows valued at $3,899. They own 676 hogs valued at $1,482. These figures are significant not only for their own values but also from the fact that they show that the Negroes are buying land, horses, mules, cows and hogs.

In a recent meeting of Negro farmers, investigation was made and it was found that 56 percent of those present had their own farms and 75 percent of them owned their own teams. This was a meeting of farmers from the various sections of Halifax, Edgecombe and Nash counties These farms have a great many things of value not listed in the inventory above. On a recent visit through the county, I saw great flocks of sheep, geese, turkeys, chickens and many colonies of bees. I saw yards and gardens that would take the prize for cleanliness and neatness anywhere. The floors, chairs and other house furniture were as clean as soap and water could make them. In any cases, the houses had been painted or white washed outside and lathered and plastered inside. In some few instances, the Negroes are connected with the central telephone exchange. They are subscribers to their church papers and many of them take several agricultural papers. The are reading and learning to think for themselves and the result of this is put into their life and work. I am speaking particularly with reference to those who own their own farms and homes. Share croppers and renters will not take care of other peoples property as they would their own. It is not human nature for them to do so. It is the exception when they do and then they must know that they will have an indefinite tenure. The story of how these Negroes get hold of this land is very interesting. Here is a man who has two farms of 182 acres. He has a six room weather boarded house on each farm and has all the necessary farm houses for his stock, tools and farm utensils. He has on one of the farms a store from which he furnishes the immediate community small supplies. He works three horses and has in his family eleven children. His house is painted white, with green blinds on the windows and he has many varieties of flowers and shrubbery about the yard. One of his sons lives on one of the farms and the father lives on the other farm and both are in splendid homes. Nothing contribute to their citizenship more than the fact that they have good homes. Further, along the same road, I met another farmer, Mr. Richard Sanders. I asked him if he cared if I used his name in connection with a short article I was writing, he said "No, use my name if you wish. I have a farm of 36 acres, bought and paid for by the sweat of my own brow and I am not ashamed of it." His house was modern in every way. It had six rooms, was painted white and had a good wide porch and a fence around the yard. There were magnolia trees, crape myrtle and other shrubbery in the yard. He has a number of out houses for his stock, tools and farm supplies. He also had a small store and owned a private school house for his own children. His crops were absolutely clean of weeds and his ditch banks were a model of cleanliness. Here is another farm owned by a man who has a six room two-story house. This farmer has three horses and 140 acres of land under very fine state of cultivation. He has all the necessary out buildings for his use and a secret order hall near the public road for the convenience of its members. Here is another farm of forty-five acres owned by a young man who lives in a six room house which is finished in good style. He own two horses and has in his family seven children. Adjoining this farm is another farm of 33 acres. This farm was a part of a six hundred acre tract of land which was formerly own by this farmer's master. A few years ago the old master died and because of this colored man's loyalty to him all these years since freedom, he gave him this home and thirty three acres. He has built his house similar to the best houses in the community and planted a fine orchard of apple, peach, pear, and plum trees about the place. He works two horses and has a number of children. He lives about four miles from town and is counted as one of the best citizens in the community.

Several years ago a certain tract of land was to be sold about seven miles away from the town of Enfield to a white gentleman with the understanding that if again sold certain colored men who wanted land were to be given a chance to buy it. Almost the same day, one tract of 92 acres was sold to a colored man on four years time. Before the time was out, the amount of eleven hundred dollars was paid and today that farmer has made improvements and has one of the best farms in his community. Last year, this man paid five hundred dollars for a pair of mules and he told me recently that he expected to sell this year, 1911, seventeen hundred dollars worth of cotton. He has grown on his farm other things besides cotton, such as: corn, potatoes, peanuts, peas, water-melons and other things. He is also interested in a saw-mill. Ten years ago, another man who had been working as a share cropper, bought 80 acres of the same tract of land paying for it eight-hundred dollars cash. He has since made good improvements and would not sell it for double what he paid for it.

In the same community about four years ago a two-thousand acre tract was sold to a company of Negro farmers. A few months after the land was bought by these men a lumber company ran a log road through the farm and bought the timber on it. The farm was bought on time but when the timber was sold it enabled the men to make the last payment at once of the entire tract of two-thousand acres. The woods and swamps are being cleared all over this large farm and log houses, probably fifty of them, will this Fall or very soon give way to neat cottages. I visited the farm recently, and was told to drive two miles East from the public road and as many miles North and I would still be on this great farm. I was told by a very prominent white gentleman who is well acquainted with the community that none of the Negroes who own the farms are educated but they were all shrewd and honest men who knew how to make a bargain. The farm as I saw it was under a fine state of cultivation. Fifteen years ago, a man with a large family moved on the Brick School farm as a renter. He had never farmed unless he had some one to "run him". That is some one to take a mortgage on his horses and crops for family provision and farm supplies until the crop was ready to be put on the market. When he had been on our farm six months he told me that since the school made no cash advances to its renters and that since he had to "run himself" that it had cost him one hundred dollars to live up to that time than any year since he had been farming. He was a man who liked to have a good time with his friends and he was fond of today. The school farm restrictions were such that he could not live on the farm, keep up these habits and be honest. He moved to another farm. Then he began to think that the restrictions were right. The more he thought about it the more he fell under his best convictions. He quit his habits and joined the church. Today he lives on his own farm of two hundred and twenty-two acres. He has four horses, seven cows, a great many hogs, a cotton gin and engine. When I was at his home some weeks ago, he had just placed an order for a saw mill. He lives in a log house which he expects to replace when he gets his saw mill so that he can saw his own lumber. He had seven years in which to pay for his farm but he made the last payment on it in five years. He has a fine crop this year and has planted a fine orchard. He has also built a number of farm houses for his stock and tools. He told me that he had not tasted a drop of whiskey in ten years. This is the part of the secret.

Some years ago, another man got the idea that he could better his conditions by going North. This man was formerly an overseer on the Brick School farm. He went to work on the public works in Jersey City. It was not long before the work closed and he was out of work. He soon ran out of money. He told me that he wrote his wife to send him railroad fare home and that the last dime he had was spent for a water-melon which he divided with another fellow. I saw him only a few days after he returned home. He rented a farm five miles from town and when I visited him I found him felling the trees in the swamps and hauling them away to town in an ox cart for firewood. Today he has bought and paid for 63 ares of land which he has literally dug out of the woods and swamps The old log hut has given place to a nice frame addition. He has every convenience for farming and has also put out fruit trees and made other improvements which put him in a class with the best farmers in the community. He never misses a farmers meeting at the Brick School and says that he is going with me the next time I go to attend the Hampton Farmers' Conference. Here is another farm owned by Mr. Hilliard Phillips. This farmer lives just across the line in Nash County. The story would be incomplete without reference to what he has done. He is probably the most unique character in the community in which he lives. When the school was organized sixteen years ago I made it my business to visit the Negro farmers in the various sections of Edgecombe county to find out for my self their progress and their possibilities. I found this farmer some twelve miles down in the county. He was little different from many others whom I visited except that he was more positive in his conceptions and was absolutely honest. His philosophy was quite original and equally sound, by getting him to put two of his children in the Brick School I was brought more into contact with him. I learned him better, He was a good renter and had rented since freedom. On one occasion he tried to buy a farm but this was in a community where the health of his family was very poor and he gave it up on account of discouragement. I persuaded him that he could buy as well as rent if he found the right man from whom to buy. I believed there were many good white men in the community who would be glad to sell him a small farm. It took him several years to find the right place and he was four years paying for his farm. He has a five room house in which he lives and has built several more houses on his farm in which his married sons live. His farm has on it 103 acres. When he bought it, it was very poor, I remember hearing him ask Dr. Taite Butler who was assisting us in our farmers' meeting some years ago, how to take an old worn out farm and make it pay for itself. Dr. Taite Butler replied "rotate", "What do you mean by "rotate" asked the old gentleman". If you ask him today how he paid for his farm he will tell you that Dr. Taite Butler's "rotation" paid for it. I said above that he was not very different from other Negroes in his community, today he would not smoke the best cigar made nor drink the best glass of whiskey produced. Turning back on these habits sixteen years ago has given his body stability, his mind counterpoise, his family a home and made him one of the best citizens in the community. He does not know one letter from another but his advice is sought by old and young, the read and the unread. Remember, he is nearly seventy-five years old and has made this wonderful progress during the last years of his life.

Negro Migration to the Cities

The matter of Negro migration to the cities will be easily solved if it can be made possible for colored people to buy small farms. In this community there are large farms being sold all the time. They average in area from two hundred to two-thousand acres. Negroes can not buy on such a large scale and expect to pay out. They need farms from twenty-five to one hundred acres. Some of them can pay cash for that size farms. They need to buy it in communities where they can add to their holdings from time to time. We could locate a hundred prosperous Negro farmers in five miles of the Joseph Keasbey Brick, Agricultural, Industrial and Normal School near Enfield, North Carolina, within a year if we could buy small farms with easy payments. All the farmers named above have large families and practically none of their boys have the city fever. They have homes and a place to work where they have a future. These boys can put out a tree on their father's farm, watch it grow, bear fruit and later build their houses near it. There is future to that. Put the schools in these centers and put in good teachers. Keep them there in spite of Negro fusses and Negro gossip. The authorities ought to know by personal communication and visitation that these teachers are what they ought to be. I know of too many communities where the school house for political reasons have been moved several miles from the Negro population. This reduces the school attendance and is a source of great discouragement to the people who want to educate their children. if Negroes can not get the best advantages in the community in which they live, they move to the cities and towns. This is good sense. Good public roads will also help to keep the best Negroes in the country. Equality in the administration of the laws will also help to retard the migration of the Negroes to the towns. Some of the worst lawbreakers in some communities are immune from arrest, trial and punishment while others are snatched up for the most trivial offenses and sent to the chain gang. Good society can not be maintained among any people when there is an inequality in the administration of justice. The ignorant know when there is an inequality in the enforcement of law as well as the intelligent. They are unrestful and resentful. Like leaven this restlessness and resentfulness permeates the society in which they move. Hence the course of least resistance they go direct to the cities and towns.

I doubt seriously if the majority of Negroes owned their farms whether such ownership would establish them in the good wishes of their white friends. Every Negro who owns his farm takes that much labor, himself, wife and children out of the labor market. This reduces the white man's help and his purse, and with the large plantations this reduction in labor would retard seriously the Southern Farm output. Truly they might bring in foreign labor but it will take many years to adjust Southern conditions to the exactions of foreign help. Certainly the men who have always had Negro help would not at once submit to such exactions. Southern society would certainly have to under go a transformation that the old fathers never dreamed of. This conglomeration introduced into Southern society would bring about such conditions that I imagine the father of the Southern Confederacy would tremble in his tomb. No, there is a better way. There are thousands and thousands of acres of land that are not in cultivation and will not be in cultivation until broken up into small farms and in possession of those who are immune to the climate and who know the conditions. These lands might be cleared and ditched by the government or by the state but they will not be kept clear until the small farmers get hold of them and depend upon them for their living. Then will they be kept cleared, ditched and cultivated. The general diffusion of agricultural knowledge and high ideals of Christian citizenship, personal respect for woman-hood and man-hood, whether white or black, engendered by a liberal academic training will bring about conditions entirely compatible and increase the southern agricultural output. I was at the state farm of North Carolina several years ago and I think I never saw such a fine farm of produce. I was told by the manager that they could grow such crops only because they could control their labor. The large planter must control his labor if he runs a thousand-acre farm economically. This can not be done unless the state passes certain laws which enable the large planters to do this. When the state passes laws to enable farmers to control their labor by certain contracts which are unintelligible to the ordinary laborer, it thwarts good government, liberty and freedom and engenders nothing but hatred toward those who seek the execution of these laws. This creates a state of peonage in substance if not in fact. It creates discontent and lawlessness on the part of the laborer. These large farms can not be run without an immense lot of help. Where a lot of people are thrown together as they are on many of the big farms there is bad sanitation and bad morals. This incubus will infest the best society.

T.S. Inborden, 1911

APPENDIX 6

Thomas Sewell Inborden walked, talked and assisted many people during his long and successful years as an educator. It was at his new home of North Carolina that he communicated and corresponded with friends, students, faculty and his bee honey customers. I have listed the names and towns that his friends lived in or were present there at one time. This detailed list should be a legacy for future years for people to know that many citizens of North Carolina, especially in the areas of the cities mentioned knew T.S. Inborden an early educator of color.

SELECTED LIST OF T.S. INBORDEN'S FRIENDS, STUDENTS, FACULTY, HONEY BEE CUSTOMERS AND CORRESPONDENTS.

FRIENDS, STUDENTS, FACULTY CUSTOMERS AND CORRESPONDENTS	CITIES AND COUNTIES IN NORTH CAROLINA (OTHERWISE STATED)
William Mitchell	Enfield
Gladys Cooper	Battlesboro
Ben Brodile	Nashville
John D.W. Ray	Greensboro
Jackson Battle	Sharpsburg
Bessie Austin	Battlesboro
Jonathan Hilliard	Nashville
Arthur Cherry	Hassell
Annie Labbs	Enfield
Alice Barrington	Nashville
Mattie Harris	Nashville
Martha Stanton	Snow Hill
Mavis Williams	Battlesboro
Henry Myrick	Ringwood
Victoria Robinson	Whitakers
Sarah Lancaster	Castalia
Johnnie Fobbs	Enfield
Ella Kimbal	Whitakers
Louise Burnette	Whitakers
Ella Harrison	Nashville
Quenesta Allen	Whitakers
Lula Woodard	Whitakers
Annie Lyon	Rocky Mount
John Watson	Whitakers
Calvin Yancey	Tarboro
Jessie Cooper	Enfield
Ida Hines	Rocky Mount
Arthur Frier	Rocky Mount
Willie Woodly	Nashville
James Hines	Battlesboro
Mary Prince	Whitakers
Bessie Ridley	Enfield
Issac Bunn	Enfield
Katie Powell	Rocky Mount

FRIENDS, STUDENTS, FACULTY, CUSTOMERS AND CORRESPONDENTS	CITIES AND COUNTIES IN NORTH CAROLINA (OTHERWISE STATED)
Blenne Powell	Rocky Mount
Lena Powell	Rocky Mount
Mamie Battle	Nashville
Ardelia Garrett	Whitakers
Lonnie Perry	Whitakers
Sarah Byrd	Whitakers
Jessie Baker	Kingsboro
Roland Smith	Corretoe
Jessie Williams	Oak City
Reddick Williams	Snow Hill
Etta Taylor	Bricks
Jake Armstrong	Enfield
Rosa Harrison	Enfield
Lucy Wills	Enfield
Oscar Haze	Whitakers
Thomas Mitchell	Enfield
John Sexton	Battleboro
Mamie Norman	Enfield
Olivia Demery	Enfield
Elnora Alston	Battlesboro
Georgeanna Bryant	Battlesboro
Sallie E. Whitaker	Enfield
Delia Holland	Nashville
Sarah Williams	Battlesboro
Luther Arrington	Bricks
Lula Manor	Whitakers
Magie Lee Williams	Whitakers
Carrie Williams	Whitakers
Arthur Cooper	Nashville
Lillie Horner	Whitakers
Middy Baker	Rocky Mount
Daniel Coley	Nashville
Milton Taylor	Scotland Neck
George Kenny	Rocky Mount
James Davis	Nashville
Lillie M. Cofield	Whitakers
Edna Peppers	Whitakers
Mamie Powell	Whitakers
Martha Bryant	Whitakers
Franker Cooper	Whitakers
Causal Robinson	Whitakers
Mary Cofield	Whitakers
Sadie Mayo	Whitakers
Hattie Taylor	Whitakers
John C. Battle	Nashville
Julius Perry	Nashville
John Brown	Liffett
Frances Cofield	Whitakers
Selma Pittman	Whitakers
Joanna Williams	Whitakers
Rena Hines	Rocky Mount

FRIENDS, STUDENTS, FACULTY, CUSTOMERS AND CORRESPONDENTS	CITIES AND COUNTIES IN NORTH CAROLINA (OTHERWISE STATED)
Lonnie Gaylor	Whitakers
Mack Sloane	Enfield
Mary Sexton	Battlesboro
Annie Battle	Castalia
Moses Hunter	Tarboro
Harry Barn	Whitakers
Jesse Perkins	Enfield
Sam Brinkley	Enfield
George Edwards	Nashville
Gertrude Byrd	Whitakers
Oscar Pittman	Scotland Neck
Johnnie Hines	Scotland Neck
John D. Baker	Kinston
Isham Coble	Kinston
James Whitaker	Enfield
Wilson Wills	Enfield
Joe Ballow	Rocky Mount
Gertrude Wesley	Rocky Mount
David L. Harris	Nashville
Buril Taylor	Whitakers
Perry Keys	Whitakers
Ella Hedgefeld	Castalia
Anie M. Lyons	Whitakers
Pearl J. Thorne	Battlesboro
Mack Baker	Kingsboro
Allene Robinson	Whitakers
Annie C. Young	Whitakers
Robert Peterson	Wilson
Angusta Freeman	Nashville
Lucile Robinson	Whitakers
James Lyons	Rocky Mount
Irene Alston	Battlesboro
Jack Hind	Scotland Neck
Bessie Duke	Whitakers
Rosa Perry	Nashville
Mary Burnette	Bricks
Ethel Sharpe	Whitakers
Jesse Edwards	Tillery
John Pittman	Bricks
Freda Hill	Battlesboro
Willie Bell	Enfield
Elbert Daniel	Bricks
Mary Kimbal	Whitakers
Norman Lucas	Enfield
Jack Pittman	Enfield
Frank Taylor	Whitakers
Sarah Rainey	Freehold, New Jersey
Henrietta Armstrong	Washington, D.C.
Silas Artis	New Haven, Connecticut
Julia Milner	Battle Creek, Michigan
Ida Belle Arrington	Kittrell

FRIENDS, STUDENTS, FACULTY, CUSTOMERS AND CORRESPONDENTS	CITIES AND COUNTIES IN NORTH CAROLINA (OTHERWISE STATED)
Mary Williams	Kennansville
Mary Gray	Williamston
John Williams	Windsor
Viola Welch	Snow Hill
Camillus Battle	Nashville
John Moore	Clinton
Katherine Mae Greene	Bridgeton, New Jersey
Flossie Bert	Washington, D.C.
Lucille Wood Cheatman	Washington, D.C.
Archilus Young	Washington, D.C.
Ida Suggs	Indianapolis, Indiana
George Bullock	Louisville, Kentucky
Dorothy Mae Hutchinson	Indianapolis, Indiana
Lena Walden	Paris, Virginia
Nello Pittman	Brooklyn, New York
Susie Adam Lighston	Chester, Pennsylvania
Leo Meyer Sultan	New Bern
Gossie Clarke	Jamaica, New York

APPENDIX 7

An inventory of the T.S. Inborden papers included a Workmen's Time Book for the school years of 1896, 1898 1897, and 1900

Brick School WORKMEN'S TIME SHEET

1896	1897	1898
James Scott	Bivens Coleman	John Arrington
Willie Taylor	Ben Macks	John Jones
Vergil Garrett	Kelly Lewis	Rufus Lewis
Ausburn Williams	James Laurence	Silas Arrington
Eddie Ross	Jenia Hunter	Henry Edward
George Wilkins	David Laurence	Willie Petway
Frank Mayo	Pleasant Wilkins	Jake Crawley
George Garrett		Sam Edmond
Cad Davis	**1900**	Ead Arrington
Oscar Garrett		
Billie Williams	Major Tillery	
	George Adams	
	William Garrett	
	Diamond Hawkins	

APPENDIX 8

One of T.S. Inborden's friends was the distinguished educator and administrator, Dean William Pickens. Pickens had worked at the National headquarters, NAACP, New York City, and was a professor and administrator at Morgan State University, Baltimore, Maryland. Pickens wrote Inborden a letter and included an interesting paper about the 60th year.

THE 60TH YEAR

"HATE ONLY HATE, FEAR ONLY COWARDICE"

BY
WILLIAM PICKENS

Not yet am I 60 years of age, but this day, the fifteenth of January 1940, I start climbing on that year; and if I live until January 15, 1941, I will have achieved it, day by day, rung by rung, -- up the ladder from the bottom to the top of the 6th decade. There is much that I could say, for in 59 years I have been very conscious of more than 50 of them. In fact, I remember since I was a little over two years old. That line of verse -- "Hate only hate, fear only cowardice"-- was written when I was 19 years old, and a Sophomore. It was the last line of a sonnet, written from the climax of an oration. This line is all I now remember of those iambic pentameters. But not once in 40 years have I ever forgotten the sincerity and the heroism of that spirit. I could write correct verse, but it was no great poetry. However, I remember that the bright teacher who heard the oration, thought that I had quoted the verses of some great poet, and was reluctantly convinced that the sonnet was my own. What have I learned in those 40 years, since that sonnet? --

That it is better to be hated than to hate,
That it is better to love than to be loved,
That it is better to receive evil than to give it,
That it is better to be lied against than to lie
That it is less disgraceful to be cheated than to cheat,
That it is less of a loss to be robbed than to commit robbery
That the trill of the open fight is not to be found in treachery, That honesty is far more reliable than shrewdness,
That it is better to forgive than to revenge,
That friends are better than things; and friendship the chief gain
That in monetary valuation, one dollar is worth 100 cents; but in other values, one honest cent is worth more than 100 dishonest dollars,
That one is not polite <u>to some</u> one <u>else</u>, but rather polite <u>out of oneself</u>. Politeness is rather of the subject than of the object; that therefore the meanest person cannot be so low that a really polite person will not feel the need of being polite to that meanest human,
That while money is certainly one of the means of living, there are many other means far more essential and valuable to a life. (If only young people could see that clearly -- and early!)
That the mind is its own hell or its own heaven, -- either more to be feared than hell or more to be revered than heaven,

That we love or we hate others for what we do toward them, and not for what they do toward us; that therefore the loving or the hating spirit is only secondarily dependent upon the object of that love or of that hate, but is primarily dependent upon the one who loves or hates. What sort of world would this world be if one started at 19 with the mentality of 59? It would be a safe world but would it be more courageous? It would be saner, but would it be as thrilling? How many people I have had trying to kill me in 40 years! But I have had equally as many standing to defend me. Therefore, I still believe in the Human Race. If at 59 I should start another 40 years, as at 19, I should at the next end reverse none of these conclusions but rather would intensify them.

"Life is real, life is earnest."

William Pickens

APPENDIX 9

Charles H. Barker wrote an early Alma Mater for Brick School,

BRICK ALMA MATER

1. Our dear Alma Mater, beloved J. K. Brick,
   Our praises shall ever be thine;
     Thou fillest the lamp, and thou trimmest the wick,
   That brighter our pathway may shine;
     Though varied our birthplace, and devious our lot,
   We came to thy portals to learn
     The requisite wisdom by which men are taught
   True values of things to discern,
     That our lives may to others with blessings be fraught,
   Wherever our footsteps may turn.

2. True wisdom, you teach, can't be purchased with gold,
   It begins with the fear of the Lord;
     And wise in the youth who doth character mold
   By the precepts contained in God's word,
     Each day should be filled up with useful employ,
   As in idleness danger doth lurk;
     For mind and for body, strength, wisdom and joy,
   All come to the people who work;
     And certainly rue it, will each girl and boy
   Who ever plain duty doth shirk.

3. Our dear Alma Mater, as forward we press
   To reach high ideals you hold,
     We're longing these virtues divine to possess,
   Worth far more than silver and gold;
     Thou teachest the richest of men here below
   Are the ones who do most for mankind;
     That the wisest are those who are striving to grow
   In tune with the Infinite Mind;
     That joy to be lasting needs out as in flow;
   And these truths in our hearts we will bind.

Charles H. Barker

APPENDIX 10

A former Brick student, class of 1907, George L. Bullock showed his respect and appreciation for Thomas Sewell Inborden. On April 2, 1960, he wrote a poem in honor of Inborden.

HONORABLE T.S. INBORDEN
(THE MODERN MOSES)

When the Civil War was nearing its end,
  and the armies were marching to and fro,
General Estes bought a tract of land
  where a great institution would grow.

And on it he grew many kinds of crops
  As most Southern farmers can,
But, in the end he failed and lost,
  For God had a nobler plan.

Mrs. Julia Brick redeemed the farm With thoughts of giving Negroes a lift, And the A.M.A. was pioneering such work In the South, so to them it was a gift.

Somewhere back in the Virginian hills
  God had raised up a man
Whom he sent in eighteen ninety five
  To transform a most heathen clan.

T.S. Inborden, a Moses of modern times
  Came down to lead the way,
Out of a wilderness of ignorance and despair,
  Into the light of a brighter day.

He slept on a table in an old dwelling house,
  While the cats and dogs had their fights,
The mosquitoes and bugs crawled over him
  And made his the most miserable nights.

And finally the dwelling house was burned,
  And the opening of school was delayed
Till money for a building could be raised,
  And five thousand by Mrs. Brick was paid.

The building was soon completed and then,
  They named it BENEDICT HALL,
There was a laundry, a kitchen, a diner and baths,
  A class room and bed rooms for all.

Two teachers came to work that fall,
  And a matron, Mrs. Davis came too,
Day pupils came from miles around
  But the boarders were very few.

Now Mr. Inborden's big task had begun,

And somewhere in his one-horse-shay
He followed a trail to some lonely home
  Tho it lead him many miles away.

And there he broke the wonderful news
  About the work he'd been sent to do,
The work that enlightened many girls and boys,
  The work that enlightened me and you.

And, as he so nobly spread the light,
  More and more students enrolled,
Many who were living in ignorance
  Came running to join his fold.

And soon new BENEDICT was capacity filled,
  The desire for knowledge was so keen,
A building must be had to house the boys,
  This need was so plainly seen.

So BREWSTER HALL was the next in line,
  Then BEARD, and INGRAHAM, then a shop,
Teacher's cottages, the principal's home,
  The chain of progress could not stop.

He made BRICK's campus a beauty spot
  In the eastern part of the state,
Those buildings and campus once kept in prime
  Alas have fallen to fate.

But, the influence which he wielded here
  Will live on and on forevermore,
Tho, years ago he passed away
  To his reward on that heavenly shore.

The lives that he touched and brought to light
  Are scattered throughout our land,
And we're proud to be his protege,
  And belong to the BRICKITE's band.

In sacred memory to his great name
  We pledge to the world our best,
Until that day when our work is done,
  And we join him up there with the blest.

So, may this cottage in which he dwelt
  Forever be to him a shrine,
And mark this spot where that great man lived,
  In the state of the long leaf pine.

By George L. Bullock
Class of 1907
4/2/60

APPENDIX 11

T.S. Inborden was very pleased with his article on "Civics and Art". He would send printed copies of this article to many of his friends throughout the years.

CIVICS AND ART

BY

T.S. INBORDEN

Civics is the science that teaches about citizenship. To be a citizen means that we should fit into the economic order of our best environment. We must have food, clothes and shelter. To obtain these necessities we must work. The theory of our government is based on intelligence in the acquiring of these necessities of life. Plato said more than two thousand years ago. "**To teach a skill is merely to train, but to teach an art is to educate.**" Teaching itself is an art. Education may be considered an applied science. Art is more than an applied science. It is the creation of the beautiful that is universally pleasing. Art is the highest expression of the innermost soul of man. If it is not in the soul it can not be expressed. It is the attaining of an ideal. It is said the French mechanic works for wages, a salary and for profits. His highest ideal is not in working for these compensations but he tries to turn out the best machine. The American works for the same wages, salaries and profits but his ideal is in the financial compensation. Both make cars, but each has a different ideal. One is in it for the financial rewards and the other works the harder to express an ideal that lends itself to artistic beauty. This fits into Plato's definition of art. "**To teach a skill is merely to train, to teach an art is to educate.**" Without skill in human mechanism we can not fit into the economic order of any environment. The Administration of civic laws is not in itself an expression of art except as the acts of administration give expression to beauty, to perfection in design, to planning, to happiness, to harmony, and to the creation of the highest ideals. The civic centre of the city of Los Angeles is a fine example of what I am trying to get to you. Here the municipal buildings are arranged symmetrically and with such utility that one who looks at them from some central point is enchanted and bewitched by their beauty and setting. The same might be said of the State House of Minnesota. The dome in the capitol of the capital city of our nation has been incomplete for many years because the painter had an ideal and died before completing his job and no other painter has been able to conceive of the same ideal. The design has never been carried out. In an art gallery in San Francisco I saw a painting. It represented a herd of stock, an undulating landscape, several valleys, great mountains in the back ground. A maid was milking one of the cows which had kicked over the bucket of milk and the stool on which she was sitting. The shadow of the cow was cast some distance away. Another cow was standing under a willow tree just across a little rippling stream. Back was the landscape on which were mountain sheep and deer, a few shrubs, rocks and other things to give the scenery a rural setting. Beyond this were some deer and elk that had been mounted. Away up in the mountain some thousands of feet away you might see other animals feeding at their leisure. All was on the canvass, of course except the mounted animals. The work was so well conceived and so well executed that the eye could hardly see where the painting stopped and the mounted pieces began. This is art in its highest conception. National parks are maintained all over the United States as a matter of civic pride. These parks include millions of acres of land. The areas are not particularly adapted for farm use but are mainly places where people may go for recreation, pleasure, recuperation, study, change in environment, which is so conducive to good health. The government is putting thousands of dollars in these reclamations. These mountain retreats are already places of natural art but a little help here and there makes them most accessible to man. These parks are all over the country. Their reservation is the finest demonstration of the civic pride of the whole country. They must be not only accessible but they must be beautiful as well. Accessibility and beauty must form the attraction. The United States government is building and maintaining highways running well into thousands of miles. They run through the most barren and some of the most inaccessible places to facilitate travel and business. The adjacent contour of the roads is being made safe, trees, shrubs, and herbaceous plants are being planted as fast as possible. In more states it is against the law for wild flowers to be plucked in two hundred feet of the road. This is a good law and should be supported by every traveler. If one has not the artistic vision he may as well be dead. At least his soul is dead already. All this adds to civic life.

Most of our cities and many of our small towns have laws prescribing the limitation and style of certain buildings. This is as it should be. Civil pride demands that our streets, houses, alleys, and everything under municipal control should be in unison and express the highest ideals. The reflection of our intelligence is at stake. The dark side of life as reflected in old ramshackle buildings, drunks in the alleys and on the front streets, chain gangs here and there do not reflect the best in our civic life. It detracts from the finest art that we might have. I saw a brick front porch a few days ago where the work was so well done that there was not a single criticism to be made. The brick, the mortar, the height, the width, the length, the cement. All of it so well matched and so well executed that it formed an object of beauty. Art and civic pride. Plato said it takes education and it does. I take one magazine largely because it is so artistically done. The printed page is a piece of art. The advertising matter, the arrangement of it, the pictures, the type, the distribution of ink, the pressure of the tape on the platen, and all so well done that the observer is lost in the contemplation or fit. The local paper should be the greatest asset to your civic pride. When artistically done it reflects your civic attitude. Lincoln's Gettysburg address will live as long as civilization. It was conceived in a temperament of the highest ideals. Four years of turmoil and excitement and emotion formed the background. The future dark and full of fore-bodings. A new order had to be created, new attitudes formed. The occasion for it was ripe. The mechanism of it was perfect. The thought of it could not have been better. All of it was spontaneity of an ardent soul. If you do not live it you can not express it. Thomas Payne wrote the "Age of Reasons." Thomas Jefferson read Thomas Payne's works and especially the "Age of Reason." He wrote the Declaration of Independence. There is nothing finer in the English language than this declaration. Theodore Roosevelt and Woodrow Wilson, both presidents of the United States and both writers of the first magnitude. They may have received their inspiration from the "Age of Reason." What they said, wrote, and did will live forever. These men were inimitable in the ethereal of human potentialities. Back of it was the artistry of the soul. Daniel Webster, Henry Clay, George W. Cable, Fred Douglass and Booker T. Washington will be satellites in every age of the world's history. Their wand was their oratory and their pen. Time will never remove the influence they had from our civic order. The subways of New York are masterpieces of civic art. Nothing adds to the civic life of any great metropolis more than these subterranean passages. They show the highest skill in mechanism and art. Most of our railroads are beautifying their lines of traffic. All transportation companies are making more beautiful every year their cars. This beauty and utility is an emanation of the artistic attitude. To be an artist one must be educated. The drought last summer demonstrated the necessity of planting trees through long stretches of the West and Southwest. Millions of them are being planted by the United States Department of Agriculture. The cost will run into millions of dollars. They are not planting these trees promiscuously. They will be selected for their utility and planted with scientific skill. This sort of conservation is the highest form of civic expression.

The artist conceives while the artisan gives expression. Both may be in one. He may be an architect, painter, sculptor, window decorator, floral designer, ceramist, musician, breeder of fine stock, a Burbank, a master gardener, a great orator like John B. Gough or Joseph Cook, G. Campbell Morgan, or he may be an inventor like Henry Ford, Edison and others. Their artistic vision has gone into ever line of endeavor. Everyone has combined art and practice. They have also given the highest expression of civic life. What they have added to our life today is absolutely incomparable. There is no single epoc in any period of the world's history to equal the civic accomplishments we are enjoying today. Only a few years ago, if you wished to go by land to Norfolk from here you had to go all the way by Richmond, Virginia. Today, if you wish to make the trip, you may choose any one of a dozen ways and have paved roads all the way and cement bridges spanning every river. The roads and bridges are the most picturesque to be found any where. A few months from now two bridges will span the San Francisco Bay, one extending East and the other North. They will cost more than a hundred million dollars. The piers will go more than two hundred feet below the surface of the water and more than five hundred feet above the water surface. Some of the single spans of these bridges will be more than four thousand feet in length. They will be wide enough for a dozen cars to travel abreast. When finished these bridges will eclipse the Egyptian Pyramids. They will be one of the few wonders of the world. Their architecture and construction were not the conception of any one man but of thousands of men who were experts, each in his line. All the mechanical intelligence of all the ages are imbibed in the construction of these masterpieces. Its artistic conception and the homogeneousness of the world will be the greatest marvel of all ages. The world will have no greater pride in any civic undertaking. It is the product of many artists and artisans. It expresses the unanimity of purpose and opinion of one hundred and twenty millions of people. The fact that we can unite on such a high project is another marvel. The United States is the greatest country in the world and we must go down in history as having done the greatest thing in the world. Talmage, the great preacher, used to say that he was not afraid to stop in any country home where flowers were in the year. The flowers showed an artistic temperament and a civic pride.

Can you vision the old New England home as described by J. G. Holland or the old Southern plantation as described by Archibald Rutledge? Both of these homes were as far apart as Springfield, Massachusetts, and Charleston, South Carolina. If you have not, you have failed to see the civic pride as engendered by millions of such men. It was this sort of inspiration that caused to be built the great railroads of our country with their spectacular bridges spanning a thousand valleys leaping from mountain crest to mountain crest as if they were ant beds. They climb the tallest Rockies or bore their way through them with electric motor, power, like a monster of life but a thing of beauty. They are facilitating our civic activities. If you happen to be in the remote west, you will see silhouetted several thousand feet on that slope five hundred bison, five hundred mountain sheep or five hundred deer and natural art greets your every mile. Again, up yonder at the very crest of the mountains overlooking the entrance to our Yellowstone National Park you will see the morning sun cover those snow-capped peaks when you will cry out as the old colored preacher did when he first saw it, "My God look at that Glory." If all the beautiful things in the world which nature and man have produced and which the greed of men have not spoiled do not appeal to your civic pride and to your own artistic vision then you are invincible. Again, **"To teach a skill is to train, to teach an art is to educate."**

March 15, 1935

APPENDIX 12

T.S. Inborden wrote an informative paper on the efforts and accomplishments of the American Missionary Association in the south especially assisting the black communities. Inborden's paper presents a who's who among many black educators and professionals who were products of "Northern Benevolence" through the leadership of the American Missionary Association. This paper is a very valuable assessment of how early black education in the south did produce some very positive results.

PRODUCT OF NORTHERN BENEVOLENCE
BY
PRINCIPAL T. S. INBORDEN

JOSEPH K. Brick School
ENFIELD, N. C.

AMERICAN MISSIONARY ASSOCIATION
287 FOURTH AVENUE, NEW YORK, N.Y.

For the last few years so much has been said about the Negro that there is now nothing new to say. Whatever one has to say seems only a recapitulation. Every phase of his life has been explored in public address, in literature and upon the stage. You have heard so much of the Russian Jew that the name has its own significance. The mentioning of the Italians suggests to you a coal mine or a lot of men digging a sewer. So with the Negro. So much has been said against him that the name suggests the worst features of the race. You see in the name only a lot of fellows half clad with a slice of watermelon in their mouths, bottles in their pockets, banjos under their arms, loitering about the street corners and stations. He has been caricatured in every conceivable way. You think of Kingston, and at once a lot of little Negroes diving for dimes are suggested to you. The mind has become so habituated to viewing the frailties of people that the sad catastrophe of the island of Jamaica a few years ago could not be made public without an intermixture of a most vivid description of the little Negroes diving for dimes. We should learn to discriminate between the worth and the worthless of all races. We must condemn any classification that includes the good with the bad. It is inimical, unjust and savage. Your missionaries who go South are good people and worthy of every imitation, but often they come home to you and inadvertently leave a sad picture. They do not mean to do so, but they do. They tell you about the one-room log hut where the family of ten cook, eat and sleep, and that room without a window; they tell you about the crude way in which everything is done; they tell you about the quack doctors, quack lawyers, quack teachers and quack preachers. There are log huts in the South by the thousands, quacks in every profession and apparently few changes in methods of doing things. Thousands of dollars spent in forty-five years and the lives of the best men you have for this work, and still these conditions? If I were supporting educational work in the South or anywhere else, and had only the saddest pictures presented to me as rewards of my philanthropy, I would get discouraged, as doubtless some of you have done. I want to show you the brighter side, to let you see that progress has been made and that your money and talent have not been spent amiss. You know that Fisk University was organized over forty years ago, with men like Dr. Cravath, Professor Bennett, Professor Chase, Professor Spence and others whose statesmanship and scholarship could no more be doubted than you could doubt the spirit that inspired Oberlin. In recent years there have been changes in the personnel, but not in the self-sacrificing spirit that has characterized it since its organization. During all these years her graduates, to say nothing about the undergraduates, have gone out into the world and created public sentiment and changed the conditions of life. They have established schools, they have preached the Gospel instead of merely an emotional religion; they are teachers of a very high order in every part of the South. They are building up the home life in the communities in which they live. instead of the one-room hut they are building cottages with rooms ranging from four to a dozen, furnished with all the paraphernalia of the most cultured homes of the country. Their courage and inspiration have been a leavening wherever they have gone. What is true of this one school is equally true of many of the other schools of the American Missionary Association. If you should make a dot on the map of the Southern States for every one who had been influenced by these schools there would not be room to note the cities, boundaries and rivers. Indeed, there would be many dots beyond the boundaries of the Southern States, beyond the Pacific and Atlantic oceans. Not all are hewers of wood and drawers of water, but they are filling places that demand the best possible trained minds and the greatest executive ability.

A few examples will best illustrate the result of your philanthropy in the South. The examples I shall give you typical of all missionary work in the South. If the truth of them is questioned they can easily be verified. Some years ago three boys presented themselves to Fisk University for an education. The mother, in order to meet the small cost, was given a job as domestic in the boarding hall. The boys had only one suit of clothes and, I believe, one pair of pants. this they changed between themselves, so that whichever one went to class might have a good pair of pants to wear. These boys graduated from the school with honors. One became president of a State University and held the job for years until his self respect and honor prevented him from subscribing to the politics of the State. All are now honest business men and influencing others for good. Some months ago when their Alma Mater needed money for a special enterprise their names were subscribed for several hundred dollars. This illustrates the fact that very many of the graduates, after getting out of school and settled in their business, do remember the financial needs of their Alma Mater. About thirty years ago an unpretentious black boy in Mississippi heard of Fisk University and walked nearly all the way to Nashville, Tennessee, where for many years he was a diligent student. After graduating he went to Oberlin, where he took a course in theology. He was immediately given work by the American Board of Commissioners for Foreign Missions and sent to Africa. He lived in Africa seven years, where he wrote books, preached and taught the people, and translated a part of the Bible into the native dialect. He came home on account of his health and is now a successful teacher and minister under the American Missionary Association in his native State. The story of his struggle when I met him in Oberlin in 1883 at the very beginning of my educational career, was an inspiration to me. Such an example is the very best basis for the encouragement of those who are looking for tangible products.

In its early history one of the present officers of the American Missionary Association was called to teach at Fisk University. He had an eye to business then as he has now to the safekeeping of the missionary funds. While waiting in the outer room of an office where he had called to see a man on business, a young colored boy was washing the windows. He observed the boy and asked if he did not want to go to school and urged him to come to the Fisk School—Fisk University. A few words from this missionary and teacher gave this lad a new vision of his own life, convinced him of the opportunities offered in a great school like Fisk University, and the great work that must be conducted by Negroes for Negroes if they would prepare themselves for it. This young boy, jovial and happy, found his way into the Fisk classes a few days later, where he spent ten or more years at persistent study until he finished the course, and, like all seekers of knowledge, he wanted more, so, in the fall after graduating, he presented himself to Oberlin to take a course in theology. When he finished in theology he was called to take a church in Washington. There he preached and labored for ten years and wrought a great work. When the American Missionary Association wanted a man to visit every church in the South under its auspices they called George Moore. When a little sweet oil is necessary to stay the friction that is sometimes engendered in this great field, when spiritual and intellectual interests are at a low ebb, George Moore is the one to help and to enliven. He is the most useful man in the Southern Congregational Church work to-day. There is not a Congregational institution anywhere in the South but what has received inspiration from him. Scores in all of our schools and churches have been converted to Christ by his preaching; thousands have been helped to live a better life. Dr. Strieby, Dr. Roy and Dr. Beard, and his name will be known in every nook and corner of the Southland where good is to be done.

About the year 1880 there came to Fisk University a boy scarcely twelve years old, the only boy of his father. This boy worked with his hands, taught in the summer schools, and when old enough and far enough in school began preaching. He was a student in Fisk University for ten years. On one occasion while yet a student, he was appointed by the oratorical association to introduce the great temperance lecturer, Dr. J.C. Price, to a concourse of Nashville's citizens and students of the colleges located there. On arising after the introduction the speaker said, "If I could make the impression on this audience which my friend has made in my introduction to you I would count myself an orator." This was said without flattery but with the utmost sincerity. A year before graduating he was appointed to preach the annual sermon to the old Central Tennessee Association of Congregational Churches. His talks and addresses as a student were prepared with such care that he always had a good audience. He graduated from Fisk University at the head of his class, and not one of his classmates questioned his place. I count myself fortunate to have been one of his classmates. Three years later he graduated from the Department of Theology at Yale University. While at Yale he had contact with the most select men of the country. His record there is one of hard work, dignity and scholarly attainments.

Soon after graduating he was called by the American Missionary Association to one of the hardest churches under its supervision, the First Congregational Church of Atlanta, Ga. Hard, because the church was in a transition period; they had always had a white minister, and it was seriously doubted if there was a colored man of the scholarship and caliber sufficient to hold the charge. Under the leadership of H. H. Proctor for fourteen years the church has been self-supporting, supporting missions in the city and outside of its own bounds. He is now building a church costing nearly forty thousand dollars, the like of which can not be found in another Negro community. The cream of the race as well as the lowly who live in that city are members of that church. When the white people in Atlanta want to show their friends from the North the best there is in the colored ministry and the best in Negro refinement and culture they take them to the First Congregational Church. This is one of the few churches in the South visited by members of the Ogden party. He has held some of the most honorable offices in the gift of the entire denomination. When the state of Georgia is ready to pass some iniquitous law infringing on the rights of her colored people the voice of H. H. Proctor is heard in unmistakable language above the noise of the rabble. Only his skin and politics bar him from the class of the matchless Grady. This is a product of the American Missionary Association and Northern philanthropy. No one can be so stupid as to ask if such work pays. Its value can not be reckoned in dollars.

In Amherst, Massachusetts, lives a lady who went South many years ago to teach and be a missionary among the needy and lowly. Her work in the school was very largely with the beginners. In order to have a full classroom she went on the streets of Nashville to seek out the lads in whom there seemed to be the greatest hope. She was keen of vision and gently in spirit, and seldom made a mistake in her judgment. Every boy whom she captured was made a Missionary to bring in others. Among the many boys who came was one in particular, a typical street lad, full of vitality and fun. Her one task was to transform the interest of this boy from the affairs of the street to the love of school and books. She like all true teachers, knew her work well. Today that she did it well expresses the fact mildly. This lad soon began to love the school, his teachers and his books. The street for him post its charms. His teachers soon learned that he was absolutely honest truthful, and reliable. These qualities are very essential to the success of students before they graduate as after they graduate. This lad went through the model school, the primary school, the intermediate school and on through grammar school. Then, he entered the preparatory department and later graduated from the college department. The intervening vacations are spent in the Pullman service. The company appreciated his worth and honesty. He proved to his fellow porters in the service that the table linen and silverware were not furnished as souvenirs to be carried away. A few years later I was surprised to meet my friend on the streets of Oberlin where he had gone to take a course in theology. After graduating in theology from Oberlin, he was called to take charge of the St. John's Congregational Church in Springfield, Massachusetts. It is the testimony of all who know him that his work there is eminently successful. The American Missionary Association has no better example of his work than William N. DeBerry. He is not only our best type of the educated ministry, but he is a builder and organizer as well, types which are not usually found in the same person. A northern paper in a recent criticism describes him as a "Southern-born man whose dark skin betokens a child of the tropics of unmixed blood, full of the elements of virile strength, whose face indicates a high degree of mentality matched with a determined will, which qualities appeared in his address upon the needs of the Negroes scattered through the North." He is a diligent student of the sociological status of the Negroes of the entire country, and he knows how to present facts regarding them with logic and force. nor long since he gave out the status of the Negroes of Springfield, Mass., which was largely published all over the country. Some of his critics said that the article was the emanation of the brain of some Yankee in the North who did not know what he was talking about. It emanated from the brain of William N. DeBerry. He was invited a few years ago to deliver a lecture to the Board of Education of New York City on the Negro. The fact of this invitation was a guarantee of his scholarship and a recognition of his sound judgment on racial issues. After he had delivered one of his characteristic addresses in one of the white churches of Springfield a few years ago a white lady who had never heard a colored man speak said to me: "Why he talks like a white man." This is a product, a living epistle, read of and known among his fellows. Does it pay? If it does not we had better call in all the missionaries, burn up the Bible and all its commentaries, count Christianity and all of its concomitant a failure. This is the kind of education that Mr. Taft had in mind when he said to the Fisk student body some months ago: "It is of the highest importance that your ministers should receive the most thorough academic education and everything that goes to make the basis of the knowledge of a minister of God."

Nearly thirty years ago a long black-haired boy came up to Fisk University from the iron section of Alabama. He had heard that a poor boy could come to Fisk University and by hard study become a great teacher. He found his place in the lower grades, of course, as most students did in those days. After many years of hard study he graduated. Just before graduating he attended a great conference of Methodist bishops. He at once became inspired with their enthusiasm, and of course wanted to be a great bishop. He had not thought that the greatest statesmen never become presidents. It is equally true that the greatest scholars in the Methodist regime seldom become bishops. When he considered this he decided to be a great scholar. He went to the University of Pennsylvania, from which he graduated with high honors and was at once called to teach at Howard University in Washington, D.C. It was not long before his ability as a teacher was noted and his scholarship rewarded with the chair of Dean of the Department of Pedagogy and Teachers' College. Recently he went abroad to study methods in the great universities of Germany. He rejoices now that he can be a bishop in the Congregational Church, as all Congregational ministers are bishops, and one of the great scholars of his time and race. I refer to L.B. Moore, Ph.D. Again, let us quote Mr. Taft: "It is absolutely necessary that your race should have leaders; it is absolutely necessary that your race should have men of advanced education, of advanced education professionally." This sentiment is entirely in accord with that which the founders of the American Missionary Association propagated fifty years ago, and which the early missionaries disseminated in founding all of our higher institution. This is a very important statement coming as it does from the President of the United States to the students of an institution which has always stood for the highest and best in Negro life and development. We thank God that we have a few such schools, and that beyond this in the north and even across the waters there is the opportunity for those who have the means and ability to get the advanced education professionally."

A great deal is being said in our agricultural papers and upon the public platform as to how environment conditions the growth of vegetation. No one knows this better than those who are trying, in our agricultural institutions and at our State experiment stations, to increase the annual output of our farms. Vegetation does not think and is responsible for no moral action; yet that environment conditions its growth is an absolute fact. Sometimes in spite of its worst environments some plants will put forth with all the characteristic elements of the best stock of the family under the best environment. Man is not vegetation but the highest and most complete form of God's creation. God has given him something to do, mental powers to develop, a moral life to perfect. He can not sit supinely still as the vegetation and let evolution change his environment. He must change it himself or go down. Yet, like the plant, here and there all over this country, in spite of his environment—the condition into which he was born—his segregation, his disfranchisement and his former servitude, we see *evidence* in the Negro's acquisition of this world's goods, in the development of his intellectual and moral life, of that which will compare well with the most favored races of the human family. Fred Douglass and Booker Washington are the best samples of thousands of our men, and I might say women also, who have outgrown their environment and made themselves in spite of it. Fifteen thousand students today are in the schools of the American Missionary Association alone, to say nothing about the other educational agencies that are operating in the South, changing the environment, not of ten millions of people, but the habitat of the entire country's population. From the jungles and swamps of Liberty County, Ga., Two boys went to Atlanta University. Their good old mother had seen a vision in the dark days of slavery, and wrapped in the folds of her old calico dress she took these boys daily out behind the weeds and hedges and presented them to the throne of God, with the petition that the vision of freedom and personal liberty which she had seen would come in her day. The culmination of events between the North and the South brought this personal liberty; Atlanta University freed them from the bondage of ignorance and gave them a new vision founded upon an intelligent conception of the spirit of Christ. These boys finished their education in Atlanta University and they have been the good leaven in every community in which they have carried the gospel. One is a very successful minister in Wilmington, N.C., and the other, George V. Clark, has recently been called to the pastorate of the Mount Zion Congregational Church in Cleveland, Ohio. He has traveled extensively with Dr. Roy to present the work of the American missionary Association, and his enthusiasm for the intelligent awakening of our people knows no bounds. He has been the moderator our State Association and an inspiration in its councils.

In the early 80's there came up to Talladega College a country boy angular in every in every appearance. I have seen somewhere that there is a principle in the science of evolution to the effect that all roses started originally with only five petals, and they poorly developed. Cultivation gives them their tints, increases their size and develops every organ. Like the original wild rose this young man had every impress of his environment, but he had besides the inherent qualities of a man. He needed only the application of the healing balm by such a college as Talladega and later Oberlin to round out his mental caliber and to enlarge his horizon in order to fit him to be the eminent teacher he is. N.B. Young is what he is because of the American Missionary Association. This is the object of the sort of philanthropy which it dispenses. If it can not change the old environments it creates new ones. It builds schools, it organizes churches where they are needed, and in doing so it creates new conditions and forms new environments. Up to this new environment, it may be Fisk University, it may be Talladega College, it may be Tougaloo, it may be Atlanta University, it may be Straight University, it may be Tillotson or Avery, or Troy, or the Brick School, these country boys come with all the angularities of body and soul. After they have been in the grind for ten years they come out a new product. Young has been the head teacher at Tuskegee and at the State College of Georgia, and he is now the President of the State College of Florida. He is the director of many of our educational associations in the South and a sane writer and counselor.

Richard Wright, a product of Atlanta University, is well known. He was the boy who sent word to the North by General O. Howard to "tell them we are rising." He has been prominent in the politics of his State, in educational work, in State and interstate councils. You send Dr. Ware, Dr. Cravath, Dr. DeForest, Dr. Andrews and others to place your impress upon Southern institutions for Negroes. These Negroes go out into every nook and corner of the Southland bearing this impress. They place this impress into the schools and churches over which they preside, and the influence of your beneficence is multiplied beyond all calculations. You have heard of Dr. Crum. You know the notoriety which the public press gave him at the instance of Mr. Roosevelt's appointment to a Federal office. The President never relinquished his purpose of appointment on account of the howling rabble. He knew the character and ability of his man and insisted that he should have the office and his appointment was confirmed. Dr. Crum is a graduate of Avery Institute, another school fostered by the American highways and hedges and bring out these dwarfed roses, these diamonds in the rough, and fit them for the habitation of the beautiful world in which God has placed us. Every literary man has heard of Dr. W. E. B. DuBois, a product of Fisk University, Harvard University and the University of Berlin. He is our foremost statistician and sociologist. He is organizer of the Atlanta University Conferences and of the Niagara Movement. Great good has resulted from the conferences, and the Niagara Movement has created an immense amount of public sentiment. When the Negro problem is settled in its entirety, absolutely settled, the principle of settlement will have to be sufficiently comprehensive to include, at least, a part of the platform of this movement. Race problems and race prejudices are seldom settled. The Jews have been a problem to the Gentiles since the beginning of their history. They are a problem to-day in every community in which they are in competition with other races. To say that race problems absolutely can not be settled is to doubt the efficacy of Christianity. A universal application of Christianity, which include the brotherhood of man in particular, to commercial, social and civic forms of life will settle all race differences. President King, of Oberlin College, said recently. "The solution of the race problem must come about with no evasion, no compromise or mechanical method, but with nothing less than reverence for the person." This sentiment is fundamental in the mind of every thinking Negro. Dr. DuBois is also an author of unquestioned ability. One of the best church buildings and one of the most intelligent audiences in the South in our connection is that at Chattanooga, Tenn. presided over by Rev. Joseph E. Smith, also a product of the American Missionary Association. He has pastored that church for almost thirty years. He has built up the church and the community and he is a leavening power in the Congregational councils of the State.

It is said by a musical critic that the only really American songs are those known as the Jubilee Songs. They had their origin in the sufferings of the race in bondage, in their striving for personal liberty, and in their desire for knowledge. They are more expressive of their inward experiences than all the orations and sermons that could be written. The one who has done more than any other man to interpret these songs and to put them to music for the educated mind is Prof. John Work of Fisk University, himself a product of that school. He has gone out to the firesides of the people, to their churches and camp-meetings and gathered them where they were sung and there wrote the music as far as it was possible for any one to do. These he has revised and dignified so that they not only touch the responsive chord of the uneducated but the most cultured and refined as well. Professor Work is not an imitator but a genius in the interpretation of these songs. No one feature of the Jamestown Exposition was more attractive than the one of rendering this Jubilee music by the Jubilee quartet of Fisk University, led by Professor Work himself. To hear him sing them himself, means for the time to be transported, so to speak, soul and body, beyond the skies "Where the Angels are hovering 'round." Hampton Institute, supported by Northern benevolence, claims the honor of educating the foremost Negro in this country and in the world. He needs no introduction here for his name is a household word in every part of this land. Fisk University, supported by this same benevolence dispensed through the American Missionary Association claims the honor of educating his wife. A heritage more noble never graced the fort of an old battlefield. Like Frances Willard, Mary Lyons and others she received in order to be spent. Maggie Murray, as she was familiarly known at Fisk, is a product of the college and asked to be excused from nothing, not even from Greek in which study she excelled most of the boys. All denominational schools, all the public schools, all the State schools, and the ministry and all other organizations that have for their object the moral and intellectual advancement of the Negro in this part of our national domain have received a wonderful impulse from Northern beneficence and brain. In the South the educational problem alone is taxing its resources beyond all precedent. let us hope that the work of educating and Christianizing shall receive no impediment until a full application of the Christian spirit permeates every vocation in life. In order for you to fully appreciate the work that this association is doing in the South among colored people it is necessary for you to have positive knowledge of their lives and homes. You can not get this knowledge by riding through the country on the trains. You may ride from Boston to Florida on the trains and know nothing about the masses of Negroes. You must visit the homes and plantation quarters if you would know the real condition. A ride through the country would give you an external view of the log cabins and a sight of a crowd of children with every appearance of squalor and poverty. I have visited thousands of such homes from Arkansas to the Atlantic Coast and I know that the conditions and influences of them are such as to invite the lowest forms of vice and sensuality. The children have nothing to associate with these homes except places in which to eat and sleep and thousands are not fit places in which to do that. It is not surprising to read of the depredations committed by them. They would be committed by any other people situated as they have been and taught by precept and example for hundreds of years. The surprise is that in very, very many of these homes there are the highest forms of chastity and virtue. Many old ignorant Negroes, inheriting the spirit of southern chivalry from their old masters, have eked out their life blood across the threshold of their old cabins, trying to maintain the purity of such cabins. When this gets into the papers the facts are so distorted that you never know the truth.

There are three difficulties encountered in the educational problem of the Negro. The first is that the Negroes have been intensely discouraged. They have had and are having today grounded into every fiber of their natures the idea that they are fitted only for the cotton field and house servant. To meet this difficulty the work of education must begin with the mothers and fathers in their cabins face to face with their little ones. The rural schools planted by the national Government, by the State Legislatures and by philanthropy to teach the people general agriculture and home economics are placing emphasis at the base of the problem. The mothers' meeting and farmers' conferences are teaching these discouraged people to look up and have confidence in themselves. To be discouraged is the worst affliction that can come to man or beast; the beast lies down to die, man loses all hope and cares not whether he lives or dies. Another difficulty is the popular prejudice on the part of a great many white people against Negro education of whatever nature. Prejudice can not be downed with argument. It is only intensified. Nothing but the grace of God will kill it. The spirit of God must dominate our schools, public and private, black as well as white. Where this sort of education progresses race prejudice will be the least. I think it's worth emphasizing that where our schools are located in healthful and intelligent communities race friction is the least encountered. It must not be thought that the Negro has no friends to education in the white South. Notwithstanding the few discordant notes you hear from various sections the South is shouldering its burden awfully. Some of the best Christian men in the entire country are directing its educational policies and the general trend is forward. The third difficulty we have is a financial one. it is a recognized fact that the South is dependent largely upon Negro labor for its sustenance. The millions of pounds of cotton, tobacco, peanuts and other produce chronicled from time to time; the fact of his owning 14,255,164 acres of land in North Carolina, Mississippi and Georgia, to say nothing about his possessions in the other States, do not prove that all the Negroes are lazy and shiftless. This is a monument to their industry, even if it is the product of ignorant labor. The system of land tenure in the South makes it very hard for the poor man, colored or white, to rise far above the absolute necessities of life. It is harder for the colored man because of the many discriminating laws and juries. The dawn of a better day has appeared above the horizon for the Negro. The elimination of the rum traffic in most of the Southern States means less vice, less jail fines, more farms for the Negroes, more and better economy in the homes, more boys and girls in our schools and higher aspirations for all the race. In ex-Governor Vardaman's State the other day, Mr. Booker T. Washington was hailed, in the midst of an address to thousands of our countrymen, by a white school official and told to advise the Negroes to put their children in the public schools. This advice may be very unusual in Mississippi but in North Carolina it is very usual. North Carolina provides one of the best equipped A. and M. Colleges in the South for her colored people and maintains three Normal Schools that are doing efficient work. Her public schools are equal to the best public schools in the South. In Alabama and Georgia, Judge Jones is seeing that the Negro gets his rights as a laborer as far as the Federal laws are concerned at least. The scarcity of labor south of Mason and Dixon's line does not mean that the Negroes are growing more shiftless but that the South is evolutionizing and the Negroes are adapting themselves to new conditions. Some, of course, are going North and West but the bulk of them are here and a very great many of those who are here are buying homes and farming on their own account and consequently are not in the labor market. The tendency is upward and forward, not backward.

What have you done? I have endeavored to show what you have done in these columns but a recapitulation for the sake of emphasis will not be out of order. You have demonstrated to the world, through the noble men and women you have sent into the South, that the Negro intellect is as active and capable of high attainments as that of any other nationality in the world. When you read in our missionary journals that the boys and girls walk ten or twelve miles daily to school and that they bring eggs, poultry, butter, milk, sugar-cane or fish, or a cart of wood with which to pay their tuition and buy books, don't think it is fiction. It is a fact that shows a determination and an enthusiasm that knows no bounds but success. It shows also where you began with these people. By your faith and patience and financial support these boys and girls have put the African dialect into English, you have made college presidents of boot-blacks, preachers of the highest order of Pullman porters and hotel boys; you have made first-class college professors out of cotton pickers. You have transformed thousands of log cabins into beautiful homes with broad lawns of find shrubbery. In many of these homes, you will find some of the same books that you read; the same papers that give life and tone to your home; the same music that your sons have studied. Instead of the rough, the sullen, the uncouth, the sour-looking, the dissipated, the furrow-faced, the half-clad boy that came up from Mississippi, Alabama and Georgia a few years ago to College, you will find a gentleman of culture and refinement whose intellectual aspirations could be satisfied only by having a diploma from Oberlin, Yale, Harvard, Heidelberg or Oxford. Let no one say this sort of education is not needed. The lower the scale of general intelligence of the masses the higher should be the attainments of the leaders in intelligence, morality, temperance, virtue, loyalty to truth, and patriotism. This alone is the plane of enlightened citizenship. The grandeur of such work as you are doing all over this country will never be fully realized until the trumpet of the centuries shall call up the generations that have been influenced in these schools. Then up from the cane farms of Louisiana, from the bottoms of Mississippi, from the swamps of Arkansas and Texas, from the black belt of Alabama and Georgia, from the rice fields of South Carolina, from the highlands of Tennessee and Kentucky, will come the testimony, overwhelming, triumphant and jubilant.

APPENDIX 13

Early education in the south around the 1900s was centered around vocational training. In recent years, some cities in these United States, have considered programs of vocational training for some youngsters who might not have an interest in an academic curriculum. T.S. Inborden, during his early years at Brick School, had some very sound and interesting ideas on Vocational Training. He wrote a paper on his views and suggestions.

VOCATIONAL TRAINING
BY
PRINCIPAL T. S. INBORDEN

Chapter I

One's vocational is the thing selected for his life work, it is the employment which takes his time and thought for his living, or for the support of his family, or for the support of some institution, society or for the State. It may be a trade, a business or a profession. It may not always carry with it the idea of remuneration. The fact is, we know a few men who get nothing from their vocation in the way of financial remuneration. They get happiness, inspiration and pleasure out of it. When we speak of Vocational Training we have reference to the training which appertains particularly to the effectiveness of our life work. Training and education are not the ends of life but they are agencies in affecting the environment and the conditions of life. In a sense, every form of education is vocational because the object of all education is the perfection of our lives for some useful purpose. There are only a few schools in all the world that are educating solely for purposes of culture and refinement. You will not find in any of our schools, among our advanced students, those who will not tell you that the object of their education is to facilitate their work, or to make the anticipated problems of their future easy of solution. This thought carries with it the idea of intellectual development, and also of character formation. It eliminates the idea of educating animals. we can not appeal to their intellects nor do we speak of developing their moral characters. We appeal to them by emotional suggestions. We elicit attention by inflicting pain or by appealing to their physical appetites and sometimes by mere kindness. If you appeal to people on the same basis, you will develop in them the same qualities of nature and the same kind of attention that you would develop in the animal. One sees evidences of this in the State prisons, on the chain gangs, and in the slums of the criminal classes. The criminal is a product of his environment, either immediate or prenatal; if the latter, he may have been influenced generations ago as the animal is being influenced today. This, as you know, is very probable and possible. When we speak of training people we include the idea of education in its most comprehensive form because our appeal to them is through their intellects and on the basis of their moral character and their free moral agency. The efficiency of our appeal and the response to it will be evidenced in proportion to the development of the intellect and the moral life of the subject to whom the appeal is made. The mule neighs at meal time when he hears the farm bell, the pigs come when certain sounds are made, the hireling, simply draws his wages. All these responses have come simply to satisfy the physical appetite. The work of neither is efficient because it is not intellectual and not thoughtful and not purposeful. The power to direct the mind and the power to control the body according to fixed principles are of the first importance in the acquisition of efficiency in any line of endeavor. This power is primarily dormant in the heart, brain and life of man; it is God-given. It is the least potent when neglected. It reaches the climax when correctly developed. Mind is to man what the bridle is to the horse; it is the lever of direction and control. With a poor bridle, you have a dangerous horse, with an illiterate and undeveloped mind you have a dangerous man. With an illiterate and undeveloped race or part of a race you will have a dangerous environment which will make dangerous conditions. Our only salvation of mind, body and life from the evil heritage and tradition of the past must come to us by education and training under the best directed Christian influences. Line upon line and precept upon precept. Here a little and there a little. Sympathetic and patient insight must characterize every step of progress. The greater the illiteracy the more careful and thorough and comprehensive should be this training and education. This must be fundamental in whatever else we may have to say on the subject of training for life work. Over at the Jamestown Exposition a few years ago, we saw what training will do for a horse when sufficient time is given to his training. The Eskimo is an expert at trapping because for centuries his food supply has depended upon that vocation. The North American Indian is dexterous and efficient with a gun because hunting has been his vocation. For thousands of years, as far as we know. The Indians were trained to accuracy with the arrow. It would be most surprising if they did not use the rifle with absolute precision. The cowboy is an expert with the lasso. The Eskimo, the Indian and the cowboy are the best examples of the training people get in their vocation. Their acuteness and dexterity were acquired, as a matter of necessity, by years of training, but without intelligent and scientific direction.

The other day, I attended a farmers' institute in our community where I heard two lectures. One of the gentlemen was a man perhaps seventy years old. He was educated as a physician but failed in health and took up the business of farming. He is an expert farmer and in the service of this State, North Carolina. His work is to go from one community to another and advise with the people as to the best methods of farming. He began life with all the antecedents of intelligence and liberty of choice and was given a liberal education with the additional training of proficiency as a physician. This training was all incidental to his life vocation as a farmer. It was the most important general preparation for life that one could receive. It was the basis for all the after knowledge he should acquire, not only on the subject of agriculture, but of any other subject. This preparation in the cultural studies and in the sciences of medicine was reserved power that would count for success in any enterprise. This man had been all of his life in training for this phenomenal success. He has lived twice the average age of man before he becomes the master of his vocation. For this important work, time has given him only one endowment which he might not have had at thirty-five; that one was wisdom. The other speaker was only about thirty-five years old. He had a farm of his own and was in the service of the State. In a competitive examination, the younger man might score the higher mark. The difference is simply this: Knowledge acquired out there in the hot sun for thirty or forty years, experimenting with crops covering a thousand acres, is a laborious and expensive thing. Most men with less education than the old gentleman had either quit or are willing to plod along with smaller result. This man was trained in his vocation. The younger man was educated and trained in an agricultural college for his vocation. He was not a theorist either, for in most of our agricultural schools, theories, most of them, are capable of the most practical demonstration. The principles which it would take years to demonstrate out there on the farm might be demonstrated in a few days or weeks in the school laboratory. This could be done by the younger man at a great saving of time and expense. This is the object of our industrial schools. They save time and expense in the preparation of the people for their life work. These opportunities for preparation for work in our schools can not be brushed aside by the wave of the hand without great loss in the productive resources of our people.

WHY SPECIALIZE IN ANYTHING?

Chapter II

The man who starts out in life with nothing definite to do is an indefinite and unsatisfactory worker. He had better have something definite in mind and try to do that better than any one else in the world, if it is only grubbing stumps and piling stones. There is an endless opportunity in this occupation for developing strength and character. One of the hardest things we all have to do in our educational work is to convince the people of the necessity of special training for special vocations. The basis of their argument is that a few people in the community have succeeded without education and special training and hence they can do the same. If one has not had the opportunity of acquiring knowledge by means of the book and the laboratory, it is a fine illustration of good sense that he acquires it by experience. This is particularly true when so many people do not get it from books, the laboratory nor from experience. They never learn. With the average Negro one needs to go to school to learn only four things. He can be a preacher, a doctor, a lawyer or a teacher. He does not need too much education if he is going to be a preacher; in some communities the less he has the better he is liked. If he has a good voice and good use of his limbs so that he can give vent to his physical emotions, this assures his success. This sort of success gives nothing to the intellect and very little to the moral life. "The proof of the pudding is in the eating." It is only recently that education has been the basis of preparation in fact for the profession of teaching. In many sections of the country today education as a preparation for that profession is a farce. I have known personally in many instances where education in the proficiency of teaching had very little bearing upon one's ability to "get a school." It is not surprising with this acquiescence the pulpit and in the classroom to find whole communities in the darkness. The men often tell me that the girls are going to marry and so there is no use educating them. I never had a man who had good preaching and good teaching tell me that. Did you? You may as soon expect gravitation to reverse its order as to expect a tract of men to advance in civilization, in refinement, in culture, in Christianity, or in any other virtue without its women. Deprive the race of efficient home life and its attractions and it becomes nomadic. The man who does not train his girls for usefulness and service in the knowledge of the necessary ordering of home life is to be pitied. He does not see into the future and cares nothing for it. He is minus the instincts that should characterize his kind.

Take the matter of financial remuneration. He who gets an education solely for the purpose of getting money has missed the aim and object of life. It is very important that we should make money. We shall never be in a position to be counted as the world's goods to lift us above the absolute necessities of life. Money will give us standing in the financial, intellectual and social world as possibly nothing else will, but money is not the end of life. It is the least of all the gods to be worshipped. The history of this country is black with suicides and failures with the craze to get money. In the hands of those who do not value its legitimate use, it is a power for evil. In the hands of those who do know its value it may be a power for good. What is the value of special or vocational training as expressed in money? Here is a young man who comes to us earning five dollars a month. At the end of one year he is able to earn for his services as much as ten dollars a month. His services are worth just twice as much as formerly. He comes to us at the age of sixteen with not money enough to pay his medical fee and to buy his school uniform. In all of his life he never saw twenty-five dollars to call it his own. The average salary for these boys would not be over six dollars a month the year round. At the end of the year, they can not give an accurate account of one-fourth of their earnings for a year. We have had a great many such boys in our school, so that I know pretty well what I am saying. We know that a good many after being in school just one year have gone out and doubled their wages. By studying four and five hundred percent. What I wish to say is this: untrained a young man will have to work ten years to earn $720. This is not money enough to purchase comfortable clothes, nutritious food and decent lodgings for that time. You will not need to go out of this community to see a demonstration of this fact. If the same young man had spent four or five years in training for some definite purpose, his earning power would have been increased, at least, to eighteen dollars a month. So, for the remaining six years of the ten, he might have earned twelve hundred and ninety-six dollars. It would be this much at least. This is a low estimate. I positively know of instances where young men have by training increased their earning power from six dollars a month to three and four hundred dollars a year. This is not exceptional either. It is the reward of merit and efficiency that results from years of preparation. As a matter of fact, you expect to hear that the men in the professions are the best paid. It is not always true that they are. Those wo are the best paid are usually those who have spent very much time in special preparation. They are those who are exceptionally well-fitted for their work. I know a number of bricklayers who earn from three to five dollars a day. There are a few artists in the trade who earn from seven to ten dollars a day. This would be impossible without great training in mechanical ingenuity. If you are looking for money here is your chance. The mechanical field is large and not crowded. One need not expect to earn threes dollars a day nor five dollars a day with only one year's preparation. He might be able at the end of a year to saw to the line that another has made and might be able to "butter a brick." I know a good many mechanics who have worked at the trade longer than two years who can not do either. Carrying a trowel or tool-chest does not constitute a mechanic any more than carrying a pile of books constitutes a scholar. Ingenuity and skill in mechanical work do not come automatically. They come with close application to detail, repetition and after many failures. The best paid men in the professions are those who have spent the most tie in preparation. They were not only trained for proficiency but they continue in training while engaged in their vocation. Many men have failed in the school-room, in the pulpit and in the trades because they thought that the end of class-room preparation was the end of preparation for success. They retrogress instead of progress.

Chapter III

It is often said that there is plenty of cheap labor in the South. I am sorry that this seems to be true. If it is cheap, it is because it is inefficient and unintelligent. But is it cheap? When a man has a beautiful farm which he can not cultivate himself and has to see it deteriorate in value year after year because of misdirected labor, I would not call that cheap labor. If one has a valuable machine to run and puts it into the hands of a man because he can hire him for fifty or seventy cents a day, and the machine costs for repairs as much as the man for his labor, and in most instances more, I would not call that cheap labor. Here is where we are losing out in mechanical lines. If you hire a mechanic and he puts paint or whitewash over your floors carpets, furniture and spoils your piano, I would call him expensive at any price. If your horse should be shod and the nails driven into the foot in such a way as to make him a cripple, I would call the smith a very expensive man. if you hired a cook because you could get her for a little money and she appropriated to her own use and without your knowledge the provisions you provided for your family, or if she did not know how to utilize the provisions you provided, I would call her very expensive, too. That would not be cheap labor. If you simply hired a girl to push your baby cab, her negligence, which is often positively bad, might be such as to prove the most expensive. This is not cheap labor. Labor that works half the time and idles half the time and wants pay for whole time is not cheap. Labor that wastes the provisions for the sustenance of your family is not cheap labor. labor that keeps you repairing machinery and picking up tools from morning until night is not cheap labor. Labor that has to be coaxed, dogged and literally cursed and that keeps one mad from morning until night is not cheap labor. labor that has no interest in the thing being done nor responsibility beyond the matter of drawing its money is not cheap labor. The cheapest mechanic we ever hired was one we paid about five dollars a day. He did his day's work in eight hours and had the rest of the time to use as he pleased. We never had to do his work over and never had to complain to his firm. The other day when I was in New York I went in to see my friend and found that he was no longer a mechanic working by the day, but he was a member of the biggest firm on Water Street. He is receiving the reward which interest, responsibility, thoroughness and efficiency merit. The kind of service which such men render can not be measured in money terms. Such efficiency in any line of endeavor which is the outgrowth of a wide knowledge, great skill and experience is one of the most important factors in economic, social and world progress. It is this kind of efficiency that must count in race evolution. Not the efficiency of one man nor a dozen men nor a hundred men, but of the race in general in every occupation.

Who receives more money for service than the men in the professions? Bricklayers, who work by the day, get more for their work than either the preachers or teachers. In North Carolina they receive almost twice as much as the teachers in the public schools. Any good bricklayer can make a good living at his trade, but is the exception when a good public school teacher can make a living at his profession. What is true of the bricklayer is true with the men in other mechanical lines. They may not receive as much as the doctors and lawyers. They have a field that is altogether unique; they dictate their own prices. Dressmakers in any of our little towns make two and three time as much as the best paid teachers in the public schools. Trained nurses receive for their services as much in one week as our teachers receive for a month's service. Trained cooks can demand for their work two and three times as much as those not trained. We are not able to find people sufficiently trained to teach these subjects in our schools, to say nothing of their filling the demand of the community in which they may live. Do not forget the object of our education. We are in training for service not for idleness We are to correlate our lives with the most intelligent laws of nature, and thus, bring ourselves into harmony with the laws of God. To be out of harmony with nature is to be out of harmony with the laws of God and at variance with the laws of man and a misfit in the world. This service which we are to render may be playing an organ for Mr. Carnegie, or singing in a vested choir, or preaching in Broadway Tabernacle or performing the same service in some State prison, or cooking for the Governor of North Carolina, or in your own humble kitchen, or cleaning the dishes, or raising the children in your own homes. I have to say that not all the people who go through the schools and engage in their chosen professions are efficient. I am sure they are not less efficient because of such training. There are certain elements of disposition which do not respond to suggestion, and of moral worth of one's personal character, aside from any consideration of education and training, which must be taken into account. The simple matter of knowing is a small item in one's preparation for life work. I would not emphasize less the matter of acquiring knowledge, but I would emphasize more the matter of personal life and character. If the growth and development of one's personal habits and character do not harmonize with the best laws of life and of society than one's knowledge is unavailable. It is a great pity that from year to year we have such finely developed intellects going out from our schools utterly incapable of doing anything, because their vision has been distorted by heredity, by association and by environment. It is not enough that a workman be able simply to demand a salary. His service should be sufficient to cover his salary and to bring in a revenue to his employer. Anything less than this will be inefficient and expensive. The people who employ labor, whether common or skilled, are beginning to look to the schools for efficiency in the kind they employ. They have a right to do this because the schools are taxing capital for their support and the community has a right to expect better service and better citizenship. Simple muscular service is not enough. Farmers and land owners do not care to rent their land to men who will not use the best methods in developing the land and retaining the fertility of the soil. If better methods are not used Negroes will find it exceedingly hard in the years to come to rent good farms. Slip-shod farmers as well as other slip-shod workers will find life very bad in the future. There will be no demand for this supply of labor at any price. The question with school authorities is, how to arrange the courses of study so as to meet the demand, and I might say the emergency that is facing us. It is not simply a matter of personal, intellectual fitness for the higher demands of life. We are face to face with conditions that demand better preparation for the most ordinary duties of citizenship and for duties which family ties have imposed upon us. We are in competition with every race on the globe; we are in a democratic country; our spirit must be cosmopolitan; our education and training comprehensive and broad.

Chapter IV

This brings us to a consideration of the various forms of handicraft. These are classed as manual training, hand work, busy work, construction for purposes of utility, domestic science, house-training, nurse-training, and the list may be continued indefinitely. All this may be included in the vary general term, *Industrial Education*. The government calls them Industrial Arts. Primarily the term manual Training had for its object the development of the mind. Its place in the course was that of a cultural study. It may be cultural but when correctly taught there is no subject more applicable to the problems of daily life than manual training, except probably the trade itself. It is broader than the trade because the principles may be applied or utilized in any vocation. Before one proceeds very far in the construction of articles under the Manual Training idea he has learned the nomenclature of tools. The chisels, the saws, the braces, the bits, the vise, the square, and hundreds of other tools become familiar objects to them. He learns the application of these tools in the construction of articles. From the beginning of the course he proceeds step by step in a series of exercises, requiring as he proceed, increased strength of mind and perfect accuracy in execution. The synthesis in the series is such as to create ingenuity and the power of personal initiative in the student and to inspire the formation of correct habits. It also gives him the power of concrete analysis. He learns in an abstract way in arithmetic or geometry that certain bodies have certain surfaces; he goes into the shop and makes the bodies with saw, plane and chisel, and studies the nature of the surfaces and the process of the construction of this article. In the thing made may be involved the fundamental principle in the repair of your typewriter or your bookcase or your bookcase or your broken chair. These processes enter into one's experience and become a part of life. They have created in the student a love for work and inspired in him a feeling of dignity toward it. The dependence of the hand upon the mind and the mind upon the hand for definite results gives him an ideal and an appreciation for the best in that line of work and quickens every fiber of his conscience. He has become an intelligent criterion. A new world has been unfolded to him. Every sense has been quickened; his ideas have been differentiated; dexterity in the movement of hand and body has been acquired; self-expression given; self-reliance created; and the moral character stimulated. These processes are not only educational but they form the basis of a trade. They are the basis not of a particular line but if a very general line. They are to all trades what the fundamentals in arithmetic are to advanced mathematics. No educated man can afford to boast of his education unless he knows the use of a few tools and can use them. This should be a part of his education and no man should be without it any more than the strictly industrial enthusiast should be without that education and refined touch which books alone can impart to him. If one masters the principles of making a box four inches square he can make one ten inches square or ten feet square. The same principles are involved. If he can make a miter for a box he ought to be able to make one for a bureau. If they are correct on a small scale they are applicable on a large scale.

The utility of this sort of work can not be questioned. Let me illustrate. Some months ago, I was traveling in "The Together Campaign" in North Dakota, in the interest of Congregational benevolences. It was my good fortune to spend the Sunday preceding our meeting on Monday at Valley City, at Oriska, a small town on one of the great trunk lines of the West, with a minister who was working under the Congregational Home Missionary Society. Saturday night I was the guest of a deacon of the church who lived four miles from the town. This deacon, let me say, was a graduate of Bowdoin College and his sons and daughter were products of Fargo College, North Dakota. All of them were farmers. I was told that they grew on their farm last year, 1908, fourteen thousand bushels of wheat alone. Sunday morning we all drove back to the town where I took part in three of the services of the day. After the night service I asked the minister if I might not just as well stay at the parsonage that night as I was already suffering greatly from Dakota cold. He said, "Well, I am just out of school and if you can put up with our fare, I shall be too glad to have you stay." We went to the parsonage, and let me say, It was one of the happiest occasions of my trip which was extended nearly three months. My cot was improvised and located in the sitting room. the story of his life gave me a new inspiration. I am sorry that I can not narrate the details of it for the benefit of the boys and girls who may read this. He had had a course in Manual Training. He and his wife were graduates of Leland Stanford University in California. They worked their way through college. He said that he had made the furniture in his house; he had repaired the church building with his own hands and I think he said that he had also built the little cottage in which he lived. His work a the University was keeping the buildings and furniture in repair. The work I saw in his home and about the church was not that of a novice but it bore the evidence of the skill of a man who knew first principles. His wife appeared to be a model young housekeeper; she assisted her husband by teaching school four miles away in the country, but if she had had no other endowment she showed remarkable good sense in marrying a man who could do something else besides preach. They are both going to China as missionaries. They have studied theology one year in Oberlin, but, running short of means, they went out on the western plains and took charge of a small church in order to replenish their funds so as to finish their education for their missionary work. This is an apt application of industrial training. When a man can go from the college into the pulpit and preach the gospel and from there on the scaffold, with saw, hammer and square, and build the parsonage and repair rents in the church and from there into the shop and make furniture for both, he has something that will bring success. when correctly taught manual training fits one mentally and physically and morally too for the necessities of any emergency. It makes available our best knowledge and our best experience. This illustration is paralleled in hundreds of cases where the boys and girls have gone out from our schools. They are building churches, schoolhouses and homes and many of them are making their own furniture. Our trouble is that we do not have enough who are willing to come into our institutions for this preparation. Some months ago a mechanic came to our school and incidentally said that his son was destined to be one of the finest physicians in New York. He has already made a reputation for himself. I remember when this young boy was working with his father, in Rocky Mount, making tobacco flues and tin cups. While getting his education in the graded schools he was at the same time learning a trade with his father who is one of the best tinners in North Carolina. If this boy fails as a doctor he need not fail as a tinner. He need not fail as either. He was primarily what every citizen of this country should have; he had a first-class general education as a foundation. If he takes after his father he also has a good endowment of common sense. No form of education will be available unless one does have a good endowment of this article we call common sense. It is always at a premium. The man who can express himself well literally and mechanically with good common sense will be apt to succeed. White boys are willing to go in with their fathers and learn but Negro boys as a rule want their fathers to hire them and pay them wages for learning a trade. In our schools they want pay for their service before they have mastered the essential principles of a trade. A boy does not stop to think that in learning a trade of any sort he wastes more stock than his labor is worth. A large part of the expense of maintaining industrial schools goes right here. It matters not what the industry is. If it is not stock, it is tools or expensive supervision.

Chapter V

I think the term industrial education is sufficiently expressive for our use. It may be and work, or busy work, or manual training, or learning the various trades. It may be educative and on the same basis of any other study, or it may be simply manual labor, and without any particular educational idea, for which the student receives remuneration in money or some other equivalent. It may take its name from the assembling of machinery that has already been made in some factory; it may be making a split or straw basket--a thing that I did before I ever saw a college. Any attempt to cover all the trades and industries and at the same time maintain a high efficiency in academic standing, with few teachers and poor facilities, in one school, is a conglomeration that usually ends in doing nothing. I know of a few such attempts. It is a waste of time and poor economy. Better select a few things that will be in demand by the community, and do them well. I do not believe in graduating girls as milliners whose knowledge extends just a little beyond the multiplication table, and who do not know, ordinarily, a correct English sentence. The English may not have anything to do with making dresses, but it has a lot to do with the ordinary culture that brings success in business. I would not graduate a boy nor a girl who was not well advanced in mathematics and literature. If a tradesman does nothing but work at his trade, he soon loses his job or becomes a serf. We are not educating and training serfs. This country does not want such a class of workers. We are training people to act and live compatibly with the highest laws of nature on their own efficiency and initiative. In order to succeed in any business, one must have relations with other people. Success depends upon an intelligent manipulation of this business. One should know the value of the various products, such as labor, tools or machinery, raw material, or whatever he handles, which are factors in the business. Competition in every line of work is too sharp for one who has only an elementary preparation to succeed very long. You see, I can not get way from the one thought, which, to me, is fundamental and at the basis of all success in business or profession. That thought is the preparation in the cultural studies. If a tradesman expresses himself with his tongue or with his pen or with finger signs, it should be done with accuracy and with elegance. I believe that if a man is going to preach, he should have the best education a college can give, preparatory to his theological study. Less preparation will put him in a large class where little or no efficiency is required. I do not want a physician to doctor my family or me whose preparation for his profession was only a normal course in some secondary school. I want the best preparation that the best college can give. I do not mean to be sentimental in this matter. I am a race man, but I want the service of the man "who can deliver the goods." If you are going to be a civil engineer, or an architect, any less than a college education or an equivalent will mean your failure. Take the men and women who are eminently successful in any line of work, and you will find that they had at the bottom a very liberal education. The term "success" is a varying term. What one man would call success, another might call a failure. I do not mean simply one's ability to accumulate money and property, or the ability to excel in business, or to get office, nor even to be a great scholar. The history of this country for the last twenty-five years shows that one can have each or all of these attainments and spend his last days in the United States prison. I would count any man successful who is able to see the truth in its relation to himself and the other man, who follows it with Christian fortitude and brotherhood. I mean by "efficiency," the power to do things that will be most effective for good in the life of the individual, in the environment of the community, and in the evolution of the race.

If one expects to be a third-class preacher, doctor, teacher, mechanic, or farmer--there a plenty of places below--then he needs only a third-class education. There are so many who want to make a short-cut to graduation. There are no short-cuts in the attainment of useful knowledge. I do not expect this article to arouse such people from their slumbers. If they have not already seen visions in the horizon of the world's advancement, I do not expect these words to bring them sight. I believe in preparation for any vocation, not that I may measure arms with the black man, nor the red man, nor the yellow man, nor the brown, man, nor the white man, but that I may be the equal of any man of any race and of all professions, trades or business. I am addressing you who have aspirations beyond the day and the dollar. The future will be what this generation says it shall be. We can not afford to barter our birthright for a mess of pottage. As those who stand in the vanguard of the situation we must not mistake the call that comes to us. It matters not what the vocation may be--special preparation, every boy and girl must be taught how to make a living. They should do the ordinary things with skill and efficiency. Those who come to our schools are learning this. If they are going to be mechanics, they should put into their work all the knowledge, skill and ingenuity available. I mean knowledge that comes from the best of books, experience and things. I know of no vocation more inviting and alluring to our people to-day than that of farming. Here they have the whole field. They have in this field no exotic competition. Here they will have an application for all the science they can get in any college. Vegetation, animal life, soil composition, chemistry, physics and allied subjects constitute a field of vital importance in farm husbandry. He who masters these subjects in their application to farm development is an agriculturist of the first rank. There is no vocation in which there is such a display of ignorance as among farmers. The majority of Negro farmers do not read bulletins; they never hear a lecture on farming; they never attend a farmers' institute. They do not attend fairs where they might see the best products of the farm, either in the way of vegetables or farm animals, and they are untrained in their business relations. Their lack of knowledge gives them an endless amount of trouble in their business affairs. Some of the best agricultural papers may be had at the rate of fifty cents for three years and one dollar for five years. Fifty Negro farmers can organize themselves into a farmer's conference at any convenient place at any time of the year, and the Agricultural Department at Washington, or the Agricultural Department of the State, will be glad to send an expert to lecture to such a group of farmers, without the cost of one cent to them. Negroes do not embrace these opportunities of knowing, first, because they do not have general intelligence and initiative to appreciate them, and, second, they can not leave their little patches long enough.

The National governments spending eleven million dollars a year to help the farmers of the United States. The State governments are maintaining, at great expense, sixty-three agricultural colleges for the purpose of improving farming methods. The number of Negroes enrolled in all the colleges for Negro youths is not any larger than it should be in any one of the State colleges. These colleges are splendidly equipped with teachers and with appliances, and it is an awful pity that they do not have three times as many applications as they can accommodate. It is a greater pity that the men have to go out and literally beg the youth to come to school. It is a sickening sight that right in the shadow of our agricultural schools Negroes may be seen plodding along with one ox or one horse or mule, and that one animal so poor that it gets one foot before the other with great difficulty, and it takes two such animals to till a one-horse crop of twenty-five acres. The suggestion of better methods elicits a reply that "I have been doing this for fifty years." They forget the fact that for as many years they have scarcely made enough to keep soul and body together. It is the same old rut which their circumstances have conditioned for them, and from which they can not extricate themselves. The cost of living has reached such proportions that only the man who uses improved methods can keep up. Our prejudice toward modern means and methods must give way to modern ideas before we can progress in any line of work. Fixed ideas of any truth precludes all possibilities of further study and growth along that line. Our farmers must be better judges of the animals they buy for farming. They must learn the utility of a wagon over that of a buggy on the farm.

They must see the utility of a garden, a pigpen full of pigs, a poultry yard, and fruit trees. This is what we are teaching in our schools and talking about in our farmers' meetings. This is why the States and the Federal government are sustaining these schools. This is why private philanthropy is sustaining educational institutions. All are trying to get the masses to develop the natural resources within their reach. When proper methods are followed, the family consumption, which now comes from the store, will be cut off. A failure to observe better methods means debt, poverty and squalor. It means elimination from the progressive, wealth-producing industrial system.

CHAPTER VI

In a great many of our schools our students are not far enough in their academic studies to take scientific agriculture beyond the merest elements, so most of them are giving that which seems the most practical along with such elementary science as can be introduced at the advancement. The work has to be very elementary, because those who come to us do not remain long enough to take advanced courses, and most of them are so low in their studies that it seems impractical to try to give them science without some literary basis. The generous support which the Southern States are giving to agricultural colleges is a guarantee of the effectiveness of even this rudimentary kind of education which our boys and girls are getting. I have already spoken of the money value of the vocation of cooking and sewing. These subjects are being taught in our schools to the girls as a most important item of household economy. In many of our schools they have been taught in a very narrow sense. I think they have been brought into great disrepute in the way they have been taught in many of our Southern Institutions. Some of the schools are probably turning out good cooks. A few are turning out good teachers of these subjects. I think that every county teacher should be able to teach her children the rudiments, at least, of cooking and sewing. I do not mean the rudiments of making candies and cookies but of the substantials. This can be done in every community if the teacher has the right knowledge and gets into the work with the right spirit. No subject is of more importance than the correct preparation of food. Poorly prepared food gives rise to indigestion and all sorts of ailments. A good cook ought to know the chemistry of foods, their simple analysis, their economic value, their dietary and nutritive value. She ought to know something definite about hygienic and sanitary conditions. It would be greatly to her advantage to know something about common plumbing and the processes of heating and lighting. They can not get more than even a smattering in our schools because they, too, are looking for short-cuts. The why and the wherefore or the correlation of the sciences should be the basis of every practical operation in our educational work. Until the students become originators and discoverers of new truth for themselves they must know the sources of scientific truth so that they can apply it to all the practical operations of life, each for himself.

It is thus that interest is simulated and practical work robbed of its drudgery. We need to know how to build houses because we need better constructed homes for our families; we need to know how to be manufacturers of the staple products of commerce so as to give employment to the unemployed among us and thus be an industrial coefficient of the community in which we live. We ought to be more intelligent farmers. Our women need more skill in the arts of domestic science. The race needs professional skill in the proportion that other races have it. These are some of the vocations that have engaged the attention of man since the beginning if civilization. Our success will depend upon our preparation for the vocation. Our efficiency will depend upon the acumen we can inject into the vocation.

APPENDIX 14

Some teachers' roll books and catalogues included the subjects and names of students who attended class at Brick School during the years of the early 1900s, 1912, 1913, 1914, 1915, 1916, 1917, 1918, and Students, Brick Junior College, 1930-1931. Brick classes enrollment 1912-1918, 1930-1931.

Arithmetic, Eighth Grade - 1912

Lucinda Pitts	Dorothy Inborden	Gussie Murrain
Hattie Little	Olivia Payton	Edward Phillips
Louise Arrington	Cora Arrington	Emma Miller
Eula Arrington	William Borden	Ella Willis
Mattie Booker	Murvin Sumner	Bessie Davis

Grammar and Arithmetic - Seventh Grade - 1912

Esther Williams	Mary Phillips	Anna Jones
Olive Bond	James Hubbard	George Weston
Plummer Richardson	Ina Price	Pensive Shaw
Charles Valentine	Jacob Porter	Mary Exum
Oliva Exum	Annie Spencer	Caroline Frazier
Edward Watkins	Corinna Edwards	Sylvester Purrington
Collin Johnson	Joseph O'Neal	Connie Joyner
William Bradshaw	Dutch Blount	Annie Colson
Jeremiah McCleod		

Algebra - 1912

Charles Hayley	Lillie Lane	Naomi Greene
Amanda Aldrich	Cenobia Ross	Luli Williams
Richard Wimberly	Tazzie Dodson	Julia Inborden
Woodie Home	Maude Chishlom	Samuel Henderson
Bennie Henderson	Lizzie Battle	John Murrain
J.H. Reeves	Willie Jones	Mansfield Ready
Lula Bullock	Etta Cofield	Lillie Lane
Joseph Bullock		

Arithmetic, Grade 8 - 1912

Marian Davis	Olive Bond	Samuel Hines
James Greene	Georgianna Scott	Winona Stevens
Charles Valentine	Annie Spencer	Caroline Frazier
Jacob Porter	Jeremiah McLean	Murvin Sumner

Thomas Sewell Inborden

Algebra, 1st Year - 1912

Dorothy Inborden	Hattie Little	Louise Arrington
Wanda Peyton	Edward Phillips	Olive Payton
Richard Wimberly	Eula Arrington	Lucinda Pitts
Mattie Booker	Gussie Murrain	
Lucy Garland		

Arithmetic, Seventh Grade - 1912

Chester Phillips	William Downer	George Weston
Pensie Shaw	Bessie Hinton	Mary Lynch
Hopie White	Sarah Pittman	Mary Phillips
Ella Walters	Peter Phillips	Irene Carlisle
Jessie Bullock	Thomas Arrington	Lillian Martin
Madge Martin	John Grundy	Nettie Hicks
Mary Arrington		

Brick School English Literature Class

Teacher, D.H. Hodges, 1913

Students

Fannie Anthony	Olive Bond	Victoria Pegram
Zenobia Ross	Dorothy Inborden	Eula Arrington
Louise Arrington	Hattie Little	Maude Chisholm
Etta Cofield	Lula Bullock	Tazzie Dodson
Foss Frederick	Olivia Payton	Lucinda Pitts
Jacob Porter	George Scott	

Teacher - Mrs. Inborden's Seventh Grade Arithmetic Class

December 1913

Phenie Anderson	Lewis Austin	Naomi Anthony
Dorsey Boddie	Powell Bernhardt	Thomas Bullock
Marie Colson	Purvis Chesson	William Dixon
Matthew Davis	Mamie Grant	Samuel Holt
Wilson Howe	Jerry Huffman	Victoria Hill
Harold Kennedy	Cornelia Lyons	Lillian Martin
Emma Mial	Sallie Murrian	Peter Phillips
Thaddeus Phillips	Lizzie Pittman	Harry Proctor
Clarissa Reid	Martha Ross	Norman Saunders
Minnie Smith	Robert Shepard	James Walls
Esther Woodard		

Arithmetic - 8th Grade   1913

Major Alston	Bessie Broadus	Wilson Inborden
Alfred leach	Walter Murrain	Rosabelle Martin
Theodore Nixon	Mary Putney	Roberta Peyton
Chester Phillips	James Reid	Ruth Somerville
Bessie Ricks	Annie Spencer	Alex Sessoms

Algebra - 9th Grade   1913

Lula Ashe	Cora Arrington	Mary Arrington
Fannie Anthony	Thomas Arrington	Jessie Bullock
Irene Carlisle	Caroline Frazier	Martha Harrison
Madge Martin	Sara Pittman	Nora Parrish
Lula Ruffin	Lucy Smith	Ella Waters
Janelle Whitaker	Hopie White	Colston White

Arithmetic - 8th Grade   October 1913

Wilson Inborden	Walter Murrain	Rosabelle Martin
Mary Putney	Roberta Peyton	Ruth Summerville
Alex Sessoms	Chester Phillips	Theodore Nixon
Bessie Broadus	Major Alston	James Read
Alfred Leach		

Algebra - 10th Year - 1913

Fannie Anthony	Eula Arrington	Cora Arrington
Mattie Booker	Olive Bond	Jeremiah McLeod
Harold Maugrey	Edward Philips	Jacob Porter
Willie Sessoms	Gertrude Wilson	Richard Wimberly
Charles Valentine		

Students - 1914-1915

Primary Department

First Grade

Student	City and State
Joseph Bryant	Bricks, North Carolina
Sylvester Burnette	Bricks, North Carolina
Harding Forney	Bricks, North Carolina
Arthur Garrett	Whitakers, North Carolina
James McKiver	Raleigh, North Carolina
Pearl Nicholson	Greensboro, North Carolina
Annette Pittman	Bricks, North Carolina
Lula Pittman	Bricks, North Carolina
Lula Mae Simms	Rocky Mount, North Carolina
Forest Taylor	Battlesboro, North Carolina

Thomas Sewell Inborden

Second Grade

Student	City and State
Elna Bryant	Whitakers, North Carolina
Addie Burnette	Bricks, North Carolina
Lee Joyner	Woodland, North Carolina
Carrie Lewis	Enfield, North Carolina
Cornelieus Lyons	Bricks, North Carolina
Rosa Belle Nicholson	Greensboro, North Carolina
Evelyn Phillips	Bricks, North Carolina

Third Grade - 1914-1915

Student	City and State
Rufus Artis	Wilson, North Carolina
Mary Battle	Whitakers, North Carolina
Eddie Bell	Whitakers, North Carolina
Alphonso Bobbitt	Enfield, North Carolina
Mary Burnette	Bricks, North Carolina
Joseph Cause	Enfield, North Carolina
Ernest Cotton	Enfield, North Carolina
Dorcas Croom	Salisbury, North Carolina
Martha Croom	La Grange, North Carolina
Richard Garrett	Bricks, North Carolina
William Garrett	Plymouth, North Carolina
Carey Howington	Enfield, North Carolina
Lucy Johnson	Whitakers, North Carolina
George Laurence	Scotland Neck, North Carolina
Eugene Lyons	Bricks, North Carolina
Joseph Murrain	Whitakers, North Carolina
Nancy Pitt	Enfield, North Carolina
Eddie Pittman	Bricks, North Carolina
Lucian Pittman	Bricks, North Carolina
George Reid	Bricks, North Carolina
Seeta Whitehead	Enfield, North Carolina
William Henry Williams	Whitakers, North Carolina
Josephus Woodward	Whitakers, North Carolina
Walter Woodward	Whitakers, North Carolina

Grammar Department

Fourth Grade 1914-915

Student	City and State
Rena Bellamy	Sharpsburg, North Carolina
Ruth Carter	Enfield, North Carolina
Raymond Chandler	Baltimore, Maryland
Redmon Drake	Rocky Mount, North Carolina
Kenneth Freeman	Rocky Mount, North Carolina
George Hilliard	Whitakers, North Carolina
Bessie Jenkins	Rosemary, North Carolina

Harriett Johnston   Thelma, North Carolina
Jennie Murrain   Whitakers, North Carolina

Fifth Grade

Walter Anderson   Middlesex, North Carolina
Benjamin Brown   East Orange, New Jersey
Harry Burnell   Norfolk, Virginia
Vera Carlyle   Whitakers, North Carolina
Anna Mae Cause   Glen Cove, New York
Curtis Cofield   Enfield, North Carolina
Maude Crenshaw   Raleigh, North Carolina
Moncy Davis   Halifax, North Carolina
Elizabeth Fletcher   Bricks, North Carolina
Milo Hicks   Detroit, Michigan
Channic Hinton   Raleigh, North Carolina
Frederick Huff   Williamston, North Carolina
Sallie Jones   Portsmouth, Virginia
William Jones   Durham, North Carolina
Blanche Lee   Hobgood, North Carolina

Student   City and State

McKinley Lyons   Bricks, North Carolina
Bertha Mack   Whitakers, North Carolina
Ethlelind Marlin   Weldon, North Carolina
Ever Beulah Martin   Aurelian Springs, North Carolina
George Murrain   Whitakers, North Carolina
Stanley Murrain   Whitakers, North Carolina
Tiney Rhodes   Greensboro, North Carolina
John Sloan   Enfield, North Carolina
Richard Williams   Wilmington, North Carolina

Sixth Grade   1914-1915

Beatrice Arrington   Bricks, North Carolina
Estelle Arrington   Bricks, North Carolina
Lillie Ashe   Raleigh, North Carolina
Eva Battle   Rocky Mount, North Carolina
Mary Battle   Bricks, North Carolina
Joseph Blount   Portsmouth, Virginia
William Blow   Wilson, North Carolina
Matthew Bond   Enfield, North Carolina
William Bowen   Williamstown, North Carolina
William Bullock   Durham, North Carolina
Marion Devereaux   Whitakers, North Carolina
James Dixon   Rocky Mount, North Carolina
Jolly Edwards   Rocky Mount, North Carolina
Arthur Elliott   Portsmouth, Virginia
Lugenia Exum   Whitakers, North Carolina
Estelle Fisher   Strieby North Carolina
Raymond Ford   Enfield, North Carolina
Benjamin Hall   Wilmington, North Carolina
Gertude Harris   Greenville, North Carolina

Maggie Hart	Whitakers, North Carolina
Dewey Haugabook	Albany, Georgia
Martha Hawkins	Macon, Georgia
Charles Haywood	Raleigh, North Carolina
Harold Hicks	Detroit, Michigan
George Hines	Greensboro, North Carolina
Morris Hunter	Enfield, North Carolina
Viola Martin	Weldon, North Carolina
Patience McKinney	Charlotte, North Carolina
Royal McLin	Rocky Mount, North Carolina
James McWilliams	Enfield, North Carolina
Emma Mial	Enfield, North Carolina
Florence Mitchell	White Plains, New York, North Carolina
Thelma Parker	Plymouth, North Carolina
Ellen Phillips	Tarboro, North Carolina
Flora Phillips	Bricks, North Carolina
Columbus Powell	Parmele, North Carolina
William Powell	Tarboro, North Carolina
James Redrick	St. Albans, Vermont
Evelyn Roberts	Washington, D.C.
Myrtle Saunders	High Point, North Carolina
Student	City and State
Bennie Smith	Scotland, North Carolina
Dennie Smith	Raleigh, North Carolina
Iona Smith	Scotland, North Carolina
Lossie Taylor	Whitakers, North Carolina
Arlee Whitaker	Enfield, North Carolina
Jesse Wright	Elm City, North Carolina

High School Department

Seventh Grade - 1914-1915

Eleanor Ashford	Clinton, North Carolina
Louis Austin	Enfield, North Carolina
Bennie Cofield	Enfield, North Carolina
Charles Davis	Philadelphia, Pennsylvania
Mason Davis	Amherst, Massachusetts
William Dixon	Durham, North Carolina
Melvin Greene	Gatesville, North Carolina
Clinton Harris	Monicure, North Carolina
Jerry Huffman	Salisbury, North Carolina
Lucille James	Scotland Neck, North Carolina
Ida Belle Johnson	Weldon, North Carolina
Margaret Jones	Raleigh, North Carolina
James Perkins	Lindsays, Virginia
Pearl Phillips	Bricks, North Carolina
Winnie Price	Littleton, North Carolina
Harridelle Proctor	Richmond, Virginia
Charles Ryalls	Richmond, Virginia
Isaac Sapp	Dunbar, South Carolina

Marion Simmons   Burlington, North Carolina
Solomon Smith   Raleigh, North Carolina
Robert Shepard   Winston-Salem, North Carolina
Carrie Williams   Weldon, North Carolina
Esther Queen Woodward   Whitakers, North Carolina

Eighth Grade - 1914-1915

Naomi Anthony   Weldon, North Carolina
George Bumpass   Durham, North Carolina
Thomasena Chavis   Wadesboro, North Carolina
Purvis Chesson   Norfolk, Virginia
Daniel Cutchin   Whitakers, North Carolina
Matthew Davis   Nashville, North Carolina
Marion Davis   East Orange, New Jersey
Osceola Edwards   Washington, North Carolina
Edward James   Hobgood, North Carolina
Annie Johnson   Norfolk, Virginia
Lillian Martin   Aurelian Springs, North Carolina
Hettie Monk   Rocky Mount, North Carolina
Bertha Parrish   Rougemont, North Carolina
Roberta Peyton   Washington, D.C.

Student   City and State

Lizzie Pittman   Rocky Mount, North Carolina
Clarissa Reed   Bricks, North Carolina
Bessie Ricks   Rocky Mount, North Carolina
Norman Saunders   Selma, North Carolina
Maria Vance   Rapids, North Carolina
James Walls   Charlotte, North Carolina
Otis Davis   East Orange, New Jersey
Henry Whitfield   Goldsboro, North Carolina

Eleventh Grade - 1914-1915

Fannie Anthony   Weldon, North Carolina
Cora Arrington   Bricks, North Carolina
Olive Bond   Enfield, North Carolina
Mattie Booker   Greensboro, North Carolina
Christopher Dobbin   Troy, North Carolina
Harold Hargrave   Salisbury, North Carolina
Jeremiah McLeod   Strieby, North Carolina
Grace Miller   Charlotte, North Carolina
William Sessoms   Nashville, North Carolina
Murvin Sumner   Salisbury, North Carolina
Charles Valentine   Roanoke, Virginia

Twelfth Grade

Eulah Arrington	Bricks, North Carolina
Louise Arrington	Bricks, North Carolina
Dorothy Inborden	Bricks, North Carolina
Hattie Little	Wilmington, North Carolina
Olivia Peyton	Tarboro, North Carolina
Maude Peyton	Washington, North Carolina
Lucinda Pitts	Wilson, North Carolina
Laura Powers	Rosemary, North Carolina
Harmon Taylor	Wake Forest, North Carolina
John Williams	Jersey City, New Jersey

Night School - 1914-1915

Hosea Arrington	Bricks, North Carolina
Luther Arrington	Bricks, North Carolina
Mabel Boseman	Dudley, North Carolina
Aaron Brown	Capertown, West Virginia
Charles Brown	Sharon, South Carolina
Maceo Burgess	Winona, West Virginia
James Burnette	Bricks, North Carolina
William Burnette	Bricks, North Carolina
David Carver	Portsmouth, Virginia
Mary Clapp	Scotland Neck, North Carolina
Rosetta Clark	Rosemary, North Carolina
Letha Davis	Ashboro, North Carolina

Student	City and State
Eljah Dean	Elm City, North Carolina
Lillian Dempsey	Whitakers, North Carolina
Mastin Glenn	Rougemont, North Carolina
Cleora Graves	Durham, North Carolina
Benjamin Hayes	Rocky Mount, North Carolina
Linwood Hill	Scotland Neck, North Carolina
Clarissa Holman	Raleigh, North Carolina
Geneva Howington	Enfield, North Carolina
Willie Howington	Enfield, North Carolina
Christena Ivey	Bricks, North Carolina
Lizzie Johnson	Durham, North Carolina
Walter Lassiter	Durham, North Carolina
Dred Lyons	Bricks, North Carolina
Bertha Macklin	Raleigh, North Carolina
Lee Ethel Martin	Rocky Mount, North Carolina
Mary Pegram	Dallas, North Carolina
Peter Phillips	Bricks, North Carolina
Thaddeus Phillips	Bricks, North Carolina
Thelma Plummer	Littleton. North Carolina
Jacob Porter	Boston, Massachusetts
Andrew Reaves	Sanford, North Carolina
Cora Roberts	Durham, North Carolina

Louis Tilly	Durham, North Carolina	
Kathleen White	Ahoskie, North Carolina	
Mary Winfield	Norfolk, Virginia	
William Lemuel	Nashville, North Carolina	

Music Department - 1914-1915

Olive Bond	Margaret Jones	Bessie Broadnax
Lillian Martin	Irene Carlyle	Viola Pittman
Martha Hawkins	Martha Powers	Dorothy Inborden
James Redrick		

Language and Geography

Fourth Grade - 1914-1915

Mary Burnett	Rosetta Clark	Richard Garrett
Cleora Graves	Beatrice Landis	Kathina Lowe
Mary Martin	Henrietta Pearsall	George Reid
David Sessoms	Nettie Whitaker	Robert Powell
Rosa Taylor	Walker Woodward	Henry Ford

Arithmetic and Spelling

Fourth Grade - 1914-1915

Callie Bellamy	Ruth Carter	Vera Carlisle
Raymond Chandler	Eddie Draughn	Madessa Exum

Student	City and State	
George Hilliard	Stephen Johnson	John Mayo
Viola Pittman	Malinda Powers	Charlotte Smith
Ralph Steven	Mattie Sugg	Nettie Thompson
Roosevelt Whitehead	Thelma Plummer	Luther Arrington
Montera Davis	Rene Bellamy	Idela Love

Normal School

Elementary 1-4, 1916-1917

Etta Lee Arrington	Bricks, North Carolina
Fannie Lee Arrington	Bricks, North Carolina
Otis Arrington	Bricks, North Carolina
Berlyn Austin	Whitakers, North Carolina
Jesse Williams	Bricks, North Carolina
Janet Williams	Bricks, North Carolina
Maria Brodie	Whitakers, North Carolina
Harding Forney	Bricks, North Carolina
Myrtle Forney	Bricks, North Carolina
Georgia Cutchin	Whitakers, North Carolina
Janie Daughtery	Bricks, North Carolina

Pennie Daughtery	Bricks, North Carolina
Joseph Dickens	Whitakers, North Carolina
Branch Harvey	Wilson, North Carolina
Edward Hill	Whitakers, North Carolina
Irene Hill	Weldon, North Carolina
Lucy Johnson	Whitakers, North Carolina
Eugene Lyons	Bricks, North Carolina
Cornellum Lyons	Bricks, North Carolina
Nathan Martin	Thelma, North Carolina
Leola Martin	Rosemary, North Carolina
Inez Nixon	Greensboro, North Carolina
Rosella Nixon	Greensboro, North Carolina
Lossie Phillips	Whitakers, North Carolina
Selma Speight	Battleboro, North Carolina
William Henry Williams	Whitakers, North Carolina
Ora Whitehead	Bricks, North Carolina
Frederick Pittman	Bricks, North Carolina
Lucian Pittman	Bricks, North Carolina

Fourth Grade 1916-1917

Jessie Battle	Bricks, North Carolina
Martha Bryant	Bricks, North Carolina
Mary Burnette	Bricks, North Carolina
Rosetta Clark	Rosemary, North Carolina
Laura Ford	Whitakers, North Carolina
Henry Ford	Ringwood, North Carolina
Richard Garrett	Bricks, North Carolina
Cleora Graves	Durham, North Carolina
Roland Gunter	Enfield, North Carolina

Student	City and State
Walter Knight	Tillery, North Carolina
Frank Kornegay	Kinston, North Carolina
Beatrice Landis	Brooklyn, New York
Mary Martin	Rosemary, North Carolina
George Myrick	Ringwood, North Carolina
Henrietta Pearsall	Farmville, North Carolina
Callie Pittman	Bricks, North Carolina
Robert Powell	Bricks, North Carolina
George Reid	Bricks, North Carolina
David Sessoms	Nashville, North Carolina
Katie Thorne	Whitakers, North Carolina
Nettie Whitaker	Enfield, North Carolina

Arithmetic

Fifth Grade February 1916

Luther Arrington	Callie Bellainey	Rena Bellamy
Vera Carlisle	Mamie Carr	Ruth Carter
Raymond Chandler	Blanche Dickens	Montera Davis

Edward Draughn
Stephen Johnson
Thelma Plummer
Ralph Stevens
Roosevelt Whitehead

Medessa Exum
Idalia Love
Malinda Powers
Mattie Sugg

George Hilliard
Viola Pittman
Charlotte Smith
Nettie Thompson

Teacher - Mrs. Fletcher
Fourth and Fifth Grades - 1916

Fourth Grade

Charles Bumpass
Dorcas Croom
Maud Laurence
Mattie Reaves
Henry Williams

Moses Bumpass
Neida Hill
Nathan Martin
Hattie Scott
Pecola Wynn

Maggie Bryant
Leah Jenkins'
Ories Merritt
Ora Whitehead
Eugene Lyons

Four and Fifth Grade

Lillie Armstrong
Arlene Joiner
Henrietta Pearsall
David Sessoms
Roosevelt Whitehead

Martha Bryant
George Lynch
Robert Powell
William Tucker
Annie Wiggins

Richard Garrett
Mary Martin
George Reid
Chester Wallace
Gerson Bullock

Sixth Grade   1916-1917

Hosea Arrington,
Roscoe Blount
Charles Brown

Bricks, North Carolina
Berkley, Virginia
Caperton, West Virginia

Student

City and State

Benjamin Brown
William Bowen
Harry Burnell
Vicenna Byers
Gertrude Bullock
James Burnette
Curtis Cofield
Lloyd Davis
Moncy Davis
Lillian Dempsey
William Alexander
Dolly Edwards
Elizabeth Fletcher
Milo Hicks
Willie Howington
Lizzie Johnson
Sandy Johnson
William Jones
Cleopatra Jones
McKinley Lyons

East Orange, New Jersey
Williamston, North Carolina
Norfolk, Virginia
Charlotte, North Carolina
Enfield, North Carolina
Bricks, North Carolina
Enfield, North Carolina
East Orange, New Jersey
Halifax, North Carolina
Whitakers, North Carolina
Berkley, Virginia
Rocky Mount, North Carolina
Bricks, North Carolina
Detroit, Michigan
Enfield, North Carolina
Durham, North Carolina
Airlie, North Carolina
Durham, North Carolina
Raleigh, North Carolina
Bricks, North Carolina

Thomas Sewell Inborden

Ethel Lee Martin	Rocky Mount, North Carolina
Beaulah Ever Martin	Rocky Mount, North Carolina
Dempsey King	Tarboro, North Carolina
Richards Mayo	Brooklyn, North Carolina
Mattie Lee Moye	Greenville, North Carolina
Ethel Myers	Berkley, Virginia
Maggie Powell	Talledega, Alabama
James Redrick	St. Albans, Vermont
Arthur Slade	Williamston, North Carolina
Molly Young	Seabridge, North Carolina
John Sloan	Enfield, North Carolina
Harry Thomas	East Orange, New Jersey
Jennie Smith	Raleigh, North Carolina
Oddie Williams	Kenansville, North Carolina

High School Department - 1916-1917

Seventh Grade

Estelle Arrington	Bricks, North Carolina
Sallie Lee Ashford	Clinton, North Carolina
Mary Battle	Bricks, North Carolina
Eva Battle	Rocky Mount, North Carolina
Joseph Blount	Portsmouth, Virginia
William Blow	Wilson, North Carolina
Matthew Bond	Enfield, North Carolina
Mary Clapp	Scotland Neck, North Carolina
Bennie Cofield	Enfield, North Carolina
Lona Daniels	Enfield, North Carolina
Marion Devereaux	Whitakers, North Carolina
Lugenia Exum	Whitakers, North Carolina

Student	City and State
Raymond Ford	Enfield, North Carolina
Hattie Ford	Whitakers, North Carolina
Maggie Hart	Whitakers, North Carolina
Harold Hicks	Detroit, Michigan
Geneva Howington	Enfield, North Carolina
Clarissa Holman	Raleigh, North Carolina
Belle Ida Johnson	Weldon, North Carolina
Culear Jordan	Seaboard, North Carolina
Patience McKinney	Charlotte, North Carolina
Florence Mitchell	Weldon, North Carolina
Flora Phillips	Bricks, North Carolina
Thaddeus Phillips	Bricks, North Carolina
Isaac Sapp	Dunbar, South Carolina
Madie Sledge	Raleigh, North Carolina
Ida Bell Smith	Jacksonville, North Carolina
Otis Taylor	Whitakers, North Carolina
Lossie Taylor	Whitakers, North Carolina
Annie Vincent	Henrico, North Carolina
Arlee Whitaker	Enfield, North Carolina

Eighth Grade

Louis Austin	Enfield, North Carolina
Edward Boykins	Sanford, North Carolina
Hattie Council	Tarboro, North Carolina
Charles Davis	Philadelphia, Pennsylvania
William Dixon	Madison, New Jersey
Melvin Greene	Hampton, Virginia
Clinton Harris	Moncure, North Carolina
Jerry Huffman	Salisbury, North Carolina
Hortense Nesbitt	Charoltte, North Carolina
Peter Phillips	Bricks, North Carolina
Pearl Phillips	Bricks, North Carolina
Harridelle Proctor	Richmond, Virginia
Marlon Simmons	High Point, North Carolina
Lewis Smith	Autryville, North Carolina
Beatrice Stanton	Charlotte, North Carolina
Madge Watson	Enfield, North Carolina
Bartel Wicker	Sanford, North Carolina
Queen Esther Woodard	Whitakers, North Carolina

Ninth Grade

Naomi Anthony	Weldon, North Carolina
George Bumpass	Durham, North Carolina
Matthew Davis	Nashville, North Carolina
Otis Davis	East Orange, New Jersey
William Dutrieville	New Haven, Connecticut
Molester Exum	Whitakers, North Carolina
Rolister Exum	Whitakers, North Carolina

Student	City and State
Lillian Martin	Thelma, North Carolina
George McLean	Greensboro, North Carolina
Roberta Peyton	Washington, North Carolina
Norman Saunders	Selma, North Carolina
Anna Spencer	Atlantic City, New Jersey
Clarissa Reid	Bricks, North Carolina

Tenth Grade

Nellie Baldwin	Dudley, North Carolina
Bessie Broadnax	Seaboard, North Carolina
Sadie Gibson	Charlotte, North Carolina
Eula Hargrove	Goldsboro, North Carolina
Wilson Inborden	Bricks, North Carolina
Alfred Leach	Moncure, North Carolina
Colston LeGrand	Portsmouth, Virginia
Rosa Belle Martin	Warsaw, North Carolina

Theodore Nixon	Vaughan, North Carolina
Mary Putney	Weldon, North Carolina
Chester Phillips	Bricks, North Carolina
Alexander Sessoms	Nashville, North Carolina
Richard Smith	Kenansville, North Carolina

Eleventh Grade

Mary Arrington	Ringwood, North Carolina
Lula Ashe	Raleigh, North Carolina
Jessie Bullock	Bricks, North Carolina
Irene Carlisle	Whitakers, North Carolina
Carolyn Frazier	Charlotte, North Carolina
Martha Harrison	Whitakers, North Carolina
Gretchen LaCour	Talledega, Alabama
Madge Martin	Thelma, North Carolina
Nora Parrish	Rougemount, North Carolina
Sarah Pittman	Rocky Mount, North Carolina
Lucy Smith	Raleigh, North Carolina
Ella Walters	Rocky Mount, North Carolina

Twelfth Grade

Cora Arrington	Bricks, North Carolina
Olive Bond	Enfield, North Carolina
Mattie Booker	Greeneoboro, North Carolina
Christopher Dobbin	Troy, North Carolina
Harold Hargrave	Salisbury, North Carolina
Jeremiah McLeod	Strieby, North Carolina
Grace Miller	Charlotte, North Carolina

Student	City and State
Jacob Porter	Boston, Massachusetts
William Sessoms	Nashville, North Carolina
Murvin Sumner	Salisbury, North Carolina
Charles Valentine	Roanoke, Virginia

Teacher Training Department

Eula Arrington	Bricks, North Carolina
Louise Arrington	Bricks, North Carolina
Lillie Lynch	Essex, North Carolina
Maude Peyton	Washington, D.C.
Laura Powers	Rosemary, North Carolina
John Williams	Jersey City, New Jersey

Music Training

Louise Arrington	Beatrice Landis
Naomi Anthony	Mecea Kornegay
Sallie Lee Ashford	Lillian Martin
Nellie Baldwin	Theodore Nixon
Mary Battle	Thelma Plummer
Cleopatra Bennett	Jacob Porter
Jessie Bullock	Maggie Powell
Vicena Byers	Malinda Powers
Bessie Broadnax	Laura Powers
Charles Davis	Mattie Suggs
Lugenia Exum	Nettie Thompson
Gretchen LaCour	Mollie Young

Night School

Thomas Arrington	Bricks, North Carolina
Cornelia Alexander	Berkley, Virginia
Bernice Barber	Raleigh, North Carolina
Silas Braxton	New York City, New York
Charles Bumpass	Durham, North Carolina
Moses Bumpass	Durham, North Carolina
Estella Campbell	Fayetteville, North Carolina
Leola Chavis	Hillsboro, North Carolina
Alice Cooper	Hillsboro, North Carolina
Pauline Devereax	Enfield, North Carolina
Samuel Daughtery	Bricks, North Carolina
George Dickens	Tarboro, North Carolina
Lucile Hardy	Charlotte, North Carolina
Jehu Hunter	Graham, North Carolina
Arthur Ham	Wilson, North Carolina
Josephine Jenkins	Weldon, North Carolina
Leah Jenkins	Weldon, North Carolina
Moses Lawrence	Ringwood, North Carolina
George Lawrence	Scotland Neck, North Carolina

Student	City and State
Maude Lawrence	Scotland Neck, North Carolina
Hampton Long	Hillsboro, North Carolina
Viola Martin	Rosemary, North Carolina
McDonald Matthewson	Tarboro, North Carolina
Lillian McDonald	Raleigh, North Carolina
Dred Lyons	Bricks, North Carolina
Theodore McLeod	Strieby, North Carolina
Henry Myers	Berkley, Virginia
Daniel Pittman	Tarboro, North Carolina
Marie Price	Portsmouth, Virginia
Hattie Scott	Enfield, North Carolina
Rhoda Stephens	Charlotte, North Carolina
Minnie Spencer	Charlotte, North Carolina

Thomas Sewell Inborden

Irene Smith	Scotland Neck, North Carolina
Bennie Smith	Scotland Neck, North Carolina
Carrie Shaw	Thelma, North Carolina
Vernon Taylor	Salisbury, North Carolina
Ellis Thigpen	Tarboro, North Carolina
Nathan Thigpen	Tarboro, North Carolina
Willie Whitaker	Whitakers, North Carolina
Belinda White	Jacksonville, North Carolina
Jonas Wortham	Warrenton, North Carolina
Dazell Wyche	Raleigh, North Carolina
Pearl Rivers	New Bern, North Carolina
Divan Reid	Bricks, North Carolina

Algebra - Ninth Grade   1917

George Baldwin	Theodore McLeod	George Elliott
Thaddeus Phillips	Bennie Cofield	Mary J. Walters
Jeannie Ryan	Laura Davidson	Charlotte Hunter
David Monroe	Flora Phillips	Raymond Ford
Pearl Phillips	Maggie Hart	George Mitchell
Lillian Reid	Waldo Falkener	Minnie Watts
Daniel Pittman	Nossie Alston	George Baldwin
Laura Davidson	George Elliott	Lugenia Exum
Raymond Ford	Hattie Ford	Waldo Falkener
Jehu Hunter	George Mitchell	David Monroe
Jeanne Ryan		

Algebra - Tenth Grade   1917

Peter Phillips	Robert Shepard	Melvin Greene
Clinton Harris	Edward Boykin	Charles Davis
John Harris	Barter Wicker	Beatrice Robinson
Madge Watson	William Dixon	Marion Simmons
Molesta Exum	Jerry Huffman	Henry Whitefield
Richard Smith		

Grammar Seventh and Eighth Grades

Seventh Grade   1917

Raymond Chandler	Boyd Rosser	Louise Peterson
Lula Walker	Lillian Williams	Viola Peterson
Eula Sessoms	George Mebane	Eleanor Johnson
Grace Jackson	William Jones	Armstrong Brandon
Vera Carlisle	Rosaline King	Henry Myers
Malinda Powers	Costina Stewart	Gertrude Bryd

Eighth Grade   1917

Grady Beall	Otis Hargrave	Elizabeth Fletcher
John E. Battle	James Pherribo	Luther Whitted
Olive Maness	Eva B. Martin	Jehu Hunter
John Hunter	Florence Mitchell	Maggie Powell
Catherine Brown	James Redrick	Rosaline King
Carrie Harvey	Henry Myers	Melinda Powers
Bennie Brown	Costina Stewart	Gertrude Boyd

Arithmetic - Seventh Grade   1918

Henrietta Pearsall	Mattie Hester	Sarah Burns
Maggie Young	Rosa Johnson	Andrew Garris
Richard Garrett	Malinda Powers	Eunice Taylor
Elton Rogers		

Algebra - Tenth Grade   1918

George Elliott	Daniel Pittman	Maggie Culp

Grammar - Seventh Grade   December 1918

Sarah Burris	Christine Frazier	Andrew Garris
Richard Garrett	Mattie Hester	Ross Johnson
Henrietta Pearsall	Boyd Rosser	Eunice Taylor
Maggie Young	Chester Wallace	Harry Cofield
Edward Peterson	Vera Carlisle	Audalene Joyner
Bettie Williams		

Algebra - Tenth Grade   December 1918

George Elliott	Lugenia Exum	Molista Exum
Hattie Ford	Pearl Phillips	Flora Phillips
Peter Phillips	Raymond Ford	Thaddeus Phillips

Arithmetic - Eighth Grade   December 1918

Louise Peterson	Victoria Walker	Eula Sessoms
Nettie Thompson	Henry Myers	Harry Anderson
Annie Whitley	Elivnora Johnson	Guthrie Turner

Arithmetic - Eighth Grade 1918

Wilson Inborden
Mary Putney
Alex Sessoms
Bessie Broadnax
Alfred Leach

Walter Murrain
Roberta Peyton
Chester Phillips
Major Alston

Rosabelle Martin
Ruth Summerville
Theodore Nixon
James Reid

Arithmetic - Seventh Grade 1918

Phenzie Anderson
Mamie Grant
Harold Kennedy
Sallie Murrain
Louis Austin

Martha Ross
Bessie Broadnax
Wilson Howe
Naomi Anthony

Dorsey Boddie
Lizzie Pittman
Harridelle Proctor
Thomas Bullock

Grammar - Seventh and Eighth Grades 1918

Seventh Grade

Brandon Armstrong
Grace Jackson
Henry Myers
Boyd Rosser
Nettie Thompson
Catherine Brown
Eunice Taylor
Gertrude Byrd

Vera Carlisle
William Jones
Viola Pittman
Costina Stewart
Sula Walker
Cleopatra Toney
Grady Beall

Elnora Johnson
Rosalie King
Louise Peterson
Eula Sessoms
Lillian Williams
Mattie Sugg
Luther Whitted

Eighth Grade

Sallie Lee Ashford
Elizabeth Fletcher
Eva Beulah Martin
Eurelia Ors
James Redrick
Calib Robinson

Bennie Brown
Otis Hargrave
Florence Mitchell
Lula Campbell
Guthrie Turner
Jehu Hunter

William Burnett
Maud Lilly
George Miller
Maggie Powell
Oscie Taylor
Willie Mae Parker

Day School Students

First Grade 1922 - 1923

Student	City and State
Wilson Adams	Bricks, North Carolina
Walter Anderson	Bricks, North Carolina
Ernest Battle	Whitakers, North Carolina

Student	City and State
Frank Battle	Whitakers, North Carolina
Walter Bandy	Whitakers, North Carolina
Eddie Bowens	Whitakers, North Carolina
Lina Bowens	Whitakers, North Carolina
Alexander Brown	Bricks, North Carolina
Amelia Bryant	Whitakers, North Carolina
Minnie Bunn	Whitakers, North Carolina
Moses Dickens	Whitakers, North Carolina
Peter Dickens	Whitakers, North Carolina
Este Fields	Bricks, North Carolina
John Forbes	Whitakers, North Carolina
Benjamin Forbes	Whitakers, North Carolina
Rose Garrant	Bricks, North Carolina
Sallie Grant	Bricks, North Carolina
Beatrice Grant	Bricks, North Carolina
Charles Hill	Bricks, North Carolina
Lucy Hilliard	Bricks, North Carolina
John Hilliard	Bricks, North Carolina
Patty Lee Horner	Whitakers, North Carolina
Bessie House	Farmerville, North Carolina
Maie McFadden	Rocky Mount, North Carolina
Henry Norman	Enfield, North Carolina
Nathaniel Peterson	Enfield, North Carolina
Ethel Phillips	Whitakers, North Carolina
Lugenia Speights	Bricks, North Carolina
Willie Mae Speights	Bricks, North Carolina

Second Grade 1922 - 1923

Student	City and State
Adam Scott	Bricks, North Carolina
Andrew Bailey	Springfield, Massachusetts
Eddie Chappen	Enfield, North Carolina
Paul Dickens	Whitakers, North Carolina
Ross Dickens	Whitakers, North Carolina
Charles Hilliard	Bricks, North Carolina
Eula Hilliard	Bricks, North Carolina
Pearl Horner	Whitakers, North Carolina
Lilie Mae Horner	Whitakers, North Carolina
Catherine Lane	Enfield, North Carolina
Joseph Pittman	Bricks, North Carolina
Mary Reid	Bricks, North Carolina
William Royster	Rocky Mount, North Carolina
Raymon Speights	Bricks, North Carolina

Student	City and State
Howard Stephens	Portsmouth, Virginia
Maude Tellery	Whitakers, North Carolina
Edward Walker	Whitakers, North Carolina
Winton White	Enfield, North Carolina
Bertha Williams	Whitakers, North Carolina

Third Grade 1922 - 1923

Otis Arrington	Enfield, North Carolina
Lucias Arrington	Enfield, North Carolina
Leather Barrett	Ayden, North Carolina
William Bowens	Whitakers, North Carolina
James Cullen Bryant	Whitakers, North Carolina
Katie Bryant	Bricks, North Carolina
Glendora Brown	Bricks, North Carolina
Tormal Epps	Rocky Mount, North Carolina
Dollie Anne Hawley	Rochester, New York
Nello Ingram	Enfield, North Carolina
Thomas Jenkins	Weldon, North Carolina
John Lowe	Enfield, North Carolina
Naomi Phillips	Whitakers, North Carolina
Andrew Reynolds	Enfield, North Carolina
Betsey Speights	Bricks, North Carolina
Johnnie Watson	Whitakers, North Carolina
Freeman Williams	Whitakers, North Carolina

Fourth Grade 1922 - 1923

Frank Adams	Bricks, North Carolina
Percy Lee Battle	Whitakers, North Carolina
Howard Battle	Whitakers, North Carolina
Georgia Bryant	Whitakers, North Carolina
Sarah Byrd	Whitakers, North Carolina
Christine Brown	Bricks, North Carolina
James Burgess	Littleton, North Carolina
William Daniel	Whitakers, North Carolina
Lonie Daniel	Whitakers, North Carolina
Joseph Davis	Whitakers, North Carolina
Hazelldell Dixon	Garretts, Virginia
Russell Forbes	Whitakers, North Carolina
James Ford	Whitakers, North Carolina
Linwood Freeman	Rocky Mount, North Carolina
Odessa Gaylor	Whitakers, North Carolina
Mary Gunter	Whitakers, North Carolina
Pauline Hawley	Rochester, New York
Carrie Hilliard	Bricks, North Carolina
Ethel Hilliard	Bricks, North Carolina
Elijah Hilliard	Bricks, North Carolina
Minnie Hilliard	Bricks, North Carolina
Callie Hill	Bricks, North Carolina

Student	City and State
Marutha Hill	Bricks, North Carolina
Frank Leak	Bricks, North Carolina
William Mason	Enfield, North Carolina
Kathy McCall	Whitakers, North Carolina
Lufenda Pittman	Bricks, North Carolina
Johnnie Pittman	Bricks, North Carolina

Lucile Pittman	Bricks, North Carolina
Mamie Powell	Whitakers, North Carolina
Joseph Powell	Rocky Mount, North Carolina
Johnnie Speights	Bricks, North Carolina
Mattie Mae Speights	Bricks, North Carolina
Royal Thorne	Rochester, New York
Edward Whitaker	Enfield, North Carolina
Charles Whitaker	Enfield, North Carolina
Myra Williams	Whitakers, North Carolina
Raymon Williams	Whitakers, North Carolina

Fifth Grade 1922 - 1923

William Alexander	Williamston, North Carolina
Ruth Arrington	Enfield, North Carolina
Bruce Austin	Arcala, North Carolina
Allen Austin	Warrenton, North Carolina
Mary Battle	Rocky Mount, North Carolina
Robert Barrett	Ayden, North Carolina
Clara Blocker	Richmond, Virginia
Pearl Boddie	Whitakers, North Carolina
Lufenda Powens	Whitakers, North Carolina
Rufus Broadie	Nashville, North Carolina
Clarence Brown	Whitakers, North Carolina
Edward Brown	Whitakers, North Carolina
Moten Brown	Bricks, North Carolina
Nathaniel Brown	Bricks, North Carolina
Herbert Carter	Warrenton, North Carolina
Boston Cherry	Hassel, North Carolina
Viola Cherry	Hassel, North Carolina
Maude Cooke	Whitakers, North Carolina
Leslie Davis	Warrenton, North Carolina
Henry Eaton	Cana, North Carolina
Margaret Eskins	Wilmington, North Carolina
Cornelius Forney	Bricks, North Carolina
Charles Exum	Bricks, North Carolina
Lucy Ford	Whitakers, North Carolina
Alden Gibson	Lynchburg, Virginia
Alfonso Hazel	Bricks, North Carolina
Eula Hilliard	Bricks, North Carolina
William Hill	Bricks, North Carolina
Edward Hill	Whitakers, North Carolina
Elvia Horner	Whitakers, North Carolina
Edith Mae Hunter	Enfield, North Carolina
Frazier Jones	New York, New York

Student	City and State
William Lancaster	Castalia, North Carolina
Jefferson Loye	Enfield, North Carolina
Annie Lyons	Rocky Mount, North Carolina
John Mack	Whitakers, North Carolina
James Manley	Conway, North Carolina

Thomas Sewell Inborden

Lossie Belle Marshall	Rocky Mount, North Carolina
Leomia McDonald	Portsmouth, Virginia
Mona Murrain	Angola, Africa
Huvesta Perry	Nashville, Tennessee
Mollie Powell	Battleboro, North Carolina
William Powell	Enfield, North Carolina
Theodore Reynolds	Williamston, North Carolina
Percy Sessoms	Wilmington, North Carolina
Mary Simmons	Wilmington, North Carolina
Janie Simmons	Bethel, North Carolina
Clarence Stancil	Whitakers, North Carolina
Annie Taylor	Whitakers, North Carolina

Sixth Grade 1922 - 1923

Irving Ashford	Goldsboro, North Carolina
Francis Adams	Fayetteville, North Carolina
Marjorie Aikens	New York, New York
Albert Aikens	Cumnock, North Carolina
Alice Batchelor	Weldon, North Carolina
Selma Battle	Whitakers, North Carolina
Gilbert Battle	Whitakers, North Carolina
Samuel Black	Wilson, North Carolina
Charles Boseman	Rocky Mount, North Carolina
Preston Bowden	Rosobel, North Carolina
Decatur Bowden	Boston, Massachusetts
Ruth Bryant	Whitakers, North Carolina
Kenella Brewington	Clinton, North Carolina
Rosa Burnette	Enfield, North Carolina
Ethel Burnette	Bricks, North Carolina
Edith Cleary	Battleboro, North Carolina
Conie Cooke	Louisburg, North Carolina
Edward Demery	Enfield, North Carolina
James Eaton	Cana, North Carolina
Christine Edgeton	Rocky Mount, North Carolina
Priscilla Exum	Whitakers, North Carolina
Christine Ford	Whitakers, North Carolina
Alice Freeman	Tarboro, North Carolina
Nina Garrett	Bricks, North Carolina
Minetta Gaylor	Whitakers, North Carolina
Annie Grimes	Williamston, North Carolina
Herbert Gilmore	Wilmington, North Carolina
Ruby Holeman	Raleigh, North Carolina
William Huff	Williamston, North Carolina
Frank Isaac	Brooklyn, New York
Georgia Lunsford	Rocky Mount, North Carolina

Student	City and State
Russell Lucas	Enfield, North Carolina
Ollie McLaughlin	Zebulon, North Carolina
Alice Morgan	Rocky Mount, North Carolina
Etta Parker	Whitakers, North Carolina

Rosa Parker	Nashville, North Carolina
Cameron Peterson	Clinton, North Carolina
Lenora Perry	Nashville, North Carolina
Mattie Powell	Rosemary, North Carolina
Donald Phillips	Whitakers, North Carolina
Westery Powell	Rocky Mount, North Carolina
Annette Pittman	Bricks, North Carolina
Irene Rolland	Scotland Neck, North Carolina
Mary Smith	Scotland Neck, North Carolina
Louise Soloman	Halifax, North Carolina
Daniel Stuart	Enfield, North Carolina
Lillian Wade	Goldsboro, North Carolina
Christine Whitakers	Enfield, North Carolina
Ernest Williams	Zebulon, North Carolina
Leah Williams	Pinetop, North Carolina
Kathy Williams	Winston, North Carolina
Mollie Wooten	Goldsboro, North Carolina

Seventh Grade 1922 - 1923

Emma Atkins	Haywood, North Carolina
Cherry Belle	Falkland, North Carolina
Clinton Boone	Weldon, North Carolina
Willard Bridges	Smithfield, North Carolina
Almon Brown	Oak City, North Carolina
Julius Brown	Bricks, North Carolina
Addie Burnette	Bricks, North Carolina
Sylvester Burnette	Bricks, North Carolina
Mary Byrd	Whitakers, North Carolina
Almeta Byrd	Whitakers, North Carolina
Elias Cooper	Castalia, North Carolina
James Crawley	Wilmington, North Carolina
Robert Dewalt	Philadelphia, Pennsylvania
Arthur Fleming	Raleigh, North Carolina
Christine Ford	Whitakers, North Carolina
Harding Forney	Bricks, North Carolina
Fannie Gorham	Enfield, North Carolina
Minnie Grady	Dudley, North Carolina
Samuel Greene	Mebane, North Carolina
Isaac Gupton	Castalia, North Carolina
Charles Hall	Wilmington, North Carolina
Lillian Hill	Bricks, North Carolina
Annie Hill	Bricks, North Carolina
Milburn Hill	Wilmington, North Carolina
Etta Hilliard	Bricks, North Carolina
Robert Hines	Norfolk, Virginia

Student	City and State
Hollis Howington	Enfield, North Carolina
Carrie Joyner	Ayden, North Carolina
Annie Key	Enfield, North Carolina

James Lyons	Rocky Mount, North Carolina
Nannie Lyons	Whitakers, North Carolina
Sarah Mason	Richmond, Virginia
Pauline Martin	Thelma, North Carolina
Robert McLain	Duke, North Carolina
Ella Mae Donald	Detroit, Michigan
Willie Ormond	Williamston, North Carolina
Carol Phillips	Whitakers, North Carolina
Sudie Phillips	Whitakers, North Carolina
Edgar Ray	Enfield, North Carolina
John Raigns	Enfield, North Carolina
William Reaves	Wilson, North Carolina
William Saunders	Wilmington, North Carolina
Ethel Smith	Conetoe, North Carolina
Iver Spaulding	Clarkton, North Carolina
Acelia Spivey	Spring Hope, North Carolina
Morris Terrell	Farmville, North Carolina
Milton Upshire	Epmore, Virginia
James Ward	Weldon, North Carolina
Bessie Watson	Enfield, North Carolina
David Warren	Clinton, North Carolina
Ruth Whitaker	Enfield, North Carolina
Stephen Williams	Portsmouth, Virginia
Eulah Williams	Littleton, North Carolina
Carlester Younger	Norfolk, Virginia

Eighth Grade   1922-1923

Blanche Adams	Fayetteville, North Carolina
Arma Bailey	Springfield, Massachusetts
Linda Baker	Kingsboro, North Carolina
Zollie Batchelor	Nashville, Tennessee
Nathaniel Cofield	Enfield, North Carolina
Augusta Coward	Weldon, North Carolina
Blanche Croom	Salisbury, North Carolina
Mary Exum	Bricks, North Carolina
Cleta Faison	Warsaw, North Carolina
Othella Faison	Warsaw, North Carolina
Myrtle Forney	Bricks, North Carolina
George Foreman	Whitakers, North Carolina
Carrie Hill	Bricks, North Carolina
Generva Jones	Scotland Neck, North Carolina
Goldia Lungsford	Rougemount, North Carolina
Robert Macbeth	Charleston, South Carolina
George Murrain	Angola, Africa
Willie Newkirk	Rose Hill, North Carolina
Mary Phillips	Bricks, North Carolina
Lula Pittman	Bricks, North Carolina

Student	City and State
Walter Pittman	Bricks, North Carolina
George Stephens	Whitesville, North Carolina
Laura White	Elm City, North Carolina

Ninth Grade   1922-1923

Zelma Allen	Godwin, North Carolina
Ernestine Bullock	Kingsboro, North Carolina
Nathaniel Byrd	Whitakers, North Carolina
Sallie Casper	Enfield, North Carolina
Vera Carlyle	Whitakers, North Carolina
Dorcas Croom	Salisbury, North Carolina
Winoa Everett	La Grange, North Carolina
Linwood Hall	Philadelphia, Pennsylvania
Fannie Mae Hamlin	Farmville, North Carolina
Ida Belle Hopkins	Rocky Mount, North Carolina
George Jones	Norlina, North Carolina
Margaret Mason	Richmond, Virginia
Henry Melchor	Gold Hill, North Carolina
Evelyn Phillips	Bricks, North Carolina
Amelia Phillips	Whitakers, North Carolina
James Richmond	Florence, South Carolina
Ira Scarborough	Nashville, North Carolina
Lizzie Sessoms	Nashville, North Carolina
Helen Thorne	Rocky Mount, North Carolina
Richard Garrett	Whitakers, North Carolina
John Stanton	Snow Hill, North Carolina

Tenth Grade   1922-1923

Belle Grady	Lexington, Kentucky
Harold Chambers	Salisbury, North Carolina
Odessa Clouse	Goldsboro, North Carolina
Asa Croom	Salisbury, North Carolina
Hattie Eaton	Winston, North Carolina
Gilbert Hill	Norline, North Carolina
George Hilliard	Bricks, North Carolina
Julia Lyons	Whitakers, North Carolina
Stephen Powell	Rosemary, North Carolina
George Reid	Bricks, North Carolina
John Sloane	Enfield, North Carolina
Lucile Stewart	Jackson, North Carolina
Sallie Mae Taylor	Scotland Neck, North Carolina
Mary Wood	Chase City, Virginia

Eleventh Grade   1922-1923

Elizabeth Bland	Richmond Virginia
Mayutha Brown	Cartersville, South Carolina
Mary Burnette	Bricks, North Carolina

Student	City and State
Sarah Burns	Dunn, North Carolina
William Childs	Washington, D.C.
Theodore Davis	Newark, New Jersey
Grace Jackson	Fredericksburg, Virginia
Audaline Joyner	Whitakers, North Carolina
Henrietta Pearsall	Farmville, North Carolina
Edward Peterson	Farmville, North Carolina
Ethel Turner	Cumnock, North Carolina
Chester Wallace	Weldon, North Carolina
Mary Watson	Enfield, North Carolina
Maggie Young	Battleboro, North Carolina

Twelfth Grade 1922 - 1923

Fletcher Atkins	Haywood, North Carolina
William Burnette	Bricks, North Carolina
William Jones	Durham, North Carolina
Gladys Quest	Springfield, Massachusetts
Carolyn Rogers	Portsmouth, Virginia
Costenah Stewart	Newport News, Virginia
Nettie Thompson	Snow Hill, North Carolina
Guthrie Turner	Cumnock, North Carolina
Marion White	Portsmouth, Virginia
Cornelia Wiggins	Plymouth, North Carolina

Brick School Night Department 1922 - 1923

First Grade

Charity Doyal	Scotland Neck, North Carolina

Third Grade - 1922 - 1923

Joseph Dawdy	Weldon, North Carolina

Fourth Grade - 1922 - 1923

Mamie Battle	Nashville, North Carolina
Sarah Hunter	Spring Hope, North Carolina

Fifth Grade 1922 - 1923

Elijah Brown	Bethel, North Carolina
Rosa Carnie	Falkland, North Carolina
Emma Hall	Snow Hill, North Carolina
Lela Jones	Whitakers, North Carolina

Student	City and State
Joseph Langely	Bethel, North Carolina
Nacy Purvis	Williamston, North Carolina
Florence Tyson	Falkland, North Carolina
Beatrice Williams	Greenville, North Carolina

Sixth Grade   1922 - 1923

Omelia Adams	Weldon, North Carolina
Ralph Avery	Columbia, South Carolina
Martha Bryant	Whitakers, North Carolina
Lemuel Croom	Salisbury, North Carolina
George Edmons	Weldon, North Carolina
McKeaver Edwards	Weldon, North Carolina
Allean Harper	Snow Hill, North Carolina
Naomi Jenkins	Snow Hill, North Carolina
Isaac Newkirk	Goldsboro, North Carolina
William Shields	Charles City, Virginia
Lenora Smith	Wilmington, North Carolina
Edward Washington	Weldon, North Carolina

Seventh Grade   1922 - 1923

Emma Battle	Castalia, North Carolina
Florence Cooper	Warsaw, North Carolina
James Faison	Clinton, North Carolina
Willie Flemons	Rocky Mount, North Carolina
George Gupton	Nashville, Tennessee
Jesse Jenkins	Weldon, North Carolina
George Matthews	Clinton, North Carolina
Catherine Slade	Williamston, North Carolina

Eighth Grade   1922 - 1923

Benjamin Ashford	Clinton, North Carolina
Bertha Blacknall	Raleigh, North Carolina
Cora Briggs	Beltsville, North Carolina
Reginald Davis	Newark, New Jersey
Pearl Dixon	Portsmouth, Virginia
Rena Belle Easter	Winston, North Carolina
Hattie Gatting	Weldon, North Carolina
Gaston Hemby	Wilmington, North Carolina
Cora Jefferson	Portsmouth, Virginia
Iver Ormond	Wilmington, North Carolina
James Williams	Wilmington, North Carolina

Thomas Sewell Inborden

Ninth Grade 1922 - 1923

Student	City and State
Isabelle Mack	Charleston, South Carolina
Marie Landers	Manor, Georgia

Tenth Grade 1922 - 1923

Dossie Ledbetter	Troy, North Carolina
Malinda Powers	Rosemary, North Carolina

Elementary School

First Grade 1929 - 1930

Chauncey Lee Bell	Enfield, North Carolina
Nell Douglass Bowen	Bricks, North Carolina
Earl Brown	Whitakers, North Carolina
Luther Brown	Whitakers, North Carolina
Quinton Brown	Whitakers, North Carolina
Colester Bryant	Whitakers, North Carolina
Louise Forbes	Bricks, North Carolina
Mingo, Forbes	Bricks, North Carolina
Osteel Garrett	Whitakers, North Carolina
Ross Garrett	Whitakers, North Carolina
Margaret Garrett	Whitakers, North Carolina
Richard Garrett	Whitakers, North Carolina
Queen Lyons	Bricks, North Carolina
Julia Gordon	Bricks, North Carolina
John Gordon	Bricks, North Carolina
Beatrice Lyons	Bricks, North Carolina
Bettie Norman	Enfield, North Carolina
Ardry Pitt	Bricks, North Carolina

Second Grade 1929 - 1930

Harold Bell	Enfield, North Carolina
Rosa Lee Bryant	Whitakers, North Carolina
Gertha Garrett	Whitakers, North Carolina
Julia Curtis Hill	Whitakers, North Carolina
Ruby Nelson	Whitakers, North Carolina
Eddie Nickolson	Whitakers, North Carolina
Geraldine Pittman	Enfield, North Carolina
Virginia Pittman	Enfield, North Carolina

Third Grade 1929-1930

Student	City and State
George Adams	Bricks, North Carolina
Mildred Bowen	Bricks, North Carolina
James Brown	Whitakers, North Carolina
Isaac Chestnut	Bricks, North Carolina
Gwendolyn Holloway	Bricks, North Carolina
Olivia Garrett	Whitakers, North Carolina
Lucian Lyons	Bricks, North Carolina
Joanna Nickolson	Whitakers, North Carolina

Fourth Grade 1929 - 1930

Robert Applewhite	Enfield, North Carolina
John Preston Barrett	Snow Hill, North Carolina
Elizabeth Brown	Whitakers, North Carolina
Ernestine Brown	Whitakers, North Carolina
George Bryant	Whitakers, North Carolina
Bertha Garrett	Whitakers, North Carolina
Rosa Garrett	Whitakers, North Carolina
Frances Gordon	Bricks, North Carolina
Virginia Joyner	Enfield, North Carolina
Ellen Norman	Enfield, North Carolina
Bernadine Pitt	Bricks, North Carolina
Dorothea Pittman	Enfield, North Carolina
Winzle Scott	Whitakers, North Carolina

Fifth Grade 1929 - 1930

Florida Mae Belle	Enfield, North Carolina
James Ford	Whitakers, North Carolina
Mary Lou Hill	Whitakers, North Carolina
Raymond Lyons	Bricks, North Carolina
Maggie Mason	Enfield, North Carolina
Samuel Mason	Enfield, North Carolina

Sixth Grade 1929 - 1930

Scott Adams	Bricks, North Carolina
Wilson Adams	Bricks, North Carolina
Almeada Bryant	Whitakers, North Carolina
John Faison	Enfield, North Carolina
Alvira Fobbs	Bricks, North Carolina
Harry Holmes	Mount Olive, North Carolina
Willie McWilliams	Enfield, North Carolina
Henry Norman	Enfield, North Carolina
Fay Tull	Jefferson City, Missouri
Annie Winnon	Vaughan, North Carolina

Annie Winnon   Vaughan, North Carolina

Seventh Grade   1929 - 1930

Student	City and State
Emily Battle	Whitakers, North Carolina
Beatrice Bennett	Charlotte, North Carolina
Lina Bowens	Bricks, North Carolina
Alexander Brown	Whitakers, North Carolina
George Brown	Vaughan, North Carolina
Katy Bryant	Whitakers, North Carolina
Clyde Cheek	Marmaduke, North Carolina
Curtis Fitts	Littleton, North Carolina
Benjamin Forbes	Bricks, North Carolina
Johnnie Forbes	Enfield, North Carolina
Jodiebelle Hill	Sparrows Point, Maryland
Milton Holmes	Mount Olive, North Carolina
Majorie Lewis	Whitakers, North Carolina
William Mann	Whitakers, North Carolina
Carey Pittman	Enfield, North Carolina
Olivia Pittman	Enfield, North Carolina
Winton Pittman	Enfield, North Carolina
Ralph Powell	Scotland Neck, North Carolina
Mary Reid	Bricks, North Carolina
Judson Smith	Enfield, North Carolina
Carranza Watson	Whitakers, North Carolina
John Watson	Whitakers, North Carolina
William Williams	Whitakers, North Carolina
Mattie Wills	Enfield, North Carolina

Eighth Grade   1929 - 1930

Martha Archer	Washington, D.C.
Howard Battle	Whitakers, North Carolina
David Belle	Bricks, North Carolina
Eddie Bowens	Bricks, North Carolina
James Cofield	Enfield, North Carolina
Jessie Cofield	Tarboro, North Carolina
Selma Davis	Whitakers, North Carolina
Clara Dawson	Elm City, North Carolina
Ernest Forbes	Bricks, North Carolina
Neal Harris	Littleton, North Carolina
Esther Holloway	Bricks, North Carolina
William Mann	Whitakers, North Carolina
Annie Mae McMillan	Bricks, North Carolina
Ida Pitt	Bricks, North Carolina
Elnora Reid	Magnolia, North Carolina
Hattie Ricks	Elm City, North Carolina
Lillie Ricks	Elm City, North Carolina
Lillian Smith	Enfield, North Carolina

Ninth Grade 1929 - 1930

Student	City and State
Andrew Bailey	Boston, Massachusetts
Glendora Brown	Whitakers, North Carolina
Christine Brown	Whitakers, North Carolina
Georgianna Bryant	Whitakers, North Carolina
Julia Cofield	Enfield, North Carolina
Hazel Dixon	New Rochelle, New York
Ruth Faulk	Roselle, New Jersey
Ada Ford	Dudley, North Carolina
Corneluis Forney	Bricks, North Carolina
Connie Hagans	Dudley, North Carolina
Gladys Kee	Seabord, North Carolina
Junius Cofield	Enfield, North Carolina
Louise Kee	Seabord, North Carolina
William Locke	Gates, North Carolina
Elvirta Mann	Whitakers, North Carolina
Viola McWilliams	Enfield, North Carolina
Mona Murrain	New York, New York
Loletta Myrick	Enfield, North Carolina
Nellie Qualls	Enfield, North Carolina
Aremetro Riche	Benson, North Carolina
Gerald Smith	Enfield, North Carolina
Wilder Taylor	Whitakers, North Carolina
Annie Tillery	Enfield, North Carolina
Estella Turnage	Enfield, North Carolina
Annie Westbrook	Rose Hill, North Carolina
Simon White	Charleston, South Carolina
Dalton Whitted	Chapel Hill, North Carolina

Tenth Grade - 1929 - 1930

Student	City and State
Gossie Clark	Scotland Neck, North Carolina
Odessa Gaylor	Whitakers, North Carolina
Rochell Hall	Zebulon, North Carolina
Bethany Hammond	Winterville, North Carolina
Robert Jones	Pennsylvania

High School

Tenth Grade 1929 - 1930

Student	City and State
Maria Lane	Jacksonville, Florida
Mattie Martin	Dudley, North Carolina
Mamie Moore	Lillington, North Carolina
Carol Philips	Enfield, North Carolina
Roderick Philips	Enfield, North Carolina
William Pretlow	Smithfield, North Carolina
Mildred Sengstacke	Savannah, Georgia
Elsie Speller	Philadelphia, Pennsylvania
Hilda Taylor	Scotland Neck, North Carolina

Student	City and State
Bessie Watson	Enfield, North Carolina
Emmaline West	Falls Church, Virginia
Theodore Williams	Littleton, North Carolina
Ida Yarborough	Broadway, North Carolina

Eleventh Grade 1929 - 1930

Inez Albritton	Franklinton, North Carolina
Halese Baxter	Henderson, North Carolina
Ernest Bloom	Florence, South Carolina
Hattie Bullock	Enfield, North Carolina
Salvadore Bullock	Enfield, North Carolina
Ethel De Brew	Scotland Neck, North Carolina
Barbara Drew	Hartford, Connecticut
Virginia Eberhardt	Athens, Georgia
Mollie Fennell	Rose Hill, North Carolina
Lottie Gunter	Moncure, North Carolina
William Harris	Moncure, North Carolina
Lillie Robbs	Wilmington, North Carolina
Frederick Shields	Enfield, North Carolina
Sadie Smith	Hobgood, North Carolina
Clarence Stancil	Bethel, North Carolina
Alberta Thomas	Savannah, Georgia
Violet Walls	Goldsboro, North Carolina
Elson Williams	Blounts Creek, North Carolina
Rudolph Williams	Kinston, North Carolina

Twelfth Grade 1929 - 1930

Gilbert Batten	Whitakers, North Carolina
Edward Demery	Enfield, North Carolina
James Eaton	Akron, Ohio
Othello Faison	Warsaw, North Carolina
Minnetta Gaylor	Whitakers, North Carolina
Ruth Jerome	Woodford, Virginia
Evelyn Johnson	George, North Carolina
Clarke Lassiter	Lassiter, North Carolina
Ella Ligon	Raleigh, North Carolina
Eleanor Murray	Washington, D.C.
Frederick Peyton	Washington, North Carolina
Vivian Richardson	Athens, Georgia
Ethel Sengstacke	Savannah, Georgia
John Sengstacke	Savannah, Georgia
Willie Strickland	Commerce, Geogria
Harry Terry	Crystal Springs, Mississippi
Hazeline Ward	Scotland Neck, North Carolina
Mary Woodfaulk	Montclair, New Jersey

Brick Junior College

Freshman   1929 - 1930

Student	City and State
Edward Aaron	Camden, South Carolina
William Alexander	Raleigh, North Carolina
John Barnard	Old Trap, North Carolina
Marietta Barnhill	Troy, North Carolina
Annie Battle	Rocky Mount, North Carolina
Pallie Brown	Troy, North Carolina
Julius Brown	Bricks, North Carolina
John Butler	Troy, North Carolina
Booker Carpenter	Albemarle, North Carolina
Susie Cheek	Dunn, North Carolina
Paul Daniels	Charleston, South Carolina
Walter Giles	Seven Springs, North Carolina
William Graves	Suffolk, Virginia
Ada Harris	Wilson, North Carolina

Sophmores   1929 - 1930

Evelyn Bethea	Asheville, North Carolina
Mabel Brewer	Thomasville, Georgia
Edith Chisholm	Charleston, South Carolina
Edna Exum	Bricks, North Carolina
Myrtle Forney	Charleston, South Carolina
Frank Gadsden	Charleston, South Carolina
Samuel Gillard	Charleston, South Carolina
Lorenzo Jordan	Thomasville, Georgia
Susie McMillan	Sarasota, Florida
Franklin Ransome	Plymouth, North Carolina

Brick Junior College

Sophomore Class   1930-1931

Edward Aaron	Camden, South Carolina
John Barnard	Old Trap, North Carolina
Annie Battle	Rocky Mount, North Carolina
Julius Brown	Bricks, North Carolina
John Butler	Hackensack, New Jersey
Booker Carpenter	Albemarle, North Carolina
Susie Cheek	Dunn, North Carolina
Walter Giles	Seven Springs, North Carolina
Ada Harris	Wilson, North Carolina
Mildred Ingram	High Point, North Carolina
Roberta Lassiter	Selma, North Carolina
Julian Lyon	Enfield, North Carolina

Callie Martin	Pinehurst, North Carolina
Elizabeth McRae	Troy, North Carolina
Violette Norcott	New Haven, Connecticut
Mary Phillips	Bricks, North Carolina
Ashton Randolph	Garden City, New York
Annie Whitehead	Rocky Mount, North Carolina
Felder Williams	Lakeland, Florida

Junior College - Freshman Class

Carlina Ausby	Halifax, North Carolina
Gilbert Batten	Whitakers, North Carolina
Lovey Bullock	Timberlake, North Carolina
Winema Campbell	Salisbury, North Carolina
John Cox	New York, New York
Edward Demery	Enfield, North Carolina
James Eaton	Bricks, North Carolina
William Ellison	Rocky Mount, North Carolina
Othell Faison	Warsaw, North Carolina
Lucy Faison	Seaboard, North Carolina
Mamie Fitts	Littleton, North Carolina
Lucy Gatling	Winton, North Carolina
Minetta Gaylor	Whitakers, North Carolina
Edwin Hardy	Enfield, North Carolina
James Harrington	Rocky Mount, North Carolina
William Holmes	Mount Olive, North Carolina
Winsor Johnson	Calipso, North Carolina
Elnora Morrison	McIntosh, Georgia
Eleanor Murray	Washington. D.C.
Penny Logan	Rocky Mount, North Carolina
Frederick Peyton	Washington, D.C,
Vivian Richardson	Atlantic City, New Jersey
Willie Strickland	Commerce, Georgia
James Taylor	Rocky Mount, North Carolina
Harvey Tillery	Raleigh, North Carolina
Mary Vann	Mount Olive, North Carolina

Junior College - Twelfth Grade

Inez Albritton	Franklin, North Carolina
Halese Baxter	Henderson, North Carolina
Ernest Broom	Florence, South Carolina
Clarice Brown	Whitakers, North Carolina
Nathaniel Brown	Whitakers, North Carolina
Hattie Bullock	Enfield, North Carolina
Gossie Clarke	Scotland Neck, North Carolina
Flaybelle Coble	Badin, North Carolina
Ethel Drebrew	Scotland Neck, North Carolina
Barbara Drew	Hartford, Connecticut
Virginia Eberhardt	Athens, Georgia
Mollie Fennell	Rosehill, North Carolina
Lottie Gunter	Moncure, North Carolina
Rochelle Hall	Zebulon, North Carolina

William Harris	Moncure, North Carolina
Robert Jones	Moncure, North Carolina
Isabella Miles	Columbus, Georgia
Annie Powell	Rosemary, North Carolina
Frederick Shields	Enfield, North Carolina
Sadie Smith	Hobgood, North Carolina
Clarence Stancil	Bethel, North Carolina
Alberta Thomas	Savannah, Georgia
Violet Walls	Goldsboro, North Carolina
Wilma Wilkins	Ringwood, North Carolina
Randolph Williams	Raleigh, North Carolina
Elson Williams	Blount Creek, North Carolina
Ida Yarborough	Broadway, North Carolina
Hilda Taylor	Scotland Neck, North Carolina

Junior College - Eleventh Grade

Lefenda Bowens	Bricks, North Carolina
Christine Brown	Whitakers, North Carolina
Julia Cofield	Engield, North Carolina
Hazel Dixon	New Rochelle, New York
Fred Gorham	Edenton, North Carolina
Ada Ford	Dudley, North Carolina
Bethany Hammond	Winterville, North Carolina
Viola McWilliams	Enfield, North Carolina
Loletta Myrick	Enfield, North Carolina
William Pretlow	Smithfield, Virginia
Carol Phillips	Enfield, North Carolina
Nellie Qualls	Enfield, North Carolina
George Reid	Bricks, North Carolina
Elisha Short	Edenton, North Carolina
Elsie Speller	Philadelphia, Pennsylvania
Leomia Wess	Kerr, North Carolina
Emmaline West	Pittsburgh, Pennsylvania

High School - Tenth Grade   1930-1931

King Boykins	Parkersburg, North Carolina
Glendora Brown	Whitakers, North Carolina
George Bullock	Rocky Mount, North Carolina
Maurice Bullock	Rocky Mount, North Carolina
George Anna Bryant	Whitakers, North Carolina
Clara Dawson	Elm City, North Carolina
Albert Dean	Miami, Florida
Quincy Devereaux	Soperton, Georgia
Pandora Eaton	Murfreesboro, Tennessee
Ruth Faulk	Westfield, New Jersey
Cornelius Forney	Bricks, North Carolina
Odessa Gaylor	Whitakers, North Carolina
Connie Hagan	Dudley, North Carolina
Lillian Hill	Battleboro, North Carolina
Westry Hill	Battleboro, North Carolina
James Quinichett	Whitakers, North Carolina

Thomas Sewell Inborden

Student	City and State
Mildred Sengstacke	Savannah, Georgia
Wilder Taylor	Whitakers, North Carolina
David Thorpe	Rocky Mount, North Carolina
Bessie Watson	Enfield, North Carolina
Dalton Whitted	Chapel Hill, North Carolina
Frederick Wilkerson	Temple, Texas
Herbert Wright	Bricks, North Carolina

High School - Ninth Grade   1930-1931

Martha Archer	Washington, D.C.
Percy Batchelor	Nashville, North Carolina
Howard Battle	Whitakers, North Carolina
Lewis Bell	Enfield, North Carolina
David Bell	Enfield, North Carolina
Eddie Bowens	Bricks, North Carolina
William Bowens	Bricks, North Carolina
Kate Bryant	Whitakers, North Carolina
Pauline Chappelle	New York, New York
James Cofield	Enfield, North Carolina
Jessie Cofield	Tarboro, North Carolina
Neal Harris	Littleton, North Carolina
Cordelia Hemmons	Bricks, North Carolina
Paul Hepler	Wilson, North Carolina
Ernestina Jones	Far Rockaway, New York
Leonard Jones	Far Rockaway, New York
Lloyd Malone	Enfield, North Carolina
Annie McMillan	Wallace, North Carolina
George Pitchford	Littleton, North Carolina
Olivia Pittman	Enfield, North Carolina
Hattie Ricks	Elm City, North Carolina
Ruby Rosser	Whitakers, North Carolina
Gerald Smith	Enfield, North Carolina
Annie Tillery	Enfield, North Carolina
Simon White	New York, New York

Eighth Grade   1930-1931

Lina Bowens	Bricks, North Carolina
Allen Brewer	Scotland Neck, North Carolina
Romine Carlisle	Whitakers, North Carolina
Peter Dickens	Whitakers, North Carolina
Callie Dickens	Whitakers, North Carolina
Samuel Eaton	Cana, North Carolina
Ernest Forbes	Bricks, North Carolina
Willie Griffin	Pittsburgh, Pennsylvania
Jodie Belle Hill	Sparrows Point, Maryland
Milton Holmes	Mount Olive, North Carolina
Laura Joyner	Elm City, North Carolina
Marjorie Lewis	Whitakers, North Carolina
Mattie Lucas	Elm City, North Carolina
Henry Lynch	Whitakers, North Carolina

Student	City and State
Winton Pittman	Enfield, North Carolina
Lillie Ricks	Elm City, North Carolina
Elnora Reid	Franklin, Virginia
Sadie Williams	Henderson, North Carolina
Carey Pittman	Enfield, North Carolina

Seventh Grade

Scott Adams	Bricks, North Carolina
Beaulah Batten	Whitakers, North Carolina
Almeda Bryant	Whitakers, North Carolina
Annie Curtis	Whitakers, North Carolina
John Faison	Enfield, North Carolina
Alvera Fobbs	Bricks, North Carolina
Harry Holmes	Mount Olive, North Carolina
Willie McWilliams	Enfield, North Carolina
Mary Reid	Bricks, North Carolina
John Watson	Whitakers, North Carolina

Elementary School 1930-1931

Wilson Adams	Bricks, North Carolina
Florida Belle	Enfield, North Carolina
James Ford	Whitakers, North Carolina
Raymond Lyons	Bricks, North Carolina
Maggie Mason	Enfield, North Carolina
Samuel Mason	Enfield, North Carolina
Ozette Pittman	Enfield, North Carolina
Catherine Young	Bricks, North Carolina
Garrett Young	Bricks, North Carolina
Geneva Young	Bricks, North Carolina

Fifth Grade

George Bryant	Whitakers, North Carolina
Bertha Garrett	Bricks, North Carolina
Frances Gordon	Bricks, North Carolina
Catherine Hemmons	Bricks, North Carolina
Arthur Jones	Bricks, North Carolina
Doreatha Pittman	Enfield, North Carolina
Muriel Young	Bricks, North Carolina
Yvonne Wright	Bricks, North Carolina

Fourth Grade

George Adams	Bricks, North Carolina
Mildred Bowens	Bricks, North Carolina
Olivia Garrett	Bricks, North Carolina
Rosa Garrett	Bricks, North Carolina
Lucien Lyons	Bricks, North Carolina
Lethia Young	Bricks, North Carolina

Student	Third Grade City and State
Harold Bell	Enfield, North Carolina
Rosalie Bryant	Whitakers, North Carolina
Mildred Hemmons	Bricks, North Carolina
Rubye Nelson	Whitakers, North Carolina
Geraldine Pittman	Enfield, North Carolina
Virginia Pittman	Enfield, North Carolina

Second Grade

Nell Bowens	Bricks, North Carolina
Edward Carter	Whitakers, North Carolina
Mingo Fobbs	Bricks, North Carolina
Gertha Garrett	Bricks, North Carolina
Richard Garrett	Bricks, North Carolina
Osteel Garrett	Bricks, North Carolina
John Gordon	Bricks, North Carolina
Julia Gordon	Bricks, North Carolina
Esther Queen Lyon	Bricks, North Carolina
Audry Pitt	Bricks, North Carolina
Evelyn Young	Bricks, North Carolina

First Grade

Chauney Bell	Enfield, North Carolina
Earle Brown	Bricks, North Carolina
Corlester Bryant	Whitakers, North Carolina
Louis Fobbs	Bricks, North Carolina
Aaron Garrett	Bricks, North Carolina
Gladys Garrett	Bricks, North Carolina
Margaret Garrett	Bricks, North Carolina
Annie Harrison	Bricks, North Carolina
Minnie Harrison	Bricks, North Carolina
Juluis Hunter	Whitakers, North Carolina
Beatrice Lyon	Bricks, North Carolina
Evelyn Nelson	Whitakers, North Carolina

Extension Classes

Education

Dorinda Anthony	Scotland Neck, North Carolina
Florence M. Arrington	Halifax, North Carolina
Thelma L. Black	Demopolis, Alabama
Roxie Brewer	Scotland Neck, North Carolina
Anna H. Brinkley	Ringwood, North Carolina
Bernadine G. Brookens	Washington, D.C.
Mrs. Bertha E. Bullock	Enfield, North Carolina
Mrs. Emma C. Cooper	Hertford, North Carolina
Mary J. Davis	Warrenton, North Carolina
Lena A. Ferrell	Enfield, North Carolina
Susie Ford	Enfield, North Carolina

Student	City and State
Maude Freeman	Fayettville, North Carolina
W.D. Gatling	Enfield, North Carolina
B.D. Hardy	Enfield, North Carolina
Elizabeth Harden	Lexington, Kentucky
Lucy Jones	Weldon, North Carolina
Susie Jones	Ringwood, North Carolina
John D. Killingsworth	Chicago, Illinois
Lillian Moore	Staunton, Virginia
Bessie Pittman	Enfield, North Carolina
Viola Pittman	Enfield, North Carolina
Mabel Robinson	Boston, Massachusetts
Ernestine Rose Saunders	Bricks, North Carolina
Blanche Smith	Scotland Neck, North Carolina
Vivian Toney	Rosemary, North Carolina
Courtney Tucker	McKenny, Virginia
Susie Wilkins	Weldon, North Carolina
Juanita Olivia Whitaker	Enfield, North Carolina

Ministerial Training 1930-1931

Rev. Charles Taylor	Whitakers, North Carolina
Rev. McKinley Nicholson	Enfield, North Carolina
Mrs. Emma Burnett	Rocky Mount, North Carolina
Hunter Stitt	Rocky Mount, North Carolina
Mrs. Lonnie Whitehead	Rocky Mount, North Carolina

Extension Class In Agriculture

Charles Adams	Bricks, North Carolina
Eddie Bowens	Bricks, North Carolina
Benjamin Fobbs	Bricks, North Carolina
Robert Garrett	Bricks, North Carolina
Richard Garrett	Bricks, North Carolina
Dorsey Gaylor	Whitakers, North Carolina
Henry Lyons	Bricks, North Carolina

Brick Center 1930-1931

Modern Educational Theme - Training For Citizenship

Dorinda Anthony	Scotland Neck, North Carolina
Annie Bell Barber	Norfolk, Virginia
Roxie Brewer	Scotland Neck, North Carolina
Bernadine Brookins	Washington, D.C.
Bertha Bullock	Enfield, North Carolina
Emma Cooper	Hertford, North Carolina
Leora Dees	Oxford, North Carolina
Emily Earl	Battleboro, North Carolina
Susie Ford	Enfield, North Carolina

Student	City and State
Baxter Don Goodall	Charleston, South Carolina
Fannie Hunter	Enfield, North Carolina
Emma Johnson	Tillery, North Carolina
Susie Jones	Enfield, North Carolina
J. Dekoven Killingsworth	Chicago, Illinois
Ella Lewis	Natick, Massachusetts
Emma Murden	Elizabeth City, North Carolina
Louise Myrick	Enfield, North Carolina
Juanita Newkirk	Enfield, North Carolina
Bettie Pittman	Enfield, North Carolina
Blanche Smith	Scotland Neck, North Carolina
Sallie Mae Taylor	Scotland Neck, North Carolina
Hattie Wills	Enfield, North Carolina

Rocky Mount Center

Mental Hygiene

Training For Citizenship

Lucy Armstrong	Rocky Mount, North Carolina
Mary Backus	Rocky Mount, North Carolina
Mary Battle	Rocky Mount, North Carolina
Louise Bost	Rocky Mount, North Carolina
Arkanna Braswell	Rocky Mount, North Carolina
Petty Brown	Rocky Mount, North Carolina
Helen Coleman	Rocky Mount, North Carolina
Beatrice Davis	Rocky Mount, North Carolina
Annie Deans	Rocky Mount, North Carolina
Nettie Drake	Fayettville, North Carolina
Ruth Evans	Goldsboro, North Carolina
Annie Flournoy	Monticello, Georgia
Ada Foreman	Rocky Mount, North Carolina
Edith Foreman	Rocky Mount, North Carolina
Corlease Frazier	Rocky Mount, North Carolina
Mary Gaynor	Tarboro, North Carolina
Cora Grant	Rocky Mount, North Carolina
Walter Grant	Rocky Mount, North Carolina
Marguerite Hall	Rocky Mount, North Carolina
Elizabeth Hilliard	Rocky Mount, North Carolina
Carrie Hines	Rocky Mount, North Carolina
Ethel Hopkins	Conetoe, North Carolina
Victoria Hopkins	Rocky Mount, North Carolina
Carrie Howell	Rocky Mount, North Carolina
Helen Howze	Rocky Mount, North Carolina
Ethel Hunter	Rocky Mount, North Carolina
Helen Hunter	Rocky Mount, North Carolina
Mattie Hunter	Rocky Mount, North Carolina
Janet Hunter	Rocky Mount, North Carolina
Lorell Lewis	Battlesboro, North Carolina
Mary McKay	Battlesboro, North Carolina
Vinie Murray	Charlotte, North Carolina

Student	City and State
Alice Nicholson	Elm City, North Carolina
Audolene Parker	Rocky Mount, North Carolina
Geneva Pittman	Rocky Mount, North Carolina
Lizzie Pittman	Rocky Mount, North Carolina
Nellie Pittman	Rocky Mount, North Carolina
Theresa Pittman	Rocky Mount, North Carolina
Zellie Pittman	Rocky Mount, North Carolina
Lillian Reeves	Rocky Mount, North Carolina
Effie Saunders	Rocky Mount, North Carolina
Causie Shelly	Rocky Mount, North Carolina
Eura Smith	Rocky Mount, North Carolina
Lillian Smith	Rocky Mount, North Carolina
Sarah Sorrell	Rocky Mount, North Carolina
Carrie Spaulding	Rocky Mount, North Carolina
Margaret Spencer	Goldsboro, North Carolina
Lillian MeBane	Rocky Mount, North Carolina
Bettye Sumner	Rocky Mount, North Carolina
Fannie Mae Taylor	Rocky Mount, North Carolina
Annie Whitehead	Rocky Mount, North Carolina
Annie Williams	Portsmouth, Virginia
Marguerite Wimberly	Rocky Mount, North Carolina
Mary Wimberly	Rocky Mount, North Carolina
Lucy Wood	Roper, North Carolina
Lendora Yancey	Rocky Mount, North Carolina

Weldon Center

Modern Educational Theme

Training For Citizenship

Florence Arrington	Halifax, North Carolina
Willie Howell Cheek	Weldon, North Carolina
Maude Freeman	Fayettville, North Carolina
Canary Hamilton	Rosemary, North Carolina
Fannie L. Horne	Weldon, North Carolina
Lucy Jones	Weldon, North Carolina
Fannie B. Kee	Garysburg, North Carolina
Dorothy Manley	Hertford, North Carolina
Lillian Moore	Staunton, North Carolina
Alice Person	Garysburg, North Carolina
Olivia Squire	Garysburg, North Carolina
Cleopatra Toney	Rosemary, North Carolina
Courtney Tucker	McKenny, Virginia
Susie Wilkins	McKenny, Virginia
George Williams	Weldon, North Carolina

APPENDIX 15

T.S. INBORDEN'S
PHILOSOPHIES AND QUOTATIONS

A Creed

Views on Education

Views on Motion Pictures

Farm Life

Views on Drinking and Smoking

People's Inheritance

Quotes - Predjudice
        Environment
        Ignorance

Miscellaneous Quotations

Quotations - Our Standards

Religion and Education

Reading Material

Influence The Farmer

A Racial Concern

Administrative Ability

Statements

T.S.' PHILOSOPHIES

T.S.' Creed, Any man who engages in the serious business of life activities who dares not have a creed is doomed to failure. One must examine himself with relation to the general activities of society and see that his creed has the background and basis of merit.

The environment in which we live is responsible for the conduct of its citizens. It is the law of nature as well as the law of plant life and human nature in particular. You grow what you plant. You do not teach what we do not exemplify in life.

The school had ceased to assume the prerogatives of home life. It was never intended that they should assume them its the beginning but we have had a tradition which was excellent life, we should preserve the best in our home life.

If you are a father or mother it is your first duty to educate and train your children. It matters not what your circumstances are. You brought them into the world and you should see that they get a right start.

If you do not give the child a chance to go to school when the child reaches the age to educate himself, he must find the will, time, and patience.

A trained head and heart will remove drudgery and bring happiness, pleasure and more valuable attributes to one's service on Christianity. Competition is too great for any young person to expect to go very far earning their own living without a Christian training.

Education

Some people have had a propaganda for many years that a little learning is dangerous thing. They have been advised that they belong to a subject group and they need only rudimentary necessities of life. It is the appeal for the glitter and glare for some youth.

No one wants to be a slacker at anything. The man who refuses to make the utmost sacrifice in time and money for the education of his boys and girls is a slacker.

Intelligence is always in the line of promotion, ignorance never.

The youth of the land, your youth ought to have a large vision of life by education and training.

We must recount the steps in our origin and growth so that the future historian may have a starting point.

If one wants to read something full of motion, emotion and fact, read the *Ex Colored Man* by James Weldon Johnson of the Crisis Staff. Read the books by Booker T. Washington, and W.E.B. DuBois' book on Africa. If youth think they must grovel in the slums for literature, it is because their standards are low and they have been ill taught. A stream can not rise above its source.

Views on Motion Pictures

Our drifting and standards are influenced by the motion picture show. The motion picture is the most potent factor in the education of our youth. A few weeks ago, I was invited to attend a motion picture show and to attempt to put into languages. What I saw would very much greatly shock my sense of modesty. Like a lot of our literature these pictures also appeal to the base element in human life.

Farm Life

The farmer must unite with other farmers in the persecution of his work. There must be cooperation by farmer in the community uniting together. We as blacks do not organize at times, possibly because we lack faith in each other. This is natural. It is about all the education that a great many Negroes have had for two hundred years. We have been schooled in credulousness. Expect the Best that it is in your neighbor and your neighbor will prove up to your highest expectations.

Views On Drinking and Smoking

To prevent these habits or indulgences, I stay away from these things especially because of association. I associate cards with gamblers and whiskey and wine with drunkards and revelers. I do not care to go where these things are going on because my personality will be felt by others who are liable to say or do something in a patronizing way. They might make say what I should not say. My attitude may be out of date but I have done the things I have done in life that have been greatly to my honor by following this philosophy and I do not expect to change now. Most of the people who have practiced the new philosophy relative to drinking, gambling had not demonstrated to me that their new philosophy has gotten them anywhere. I get no where tantalizing people for their differences.

People's Inheritance

There is not a human being on earth that has not had some ecentricities or some abnormalities according to the treaties on these subjects. It is not best to dwell on these abnormalities too much. when it is an affectation of the human race, one must take human nature at its best and not at its worse. It is best when one has a summary of all the best qualities of what we conceive to be the best qualities or that has the approval of the best people. Our physical condition is largely a matter of our mental atmosphere. The expression of our personality which is only a matter of character and is also a matter of our thinking. Some one can pick out an exception and dispute even this statement because they have found an exception. If I take the time, I could write out the mental and physical characteristics of every person I know and giving almost their entire horoscope and it would be indisputable. No two people are alike and they are not going to act alike. We cannot get away from the facts of our inheritance. Fifty percent of our inheritance come from our parents and fifty percent from our grandparents. One never knows when there will be some cropping out from the fourth generation back on the tenth back. I cite a situation where a lady who was selling eggs (Mrs. Bunn). Years later she got from selling eggs two white rock chickens. In all the years I have been growing chickens, I never had that to happen but it does happen.

The world would be very meritorious to live if everything was like other things and so we have to take our lives as we find them and live it the best we can. Our heritage and our environment contribute more than anything else to our attitudes. If we are weak in our inheritance and most of us are as we are not responsible for our fore parents. We must look to our environment. This means so much. Personally, my own inheritance was not a bad inheritance. I am made up of Indian for the most part, southern white aristocracy and some French extraction. Through my grandmother, some white Dutch, on my father's side. These inherent qualities have given me the stability and tenacity and personality that has made me but more than any other factor has; perhaps been my environment, I have put myself with people who were looking upward and onward and who wanted to be somebody. I have tried to make my own environment. We have got to take what we have and make it the best we can. The one thing to consider is whether our course is going to lease us to weal or woe. That must be decided by the individual.

Commentary

T.S. Inborden wrote these very knowledgeable and personal thoughts some sixty years ago to his daughter, Dorothy Viola Inborden Miller. He placed a serious premium on the significance of one's genetic inheritance from parents and grandparents. However, he stated one's environment, attitude and personal wishes to succeed and obtain a place of positive survival in this world plays an integral part of an individual survival. I pose this question, has these remarks of many years ago played an integral part in his daughter's longevity along with her possible genetic inheritance to be blessed with 98 years of life in this flesh?

T.S. Quotes

Racial Prejudice is due to tradition, environment, ignorance, tradition, days of slavery with all its factors. That is debauchery separation of families, inhumanity, loss of personal respect and moral let down.

<u>Environment.</u> A stream can not rise above its source. All life partakes of its surroundings. This is evolution. All evolution is of slow growth. This is best illustrated in the vegetable kingdom. All roses were developed from the plain wild rose. It had only five petals at first but by care and the best environment in color and growth.

<u>Ignorance.</u> Enlightment is the best cure for all of racial troubles.

This comes by travel, schools and the largest possible contact. This can be enlarged very much. Character is developed in the struggle to achieve. We can not measure the sweetness and purity of soul that comes from achievement. Yet, it is the biggest produce of all of our agriculture procedure.

Miscellaneous Quotations

Many Negro farmers needed to take an initiative, self assertive to obtain knowledge of the sod, plant life, soil fertility, predacious life (insect)

The man who produces what foods he needs, who knows when and what to plant and how to cultivate and market his products is a superior type.

If you want to change the conduct of people you change their psychology that is all.

Take away our Christian institutions, and you take away the most vial asset for good that a community can have.

Institutions did not stand still. They move upward and onward or they retrogress.

Many of our best schools have closed because of local apathy and lack of appreciation what they were doing.

Our Standards

Trueisms are taught by example rather than precept. Are we teachers setting up a higher standard of the moral life than the parents of our students? If we are short in our ideals, we should see to it at once that we make the sacrifice necessary to the perfect *exemplification* of the highest life. we are lost among ourselves as to what is the best. We do not need to be lost.

Habits

We form our habits than proceed to build about as our philosophy of life to sustain us in our habits we build in the sand.

Concern For Common People

Some of our pulpits are not reaching the people. Listen on the air and hear what you are getting. I know there are millions of fed up intellectual souls who want only the appeals to their highest intellectual level, but their lives are fixed in their habits and growth and the great mob outside gets some thing unless they happen to drop into the salvation.

Religion and Education

I regard preaching and teaching as two coordinated professions that have to do with the human soul and the future destiny of man and woman.

Reading Material

What are we reading? Why would I want to sit for weeks and months pursuing the literature of the slang, slough of the underworld. Yet the newstands are loaded with this material and sales are great. Too much of it appeals to the base element in human life. The fact is if it did not appeal to the emotion very strongly it would have not sold.

Small men cannot do big jobs. It takes big men to do big things. I mean of course mental calibre you have the blood and background. They are assets and assure success.

Influence the farmer and the teacher as much as the students. If you want to change the conduct of a person you change their psychology, that is all.

A Racial Concern

During the First World War, I was credited with having Negroes to buy 48,000 dollars of war stamps and government bonds in making the world safe for democracy. Is it safe yet? Not with the lynching record this county made last year.

Administrative Ability

A college degree, a master's degree, a doctor's degree is no guarantee of one's administrative ability. Common sense must dictate any departure from office routine that brings success.

Statements

I had to shear my life and soul of the attitudes that were incompatible with the highest and best things that I had set out to do. I have always had a mind of my own and follow largely and my own beckonings when I know I am correct.

The efficacy of any philosophy is in the efficiency of its product. That is the measure of success.

It means very much to any human being or life to be born with the correct heritage. Without the correct heritage one has a hard road to travel.

The knowledge of how to extract from the soil the largest and best products which the community may need for its consumption is an asset in which any group of people may well take pride.

The mind is the master and unless that has training and poise, the hand fails. The academic course is to meet this condition.

APPENDIX 16

A TRIP TO CALIFORNIA
BY
THOMAS SEWELL INBORDEN

April 22, 1922

My Dear Friend:

You will be interested to know that I am again back from my five months trip to the north and Northwest. While away I covered, according to the railroad time tables, about twelve thousand miles. This took me through most of the Northern states and the New England States and in the Western States. I left Chicago the 21st of January and visited and stopped at the following places: St. Paul and Minneapolis in Minnesota; Aberdeen in South Dakota; Marmarth in North Dakota; Miles City, Three Forks, Butte and Gerson Hot Springs in Montana; crossing Idaho into Spokane, Washington. We crossed the Continental Divide a few miles east of Butte in four or five feet of snow in an elevation of six thousand feet above sea level. This train was pulled by powerful electrical engines for six hundred miles over the most picturesque mountains in the world. We crossed the tributaries of the great Missouri River more than a score of times, and scaled many mountains, from the highest elevations and glided down into Seattle, Washington, into an elevation of fifteen feet on Puget Sound. Trees were budding and many flowers were already in bloom. After a few days we went to Tacoma in Washington and Portland in Oregon. Then we were off to Sacramento, San Francisco in California. The course took us from the beginning of the Sacramento River in the Siskiyou and Shasta Mountains to its mouth at San Francisco Bay or to the Straits of Carquinez, landing us at Port Costa for Richmond, Berkley and Oakland in Alameda County. At the fine Oakland pier we disembarked from the train and took the ferry boat four miles to San Francisco, passing the Government Island to the lest looking right into the setting sun through the Golden Gate. A few days here in this beautiful setting and we were off for Los Angeles, five hundred miles to the south still. Fresno, Bakersfield, Tehachapi, across the snow-clad Sierra Madre ten thousand feet elevation and in sight of Mount Whitney four thousand feet higher. Down a Valley and to San Fernado and Burbank and Los Angeles. Then to the orange show at San Bernardino, passing on our way Pomona, San Gabriel, Claremount and Garrett & Co.s grape vineyards, one of the homes of the Virginia Dare Extracts. Mr. Garrett is an Enfield man. We could spend only a few days at Los Angeles, then we were off the Coast Route to San Francisco again. Santa Barbara, Ventura, Gaudaloupe, San Lois Obispo, Delmonte, Santa Cruz, San Jose, Santa Clara, Red Wood Cities are familiar names. It took three steam engines to pull the train over the mountains coming north. A few days later we were off again for Sacramento and Salt Lake City in Utah, and Glenwood Hot Springs in Colorado. Passing Florence we came into sight of Pikes's Peak more than a hundred miles east of us, and passing the water swept city of Pueblo and Colorado Springs into Denver the mile high city. A few days spend here and I was off again for Phillipsburg and Des Moines and to Chicago, coming through Nevada, Utah, Wyoming, Colorado, Nebraska, Kansas, Iowa and Illinois. I spent a few days in Chicago, was held up on my arrival from the station to my stopping place in Chicago, but was not robbed. My outcry for "Police and help!" thwarted their plans. Then I was off to Washington City and home on the 22nd of March. At the station I was overwhelmed by the students, teachers and friends in the community who had come to welcome me home with school yells and band music.

I traveled two thousand miles in California alone. I gave twenty-eight addresses, attended eight recitals, fourteen lectures, four theaters where persons of color were the stars, three ministers' meetings, one annual conference, the meeting of the American Missionary Association, the annual meeting of the Connecticut Congregational Association, visited ten colleges and schools, nine state capitals, seventeen city, state and municipal and school museums, twenty public markets. In addition, I talked with Japanese and Chinese farmers, fruit growers, cattle men, sheep men, miners, Negro ranchmen. I met them on the trains, on the farms in the hotels and restaurants, on the boats, on the streets, in the stores, markets, and everywhere. I came back with a few pounds less in weight, but with a vision that money could not buy. I am very truly, T.S. Inborden.

Just A Minute

I am here for only a couple of days. It is a long ways from Bricks, North Carolina, to Seattle, Washington. I still have two thousand miles before me before I turn my face eastward. One gets an idea of this great big country only by traveling over it, as I have done for the past three months. He can get it no other way. Such a trip ought to condition every young man graduating from an Eastern college. Here we go from Bricks in the eastern part of North Carolina to Washington City. The Atlantic Coast Line train takes us through the most historic setting of the Coastal Plains of that eastern section into the foothills of the Old Dominion, through the Civil War battle grounds of national fame, up the historic Potomac, passing Richmond, Fredericksburg, the rustic triangular monument to the great general who in his unfortunate retreat met death at the hands of his own men, into Alexandria, the most historic and conservative town of the pre-war days. Alexandria, the other end of the old pike leading from the "far west" through Winchester Town seventy-five or more miles away. this old pike was put in history by Sheridan's ride, twenty miles away from Winchester Town. Well, we cannot stop in Washington City. It needs nothing that I can say. from Washington we went up into Old Virginia. Taking the Southern train we went through the Virginia Valley and the Shenandoah Valley. The trip took us right through the heart of the battle-fought country of Manassas, Bull Run, over "Goose Creek," "Painter Skin," "Jeffries" - creeks that are well known to all Virginians. We went right into the heart of the Old Blue Ridge, and looking down on Harper's Ferry, Winchester, Middleburg, Leesburg, Upperville, Berryville, the Shenandoah River, on to Washington itself, sixty miles away. Here are five counties: Fauquier, Loudon, Warren, Clark, Jefferson and others in the distance, covering an area of more than ten thousand square miles of the finest country in the world, all to be seen from one level space without moving ten feet on this historic old mountain. Corn, wheat, cattle, and sheep, fill her valleys.

There is no part of these valleys and mountains that cannot, and that do not, grow the finest apples and peaches that are grown in the world. (I am saying this in Seattle, Washington.) I went back to Washington from this fine country, and from Washington to Jersey City. from there I went over to New York and Brooklyn, and out on Long Island Sound. From New York I went to Springfield, Massachusetts. From Springfield I went to the great meeting of the American Missionary Association, which was held at New London, Connecticut. From there I went back to New Haven for Armistice Day and to see Marshal Foch receive his degree from Yale, and the great football game where there were eighty thousand people. I went back to New York again, where I put in two very profitable weeks studying racial and living conditions. From New York City I went to Rochester and put in several days speaking here and there to small groups of people. From there I went to Batavia for only a few hours, and then to the city of Buffalo. From Buffalo to Cleveland and Oberlin, Ohio and in two weeks on to Detroit, Michigan. A few days in Detroit, and I was on my way to Ann Arbor, Jackson and Kalamazoo, Michigan. I reached Chicago a few days before the Christmas holiday. After the Christmas vacation I visited the high schools of Gary, Indiana, and put in another week attending the Mid-Winter Conference of Congregational Workers of the United States. Only three other colored men were in attendance at this conference. They were Dr. Alfred Lawless, of New Orleans; Dr. Kingsley, of Cleveland; and Dr. C.W. Burton, of Chicago. We learned in this great Mid-Winter Conference that there are other problems besides the Negro problem. Indeed, he was scarcely discussed at all. Immediately after the Conference, I turned my face westward. It did not seem safe that I should go alone to buy my ticket and to have my money put into travelers cheque before leaving, so our good friend, Mr. J.E. Wade, of the police force, offered his services and accompanied me to the bank and ticket office. Mr. Wade was formerly from Elerby, N.C. He and his nephew from Richmond County are giving fine services on the police force of Chicago. I was told that they have about a hundred colored men on the police force. All of these men are giving excellent service. I was surprised and glad to see in many of the largest business houses in Chicago our colored men and women doing business over the counters. I saw them in the shipping houses and in the ticket offices. In the city post office of Chicago I was told by one of the "checkers" that out of about eight thousand or more employees that nearly two thousand were colored. I was escorted through every department of the great post office and saw the men handling the nine hundred tons of mail that go through the office every day. Many of the men I knew personally, and some were relatives. Most of the men were experts at their job. A very large number of them are graduates from our best colleges. All of them were fine looking, well groomed men. They were not the least in appearance when compared with the other racial groups. From Chicago I took the Chicago, Milwaukee and St. Paul train to St. Paul. The glacial swept areas of Illinois, Wisconsin and Minnesota abounds with natural resources aside from the farm products. This is a community of wheat, corn and flour mills. It is the home of the world's best packing houses. Minnesota is the synonym for "Gold Metal"; it also says the last word on poultry feed and products. I was shown through a sanitary packing-house where nearly or quite a thousand people were given employment. Coffee, tea, spices and sugar and other commodities are shipped in daily by the train loads and made into new products, repacked and shipped out daily to all parts of the world. The amount of all sorts of candy, cakes, etc., handled was a revelation. Machinery has taken care of every operation in this great establishment, except the absolute thought of man. To the unitiated it might seem to think also. The world's best brand of cheese comes from these parts also. I was surprised to learn that one little community east of St. Paul, in Wisconsin, called Rio, shipped two years ago more than two hundred and twenty-five thousand dollars worth of the finest grades of tobacco. Some of the soldier boys will be interested to know that some of the buildings, probably most of them, at Camp Douglass were still intact as we sped by them through the cliffs and dells.

From St. Paul we turned our face westward for a two thousand mile jaunt on one of the best equipped and finest trains that ever rolled the iron. Nor a minute late on its own account, up hill, down grade, across deep canyons, under the mountains, over the top of the mountains, spanning valleys, across the river beds and lowlands, with the same speed, whether in eight feet of snow on the Cascade Mountains of whether there is no snow, and on to the Pacific Coast. Pulled by the most powerful electric engines in the world, she leaps onward by the touch of her engineer like a thing of life and thought. Our first stop was in Aberdeen, in South Dakota. It was night on our arrival, and I left the train to spend the night for the rest, so that I might have the day to see - yes, just to see. I had been to Aberdeen in 1909 and knew what to expect. The porter advised me not to go out without wrapping up well, as it was about twenty degrees below zero. I went to the first place where the sign read "hotel." I was comfortably located, and after I had gotten a lunch thought I would find the school where I once spoke, but before I had gone very far I decided that my room was the best place for a stranger in that sort of weather. My face could not have been colder if it had been buried for twenty minutes between two blocks of ice. This particular community is noted for its fine quality of white potatoes. They are grown in great quantities, and they are the last word in potato growing. There are none any better anywhere else in the world for flavor and texture.

In a country so cold and bleak one would not expect to find much vegetation. Quick maturing crops of wheat and corn are grown. Hogs, cattle and sheep abound. For hundreds of miles in every direction there is absolutely nothing but a barren track of land which affords a great quantities of the finest hay, which grows naturally. Every mile looks for the world just like the one from which you have just come. There is nothing to break the monotony of the landscape except the monotony of another one. The porter or conductor comes in and says, "Twin Brooks," "Stone Falls,""Odessa," etc., and you lookout when the snow does not blind the view and you see nothing but a few houses, a wheat elevator, or a lot of sleds drawn by two or four horses; not a tree except perhaps a few planted by the government agents. As you reach the North Dakota line not a tree to mark even the site of the little towns that may be more pretentious.

At Marmarth we come into Montana at an elevation of 2700 feet, having put behind us nine hundred and ninety-five miles since leaving Chicago. We have already passed Wakpala, an Indian Reservation, and school. These are easily in sight. We have also left the Missouri River and the Little

Missouri River behind. We come into Musselshell Division, and soon cross the Yellowstone River. Miles City is our station for the night. It is nearly twelve hundred miles out of Chicago with 2300 feet elevation. Several smaller tributaries to the Yellowstone River are passed. Small shrubbery and a few trees in the river courses are a great relief to the landscape. But before we reach the "City" to which we are destined for the night we come into "Bad Lands." Here nature went into contortions and left an awful frown upon her face. I asked the white porter, a very fine fellow (a Lutheran by faith), what was the matter with the country. He said "This is Bad Lands."

Miles City was not a bad looking city. It had all the modern improvements. For several hundred miles we followed the valleys of the Musselshell River and the Yellowstone River, crossing and recrossing the rivers and valleys, sometimes over a high mountain and then almost precipitously down and under another mountain, only to rejoin the river again through another tortuous valley. We reached the Rocky Mountains Division at Harlowton, Montana, thirteen hundred miles west of Chicago at an elevation of 4,000 feet. If you have any heart trouble, you will know that something outside in the physical world has happened before you get here. On we go over the "Summitt of Big Belts" literally up, up, up, around this curve, across that ravine, up by this tall hill, finally on the top, and you look back for five, ten, fifteen or twenty miles and you see the ribbon of track you have spun out. You see the thousands of waste acres of snow and the cattle hugging the hills for protection against the winter's cold. They are inured to it. Ours would die the first night out. The reader would get sleepy before he had spent one hour out there. That is the way you freeze to death; you just get sleepy. We pass Ringling, the Montana Canyon, and again miles further we speed along and cross the great Missouri River seven hundred miles above where we crossed a few days ago. Near Eustis we cross the Jefferson, Madison, Gallitin Rivers forming the Missouri River. Bull Mountains have been left three hundred miles behind and still we speed along. Our horse neither tires nor pants. They feed him "white coal" generated at great substations from fifty to a hundred miles apart. Generated by mountain streams in their mad rush to the great bosom of waters. At dark, I wanted to stop at some small mining town for the night so as not to miss any scenery. The conductor advised against this because of the condition of the people and their accommodation for strangers. I listened, and stopped at his advice at Three Forks, almost fifteen hundred miles out from Chicago, and still 4,000 feet elevation. This was in a valley of farming land of more than three hundred thousand acres of the best farming land in Montana. The great valley was very beautiful, with the mountains ten, twenty, thirty, fifty and a hundred miles away in every direction, silhouetted above the clouds, and dotted with its own shadows. As the sun came up from the east and spread its majesty over the snow-clad peaks, every one was made a diamond of beauty. But we were not to stay at Three Forks over Sunday. We are traveling on trains 15 and 17 every day. At 8:50 we departed in very cold weather - ten degrees below zero, they said. It was only three hours ride from Butte, Montana. I did not want to pass the highest point reached on the whole trip in the dark. I wanted to have my eyes open and see when I went over the real top. Well I did. It was 10:53 by my watch - 1,505 miles out from Chicago, 6,322 feet elevation.

The writer of the "Ex-Colored Man" said when he was in Paris with his landlord he was very fond of music, etc., and so one night he went to one of the finest theaters in the city. Soon after he had taken his seat a very aristocratic looking gentleman came in whom he had at one time seen at his mother's house in the state of Georgia. He was very small at the time he saw him in Georgia, and he was sure it was the same gentleman. He had with him his beautiful wife and a more beautiful daughter. To his amazement they sat almost adjoining him in the theater so close that he might have touched them. They did not know him. He knew that it was his own father, and this beautiful girl just finishing high school was his own sister, flesh and blood. He wanted to speak, but conventionality and tradition had closed his mouth, and to save tragedy he arose and left in silence.

I have looked forward all my life for just such an opportunity to see this great country, as I have now had, and as I am having, because I still have 5,000 miles ahead. Most of my younger life was spent in missionary service on small salary, and with a family of children to educate and prepare for a larger life than I had the opportunity of having. This opportunity now comes to me through the officals and friends of the American Missionary Association under whose auspices I have worked for thirty-two years. It comes as an appreciation of their part for my long service. I may not have done everything they wanted me to do, but I have tried to follow the dictates of an honest conviction.

When I passed over the great *Continental Divide*, I remembered my dream of forty years. I knew no one and had no one to talk to about it. I looked into space and thanked the Lord of all of us that I had cast my lot where the rewards had been faithful and abundant. I felt like crying out in paroxisms of joy.

We still "a-going." We reached Butte, Montana, at noon Sunday, January 29th. It was very cold, but I found a good hotel near the station, so that I did not have to be in the cold very long. I was advised and was quick in deciding that I would in an hour take the trip to Gerson Hot Springs, eighteen miles away. Several miles from the place I saw what seemed to be smokestacks with steam pouring out each one. I found on arrival that these were just openings in the roof, forming vents for the steam from the hot water as it comes from the mountains at a temperature of 195 degrees. The water has wonderful healing properties. I did not take the bath because of the extreme temperature outside. The hot springs are very numerous in these parts of the country. All the rivers were frozen several feet deep but here and there where the streams pass very close to the mountain gorges one can see the temperature of the waer change by the warmer currents coming right out of the hills. Butte is the largest mining center in the world. One hill is the richest hill in all the world - is worth more than all of Wall Street, New York. The bar-iron, copper, silver, gold, and other by-products probably go down to the center of the earth. I went 2,200 feet down, and I was then 800 feet from the bottom of it. I was donned in a real miner's outfit, including a miner's acetelyne lamp. Our decending cage was about four feet square, and held four men. It was built to bring up twenty tons of ore about every minute of the day. State laws define how fast human beings shall be brought up or taken down. The installation that operates this mine cost more than a million dollars. It is the finest electrical outfit I ever saw. The house in which the machinery is located that operates the pulleys, under air pressure, is more than a hundred feet square. When the signals are given, twenty-eight feet down, one man brings the load to the tenth of an inch exactness to any level in the pit or on top of the ground, a hundred feet high if necessary. Thousands of wheels, belts, pulleys, pistons, etc., move in every part of this building to the touch of one man. If he makes a single mistake it may cost one life or a thousand in the mine. It may cost a mint of money in destruction. Efficienty, absolute efficiency is the only thing that counts.

Five very large pumps about twelve feet square each bring up the surplus water from below. They are located many feet below the surface of the ground, and it is never cold down there. The water is charged with copper, and this disintegrates any other metals, so that the long troughs over old tin cans and iron waste, where the copper is deposited and afterwards taken off. I did not have time to get all the details of the process. Mr. J.D. Rockefeller, I was told, owned most of the stock of this particular mine. In the morning of the same day, I visited one of the best schools in this country. It was a city high school. Everything taught in this school leads to mining. That is the big job there. The youths are prepared to do the things they will have to do when they leave school. Boys ten to fifteen years old are experts already in the machine shop. We left at noon Tuesday, and my destination was Spokane, Washington. We crossed the Missouri River, the valley of the same name, and Summit and Bitter Root Valley, also made famous by its fine apples and vegetables. We passed again under the mountains two miles. Here we were eighteen hundred miles from Chicago in an elevation more than 4,000 feet. At Superior we were delayed several hours in the night on account of a freight wreck. We arrived in Spokane about noon Thursday. We crossed the Cascade Mountains in eight feet of snow. This was after leaving Spokane. We visited the Spokane Valley, another valley made famous by its apples. I talked with a banker about the products of the community. They are trying to get emigrants from the East to come into the community. It is a farming and lumber community. I visited the exhibits of farm products kept by the chamber of commerce of the city. They are wide awake. I saw all sorts of vegetables grown on irrigated land and by dry farming methods that would make our farmers take notice. I never saw finer vegetables anywhere. They are grown under great pressure. From Spokane 1,900 miles west of Chicago, in an elevation of 1882 feet, we dropped down here (Seattle) in a few hours to 2,200 miles west of Chicago and to sea level. From eight feet of snow crossing into a temperature of 36 degrees above zero. No snow and no ice.

February 2nd we arrived at Seattle. Twelve days and about twenty-two hundred miles from Chicago. This is considered the chief city of all this part of the country. It has a population of about 350,000 people. Its scenic environment, with its backgroun of mountains and its valley intersected by sounds, bays and rivers, make it the most beautiful city in the world. It is called the "Floral Paradise." I saw many flowers blooming in the open. It is said to be the cleanest and best lighted city in the world. I wanted to see Puget Sound, so the next morning bright and early, I found my way over the network of railroads on a high elevation above the streets to the fine pier several hundred feet above the water. Here I had a fine view of the Sound and the great expanse of water and mountains yonder a few miles, and literally thousands of boats of every kind and from everywhere in the world. The place from which I made the observation was a fine room with large glass windows, leather seats, heat, restaurant, etc., to make the weary traveler rested and welcome. This was Puget Sound. This is where literacy has the highest rating of any American city. If any city is cleaner or better lighted, I have yet to see it.

In these parts there are billions of feet of lumber untouched by the despoiler. I saw fir trees measuring four and six feet in diameter. I was told they were three and four hundred feet tall. I saw two men sawing with a cross-cut saw, one on one side and one on the other side, and the diameter was so great that only one man could be seen below his head. The sound itself is said to be large enough to contain all the navies of the world and still have more room. The diversity of scenery, its climate, air, beautiful sunshine, mountains, sound, and inland waterways, woods, flowers, parks, fine hotel, theaters, public markets, and city railway system, post office, and the State University, give that place a setting hard to describe in this limited space. The three or four public markets are works of art. One on Second Street was terraced, and is the cleanest market I ever saw, and I have seen a great many. The markets will generally indicate what the farmers are doing. They show the best products raised in the community. The arrangement of these country products will give you an idea of their artistic values. The Japanese were in evidence everywhere. They were universally polite and clean. They may be ubiquitous, but they are certainly utilitarian. They know how to get the best results from the soil as farmers. They had the best things I every saw from the farms. They are credited with having a lot of sense and of being very industrious. These are very important assets in the development of any community, whether in California or in North Carolina. Having sense means having efficiency, knowing how to do. Industry means power and wealth. As much as I would have loved to linger here longer, I had to divide my time with other points of interest. I left there early Sunday morning, the fifth of February, for Tacoma, about forty miles away. Through miles and miles of orchards of raspberries, loganberries and blackberries, apples and pears and walnuts, passing great canning and packing houses, irrigation projects, mining sections, etc., and at 10 o'clock the Olympian rolled into Tacoma. Mount Rainier, Mount St. Helena, Mount Hood, and Mount Adams, off in the distance had already come into view. You are overwhelmemd by their vastness and grandeur. Their snow-capped peaks, timbered inclines and fertile valleys cannot be equaled anywhere else in the world. We are still on the Puget Sound. The city has a population of more than a hundred thousand souls. They represent every nationality under the sun. It has the finest harbor and the most equitable climate in the world. The rainfall is around thirty-five inches a year, which insures better farming conditions. The Chamber of Commerce of Seattle and Tacoma are vieing with each other as to which will show the best exhibits of the state. Their great varieties of wheat, corn, flax, rye, oats, grasses, barley, buckwheat, apples, pears, small fruits and nuts, and their by-products: honey, preserved fruits, tomatoes, and manufactured products, views and paintings of cattle and sheep raising, lumbering, e.g., simply baffle the imagination.

You want to sit and look for hours and write impressions in your notebook, and then go out and come back again and do the same thing as long as you have a minute to spare.

Tacoma has a stadium that seats forty thousand people. Nothing else like it in the United States except the college stadium at Cambridge and New Haven. Schools and churches are the finest in the whole country. It was my pleasure to speak twice the Sunday I was there in one of the largest and finest churches in the city (white), and in the evening to one of our colored churches. The museum contains pictures of the early pioneers and Indian history curios. It was in this community where the earliest white settlements were made. The stadium and Stadium High School are located on one of the highest points in the city overlooking Puget Sound, which is precipitously, several hundred feet at the base of the hill. Trains may be seen for miles and miles coming from the East and North, and boats from Alaska, Seattle and Vancouver as they turn the western promontory. I traveled with an elderly gentleman who built almost the first house in that part of the city for the father of the present occupant, and I also had dinner in that house overlooking the stadium and the Sound. The minister living in the house is an eastern man, and his wife is the daughter of a missionary to Honolulu. She went over the Morning Star soon after its construction forty years ago, in company with President Fairchild of Oberlin College. At that time she was a small child.

The state of Washington produced in 1921 28,000,000 bushels of apples alone that were worth more than $30,000,000. At the same time New York is said to have produced 14,000,000, California 6,000,000 and Michigan 6,000,000 bushels of apples. At the time Spokane County, in which Spokane is located, is said to have produced 80,000,000 bushels of wheat. I went through this valley, a part of Yakima and a part of Wenatchee valleys. One wonders at the great productivity of this country when he thinks of the great mountains almost everywhere - mountains where absolutely nothing can grow. The valleys are protected by these mountains. They are for the most part virgin soil. Irrigation projects have brought the melting snow to the ripening fruit and grain. The sun, penetrating into these mountain recesses have brought color and flavor equaled by no other community.

Pity it is that we cannot stay here to see more of this environment. We must go to Portland, Oregon. We pass Rainier National Park on the left closed to winter tourist, and the towering sentinels already mentioned. We are in sight of them until we get to Portland, nearly two hundred miles away. Portland is a fine city of unusual wealth, fine houses, parks, hotels, banks, more than two hundred miles of street car lines. beautiful stores and public buildings, and flowers, flowers, everywhere flowers. The mountains back of the city are circled by beautiful drives and street carlines and every sort of house that can be built on the face of the earth, terraced from top to bottom, trees, ferns, flowers, vines, form the most perfect menagerie of vegetation and of art that one can conceive. It looked like the composition of one mind. It was the cooperation of many minds for civic beauty. The view from Council Crest - see it once and you will never forget it if you have any imagination. The Columbia River cutting in half and stretching away for miles in the distance, the towering snow-capped mountains already named above, the beautiful Willamette River whose course for several hundred miles we shall soon follow, the Cascade Range, thousands of acres of find farms and beautiful farm homes spreading out in every direction as far as the eye can see, a flock of sheep, a few thousand cattle, a herd of ponies and horses, the weird whistle of steamers coming up the river, and trains passing up the several valleys, all seen from Council Crest give you a feeling of scenic beauty that you cannot overcome. What a paradise for botanists. How I would like to have lingered in that environment until the foliage came into their glory! The markets are again gems of beauty. One has to buy whether he needs anything or not. The sellers are so courteous and polite. The arrangement of the products are so unique and artistic; they have so much and so great a variety; the people handling the goods were so clean in their pure white garbs; the tables and stands were immaculately clean; everything put on the market was absolutely clean and pretty. You just had to stop and taste here and there and buy. I brought here several kinds of honey for samples, which I brought six thousand miles home. I carried it all the way. Sage honey, clover honey, alfalfa honey, apple honey, orange honey, olive honey, raspberry honey, etc.

At night I saw a big roller machine actually scrubbing the streets. Beat that if you can. I saw it. The Chamber of Commerce gives out every year free literature telling about the products of the state, and they have a show of the farm and mineral products that simply cannot be equal anywhere. The market stands I was told were owned by the city and are rented to the farmers and others on condition that only farm-grown products produced by themselves were to be on sale in them. The rent was just a nominal rent to encourage the farmer to bring his wares and sell it. The Southern Pacific train took us south from Portland. The road leads for many miles up the Willamette River through the most beautiful valley, then up the Umpqua River, and the Umpqua River Valley, and into the Rogue River Valley. The climate conditions are well adapted for grains, grasses, fruits and walnuts. The growing seasons are especially long, and there is not much danger from frost. The fruit orchards yield from five hundred dollars to a thousand dollars an acre. Some of course with less care, yield much less. The higher figures show the possibilities under the best care. On my way south I saw a great many apples thrown out in the fields. I was advised that the fruit association were not getting their prices, and they were thrown away to save cheap sales. They picked last year 2,650,000 boxes of apples valued at $2,600,000. These apples were the Spitzenbur, yellow Newton Pippins, Jonathan, Rome Beauty. These are the varieties prized for their color, keeping quality, flavor and conformity to the best types. The trees come into bearing the fourth and fifth years, and increase their yield from one bushel to seven a year. Their apple pests are the same as ours. They must spray to get the best results. The trees are not large. The average yield to the acre is from three hundred to four hundred bushels, at a total cost of about forty and sixty cents a bushel. Large acreages of pear tress of the standard varieties are grown, and they are more prolific bearers. The yield is said to be higher per acre than that of apples. I saw scores and scores of very large pear orchards. The trees are less trouble to care for than apple trees. I saw thousands and thousands of trees in the Willamette, Umpqua and Rogue River valleys that baffled me to know what they were. They did not look like any sort of trees I had ever seen, and yet I did not want to appear too ignorant to my fellow travelers. I had only one way to find out, and that was to ask somebody who knew. They were *prune* trees. The cost of caring for a prune orchard is said to be from five to seven dollars an acre. The average crop an acre is about five tons. The average value per acre is from $75 to $250. About thirty million tons are produced and the demand is growing. They have not begun to fill the demand. People are learning more than ever the food and medicinal value of this fruit.

Nearly fifty million pounds of cherries are produced annually at a value of more than two hundred thousand dollars. They yield about six thousand pounds to the acre at a profit of from one hundred to eight hundred dollars an acre. In Western Oregon, the Upper Columbian Valley, and the southwestern part of the state peaches are grown on a large scale and at great profit. Grapes, strawberries raspberries, blackberries, loganberries and currants are grown in great quantities. At La Grande, Oregon, there is a sugar beet factory whose capacity is three hundred aand fifty tons daily. Beets are grown largely in that section. French walnuts are grown in large quantities. Seedlings are grafted with improved varieties. The largest I ever saw were in the markets. I stopped one night at Grant's pass and saw some of the largest and finest pumpkins that can be grown in the world. Stock raising probably stands at the head of the productive resources of the state. Great quantities of cattle, sheep, horses, mules, hogs, and even goats are raised. The income from this industry would be many millions of dollars. Poultry is grown all the year, and millions of dollars are realized yearly from dairying. The annual output of honey is around two million poounds, averaging more than three hundred thousand dollars. I have said nothing about the fisheries, the fertility of the rivers, lakes and bays, and the lumber conditions. There are about twenty million acres of land in Oregon unappropriated, waiting for brain and brawn. It belongs to the government. You may have it if you will qualify and meet the conditions.

On my way to San Francisco, I had planned to stop at Eugene and see the State University, but I found that I could not do so without very much delay, and also because the weather conditions were bad. It is a railway center of considerable importance. Passing Cottage Grove, we crossed the Umpqua River and went up the valley some distance, and up the Rogue Valley close by the river of the same name into Grant's Pass. Here I preferred to stay all night so as not to miss any view or things of interest. We were never out of sight of picturesque scenery and mountains of great height and beauty. Orchards and fine gardens of vegetables were ever in sight. Our train has taken us into Cow Creek Canyon, beautiful and picturesque. Grant's Pass is the fruit shipping center for this part of the state, and I saw many packing houses. On to Ashland at the foothills of the Siskiyou, where the lythia water and mineral spings attract your attention as you pull into the station and all get out to try the water as it comes fresh up into the glass receptables for you to drink. Ahead and around you on every side nothing but mountains towering a mile high. You wonder how you are to scale that tower in your front. Your train takes on another engine, possibly two, and off you go up the Rouge Valley until the Rogue River is lost in the mountain stream. When you can go no further your train cuts across the head of the valley on a high bridge and climbs the oposite mountain parallel to the track you have just come on the other side, going directly north, exactly reversing your course. We zig-zag up the mountain for an hour till we reach an elevation of nearly ten thousand feet. All this time we are in sight of Ashland, fourteen miles below, lying placid, warm and quiet. The snow plows are busy keeping away the snow and the men are clad in the warmest sheep skins from head to foot. A mile off to the left, a thousand feet higher, is "Pilot Rock," lying as if it had been hurled by some powerful giant. This is the landmark that guided the early pioneers and Indians in their early explorations through that unknown country. Freeing our train from her extra engines, we sped off at a tangent through a fine growth of timber and cut over land. This is the Shasta route, and we have just scaled the Siskiyou Mountains. Now we start down the slope, entering the Cantara Loop and crossing at the very head of the Sacramento River. Now we have crossed the line into California. Mount Shasta, the most majestic peak of the western continent, fourteen thousand feet and more, towers above us, and off at some distance. We enter Sacramento River Canyon and stop at Shasta Springs, which is a source of this river. There we got off the train and drank the finest water that ever came from the earth. This is probably the greatest summer resort on the Pacific Coast. I saw one rabbit sitting in his burrow on the side of the hill. The snow was falling terrifically. Miles and miles down this canyon we go, passing ferns and moss hanging from a thousand crags. We pass Castle Crags away to the west like sentinels guarding our entrance. More than four hundred miles we go, following this tortuous river valley until it spreads out into San Francisco Bay. We pass Chico, a community of fruit interest and great vineyards. It one will look at the map of the state of California, he will see that almost all the state is included in two great valleys, especially in the northern part of the state called Northern California. These are the valleys of Sacramento adjacent to the Sacramento river, which runs the entire length of the valley and into the Straits of Carquines and into the San Francisco Bay. The other valley is San Joaquin. In the first of these is located Sacramento, the capital of the state, and in the second valley is Fresno, near the southern part of the valley, and also Bakerfield. We are told that about half of the cultivated land in California, or that which may be cultivated, is in the valleys. They form more than fourteen million acres. They are about four hundred and fifty miles long and more than forty miles wide. The Sacramento and San Joaquin rivers are the drainage for this great basin. These two great rivers come together near Walnut Grove, one from the south and one from the north. I traveled the entire valleys of both these rivers. There are almost three millions of acres in the Sacramento Valley alone, and from my observation not more than half of it seems to be in cultivation. Thousands of acres of its are in citrous fruits and other fruits and walnuts. At the same time of my visit large areas of the two valleys were under water. The lands are rich and yield radily to various kind of cultivation. When the overflow from the rivers during the rainy season is controlled, there is no reason why these lands should not be more valuable to the state. Large areas are still in the formulation, and look as if they might make great rice plantations. I heard while out there that something was being done to get Japanese farmers to work these low areas into rice farms.

I stopped one night at Redding. This is only a few miles inside of the state line. It was here that the "Gold Rush" was made in 1849. Some of the old settlers are still here and remember the "rush". I was told that two per cent of our gold still comes from this community. It was here that I really saw the first sign of California. The next morning after my arrival, while waiting for my train, I saw oranges in the parks and about the homes near the central part of the town. Magnolia trees and palm trees showed that we were in a new and strange country. Tropical plants of one sort or another can be grown from one end of the state to the other. One man said that he could pick oranges at the same time watch the melting snow on the nearby mountains. The rainfall varies from fifteen to thirty inches, whether in the lower or upper part of the state. Irrigation projects are on foot, and furnish all the water needed for the crops. As the acreage increases, these projects will grow. Sacramento river and Feather River are the main sources of water for this upper country. I traveled through both of these valleys and to the very mouth of the rivers. We arrived at Benecia late in the afternoon, and the entire train is put aboard the largest ferry boat in the world, and carried across four miles to Port Costa, across the Strait of Carquines. We pass Richmond, Berkeley, Oakland. At Oakland we pull into the Oakland ferry and disembark again to a large ferry boat, and in twenty minutes we are in the city of San Francisco. We are here for only a few days, then we leave for the sourthern part of the state. We reserve our impressions of the city till our return. The other valley further south is supposed to be eleven thousand square miles, and has about seven million acres of arable land. It is a boundless area and productive of the greatest quantity of oranges, olives, grapes, etc. We spent a part of two days at Fresno, and addressed the colored Baptist Church at night. There are some colored farmers in that section who are doing well on their farms. We regretted very much that we could not count them by the thousand. They are altogether too few. Bakersfield, which is in the southern part of this valley, is a great oil section of the state. There are four such centers in this state. Their combined output a few years ago was ninety-two million barrels. Oil has taken the place of coal in almost all the industries of the state. The refineries are seen almost everywhere. Stock raising, grapes, orange orchards, peach orchards, olive orchards, fig orchards border every road. I saw at least one flock of sheep numbering more than three thousand. We crossed the Sierra Madre over the Tehachepi loop at an elevation of more than seven thousand feet. Going down the mountain we passed into the great Mojave Desert. Death valley, 290 feet below sea level, forms a part of this desert. There must be several thousand square miles of country in this area, and I would not give fifty cents for the whole of it. The discovery of oil may give value or the irrigation projects may save it for farm developments. Yucca, sage and sand seemed to be its chief products at present. Mojave, Lancaster and San Fernado are our next stop. A few ours later we are in Los Angeles.

The object of my trip West was to study farming conditions with reference to the colored people and to acquaint myself with living conditions in that part of the country. There is little that I can say about Southern California, and Los Angeles especially, that the world does not know. It is separated from the northern part of the state by the range of mountains already referred to, known as the Tehachepi

Mountains, which are a part of the Sierra Madre. There are seven counties south of this mountain divide. It has a reputed population of more than six hundred thousand people. They represent every nationality. There are forty-five thousand colored people in the city. The state as a whole is the most cosmopolitan I ever saw. I wanted to take some data from the printed matter sent out from the Chamber of Commerce. The products of the county must measure in a very large way the industry and happiness of the citizens. It is the leading county in the United States in the value of all crops. It ranks first in the value of farm property, in the value of all farm crops, in the value of fruits and nuts, hay and forage, dairy products, bearing lemon trees, beet sugar production, and in bearing olive trees. It ranks second in poultry, bearing orange trees, irrigation enterprise, and walnuts products. The conduit which brings the city water for more than two hundred miles was build at a cost of twenty-five million dollars. There are four trans-continental railways that enter the city of Los Angeles, and probably a dozen other smaller lines. They have more than twelve hundred miles of improved streets and more than nine miles of sewer. There are twenty-five public parks. I visited a number of them. They have more than five hundred miles of electrical car lines and more than a thousand miles of electrical lines running to all parts of the county. Their schools are the best in the whole country. They have hundreds of churches that are well attended. I took daily tours to many of the surburban towns in twenty and thirty miles radius. Culver City, Santa Monica, Venice, Beverly, Hollywood, Long Beach, Redondo, Pasadena, Pomona, Claremont, Ontario, San Gabriel, Burbank, etc. These are all beautiful spots. Some of them are real little cities with every modern facility. I thought at the time of my visit that if people who live under such an environment as I saw were not happy, they have no need to go to heaven when they die. They told me that I ought to have made my trip in the summer when I could see the country in its glory. I went in an auto bus to San Bernardino seventy miles through the country to the orange show. It is called the Gate City to Southern California. The county itself is a wonder in its output of fruits and walnuts; oranges especially. I saw millions of bushels of the yellow fruit everywhere for miles and miles till the eye tired of seeing what I called an awful waste of nature's products. The city is called the commercial center of the orange belt. It is a beautifully laid out city with semi-tropical plants growing everywhere, luxuriantly beautiful. The show takes up more than an acre of ground, and oranges were blended in the most gorgeous display in every conceivable figure. Oranges, lemons, grape fruit and their by-products by the millions. The trip through the valley took me over the finest roads in the world. They could not be finer. I was more than interested to pass "Garrett and Company's" vineyards, one of the homes of the Virginia Dare products. Mr. Garrett himself is an Enfield, N. C., man. The extracts are bound to be right if it is "Virginia Dare." What is said of any one of the southern counties may be well said of any other, except perhaps the "Imperial Valley County." I did not go to that county, but from what I heard about the county it looks as if a special edict was issued from the maker of all the counties to do some special work on that county alone. It was the last county formed in the state and its area is more than four thousand square miles. It is in the extreme southwest part of the state. The lay of the land, the soil itself, the climate, location, altitude make it the best place in the world for stock raising and fruit production. There are more turkeys grown in this one county than in other similar sections in the world. I was very much impressed with the fine school houses and churches. No money or care seemed to be lacking in the construction of these important centers. Every one I saw in the country or city was decked with profusive growths of shrubbery and flowers. While I was in Spokane, the city claimed the lowest death rate per thousand of its populations. When I was in Seattle that city claimed the same thing. When I was in Tacoma they claimed they had the lowest death rate; when in Sacramento they claimed to have the lowest death rate. In San Francisco they claimed the lowest death rate; Oakland claimed the same; Los Angeles claimed the lowest also. When we were crossing the Techachepi mountains ten thousand feet elevation I saw a fine graveyard up further on the side of the hill, and I was surprised. They might have been soldiers killed in the war. One almost wonders why folks should ever die in such a beautiful country. Conditions are so good for living right along. Good churches, excellent schools, clean cities perfect climate all must contribute greatly to long life. They ought to be happy, but happiness cannot be bought with luxuries; it contributes more than anything else to long life when other conditions are good. The city of Los Angeles is twenty miles from the Pacific Ocean, and I venture to predict that in less than twenty years the city will extend and include Venice, Santa Monica, Long Beach and all the little coast towns along the water front, and the largest ocean vessels will be doing business in the heart of the business section as they are in Seattle, Tacoma, Portland, San Francisco, Oakland. Their population will soon be in the millions. It is growing by leaps and bounds every day, every week and every month. Fourteen thousand people come there every year. The people are busy everywhere. They have the secret of getting a larger population. Create industrial interests and the folks follow. Good schools and good churches; a community in which there is compatibility between all classes and not hatred. These are the best drawing cards. One does not travel many miles in California without asking questions. Many of the questions will have to be answered by history. Cortez, Juan Rodriguez, Cabrillo, Don Gasper de protola, Fray Junipero Serre are familiar names in its early history. The country was known as Alta' and Baja, which was upper and lower California. It began in the extreme southern part of the state and went as far north as the foot of man could tread. The old maps show the southern part of the state as being a part of Mexico. It was sometimes called the land of the Heart's Desire. To use the words of another it was in 1769, "That destiny marked Southern California for its own, ordering the fig and the vine to make soft the dessert wastes, lemon and orange bloom for the upland slopes, herds for a thousand hills, living water to make green the sunbrowned land; and, last, not the dream of seven mythical cities of gold, but the bright reality of thrice seven times seven golden cities that now throb with the tides of commerce and the tread of countless feet." At the beginning of its history the King of Spain ordered that in order to make the country safe for Spain and its religion, that missions should be established. Under the orders of the great Catholic church fifteen or more missions were established--fifteen of them along the coast. My trip back to San Francisco, five hundred miles north, took me along the Pacific coast in sight of many of these missions. We follow what was called the "Highway of the King." Those we passed were San Buenaventura, Santa Barbara, San Miguel, and Santa Clara. The southern part of the state especially owes a lot to these early missionaries. They gave harbor to the traveler, irrigated the land and started the early settlers and Indians to farming.

From San Francisco to Los Angeles along the coast is a country backed by mountains of great height and beauty with slopes and valleys surpassing any description. For hundreds of miles our train slipped right along the edge of the Pacific waters, sometimes forty or a hundred feet above these waters, sometimes nearer, then off on a hill top, then across an arm of the seas then headlong toward the water as if to go right into it, only to swerve around some high hill and then out into some beautiful valley. You have to see it to appreciate it. Passing San Fernando, Oxnard, Ventura, we come to Santa Barbara in Santa Barbara County. The county is mountainous and has four large valleys. The valleys are the Santa Ynez, Los Alamos, Lompoc and Santa Maria. The last named valley is said to have four hundred square miles, and can support ten times its population. Mustard seed is the leading agricultural product in the county. The whole county is well adapted to all vegetables and fruits that are common to that part of the state. I saw many orchards of great size. It is said that three fifths of the prunes and three-fourths of the apples grown in the state grow in these valleys adjacent to the coast. This is due to the fact that perhaps the rainfalls is greater-than further inland. Printed matter on this section tell us that the products of this coast range are the following: beet sugar, wheat, barley, hay, garden seed, oil, coal, asphaltum, cement, lime, live stock, butter and cheese, fruits, berries, vegetables, olive oil, walnuts. I saw great flocks of sheep, cattle and horses. Millions of wild ducks, and we were never out of sight of sea gulls. They are the scavengers on land and water. I was fortunate in meeting people here and there who could give me lots of the sort of information I wanted. As our train rounded the coast of Santa Barbara we caught sight of the Islands of Santa Cruz, Santa Rosa, San Miguel. They may have been thirty miles to our left. Passing Point Conception, a lighthouse here and there, a large open field in the actual making, or a sandhill thrown up in the past few months, crossing Santa Maria River, leaving Lompoc and Ynez Valleys behind, we came to San Louis Obispo. Great quantities of oil are delivered to this port for shipment. It is also the seat of the state polytechnic school. The rainfall here is very light, so that farming is not profitable. The western slopes of the mountains for nearly a hundred miles afford good grazing for cattle and sheep. The water is largely mist from the Pacific Ocean with a very low rainfall. At this point our train leaves the sight of the coast and we climb the Coastal Range, being pulled by three powerful steam engines up an elevation of great height, more than seven thousand feet, and head into the Salinas and Santa Clara Valley. Salinas Valley has an area of 500,000 acres and the two valleys are almost 150 miles in length and fifty miles wide. We head toward "Bishop Peak" no less than four times climbing this mountain. We go down into Monterey County and follow the Salina River till we get to Monterey Bay near Del Monte. Santa Cruz is our next stop. We pass the Lick Observatory. We enter Santa Clara Valley crossing the mountains by the same name. We also pass Stamford University. We leave San Mateo County on the left and we speed along. We pass San Jose. Dark covers us, but at Redwood City we come into sight of San Francisco Bay and thirty miles further we are in San Francisco again.

Five hundred miles are covered in about fourteen hours. The mountain ranges on both sides for several hundred miles, and the mountain on one side and the Pacific Ocean on the other for several more hundred miles with an ever changing view of mountain inclines, rivers, valleys, irrigation projects here and there, the excitement of high elevation, crossing some divide, farming operations throughout the entire course, fruit orchards, vineyards, gardens, great flocks of sheep, cattle, etc., chateaux, villages, mining operations and oil wells. This is the panorama that simply bewitches the brain. It was such as this that the old colored preacher saw when he could no longer contain his emotions when he said, "My God, look at that Glory." It is glory, and the man whose soul does not feel it is dead. Add to this the ocean scene with every angle the train makes, the steamers away out, the sunset behind these beautiful waters, and do you wonder that I have been dreaming this thing every night since I had the experience of it. It gets into your soul in some way. Some one has said, "Its all California from east to west, from north to south." I traveled two thousand miles in the state alone in every direction. The inspiration is the same. I spoke in one of the largest churches out there, heard some of the finest speakers in the world, saw some of the best shows, tramped over some of the orange, apple, fig, prune and berry orchards, bee and poultry yards. I visited soldiers' homes, city parks, city museums and farms in the country. I visited some of the best schools in the West and Northwest, including the state universities where they are really doing things.

Our eyes are now set toward the east and home. We are at San Francisco. Before we leave here we must revert to the lower part of the state again. The city of Los Angeles gets its water from a distance of more than two hundred miles from the snow-capped slope of Mount Whitney. They are the highest mountains in the United States except in Alaska. The aqueduct is the largest in the world. The reservoirs are located in the San Fernando Valley. The pipes taking this water from its source to its outlet are eight to ten feet in diameter. Forty miles of this water is run in open lined canals. The line was pointed out to me many miles out of Los Angeles by a fellow traveler who knew the history of its construction. As one travels from north to south in this state and from east to west he is very much impressed with the great network of wires stretched everywhere, apparently reaching every farmhouse and factory. These are high-powered electric wires carrying power to the industrial centers and to the farms for light and power for power more than light. Water has to be supplied to all the farms by irrigation. Where gravity does not do the work they must depend on pumps. The electric power is used to run the pumps. This power is generated by the mountain streams hundreds of miles away. The great power plants are largely owned by companies in the East. The irrigation projects, I presume, are the most wonderful in the world. I was advised that it cost about eight dollars an acre to get the canals into operation. Another interest of great importance in the growth of a country is the public roads. The roads were universally good. I traveled several hundred miles over the public roads in Los Angeles and San Barnardino counties, and for the long stretches I never saw better roads.

Hollywood, which is really a part of the larger city, is a very pretty place. The streets are paved and there was not a shoddy nor a cheaply constructed house to be seen. I counted seven moving picture studios. I had no idea that these studios were built on so vast a scale. It seems that all the stars in the moving picture world have their studios here, and their fine home--Charlie Chaplin, Douglass Fairbanks, Mary Pickford, and others. Many of the great meat packers of Chicago, Omaha and Denver have million dollar homes in or near this little suburb. The south side of Beverly Hills is covered with these expensive homes. There are a number of these studios in Culver City. This is a small place about fifteen miles toward the Pacific from Los Angeles. The dominating genius of it is Mr. Harry Culver. Ten years ago it was not born, and today it has a population of about two thousand people. The little railroad station, the little homes, the well paved streets and business houses, all show signs of taste and industry. Here is where "Fatty Arbuckle" got his start, and his studio is still there as a reminder. Several boulevards and electric lines pass through the town from Los Angeles to the Pacific Ocean, which is only five miles away. Venice, with a dozen other settlements along the coast for ten or more miles, is the Coney Island of Southern California. Street cars and boulevards give one ready access to every part of the beach. They have all the eating houses, cheap shows, swindling games and junk shops for the attractions. The building lots in some of these little villages are sold under restrictions. I was curious to know the restrictions. Houses that are put on them must not cost less than twenty-five hundred dollars, and no lot shall be sold to any one except purely Anglo-Sagon--a fine opportunity for unanimity of spirit and exclusiveness if not tested under the state law by some ubiquitous spirit.

The problem of racial identity is a complex one in that country. I saw Mexicans who looked all the world like Negroes, and Negroes who looked all the world like Mexicans. Their language was the only distinguishing features, and in many cases the Negroes were better clad and better groomed. Negroes spoke the unadulterated English language. Their Alabama, Mississippi, Georgia, Louisiana or Texas previous environment may have given them more of the Southern brogue. The Mexicans have clung to their Spanish tongue or some broken dialect. Japanese, Chinese, Filipinos, Porto Ricans and others form another group. Then there is another group from northern Europe and southern Europe belonging to the white races, and all these units speak a language of their own and follow largely the customs of their country. I wondered who was fit and who could qualify under "The Restrictions."

I will say nothing about Chicago, but let me start at Butte, Montana. From Butte, Montana, to Spokane, Seattle, Portland, Sacramento, San Francisco, Oakland, Fresno, Los Angeles to the least city in the West there are all sorts of secret organizations and labor unions, selfish and otherwise, cliques and clans, to whom you must pay obeisance. Add to this the rankest Bolsheviki spirit, from the four ends of the earth, and you have a problem worth the attention of our best statesmen. I have been trying to get away from San Francisco, but it is hard to leave a community of so inviting environment. I can only name a few places now that are strikingly full of interest. Here is the Golden Gate Park, over yonder a short distance the Presidio, a little further around on the bay the Art Palace. Here is where the exposition was held. Down on the beach are the Sutro baths and cliff houses. From this fine eminence I saw seven seals, some sleeping, some bathing, some growling. They were on the rock a four hundred feet off the beach. Rural paintings in the museums, depicting wild animal life in their natural setting with the mountain background, etc., were very real. The Southern Pacific station, located between Third and Fourth streets, and the ferry at the foot of Market Street, or at the head possibly, are worlds of art. They are the last word on station building. Market Street has four electric lines, and it is the leading thoroughfare of the city. Practically all the other streets of the city run into it at some angle. Sixteen blocks from the ferry is the civic center. Here are located the city auditorium, which seats ten or twelve thousand people, the courthouse, one of the finest buildings in the state next to the capitol itself, the city library, and one of the high schools. These are circled about a square which has a large fountain of flowing water. A very large area of the city was burned when the earthquake was some years ago, but this has been rebuilt so well and completely that one would never know it. I went over most of this area.

I visited the University of California, which is located in Berkley, and had only time to go through the library and agricultural building. They have a campus of 264 acres and an enrollment of ten thousand students. They have a theater that seats ten thousand people. They have a tower 302 feet high built of white granite. In this tower is located the clock and chimes. They have in mind a large project for an athletic field and stadium. This will be located back of the college in the hills, which is the property of the college. Oakland is the San Francisco terminal of three transcontinental railroads. They are the Southern Pacific, the Western Pacific, and the Santa Fe. We take the Western Pacific for Sacramento at 9 o'clock in the morning. At 2 o'clock in the afternoon we have made the trip of more than a hundred miles through the San Joaquin Valley and again into Sacramento Valley. We spend a part of two days here. The state capitol is a very fine building. The ground adjoining the building forms the finest park in the world. They have searched all the world to find trees and rare plants for this wonderful park. They have them from every known country and from every accessible community. Many of these trees were in full bloom the 28th of February when I was there. An officer of the grounds told me to find the keeper and he would give me all the cuttings I wanted, but unfortunately I could not find him. The city is located in rather a flat country. It has not been a great many years, geologically, since this was all under water and a part of San Francisco Bay. The two large rivers intersecting this valley have done their work in transporting silt, sand and debris from the mountains so well that most of the community is inhabited. The periodical overflow of these rivers still gives the traveler an idea that it is a part of the bay. I saw nearly a hundred miles of it under water, when I wondered how the farmers got from the house to the barn. We leave Sacramento at midnight on the Western Pacific Railroad for Salt Lake City, Utah. We pass Marysville, which we have already seen on our southern journey, Oroville a little further north, and we follow the Feather River and the Feather River Canyon. At daylight we find ourselves climbing the mountains again in snow several feet deep. The canyons are narrow and deep. The mountains above are beautiful, rugged. Vegetation and all sorts of timber come into sight again. The mountain streams are beautiful and clear. We arrived at Reno Junction about 10 o'clock in the morning. At Paxton we pass the little narrow gauge road leading into Indian Valley. The canyons look too narrow for another railroad, but just below us clinging to the rocks and the mountains the little road leads off into another mining section and through gorges that look impassable. Of the more than two hundred stations along the way a great many of them are scarcely stopping places. A few are only places for the train crew to examine the cars. At Reno Junction, Nevada, we come into a country that is more open, and where the population is larger. We cross Honey Valley, Winnemucca Valley, scale the Virginia Range, and come into Smoke Creek Desert, pass to the right of Granite Peak, and we come into Black Rock Desert. We pass what is called the Alkali Flats. This is a vast area of country with no vegetable growth of any sort. Nothing can grow on it. This reminds one of a very large bowl. We are moving along with great speed through the valley with the side of the bowl towering up at a tremendous height. We cross the Antelope Range in the Northern part of Granite Spring Valley. A few miles further we come into the little town of Winnemucca. This is a railroad center and a cattle country.

We are in Humbolt County and follow Humbolt River. We have passed Winnemucca Peak, Black Butte, the Eugene mountains, and other points of interest and beauty. It would tire the reader to follow us for the next several hundred miles through this tortious river course, through large and small valleys, through mountain gorges, up the side of mountain ranges, over some of the highest peaks, under the tunnels and through great banks of snow. At Sulphur we passed several men and their horses with a big mountain lion they had just killed. The government pays twenty-five dollars for each lion killed. They are destructive to sheep. The Denver Sunday papers had the incident written up in the papers Sunday following the killing. We cross the Desert Range at Wendover, Utah, and strike out for forty-eight miles through the Great Salt Lake Desert, leaving Grass Mountain Summit to our left, we enter another range of mountains to emerge near the south end of Salt Lake. I do not know the area of the Great Salt Lake Desert, but it is a very large area numbering perhaps several thousand square miles of country. Water and irrigation would do it no good. It looks like desolation carried to the tenth degree. It must have been at some time a part of the Salt Lake. It supports absolutely no vegetation of any sort. It is a barren waste. There is no other place in the world exactly like Salt Lake and Salt Lake City. The city is eighteen miles from the Lake. One cannot drown in the water of this lake because of the density of the water. The city is one of the best laid out in the world. The mentioning of Salt Lake City suggests to you at once the Mormon Church. This church was organized in 1830 in the state of New York. The Mormons located later in Kirkland, Ohio, and there erected a temple which is said to be standing today. The church was persecuted, and Joseph Smith was martyred. It was moved from place to place, and finally Brigham Young, its President, had a Mission. He saw a land in the far west, and was directed to go to this remote country, far away from persecutions, where the colony might worship in their own way. They started out for this far country, and were many months making the trip. The party was composed of 143 men, three women and two children, and three colored servants. The names of all are on the fine monument at the head of the principal street of the city. When they had reached the place the President said, "This is the place I saw in the vision." The men were advised to go to work at once on small farms. The first year they grew a good crop by irrigation, but about the time the crops matured the crickets came and almost ate the crops. The sea gulls from the lake eighteen miles away came and ate up the crickets. This saved the pioneers. They have in the sacred square a monument to the sea gulls. It is known as the Temple Square. The temple is the most unique building in the world. It was forty years in construction, and it cost a million dollars. It is built of nature gray granite which was hauled by teams for more than twenty miles away. The Tabernacle standing in the same square is also a unique construction. It will seat ten thousand people and has in it one of the best organs made. The building is a "long, oval shape, dome top. The hearing qualities are perfect. One may drop a pin in a hat or on the floor, and two hundred feet away, at the other end of the auditorium, hear it fall." No nails are used in its construction. Pillows support the arches, while wooden pegs tied with raw hide support the individual pieces. The gray stone Assembly Hall, where relics and art collections are kept, is also in the same square. One should visit the state capitol. It is located on one of the nearby mountains. This mountain is at the head of several streets and had an electric line running around it and to the top. The building itself is one of the finest in the country. It has large granite supports measuring three or four feet in diameter, twenty or more feet in length, of Georgia marble, polished to a finish, each weighing twenty-five thousand pounds. These great pillows were brought from Georgia on forty-six cars. One could spend weeks in this fine building studying the art of it and the great display of relics of the early pioneer life. Several Mormon sisters have charge of the collections, and they are very interesting as well as very entertaining.

We leave Salt Lake City, and forty miles east we come to Provo. We are more than four thousand feet in elevation. It is called the Garden City. It is near the Wasatch Mountains. We pass through the Provo Canyons. This is unlike anything else we have seen. We climb the mountains overlooking a most beautiful valley off to the left with a very fine stream said to contain trout. There are fine homes and orchards and many flocks of sheep and cattle. There is some mining a few miles across the valley on the opposite mountain side. A railroad stretches across the valley to connect with this mine from the main line. A few apple orchards. Some fine red barns. The meadows evidently afford a great deal of hay. Hundreds of stacks of hay, as green as if just cut, dotted the valley. We are in several feet of snow and being drawn by several massive steam engines. Up, up, up we go till we reach Soldiers' Summit, seven thousand and four hundred feet high. Your heart begins to beat a little faster, some one has the headache, another has bleeding of the nose. If you have slept all the way through the valleys and up the mountains you will begin to wake up when you reach this high elevation. Unless your heart is seriously affected you do not need to worry, for you are in this elevation only a few minutes when you begin to drop to normal altitude for these parts. The snow is about six feet deep and sparkling. The air is fine and pure, and your mouth grows dry for some of the crystal liquid you have just passed. It comes from crags and crevices for more than a half mile above you, scarcely missing the sides of your train as it passes its narrow channel. A crowd of a dozen or more school girls get on the train. They are all the world like our own girls, only they were white, every one of them. They sang songs made speeches, moved from place to place on the train, recited their lessons, talked kindly of their teachers and their fellows, of the loved ones they have left behind for a few months these were just school girls, that was all. The tourists, including my lonely self, were glad to have this merry bunch--this innovation to break the monotony. They leave us at Green River, and we settle down again to our usual response when we are soon disturbed by the news butcher saying, "The mountain ahead is one-half mile high, the canyon ten feet wide, just wide enough for the train to pass." "It is Castle Gate." The walls of the red stone stand up like the walls of a sixty-story sky-scraper. On both sides these walls tower up till your neck tires looking up at them. Here the engineers have defied nature. You follow the river and the canyon, sometimes on this side, sometimes on that side, rising and falling in elevation till you reach Mack, near the state line of Colorado at an elevation of four thousand and five feet. You pass through a valley widening out from a ten-foot gorge to forty or fifty miles, and absolutely fenced all around by these massive walls for fifty or more miles as effectively as if done by the master hand of some giant. We follow Hog Back Canyon and a tributary of the Colorado River. We arrive at Glenwood Hot Springs at 10:30 at night, four hundred miles from Salt Lake City in an elevation of five thousand and seven hundred feet. We stop here for the night and take the 6 a.m. train the next morning for Denver. We are on the Denver and Rio Grande Railroad. We pass up the Colorado River Canyon. The road is tortious, the stream abounds like the waters of "Galore," the mountain crags are high and precipitous, every foot has tested the skill of the engineer. It is wonderful. We go through Tennessee Pass, sight Mount Jackson toward the west. Mount Elbert to the left more than fourteen thousand feet high is seen. We leave Readville to the left and pass through the richest mining region in the world. Georgetown, Red Cliff, Fair Play, Platt Ranch, Buena Vista, Cripple Creek, Anaconda Goldfield. All these are centers of mining interests. They abound in gold, silver, lead, copper, zinc, etc. We come south from Glenwood Springs to Salida nearly a hundred miles and into the Arkansan River Valley and follow this river to Florence and Pueblo. It will be remembered that in the summer of 1921 there was a cloudburst in that section of the country, and Pueblo was in the midst of the washout. Hundreds of lives and millions of dollars worth of property were lost. The valley still shows great evidence of that destruction everywhere you look. This was particularly true of the city itself. I stood under the pier of their fine station, and the high water mark was two feet above my head. We are seven hundred miles from Salt Lake City and still seventy-five miles from Denver. We are at Colorado Springs. Denver is our destination for the night. As we leave Cannon City and Florence we sight to our north perhaps a hundred miles Pike's Peak. This is early in the afternoon, and we do not lose sight of that majestic wonder of the world until we have passed Denver for almost another hundred miles.

We spend four days in Denver very pleasantly and profitably. It is the "Mile High City." We have left all the mountains behind. The community, including Colorado Hot Springs and Denver and Pike's Peak need no description from me. They are too well known. It is the healthiest place in all the world. I saw no graveyards, and I presume they are few and very far between. The elevation is more than five thousand feet.

We are now seven hundred and fifty miles east of Salt Lake City. Denver is a fine place in which to live. I am not so sure about the conditions of earning a living. We leave Denver at 10 in the morning and stop for the night at Phillipsburg in Kansas. The country is practically all prairie land suited for cattle, horses and sheep, corn, wheat, and the grasses. It is an open country with few trees excepting the low sections and river bottoms. We pass Lincoln City in Nebraska and later the city of Omaha. We have already crossed the La Platte River and now at Omaha we cross the Missouri River. Passing Council Bull in Iowa we speed along to Des Moines, Iowa, where we plan to spend the next night. We arrived late in the evening and left early the next morning for Chicago. The country was largely given to farming and stock-raising. We were in Chicago about two weeks, and were then off for Washington City, where we spent another week, then we came home, arriving here at Bricks the 22nd of March. A most cordial reception awaited me here. I was met at the station by teachers, students and friends of the community, all led by the school band.

Not many colored people on the Pacific Coast as compared with our eastern country. They are scattered here and there throughout the middle west. Most of those I saw looked as if they had good jobs and were busy. I saw a great many very nice homes of our colored people. I visited a great many places of business entirely colored. The colored ministers were all educated men. The colored churches were up to date. I spoke in a number of them, and the audience looked well groomed and happy. I quizzed the professional men, and they advised me that the outlook for the colored people generally was good. All advised that colored men going west ought to have some money to start a business. If colored men would go west and enter farming their opportunities would be unlimited. They ought to have money enough to carry them till their crops come to maturity. If they grow fruit it takes the young trees five years to come into bearing, and they must have something to depend upon during that time. At the same time there is no time of the year in California when a farmer cannot grow vegetables. There are fruit growers' associations that take care of everything the farmer grows. He can become a member of any of them irrespective of his color. He must have some money and some farming sense. There are forty-five thousand colored people in Los Angeles. Only a few are farming. There are not enough farmers to attract any attention. I am always sorry to see so many of our folks flock to the cities when the farms are offering so many opportunities for independence and a better living. There is nothing needed in the west so much as water and people--*water and people*. If they get the people the irrigation projects will soon give the water. They need not only people who are not dependent upon others for every move they make, but people who are industrious and who have the brain.

We hear in the East a great deal about the Japanese. I hear more about them here than I heard on the coast. Out there they have the reputation of being industrious, smart and great organizers. I do not think those are bad qualities. They are qualities that we have been taught to prize. There is no reason why we should prize them in one race and despise them in another. They are universally courteous. Some Northern people think they will get all the land. I saw millions and millions of acres of land in California alone that somebody needs to get and put to use. Then I saw other millions stretched four thousand miles and more across the American Continent that will feed all the world when brought under cultivation and development. They tell us out West that all the mountains in that country are full of minerals. If that is true we have not touched the world's supply. From the unoccupied land I saw there must be enough to feed a hundred times our present population. In some of these states one can travel almost a hundred miles and not see a sign of human life except the little station settlements. New York, Cleveland, Detroit, Chicago, and a few other cities are too congested for healthy environment, and some propaganda ought to be started by some organization or somebody to popularize the country and the farms. The spirit of competition in our large cities in any occupation is virulent. It is not worth the struggle. Manhood and womanhood is stagnant. It is truly the survival of the fittest. I never saw a Negro farmer in the South begging bread. Vast areas of our best farming land ought to be bought by this congested crowd filling our large cities. Our people go to the city because of the lack of compatibility of people in the community where they want to live. They may not like the other race out West, but there was great silence and a unanimity of opinion relative to an open expression of their hatred. Poor education of the laws, open expressions of hatred, fear of personal molestation. These were the expressions I met in Cleveland, Detroit and Chicago. Norman Angell expresses it in his book, "The Fruits of Victory," when he gives the cause of the world's restlessness and war. He says they have resulted from our wrong thinking. We have got to be big enough to forget some things and start off right. Correct our thinking. I attended a Christian Science Church in St. Paul, Minnesota, and one of the tenets of their church is that if you have a pain just forget about it and it goes. It seems to work, for that church is doing a great business all over the country. That is what we have got to do in the political world and in the world where our relations interlock. We do not get anywhere by hatred and fighting.

Every city and every town I visited from Spokane to Seattle to San Barnardino, seventeen hundred miles south is on a boom and every one you meet is a boomer. That is the way to build up a community or a city or a town, or anything else. I was not supposed to give any addresses while on this trip, unless there was some fine opportunity to make friends for the American Missionary Association and for Brick School. I could not afford to let such opportunities pass even though I was out seeking recreation and rest and change. This opportunity came to me at least twenty-eight times. I was invited to speak twice in Dr. H. H. Proctor's Church in Brooklyn, N. Y. Dr. Proctor was a classmate of the writer at Fisk University. He had one of the largest churches in all the South, the First Congregational Church in Atlanta. Then the migration of colored people began to be a problem in the Northern centers, Dr. Proctor was called to Brooklyn to meet the impending on rush. He has projected one of the largest church enterprise in Greater New York, and his bringing the enterprise to a successful fruition will mean great things for New York and for the colored people generally. Dr. Proctor is a large man, mentally and physically, and he has a large vision. His vision is not larger than the times are demanding. Our church people are demanding a larger programme. Some of our churches, perhaps all of them, have been too reticent and conservative, holding on to the dead past and lost prestige with the masses. Dr. Proctor is planning a progressive and constructive programme. I could not lose the opportunity which his kind invitation gave me to tell our Northern friends what our Southern brethren are doing along many lines. I also had the invitation to address a large Baptist Church in Brooklyn where more than a third of its membership of more than three hundred members were from Gloucester County in Virginia. A former Brick School boy was the shepherd of this flock.

Out on Long Island we had the pleasure of addressing a small Congregational Church under the leadership of Rev. G. W. Hinton. We found here a goodly number of our North Carolina friends, and they were glad to hear from their friends here in North Carolina. Later the Fisk University singers from Nashville, Tenn., met with the Greater New York Fisk Club at the Y. W. C. A. in a Harlem Cafeteria, and a fine programme was given. I was invited to speak at the Baptist Ministers' meeting in New York in one of the largest Churches in the city. If the size of the church, the furnishings, etc., and the appearance of the men meant anything it certainly looked at if our friends in New York City were very prosperous. The young lady who directs all the work of the Y. W. C. A. on 137th Street is a Brick School girl who later graduated from Pratt, and we have every evidence that she is making good in that great city.

At Springfield in Massachusetts we had the pleasure of speaking three times for Rev. William N. DeBerry. Dr. DeBerry is a product of Fisk University and Oberlin Theological School. He has the finest work of any of our men. His church organization is unique; he is progressive and constructive, at the same time scholarly and conservative. He is the most aristocratic Negro preacher we have today. His spirit is contagious and he has the finest cooperation of his members from the oldest to the youngest.

At Rochester we had the invitation to address a very fine gathering of friends who had met at a reception to the teacher of their Sunday-school Class and to the minister of their church. At Buffalo we also gave an address at another Baptist Church. In all of these places we met scores of people from North Carolina. In Cleveland, Ohio, I had the invitation to speak several times at the Mount Zion Congregational Church. Rev. Harold Kingsley is the present pastor. Rev. Kingsley is a product of Talladega College, Ala. His wife was a former teacher here at Bricks. We had a most cordial reception at his church and at his home. It was in this church where I read my first essay nearly forty years ago. Its pastor at that time was Rev. Dr. S. N. Brown, who is now Dean of Theology at Howard University. The church has had a great history. The former pastor was Rev. George V. Clark, of Charlotte, N. C. Dr. Clark was a Liberty County (Georgia) boy and a product of Atlanta University. The church is now in the most congested Negro section of Cleveland and has before it a great destiny and future. The present minister is a young man of great enthusiasm and well prepared to meet its growth. The city of Cleveland has a congested Negro population. I saw a statement in the Cleveland papers from the head of the Cleveland "Community Chest" that of all racial groups in the city the colored people had more than done their part with the least expenditure of effort. I visited several of the larger churches Baptist and Methodist churches. All the Cleveland churches seem to be in the most progressive state. Their church buildings are among the very best in the country. Their membership and attendance are very large. In Detroit we attended Rev. Dr. Bradby's church, which is said to have a membership of four thousand people. I also spoke at one of the services. They had four services going at the same time. About a third of these people held up their hands indicating that they were from North Carolina. The day was very cold, but their spirits were very warm. Dr. Bradby is a Canadian, but understands thoroughly the Negro temperament, and gives them exactly what is best fitted to that temperament. He speaks with authority. At night I attended one of our churches ministered to by Rev. Brooks. The church has some institutional feature and is doing excellent service for the community. Mrs. E. E. Scott, of Montgomery, Ala., is assistant in these civic service features. In Kalamazoo, Mich., we attended a revival meeting in the Methodist Church. The temperature outside did not disturb the emotional elements the least when the several ministers put on the "arousements.' I had to wonder whether I was in northern Michigan or in North Carolina. I spoke in a Baptist Church in Chicago where they are said to have a membership of ten thousand people. Several services were going on at the same time. I also addressed a congregational audience in Chicago presided over by Rev. Dr. C. W. Burton. Dr. Burton is a product of Talladega College, and Yale Theological School. He is a fine type of minister and is doing great good.

In Butte, Montana, I was told there are about five hundred colored people and three colored churches. These churches had no regular ministers at the time of my visit. The colored men work as porters and miners. They have mixed schools. They have several social clubs and secret orders, such as the Masons and Odd Fellows.

In almost all of the cities I visited mixed schools are the rule, and many of them have a percentage of colored teachers. In Cleveland especially I was told that the colored teachers are liked very much by their students and parents of the opposite races. In many places it would be most difficult to tell who are colored and who are white. Most of the teachers I met are very efficient and alive to their job.

In Tacoma I spoke to the Sunday-school in the morning and in the evening I spoke at the evening services of the First Congregational Church, Rev. Dr. Edgar C. Wheeler, minister. Prof. Oliver E. Richardson, of the University of Washington, followed me with an address on the "Study of International Relations." The subject of my address might have been "Inter-Racial Relations." At the close of this address I visited the colored Methodist Church, and also spoke there. The church was well filled, and the services were full of interest. The minister was a well trained man, and had the best order and system in the church.

In Portland I attended a meeting of a select group of ladies and gentlemen of the Theosophical Society. I did not speak, but went primarily to hear an old friend speak on the subject of "Racial Unity." His lectures covered a number of cities on the coast, and his subjects, "The Unity of Religions," "Seven Valleys," "Inter-racial Amity," "Harmony Between Religion and Science," "The Mashrak; Ulkar or Universal Science," "What is a Bahai?" "Four Stages in Man's Growth." All of these different lectures are summed up in the one thought, "The Fundamental Unity of

Races and Religion." The object of the lectures are the promotion of universal brotherhood, international cooperation, universal education, the abandonment of prejudices. The lecturer was a colored man, a product of Fisk University, and of the law school of Howard University. He has traveled through Europe, Egypt, and Palestine. His thought and language is clear and convincing. Our friend Dr. Gregory proved himself a master with these subjects.

The subjects above are very suggestive. There is nothing else to be said when the speaker has finished his address. What does it mean? In New York, Buffalo, Cleveland, Detroit, Chicago, St. Paul, and all our large centers there are the finest temples and edifices built to the new cult, new thought, new religion. Many of our traditional churches in these large centers have a hard fight to get a hearing. I attended one of these new thought Churches in St. Paul where the interest was at white heat with an attendance of more than seven hundred people. The temperature outside was fourteen degrees below zero. This was at night. All these cults are based in one way or another on the Bible, but we seem to have adapted for our own spiritual edification and practice that which fits our own mind and temperament. We then argue that everybody else is dead wrong. Some of the finest minds I know are lined up with these new cults. Surely they must have some basis for their mental attitude.

I was asked by the Secretary, Rev. Dr. George Hinman, of the American Missionary Association office in San Francisco, to fill an appointment for him in Berkley, Cal., February 26th. This was at the North Congregational Church at Berkley. This church was right under the shadow of the University of California, and I counted it a great honor to be asked to speak there. The minister of the church was Rev. Mr. Ralph Baxter Larkin. He was sick the day of my visit, and I was introduced by Rev. Dr. Sargent. The printed programme announcing the service for the day with my address had this on the first page, "A Church of Reverent Worship, open mind, intellectual freedom, social conscience, spiritual aspiration and human sympathy. It seeks to discover and interpret the meaning of life in the life of the eternal." This expression gave me great poise for what I had to day. I was at once at ease.

It is fine to speak to people who have a sympathetic spirit especially when you have a feeling that you have an unpopular subject. My racial identity was not clear in the mind of the gentleman who introduced me. He said something like this: "Professor Steiner, of the University of California said somewhere that if he had to be born again he would like to be born a colored man, so that he might be able to study the colored problem from the inside. We have with us today a gentleman who understands the colored problem, and who did not have to be born colored either." These may not be the exact words, but it is the thought. The first thing that I had to do was to dispel the mind of my audience of the fact or statement just made, that I did not have to be born a colored man, and that I wanted them to know that the traditions of our country and the laws in many, if not all the states, had said that any man is colored who has one iota of Negro blood in his veins. I am glad to have the honor to address you as a colored man." Those who know me best tell me that I do not have many stopping places. So I forewarned my friends in the front of me that sometimes my address was three in one and sometimes one in three. Three in one when I have only one hour in which to speak and one in three when I have three hours in which to speak. Speaking to a congregational Church, and a white church, too, one has to observe the traditions very closely. These traditions limit us to about thirty minutes, and unless one is very interesting he had better stop in twenty-five minutes. So my address had to be three in thirty.

The audience was scarcely dismissed when a large crowd gathered at the corner of the church to ask more about certain topics which I had only the time to touch. They were seeking to discover and to interpret the meaning of life. I was invited to go home with many friends, but I could not go with all, so a compromise was effected, and several families joined, and I was the guest for the afternoon of these families. One of these families had been missionaries in China. Others had worked among the Japanese. There we were exchanging our experiences each for the edification of the other. We were all happy that our lot had been cast in these divergent directions.

I cannot continue this without becoming monotonous. I was most happily received in a great many other churches, colored as well as white. My message was generally, "The Amistad," "The American Missionary Association," "General O. O. Howard and Reconstruction," "The Schools of the American Missionary Association," "The Progress of the Colored People," "Inter-Racial Relations," etc. One can see a wide latitude in these subjects. At the theaters we saw several colored stars. In Buffalo Charles Gilpin in "Emperor Jones." Gilpin is an artist of the first magnitude, but I did not like his selection. I am not a critic of such matters, but it did seem to me that his piece was coarse. It was very popular. One could hardly find seating room in the large house where the play was given. In New York "Shuffle 'Long" was exciting great interest. There must have been twenty or more taking part in the play, and every character was an artist. I never saw anything finer. These people played in New York in one house for nearly a year, and while the entrance fees were high the house was packed every night. In Chicago Bert Williams was the whole attraction. I saw him at the Studebaker in "The Loop" just before his breakdown. I was told that after his death the company broke up. They could not find another "Bert Williams." In his death the race has lost one the greatest stars in the theatrical world, irrespective of color. It is an awful tragedy of our times that racial prejudice is blind to art when the artist happens to be colored. It is no fault of the artist that he was born colored. The theatrical field has been rather restricted so far as our colored artists are concerned, but wherever they have had the opportunity they have not been found wanting. "Broadway Rastus and Sambo" are in a class by themselves. The play is clean and fine, every whit of it. It will cure the blues. The singers are the best of the American stage. The vaudeville is equal to any I have seen in the best white theaters. Every place visited we met very prominent colored men and women who were formerly from North Carolina. We are compiling some interesting data on them which we hope to give to the public later.

In Cleveland we met our old friend Lawyer J. P. Green. He has been a lawyer there for forty years. He has written a splendid book of his life. He has been Recorder of Deeds in Washington, and for several terms member of the Ohio Legislature.

Mr. Charles Smith, whose parents were North Carolina people, has served on the Cleveland police force twenty-five years, and is now retired. His parents lived at Chapel Hill this state, and migrated to Oberlin where he, with several other brothers and sisters, were educated.

Mrs. Mary Talbert, of Buffalo, is President of the Negro Women's League, which is a national organization of women. She was educated in Oberlin. Her parents migrated there before the Civil War from this state. It would take a chapter to tell what great things she has done for the colored women and what she is now doing. She is a traveler, lecturer and scholar. She has recently raised the money to have the Fred Douglass Home in Washington City as a Memorial to the greatest Negro who ever lived. It will be dedicated the 12th of August, 1922. Her husband, Mr. William Talbert, is a city official in the treasurer's office, of Buffalo, New York.

Mrs. Clara Hardy, of St. Paul, Minnesota, a sister of Mrs. Talbert, is also a graduate of Oberlin College. She has held many places of honor in her adopted city. She is now a Court Bailiff. She is a writer and speaker of no mean ability. Her home was a perfect model.

In California it was my pleasure to stop with Dr. R. R. Robinson. He is a Halifax County man. He was a student here for a number of years working his way with his hands. He laid out our walks, planted many of our older trees and helped to "Start Bricks." He took an agricultural course at the A. and T. College in this state and went to Tuskegee, where he taught several years. He married a North Carolina girl from Bethel, who was a trained nurse. Later he went to Nashville, Tennessee, and took a course in medicine. After graduating he practiced medicine in Brunswick, Ga., through the flu, and was very successful. After the world war he went to Tulsa, Oklahoma, and was there when the riot broke out. He saved his life by hiding in the woods three days, he and his wife. He lost all his office fixtures and medical instruments, and every remnant of personal apparel. He is now a very successful physician in Los Angeles, California.

I have given only an outline of some impressions of my trip to California with the hope that it may inspire some reader to know, to go, and to acquire a larger vision of the world and of life.

APPENDIX 17

FARM LIFE

For many years the farmer has been the laughing stock of the country. The conduct of his farm and his business methods have brought him more gibes and thrusts than are brought to any other professional class. The late Booker T. Washington described the characteristics of his class many years ago. The poor old mule or horse and often the ox, hitched to a single plow, scratching the earth with as much effectiveness as an old Plymouth Rock rooster would scratch for newly planted oats. The farmer follows behind this slow plodding plow in tatters and rags, illy fed, too often diseased with hook worm or some other infectious malady. His road sides and ditch banks for ten or twenty feet back are filled with weeds and shrubby growth to sap the vitality from the glowing crops in their proximity. He has stagnant pools all over his patch in wet weather to further deplete the growth of his crops that may be left from the weeds by the roadside and ditch banks. His home, the home of the old farmer, is the last thing to which any attention need be given. He has followed his methods for "Fifty years or more." He has cotton right up to the door, potatoes, peanuts or corn filling the yard. No place is left for flowers or ornamentation of any sort. The old log house, just a place in which to sleep and in which to hide when it storms outside. It has only two rooms for a large family. The old man is in tatters, the wife is in tatters and the children are in tatters. I have seen many, the least of the little ones, as naked as they came into the world. The implements of such a farmer never saw shelter or protection from the weather from the time they were bought from the store until they had been disintegrated by rust and rot and had gone back into the original mother earth to rest forevermore. The farmer himself had a personality that was uninviting and dirty. He thought the good Lord had created him for just the sort of life he was eking out, and he eschewed all progress. Good roads and decent schools were things he never needed and he would not consent for such improvements if they cost him anything. The old mongrel hen was good enough because she could roost in the trees and lay at the same time. The pinewood rooters were all right because they could make their living by eating pine roots and other people's crops. A half dozen dogs were useful to feed. The old cow was still kept in the family because of the ancestral history and not because of her utility. Slipshod methods in business have been the handicap of more farmers than all the evils attending them. We very often receive congratulatory letters from business men on our farmers' programme and at the same time these business men lament the fact that our farmers' business methods are so poorly managed. Not long ago we received notice that two of the wealthiest farmers, Negro farmers, in Georgia had died. They were reputed to be worth more than a hundred thousand dollars in cash besides the great land holdings and other property they owned. Later when their estates were settled up their business was in such a tangled condition, all interwoven with that of their neighbors', that there was nothing left for the wife and children. I hope that we do not have in North Carolina such tangles as the above. Whatever else the farmer does he ought to keep his business straight. We have found out through our Federal Farm Loan Organization that many farmers have bought and paid for farms and have paid taxes on these farms for twenty years but it would take a "Philadelphia Lawyer" to find out whether the legal owner was the farmer, the banker, or the land company, or the merchant. That is bad business. Any man who mortgages his farm after he has paid for it seriously jeopardizes his future as far as his farm is concerned. If you have debts that must be met you had better sell a portion of your farm outright and keep the other clean and clear. The mortgage business is a bad business for the average farmer to take into his partnership. The merchants, the business men, the state government and national government, are all emphasizing every movement tending to the exit of this mortgage system. The farmer, first of all, should give it a hard kick.

It is a matter of education first. These farmers' meetings give us an opportunity to inform ourselves. Our schools and our colleges are helping us to get informed. The local conferences have no other purpose than to help you to be informed on farm and business matters relative to your farm. Bulletins sent out by the State and National governments are among the greatest educational agencies. They are all practically free. The farmer *who does not and will not* take advantage of such agencies of information is certainly destined to be at the foot of the ladder; and there is where he belongs. The farmer who is given all the agencies and Says he will not pull himself up ought to go down the sooner he goes with that spirit the better, so that some other man can take his place and make good. I still see some of these old timers carrying water across the field a half mile away, still taking care of the family wash down by the river side, still holding on to the old ash pile. These relics have been heirlooms in the family and we are reluctant to let them go. It takes some spirit, some purpose and a great will to tear away from these old traditions. It must be done if we are going to advance. We must learn the lessons of experience. They have been sad lessons to many farmers. These farmers' conferences are bringing to you lessons of scientific farming. Let the traditions go to the wind and take hold of the new problems in your farming and farming business that will bring success, happiness and a life. Today as never before the farmer is coming into his own. Watch the agricultural papers and magazines. Visit our county and state fairs. See the interest and note the comparisons in our community fairs. Progress is in the air. If there are those who do not believe it, they will believe it, and feel the impress of the upward move, or they must get out of the business. Any farmer, white or colored, who does not line up with the best farming methods of the community is bound to lose out on his farm. The lessons may be hard, but as a class of farmers you must get these lessons. The first lesson that must come to every farmer is that he must line up or unite with other farmers in the prosecution of his work. Every industry is organized except that of farming. The farmer produces his crops, and, unorganized, sells them to any bidder who comes along and takes his price or nothing. Organization will help the farmer to get the best price for his products. No man works very long by himself at anything. You cannot make it alone. Cooperation in the word. You get cooperation by organization. Every industry that is worth the name is organized. Organization helps you to buy as well as it helps you to sell. It will get you the lowest prices for what you have to buy, and the highest prices for what you have to sell. Single handed you pay what is charged and sell it for what you can get, much or little. The government is fostering the Federal Farm Loan Organization in order to put the farmer on his feet. Are you using that organization? The state is encouraging farm unions. They can be formed in every community where you can find ten men, ten real men. Are you using this organization? Some communities are using them very effectively. Our own Federal Farm Loan Organization, the Tri-County Federal Farm Loan Organization, of Bricks, N. C., has put into Negro farms and farm improvements about seventy-five thousand dollars and has applications for nearly as much more. Do we have your application? Let us illustrate what we want to impress relative to cooperation and organization. A few years ago two renters came to the Brick School farm. Each had one horse. The wives had a lot of small children and could not be expected to do very much on the farm. One day I saw a team of two horses plowing. The two men had united their horses and were plowing their ground with a double team. One was plowing and the other man was clearing up the ditch banks. They worked tandem all summer and seemed to get fine results. They were happy in their work and each was company for the other. A few years ago we needed here on the Brick School farm a peanut thresher. No one could get the thresher alone, so an organization was perfected and a peanut thresher was bought for two hundred dollars. This thresher did fine work for many years, and brought the stockholders a nice little revenue as long as it was in service. I cannot see why a few men in every Community cannot unite their efforts and get everything they need on their farms. Every time I go to Rocky Mount I see scores and scores of wagons on the road hauling tobacco to market. These wagons go in groups for company and mutual help. I have counted as many as twenty in one group, and I am sure the different groups represent a certain community. These communities of small farmers ought to unite and buy jointly a truck. Some of these grouped teams travel, to my personal knowledge, thirty miles with their tobacco. This trip takes two days and one night to land the sale. The teams and the men alike are unfit for work for several days thereafter. Count the cost of man, wagon and animals. The automobile will do the same work in a few hours and be ready instantly for other work. If the farmer drives his wagon half of his time on the road is lost driving this way and that getting out of the road for trucks and automobiles you cannot put your products on the market as fast as your neighbor you cannot compete with him. That is all. If you cannot do it single handed unite your forces. That is the commonest of common sense. Farmers cannot hire ditching done any more. Ditching with pick and shovel is a past art. You cannot pay the price, and you cannot find the ditcher. Ditching is now a profession. The last time we had our work done by hand the gentleman came in a large Buick, worked a few hours for a few days and the job was done. The element of drudgery is too great. We are living in an age of steam and gas and power. Why strain the muscles when you can turn the throttle with the weight of one finger and the work is done. You can buy a machine ditcher, drawn by horse power, for as little as forty dollars. If done with hired help it does not take but a few yards to cost forty dollars. Two mules and a machine ditcher will make more ditches in a day them ten men can make in a week. Here the drudgery is eliminated. Any boy can drive the team. Why not join your forces and buy a ditcher or buy it by yourself? A dozen peanut growers will pay more to thresh their peanuts in one year than a whole peanut outfit will cost. At the same time it is yours and you can thresh your peanuts when you please to do it. You will have the outfit for many years, depending upon the care you give it. We are paying now around ten dollars a cord for cutting wood. The best woodcutters cannot cut more than two cords of wood in the woods a day. Do you know that you can buy a wood saw that will fell the tree and cut up the wood, and that one man can cut as much as fifteen cords in one day? Muscular strength and drudgery are again eliminated. Why not a few of you unite your forces and buy a machine, and in a few days lay in all the wood you need for the winter and summer use? Do you like to trudge along the old way because it is traditional? I do not know of anything more annoying than to have to run to the woods or wood pile morning, noon and night, to cut wood for the preparation of the meal. To me it would be enough to spoil the temper of a saint.

Here is a fine proposition suggested to me by a former Brickite. I am not sure that it is original with him, but it is a fine proposition and I am passing it along: The average farmer who is working on his own farm or farming on his own account must grow not less than four or five hundred bushels of peanuts yearly or more. Some, to my knowledge, grow eight hundred and a thousand bushels. It usually costs twenty-five cents a sack to thresh this amount. One sack holds about four bushels. It will cost twenty-five dollars to thresh one hundred sacks or four hundred bushels. Form a company of sufficient numbers and let them pay for their stock exactly what they would pay to an outsider for threshing their peanuts. If properly handled it would pay for itself in one year and after that it ought to clear a dividend. There is one outstanding difficulty in this as in nearly everything in which we engage in cooperate manner. That one man who will take the leadership. Where is he? He must be unselfish, honest and levelheaded. I am speaking especially with reference to farmers who have limited means and not much help. Cooperation and organization ought to mean more than a little partnership. To organize and cooperate for community uplift and progress takes a lot of intelligence and honesty. I would not impugn your citizenship and standing in the community to say that you lacked either as farmers. It is a fact that most of us as farmers are hard to understand some of the simplest business relations. When the business demands that we shall pay our bills by a bank check and require a receipt, and that all these operations should be booked, and when an auditor is called in to balance our accounts and check up our mistakes we are too quick to think that our honesty is questioned. There is no other way to do business when others are involved in that business. *The honest man wants to be checked up*. It gives him a standing that nothing else will. Treasurers and secretaries of any organization whether churches, Sunday Schools, secret orders, debating societies, or what not, have no business keeping other people's money in their personal possession. The banks are the national depositories for all such organizations and other people's money ought to be kept there.

It should not only be put in the bank, but it ought to be put there to the credit of the institution to which it belongs. This may not be good farming, but it is good business. I know of at least one man who went to the penitentiary for using other peoples money for only a few days and could not replace it. Organizations and companies should demand canceled checks and receipts for all expenses every so often in a joint meeting. If officers count this an infringement upon their personal integrity dismiss them and get officers who do not so regard it. It is the only way to do business. We do not organize more and do not succeed better because we lack faith in each other. This is perfectly natural. The Negroes have been schooled in credulousness for a great many years. The encumbrance of so long an inheritance cannot be so easily thrown off. Expect the best that is in your neighbor and your neighbor will prove up to your highest expectation. You not only make your neighbor better by your good thoughts of him, but you add to your own spiritual and mental growth incalculably. You grow yourself. Farmers must buy modern machinery for their farm. It is the best investment you can make. Corn planters, cotton planters, gang plows, and machinery of every sort that will save you worry and steps should be bought. You cannot afford to farm without these implements. If you do you must be left behind in the occupation of farming. You can not make it. I think a farmer who can buy an automobile ought to be able to buy a tractor engine. With a tractor engine you can plow, harrow, and plant your ground while your neighbor is breaking his ground, and you have beaten him a hundred miles in the manner in which you have prepared the soil. At the close of the day you are not too tired to go with your family to the moving picture show or to some community entertainment where you may get an inspirational uplift for the next day's work. Look at your neighbors. That is what they do and keep ahead of you. I think the farmer who is making good ought to buy a Ford car. I saw a big farmer the other day who lived out about eight miles from Rocky Mount. He was driving a horse and buggy. I asked him how much money he had cleared the year before on his farm and he said that he had cleared over and above all expenses about three thousand dollars. It took him a good half day to drive to Rocky Mount for his plow point. He might have saved the trip or run over there in twenty minutes and made his purchase and had the rest of the day for work on his farm if he had owned a Ford car. I am not arguing that one should purchase modern machinery with which to facilitate his work in order to give him more time to be idle. It will give him more time to do the things that machinery cannot do. The good farmer never has idle time. Time spent at a farmers' conference is not idle time. The matter of getting the latest and best information on farming methods is the most important thing that a farmer can do. One cannot put into practice on his farm or anywhere else what he does not know. Improved machinery means more intelligence on the farm. Farming is the most complicated and diversified occupation there is in the world. It takes a horticulturist to grow apples to perfection. It takes a dairyman of the best type to put milk and butter on the market to meet state and county inspection and public approval. It takes a mechanic of the highest quality to keep up repair on the farm of fences, houses, and machinery. It takes a bookkeeper to keep farm accounts and records. He must be something of a Wall Street broker to keep up with market prices so that he will know how and where to sell his farm products. He must be an electrician and an engineer as well if he is going to compete with his neighbor who lights his house with a Delco light and runs all of his machinery with power. When you come to live stock you have a world without end of necessary information for your success. Cattle, cows, sheep, hogs, horses, poultry, bees, and scores of special strains of each, every one of them requiring special treatment and expert knowledge. If the farmer has the inclination and the will he can become specialist in any one of these lines. There are men who do nothing but breed the special brands of high bred stock. There are those who breed bees and who supply the world's demands of purebred queen bees. The higher you go in this specialization the more you become the world's greatest benefactor.

I have been studying about the value of limes upon the soils. To be a first-class farmer you must be a chemist of the first magnitude. You as farmers, have no idea of the part that chemicals must play in the production of your crops. The fertilizer that will bring to perfection one crop will kill another. You must know the fertilizer and know the nature of the soil on which this fertilizer is to be used and you must know how well a certain grade of fertilizer is adapted to the seed you want to produce. Every first-class farm is a chemical laboratory and the farmer is a chemist. Every first-class farmer must be something of a physicist as well. Every first-class farmer must be something of a doctor as well for all animals are subject to bodily disorders that must be corrected by medical advice. He must also be a weather prophet. You cut your hay and let the storm come on it and see where your profits go. You must be able to read the signs in the heavens and the published directions. Your job is a big one requiring as you go up the most complicated knowledge about every thing under the sun. I have said nothing about plant diseases and insect life affecting the success of the farmer nor that world or destruction hid in the unseen bacteria. As farmers you may be sluggards moving along on the lowest possible level of life or you may be a prince living in a palace. There are a lot of us on the lower levels who ought to move up to the higher gradations. You can get more out of your farm life but you must *know how*. If you expect to work simply as a hireling you will not need this information to any great extent. You only have to do as you are told to do as a hireling. You may never as a hireling be asked to use even your own initiative in an emergency. If you expect to manage a farm you must have initiative and some executive ability. Twenty acres or more constitute a farm. If you have that much land you are a farmer and you must move on your own initiative. The days of ignorant farming are passing. The government cannot and does not encourage ignorant farming. The times are demanding better schools and better roads. These two improvements are here and the farmers must pay the bills. Your farm must make you a living and enough more to meet, these public expenses. If your intelligence will not make the ends meet, then before a great while the taxes will eat you up and your land will go into the ownership of men who have the intelligence to make the land meet the bills for pubic improvements. As farmers you must subscribe to every public improvement that comes into your community. You must buy stocks, bonds and meet public taxes. These improvements all increase the value of your farm. Selfishness and personal ends must not hold back community progress in any line. You are a part of the community and when you hold back its progress you defeat yourself. Not to know is no longer an excuse. *You must know*. You cannot stay at home and pride yourself that you never go to a farmers meeting and expect to know. Wherever people are gathered together to discuss public problems there you may go to learn. There is where you get in the spirit of things. There is where you get knowledge. There is where you get the inspiration. The spirit of rivalry and competition will go a long way to help us in our farm operations. There is a farmer in Nash County who thinks he can beat every one else in the county growing watermelons. There is a score of farmers in his community quietly trying to beat him. The result is that there are better watermelons grown in that community than in any other community in the county.

FARMERS' CONGRESS, AUGUST 16, 17, 1921

It is worth very much to any man who is interested in agricultural operations to take a leisurely trip four hundred miles through North Carolina in an automobile. A party of us left Bricks July 11th and joined Rev. P. R. DeBerry in Raleigh. Taking his big Studebaker car, we were off the 12th for a two days trip among the colored farmers of the central and western part of the state. We were not touring, nor sightseeing, nor joy riding. Our one purpose was to study the land, the people and the conditions under which our colored farmers were living. We wanted to see what conditions were compatible and what were not compatible. The trip took us through about eighteen counties. We started our study in Edgecombe County. This is the county in which Brick School is located. This county should be the first in all of its operations because of its educational advantages and the inspiration it ought to receive from this institution. There are in the county now about 25,000 Negroes. These Negroes own 4,000 farms and homes, numbering about 17,000 acres of land. Some individuals own as much as 500 acres. We are sorry to say that most of this land is not under the most improved condition. We have not been able to have in this county a full time farm demonstration agent. The Brick School and our farm meetings have given very much impulse to farm operations, but even this has not reached all the farmers in ways to stimulate them to their greatest efforts. We lack time, money and authority that ought to come directly from the state. It has been demonstrated in other counties that nothing is so valuable in stimulating the farmers as a real, live, wide-a-wake farm demonstration agent who lives and works among the farmers every day. A farm not half developed and not improved is not an asset to the state nor to the owner. It ought to come into the highest state of production, then only does it become wealth. The school population of this county is about 7,000 children with an enrollment of about 5,000 children, whose average attendance is about 3,000 under the compulsory law. The county has a colored school supervisor who gives the work all of her time. Mrs. Carrie Battle has revolutionized the school work under her charge. She is insistent and tireless. Every one knows her and respects her. Her office is in the courthouse at Tarboro. The white county officials hold her in the highest esteem. The teachers and schoolhouses rank among the best in the state for colored people.

I do not know anything that affects public improvements and progress more than good roads. The farmers are generally slow to vote for good roads, but no class of people appreciate them more than the farmer when they are built. The area of the county is 515 square miles and yet I have traveled over every part of the county and over some of the best roads in the state. The local papers tell us that a cement road leading across the county is now in process of construction. This road will eventually lead into Raleigh, some fifty miles away.

   Halifax County has an area of 681 square miles, with a colored population of nearly 30,000 souls. They own 70,000 acres of land. Their school population is around 10,000, with an enrollment of about 7,000, and an average attendance of about 3,000 children. This county has a colored school supervisor who has done a very fine work among the colored people. The colored people meet every condition set by the state and county for the erection of colored schoolhouses. A few months ago they had raised their part for twelve Rosenwald schoolhouses, and had to wait on the county and state to recoupe their part. They will meet any condition set for them. The colored population is not congested in any one part of the county. They are located in every direction of the county and about evenly distributed. Their homes, for the most part, are clean, and their houses are well constructed and show signs of thrift and happiness. Very few colored farmers have migrated from this section of the state. Those who have gone from Halifax county can hardly be missed. This in itself shows that the racial equilibrium is not much disturbed. Nash County, which joins us on the west, is one of our best farming communities. The fifteen thousand Negroes in the county own more than 25,000 acres of land and more than 2,000 farms. They are a progressive lot of colored people. They have a number of independent schools aside from the public schools. They have excellent churches, and their homes are being built on modern lines. This county has twelve miles of cement road running from Rocky Mount to Nashville, the county seat. The contour of the county is rolling and red clay. The important towns are Nashville, Spring Hope, Middlesex, and let us say a part of Rocky Mount. There is a great deal of the land in this county uncultivated and developed. It waits only for the man who has the brain and the energy. The county has no county farm demonstration agent nor colored school supervisor. I do not know what can be more advantageous to the success of the colored farmer than the addition of a colored farm demonstration agent and a colored school supervisor. While the preachers are ministering to the spiritual needs of our folks and the teachers are directing their intellectual life, and the state and county health offices are looking after the health of the masses, the farm demonstration agents and the colored school supervisors are daily giving inspiration and purpose to rural life everywhere. The state and county are the direct beneficiaries of the work of these two agents. Having five children go to school every day from one family where formerly only three went means very much for the literacy of the state. Teaching boys how to grow forty bushels of corn on the same acreage where their fathers could grow only ten is adding very much to the wealth of the state. The community which does not appreciate and recognize this truth is impervious to eternal values. Every farmers' conference tells how much increase there has been in corn, peas, cotton, peanuts, oats, rye, tobacco, and other things under the direction of our farm demonstration agents.

   We past through Franklin County into Wake. Every one knows that Raleigh is in Wake County. As soon as you arrive in Wakefield or Zebulon, both small country hamlets, you know that you must be about fifteen miles from the capital city. Hard-surfaced roads present such a temptation to touch the accelerator just a little, and little, and again a little more, and again, if you do not happen to see any motorcycles lurking about. The colored population of this county is less than 30,000, and they own less than 6,000 farms. They own about 60,000 acres of land. Their school population is about 10,000, with an enrollment of about 7,000, and an average daily attendance of about 4,000 children. We ought to expect the school average to be higher, of course, being adjacent to the seat of state authority. Wake County has had for a number of years two colored agents, in the person of Miss Delany for the schools, and Professor Roberts for the farmers. They have gone in and out of the farm homes daily carrying inspiration and encouragement and inspiring hope. The daily contact with these personalities has been the leavening power in the county. We have seen for a number of years the finest products that could be produced on exhibition in our colored State Fair. In the city market in Raleigh every day in the year one will see these same fine farm products. They will do justice to any racial group. Here one will see what the agents are doing to help the farmers to conserve and preserve their products. The homes of the farmers show neatness and cleanliness. We have been greatly surprised to see how far some of our farmers have gone in beautifying their homes and premises. *This is as it should be.* The excellent public schools of Raleigh, the fine institutions represented by St. Augustine School and Shaw University have given the colored rural population a great inspiration. The well ordered homes of some of their city cousins have also been an inspiration to the colored rural population. There are so many opportunities, educational and inspirational, about the state capitol, that it is almost like living under the shadows of a great university. Then the main thoroughfares are so fine that those living in the most remote parts of the county ought to have no difficulty or count it no hardship to go to the city for lectures, recitals, conventions, conferences, and for general consultation with those under state authority. These opportunities are the best sort of unearned increment.

We pass from Wake County to Chatham County. There are no less than 8,000 colored people in Chatham County. They own about 2,000 farms and homes, and about 30,000 acres of land. The two small towns, Moncure and Haywood, have quite a settlement of colored people. At Haywood they seem rather isolated and some of the homes had a progressive appearance. The disadvantages under which we started, the social, industrial, business and educational status, in which we find ourselves should not be allowed to differentiate from other people who live in the same community and in the same environment. If other racial groups living in the same community have their homes painted, flowers in their gardens and other ornaments that add to home life and beauty, it is perfectly right that we should catch the inspiration. If we cannot be leaders in these matters, we ought to be good followers. We have the labor, and a gallon of paint and a paint brush will work wonders in a few hours. If we cannot keep the yard fence looking decent and in repair let us move it. We must take personal pride in the community in which we live. It is the best sort of civic pride. In this community we ought to prove our best selves. Chatham County has disgraced itself recently with a lynching bee.

Crossing the river into Lee County we were very much impressed with the sign, "You are welcome to Lee County." This large sign was in a most conspicuous place and we interpreted it to mean what it said, and that we were included in the invitation. We stopped to ponder and to contrast the difference. We have been in parts of our country where the overhead signs read, "Niggers and dogs not wanted." We have seen in other parts where land was advertised for sale and the biggest asset in the advertisement was the absence of Negroes from the community. There are less than 4,000 colored people in Lee County. They own about 700 farms and about 8,000 acres of land. The area of the county is very small, and the entire population less than 15,000.

I have been for several years on a local inter-racial committee. Since the world war it has been necessary to have such a committee in the South on inter-racial relations. I am also on the state inter-racial committee. That means that I am always looking out for the small things and the larger things, too, as we make our daily rounds, that count for good will and peace between the two racial groups. At Sanford we saw a large number of colored men at work as carpenters and bricklayers on some of the finest buildings going up in the city. I was shown others and advised that they were the work of colored carpenters, under colored contractors. A former Brick School boy was foreman on one of the jobs. These contractors and workmen were personal friends of mine, and later I had the pleasure of seeing some of their own homes and business. They were among the best in the community. Broadway, Cumnock, and Jonesboro are progressive communities in which the colored people are doing well. I was advised that only a few of the colored people had migrated from this part of the state. It means that they are happy and that they can buy homes in communities that are compatible. After all, we must have compatibility in our homes and in our neighborhood, in our community in our relations with the outside world. I would not live a week in a community that was not compatible. To receive a gibe and a thrust every time one steps on the street, or into a corner grocery, or on the public highway, by other racial groups is contemptible~ and especially so when one knows that there is absolutely no redress for that sort of contempt. One wonders what the preachers are preaching or what the schools are teaching. Patriotism, love of community, social and personal progress are of slow growth in such communities where there is so much incompatibility.

All the world has heard of Moore County. It is an area of 798 square miles. The main line of the Seaboard railroad crossed it from north to south. It is crossed and recrossed by Page's railroad. Here is Southern Pines, Pinehurst, Jackson Springs, Carthage, and scores of other smaller towns. The names are common to the resorter and tourist. It has a population of less than 6,000 Negroes, who own about 16,000 acres of land. Excluding the villages and towns, twenty,five years ago I would not have paid the taxes for all the rest of the land. Twenty-five years ago I went all over the county, and one could scarcely get anywhere for the sand and roads were practically unknown. Sand, sand, sand--everywhere sand. Moore County is now the veritable garden spot of the state. The local intersecting railroads have changed hands. Fine public highways have been built in every direction. The tourist and capitalist, making their annual visits to this section, have discovered in that vast land undiscovered possibilities of wealth. Thousands and thousands of acres of this waste have been converted into peach orchards. Peach packing stations have been built all along the track for the convenience of the peach shippers. I was told that several trains of peaches were shipped daily to the Northern market. Where the land was not already planted I saw the Fordson tractors getting it ready for fall planting. Most of this undeveloped land was what is called cut-over land. It is absolutely barren except for a lot of shrubby pines shrubby oaks and some native tough grasses and wild composite flowers. Tupelle and poplar may be found in the swamps and lowlands. I wondered as I passed along to get a bit of information here and there, if our colored people were learning to do by doing. I wondered if they were getting the inspiration. Sixteen thousand acres of land ought to be the nucleus of an industry. A hundred acres ought to make a good peach farm. What an opportunity for the colored man who has brain and industry and some little money and a great ambition. We have not the faintest idea of the wonderful opportunities in the millions of acres of the waste lands of our southern country. These lands are just begging the capitalist to come and invest in the undeveloped resources of its bosom. It is there, but it just needs the brain and some little money. The brawn is there, too; it just needs the intelligent direction. Compatible conditions will keep it there. The land in Moore County will never again sell for one dollar an acre while peaches are selling for three dollars a bushel at the tree. Most of the trees bear from two to five bushels of peaches. They are planted about fifteen feet apart. It takes about 150 trees to the acre. Any one can figure the income at that rate. These peaches ought to begin bearing in three years. There is nothing so fabulous as the income per acre from such an investment. There is nothing so sure. Some of the rows as we viewed them seemed endless. Greensboro, sixty miles away, was sending trucks to the peach area daily for loads of peaches for the local market, in Greensboro. A little while back one of these peach orchards sold for $85,000.

The business of supervision has become so important that many of the growers combine and employ an expert from the State Department of Agriculture. They can pay more than the state can pay for such expert supervision. The work is as yet in its infancy. We are advising our Negro boys to go to our best agricultural schools and specialize in this department of fruit cultivation so that they can manage such enterprises as these large fruit farms. They do not seem to get the vision. As long as our folks are buying farms, and they are increasing their holdings every year, there are vast opportunities for their services as horticulturists. Ten Negro farmers in Moore County, North Carolina, ought to be able to get together and make peach-growing worth while to the group. Their traditions and the local environment have taken away their inspiration. They also lack knowledge. They have not been schooled in initiative of this sort. Cooperation with most of us has been a doubtful experiment. We must learn and grow more before we can take hold of the larger industries that require large cooperation. Experience and knowledge are vital to the success of any enterprise. The great enterprises of the North have been growing cooperatively since the country was discovered. The South has been giving its time to matters of social adjustments. The adjustment of its racial groups has been its nightmare by day as well as by night. Hatreds, jealousies, prejudices, have entered too much into our daily contact and relations to allow us to grow nationally. The conditions of all progress are in education, industry, compatibility. I read somewhere that the conscious mind may not get a true perspective and may error. Still it is conscious. When I read in the papers every day and note all the deviltries perpetrated here and there all over the South, I wonder that we have all gotten along as well as we have, and especially do I wonder how the Negro has made such progress. Then I hear that the subconscious mind never errors. The conscious mind would have me riled and leaving the country, boot and baggage, when I read what is happening somewhere else outside of North Carolina. The subconscious mind comes in and says to me, when I am quiet and alone and perhaps when I am half asleep, "No, do not get discouraged." The South is the garden spot of the world. It has the prettiest moons, the brightest days, its florescence on a thousand hills and in as many vales scatters its fragrance and beauty three hundred and sixty-five days in the year. Its cataracts, rills, and springs sparkle with diamonds of beauty and health. The woods and swamps are filled with every sort of game, her rivers and lakes abound with every known fish for the sportsmen, her climate is the most equitable in the world, the rainfall the most evenly distributed, the storms not so awfully destructive, the exotic population the least of that of any other similar area, with an adapted vegetation from the highest altitudes to the equator. The contour of the surface is high or low as one likes it. Smooth or rough. The Blue Ridge Mountains afford a retreat from the Northern winters as well as a retreat from the Southern sun. Her altitude, pine forest and splendid waters are an asset that no other country in the world can equal. In the next few years more than fifty millions of dollars will be spent in North Carolina alone for public roads. Steam roads and electric cars will soon intersect every nook and corner of the state. The most inaccessible parts of the state and the South will become the public highways. Automobiles and trucks will bring the most remote farms to the city markets daily. The telephone and radio are already available in our country homes. In the next two years North Carolina will spend four millions of dollars for Negro health and education. This has already been passed by state legislature. This amount of money put into health and education in any community will make a change. It shows an enlightenment of public sentiment and a change of attitude on the part of the citizens of the state. Progress cannot and will not be thwarted. Education, enlightenment, Christianity--this trio is the saving grace of any community. I do not know of any place better than North Carolina. *This is my subconscious mind.* It never errors. We leave Moore County and cross into Montgomery County. This is what we call a hickory country. The land is rocky and red with hills almost precipitous. We could not visit many of the colored people because of the inaccessibility of most of the rural homes. The colored population is about 4,000, and they pay taxes on about 8,000 acres of land. They are engaged in general agriculture, corn, tobacco and cotton being their prevailing crops. They have a few cotton factories in the town of Troy and more in the county, and many lumber mills. The Pedee River and its tributaries furnish a large part of the power for the factory work. The county has a real gold mine which was profitably worked a few years ago. It was my pleasure to visit it some years ago when it was in operation. It has been abandoned, and the machinery and buildings show signs of a past prosperity. The town of Troy has one of the two wooden courthouses left in the state. It was being replaced by a modern stone structure. It will cost when finished about $200,000. I am told that the stone in the construction of this building was taken from the site on which the building stands. It rather reminds one of our Northern centers in that it stands at the juncture of a number of the public roads leading into the town. The Peabody School, under the auspices of the American Missionary Association of New York, is the only institution in all of that part of the country giving anything like a high school education to the colored people in all of that section of the country. The school is beautiful for its location just out of the city. It fronts a public road and is on high ground with splendid drainage. Several of their buildings are new and up-to date for school purposes. A hard-surfaced road is in construction from Charlotte to Raleigh. The distance is nearly two hundred miles. It will probably pass through nine counties. It will open up a country of immense possibilities. A cement bridge connecting up this road is already in construction across the Yadkin River. This bridge will be nearly or quite 2,000 feet long. It would ornament the approach to any Northern city.

From Troy we went to Biscoe, Star and Ashboro in Randolph County. This is also an oak and hickory county. The roads took us through a very fine section of the country. The country looks very undeveloped. The roads were very fine. The rural homes appeared rather small. Many of the women along the roads were seen bottoming chairs. Chair-making seemed to be one of the main industries in that section. The frames of the chairs were made at the factories and sent out to the country women to have the bottoms put in them. These bottoms were made of white oak splits. The absence of colored people engaged in this business seemed very noticeable. The town of Ashboro had all the appearances of being a hustling town. More than a half dozen buildings were going up. We saw no colored carpenters or bricklayers on the job anywhere. We were advised that no colored men were allowed to work at their trade in the town. We saw several colored mechanics with their kit of tools packed, leaving the town. Some of them we knew to be the equal of any mechanics in any other group of workers. Still their mechanical efficiency counted nothing. It was their unfortunate tradition, and their black faces which counted them out. Here my conscious mind came up again. We did not have the feeling that we had when we left Lee County. A man ought to be passed on his merits and not on his color. They wanted mechanics but not black mechanics. These men would do well to migrate. Wherever they went I know they were in the frame of mind to swear vengeance against any community that would tolerate that sort of condition. That is what makes socialists, bolsheviks, and Catholics out of us. We soon find ourselves in Guilford County. We arrive in High Point and remain long enough to see friends and inquire about the conditions of our farmers.

I think it true that there are more manufacturers of furniture in this county than in any other county in the state. The Brick School has bought furniture in New York only to await shipment from High Point. Later we have gone to High Point and seen this furniture in the making. These two cities are in the oak and hickory sections of the state. I have seen its street cars in Philadelphia, New York, Baltimore, Washington, Asheville, Atlanta, Ga., Birmingham, Ala. Of course a business of this size will give work of one sort or another to a great many of our colored laborers. There are 15,000 of our people in Guilford

County. They own 3,000 homes and farms. They are paying taxes on 17,000 acres of land. The Negroes in Guilford County have the inspiration of one of the best state colleges for Negroes to be found in the South. The college ought to be the center of all the best influence for farming in a hundred miles about it. If they are found to be using poor farming methods they ought to be fined. Alamance, Orange and Durham counties are rather small counties, but they have some of the best farms and form some of the best farming and industrial communities to be found in the state. Durham is really the emporium for Negro enterprise and thrift. Tobacco, cotton and corn, and some wheat are the leading farm products in this section of the state. Gibsonville, Burlington, Graham and Hillsboro are thriving towns. They are centers of cotton and furniture manufacturing interests.

This study took us through about fifteen counties. We were not investigating the town and city conditions, but the farming interests. In counties where they had rural supervisors there was a marked difference in the attitude and progress of the farmers. Their outward appearance was different from what we saw several years ago. The farmers were better clad; their work animals were in better condition; their teams were not all dilapidated; many of them are using improved machinery; their barns and houses were more orderly built and better maintained; the houses in which they live are a decided improvement over the old houses we usually see along the railroad. They are giving more care to their wells and pumps. They are learning to screen their windows. The ancestral waste barrel in many cases are being removed from their kitchen windows. They are using more paint not only to save their houses, but because it adds beauty to their premises. They are planting flowers. They are putting out fruit trees and investing in thoroughbred chickens, hogs and cows. These are all good signs. They are really coming. Some have had to come from so far down the road that it may appear that they have not made any progress. They are coming nevertheless. At no place where we stopped did we have to confine our diet to sweet potatoes and boiled eggs in order to preserve our health by the osmos process. We saw in many places attempts made to improve the soil. We found alfalfa, red clover and crimson clover in the red clay sections. Peas were grown generally. The farm demonstration agents and the farmers' conferences have been an inspiration to the farmers to grow legumes to help the land to bring forth its fruit. They are learning that they can not use up the fertility of the soil and still have it. They are learning that an investment in legumes is one of the best they can make for crop productions. The papers have been saying that one man in four in the American army is uneducated. If that is true it is a sad comment on the conditions of this country. There is no power in the world to equal that of education. We cannot exaggerate its power and its importance. A trained mind, a trained hand and a trained heart are indomitable. An unlettered man lives in isolation. He cannot appreciate the creation of nature. There is no progress in isolation and a static mind atrophies. Whatever be the proportion of illiteracy, those of us who move about among the masses know that notwithstanding our private schools and public schools, ignorance and superstition are simply appalling. It is not only appalling, but it is dangerous to any environment. It is a menace to the state and government.

Brick School IN PERSPECTIVE

Work began at the Brick School in 1895 under the auspices of the American Missionary Association. The "Estes Farm," named after the owner, General Estes of the Civil War, came into the possession of Mrs. Julia E. Brewster Brick, of Brooklyn, New York, who found it a burden on her hands. Mrs. Brick had visited the community, and her heart had been made sad by the sights which greeted her on every side. The sad faces and depressed spirits in a large environment of Negro congestion appealed to her heart. She was responsive to this appeal. It was the voice of God which she did not mistake. Her life and thoughts and heart had been attuned to this appeal, and so she sought how best she might help the situation. The advice of General Oliver O. Howard was sought. He introduced Secretary A. F. Beard and Mr. H. W. Hubbard, at the time Treasurer of the American Missionary Association. The result of this counsel was that a large farm of 1,129 1/2 acres of land in North Carolina three miles from the town of Enfield was given to the American Missionary Association for Negro education. With the gift came also from the same source $5,000 for the first building. There followed other gifts from Mrs. Brick and from the American Missionary Association, so that the farm was soon stocked with hogs, horses, mules, cows and farm implements. Houses of various sorts, including school buildings, dormitories, teachers' cottages, tenant houses and barns have been put up, valued at several hundred thousand dollars. This beautiful munificence has been our saving grace during the last twenty-seven years of stress and strain in the financial world. We began work with the modest number of five teachers. We now have about twenty teachers and a few less than 400 students. The students come from a dozen states and from nearly all the counties in North Carolina. The larger number of them comes from a radius of fifty miles.

The purpose of the institution is to teach the students to do the things the best way in the community where they may live. Being rurally situated, the first and greatest appeal must be made along the line of an agricultural education. The knowledge of how to extract from the soil the largest and best products which the community may need for its consumption is an asset in which any group of people may well take pride. Most town and city boys coming to us have an aversion to this form of education, and especially to the strenuousness necessary to an efficient application of the most vital principles of agriculture. Horses have to be shod, and farmers have to have houses in which to live and under which to shelter their stock. So we have to teach the boys to work in iron and wood. Along with this goes some drawing and planning. Tools and wagons must be kept in repair. Boys going back to their communities ought to be later the real leaders in the community. In many instances they are the leaders. While the boys are investing their time in the farm crafts and the shop crafts the girls are learning to do needlework and house cleaning, washing and sewing. They learn the home life by getting some of the conventionalities of it here in the classroom under teachers who get from Pratt and Columbia and other good schools the best they have to offer. These teachers are themselves largely the products of our American Missionary Association Schools. They have not been satisfied to "graduate and quit," but they have continued to study. In addition to giving the boys work on the farm and in the shop, and the girls work in the kitchen, laundry, dining-room and sewing-room, and general house cleaning, all are offered a first-class high school course covering six years, preceded by six years of elementary education.

The writer of these notes is himself a product of Oberlin and Fisk University. He knows how to do a great many things, including type-setting, printing, farming, plumbing, some work in wood, poultry-raising and agriculture, stock husbandry. He lectures, preaches sometimes, and writes for newspapers. He counts himself a fair judge of artistic values wherever they are on exhibition. He knows how utterly impossible it is to try to do any one of the above things with any degree of efficiency or even ordinary skill without mental training. The mind is the master, and unless that has training and poise the hand fails. The academic course is to meet this condition. Many of the boys and girls stay to finish it, but the bulk never finish. Many of them do not stay for the full course--not that they do not have the money in money cases--but because education among the masses it not popular. They have had a propaganda for many years that a little learning is a dangerous thing. They have been advised that they belong to a subject group, and that they need only the rudimentary necessaries of life. A fine horse and buggy or a car and nice clothes make an appeal above any sacrifice for study. It is the appeal for the glitter and the glare. This false notion comes to the half grown youth because they got a bad start. They were neglected in the public schools--parents ignorant of the necessity of education on the one hand, and poorly prepared teachers on the other hand, and poorly furnished and constructed schoolhouses. The whole school environment has not been psychological. It has rather been repulsive. Some who return to their homes are making good farmers, as evidenced by their better crops, better fertility of their soil, better kept work animals, better kept machinery, better homes, yards, and community life.

Many of those who finish the high school course attend other schools and later enter the ministry, dentistry, or become physicians, teachers, Y. M. C. A. or Y. W. C. A. workers, or instructors in agriculture either in our schools or as county farm demonstration agents. The best examples are Isaac Bunn, farmer, and owns his own farm of 250 acres bought and paid for in Halifax County; Benjamin Bullock, under the Smith-Lever Fund, in charge of agriculture in the colored state college in Texas; Rev. A. S. Croom, Baptist minister, Salisbury, N. C.; Dr. Joseph Harrison, physician, Kinston, N. C.; Dr. Willie Sessoms, dentist, Rocky Mount, N. C.; Dr. R. R. Robinson, physician, Los Angeles, Cal.; Miss Hattie Green, Miss Lucy Richmond McCoy, Miss Susie Adams, Young Women's Christian Association work, New York; Miss Annie Rhodes, teacher in the city schools of Chicago; Miss Lula Bullock, teacher in city schools, Louisville, Ky.; George Bullock, manual training in city schools of Louisville, Ky.; Joseph Bullock, a captain in the army, and now a student of dentistry. More than a hundred have gone out as graduates, and all are a leavening in the community in which they live. The influence of the Brick School has counted in the community life of the masses more than any other agency in operation. We mean by "Community" the area of a circle of which the school is the center and whose radius ia twenty-five miles. We have three counties virtually inside of this circle whose

Negro population is more than 60,000. The circle cuts into six other counties whose combined population is more than 148,000 Negroes. The nearest institution under private auspices doing anything like high school work is exactly sixty-three miles away. We have a field all our own. The area in this circle is "our community." We have sought all these years to better the community life by reaching the farmers directly. To this end we have annually and semi-annually farmers' meetings. They come and spend one or two days at our expense for entertainment, where they have contact with our teachers and with men and women sent by the State Department of Agriculture at Raleigh, who lecture on the best methods of farm and home life.

We must do more than talk. We must help them. We have here a local Federal Farm Loan Organization, and this organization in the last three years has put into Negro farms more than $130,000. This money is let by the United States government and on conditions that can be met without hardship to the borrower. Titles are investigated, deeds are properly made, and a new spirit is put into the farmers of the community. We are encouraging our colored men to buy small farms of twenty-five and fifty acres and build for themselves modest homes near their public schools as far as they can, and not too far from their local churches. We advise them to patronize these institutions freely and to build up their community life. The vision has been a long ways off, like the rainbow, but they have begun to catch it. In these three counties they are paying taxes on more than 100,000 acres of land. Their homes are very much improved. Their churches are excellent for rural communities. They are contributing largely for the Rosenwald schools. In Halifax County they have twelve, and more are now in construction, the colored people paying one-third of the cost. They have helped us generously to erect several teachers' cottages here at Bricks, and $5,000 is now pledged for further improvements, which will be paid as soon as farming conditions and prices enable them to do so. Righteous public sentiment is of slow growth, and one cannot expect to change traditions quickly whose roots have penetrated every strata of society. It takes sympathy patience, years, work, and some money.

T. S. INBORDEN.
May 17, 18, 1922.

A PICTORIAL REVISIT

Harriet Proctor Smith
Mother of T.S. Inborden
At Her Home In Blue Ridge
Mountains, Virginia

T.S. Inborden's
  Childhood Home
  Upperville, Virginia

T.S. Inborden's
  Sister, Cecelia
  Smith

T.S. Inborden's Sister, Cecelia
Her Two Daughters, Son And Grandchildren
Middleburg, Virginia

Willie Carroll And Family
Upperville, Virginia
T.S. worked for his father when
he was 8 years old

T.S. Inborden's Oberlin Classmates,
Left To Right, Attorney Loeb, T.S. Inborden
And Dr. John Hunter

Wilson Bruce Evans
Free Man Of Color
Sarah Jane Inborden's
Father

Children Of
  Wilson Bruce Evans
  Oberlin, Ohio

Thomas Sewell Inborden

Wilson Bruce Evans' Home, Oberlin, Ohio. He Built It in 1856.

Sarah Jane Evans Inborden

Sarah Jane Evans Inborden

Sarah Jane E. Inborden

Sarah Jane E. Inborden

Sarah Jane E. Inborden

Cornelius B. Evans,
Sarah Jane's Brother

C.B. Evans, Far Right End

Julia Evans Johnson and Children, James Cornelius, Daisy Viola, Sarah Jane, and Susan Sunbeam Johnson. Julia Was The Sister Of Sarah Jane Evans Inborden.

Daniel Murray

Evans − Murray Family
Front Row Middle
Anna Evans Murray

Carmen Murray Bonde
Cousin Of Sarah Jane Inborden And
Great Grandaughter Of Henry Evans

Thomas Sewell Inborden

Sarah Jane E. Inborden

T.S. Inborden, Julia, Dorothy,
Wilson Bruce, and Sarah Jane Inborden

Julia Inborden Gordon
T.S. Inborden's Daughter

Julia E. Inborden Gordon and
Her Mother, Sarah Jane Inborden

A Musical Arrangement By
Julia I. Gordon

A Prayer for a Little Home

This arrangement of poem with the Minuet by Mozart, was made especially with concern for those 4 H Club girls and boys whose parents or guardians own no home or land.

Arr. by JULIA GORDON

God send us a lit-tle home
To come back to when we roam.
Low walls and flu-ted tiles,
Wide win-dows, a view for miles;
Red fire-light and deep chairs;
Small white beds up-stairs;
Great talk in lit-tle nooks;
Dim col-ors, rows of books.

© Copyright MCMLVIII by Julia Gordon
International Copyright Secured
Printed in U.S.A.

Arrangement By
Julia I. Gordon

Arrangement By
Julia I. Gordon

Left To Right, Doris E. Hughes, Shakespeare Kent, Edward Kent, Sylvia Kent, Camille Early Grooms and Francis Gordon Early Kent

T.S. Inborden's
Granddaughter
Julia Gordon Jordan

T.S. Inborden's
Grandchildren

Dr. Doris Early Kent Hughes
D.V.M
T.S. Inborden's Great
Granddaughter

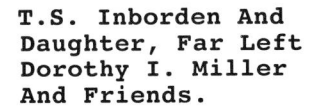

T.S. Inborden And
Daughter, Far Left
Dorothy I. Miller
And Friends.

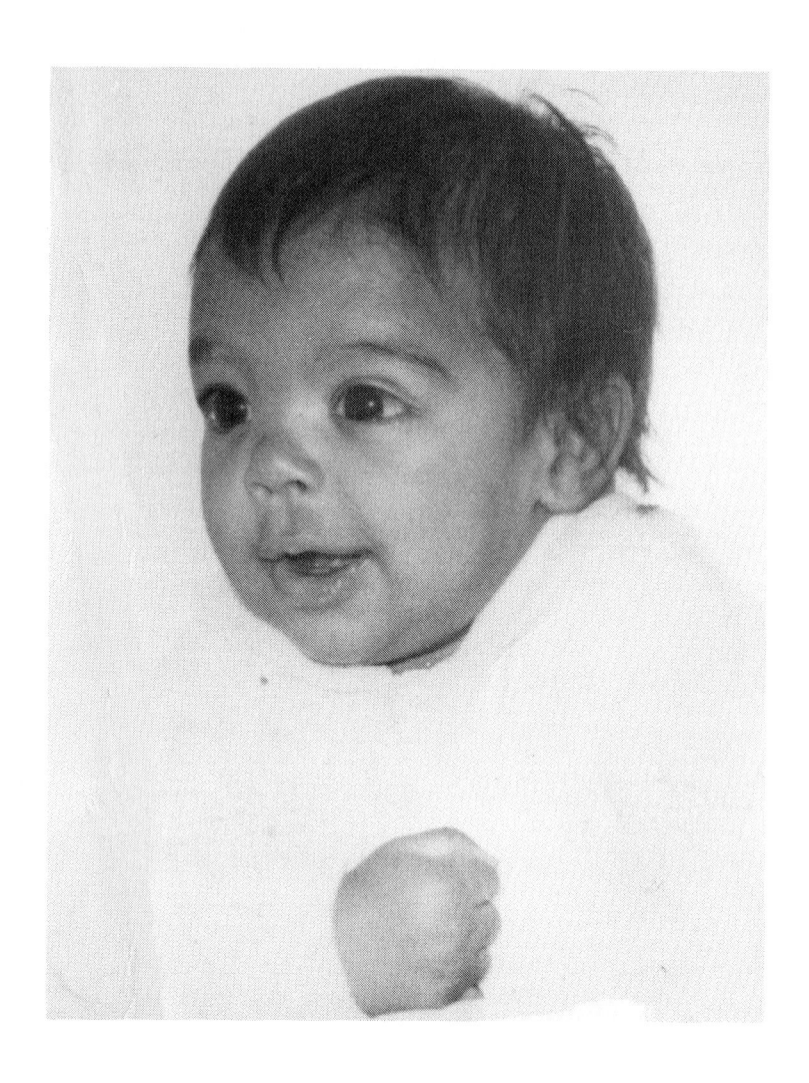

**T.S. Inborden's Great Great Grandchild
Zayne Grooms**

Zayne Grooms

Dorothy Inborden Miller

Dorothy Inborden Miller

T.S. Inborden And Daughter
Dorothy Inborden Miller,
Institute, West Virginia

Dorothy Inborden Miller

Thomas Sewell Inborden

Wilson Bruce Inborden

Wilson Bruce Inborden
Student Army Training
Cadet, 1918

Walker Doyle Miller
Husband Of
Dorothy I. Miller

Nan Inborden
Wife Of
Wilson B. Inborden

Thomas Sewell Inborden

Helena Normal School
Helena, Arkansas
1892

Albany Normal School, Georgia
1894
T.S. Inborden, Back Row Left

Joseph K. Brick
Benefactor Of Brick School

Julia Elma Brewster Brick
"She Made Brick School Possible"

Left To Right, Julia Brewster Brick, Her Niece,
Miss Lydia Benedict, And Dr. A.F. Beard,
Secretary, American Missionary Association

Thomas Sewell Inborden

Benedict Hall
Destroyed By Fire, February 5, 1904
Brick Campus

Benedict Hall (Rebuilt)
Girls Domitory
Brick Campus

Elma Hall
School Administration
Brick School

Brewster Hall
Brick Campus

Beard Hall
Brick Campus

Dining Hall
Brick Campus

Ingraham Chapel
Brick Campus

A Scenic View Of Brick Campus
Looking From An Area Of
Ingraham Chapel

Model School
Brick Campus

Teacher's Cottages
Brick Campus

Teacher's Cottages
Brick Campus

**Inborden House
Original Principal's Home
Brick Normal School**

Brick School Farm Barns

Brick School Farmer's Day Exhibit

Farm Barns Brick School

Store House Brick School

Steam Laundry Brick School, 1916

Thomas Sewell Inborden

T.S. Inborden, Back Row, Center
And Teachers' Brick School.
Sarah Jane Inborden, Second Row Right.

Front Row: Miss Little, Miss Sadgewar, Mrs. Forney
Second Row: Mrs. Inborden, Mrs. Martin, Mrs. Davis, Mrs. Williams, and Mrs. Baker
Third Row: T.S. Inborden, Miss Mary Robinson, and Mr. Martin.

T.S. Inborden And Brick School Faculty

Mrs. Lord, Center and Friends. She Sent The
Pictures To Brick School. The Picture Was
Taken In Batavia, New York, 1896.

Mrs. Lord

Brick School Woodworking Class

**Domestic Science Class
Teacher Emma Baker**

Brick Students
First Row, Left To Right,
Two Girls, Julia And Dorothy Inborden

T.S. Inborden With George W. Moore,
Katie Dowdell, A.H. Brown,
William Sinclair And Others, Brick School.

Students Brick School,
T.S. Inborden, Center Back

1900's North Carolina
Education Meeting
T.S. Inborden, Third Row, Far Right End

Brick School Ladies Played Tennis, 1916

Thomas Sewell Inborden 395

Farm And Garden Industries
Brick School, 1916

YWCA Activities
Brick School, 1922

**Young Women's Christian Association
Activities, Tennis, Brick School, 1922**

Young Women's Christian Association
Activites, Brick School, 1922

Thomas Sewell Inborden

Classes in Agriculture, Brick School, 1916

Brick School Graduating Class, 1924

Brick Boy's Basketball Team, 1926

Brick Girls' Basketball Team, 1926

Thomas Sewell Inborden

T.S. Inborden With Friends
In Northfield, Massachusetts

**T.S. Inborden
First Row Middle And
AMA Missionaries**

T.S. Inborden And Friends

T.S. Inborden

Dr. George Moore
And
T.S. Inborden

Left To Right, T.S. Inborden
Della Jacobs And Sarah Jane Inborden
Bricks, North Carolina

An Early Black Business
Coopers' Electric Shoe Factory

T.S. Inborden, Right With
Grandchildren (Gordons)
And Their Friends

T.S. Inborden
With Chickens

Allen Davis'
Grandchildren
Upperville, Virginia

T.S. Inborden Visiting Relatives
Upperville, Virginia

Left To Right, Jennie Conner (Clarence White's Mother)
Mrs. Curtis And Her Daughter

T.S. Inborden's Young Friends

West Wilkins And Her Sunday School,
St. Chapel Church, North Carolina

Left, Benjamin Hayes, And Right His Uncle

Bullock House
Bricks, North Carolina

St. Chapel's Church
Halifax County, North Carolina

Mr. And Mrs. Wiggins
North Carolina

Second From Left, Benjamin Bullock
And His Friends

Captain Bullock, DDS

Joseph H. Douglass
Concert Violionist And Teacher
Grandson Of Frederick Douglass

John W. Davis
Former President, West Virginia
State College, Institute, West Virginia
(Friend Of T.S. Inborden)

Richard B. Harrison
Actor
Visited Brick School

ORCHESTRA

GLEE CLUB

PHYSICAL CULTURE

HEALTHY SPORTS

**Brick Junior College
Activities**

Brick Junior College
Dining Room

Brick Junior College
Chemistry Laboratory

Brick School Alumni Reunion
August 23, 1951
Brick Campus, North Carolina

Principal, Inborden School
Escorts Dorothy I. Miller To School
Enfield, North Carolina

Dorothy I. Miller Talks With
Principal, Inborden School

**Dorothy Inborden Miller
At Inborden School**

Dorothy Inborden Miller
Admires Painting Of Her Father
By T.S.' Great Granddaughter, Dr. Doris Hughes

Frances Gordon Kent And Her Grandchildren
Visit Inborden School. Her Daughter Camille's Children are
Catherine and Jerry. Her Daughter Doris' Children are
Richard Jr., Melany, Candyce, Wilson and Lewis.

NOTES

CHAPTER 1

[1] T.S. Inborden to Julia Inborden Gordon, Richmond, Virginia, 1930. Personal biographies of T.S. Inborden, Inborden Papers, 1850 Census, Fauquier County, Virginia.

[2] Personal Notes, T.S. Inborden, Inborden Papers and Robert Ewell Greene with the assistance of Dorothy Inborden Miller. *Branches of Harriet Proctor Smith.* Unpublished manuscript, 1980.

[3] Telephone interview with Mrs. Connie Travis, Canada, November 1993. Connie Travis to Robert E. Greene, Fort Washington, Maryland, November 10, 1993.

[4] Telephone interviews with T.S. Inborden's relatives, Middleburg, Virginia, November, 1993.

[5] Ibid.

[6] T.S. Inborden to Julia Inborden Gordon, Richmond, Virginia, 1930, Inborden Papers.

[7] Personal biographies of T.S. Inborden, Inborden Papers.

[8] Ibid.

[9] Robert E. Greene, *Leary Evans Ohio's Free People of Color*, Washington, D.C. 1989 pp 45-46.

[10] Ibid., p.25.

[11] Ibid., pp 28-30.

[12] Ibid., pp 11-22, 23-24, 28-31 and John Sinclair Leary Perry, *The Leary Family The Negro History Bulletin*, (November 1946).

[13] Oberlin High School, Graduating Exercise Program, 1886.

[14] Robert R. Church to Wilson Bruce Evans, Oberlin, Ohio, 1880's, Inborden Papers.

[15] T.S. Inborden to Sarah Jane Evans, Oberlin, Ohio, September 5, 1887, Inborden Papers.

[16] Ibid., October 21, 1887.

[17] Personal Notes, T.S. Inborden, Inborden Papers.

[18] Fisk University, Graduation Exercise Program, 1888, Inborden Papers.

[19] Harriet Proctor Smith to T.S. Inborden, Fisk University, Nashville, Tennessee, June 16, 1888, Inborden Papers.

[20] Class Report, September 5, 1889, T.S. Inborden, Fisk University, Report Card, Inborden Papers.

[21] Augustus Field Beard, *A Crusade of Brotherhood* (Boston: The Pilgrim Press, 1900)

[22] Professor W.G. Waterman, *Fisk University and some of its Graduates*, (Nashville, Tennessee, 1900).

[23] Personal Notes, T.S. Inborden, Inborden Papers.

[24] Personals, *The Fisk Herald, Nashville, Tennessee* (October 1893) V.Xl.

[25] Personal Notes, T.S. Inborden, Inborden Papers.

[26] M. Saunders to T.S. Inborden Bricks, North Carolina, July 24, 1895, Inborden Papers.

[27] T.S. Inborden to Sarah Jane Inborden, Albany, Georgia, October 24, 1894, Inborden Papers.

[28] *Program*, Sixteenth Annual Session, Georgia Congregational Association, Thomasville, Georgia, November 14-18, 1894, Inborden Papers.

[29] L.J. Saunders to T.S. Inborden, Bricks, North Carolina, 1895.

[30] Personal Notes, T.S. Inborden, Inborden Papers.

CHAPTER 2

[1] Personal Notes, History of Brick School, T.S. Inborden, Inborden Papers.

[2] Ibid.

[3] Ibid.

[4] Ibid.

[5] Personal Notes, T.S. Inborden, Inborden Papers.

[6] Ibid.

[7] Reverend George W. Moore, "A Plantation School, North Carolina," *The American Missionary* (October 1899): 106-107.

[8] Family Bible of Sarah Jane Evans Inborden. The births of the Inborden children were recorded in the Bible. Sarah Jane Leary Evans to Sarah Jane Evans Inborden, Bricks, North Carolina, December 21, 1897, Inborden Papers.

CHAPTER 3

[1] Personal Notes, History of Brick School, T.S. Inborden, and School Brochure, 1895, Inborden Papers, and Selected Curriculum Brick Normal School, 1901, Inborden Papers.

[2] Reverend R.R. Johns "What They Ring For:" *American Missionary* (May 1904): 133-136.

[3] Jeannette Norvell Keeble to Sarah Jane Evans Inborden, Albany, Georgia, April 27, 1901, Inborden Papers.

[4] Personal Notes, Early Years, Brick School, T.S. Inborden, Inborden Papers.

[5] Julia A. Johnson to T.S. Inborden, Bricks, North Carolina, March 16, 1903, Inborden Papers.

[6] Editor, "The History of Brick School" *The Joseph K. Brick News VII* (January 1904).

[7] *The Bostian Guardian*, April 23, 1904. This newspaper was published by Monroe Trotter, a Civil Rights journalist who believed in the upward mobility of people of color.

[8] Francis J. Grimke, "Brick School", *American Missionary* (May 1904).

[9] Personal Notes, T.S. Inborden, 1904, Inborden Papers.

[10] Jesse Lawson *How to Solve The Race Problem* (Washington, D.C., Beresford Printer, 1904) 27-28.

[11] T.S. Inborden to Mr. George Eastman, Rochester, New York, June 6, 1904, Inborden papers.

[12] T.S. Inborden to Secretary Beard, New York, December 9, 1904, Inborden Papers.

[13] T.S. Inborden to Julia Lowe, Springfield, Massachusetts, July 24, 1904. Inborden Papers.

[14] T.S. Inborden to Reverend W.E. Mann Indian Chapel, Massachusetts, 1904, Inborden Papers.

[15] Personal Notes, T.S. Inborden, 1904, Inborden Papers.

[16] T.S. Inborden to Annie Upperman, Washington, D.C., October 17, 1904, Inborden Papers.

[17] T.S. Inborden to Lydia Benedict, Brooklyn, New York, November 7, 1904, Inborden Papers.

[18] T.S. Inborden to Dr. H.B. Frissell, Hampton Institute, Virginia, 1904, Inborden Papers.

[19] T.S. Inborden sent letters with information and brochures on Brick Normal School to: Reverend J.A. Jones, Sedalia, North Carolina (N.C.); J.E. Clayton, Brooklyn, N.C.; Cordelia Coldwell, Charlotte, N.C.; Louise Robbins, Quincy, Illinois; Mrs. W.D Blackman, Hinsdale, Illinois; Susan K. Robbins, Enfield, N.C.; Mary Young, Raleigh, N.C.; Ella Saunders, Wilmington, N.C.; Eva V. Coleman, White Plains, Virginia, Ella Whitfield, Washington, D.C.; Mrs. E.A. Johnson, Alexandria, Virginia; Noah Hill, Sparrows Point, Maryland; Reverend G.V. Clark, Charlotte, N.C.; W.J. Hayward, Sherborne, Massachusetts; Ransom Harris, Aurora, N.C.; James Edmonson Scotland Neck, N.C.; F.C. Sadgwar, Wilmington, N.C.; and Allen Nixon, Pikesville, Tennessee. T.S. Inborden sent letters to the School benefactors who gave money, clothing, supplies and books. He acknowledged the generosity of Reverend T.H. Hanks, Springfield, Massachusetts; Herbert S. Rainey,

Springfield, Massachusetts; Alfred Swan, Palmer, Massachusetts; Mrs. M.C. Hastings, Warren, Massachusetts; Reverend William Excell, Livenis Cantre, New York; Eleanor Little, Bryn, Mawr, Pennsylvania; Mrs. G.H. Demlay, Conrad, New Hampshire; Mrs. J.M. Hitchcock, Palmer, Massachusetts; Mrs. C.M. Carpenter, Oxford, Massachusetts, and Mrs. L.P.H. Putney of Atlanta, Georgia. Letters, Brochures, Notes, December 1904, Inborden Papers.

[20] Ibid.

[21] T.S. to Dr. Beard, New York, December 13, 1904, Inborden Papers.

[22] *The Joseph K. Brick News*, May, 1905.

[23] *The Joseph K. Brick News*, February, 1905.

[24] Ibid., May, 1905.

[25] Ibid., June, 1905.

[26] Dr. A.S Harrision to T.S. Inborden, Brick School, April 20, 1905, Inborden Papers.

[27] *The Joseph K. Brick News*, May, 1905.

[28] T.S. Inborden, "Suggestions for the Teacher", *Brick News* 6 (April 1907).

[29] T.S. Inborden to Sarah Jane Inborden, Bricks, N.C., August 15, 1908, Inborden Papers.

[30] T.S. Inborden "The Values and Limitations of Industrial Education, *American Missionary* (December, 1908).

[31] Personal Notes, T.S. Inborden, 1909, Inborden Papers.

[32] Ibid.

[33] T.S. Inborden, "Abraham Lincoln" *American Missionary* (February 1909): 35-38.

[34] Personal Notes, Farmers Day, February 12, 1907, 1911 and 1912, Inborden Papers.

[35] T.S. Inborden "Progress of Negro Farmers in Brick Community" 1911, Unpublished paper, Inborden Papers.

[36] List of Black Teachers, Scotland Neck, N.C., 1912. Inborden Papers.

[37] Personal Notes, T.S. Inborden, 1913. Inborden Papers.

[38] T.S. Inborden "Form Letter", 1913 Inborden Papers.

[39] Catalogue, Brick School, 1914-1915, Bricks, N.C., Inborden Papers.

[40] *The Joseph K. Brick News* XVI, 3,4,7, February, April and November 1915.

[41] Ibid.

[42] Ibid.

[43] Ibid.

[44] Personal Notes, T.S. Inborden, Inborden Papers.

[45] T.S. Inborden to Susan Beam, New York City, New York, July 10, 1915, Inborden Papers.

[46] H.P. Douglass to T.S. Inborden, Brick School, N.C., September 7, 1915, Inborden Papers.

[47] T.S. Inborden to Paul H. Douglass, New York, October, 1915, Inborden Papers.

[48] Personal Notes, T.S. Inborden, November, 1915, Inborden Papers.

[49] Personal Notes, T.S. Inborden, compiled brief sketches of the Inborden extended family and interviews, Inborden Papers.

[50] Dorothy Viola Inborden to Mr. and Mrs. T.S. Inborden, Bricks, N.C., January 2, 1916, Inborden Papers.

[51] Dorothy Inborden to Mrs. and Mrs. T.S. Inborden, Bricks, N.C., March 5, 1916, Inborden Papers.

[52] T.S. Inborden "Results, *American Missionary*, (March 1916) 3: 729-731.

[53] Julia E. Inborden to Mr. and Mrs. Inborden, Bricks, N.C., May 8, 1916, Inborden Papers.

[54] Dorothy Inborden to Mr. and Mrs. T.S. Inborden, Bricks, N.C., May 9, 1916, Inborden Papers.

[55] Lydia Benedict to T.S. Inborden, Bricks, N.C., December 10, 1916, Inborden Papers. Lydia Benedict was the niece of Mrs. Julia B. Brick.

[56] Dorothy Inborden to Mr. and Mrs. T.S. Inborden, Bricks, N.C., March 25, 1917, Inborden Papers.

[57] Ibid., May 6, 1917.

[58] George E. Haynes to T.S. Inborden, Bricks, N.C., May 17, 1917, Inborden Papers.

[59] C.B. Evans, to Sarah Jane Inborden, Bricks, N.C., June 19, 1917, Inborden Papers.

[60] Sarah Jane Inborden to Julia Inborden, Fisk University, Nashville, Tennessee, October 1, 1917, Inborden Papers.

[61] *The Joseph K. Brick News* XIX, October 1918.

[62] Ibid.

[63] Ibid.

[64] Ibid.

[65] T.S. Inborden To Parents and Friends of Brick School, N.C., November 25, 1918, Inborden Papers.

[66] *Memorandum* To Parents and Friends, Brick School, N.C., from T.S. Inborden, 1919, Inborden Papers.

[67]*Memorandum,* Farmers Day Bricks, North Carolina, March 26, 1919, Inborden Papers.

[68]Dorothy Inborden To T.S. Inborden, Bricks, N.C., May 12, 1919, Inborden Papers.

[69]George L. Cady. *Planting Ideals in Soil and Souls,* (New York: American Missionary Association, 1920) pp 3,7,8 and 14-19.

[70]Personal Notes, T.S. Inborden, 1920, Inborden Papers.

[71]Personal Notes, Writings on Brick School, 1920, Inborden Papers.

[72]Julia Ella Inborden Gordon to T.S. Inborden, Bricks, N.C., January 4, 1920, Inborden Papers.

[73]Personal Notes, T.S. Inborden, Telegram, 1920, Inborden Papers.

[74]Ibid.

[75]Ibid.

[76]American Missionary Association to T.S. Inborden, Bricks, N.C., November 13, 1920, Inborden Papers.

[77]Personal Notes, T.S. Inborden Papers.

CHAPTER 4

[1]*American Missionary* (July 1921): 162-163. Observations by T.S. Inborden when he visited Wilmington, N.C.

[2]*Program,* Twenty-Sixth Anniversary YMCA, Brick School, March 21, 1924, Inborden Papers.

[3]T.S. Inborden "Rural Life In North Carolina", *American Missionary,* (January 1922): 462-464

[4]Personal Notes, T.S. Inborden, February, 1922, Inborden Papers.

[5]T.S. Inborden to Sarah Jane Inborden, Bricks, N.C., February 14, 1922, Inborden Papers.

[6]Charlotte Brown Hawkins to T.S. Inborden, Bricks, N.C., April 19, 1922, Inborden Papers.

[7]T.S. Inborden to the Friends of Brick School Community, N.C., 1923, Inborden Papers.

[8]Ibid.

[9]T.S. Inborden to Members, North Carolina Industrial Association, October 27, 1923, Inborden Papers.

[10]T.S. Inborden to Selected Friends, N.C., December 17, 1923, Inborden Papers. There was scheduled a Patron's meeting on December 28, 1923 concerning the state's taking over all elementary schools to include private schools. The

grades below seventh grade would be eliminated. T.S. told his friends please attend the meeting and discuss these matters.

[11]*Program*, Semi-Annual meeting, The North Carolina Negro Farmer's Congress, Clinton, N.C., January 22-23, 1924, Inborden Papers.

[12]Dorothy Inborden Miller, "State Cooperation with Joseph K. Brick School in North Carolina", *American Missionary* (February 1924): 611-612. This article was written by T.S.' daughter.

[13]Reverend Henry S. Leiper, "As Others See Us", *American Missionary* 78, 80 (September 1924): 203-207

[14]Ibid.

[15]Personal Notes, T.S. Inborden, 1925, Inborden Papers.

[16]Ibid., article by T.S. Inborden on Farmer and their farms, 1925.

[17]*Memorandum*, Student Unrest, Fisk University, Nashville, Tennessee, February 12, 1925, Inborden Papers.

[18]Ibid., reference L.H. Wood's remarks to students.

[19]*Minutes*, Meeting of Greater Fisk Committee, Nashville, Tennessee, February 16, 1925, Inborden Papers.

[20]George N. White to F.A. McKenzie, Fisk University, Nashville, Tennessee, February 13, 1925, Inborden Papers.

[21]Memorandum, Remarks by President McKenzie to the Greater Fisk Committee, February 19, 1925, Nashville, Tennessee, Inborden Papers.

[22]H.H. Proctor to T.S. Inborden, Bricks, N.C., February 25, 1925, Inborden Papers.

[23]Addie Sweet to T.S. Inborden, Bricks, N.C., February 25, 1925, Inborden Papers.

[24]T.S. Inborden to Hollingsworth Wood, New York City, New York, March 27, 1925, Inborden Papers.

[25]F.A. Stewart to T.S. Inborden, Bricks, N.C., April 4, 1925, Inborden Papers.

[26]Mary E. Chamberlin to T.S. Inborden, Bricks, N.C., April 9, 1925, Inborden Papers.

[27]Personal Notes, T.S. Inborden, Great Fisk Committee, Final Report, April 18, 1925, Inborden Papers.

[28]Ibid.

[29]*Program*, Semi-Annual Meeting, The North Carolina Negro Farmers Congress, St. Augustine College, Raleigh, N.C., July 30-31, 1925, Inborden Papers.

[30]F.B. Lathan to T.S. Inborden, Bricks, N.C., August 15, 1925, Inborden Papers.

[31]*Schedule*, Church visitation dates, missionaries, American Missionary Association, September 1925, Inborden Papers. *Program Church Bell*, First

Congregation Church Great Falls, Montana, September 25, 1925, Inborden Papers, and *Helena Montana Newspaper*, September 27, 1925, Inborden Papers. Brochure "Fresh Facts from Missionary Fields", November 1925, Inborden Papers, and *Tomaket Times (Washington)* December 4, 1925, Inborden Papers.

[32] Ibid.

[33] *News and Observer (Raleigh, N.C.)*, March 21, 1926.

[34] *Memorandum*, Farmers Day, Bricks, N.C., February 19, 1926, Inborden Papers.

[35] Mrs. N. Cresap to T.S. Inborden, Bricks, N.C., April 19, 1926, Inborden Papers. T.S. responded to Mrs. Cresap in Scarlsdale, New York on April 23, 1926.

[36] Reverend H.H. Proctor to T.S. Inborden, Bricks, North Carolina, March 18, 1926, Inborden Papers.

[37] Ibid., May 11, 1926.

[38] A.L. Davis to T.S. Inborden, Bricks, N.C., May 23, 1926, Inborden Papers.

[39] Reverend Clarence Hall Wilson to T.S. Inborden, May 24, 1926, Inborden Papers.

[40] Ida B. Arrington to T.S. Inborden, Bricks, N.C., May 25, 1926, Inborden Papers.

[41] Maggie Young to T.S. Inborden, Bricks, N.C., May 25, 1926, Inborden Papers.

[42] F.A. Stewart to T.S. Inborden, Bricks, N.C., May 29, 1926, Inborden Papers.

[43] T.S. Inborden to N.C. Newbold, Raleigh, N.C., 1928, Inborden Papers.

[44] T.S. Inborden to Professor W.A. Robinson, Raleigh, N.C, May 31, 1928, Inborden Papers.

[45] T.S. Inborden to Attorney, R.C. Dunn, Enfield, N.C., June 7, 1928, Inborden Papers.

[46] T.S. Inborden to *Journal and Guide Newspaper*, Norfolk, Virginia, 1928, Inborden Papers.

[47] T.S. Inborden to Mr. Petway, September 27, 1928, Inborden Papers.

[48] *Memorandum*, Eagle Life Insurance Co., November 8, 1928, Inborden Papers.

[49] Jesse Edward Moorland to T.S. Inborden, Bricks, N.C., April 22, 1929, Inborden Papers.

[50] L.E. Graves to C.B. Austin, New York City, New York, July 3, 1929 (copy), Inborden Papers.

[51] Charles B. Austin to L.E. Graves, Raleigh, N.C., July 5, 1929, Inborden Papers.

[52] Knights of the Ku Klux Klan to Professor T.S. Inborden, Brick School, Enfield, N.C., July 18, 1929, Inborden Papers.

[53] *Catalogue, The Brick Bugle* 1929-1930, Inborden Papers. A catalogue prepared by Brick Junior College Faculty and staff. Reference selected students high school, elementary school, campus buildings and curriculum.

[54] Ibid.

[55] Personal Notes, T.S. Inborden, Student Strike, 1929, Inborden Papers.

[56] Personal Notes, T.S. Inborden, Brief Biographical sketch of John C. Wright, 1929, Inborden Papers.

[57] T.S. Inborden to R.C. Dunn, Enfield, N.C., September 8, 1929, Inborden Papers.

[58] T.S. Inborden to Dr. Carnegie, Rocky Mount, N.C., September 29, 1929, Inborden Papers.

[59] T.S. Inborden to Dr. Dubissette, October 1, 1929, Inborden Papers.

[60] T.S. Inborden to members of the Executive Committee Health and Hospital Board, October 5, 1929, Inborden Papers.

[61] T.S. Inborden to Julia Inborden Gordon, Richmond, Virginia, June 22, 1930, Inborden Papers.

[62] Fred L. Brownlee to T.S. Inborden, Bricks, N.C., February 4, 1933, Inborden Papers. Executive Secretary, AMA, Brownlee asked T.S. to select names of people who desired to contribute to Dr. Beard's Endowment, dedication of former AMA Executive Secretary's 100th birthday. A form letter was sent.

[63] Walter White to T.S. Inborden, Bricks, N.C., April 25, 1930, Inborden Papers.

[64] T.S. Inborden to L.E. Graves, Raleigh, N.C., May 30, 1930, Inborden Papers.

[65] T.S. Inborden to Benjamin Exum, Whitakers, North Carolina, April 15, 1930, Inborden Papers.

[66] L.E. Graves to T.S. Inborden, Bricks, N.C., June 3, 1930, Inborden Papers.

[67] James C. Evans to T.S. Inborden, Bricks, N.C., June 20, 1930, Inborden Papers.

[68] T.S. Inborden to Mrs. Wilson Bruce Inborden, Raleigh, N.C., December 8, 1930, Inborden Papers.

[69] Personal Notes, T.S. Inborden, April 21, 1931, Inborden Papers.

[70] New York Herald Tribune, August 23, 1931.

[71] Carl Murphy to T.S. Inborden, Bricks, N.C., July 31, 1931, Inborden Papers.

[72] T.S. Inborden to R.R. Moton, Tuskegee, Alabama, August 29, 1931, Inborden Papers. Major R.R. Moton was President, Tuskegee Institute. He was also at Hampton University, Virginia.

[73] Agreement, T.S. Inborden and Mr. and Mrs. Benjamin Fobbs, Bricks, N.C., September 29, 1931, Inborden Papers.

[74] T.S. Inborden to Dr. M.E. Dubisette, New York, September 29, 1931, Inborden Papers.

[75] T.S. Inborden to President Wright Brick College, N.C., September 4, 1931, Inborden Papers.

[76] T.S. Inborden to Nan Inborden, Raleigh, N.C., 1932, Inborden Papers. Inborden wrote a letter to his daughter-in-law, Nan Inborden and discussed some of his best accomplishments.

[77] T.S. Inborden to B.D. Mann, February 12, 1932, Inborden Papers.

[78] T.S. Inborden to Mr. Jackson, February 21, 1932, Inborden Papers.

[79] T.S. Inborden to Attorney Andrews, North Carolina, February 28, 1932, Inborden Papers.

[80] *Memorandum* to J.C. Wright, Brick Junior College, N.C., from T.S. Inborden, June 24, 1932, Inborden Papers.

[81] T.S. Inborden to Governor O. Max Gardener, Raleigh, N.C., October 26, 1932, Inborden Papers. Inborden was very concerned about the problems of black people and their need or some relief after the 1930 depression.

[82] Personal Notes, T.S. Inborden, November 4, 1932, Inborden Papers. Inborden was very active in assisting local residents in community welfare problems.

[83] T.S. Inborden to Mrs. H. H. Proctor, Brooklyn, New York, 1933, Inborden Papers. Inborden wrote a personal letter to Mrs. H. H. Proctor, widow of his friend and former Fisk classmate.

[84] Lucinda Smith to T.S. Inborden, Bricks, N.C., 1933, Inborden Papers.

[85] R.C. Lucius to T.S. Inborden, Bricks, N.C., 1933, Inborden Papers.

[86] T.S. Inborden to W.C. Jackson, Chapel Hill, N.C., March 27, 1933, Inborden Papers.

[87] T.S. Inborden to the children of Mrs. Maggie Speight, Bricks N.C., March 31, 1933, Inborden Papers.

[88] *Program* Fifty Second Annual Meeting, N.C., Negro Teachers Association, Raleigh, N.C., April 14, 1995, Inborden Papers.

[89] Mr. and Mrs. Benjamin Young to T.S. Inborden, Bricks, N.C., May 31, 1933, Inborden Papers.

[90] Personal Notes, T.S. Inborden June 31, 1933, Inborden Papers. Inborden attended a June Howard University Commencement.

CHAPTER 5

[1] James Sanford to T.S. Inborden, Bricks, N.C., July 7, 1933, Inborden Papers.

[2] Fred L. Brownlee to T.S. Inborden, Bricks, N.C., July 12, 1933, Inborden Papers.

[3] T.S. Inborden to County Superintendant of Edgecombe and County Officials, Tarboro, N.C., July 15, 1933, Inborden Papers.

[4] T.S. Inborden to N.B. Young and Family, Tallahasse, Florida, July 19, 1933, Inborden Papers.

[5] A.E. Akers to J.A. Abernathy, Tarboro, N.C., July 26, 1933, (copy) Inborden Papers.

[6] W.L. Horne to R.C. Dunn, Enfield, N.C., July 27, 1933, Inborden Papers.

[7] Reverend J.W. Blackwell to R.C. Dunn, Bricks, N.C., July 29, 1933, Inborden Papers.

[8] T.S. Inborden to W.W. Saunders, Louisville, Kentucky, July 30, 1933, Inborden Papers.

[9] Joseph L. Peacock to R.C. Dunn, Enfield, N.C., July 31, 1933, Inborden Papers.

[10] T.S. Inborden to Mrs. Bratcher, August 4, 1933, Inborden Papers.

[11] Harold D. Cooley to R.C. Dunn, Enfield, N.C., July 31, 1933, Inborden Papers.

[12] T.S. Inborden to James E. Hilman, Raleigh, N.C., 1933, Inborden Papers.

[13] Jeannette Keeble to T.S. Inborden, Bricks, N.C., August 5, 1933, Inborden Papers.

[14] John W. Davis to T.S. Inborden, Bricks, N.C., August 9, 1933, Inborden Papers.

[15] Nan Inborden to T.S. Inborden, Bricks, N.C., August 10, 1933, Inborden Papers.

[16] Lugenia G. Exum to Thomas S. Inborden, Bricks, N.C., August 15, 1933, Inborden Papers.

[17] Evelyn Forney to T.S. Inborden, Bricks, N.C., August 16, 1933, Inborden Papers.

[18] J.H. Bias to T.S. Inborden, Bricks, N.C., August 18, 1933, Inborden Papers.

[19] W.A. Holmes to T.S. Inborden, Bricks, N.C., August 19, 1933, Inborden Papers.

[20] Julia P. Johnson to T.S. Inborden, Bricks, N.C., August 25, 1933, Inborden Papers.

[21] T.S. Inborden to J.L. Peacock, East Northfield, Massachusetts, August 25, 1933, Inborden Papers.

[22] T.S. Inborden to Fred L. Brownlee, New York City, New York, August 25, 1933, Inborden Papers.

[23] Job applicants to T.S. Inborden, Bricks, N.C., Inborden Papers. With the reopening of Bricks School in 1933. T.S. received letters from numerous applicants requesting teaching positions. They were: W.A. Holmes, Mt Olive, N.C.; Pearl Johnson, Orange, New Jersey; Frederick Cooper, Kenly, N.C.; Dorothy Latham, Tarrytown, New Jersey; Emily May Harper, Raleigh, N.C.; and Julius C. Garnes, Henderson, N.C., and Sallye Taylor.

[24] T.S. Inborden to J.W. Pittman Enfield, N.C., September 2, 1933, Inborden Papers.

[25] Secretary Brownlee to T.S. Inborden, Bricks, N.C., 1933, Inborden Papers.

[26] Mary V. Little to T.S. Inborden, Bricks, N.C., 1933, Inborden Papers.

[27] T.S. Inborden to Friends and Patrons of Brick School Tri Counties, N.C., September 10, 1933, Inborden Papers. T.S. was discussing the restructuring of the Tri County School.

[28] Cora E. Black Grant to T.S. Inborden, Bricks, N.C., September 11, 1933, Inborden Papers.

[29] Personal Notes, T.S. Inborden September 25, 1933, Inborden Papers.

[30] T.S. Inborden to Dr. Thomas October 6, 1933, Inborden Papers.

[31] T.S. Inborden to Robert Elzy, October 9, 1933, Inborden Papers.

[32] Reverend G.T. Thomas to T.S. Inborden, Bricks, N.C., October 2, 1933, Inborden Papers.

[33] L.S. Inscoe to T.S. Inborden, Bricks, N.C., November 1, 1933, Inborden Papers.

[34] Fred Brownlee to T.S. Inborden, Bricks, N.C., May 18, 1934, Inborden Papers.

[35] Thomas E. Jones to T.S. Inborden, Bricks, N.C., April 27, 1935, Inborden Papers.

[36] *Program* Commencement Exercises, Bricks, N.C., May 19, 1935, Inborden Papers.

[37] Dr. C. Hawkins to T.S. Inborden, Bricks, N.C., July 15, 1935, Inborden Papers.

[38] *Memorandum*, Conference with N.C. Newbold, Fred Brownlee and educators, July 19, 1935, Inborden Papers.

[39] T.S. Inborden to Joseph H.B. Evans, Washington, D.C., October 9, 1935, Inborden Papers.

[40] T.S. Inborden to J.D. Reid, Wilson, N.C., September 23, 1935, Inborden Papers.

[41] Joseph H.B. Evans to T.S. Inborden Bricks, N.C., September 24, 1935, Inborden Papers.

[42] Honorable J. Reid, M.C., to T.S. Inborden, Bricks, N.C., October 5, 1935, Inborden Papers.

[43] Joseph H.B. Evans to T.S. Inborden, Bricks, N.C., October 9, 1935, Inborden Papers.

[44] W.R. Gregg to T.S. Inborden, Bricks, N.C., February 10, 1936, Inborden Papers.

[45] Personal Notes, T.S. Inborden, The Honey-bee culture activities of Inborden, Inborden Papers.

[46] Personal Notes, T.S. Inborden, 1936, Inborden Papers.

[47] Ibid.

[48] Doris M. Dubissette to T.S. Inborden, Bricks, N.C., May 11, 1937, Inborden Papers.

[49] G.W. Bullock to T.S. Inborden, Bricks, N.C., July 2, 1937, Inborden Papers.

[50] N.E. Greshman to Principal, Brick School N.C., July 1937, Inborden Papers. There was a meeting with school employees on a segregated basis by the state Board of Education. Sometimes, I believe it would be good for young people today and even some young adults to read about the trials and tribulations black people experienced during the era of segregaton in America. These past reflections will bring to them how some senior citizens of color paved the way for them to enjoy some equal opportunities.

[51] C.A. Hudson to T.S. Inborden Bricks, N.C., July 1937, Inborden Papers.

[52] T.S. Inborden to Superintendent of schools, Tarboro, N.C., September 15, 1937, Inborden Papers.

[53] The *Bricks Bugle (Brick, N.C.)*, December 1937. The December issue of the Bugle had some articles related to the student enrollment, home economics, dog show, Armistice Day Celebration, teachers lectures, comments by T.S. Inborden, Papers Staff, Christmas Spirit, Program of events, visitors and socials. Basketball was played by the students, but not a dominant factor in their daily lives. The newspaper also had articles on the dramatic club, senior recitals, school movie, health and local advertisers that supported the school.

[54] Clyde Hoey to T.S. Inborden, Bricks, N.C., January 15, 1938, Inborden Papers.

[55] Program, "Dedication of School Gymnasium" Spring Hope, South Carolina, January 17, 1938, Inborden Papers.

[56] William John Clark to T.S. Inborden, Bricks, N.C., March 31, 1938, Inborden Papers.

[57] Sigmund Meyers to T.S. Inborden, Bricks, N.C., April 6, 1938, Inborden Papers.

[58] T.S. Inborden to Superintendent, N.E. Greshman and the County Board of Education Edgecombe County, Tarboro, N.C., May 1, 1938, Inborden Papers.

[59] T.S. Inborden to N.C., Newbold, Raleigh, N.C., June 4, 1938, Inborden Papers.

[60] Fred Brownlee to T.S. Inborden, Bricks, N.C., June 9, 1938, Inborden Papers.

[61] N.E. Greshman to Attorney R.C. Dunn, Enfield, N.C., June 25, 1938, Inborden Papers.

[62] T.S. Inborden to Professor Trigg, N.C., June 18, 1938, Inborden Papers.

[63] T.S. Inborden to Professor Evans, Washington, D.C., June 26, 1938, Inborden Papers.

[64] M.V. Barnhill to C.M. Eppes, Greenville, N.C., June 29, 1938, Inborden Papers.

[65] T.S. Inborden to Lawyer Dunn, Bricks, N.C., June 30, 1938, Inborden Papers.

[66] J.W. Wiley to T.S. Inborden, Bricks, N.C., July 1, 1938, Inborden Papers and Queen E. Lyons, North Carolina College for Negroes, Durham, N.C., July 27, 1938, Inborden Papers.

[67] T.S. Inborden to Mr. Dreyden, September 19, 1938, Inborden Papers.

CHAPTER 6

[1] D.B. Fearing to T.S. Inborden, Bricks, N.C., August, 1939, Inborden Papers.

[2] Francis Gordon to T.S. Inborden, Bricks, N.C., February 6, 1940, Inborden Papers.

[3] William Pickens to T.S. Inborden, Bricks, N.C., January 3, 1940, Inborden Papers.

[4] Personal Notes, T.S. Inborden, 1940, Inborden Papers. Inborden wrote some notes on Evaluation In Human Life, Negro farmers, Aristocrats of the comunity, boll weevil, economic scare and the appointment of Black Farm Agents.

[5] Emily Mae Daniels to T.S. Inborden, Bricks, N.C., April 28, 1940, Inborden Papers.

[6] N.C. Calhoun to T.S. Inborden, Bricks, N.C., May 24, 1940, Inborden Papers.

[7] Progam, "Commencement Exercise" Brick Tri County High School, Bricks, N.C., May 26, 1940, Inborden Papers.

[8] Susie Green to T.S. Inborden, Bricks, N.C., February 12, 1940, Inborden Papers.

[9] Daisy A. Fox to T.S. Inborden, Bricks, N.C., July 18, 1940, Inborden Papers.

[10] Ashton Smith to T.S. Inborden, Bricks, N.C., September 1, 1940, Inborden Papers.

[11] T.S. Inborden to Govenor Clyde R. Hoey, Raleigh, N.C., August 22, 1940, Inborden Papers.

[12] Mattie Burwell to T.S. Inborden, Bricks, N.C., August 28, 1940, Inborden Papers.

[13] T.S. Inborden to Mattie Burwell, Oberlin, Ohio, 1940, Inborden Papers.

[14] Ashton Smith to T.S. Inborden, September 1, 1940, Bricks, N.C., Inborden Papers.

[15] Clyde R. Hoey to T.S. Inborden, Bricks, N.C., September 5, 1940, Inborden Papers.

[16] Minnie Gregg to T.S. Inborden, Bricks, N.C., October 9, 1946, Inborden Papers.

[17] William Pickens to T.S. Inborden, Bricks, N.C., October 15, 1940, Inborden Papers.

[18] T.S. Inborden to Thomas Pearsall, North Carolina, 1940, Inborden Papers.

[19] Olivia Street to T.S. Inborden, Bricks, N.C., 1940, Inborden Papers.

[20] T.S. Inborden to Howard Gordon, Raleigh, N.C., November 10, 1941, Inborden Papers.

[21] Personal Notes, T.S. Inborden, Inborden Papers, 1943. When Inborden's brother died, he wrote the eulogy, expressing Ashton's roots and the love for his brother.

[22] Jeannette Keeble Cox to T.S. Inborden, Bricks, N.C., January 14, 1944, Inborden Papers.

[23] Honorable R. Hunt Parker to T.S. Inborden, Bricks, N.C., 1944, Inborden Papers.

[24] Reverend F.L. Bullock to T.S. Inborden, Bricks, N.C., May 12, 1944, Inborden Papers.

[25] Julia Gordon to T.S. Inborden, Bricks, N.C., September 23, 1944, Inborden Papers. Inborden's granddaughter Julia (Sister) had a pleasant and warm concern for her grandfather.

[26] Julia Gordon to T.S. Inborden, Bricks, N.C., September 27, 1944, Inborden Papers.

[27] Francis Gordon to T.S. Inborden, Washington, D.C., October 3, 1946, Inborden Papers.

[28] Personal Notes, T.S. Inborden, 1945, Inborden Papers. Inborden had a medical problem with his prostate gland. He recovered from his illness with some minor complications and follow up treatments.

[29] Daisy A. Fox to T.S. Inborden, Washington, D.C., October 22, 1946, Inborden Papers and Charles G. Tollafield to T.S. Inborden, Washington, D.C., 1946, Inborden Papers.

[30] Lela Gordon to T.S. Inborden, Washington, D.C., January 12, 1946, Inborden Papers.

[31] John W. Mitchell to T.S. Inborden, Washington, D.C., February 4, 1946, Inborden Papers.

[32] Rose Leary Love to T.S. Inborden, Washington, D.C., March 7, 1946, Inborden Papers. Love was a cousin of Sarah Jane Evans Inborden.

[33] The *Enfield Progress*, August 1946.

[34] Fred L. Brownlee to T.S. Inborden, Washington, D.C., September 20, 1946, Inborden Papers.

[35] Silas A. Artis to T.S. Inborden, Washington, D.C., October 22, 1946, Inborden Papers.

[36] Daisy Fox to T.S. Inborden, 1946, Bricks, N.C., Inborden Papers.

[37] Jessie Stoudmier to T.S. Inborden, Washington. D.C., November 4, 1946, Inborden Papers.

[38] Maggie Grant to T.S. Inborden, Washington, D.C., December 8, 1946, Inborden Papers.

[39] John W. Mitchell to T.S. Inborden, Washington, D.C., to January 4, 1947, Inborden Papers.

[40] T.S. Inborden to J.W. Reid, Whitaker, N.C., January 18, 1947, Inborden Papers and J.W. Reid to T.S. Inborden, Washington, D.C., January 20, 1947, Inborden Papers.

[41] T.S. Inborden to Anna E. Murray, Washington, D.C., March 2, 1947, Inborden Papers.

[42] T.S. Inborden to Fred L. Brownlee, New York, March 4, 1947, Inborden Papers.

[43] Emmaline West McMillon to T.S. Inborden, Washington, D.C., March 11, 1947, Inborden Papers.

[44] Jeannette K. Cox to T.S. Inborden, Washington, D.C., April 4, 1947, Inborden Papers.

[45] Daisy Fox to T.S. Inborden, Washington, D.C., April 16, 1947, Inborden Papers.

[46] O.H. Bellamy to T.S. Inborden, Washington, D.C., April 19, 1947, Inborden Papers.

[47] T.S. Inborden to County Treasurer, Lorain County, Elyria Ohio, August 17, 1947, Inborden Papers.

[48] Personal Notes, T.S. Inborden, 1947-8, Inborden Papers.

[49] Fred L. Brownlee to T.S. Inborden, Washington, D.C., October 28, 1947, Inborden Papers.

[50] T.S. Inborden to Flossie Parker Tarboro, N.C., October 30, 1947, Inborden Papers and Julia E. Gordon to T.S. Inborden, Washington, D.C., October 31, 1947, Inborden Papers.

[51] Nora E. Morgan to T.S. Inborden, Washington, D.C., August 28, 1948, Inborden Papers.

[52] John N. Gordon to T.S. Inborden, Washington, D.C., August 5, 1949, Inborden Papers.

[53] Edna Lewis to T.S. Inborden, Washington, D.C., 1949, Inborden Papers.

[54] G.E. Davis to T.S. Inborden, Washington, D.C., June 14, 1949, Inborden Papers.

[55] Myrtle L. Forney to T.S. Inborden, Washington, D.C., February 13, 1949, Inborden Papers.

[56] Julia Evans Inborden Gordon to Dorothy I. Miller, Washington, D.C., March 3, 1949, Inborden Papers.

[57] Daisy Fox to T.S. Inborden, Washington, D.C., September 18, 1949, Inborden Papers.

[58] Edna Lewis to T.S. Inborden, Washington, D.C., April 21, 1949, Inborden Papers.

[59] Personal Notes, T.S. Inborden, 1951, Inborden Papers. Thomas Sewell Inborden, and educator, teacher, principal, botanist, aspiarist, agriculturalist and loving father and grandfather had completed 86 years of his fruitful life in the flesh at 11:15 on Saturday, March 10, 1951. His accomplishments in life were well done and he was called to God's everlasting paradise after a successful life. Sympathy gestures by T.S.' friends and list of names. *Oberlin News Tribune*, March 15, 1951, article reference T.S. demise.

BIBLIOGRAPHY
PRIMARY SOURCES

Manuscript Collection

Thomas Sewell Inborden papers
Moorland Spingarn Research Center, Howard University, Washington, D.C.
Mary Ann Shadd papers

National Archives, Washington, D.C.

Military Pension Files, RG15 of the Adjutant General's Office
Military Pension File, Wilson Bruce Evans, RG94
Special Veterans Census, 1890, Lorain County, Ohio. Roll 72. Microcopy 123.

State Archives

North Carolina State Archives
Governor Reid papers

Journals

Negro History Bulletin
Journal Negro History

Newspapers

Afro American (Baltimore)
Boston Guardian
Enfield Progress
Helena Montana Newspaper
New and Observer (Raleigh, N.C.)
New York Herald Tribune
News Tribune (Oberlin, Ohio)
Rocky Mount Telegram (North Carolina)
Southern Workman
Tomaket Times (Washington)

Magazines

Crisis
Fisk University News

Interviews

Miller, Inborden Dorothy, *Conversations with Dorothy Inborden Miller and interviews by Robert Ewell Greene, 1976-1995,* Oberlin, Ohio and Washington, D.C.

Personal Notes

Unpublished and published manuscripts, Class lectures and photographs from the Library of Robert E. Greene.

Secondary Sources

Books

American Unitarian Association, *From Servitude to Service.* Boston: American Unitarian Association, 1905.

Beard, Augustus Field. *A Crusade of Brotherhood.* Boston: The Pilgrim Press, 1909.

Bigglestone, William E. *They Stopped In Oberlin, Black Residents and Visitors of the Nineteenth Century.* Arizona: Innovation Group Inc., 1981.

Brown, Sterling, Davis, Arthur P. and Lee, U.S. eds., *The Negro Caravan.*

Douglass, H. Paul. *Christian Reconstruction In The South.* Boston: The Pilgrim Press, 1909.

Fleming G. James and Burckel, Christian E., *Who's Who In Colored America.* New York: Christian E. Burckel and Associates, 1950.

Freeman, Douglas Southall, *R.E. Lee A Biography Volumes III, IV* New York: Charles Scribner's Sons, 1936.

Freeman, Douglas Southall, *Lee's Lieutenants A Study In Command Volumes 1* New York: Charles Scribner's Sons, 1943.

Government Printing Office, *The War of the Rebellion: A compilation of the official records of the Union and Confederate Armies Series I- Volume XI.* Washington: Government Printing Office, 1884.

Greene, Robert E. *Black Defenders of America, 1775-1973.* Chicago: Johnson Publishing Co., 1974.

Greene, Robert E. *Leary-Evans, Ohio's Free People of Color.* Washington, D.C.: Hickman Printing, Inc., 2nd edition, 1989.

Greene, Robert E. *They Did Not Tell Me True Facts About African Americans In the African and American Experiences.* Fort Washington, Maryland: R.E. Greene Publisher, 1992.

Hare-Cuney, Maude. *Negro Musicians and Their Music.* Washington, D.C.: The Associated Publisher, Inc., 1936.

Hickok, Charles Thomas, *The Negro In Ohio 1902-1970.* New York: AMS Press Inc., 1975.

Hodder and Staughton, *The Story of the Jubilee Singers With Their Songs.* London: The Gresham Press, 1875.

Holy Bible. Cambridge: C.J. Clay and Sons, University Press, N.C. (Family Bible of Sarah Jane Evans.)

Lawson, Jesse, *How To Solve The Race Problem.* Washington, D.C.: Beresford Printer, 1904.

Lee, Robert E. Captain. *Recollections and letters of General Robert E. Lee.* New York: Garden City Publishing Co., Inc., 1924.

McDougall, F.C., *A Key To Some Common Plants of the Eastern United States.* Chicago: Western Publishing House, 1902.

Moore, George H., *The Treason of Major General Charles Lee.* New York: Charles Scribner, 1858.

Office of Alumni Affairs, *Alumni Directory of Fisk University.* Nashville, Tennessee: Office of Alumni Affairs, 1971.

Quarles, Benjamin, *Allies for Freedom, Blacks, and John Brown.* New York: Oxford University Press, 1974.

Rhodes, Charles Dudley. *Robert E. Lee The West Pointer*. Virginia: Garrett and Massie Publishers, 1932.

Root, A.1. *The ABC of Bee Culture*. Ohio, Medina: A.1. Root, 1883.

Shepherd, Jacob R. Camp. *History of the Oberlin Wellington Rescue*. Boston: John P. Jewett and Company, 1859.

Simmons, William. *Men of Mark*. George M. Rewell & Co., 1887.

Thomas, John W. Jr. *Jeb Stuart*. New York: Charles Scribner's Sons, 1934.

U.S. Department of Agriculture, Weather Bureau, *Instructions to Special River and Rainfall Observers*. Washington, D.C.: U.S. Government Printing Office, 1915.

Waterman, W.G., *Fisk University and Some of Its Graduates*. Nashville, Tennessee, 1900.

Wilkinson, Frederick (ed.) *Directory of Graduates Howard University 1870-1963*. Washington, D.C.: Howard University, 1963.

INDEX

A

Abernathy, J.A., 118
Abbott, Lyman, 115
Adelphian Literary Society, 35
AFRO American Newspaper, 105
Agriculture Classes, 399
Aker, A.E., 49, 54, 118
Akins, Superintendent., 53
Albany Normal School, 15, 25, 365
Albritton, Inez, 94
Alpha Phi Alpha Fraternity, 8
Alsop, Mr., 142
Alumni Reunion, 422
Alvarez, Jerry, 50
American Missionary Association, 13, 14, 15, 16, 21, 29, 40
Anderson, C.T., 90
Anderson, Harriet, 4
Andrews, Attorney, 109
Archer, Aaron, 168
Arrington, Bascom, 6, 35
Arrington, Fannie, 162
Arrington, Ida B., 87
Arrington, Luther, 62
Arrington, Samuel, 49
Artist, Davis Mabel, 139
Artist, Silas A., 159
Atkins, J. Altson, 88
Atkins, Jack, 51
Austin, Charles, 103
Austin, Charles B., 93

B

Bacon, John G., 8
Bailey, J. W., 49
Baker, Erma, 387
Baker, Lula, 94
Baker, Mrs., 384
Baker, Rev., 80
Balkey, Julia, 115
Banks, F., 99
Bannister, Gabriel, 17
Barbour, John Lemuel, 14
Barnhill, M.V., 141, 142
Battle, Cullen, 21
Battle, Ida, 168
Battle, Kemp, 21
Battle, Mark, 21, 117
Battle, Mary, 49
Battle, Richard, 32, 33, 148
Beam, Miss, 48, 49
Beard, Augustus F., 14, 15, 16, 18, 21, 29, 32, 114, 115, 160, 368
Beard Hall, 20, 373
Bee Culture, 134, 145, 159
Beebe, H., 11
Bell, Alexander Graham, 8
Bellamy, O.H., 159, 161
Benedict Hall, 20, 369, 370
Benedict, Lydia, 18, 31, 44, 56, 368
Berry, Louis, Rev., 46
Bias, J. H., 122
Black, Arnold, 4
Black Diversity, 60
Black, George P., 3
Black, Gordon, 4
Black, Horace, 3
Black, Horace Greely, 3
Black, Julia, 3
Black, Sidney, 4
Black, Stanley, 4
Black, Thelma L., 94
Black, William Herbert, 3
Blackwell, J. W., 119
Bliss, Principal, 104
Blount, Joe, 62

Bluford, F.B., 122
Boaz, Sophia, 79
Boll Weevil, 147
Bonde, Murray Carmen, 345
Borders, T.K., 136
Boston Guardian, 26
Boulder, Cora, 57
Boykins, Edward, 62
Boyston, Miss, 79
Boy's Basketball Team, 401
Bradford, Nan, 52, 53
Brantley, Mrs., 37
Braswell, Mac, 151
Bratcher, Mrs., 120
Brewster Hall, 28, 372
Bruce, Eugene A., 135
Brick Alumni, 1902-1914, 44-45
Brick, Brewster, Julia, 18, 19, 26, 117, 168, 367, 368
Brick Bugle, 136
Brick Glee Club, 393
Brick, Joseph Keasbey, 18, 19, 366
Brick Jubilee Club, 43, 44, 393
Brick Junior College, 76, 77, 94, 95
Brick Junior College Activities, 420
Brick Junior College Chemistry Laboratory, 421
Brick Junior College Dining Room, 421
Brick News, 1915-1920, 44, 45
Brick New York Alumni, 127
Bridges, John, 21
Broome, Ernest, 95
Brown, A.H., 24, 389
Brown, Hawkins Charlotte, 71, 186, 129
Brown, J.E., 129
Brown, John, 10
Brown, Roy, 131, 132
Brown, Sterling, 80
Brownlee, Fred L., 93, 107, 111, 116, 124, 125, 129, 130, 139, 158, 160, 162

Bruce, Eugene A., 129
Brumfield, Professor, 80
Buckingham, Ruth E., 94
Bullock, Benjamin, 104, 128, 416
Bullock, Captain, 416
Bullock, F.L., Rev., 155
Bullock, George, 30
Bullock, George Sr., 66, 67
Bullock, G.W., 135
Bullock House, 414
Bullock, Jessie L., 61
Bullock, Joseph, 61
Bullock, Lula, 45, 55
Bullock, Mr., 48
Bunn, Isaac, 108
Bunn, Mr. and Mrs., 37
Burwell, Mattie, 150

C

Cabell, Smith Mattie, 1, 153
Cable, George W., 154
Cady, George L., 64, 65
Cahill, A.M., 13
Calhoun, N.C., 148
California Trip, 71
Caliver, Professor, 80
Calloway, James N., 14
Calloway, Thomas J., 14
Carr, Ethel, 61
Carroll, Havens Miss, 49
Carroll, Willie, 334
Carnegie, Dr., 96
Chamberlain, Mary E., 83
Champ Family, 22
Chase, Black Julia, 3
Cherry, John, 90
Chicago Fisk Club, 80
Chicago Visit, 1922, 70, 71
Chisholm, F.S., 7
Church, Mary Eliza, 11
Church, Robert R., 11

Clark, W.G., 154
Clark, William J., 138
Clarke, Madge Hockaday, 152
Cleveland, Ohio, 6,7,8
Coel, Eliza, 155
Coel, Mildred K., 115
Coel, Rev., 115
Cofield, Junius Rev., 138
Coleman, L. Zenobia, 94
Collins, Miss, 79
Colson, John, 62
Commencement Exercise, 1915, 45,46
Commencement Exercise, May, 1905, 34
Commonwealth Newspaper, 142
Conner, Jennie, 411
Conrad's Store, 5
Cooley, Attorney, 120
Cooper's Electric Shoe Factory, 408
Copeland, Fred, 53
Copeland, John Anthony, Jr., 10
Copeland, John Anthony, Sr., 10
Copeland, William, 10
Cornish, S.E., 13
Cox, Jeanette Keeble, 122, 154, 160, 161
Cravath, E.M. Rev., 115
Cravath, Paul, 64
Cravath, President E.M., 13, 16
Creech, Oscar, 49
Crisap, Miss, 86
Croom, A.S., Rev., 35, 66
Cross, Grayson, 164
Cross, Jim, 164
Crosthwait, Mrs., 54
Crum, W.D., 36
Curriculum, 1901, 23
Curtis, Mrs., 411

D

Daniel, S.I., 81

Daniels, Emily Mae, 148
Davis, Alice, 15, 34, 87, 139, 140
Davis, Allen, 410
Davis, A.W., 80
Davis, G.E., 103, 163
Davis, John W., 122, 418
Davis, Mrs., 384
Davis, Otis, 62
Dawson, Hopie, 124
Dawson, William, 64, 167
D.C. Brick Alumni Club, 161, 162
Dean, C.E., 147
Deberry, W.N., 44
DeLaney, Sadie, 47
Denton, Cicerco, 49
Desmukes, Alberta, 49
Dewitt, J.H., 80
Dining Hall, Brick Campus, 374
Domestic Science Class, 387
Douglass, Frederick, 16, 35, 115
Douglass, Joseph, 35, 417
Douglass, Paul, 49
Douglas, Ruth, 94
Dowdell, Katie, 389
Dowell, Miss, 21
Dowtin, Mamie, 124
Draughn, Eddie, 136
Dreyden, Mr., 144, 158
Dubissette, Doris, 135
Dubissette, Dr., 88, 90, 91, 96, 106
Dubois, William E.B., 12, 14, 78, 80, 84
Dunn, R.C., 89, 95, 118, 199, 120, 124, 139, 140, 142
Dunston, Dorothy, 162
Dunston, Frank., 96

E

Eagle Life Insurance Company, 91
Early, Camille, 50
Early, Doris, 50

Early, Edward Jr., 50
Early, Edward Dr., 50
Eastman, George, 25, 28, 29, 159
Eaton, James, 98, 140
Eaton, Mr., 139
Edgecombe County Fair, 133
Elam, Chauncey L., 94
Ellis, John M., 11
Elma Hall, 20, 371
Elzy, Robert, 127
Embrie, Mr., 88
Enfield Progress, 142, 158
Epilogue, 166, 167, 168
Epps, C.M., 141
Estes, General, 18, 120
Evans, Anna, 8
Evans, Cornelius, 10, 25, 53, 58, 148, 150, 151, 341, 342
Evans, Corrie, 7
Evans, Delilah, 7, 8, 10
Evans, Elizabeth, 8, 10
Evans, Frances, 10
Evans, George Dr., 163
Evans, Henrietta, 9
Evans, Henry, 7, 9, 10, 159
Evans, J. A., 74
Evans, James C., 101
Evans, Jane, 8
Evans, John, 8
Evans, Joseph H.B., 9, 130-133, 141
Evans, Julia, 8
Evans, Julia Ann, 10
Evans, Leary Sarah Jane, 10, 11, 12, 14, 15
Evans, Lillian, 9
Evans, Mary Patterson, 8
Evans, Matthew, 8
Evans, Rosa, 7
Evans, Sarah Jane, 9, 11, 15
Evans, Sheridan, 8
Evans, Wilson, 8

Evans, Wilson Bruce, 7, 8, 10, 11, 15, 22, 134, 336
Evans, Wilson Bruce's Children, 336
Evans, Wilson Bruce's Oberlin Home, 337
Evans, Wilson Bruce Dr., 9, 31
Evanti, Lillian, 36, 158
Exum, Benjamin, 100
Exum, Lugenia, 100, 122, 162
Exum, Priscilla, 100
Exum, Virginia, 162
Exum, William, 100

F

Faculty and Staff, 1915-20, 44
Fairchild, James, 160
Falkener, E.L., 34
Farm Barns, 381, 382
Farm and Garden Industries, 395
Farm Life, 69, 70
Farm Security Administration, 144
Farm Tenants, 42
Farmers Day, 1910, 41
Farmers Day, 1915, 46, 47
Farmers Day, 1919, 63
Farmers Day, 1923, 73
Farmers Day Exhibit, 381
Farmers' Meeting, 1900, 25
Fearing, D.B., 145
Federal Farm Loan Organization, 77, 78
Ferguson, Meredith G., 81
Finch, H.M., 49
Finney, Dr., 160
Fisher, Isaac, 79
Fisk Herald, 15, 82
Fisk University, 168
Fisk University Student Unrest, 1925, 78, 79, 80
Fletcher, Mr., 29, 34
Flood, Tillery Area, 149, 150

Fobbs, Benjamin, 106
Ford, W. Dr., 80
Foreman, Clark, 132
Forest City Hotel, Cleveland, 7
Forney, Evelyn, 122, 124
Forney, Mr., 34, 37, 104, 120, 127
Forney, Mrs., 384
Forney, Myrtle L., 163
Forten, Charlotte, 27
Foster, Frank Hugh, 92
Fountain, R.T., 129
Fox, Caroline, 4
Fox, Curtis, 4
Fox, Daisy, 4, 145, 148, 149, 157, 159, 161, 164
Fox, George, 4
Fox, Hebie, 4
Fox, Henry, 4
Fox, Leslie, 4
Fox, Lillie, 4
Fox, Rose, 4
Fox, Waynefield, 4
Freeland, Smith Frances, 1, 153
Frissell, H.B., Dr., 31

G

Gandy, John H., 79
Gardener, O. Max, 111
Garfield, President, 6
Garner, Dr., 76
Garren, Mr. and Mrs., 46, 47
Garrett, Charles, 18
Garrett Farm, 18
Garrrett, Joe, 18
Garrett, Paul, 18
Garrett, Richard, 163
Gates, Merrell E., 115
Gates, President, 16
Gaylord, Irving C., 48
Georgia Congressional Association, 16

Gilbert, Lucille, 61
Girls' Basketball Team, 402
Gordon, Frances Camille, 50, 145, 146, 150
Gordon, Howard, 152, 153
Gordon, John H. 50, 67, 94, 124
Gordon, John Newton, 50, 51, 148, 150, 157, 162
Gordon, Julia Evans, 50, 51, 145, 150, 155, 156
Gordon, Julia Inborden, 67, 97, 98, 161, 163, 348, 349, 350, 351, 352
Gordon, Lela, 157
Gottenger, Dr., 121
Graduating Class, 1924, 400
Graham, Frank P., 145
Grant, Cora Black, 125
Grant, Exum Rebecca, 100
Grant, Maggie, 151, 159
Grant, Martha Archer Crichlow, 168
Grant, Mrs., 162
Graves, L.E., 91, 93, 99, 100
Gregg, Minnie, 151
Gregg, W.R., 134
Green, Hattie, 30
Green, Katherine, 135
Green, Ned, 137, 151
Green, Susie, 148
Green, W.W., 139
Gresham N.E., 135, 139, 140
Griffin, Ada Bell, 49
Grigsby, Alice, 145
Grimke, Angelina W., 27
Grimke, Archibald H., 27
Grimke, Francis J., 27
Grimke, Henry, 27
Grimke, Sara M., 27
Grooms, Early Camille, 50, 156, 353
Grooms, Catherine, 50
Grooms, Henry, Dr., 50
Grooms, Ian, 50
Grooms, Ivan, 50

Grooms, Nina, 50
Grooms, Zayne, 50, 356, 357

H

Hall, Agnes, 153
Hall, L.E., 11
Hall, Mr., 107
Hamlin, C.H. 129
Hardin, Elizabeth, 124
Harding, J.M., Miss, 34
Harpers Ferry Raid, 10
Harris, Susan M., 14
Harris, Thomas Porter, 14
Harrison, A.S., 34, 35
Harrison, Richard, 36, 419
Hart, James, 145
Hawkins, J. Leon, 94
Hawkins, M.E., 129
Hayes, Benjamin, 62, 413
Haynes, George E., 58
Helena Normal School, 364
Hemmons, L.W., 125
Hickman, Louis M., 145
Hicks, Essex I., 162
Highsmith, E., 124
Hill, Joseph, 35
Hilman, James E., 121
Hinman, George W., 49
Hoey, Clyde R., 137, 138, 145, 149, 151
Holloway, William 4, 93, 94, 95, 123, 128, 154
Holmes, Henry, 95
Holmes, Oliver W., 123
Holmes, W.A., 122
Horne, Joshua Jr., 21, 117
Horne, W.L., 118, 119
Howard, Oliver O. Gen., 2, 18
Howard, Smith Virginia, 1
Howard University, 78, 81
Hudson, C.A., 135

Hudson, Mr., 107
Hughes Early Doris, 50, 156, 353, 355
Hunt, Eugene B., 94
Hunter, Dr., 7, 11, 335
Hunter, Jehu, 168
Hunter, Nell, 145
Hunton, W.A., 35

I

Imboden, John, 3
Inborden, Dorothy V., 4,5, 22, 25, 32, 51-53, 55-58, 63, 74, 75, 134, 347, 388
Inborden, Evans Sarah Jane, 16, 22, 25, 34, 37, 38, 58-61, 63, 65-68, 71, 92, 94, 121, 130, 158, 159, 161, 164, 338-341, 346-349, 383, 384, 408
Inborden, George Martin, 22
Inborden, Hospitalized 1945, 157
Inborden House, 380
Inborden, Julia Ella, 5, 22, 25, 32, 50, 59, 388
Inborden, Nan, 52, 102, 107, 108, 137, 161, 362
Inborden School, 155
Inborden, Sewell, 22
Inborden, Thomas, S., 2, 3, 5, 6, 7, 11, 14, 15, 16, 19, 21, 22, 23, 26, 28, 40, 53, 54, 55, 62, 63, 70, 71, 72, 73, 79, 81, 82, 84, 85, 91, 104, 105, 126, 138, 139, 141, 149, 150, 164, 165, 166, 167, 168, 335, 346, 347, 359, 363, 383, 385, 389, 390, 391, 403, 404, 405, 406, 407, 408, 409, 410, 411, 412
Inborden, T.S. Childhood Home, 332
Inborden, Wilson bruce, 22, 52, 53, 88, 89, 108, 347, 361
Industrial Education, 38, 39
Ingersoll, Mr., 7, 11
Ingraham, George, 20
Ingraham Hall, 20, 375, 376
Inscoe, L.S., 120, 128

Irwin, Clyde R., 145

J

Jackson, A.L., 81
Jackson, T.S, 108, 109
Jackson, W.C., 113
Jackson, W.G., 109
Jackson, William, 13
Jacobs, Della, 408
Jamestown Exposition, 36
Jefferson, Dr., 80
Jennings, Anderson, 8
Jocelyn, Simeon S., 13
Johns, R.B., Rev., 23, 33, 34
Johnson, Charles S., 84, 158, 162
Johnson, E.A., 34
Johnson, Hilda, 9
Johnson, Evans Julia, 25, 67, 343
Johnson, Julia P., 123
Johnson, William R., 149, 150
Joint Missionary Campaign, 39
Jones, John, 20
Jones, Thomas J., 63, 64, 84, 87, 129
Jordan, Gordon Julia, 354

K

Keeble, Jeanette, 25
Kelly, Berry O. 47
Kendall, H.W., 86
Kenslow, Jim, 4
Kent, Edward, 353
Kent, Frances Gordon Early, 156, 353, 427
Kent, Shakespeare, 50, 353
Kent, Sylvia, 50, 51, 353
Kerr, John H., 136
Kerr, Judge, 132
Killingsworth, J.D., 124
Kimbro, Harriet F., 14
King, Cornelius, 147
Kittrell College, 146, 147
Knop, Dr., 147
Ku Klux Klan, 81, 94, 96, 107, 124

L

Langston, Charles, 8, 10
Langston, John M., 10
Latham, F.B., 85
Latham, Nannie B., 9
Latimer, Helen C., 122
Lawless, Dr., 76
Lawson, R. Augustus, 81
Leach, Alfred, 62
Leary, Henrietta, 8, 9
Leary, John, 9
Leary, John Sinclair, 9, 158
Leary, John S. Jr., 10
Leary, Lewis Sheridan, 9, 10
Leary, Libby, 9
Leary, Louise, 10
Leary, Lucy, 9
Leary, Mary Elizabeth, 9
Leary, Matthew Nathaniel, 9, 10
Leary, Matthew Nathaniel Jr., 9
Leary, Matthew Nathaniel IV, 10
Leary, Patterson Mary, 10
Leary, Sarah, 9
Leary, Sarah Jane, 8
Lee, Asher, 3
Lee, Frank, 60
Lee, Horace, 3
Lee, Martha, 3
Lee, Robert E., 2, 3, 4, 149
Lee, Rosa, 145
Lee, Rosella, 153
Leigh, M. Gertrude, 94
Leiper, Henry S. Rev., 75, 76
Leventhal, J.L., 80
Lewis, Charles S., 80
Lewis, Clarence, 9
Lewis, Clarence Jr., 9

Lewis, Edna, 1, 153, 160, 162
Lewis, Evans, Hilda, 9
Liberia, 157
Lightener, C.E., 91
Lightener, R.H., 47
Lincoln, Abraham, 40
Lincoln Temple Congregational Church, 28
Lincoln University of Missouri, 119, 147, 148
Little, Hattie, 46
Little, Mary V., 94, 125
Little, Miss, 384
Little, M.V., Miss, 34
Loeb, Attorney, 7, 11, 335
Lord, H.K., 158
Lord, Mrs., 386
Louis, Julia, 4
Louisville Fisk Alumni, 81
Love, Rose G., 10
Love, Rose Mary Leary, 158
Lowe, Julia, 30
Lucius, R.C., 113
Lyman, Homer C., 60
Lyons, McKinley, 62
Lyons, Queen E., 144
Lyon, Rubye, 94

M

Mann, B.D., 108
Mann, Mr., 106
Mann, W.E. Rev., 30
Marrow, Emma L., 124
Marsh, Rev., 115
Martin, Isadore, 34, 161
Martin, Max, 161
Martin, Mr., 37, 384
Martin, Mrs., 384
Maryland, Dr., 80
McCall, James Dickens, 14
McDougold, Emma, 85

McDowell, Fay, 157
McKenzie, Fayette A., 78-83
McKinney, Louise R., 94
McLean, George, 62
McMillian, Mrs. 160
McMundy, Judge, 63
McNier, F.A., 49
McWilliams, James, 62
Meimoriel, Juliette Anna, 9
Meimoriel, Willard Colostic, Mariette, 9
Merrick, N.C., 144
Metropolitan AME Church, 28
Meyer, Max, 86
Meyers, Sam, 18, 69, 86
Meyers, Sigmund, 138
Milholland, Jean M., 106
Milholland, John E., 106
Miller, Inborden Dorothy, 2, 68, 144, 150, 151, 155, 157, 158, 161, 163, 164, 168, 355, 358, 359, 360, 423, 424, 425, 426
Miller, Kelley, 33, 40
Miller, Walker D., 52, 362
Missionary Training Institute, 153
Mitchell, John, 152, 158, 159
Mitchell, Sadie, 61
Model School, 377
Monroe, James Rev., 15
Moody, Chairman, 30
Moore, Ella Shepard, 68
Moore, George Rev., 22, 36, 67, 68, 389, 407
Moore, John, 92
Moore, T. Clay, 80
Moorland, Jesse, 36, 92, 93
Morgan, Nora E., 162
Morrison, Fred, 112
Mosby, John S., 2
Mosley, Virginia, 135, 153
Moton, R.R., Major, 63, 76, 107
Murphy, Carl, 105

Murray, Anna Evans, 159, 160, 344
Murray, Daniel, 8, 160, 344
Murray, George Henry, 8
Murray, Mary, 153
Murray, Smith Mary, 1
Myrick, Frankie, 124

N

Napier, J.C., 36, 64, 79, 80, 87
National Conference of Congregational Workers, 1915, 44
National Sociological Society, 28
Neely, Winnie, 113
Neill, Andrew P., 14
Neville, E.K., 49, 130
Newbold, N.C., 49, 75, 87, 114, 129, 133, 139, 141
New Farmers of America, 137
Nicholson, B.M., 150
Nineteenth Street Baptist Church, 28
Norfolk and Guide Newspaper, 90
North Carolina Industrial Association, 73
North Carolina Negro Farmers Congress, 1924, 74
North Carolina Negro Farmers Congress, 1925, 84
North Carolina Negro Teachers Association, 114
North Carolina Race Relations Committee, 111

O

Oberlin Anti-Slavery Society, 10
Oberlin College, 7, 8, 10
Oberlin High School, 10
Oberlin, Ohio, 7, 8, 164
Oberlin-Wellington Rescue, 8, 10
O'Kelly, Berry, 96, 107
O'Kelly, Roger, 91

O'Leary, Jeremiah, 9
Oxly, Mr., 131

P

Parker, Fletcher, 151
Parker, Flossie, 162
Parker, R. Hunt, 154
Parks, Dr., 80
Partch, A.W., 80
Patterson, Mary Simpson, 10
Payne, Clarence H., 80
Payne, Mr., 7
Peacock, Joseph L., 120, 123, 124, 139
Pearsall, Thomas, 151
Pease, Hiram A., 7
Pegues, A.S., Dr., 91
Pennington, J.W.C., 13
Perry, Dallas, 9
Perry, Dallas Leary, 9
Perry, Davis Henrietta, 9
Perry, Hattie B., 9
Perry, John Sinclair Leary, 9
Perry, Mary Elizabeth II, 9
Perry, Matthew Nathaniel IV., 9
Phelps, Amos A., 13
Phillips, Chester, 62
Phillips, Dr., 79
Phillips, J.T. Dr., 80
Phillips, Joe, 137
Phillips, Mr., 37
Pickens, William, 146, 151
Pillow, William H., 13
Pinchback, Nettie, 162
Pittman, C., 96
Pittman, Gary, 124
Pittman, J.W., 124
Pittman, Mrs. 37
Poindexter, Maria, 3
Pope, M.T. Dr., 47
Price, Cyril, 94

Price, John, 8
Price, Ruby, 94
Proctor, A.M., 49
Proctor, Caroline, 1
Proctor, Hannah, 1
Proctor, Henry, Hugh, 14, 16, 76, 79, 80, 81, 82, 87, 104, 112, 113
Proctor, Jane, 1
Proctor, Levi, 1
Proctor, Nathaniel, 1
Proctor, Thomas Sewell, 1
Putney, Mary, 61
Pynchon, Dr., 132

Q

Quackonon, James, 13
Quinchett, Olivia, 100
Quinn, Dave, 148
Quinn, Minnie, 148

R

Ragland, Fountain W., 33
Rainey, Smith Sarah, 1
Ramey, Smith Sarah, 1, 153
Ray, Charles B., 13
Reconstruction Finance Corporation, 110
Redding, Katheryne, 90
Reed, J.W., 159
Reid, Governor, 7
Reid, Professor J.D., 131
Revels, Aaron, 9
Revels, Hiram, 9
Revels, Sarah Jane, 9
Reynolds, L.R., 145
Rice, A.N., 119
Richardson, Daisy, V., 67
Richardson, Edward, 157
Riddle, Gladys, 4
Roanoke Island Historical Association, 145
Roberts, M.A., Miss, 34
Robinson, Florida P., 94
Robinson, James N., 79
Robinson, Mabel, 94
Robinson, Mary, 384
Robinson, W.A., 88
Robinson, William H., 94
Rocky Mount Hospital, 137
Roosevelt, Eleanor, 9
Rosenwald, Mr., 87
Ruffin, Winfield, 21, 117
Ryder, C.J., 16

S

Sadgewar, J.A., Miss, 34, 384
Saint Chapel's Church, 414
Sanders, Richard, 42
Sanford, Alcinda, 4
Sanford, James 116
Sanford, Oscar, 4, 6
Sargent, Charles F., Rev., 16
Saunders, Ernestine, 94
Saunders, L.J., 16, 17
Saunders, Joseph W., 94, 96
Saunders, M., 15
Saunders, Mary, 15, 16, 17
Saunders, W.W., 119
Schmokes, Pearl, 96
Scott, Emmett, 106, 146
Scott, John, 8
Sengstacke, J.H.H. Rev., 16
Sessoms, A.H., 92
Sessoms, William M., 115
Shaw, Professor, 81
Shepherd, Marjorie, 51, 57
Silver, Joseph, 144
Silver, Mr. and Mrs., 65
Simmons, S.B., 132
Sinclair, William, 18, 389
Slade, C.W., 90

Sloan, Mr., 37
Small, A.L., 80
Smead, Edith E., 4
Smith, Cecelia, 1, 332, 333
Smith, Edward Ashton, 1, 135, 149, 151, 153
Smith, Frank Gatewood, 14
Smith, Helen, 124
Smith, Helen B., 120
Smith, Laura, 61
Smith, Lucinda, 113
Smith, Luther, 153
Smith, Proctor Harriet, 1, 2, 6, 12, 13, 331
Smith, Robert Edward, 1
Smith, Rosella Lee, 1
Smith, Thomas Clarence, 1
Smith, Turner, 1
Smith, Walter, 153
Smith, Willie, 153
Snype, Jefferson R., 122
Southern Interracial Committee, 129
Spaulding, C.C., 104
Speight, Maggie, 112, 113
Spellman, C.L., 152
Spinney, Dorsey, 1
Steam Laundry, 382
Stevens, Matthew Elliott, 14
Stewart, F.A., 79, 82, 83, 87
Stokes, Brown Ora, 152
Storehouse, 382
Storey, Lucy C., 34
Streator, Miss, 80
Street, Olivia, 152
Student Labor, 32
Suggestions For Teachers, 36
Sumner, Charles, 15
Sutton, H.E., 152
Sweet, Addie, Miss, 81
Sweet, A.F., Miss, 80
Syphax, Leary Nannie Ethel, 10

T

Talley, T.W., 14, 80
Taft, President, 56, 57
Tappan, Arthur, 13
Tappan, Lewis, 13
Taylor, Harrison T., 62
Taylor, Lizzie, 124
Taylor, Maude, 61
Taylor, Mr., 48
Taylor, Robert, 123
Taylor, Roy, 132
Taylor, Sallye J., 124
Teachers, Community, 1912, 43
Teachers' Cottages, 378, 379
Tennis, 394, 397
Terrell, Mary Church, 25, 36
Terrell, Mr., 7
Terrell, Robert Heberton, 11
Terry, Emma, Jean, 14
Thomas, Attorney, 21
Thomas, D.A., 138
Thomas, G.T., 127, 128
Thornton, Robert A., 66
Tibbs, Elizabeth, 9
Tibbs, Thurlow Jr., 9
Tibbs, Thurlow Sr., 9
Tillery, L.F., 49
Tillery Mutual Association, 141
Tillery Rehabilitation Project, 130, 131
Tillery Settlement, 144, 152
Tobias, Channing, 60
Tollafield, Charles G., 157
Travis, Connie, 3, 4
Tri County Brick School Activities, 136, 137
Trigg, Professor, 140, 145
Trotter, Monroe, 26
Tull, Alice J., 94, 148
Tull, Irving C., 94, 148
Turner, Guthrie L., 167, 168

U

Upperman, Annie, 30

V

Vicks, W.W., 49
Vines, E.L., 49
Voss, Rufus N., 91

W

Wall, O.S.B., 8
Warren, John Turner, 14
Washington, Booker T., 76, 106
Washington Murray, Margaret, 79, 81, 114
Washington, Sarah, 61
Watkins, J.L., 20
Watkins, Susan S., 67
Watts, Julia, 4
Watts, Martha, 3, 4
Weather Observer, 133, 134
Weed, Edward, 13
Welfare Committee 1931, 112
Wesley, Charles, 80, 123
Western Association Congregational Churches, 85
Weston, Nancy, 27
Whipple, George, 13
Whitaker, Michael, 49
White, Clarence C., 20, 36
White, Dominance, 111
White, George, 80
White, George Congressman, 142
White, George M., 103
White Strawberries, 6
White, Walter, 99, 103
Whiting, William E., 13
Wiggins, Mason, 18
Wiggins, Mr. and Mrs, 415
Wiggins, Winnifred, 112

Wiley, J.W. Jr., 129, 143
Wilkins, West, 412
Williams, Mrs., 384
Williams, Orman, 21, 117
Williams, Ruby, 96
Williams, Sarah L., 85
Williams, T.B., 36
Williamson, C.H., 124
Wilson, Clarence, 87
Wimberly, Exum Rolista, 100
Wood, L. Hollingsworth, 79, 82
Woodbury, Dr., 16
Woodworking Class, 387
Wooten, William, 113
Wray, John D., 74
Wright, John Clarence, 95, 106, 111, 127
Wright, Theo S., 13

Y

Yeargen, Max, 60
Yeamans, Francis, 33
YMCA Cabinet, 392
Young Boys Christian Club, 392
Young, Maggie, 87
Young, N.B., 118, 119, 120
Young, Nathan B., 115
Young, Smith Nellie, 1, 2, 153
YWCA Activities, 396, 397, 398